THE SOVIET CITIZEN

Daily Life in a Totalitarian Society

by

Alex Inkeles *1920-* and Raymond A. Bauer

with the assistance of
David Gleicher and Irving Rosow

HARVARD UNIVERSITY PRESS

Cambridge, Massachusetts

1961

Distributed in Great Britain by
Oxford University Press, London

This is study number 35 in the Russian Research Center series and a
report of the Harvard Project on the Soviet Social System.

This volume was prepared under a grant from the Carnegie Corporation of New York.
That Corporation is not, however, the author, owner, publisher, or proprietor of this
publication and is not to be understood as approving by virtue of its grant any of the
statements made or views expressed therein.

Library of Congress Catalog Card Number 59–9277

Printed in the United States of America

TO CLYDE KLUCKHOHN

Preface

The proper period of gestation for a book has never been established. Suffice it to say that by any standard this book has been long aborning. The Harvard Project on the Soviet Social System was organized in the spring of 1950. Our interviews and questionnaires were completed by Soviet refugees in Europe and America during 1950–51. Processing of these materials began in 1951, and the analysis of them started in 1952. The first drafts of the early chapters of this book were written during the summer of 1953, when we sneaked away from our administrative duties to work together in New Hampshire. In the meantime, three other books based on the materials of the Harvard Project have appeared. Two are specialized studies of a single topic: *Doctor and Patient in Soviet Russia,* by Mark G. Field; and *Factory and Manager in the USSR,* by Joseph S. Berliner. The third, *How the Soviet System Works,* by R. Bauer, A. Inkeles, and C. Kluckhohn, was, however, a rather general study of Soviet society. A discussion of the relationship of this book to *How the Soviet System Works* should illuminate the nature and background of the present volume.

How the Soviet System Works was an attempt to use the perspective gained by our experience on the Harvard Project as the basis for a fresh overall view of the Soviet system. The greater part of that book was not based *directly* on our interviews and questionnaires, but on standard sources of material which we reinterpreted in the light of our data. It concerned itself with the dynamics or "operating characteristics" of the Soviet system, with broad socio-political processes. Insofar as we reported results arising directly from our field work, they were largely summary comments without citation of detailed evidence. This volume, *The Soviet Citizen,* presents the main body of statistical data from the Harvard Project. In a sense it contains much of the evidence on the basis of which *How the Soviet System Works* was written several years earlier. But it would be misleading to describe it mainly as a delayed publication of "supporting evidence" for its predecessor. On the contrary, this volume stands quite independent of the earlier book. It arises from a rather distinct conception, and is meant to fulfill different functions. Whereas the earlier book was concerned with Soviet institutions and politics, broadly conceived, this volume is concerned with the people and with their daily lives. The earlier study aimed at an assessment of the strengths and weaknesses of the *system,* while this seeks to discern continuity and change in the life experience of individuals and groups. It is basically a book about the social-psychology of Soviet life. The first study stressed the distinguishing or distinctive features of Soviet society, whereas here we call particular attention to striking parallels between the attitudes and life experiences of Soviet citizens and those in other large-scale industrial societies. Finally, it is true that *How the Soviet System Works* carried a rather large volume of interpretation and assertion relevant to the amount of evidence it presented, whereas in this book we have based ourselves very closely on the mass of data collected in our interviews and questionnaires. Subjects to which we could earlier give only a paragraph or two of bold assertion have in this book often become the topic for an entire chapter of fully documented material.

In this book, as in all the work of the Harvard Project, data from Soviet refugees have been used in conjunction with standard Soviet and American sources. Both authors spent a month in the Soviet Union after the thaw opened Russia to foreign travel, one in 1956 and the other in 1957. We have carefully weighed our firsthand impressions as a counterbalance to the report of the refugees. Some critics of earlier reports of the Project implied that we have relied exclusively on "tainted" refugee data, or that we prefer it to other sources of information. This is far from being the case. Our own position is that we have had the good fortune of being able to add information from Soviet émigrés to our other sources of information. Each source has its advantages and disadvantages and should be judged against all the others available. As valuable as is a visit to the USSR, it too has its limitations — and on this score we have had the chance to check our impressions with many dozens of other visitors. Apparently everyone realizes that a Soviet refugee may give "biased answers" to an American interviewer. But the same is true of Soviet citizens and American visitors talking to each other — as one of us realized when he found himself defending some questionable features of our own foreign policy. Even though any single source of data might have its own difficulty, the convergent cumulative impact of several sources may be highly convincing. In going from our findings to an assessment of their social and political significance, therefore, we have sought to give proper weight not only to our unique refugee data, but to all the sources of information and interpretation which are relevant.

What has been said of the use of several sources of information converging on a given point also has relevance to work *within* the framework of the refugee data itself. As we point out in the early chapters of this book, we gathered a wide variety of data and utilized a number of different approaches in analyzing it. Although a surface impression may suggest that our approach was coldly statistical, we actually spent a great deal

of time in qualitative analysis, which at every point influenced the interpretation of our statistical findings. In many instances an individual
batch of data or an individual mode of analysis had its ambiguities, but
several batches of data or modes of analysis all pointed to the same conclusion. To expose the reader to the full range of data which furnished
the background for a particular conclusion would often put an intolerable
burden on both him and the publisher of the book. The past several years
have been devoted not only to writing, but to more intensive analysis and
checking of our statistical findings, and subsequent rewriting in order to
insure that our results would be presented as compactly, clearly, and unambiguously as possible.

Since by professional training and natural bent we regularly *read*
tables, we drew on our experience and past frustrations to guide us in
developing devices to aid our readers in the assessment of the data. In
our Appendices will be found the full translation of the more important
questionnaire and interview forms we used. They also contain an explanation of how all of the major special measures, such as the "Index
of Anti-Soviet Sentiment," were developed. Furthermore, each statistical
table has a special note, which indicates the question used to gather the
data and methods used in constructing the indices employed, as well as
the conventions used in treating the data for tabular purposes. In the
regular notes to each chapter we have also given question wordings or
other technical information to explain points from the text which could
not appropriately be elaborated within it.

Probably only the most technical readers will be interested in all the
guides we have provided. However, it has been our intention to encourage
all readers as much as possible to attend to the technical aspects of this
study. It is for this reason that we have gone against some earnest advice
and presented our main methodological discussion at the beginning of the
book, rather than relegating it to an appendix. It is true, as we indicated
above, that our conclusions are by no means exclusively based on data
received from Soviet refugees. To the extent that émigré data is involved,
however, methodological considerations are much more central to the
entire study than in many other social science investigations. Furthermore, it has been our experience that a disquieting proportion of readers
come to such a study with fixed conceptions about the social and political
composition of the refugees, the degree of bias they manifest, and the
sophistication (or lack thereof) of the users of such data. While the interested reader could go as well to an appendix as to the first three chapters of the book, we feel that symbolically the methodological discussion
belongs at the beginning. The reader who is convinced that he is not
interested in methodology may begin the book with Chapter IV, the
first topical chapter. However, if he does so the responsibility for mis-

understanding our approach to the data lies with him, and not with us, since we have done everything we can to alert him to it.

Since living conditions of the Soviet citizen have been in constant transition, the reader may raise questions about the currency of our findings. Admittedly the main body of statistical data, insofar as it was gotten from refugees, pertains to the period before World War II. Undoubtedly, also, some at least of our findings are primarily of historical significance. While we deal with the general problem of the currency of our findings in Chapter I, we feel that at the risk of repetition we should ask the reader to withhold judgment. He will find that this crucial issue is one of our central concerns, and that we have taken special pains in supplementing our interviews with other sources of information and in tempering our conclusions wherever the problem of change is particularly relevant. There has been continuity as well as change in Soviet life; and even where there has been change the refugee data often aided us in assessing that change. Almost every one of our chapters, therefore, ends with a section in which we summarize late developments, evaluate our findings in the light of those developments, and seek to assess their relevance for the future.

Giving proper acknowledgment to all who have contributed to the final report of a large-scale social science project is a bit like assigning the credits for a movie. The director and the author of the screenplay obviously deserve credit. But the cameraman, the actors, the composer of the score, to name but a few, all have made significant contributions. Our problem is not so acute, since the conception and design of this book are entirely our own, and with the exception of one chapter no one else took any part in writing it. But it is nevertheless true that if ever there was a "group project," ours was it. Literally dozens of persons including interviewers, coders, research assistants, analysts and specialist consultants were in some way essential to making the Project and this book possible. In the preface to *How the Soviet System Works* we tried to make as complete an acknowledgment of our indebtedness as is possible. Everyone listed there as contributing to the Project also contributed thereby to this book, and we wish here to reiterate our appreciation. Here we have limited ourselves to mentioning those whose contribution bore directly on this particular work. There are unfortunately many whom we cannot attempt to mention even though their indirect contribution may have been appreciable. To these we tender our apologies, and offer our gratitude for their many services.

To begin we must acknowledge our special debt to David Gleicher and Irving Rosow. They did not share responsibility for the design of this book, and took no part in writing it, except for Chapter XIV which is a condensed version of a memorandum written by Mr. Gleicher. But their intellectual and technical contribution to the Project and to this book was so extensive we felt we must call attention to it by citing them on the title page. Although Mr. Gleicher was not associated with the Project until the field team returned from Europe, he was from that point on a central person in its activities. He organized and supervised the coding of our materials, often on codes devised by him, oversaw our entire machine room operation, and was constant technical adviser and intellectual guide to weary analysts in their moments of despair. Yet he found time to write numerous memoranda on a number of vital methodological and substantive problems which greatly influenced our understanding of our data and our approach to it. The contribution of Dr. Irving Rosow was different but equally valuable. He was free of the administrative burdens carried by Mr. Gleicher, although he also gave constant aid and comfort to the analysts we harried and puzzled. He too wrote numerous important topical memoranda. His distinctive contribution, however, lay in his service over several years as a personal assistant to the senior author. In that capacity he did the initial survey of many topics, solved "problems," clarified ambiguities, and resolved contradictions. He is a keen analyst, and once he has touched a body of material no subsequent interpretation can be entirely new or fresh. His mark is therefore on almost every page.

Almost every one of the other analysts on the Project did work which in some way contributed to our own effort. To acknowledge our debt to them we have called attention to their relevant reports in the notes to each chapter. We feel it necessary, however, to indicate several whose contribution was either very extensive or whose work influenced a major section of this book: Alice Rossi, for her work on generational differences, which touched on almost every topic in our study; Sylvia Gilliam, for her analysis of the nationality materials and the wartime occupation questionnaire; Babette Whipple, for the comparison of the samples interviewed in Europe, as against the United States; Robert Feldmesser, for his work on social stratification; and H. Kent Geiger, for his study of the family.

Edward Wasiolek, John Zawadsky, and Anna Weintraub were energetic and intelligent research assistants. Nancy Deptula handled the main editorial and secretarial work in getting the final manuscript into form, and in the process rendered conscientious service as a statistical research assistant. Rose Di Benedetto was our able typist. Helen Parsons, administrative assistant of the Russian Research Center, smoothed many an administrative hurdle for us, as did Elizabeth Fainsod in earlier stages of the work.

The initial support for this study came, of course, from the United States Air Force, which underwrote the Harvard Project on the Soviet Social System. In *How the Soviet System Works* we gave thanks by

Contents

XV. The Nationality Problem   338

Life Chances of Ukrainians vs. Russians. Basic Attitudes and
Evaluations of the Regime. The Salience of the Nationality Prob-
lem. Patterns of Nationalism Among Ukrainians. The Issue of
Ukrainian Independence. Summary and Conclusions.

PART FIVE: CONCLUSIONS

XVI. The Future of Soviet Society   377

APPENDICES   401

List of Tables

XIII

PART ONE: OBJECTIVES AND METHODS

I

The Harvard Project on the Soviet Social System

There are three major respects in which the authors of this book may, without too greatly violating the canons of modesty, declare it to be unusual. The first is that it reports one of the very few researches which have sought to study a large-scale industrial society primarily through the people's own report of their experiences and attitudes as they pursued the round of daily living at home, in school, on the job, at play and in politics. There are, of course, many excellent books describing the history of the Soviet Union, and the formal structure and functioning of its institutions, but we know almost nothing about the attitudes, values, and experiences of its citizens. Even in the case of the United States, whose population has probably been surveyed and polled on more questions than any other nation, there is no *single* study in which one can find recorded the experiences and attitudes of the population at large over a wide range of the major areas of American social life. There are, of course, excellent studies of particular topics, such as attitudes toward civil liberties, national politics, military life, and stratification and mobility, but these are nowhere drawn together to give a composite picture of the round of daily living in America as experienced and evaluated by its citizens.[1] And even if we were to "compose" such a book from the individual studies, the fact that each used a different sample would greatly limit our ability to see the different areas in proper relationship. For example, we would have no way of telling whether those who were dissatisfied with their jobs as reported by the study of making a living, were also the ones who were most radical in their political attitudes, or most consistently reported having trouble getting on with their families.

In our study of how Soviet society impinges on the individual and how he fits into the functioning pattern of Soviet life, we therefore attempted to discover the experiences of people from all walks of life as they pursued the round of daily living in the family, at school, in work, recreation, and politics. We sought to explore not only their experiences but also their

values and beliefs, their desires and frustrations. Among the questions
to which we addressed ourselves were these: Who are the people who get
ahead, who lags behind in the race for success, and what are the consequences? Who gets educated, who does not, why are there such differences
in educational opportunity, and how do people feel about them? Which
are the more stable families and what are the conditions which make for
and the consequences which follow from family stability? How are those
who fall victim to the political terror and their families affected in their
chances to earn a living and to advance themselves? Who enjoys his job
and why, and what effect does not liking his work have on one's evaluation
of Communist society? We treat, as well, a series of political questions.
What do people find good, as well as bad, in the Soviet system? What
experiences make for loyalty, which for disaffection? How do people
handle their hostile political feelings under conditions of totalitarian rule?
And we try to assess the problems of the system with regard to the major
sources of social cleavage, including that between the Communist minority
and non-Communist majority, the upper and the lower classes, the Russians and the non-Russian nationalities, the old generation and the newer
Soviet generations. These and other problems we try to see in relation to
each other and to the larger framework of Soviet society in which they are
set.

We feel this book also breaks new ground by its systematically comparative emphasis. Although we have never allowed the Soviet Union
to be lost sight of as the main object of our attention, we have at every
point sought to find comparable data from other industrial countries
and particularly the United States. It will perhaps come as a great surprise to many that there is an extraordinarily close correspondence between
the pattern of experience and attitudes of Soviet citizens and their counterparts on the same level of education or occupation in a variety of other
large-scale industrial societies having a markedly different culture and
history and possessed of quite dissimilar political institutions. We hope
thereby to place on a more firm footing some of the rather speculative
arguments about the relative compatibility of industrialism and totalitarianism, and to take a few small steps towards development of a general
social-psychology of industrial society.

The third respect in which our study is unusual is much less a virtue, and was certainly not a distinction we consciously sought. That
distinction lies in the chief source of our information, which is not a
scientifically drawn sample, but rather a group of refugees from — or,
as they prefer to call themselves, "non-returnees" to — the Soviet Union.
Naturally, we would have been delighted to interview a scientifically
adequate sample of Soviet citizens within the Soviet Union, but it is obviously impossible to conduct a scientific survey under conditions of

Soviet totalitarianism. Indeed, even if we were allowed to ask our questions inside the Soviet Union there would have been most serious doubt as to how honestly we would have been answered by people still living in the land of the secret police. Be that as it may, we were of course not free to conduct our investigation within the Soviet Union with citizens still living there. We had no choice, therefore, but to take advantage of a "once in a lifetime" opportunity, namely the presence in Western Europe of between a quarter and a half million former Soviet citizens who succeeded in escaping repatriation and remained in Western Europe after the war. These people had lived all or most of their lives as Soviet citizens, until recently under Soviet jurisdiction. Since they represented all walks of life, all ages, occupations, and nationalities, it was possible to draw from their midst a sufficient number of informants to permit us to study a great variety of problems concerning life in the Soviet Union. It is material from 764 long interviews, and detailed questionnaires from almost 3,000 different respondents woven together with relevant facts drawn from official Soviet sources and traditional Western scholarly studies of Soviet society, which constitute the main source on which this book is based. Lest there be a misunderstanding we hasten to stress that such information is far from being our sole source of material. On the contrary, we have attempted to give a fairly rounded picture of the sociology and psychology of daily life in Soviet society. We have, therefore, given a brief historical account of the development of Soviet policy and institutions in each of the major areas with which we deal. We have also sought to bring information on recent and current developments in the Soviet Union to bear on our interpretation of the report former Soviet citizens gave of their experiences and attitudes. The information from the refugees is always used against this background of other material, to increase our understanding of what happened, of how people reacted, and how in their turn, institutions changed, are changing, and will yet change. Although the refugee interview data is the main "new" material we introduce, we have sought to use it so that it contributes to our store of knowledge not merely in and of itself, but also by casting new light on "old" facts and permitting a fresh interpretation of long established theories and assumptions.

Two important questions are repeatedly raised with us concerning the use of our interview. The first concerns the representativeness, the reliability and validity of the information given by "political" refugees. The question is often put as follows: "How can you expect to learn anything about ordinary, average Soviet people and their lives by talking to a lot of disgruntled refugees who ran away from their home country?" This is so important a question, and our materials pose so many unusual problems for analysis, that we have devoted the first three chapters of our book to a rather exceptionally full account of the methods we used in gathering and analyzing these data. We feel the issue to be so important that we have placed these chapters in the front of the book rather than in the more usual methodological appendix. Readers to whom the questions of method and methodology are not of central concern, and who are more interested in what we do with what we have at hand, may choose to proceed directly from the end of this section to the presentation of substantive findings beginning with Chapter IV.

The second challenge to our data with which people most commonly confront us has to do with its relative "age." Especially after the apparent rejection of Stalin as a leader and of some aspects of Stalinism as a style of governing, our audiences are inclined to say: "Well, even if you can rely on the report of these people for some purposes, isn't that all past history now?" It is indeed the case that most of our interviews were conducted in 1950 and 1951, before the death of Stalin and his subsequent denunciation. More important, most of our subjects left the Soviet Union quite a bit earlier, mainly between 1943 and 1946, although some escaped as late as 1950–51. As of this writing, therefore, the information most of them gave us is at least ten and often thirteen years behind the times. Finally, much of what they described was experienced under conditions which clearly cannot recur again in quite the same form in Soviet society. For example, the forced collectivization of the farms was an event which by its very nature was not recurrent.

We wish to stress that we have no objection to accepting the role of "mere" reporters of "past history," especially when the history involved is important in human terms. But reporting history is *not* our prime purpose. On the contrary, we are convinced that the great majority of our findings have more than historical interest, and are of considerable relevance for understanding the present and assessing the probable future development of Soviet society. Confusion on this score stems mainly from the mistaken assumption that since our informants were in some sense "political" refugees we spent our time questioning them more or less exclusively about their political opinions and experiences. This is not the case. The overwhelming majority of our questions dealt rather with what individuals routinely experienced and felt in their daily lives as they grew up, went to school, worked and played. With or without Stalin the Soviet Union continues to be a large-scale industrial society, with collectivized agriculture, governed by stringent economic planning and run by a one party dictatorship which has the power to apply terror against the population and sometimes still does. These institutions have persisted substantially in their present form since the early thirties, and there is every reason to expect their continued existence for some time in the future. Consequently, insofar as our findings deal in large measure

with experiences in and attitudes towards the relatively enduring features of Soviet society, they may have considerable relevance for understanding not only the past but the present and future as well.

Of course, certain other features of Soviet society have been especially
distinctive of the Stalinist era. Our study of them not only serves to fill
out the picture of the nature of the Soviet system under Stalin, but offers
us a base line against which to assess changes in Soviet life. The very
extensive studies which Western students of the Soviet Union have made
in recent years, together with the evidence of trends within our own data,
make it possible to identify the direction and areas of change in Soviet
life. It is a major intention of this work to make such an assessment, and
to indicate in each instance what the changes have been and probably
will be. For example, the opinion is widespread that the post-Stalin
leaders dare make only the most insignificant changes in the stringent
Stalinist style of ruling because of the danger that such concessions
would so whet the appetites of the Soviet people as to force the democratization of the Soviet system. We suggest that this hope must be greatly
tempered on the basis of our finding that Soviet citizens seem much less
concerned with winning political rights and constitutional guarantees
than with gaining more personal security and an improved standard of
living. In short, we believe our findings are of considerably more than
historical interest. However, it has regularly been our contention that
neither the problem as to the quality of our data or its "age" can be evaluated properly except in terms of the full range of conclusions we have
reached, the evidence we have used, and the modes of inference we have
employed. This book is in its entirety an answer to these questions, and
the reader must ultimately decide for himself whether or not what we
have to say is relevant to the Soviet Union yesterday, today or tomorrow.

Origins of the Project

For various reasons — its size, its possible practical importance for
the future welfare of Soviet émigrés, its potential implications for United
States policy — the Harvard Refugee Project attracted a good deal of
attention among some groups, and a considerable body of folklore developed about it. Since some of this folklore bears on the acceptability or
unacceptability of our findings, we present a relatively detailed account
of the background and history of the Project in this chapter. This chapter
has the further function of giving the reader a picture of our working
conditions, particularly in the field. Since with research such as this
one inevitably compromises between some ideal notion of how to proceed and the practical exigencies of the situation, an understanding of the
conditions under which we were working will give the reader a basis for
appraising the decisions we have made.

During the Second World War a considerable proportion of the Soviet population was at one time or another under the jurisdiction of some power other than the government of the USSR. From the time of the German attack on the Soviet Union in 1941, until German troops and their military allies were driven from Soviet soil, tens of millions lived, for at least a brief period, under German or German-affiliated control. The Germans conscripted from the population under their control large numbers of forced laborers, "Ostarbeiters," whom they later sent back to Germany. As the Germans withdrew from the territories they occupied, they evacuated forcibly still more people, who were compelled to retreat ahead of the German army to become workers in the West. Additionally, large numbers of Soviet citizens who had lived under the Germans fled voluntarily before the advancing Red Army. As a result several million civilian citizens were in German-held Europe toward the end of the war. In addition to this group, German and affiliated armies are estimated to have held another "several millions" of Soviet prisoners of war at the end of hostilities. At the close of hostilities the total of Soviet citizens under German jurisdiction was probably over five million.[2]

At the end of the war, the bulk of these people returned to their Soviet homeland. There is considerable confusion and disagreement as to the extent to which their return was voluntary or coerced. Similarly, the question of why and under what circumstances a considerable portion did not return to the Soviet Union is an equally complicated one. To some extent our later analysis will be concerned directly with this problem. Here we are interested only in the fact that after the period of immediate postwar adjustment several hundreds of thousands of former Soviet citizens remained in Western Europe under Allied jurisdiction.[3] This group was supplemented by an appreciable but generally decreasing flow of persons fleeing from the Soviet occupation forces, from Soviet missions in Western countries, and by an occasional person who fled directly from the Soviet Union, crossing through the intervening Iron Curtain territories in the course of his flight. Again, the estimates of the numbers of persons involved are confused and contradictory. But certainly it is safe to say that many hundreds of such refugees fled into Western countries between the end of 1945 and the end of 1950.[4]

There was confusion not only with regard to the numbers of persons involved, but also the circumstances of their leaving the Soviet Union, the nature of their relationship to the German Nazi government, and the conditions and reasons for their remaining in Western Europe. Nevertheless, American scholars on the Soviet Union recognized from the end of the war that these non-returners and refugees were under any circumstances a potentially valuable source of data concerning the Soviet system. Even if one granted the worst concerning the biases to be expected in these people and the sorts of answers they would give — a topic to which we shall return shortly for detailed consideration — it was obvious that their testimony, taken together with what could be garnered from more ordinary sources of information, should be a valuable asset in understanding those aspects of the Soviet system about which we had the least good data. Here at last there was some hope of studying the day-to-day functioning of the system mediated through the feelings and aspirations of the human material of which the system is constituted.

This source of data did not go entirely unexploited in the years immediately following the war. Various agencies of the Western governments interrogated these people for intelligence purposes. The émigrés themselves published memoirs and essays, and wrote in their own journals and newspapers. David Dallin and Boris Nicolaevsky, émigrés from the early period of the Soviet regime, interviewed the newer émigrés on the subject of forced labor.[5] An American survey organization, the Survey Research Center of the University of Michigan, conducted a series of interviews for the United States Air Force. As valuable as each of these studies was, they were all either of rather limited scope or the results had security classifications and were thus unavailable to the public and to the scholarly community.

In the summer of 1949, therefore, the Russian Research Center of Harvard University explored the possibility of a more general exploitation of this source from the point of view of a wide range of social science problems. Professor Clyde Kluckhohn, then director of the Russian Research Center and later to become director of the Project on the Soviet Social System, and Professor Talcott Parsons, a member of the Executive Committee of the Center, conducted preliminary investigations in Germany and Austria. Professor Merle Fainsod, also a member of the Center's Executive Committee, and Mr. Paul Friedrich carried out a series of interviews which established the feasibility and value of a large-scale interviewing project.[6] This pilot phase of the Project was carried on without government funds, but with important facilitation by the United States Air Force. On the basis of the success of this exploration, the Russian Research Center negotiated a contract with the Human Resources Research Institute of the United States Air Force in the spring of 1950 for the execution of such a project. Although this sponsorship was exclusively for basic research, and the Air Force in no way took responsibility for the Project's findings nor in any way sought to influence the direction of its conclusions, this support did create suspicion among refugees, both as to our "motives" and our freedom of action.

It is important to pause for a moment to consider the time at which this project was launched. The summer of 1950 was slightly more than five years after the end of the war in Europe. Almost all of the émigrés had left the Soviet Union between 1942 and 1944, from six to eight years previously. A considerable number of them had left Germany for other parts of Western Europe, and many were already scattered so thinly over the more distant countries of the Western World as to be virtually inaccessible. Whatever may have been the reasons for the delay between the end of the war and the inauguration of this research in 1950, it is extremely fortunate that the delay was not longer. The years 1950 and 1951 were the last in which an efficient program of interviewing Soviet émigrés could be carried on in Western Europe. During the very period in which the interviewing part of the Project was carried out, the various refugee camps were in the process of being dissolved. Some of the camps were passed over into German or Austrian jurisdiction, but most of the émigrés either became scattered throughout the German and Austrian population or emigrated a second time and moved to the United States, Canada, Australia or the various countries of South America. By the summer of 1951, physical access to these people had become considerably more difficult. The Project was, therefore, conducted under conditions which demanded quick action, and its directors and staff were driven by a sense of urgency in seeking to reach the refugees before they dispersed to the far corners of the world.

Contacts with the Refugee Community

When the Project was initiated, it was recognized that one of the most important problems in the early stages of operations was to establish effective liaison with the émigré community in order that we might be able to procure respondents for interviewing with a minimum of difficulty and under conditions which would not impair the quality of the interviews nor systematically bias our access to the many segments of the émigré community. Through Dr. George Fischer, an associate of the Russian Research Center, we established a series of contacts with the émigré community, and arranged with the Council of the newly formed Institute for the Study of the History and Culture of the USSR in Munich to sponsor us to the community of Soviet émigrés in Western Europe. The Munich Institute was composed of Soviet scholars of the wartime and postwar emigration, and included persons of the widest range of political and nationality affiliations that it appeared possible to assimilate and hold together in a single group. We realized from the start that the magnitude of political tensions in the emigration, and the extent of cleavage between the members of the several Soviet nationalities might present a serious problem in the recruitment of respondents. The Munich Institute represented at that time the nearest approximation to a representative, nonpolitical organization which could facilitate our entree into the émigré community.

While the decision to establish this relationship with the Institute may indeed have been the best possible compromise, it was not without complications. Members of ultraconservative political organizations indicated that they would not cooperate with an Institute in which so prominent a role was played by persons they dubbed "Marxists" and "Soviet agents." Similar objections were hinted at by some of the more extremist representatives of the national minorities, who feared that the Project would be biased in its approach to the nationality question because the majority of the Council of the Institute was composed of men of Great Russian nationality. This despite the fact that there were some very prominent representatives of non-Russian nationalities on the Council. A further complication was introduced by the fact that Mr. Boris Yakovlev, president of the Council, was an outstanding figure in émigré politics. In our opinion, Mr. Yakovlev conducted himself with eminent fairness and discretion in order that his own political affiliations should not bias the work of the Project, and offered to resign his post as president of the Council in order to facilitate the work of the Project. Nevertheless, his association with the Project was a focus of complaint from a number of groups in the emigration.

In order to offset these complications we took several additional steps in establishing our relations with the refugee community and our potential informants. Most important was the establishment of an effective "contact system," which was selected and organized independently of the Munich Institute. The system was organized by a member of our staff, Mr. Frederick Wyle, who previously had had extensive firsthand contact with refugees in Germany. Mr. Wyle's task was to organize a contact system, described more fully below, which would be free as possible of political bias, and to establish good relationships with the groups not embraced in the Council of the Institute. As a supplement to Mr. Wyle's work, Mr. Marc Raeff [7] devoted several weeks to contact work with members of the non-Slavic minorities, briefing them on the nature of our work, and requesting their cooperation.

Despite these early efforts to establish optimum relationships with the émigré community, this continued to be a problem throughout the data gathering phase of the Project. Although the bulk of the émigré community were warmly receptive, isolated groups made repeated attacks on the Project, mainly in their own press. These attacks stemmed from certain obvious anxieties. It was feared that we were, on the one hand, agents of the American immigration authorities checking on the refugee's account of himself, and on the other hand, agents of the Soviet secret police. We believe there were also some instances of an obvious attempt to influence or discredit the work of the Project, undertaken by agents of the Soviet secret police in Germany. A significant proportion of such at-

tacks, however, was based on simple misunderstanding. We call attention to this problem because our adverse "press" in the émigré community may have induced some groups or segments of opinion to avoid,
and others to seek out, the Project. We do not, however, believe that any
systematic biases of sufficient magnitude to affect our conclusions resulted
from these difficulties. Our general reception in the émigré community
was very positive and there were many detailed and sympathetic reports
in the émigré press describing our "scientific expedition." Furthermore,
when on our written questionnaire we asked which émigré political group
our respondents favored, we found all shades of political opinion widely
represented.[8]

Collecting the Data

Although the project had originally focused its interest on Soviet
émigrés as a source of information, its objectives were only partially that
of the exploitation of an unused data source. Its ultimate goal was the
synthesis of this new information with existing information so as to provide new insights into the nature of the Soviet system. With this goal
in view, the staff that was assembled in the summer of 1950 consisted of
scholars already active in the Soviet field. Each had some special area
of interest related to the objectives of the project. They came from a
variety of institutions: Columbia, Princeton, Champlain College, Harvard; from government agencies, and private clinical practice. They also
represented a wide range of disciplines: history, economics, political
science, literature, sociology, anthropology, and clinical and social psychology. Each scholar participated in the design of research and in the
interviewing and took the responsibility for preparing a report covering
his special area of interest.[9] It was this group, together with a group of
consultants from the Bureau of Applied Social Research of Columbia
University, which prepared the interviewing schedules during the summer
and administered a number of pretest interviews in New York during
the month of August, 1950.

The broad objectives of the Project and the wide range of interests of
its staff led to the development of a complex program of field work. One
major interest of our group was to learn in more intimate detail the
workings of certain basic Soviet institutions including some small groups
like the family or larger ones such as the factory and the hospital or
medical clinic. Another was to learn in depth the otherwise concealed
history of certain important historical events, such as those involving the
changes in Soviet nationality policy in the thirties, or the pattern of reaction of the Soviet population to the Nazi invasion and occupation of their
land. To learn more about these topics we conducted a series of 435
specialized interviews with people selected primarily on the grounds that

they had particular knowledge about the subject. For example, we interviewed almost sixty former managers, engineers, bookkeepers and other industrial specialists about the functioning of Soviet factories and their relation to other factories and to the ministries under which they operated. The results of those special series of interviews, woven together with material from more traditional sources, are being reported in a series of separate volumes written by the specialist staff members of the Project.

A quite different interest of the Project was to learn in great detail the life experiences and attitudes of representative individuals with regard to the routine details of their daily lives as Soviet citizens. For this purpose we wanted not a narrow range of specialized informants, but a wide spectrum of average individuals from all walks of life, of all ages and backgrounds. And we wished to talk with them not mainly about what they knew as specialists, but how they *felt* and *experienced* their daily existence in all areas of Soviet life. To gather this material we relied on the more usual methods of the opinion survey. In particular, we utilized a lengthy personal interview following a set but flexible outline, and a detailed self-administered paper and pencil questionnaire. Since each posed special problems with regard to the content and design of the instrument, the conditions of its administration, and the nature of an appropriate sample, each is briefly discussed below.

Decisions as to which interviewing procedures to use were made on the basis of an attempt to reconcile the Project's objectives with the practical conditions under which the interviewing team would be operating. Foremost among these was the nature of Soviet émigrés as interview subjects. American scholars who were familiar with the émigré community, members of the émigré community themselves, and our own representatives in Europe all stressed the difficulties of interviewing these people. We were told they were fearful and suspicious, and would refuse to be interviewed. Furthermore, if they consented to talk they would lie to cover up their past. Several of our advisers said categorically that it would be impossible to use a fixed interview schedule, and that the sight of a printed form would be reminiscent of a secret police interrogation and would cause them to freeze up. One of our own representatives went so far as to insist that it would even be highly inadvisable to take notes during the interview. The realization that their words were being recorded would, he said, arouse in them the fear that compromising facts would be handed over to agencies which might do them harm.[10]

Complete concession to this pressure for an informal type of interview would have jeopardized seriously our goal of gathering data which was comparable from interview to interview and which would permit systematic statistical analysis. Furthermore, the many sources of bias which had to be anticipated were so complicated that they argued for the use of the most rigorous possible controls over the interviews. It was decided, therefore, to run the risk that respondents would rebel at the set interview form. But by way of compromise, our initial interviewing guide was organized so as to make maximal concession to flexibility with minimal sacrifice of the goal of gathering comparable data. The possibility of employing a self-administered pencil and paper questionnaire was temporarily not tested since advice given by those persons who had had most contact with the community was so strongly opposed to it.

The main outline of our personal interview was developed in Cambridge during the summer of 1950. It was pretested in the United States, revised and then used for a month in Germany before being reduced to final form in October. In this final form, a copy of which is given in Appendix I, it sought to elicit from the respondent a life history covering his education and work experience, family background, relations to and participation in the Soviet government, communications behavior, political and social attitudes. At the end of the interview the individual was asked briefly to recapitulate the history of the development and changes of his attitudes toward the Soviet regime and the Communist system. As a supplement to the oral interview each respondent filled out a number of written forms. These included: (1) a psychological test, consisting of sixty sentence fragments, which the respondent completed, and which were devised to obtain certain personality data; (2) a family budget, describing the income and expenditures of his household unit; and (3) a series of written questions requiring only check off answers, and designed to assess certain attitudes and to test the extent to which the respondent seemed prone to distort information or sought to flatter the interviewer. The last of these forms, developed by the affiliated group from Columbia University, established the feasibility of employing self-administered questionnaires with Soviet refugees. In this form the personal interview required from six to twelve hours of time, depending on the background and articulateness of the respondents. We completed a total of 329 such interviews, 276 collected in Europe and 53 in eastern United States, as further described below.

The methods we used to reach these people and to induce them to undertake the interview are, of course, important to an assessment of the information they gave us. Since our next two chapters are devoted to an evaluation of our sample and the information they gave, we restrict ourselves here to indicating our general procedure for selecting informants and inducing their cooperation. For such a long interview as the personal life history it was obvious that the usual survey methods would not serve. In any event, the fear and suspicion of the refugees ruled out such an approach. We had no choice, for this phase of our work, but to rely on volunteers. One group of such volunteers were individuals who had heard of the Project and had written or come to its headquarters to volunteer their cooperation. The great majority of interviewees, however, were selected from a list of volunteers solicited by the previously mentioned "contact" system. It consisted of about forty-five contact men, themselves displaced persons resident in refugee camps in which there were substantial numbers of Soviet émigrés, or living in German communities in which there were concentrations of potential respondents. Their assignment was to explain to other émigrés the objectives of the Project, to persuade them to volunteer to be interviewed, and to forward to the central office in Munich a card containing a description of each volunteer with respect to his or her age, sex, regular occupation, and several other bits of data. The names of the respondents were, however, not sent to Munich, in order to guarantee the anonymity of the volunteers. Our selection was made solely on the basis of the individual's formal characteristics.

Since an obvious source of potential selective bias in our sample lay in the differences between people who would and those who would not volunteer to be interviewed, the contact men were asked, for a brief period, to submit data on those persons who refused to be interviewed, so that they might be compared to the volunteer group. The contact men reported an exceedingly low rate of refusals. We knew in the light of other information that they must be concealing the true rate of refusals for fear it might reflect badly on their persuasive abilities. This procedure had to be abandoned since the information we were getting was obviously inaccurate.

The information sent in by the contact men was kept in the office of the Munich Institute. Here three men organized the data, carried on correspondence with the contact men, and prepared to take care of respondents who came into Munich to be interviewed. This office was directed jointly by Mr. Yakovlev, for the Munich Institute, and by Mr. Wyle for the Project.

The entire procedure involved in administration of such an interview was the following: Since many more volunteered than could be interviewed, an individual who met the requirements of our sample design would be selected randomly from the files of volunteers. A letter would be sent to the contact man who had recruited him in which he would be identified only by the code number which the contact man had assigned him. The letter would request that the respondent appear at the office of the Munich Institute on the morning of a given day. If he lived out of town, a railway ticket would accompany the letter. Upon his arrival at the Institute he would be transported to our interviewing rooms, where he would be interviewed for two hours in the morning and two hours in the afternoon. Between interview sessions the respondent would be given the short questionnaire, the sentence completion test, and the budget form to fill out. The interviewer, in the meantime, would be recording his interview notes on a recording machine. This was the norm at which we aimed. However, such practical problems as the mechanical failure of recording machines upset this ideal routine, and on occasions notes were recorded several days after the original interview.

The vast majority of the interviewing was done in Russian; some interviewers also used Ukrainian, and, on occasion, German and English. Most of the interviewers wrote their notes, however, directly in English. The recording consisted of elaborating the content of the notes on the basis of the interviewer's recall of what had been said. This routine would be followed for two or three days, depending on the length of the interview.

At the end of each day the respondent would return to the Institute, where he would be assigned lodgings, given a food allowance of five German marks, and a day's pay of ten German marks. This amounted to quite a good day's pay and was unquestionably a factor in some persons' consenting to be interviewed, although it was certainly not the only motive. Many respondents were obviously anxious to "tell the West" about the Soviet Union, apart from any remuneration for their time.

The length of time it took for a single personal interview clearly meant that it would be impossible to complete more than a few hundred such interviews within the limitations of time and personnel available to the Project. The desirability of developing a pencil and paper questionnaire which would make it possible to get data from large numbers of persons had been obvious from the beginning, but as we reported earlier, it did not at first seem feasible. After experience with a short questionnaire following the personal interview, our associates from Columbia University ran a small experiment to test the comparability of information gotten on the same interview form when it was orally administered by an interviewer on one hand, and when it was self-administered on the other. Fifty pairs of subjects, matched for age, sex, and occupation, were used in this study. The experiment indicated that high comparability of response did indeed result, and on this basis an extensive battery of self-administered questionnaires was developed.

The main written questionnaire paralleled the personal life history interview in most major respects. Obviously it could not in the same way cover an individual's experiences in detail, but it was designed to elicit at least a skeleton outline of them. It also dealt with attitudes and opinions in a systematic way. Like the personal interview it covered the family, education, communications patterns, social stratification and mobility, experience on the job, contacts with the government and broad issues of personal and social philosophy or ideology. In each of these areas the wording of the question, and the alternatives offered on check lists were largely based on our extensive prior experience with the personal interviews.

The basic written questionnaire was completed by 2718 people, the great majority in Germany. In addition, supplementary questions on special topics were completed by those who had more time or had special characteristics. The more general supplementary questionnaires yielded a detailed family budget, an evaluation of a set of thirteen representative Soviet occupations, and a report of experiences in and opinions about the Soviet system of medical care. The more specialized units included one for those who had lived under the Germans in Soviet territory occupied by them, and one for Ukrainians on the nationality problem as they had experienced it. Although we make some use of these more specialized materials, they are not systematically reported in this book, except for the data on the nationality problem. The others will be reported in more specialized studies by members of our Project staff.[11]

The standard practice for the administration of these questionnaires was quite different from that used in conducting the personal interviews. Since the investment in any single questionnaire was extremely small, compared to the cost of conducting one of the personal interviews, we could count on collecting a large number. This fact of numbers, furthermore, made it much less important that we worry about finding a person with the precise characteristics required by our sample design, a problem further discussed in the next chapter. As a result we decided as a standard practice to administer the questionnaires to assembled groups of refugees. This was generally done in some public room, such as the dining hall, of the refugee camps in which most still lived. Questionnaires were collected at twenty different locations. The number obtained varied with the size of the camp and other factors. The smallest contribution at any one location was 12, the largest 257, the median 77. Before the arrival of the Project representative, contact men would seek to publicize the coming event, to explain its purpose, and solicit cooperation with the Project. They also announced that aid in filling out the questionnaire would be provided for illiterates. As in the case of the personal interview, we felt that we had to pay the refugees for their time, since it required the greater part of a day to complete filling in the lengthy questionnaire.[12]

Once again we faced some of the problems of misunderstanding which our earlier efforts at personal interviewing had prepared us for. One refugee newspaper went so far as to suggest that we really intended to use the IBM machine for pinpoint identification of individuals despite the fact that they did not give their names. Again we do not believe that such comments made a serious difference in the composition of the group who cooperated or in the nature of the information they gave us.

We do feel, however, that we are obliged to call attention to these facts. Their implications are further discussed in our chapters on the sample and on methodology.

Another problem, this time a new one, posed by the written questionnaire was the possibility it created that the same individual would complete more than one questionnaire. At the very outset of our work with the written questionnaire about 100 were administered under conditions which would have made this possible. And we had evidence that it was in fact happening. These were, therefore, identified as a block, set aside for special scrutiny. In approximately two dozen cases the handwriting was seemingly repeated on more than one questionnaire, and these "suspicious" forms were discarded outright. Beyond this, despite rumors to the contrary in the émigré community, the method for administering the questionnaire largely precluded such "double voting." We cannot guarantee, of course, that there were not some people who traveled from town to town or city to city to be present at the local refugee camp when our questionnaire was administered. We rather doubt, however, that the number who would have attempted this, and who would not have been detected (and could have afforded it) could have been very large.

We have already noted that some of our interviews and questionnaires were secured not in the main center of refugee concentration in Germany, but rather in the United States. Since all our informants were being seen not in their usual natural context, but rather far from home in strange surroundings, we were concerned lest the image of the Soviet Union they reported be unduly influenced by the somewhat depressed conditions they found themselves in, and by other aspects of their setting in occupied Germany. We therefore established a smaller "operation," working out of New York under the direction of Dr. Ivan London, to secure a set of "control" interviews and questionnaires from refugees who had already emigrated to the United States and had had the benefit of one year of residence in this new and presumably different environment. Fifty-three Soviet refugees were, therefore, interviewed in the United States who were "matched" in age, sex, and occupation to an opposite number already interviewed in Germany and alike in every respect except emigration to the United States and the advantage of one year of residence in this country. In addition, 638 written questionnaires were collected in this country for the same purposes. Since the personal interviews in the United States were not anonymous, we were later able to locate 46 who had the personal interview and persuade them also to complete the written questionnaire, thus enabling us to compare for the *same* individuals the differences in results obtained by the two approaches. Instead of contact men and the camps, Dr. London worked through religious, fraternal, political, and church groups which the émigrés had established in this country. The general approach was otherwise broadly similar to that used in Europe, as were the interview guides and questionnaires.

A final group of interviews was done on a group of 100 Americans matched with 100 of the Soviet émigrés. The purpose of these interviews was to offer a comparison or criterion group particularly for a number of psychological instruments which had been devised specially for our project, and which had never before been tried on another population. These American control interviews do not play an important role in the present analysis, but some of the results are used from time to time. They were done between the summer of 1951 and the summer of 1952, at which point the data-gathering phase of the project came to a close.

TABLE 1 [12A]

NUMBERS OF PERSONS FROM WHOM DATA WERE COLLECTED BY THE HARVARD PROJECT ON THE SOVIET SOCIAL SYSTEM: BY TYPE OF INTERVIEW

Type of data	West Germany and Austria	Eastern United States	Total
Extended life-history interviews, including personality and methodological tests	276	53	329 [a]
Interviews on topics about which the subjects had special knowledge	418	17	435
Sets of protocols on individuals who were interviewed at great length and given five sets of clinical psychological tests	55	5	60 [b]
Basic written questionnaires	2080	638	2718
Supplementary questionnaires			
(a) Occupational ratings	1505	641	2146
(b) Family budgets	1872	—	1872
(c) Medical care	1033	624	1657
(d) Nationality	479	32	511
(e) Wartime occupation experiences	888	14	902
Interviews and psychological tests administered for control purposes to a matched group of Americans	—	100	100

a. Includes 91 interviews with postwar refugees.
b. Includes a few incomplete cases of clinical subjects who were not given the full range of psychological tests, or who took the tests but not the interview.

It will be apparent from this brief review that we collected a great deal of data. The basic facts are summarized in Table 1. It will be equally apparent that the stringent practical limitations by which we were frequently constrained were such that the degree of rigor and "neatness" which one would ideally like to approximate in an opinion survey were manifestly impossible. Yet, even under such conditions, a good deal can be done to control potential sources of error. The efforts we made to uncover and control such potential sources of error are described in detail in the next two chapters, Chapter II dealing with problems inhering in our sample, and Chapter III dealing with problems arising from the nature of our data.

With data such as ours, and problems such as those with which we are concerned, it will ultimately be the weight of a mass of evidence, rather than any one bit that will prove persuasive. Despite our methodological assurances, the reader unquestionably will not want to make up his mind about these data until he has plunged into the substantive chapters; nor would we, on our part, want him to make this judgment until he has seen the substance of some of our findings, and become acquainted with the types of inference we make. Nevertheless, we hope that the information contained in the following two chapters will be of some assistance in the making of that judgment.

II

The Sample

The major objectives in the selection of a sample of respondents from among Soviet refugees were that we should get an adequate number to suit our analysis objectives with a minimum expenditure of our resources, and that the information given by the sample be as "correct" as possible. The latter of these objectives relates to the problems of sample bias and response bias, which will be discussed in the second section of this chapter and in Chapter III, respectively. For the moment, we pass by the vital question of whether or not we got "correct" information and briefly discuss the adequacy of our sample as to size, that is, is it large and diverse enough to support the kind of analysis we do?

The Adequacy and Efficiency of the Sample

From the outset it must be realized that our sample neither is nor was intended to be identical in composition to the "parent" Soviet population. The ideal sample at which we were aiming was *not* one which would be a representative cross section of the Soviet population from which (again for the moment begging the question of bias) we could make inferences directly to the distribution of traits in the Soviet population. Quite apart from its being unattainable, such a sample would have been grossly inefficient for our purposes. Our plan of analysis, from the beginning, concentrated on the comparison of subgroups within our sample. We wanted to know whether and in what ways young people were different from old people, highly educated different from lowly educated, men from women in their attitudes and life experiences. The most efficient sample for our purposes was one which had equal numbers of cases in each of the subcategories with which we were concerned. A case might even be made for an overrepresentation of the very groups which would be underrepresented in a cross sectional sample, such as those in more responsible positions in Soviet society, since in many instances one would want to make more refined discriminations within such groups. In any event, the *ideal* sample design on which we settled was one with equal numbers of cases within each category.

The question of sample efficiency was most acute with respect to the personal, life-history interviews. Each represented about three days of interviewing time. Therefore, it was obvious from the beginning that we could not afford to procure a very large number. Accordingly the sample design for the personal interview was drawn up to give us equal numbers in each of eight occupational categories (a close approximation of social class), in five age categories, and in the two sex categories. The ideal of this sample design was not realized for several reasons. The most important — and least unfortunate — was the high premium we placed on getting personal interviews with postwar refugees or "current defectors," that is, with those who had escaped from Soviet control after the cessation of hostilities in 1946 and preferably who had left Soviet control within the last year (1950–51). Their value as sources of recent information so far offset any other consideration that it was decided to accept *all* postwar respondents regardless of whether or not they threw our ideal sample design out of balance. The design also failed of fulfillment because certain types of people were extremely scarce in the Soviet emigration, and in some instances presumably in the Soviet population (for example, women skilled workers, or students beyond a certain age). Others, especially women of rural background, were extremely reluctant to face a personal interview of great length. In time we could have located sufficient people in every category, but under the field conditions we faced we often had to take people from the more "populous" categories simply because they were available and our interviewers waiting. For this combination of reasons, there is a considerable imbalance in the number of cases in the various categories of the interview sample. Nevertheless, the utilization of a "model" sample design did serve to make the selection more efficient and, within the limitations of the considerations just mentioned, minimized the maldistribution of cases.

The problem of sample selection for the written questionnaire was quite different. The cost of administration of each questionnaire was small, providing that this administration could be done on a sufficiently large scale to keep down the overhead involved in securing respondents and supervising the filling out of the questionnaires. Therefore, it was decided to administer as many as possible wherever large concentrations of respondents were available. No attempt was made to reject people in any category providing they met the general criteria for inclusion in our sample. By and large it seemed more economical to secure an excess number of respondents in some categories than to become involved in elaborate administrative machinery for preselecting them. It became immediately clear, however, that we were running a danger of not getting a sufficient number of respondents of very low education, since the burden of six to eight hours of reading and writing on the questionnaire discouraged many of them. Despite aid which was provided for illiterates and semiliterates, and special efforts which were made to recruit such respondents, they are nevertheless proportionately poorly represented in the questionnaire sample. Their numbers, however, are adequate for most types of analysis.

Still leaving aside for the moment the question of sample bias, which will be discussed in the immediately succeeding pages, the main question concerning the adequacy of our sample is whether or not we have sufficient numbers of persons in various categories to permit us to make meaningful statements about subgroups within our sample. There is obviously no simple criterion for a "sufficient number," since the adequacy of the size of any subsample will depend on the degree of rigor which one insists on in evaluating statistical results, the magnitude of differences between subgroups, and the amount of additional information that can be brought to bear in assessing any one statistical result.

Table 2 summarizes the distribution of both our interview and ques-

TABLE 2 [A]

AGE, SEX, AND SOCIAL CLASS DISTRIBUTION OF SAMPLE

	Men				Women			
	Under		Over	Total respond-	Under		Over	Total respond-
Social class	31	31–45	45	ents	31	31–45	45	ents
Part 1: WRITTEN QUESTIONNAIRES								
Intelligentsia	68	159	133	360	89	86	72	247
White-collar employees	43	129	201	373	62	102	101	265
Skilled workers	43	136	53	232	6	13	9	28
Ordinary workers	92	157	102	351	48	34	21	103
Collective farm peasants	76	123	72	271	41	27	7	75
Students	23	5	0	28	30	1	0	31
Other	3	15	12	30	1	5	7	13
Total respondents	348	724	573	1645	277	268	217	762
Part 2: PERSONAL (LIFE-HISTORY) INTERVIEWS								
Intelligentsia	11	47	29	87	11	9	7	27
White-collar employees	8	13	12	33	8	10	9	27
Skilled workers	7	18	9	34	0	1	0	1
Ordinary workers	26	18	6	50	6	4	5	15
Collective farm peasants	11	8	8	27	3	3	6	12
Other	9	2	1	12	3	1	0	4
Total respondents	72	106	65	243	31	28	27	86

tionnaire samples by age, sex, and the social group with which they are identified. A first glance at this table shows that despite our goal of an even distribution of cases in the various categories there is, for reasons referred to above, a marked unevenness in this distribution. This is less evident in the interview sample, but is noticeable even there. Nevertheless, in the questionnaire sample in particular, there are in most instances adequate numbers of persons in each subgroup to permit meaningful statistical comparisons. Apart from the obvious fact that there are few students over thirty, the smallest number in a single category is six female skilled workers, thirty years of age or under. The total number of female skilled workers in the questionnaire sample is only twenty-eight and there is only one in the interview sample. Therefore this is a group about which we cannot say much except that female skilled workers appear to be scarce either in the emigration or the Soviet population, or both.

It must be remembered, however, that we are seldom concerned with individual categories, as refined as those by which this table is organized. In most instances, our knowledge of the data makes it possible to combine cases within at least one of the variables by which they are separated in the table. Staff studies of the relation of such factors as age, sex, and social group membership to the various questions in which we are interested afford this knowledge. The reader will notice in succeeding chapters that except for the more complicated analyses requiring simultaneous control of several variables, we seldom have less than a hundred questionnaire cases in each of the major categories with which we are dealing. There are, of course, instances in which the complexity of analysis reduces the number of cases in some categories even below those found in this basic table. Such analyses have been pursued, and conclusions drawn from them, only when there are such strong trends in the data that they persist in the face of the handicap of small numbers.

The interview sample, by virtue of its overall size of 329 cases, is by no means as adequate for statistical analysis as is the questionnaire sample. The main burden of statistical evidence in this study therefore lies with the questionnaire sample. The interview schedule, however, often provides data not available on the written questionnaire. Some of the trends which are revealed in such data are of such strength that they would meet rigorous criteria of statistical significance despite the small numbers involved. In other instances they are bolstered directly or indirectly by information from both our data and outside sources of information. There are, of course, still other instances in which, despite the interesting nature of statistical patterns in the interview data, the conclusions which we attempt must be regarded as very tentative. Finally, the interviews provide us with a good deal of qualitative information, which must be evaluated not by criteria of statistical significance, but on its coherence with other sources of information and its inherent plausibility.

There is never any simple answer to the question of the adequacy of the size of any subsample as a basis for drawing conclusions about some parent population. Therefore, the reader will discover throughout this book that various combinations of criteria are invoked for assessing the firmness with which a proposition may be put forth. The main point we wish to stress here is that our sample, especially that for the written questionnaire, had a sufficient number of cases in the appropriate age, sex, and social group categories to support the type of analysis ordinarily undertaken in survey research.

The Problem of Sample Bias

Obviously one of the most important questions that must be asked of data derived from Soviet émigrés is the relationship of the sample to the population from which it was drawn. The ideal most social science research has sought to attain is a random sample, free from selective bias, and representative of the "parent" population in such a way that the characteristics of the sample may within certain specified limits of error be projected directly onto the larger population. Perhaps we are taking liberties in applying the word "sample" to our respondents, even in a loose sense of the word. The technical usage of the word "sample," and even the ordinary dictionary definition, contains an implication of representativeness — precisely the issue under discussion. However, we know of no more neutral way of describing our group of respondents without resorting to elaborate and cumbersome circumlocution.

In general the disposition of social scientists in recent years has been to question offhand any inferences based on a sample which might be suspected of any systematic bias. In the case of our sample, however, we were in difficulty on two counts. In the first place, it was impossible to evaluate how representative it was of the total refugee population since there was no way of knowing the composition of that group. In the second place, we were faced with the necessity of assuming that Soviet émigrés were almost certainly selectively different from the remainder of the Soviet population by virtue of the fact that they ran away from the Soviet system, or at least decided not to return to it. It was, of course, only because the refugees were beyond Soviet control that we had any "sample" of the Soviet population at all. Even in the relatively relaxed atmosphere of the post-Stalin era it does not seem conceivable that Western scholars will soon be permitted to draw a random sample directly from the Soviet populace.

Since we could not define what would be representative of the refugee population as a whole, we concentrated instead on getting substantial representation from all the major subdivisions we knew to characterize the refugee community. This had the further advantage, of course, of fitting in with our analysis plan, which stressed the exploration of similarities and differences between major subgroups of the population. The sample characteristics already mentioned, such as the substantial representation of women as well as men, of all categories and all levels of occupation and education, serve in part to demonstrate that we were drawing on all elements of the refugee community. The same point can be made about other social characteristics of the sample to be noted below, such as its nationality composition. Finally, we may note that a number of factors specific to refugee status were well represented. These include the wide range of political affiliations and the geographical dispersion of the camps cited in our first chapter.[1] Other important differentiations within the refugee community such as that between wartime and postwar escapees, and between those located in Europe as against those who had reached the United States were also taken into account. These subdivisions of our sample are more fully discussed below.

Since our sample can in no event be deemed representative of the Soviet population, the crucial question is whether or not it is possible to draw valid inferences from such a presumably biased sample, and, if so, what limitations there are on such inferences. Any sample of former Soviet citizens will be fundamentally different from the Soviet population from which it was drawn, and therefore unrepresentative of it in some sense. On the other hand, any sample, no matter how drawn, shares certain features with the parent population. We should like, therefore, to affirm here a principle that underlies all of our use of this data. The question of the importance of sample bias can be answered only in the context of the specific type of analysis which is made, and the specific inferences which are drawn.

This point is so fundamental we must digress for a moment to illustrate. Our sample must be assumed to be *more* anti-Soviet than the parent Soviet population.* Hence, if we were to project directly on to the Soviet population the degree of hostility which our respondents express toward the Soviet leaders we would be on very poor ground. On the other hand, when, as happens to be the case, a minimum of 80 per cent of the persons in almost any category of our sample indicates approval of state ownership of heavy industry, we feel warranted in assuming that this institution finds strong support in the Soviet population, since we are reasonably certain that any bias in our sample would tend

---

* Terms like "anti-Soviet sentiment," "hostility to the regime," and "hostility to the Soviet system," are not always used in a restricted and technical sense, as they are in the opinion indices discussed below, and the meaning in each instance should be clear from the context.

to suppress the expression of pro-Soviet sentiments. Some scholars have raised the question of whether our respondents might be pro-Soviet in bias on the basis of nostalgia. Surprisingly, this question turns out to be reasonable for certain topical areas. Our respondents did show a good deal of nostalgia for "the Russian people" and "Russian culture" (if they were not members of minor nationalities). In addition, after meeting the costs of medical care out of their own pockets, the refugees interviewed in the United States seemed stimulated to describe the Soviet socialized medical care system in exaggeratedly glowing terms when compared with the description given by those interviewed in Germany. But this was definitely an exception. It was extremely rare for our respondents to allow their nostalgia for home to bias them in the direction of giving us exaggeratedly pro-Soviet evaluations of any specifically *Soviet* institutions.

The question of hostility to the regime further enables us to illustrate the extent to which our ability to make inferences follows from our main mode of analysis, namely the comparison of subgroups in the population. We have already indicated that we would not attempt to assert on the basis of our sample anything precise about the *absolute* degree of hostility to the regime found in the Soviet population or in any particular group. But what of the relative degrees of hostility in groups within our sample? We find that there is a consistently stronger expression of anti-Soviet sentiment among the lower socio-economic groups. Not only does this hold on a wide variety of issues, but there is a steady and generally unbroken progression from one social class to another, with each successively "higher" social class exhibiting less marked sentiments of hatred for the regime. We accept as a point of departure that the strength of anti- Soviet sentiment expressed by the members of each social group is probably stronger than that of their counterparts remaining in the Soviet Union. It is reasonable to assume that whatever selective factors account for the anti-Soviet bias of our sample operate relatively uniformly on all the subgroups in our sample, and that comparable groups in the Soviet population will stand in the same *relationship* to each other as do the members of our sample. It would, therefore, take a very tortured set of assumptions concerning the differential impact of sample bias on each of our subgroups to cause us to exhibit major hesitation about the main conclusion to be derived from these data, namely that the lower classes are *relatively* more categorical in their opposition to the regime than are the upper classes.

Having stated with some emphasis our contention that the question of sample bias can be considered only in the context of specific analysis problems, we turn now to a fuller discussion of sample characteristics which could have a direct bearing or effect on our findings. We have already noted that we did not desire or attempt to develop a sample that was "representative" of the Soviet population in its general composition. What we wanted was a sample which provided a sufficient number of cases in relevant categories to permit fruitful analyses to be made. Meeting this goal, however, gave us no assurance that the respondents who fell in our various "typical" cells or categories were not otherwise and as a whole so peculiar that they could not be considered reliable sources of information. In other words, are not the refugees so unusual a group of people, so "deviant" in Soviet society as to be like their compatriots still at home only perhaps in being Russians, or Ukrainians, etc., of given sex and age, but otherwise totally different kinds of people? This is, of course, a very serious challenge. One simple way of approaching it is to pose and answer a series of the questions about the refugee group most commonly put to us by scholars and lay audiences to whom we have described our work.

The most common assumption about Soviet refugees is that they are a highly homogeneous rather than a broadly representative group, and in particular are alike in being mainly holdovers from the old tsarist regime, rejected people who could find no place in the new Soviet society. One test of the diversity of background among the refugees has already been indicated in the class composition of our sample. In particular the written questionnaire, for which we made no selection of respondents, but rather tried to include whole camps, came by chance to include 24 per cent from the intelligentsia, 25 per cent from the white collar employee group, 10 per cent of skilled workers, 18 per cent whose class identification was that of ordinary worker, and 14 per cent who considered themselves collective farm peasants,* 2 per cent who were students and 7 per cent who could not be classified.

Although it is apparent that all *Soviet* social groups were well represented in the emigration, it might still be true that in *origin* they were descended mainly from disfranchised prerevolutionary groups, in particular from those elite social classes who suffered most from the Revolution. However, a study of the social origins of our respondents showed that less than one fourth of their fathers were members of the so-called "exploiting" or "enemy" classes — the nobility, landowners, merchants, middle class, clergy and the tsarist military. It is a striking fact that the proportion of respondents' fathers who belonged to the "exploiting" classes *is quite close to the proportion which those groups constituted in the total Russian population in the period just preceding the revolution.*

Official Soviet sources describe the composition of the total population

* Throughout we use the terms collective farmer and peasant interchangeably, except of course when the precollectivization period is referred to.

in 1913 as including 16 per cent "exploiting" classes, 17 per cent workers and employees (presumably including the intelligentsia), and 68 per cent peasants.[2]

Now, in our sample there is an exceedingly heavy representation of the intelligentsia and employees, and the members of those groups we know more often had fathers from an "exploiting" class background. This imbalance can be adjusted by weighting each of the groups in our sample to count only for the portion it constitutes in the parent Soviet population, then applying for each weighted subsample the observed rate at which it contributed fathers from the exploiting classes. When this is done, the representation of fathers of "hostile backgrounds" in our appropriately weighted sample is only about 15 per cent. This is almost the exact percentage constituted by such "alien" groups in the Russian population in 1913.

We were not quite so fortunate, however, in escaping an imbalance at the other end of the social scale. Among our respondents who were peasants by social origin, almost three fourths reported that they came from "dekulakized" families, that is, the presumably well-to-do peasants who had been repressed during the forced agricultural collectivization. This proportion is obviously many times that which can be assumed to exist among all peasants in the Soviet Union. By official Soviet definition a maximum of 10 per cent of all peasant households of the precollectivization period had been classed as *kulak*. Even if we acknowledge that the label kulak was liberally applied during collectivization, the proportion of kulak families so treated could scarcely have exceeded 25 per cent.

This disproportionate number of peasants of alleged kulak origin suggested that we investigate the differences between kulak and non-kulak peasants as a potential source of bias in our sample. The first result of this study was to reaffirm our faith in the data. For example, 50 per cent of the respondents whose fathers had been rich peasants and were later dekulakized said that during their childhood their family's material position had been better than average, whereas only 33 per cent of the respondents of ordinary peasant background gave this answer — a finding that is consonant with the known better material conditions of the kulaks before collectivization. Similarly, 56 per cent of the dekulakized reported that their social origin was a barrier to their getting as much education as they wanted in contrast with 27 per cent of the non-dekulakized. The regime did in fact restrict the educational opportunities of kulak children. These answers, therefore, indicated that those who asserted they came from a kulak peasant background indeed had more experience with the conditions of life we know to have been common for persons of their status. Our respondents who reported kulak origin then were probably the real thing. And, on issues about which we have knowledge from other sources, they reported experiences which fit with the known facts.

Such findings as those just mentioned reinforced our confidence in the data as a whole, but we were still faced with the question of whether on other issues such as attitudes toward and evaluation of the Soviet regime our kulak peasants were markedly different from those of persons whose families had not been dekulakized. Studies revealed that there was a persistent difference between the two groups, the dekulakized reporting themselves as more frustrated in their career aspirations, less satisfied in school and on the job, more opposed to Soviet institutions and more hostile to the regime. The difference was modest, however, generally not exceeding 10 per cent. While this difference is in itself of interest, its magnitude is so small in relation to other effects with which we were concerned that for most of our analyses all peasants could be grouped together. For example, the occupation, education or attained social position of the respondent, rather than his origins, were the prime determinants of the individual's life experiences and attitudes. A difference of the magnitude found between our two peasant groups would not have a significant effect on any of our major conclusions. Consider, for example, the data in Table 3, which compares the job satisfaction of those of peasant origin both according to their early home status as kulak or non-kulak and according to the occupation they attained. It is apparent that among those from kulak background there is somewhat less frequent acknowledgment that one's job was satisfying. But the differences in satisfaction between the children of dekulakized peasants and those who did not suffer that experience are minor indeed compared to the differences in satisfaction associated with attained occupational level regardless of social origin.

TABLE 3 [2A]

EFFECT OF KULAK ORIGINS ON JOB SATISFACTION:
BY OCCUPATION

Respondent's occupation	Status of respondent's parents			
	Dekulakized		Not dekulakized	
Nonmanual	54%	(82) [a]	57%	(49)
Worker	37	(170)	38	(68)
Peasant	10	(189)	15	(80)

a. Figures in parentheses represent the total number of respondents on the basis of which the percentage is computed.

Finally, we must note that the "warp" in the sample produced by overrepresentation of kulak origins among all of those of peasant origin, could not be a very great source of distortion among the total subsample of non-manually employed. Among professional, administrative and white collar personnel, those from both types of peasant origin together were no more than 18 per cent of the total. Among our subsample of ordinary workers, however, and of peasants, those whose origins were in dekulakized peasant homes were 32 and 64 per cent respectively. Since they were generally less happy and more hostile to the regime this may have had a consistent although modest effect on the reported opinion of the worker and peasant groups as a whole. We have at several points in our text, reported specific tests for such influence where it seemed most likely to make a difference.

Related to the often-made assertion that we saw too many of the holdovers from the old days is the possibility that we did not see enough of the new types who make up Soviet society. The wide range of occupational types, and the large proportion of people who were occupationally upward mobile, which we will note more fully below, indicate that this was probably not the case. Specifically with regard to political involvement in the system, however, we wish to point out that there were apparently more former Communist political activists in the emigration than is generally realized. There were many reasons why refugees would disguise their former political affiliations, most prominent being the fact that former membership in a Communist organization generally barred one from emigration to the United States. Considering this we feel it quite notable that nineteen of those who undertook the life-history interview admitted having been in the Communist Party, eleven as full members and the remaining eight as "candidate" members.[3] Sixty admitted they had been members of the Young Communist League (*Komsomol*). At the highest point of its development in the immediate postwar period the Communist Party had a total of about six million candidate and full members, who then constituted 3 per cent of the population of some two hundred million. The nineteen members we interviewed made up almost 6 per cent of our total sample. One should not make too much of these percentages, since our total sample obviously contained only adults, and included a disproportionately large number of better educated professional and semiprofessional people who are more likely to be drawn into the party. Nevertheless, when we allow for the pressures to concealment of such membership, it certainly seems not unreasonable to conclude that the rate of Communist Party affiliation among the refugees may not be far from that in comparable groups in the Soviet population for the period in question. Of course, the fact that party members are a very small proportion of every social class means that their underrepresentation in a sample would still not greatly affect the average opinion or expression for the group as a whole. Nevertheless, we were pleased to find that even in this respect, where common sense might lead one to expect very few Communists, the refugee groups proves a much less biased sample than many believe it to be.[4]

Another challenge frequently raised is that Soviet émigrés are mainly persons who were malcontents or underprivileged in Soviet society. There are several answers to this question.

Soviet émigrés left the Soviet Union under a variety of circumstances, and with diverse reasons for not returning. Both the testimony of our respondents, and other sources of information such as captured German documents and the statements of German personnel associated with these events, indicate that a very large proportion of Soviet émigrés left their homeland under very substantial duress. In one not atypical instance, a young woman collective farmer told us that she volunteered to go to Germany as an Ostarbeiter as a substitute for her father so that he might remain behind to care for her younger brothers and sisters. Many of the former Red Army men described fighting the Germans with all their strength up to the moment of capture. It is doubtful that there should be large-scale conscious falsification in these accounts, since at the time the interviews were conducted our respondents were all aware of the fact that the sympathy of Americans could best be enlisted by asserting that one had always been irrevocably opposed to Communism and anxious to flee the USSR. In our questionnaire sample, 16 per cent of our respondents reported that they had been taken prisoners of war, 4 per cent indicated they were "deserters" from the Red Army, 43 per cent said they were forcibly evacuated from the USSR by the Germans, and only 37 per cent claimed to have left the Soviet Union voluntarily with the retreating German army. In other words, only 41 per cent of this sample claim to have left Soviet control voluntarily. Incidentally, the fact that we have in the sample large numbers both of persons who left voluntarily and of persons who left involuntarily, offers us a powerful tool of analysis, since it enables us to compare on many important issues persons who differed in the intensity of their reaction to the regime.

The reasons for not returning to the Soviet Union are similarly varied. Both the refugees and Americans who were connected with the repatriation of Soviet citizens after the war testify to this diversity of motives.[5] It seems quite clear that a large portion of those persons who remained in Western Europe would have preferred to return to the Soviet Union. Some feared punishment for actual collaboration with the Nazis. Others, having been captured or evacuated forcibly by the Nazis, were caught in a web of circumstances which they feared would place them under suspicion. Reports by émigrés who were repatriated and later escaped, or

who observed the treatment of repatriates, indicate that these fears were
well founded. Nevertheless, even in 1950 and 1951, it was not unusual
for refugees to admit to Americans in whom they had confidence that
they would still like to return to their homeland if they could resume
their normal life. Two of our respondents, even while being interviewed
by us, were in the process of arranging to be repatriated. The reasons for
wanting to return were not, of course, love of Stalinism, but rather a
desire to live under familiar conditions, among a people whose culture
they shared. Indeed, such factors eventually yielded Soviet authorities
some successes in urging former Soviet nationals to return to their homeland.[6]

Perhaps no single popularly held belief about the Soviet émigrés is
more erroneous than the notion that they are people who were failures
in the Soviet system. It would not be relevant to judge their success in
the Soviet system by the status and occupation of our respondents as a
whole, since the methods of procuring the several samples produced a
disproportionate number of relatively highly placed persons. It is relevant, however, to ask how well our respondents fared, considering their
points of origin in the system. Did they do as well as other persons of
the same origins? There is no particular reason to suspect that our respondents would exaggerate how well they had fared under the Bolsheviks. Indeed there was good reason for them to play down their success
under the Communists. But even if we were to make a considerable allowance for the possibility of such exaggeration, it is obvious that our
respondents were, by and large, a successful group. Detailed evidence of
individual mobility will be presented in Chapter IV. For now we restrict
ourselves to a simple comparison of the overall occupational distribution
found among our respondents with that of their parents of the same sex.
It is apparent from Table 4 that the younger and hence more "Soviet"
generation represented by our sample was on the whole better placed
occupationally than was the generation represented by the fathers and
mothers of our respondents. In particular professional, administrative
and semiprofessional jobs are much more common among our respondents
than was true in their parents' generation.

It is true that these figures to a great extent reflect increased opportunities for mobility in an expanding industrial society, but in that
case they also indicate that those in our sample were not excluded from
a share in that general improvement. But beyond this, a staff study by
Robert Feldmesser demonstrates that the rate of mobility in this group
was greater than the theoretical maximum of the Soviet population as a
whole. These people, then, were *more* successful than the comparable Soviet citizens who remained in the USSR.[7]

An additional point on which the émigré populace is less one-sided

TABLE 4 [6A]

OCCUPATIONAL PLACEMENT OF OUR RESPONDENTS
COMPARED WITH THAT OF THEIR PARENTS: BY SEX

	Men		Women	
Occupation	Our respondents	Their fathers	Our respondents	Their mothers
Professional	21%	11%	18%	5%
Semiprofessional	9	6	17	21
White-collar employee	13	11	31	25
Worker	41	30	18	35
Peasant or collective farmer[a]	16	42	16	14
Total number of respondents	1397	1448	473	326

a. The older generation were peasants in the traditional sense, whereas our respondents identified themselves as collective farmers.

than is sometimes supposed is the extent to which they admit to have been supporters of the Soviet regime at one time. About 30 per cent of our questionnaire sample indicated that they were "once in favor of the regime." Again, if we consider the strong situational pressures that our respondents were under to affirm their eternal, implacable hatred of the Soviet order, these figures suggest a considerable proportion of the refugees were at one time quite loyal citizens of the Soviet regime rather than lifelong enemies.

Perhaps they were "personality problems," people who were fairly normal in all the respects mentioned above, but who were psychically unstable, and therefore more likely to flee their homeland? So runs another of the questions commonly raised about the refugee group. The variety of conditions under which they left the Soviet system in itself indicates that they cannot be considered a homogeneous group of psychologically maladjusted persons. The general impression which members of the interviewing team had of the émigrés was that they were, by and large, "normal" people despite the difficulties of their existence as displaced persons. Drs. Beier and Hanfmann[8] who administered and analyzed the clinical psychological interviews concluded that 70 per cent of their respondents displayed good or adequate adjustment. The remaining 30 per cent who were judged maladjusted is perhaps a somewhat higher proportion than one would expect in an ordinary "average" group of that size. This disproportion was, however, predominantly attributable to one group which demonstrated a markedly higher degree of maladjustment. These were the postwar refugees. Only an extremely small portion of our

written sample, 57 out of more than 2700 persons, were postwar refugees, so that they could not affect any of the statistical conclusions
reached on that instrument. In the interview sample, however, they com-
prised more than a quarter of the total. For this reason we made a
special study to compare the responses of "matched" postwar with wartime refugees on a series of important topics.[9] As we shall see below,
there were no important differences in the way in which the two groups,
whatever their emotional adjustment, viewed and reported the Soviet
system.

The comparison of postwar refugees with wartime émigrés also answers another question that is often raised. It is said, and quite reasonably, that wartime émigrés last saw the Soviet system when it was shaken
by military defeats and suffering all the disadvantages and discomforts
of the impact of the war. We may presume, therefore, that in retrospect,
they see the system in a different perspective than do those people who
lived in it after the war ended in victory for the regime. Likewise, the
argument continues, the length of the time between leaving and being
interviewed will result in a considerable distortion of memory. On an *a
priori* basis there is every reason to believe that such factors would be
at work. Nevertheless, our staff study comparing postwar and wartime
refugees offers strong evidence that both groups have essentially the same
attitudes toward the Soviet system.

The study was done by matching fifty-one pairs of wartime and postwar émigrés on age, sex, and education, and comparing their answers in
several major attitudinal areas: assessment of strengths and weaknesses
of the Soviet regime; attitudes toward certain aspects of Soviet political,
social, and economic organization; opinions about the best forms of economic organization; position on civil liberties; images of mobility and of
leadership in the Soviet Union; and a few miscellaneous attitudes. It
will be seen from the representative findings given in Table 5 that there
are no consistent differences between the wartime and postwar émigrés,
although there are differences between the upper and lower educational
groups. There are some differences, but their pattern does not appear to
be systematic. As a matter of fact, the degree of similarity which the two
groups exhibit is all the more remarkable in view of the relatively small
number of cases.[10] The differences by education are invariably greater.

A comparable problem arose due to the high incidence of political
arrest those in our sample claimed to have experienced. Even though he
was "of good social origin," a well-adjusted devotee of the regime, and
doing well in his job, a person who had suffered at first hand from the
political terror might be expected to be unusually bitter and prone to
distort his memory of Soviet life. About a quarter of our sample reported
themselves arrested while living in the Soviet Union, and a still larger

TABLE 5 [10A]

SELECTED ATTITUDES:
BY TIME OF DEPARTURE
AND BY EDUCATIONAL LEVEL

Attitudes and Experiences	All educational levels[a]		All refugees	
	Wartime departure	Postwar departure	Low education[b]	High education[b]
Interests of Soviet intelligentsia and workers coincide	63% (35) [c]	62% (34)	52% (37)	69% (42)
Active Communists are most likely to get ahead	49 (45)	50 (40)	55 (38)	45 (47)
Had a chance for a career	35 (49)	42 (45)	27 (45)	49 (49)
In favor of freedom of political organization	51 (47)	45 (47)	33 (45)	61 (49)
Nothing reliable in Soviet press	31 (45)	18 (45)	37 (43)	13 (47)

a. The effect of differences in educational level between the two groups is controlled automatically by the original matching.

b. "Low" education includes all with zero through seven years of schooling; "high" education all with eight or more years.

c. Figures in parentheses represent total number of respondents in each cell on the basis of which the percentage is computed.

proportion had had some member of their family arrested. Approximately four out of five of all our respondents reported that either they or some member of their family had been arrested at some time. From any other population than the Soviet one, such a sample would be clearly and unequivocally deviant. In the Soviet population, however, the rate of political arrests has been extremely high and no one knows the average for the population. Nevertheless, it did seem that the rate of political arrests among our respondents and in their families was probably higher than for the population at large, and as a result another of our series of comparative studies was made.[11]

The results yielded were somewhat like those emerging from our study of dekulakized and non-dekulakized peasants. On basic social attitudes not specifically labelled Soviet or Communist those who had experienced arrest were indistinguishable from those who had not. For example, they were equal in their support of public ownership of heavy industry. The same was true of their images and assessments of the Soviet system. Thus, they were alike in their approval of the Soviet educational system, its socialized medicine and its guarantee of employment. As was true in the case of kulak peasant origins, the role of arrest experience with regard to almost all such questions was minor compared to the influence of one's education or occupation. For example, Table 6 summarizing the respondents' estimations of the reliability of the Soviet press reveals that exposure to arrest is in no way correlated with our respondents' attitudes, while education appears to have a great deal of effect, accounting for differences of up to 58 per cent.

TABLE 6 [11A]

PER CENT SAYING "NOTHING RELIABLE" IN SOVIET PRESS:
BY ARREST EXPERIENCE AND EDUCATION

Arrest experience	Education		
	0–4 years	5–10 years	Some college
Respondent arrested	70% (126) [a]	39% (129)	16% (134)
Family arrested	60 (250)	36 (500)	18 (253)
Neither arrested	75 (79)	38 (134)	17 (59)

a. Total number of respondents on the basis of which the percentage is computed.

It should be said at this point that certain aspects of the impact of arrest on our respondents came to us as a surprise, and in fact were stubbornly resisted for some time. We found it hard to believe that the experience of having been arrested or of having a member of one's family arrested would not have a profound effect on the full range of one's political and social thinking. For this reason, several members of the staff attempted at various times to punch holes in our findings. Despite these efforts to prove ourselves wrong, we eventually came to accept the conclusion that although arrest affected one's hostility toward things specifically Soviet, prejudiced somewhat his job chances, and increased the probability of his fleeing the Soviet Union voluntarily, it had virtually no effect on his generalized political and social attitudes, for example, his notions of the type of society he would like to live in and a host of related questions. This does not mean, of course, the people who had not experienced arrest were in *all* respects similar to those who had experienced an arrest either personally or to a member of their family. There were differences in sex, degree of administrative responsibility associated with one's job, hostility toward things explicitly Soviet, and tendency to report that one had (or had not) left Soviet jurisdiction voluntarily.

This meant that in our investigations of general political and social attitudes arrested and nonarrested persons could be treated as one. On other issues, however, we had to distinguish between them. As a matter of fact, this distinction became one of the main foci of a portion of our analysis.[12]

We may mention one last charge of unrepresentativeness which is made against the refugees as a potential sample, namely that they are mainly people from the fringe areas of the Soviet Union and do not really speak for the hard core of Great Russians who are assumed to make up the main support of the system. We should point out, in this connection, that there was a vast pool of potential refugee informants we did not tap for precisely this reason. Only those who had been living in the Soviet Union either since its formation or since their birth were included in our sample. Thus, we explicitly excluded those people from the Baltic states and those from Western Ukrainian areas who lived as Soviet citizens for only a short period following Soviet annexation of their home territories during World War II. Even with this exclusion the fact that the German occupation involved predominantly the Ukraine meant that a disproportionately large segment of the refugee sample was Ukrainian by nationality. Although definitely a minority in our total sample, the fact that they account for 35 per cent of our respondents gave them twice the weight in our sample they had in the Soviet home population according to the prewar 1939 census.

Again we undertook a detailed study to assess the possible biasing effects of this large Ukrainian minority. Since these and other aspects of the nationality problem are dealt with at length in Chapter XV, we will only say here that there are certainly some hard feelings between Ukrainians and Russians as national groups, and they see the *nationality* problem differently. But with regard to most of the questions which are the central concern of this book, especially life experiences, values, and political attitudes, a Ukrainian lawyer or doctor is much more like a Russian lawyer or doctor than he is like a Ukrainian peasant. This holds true for literally hundreds of questions on our many instruments. Tables 94 to 96 in Chapter XV show such homogeneity of attitudes between Ukrainians and Russians on several questions, accompanied by large differences among those of different social class.

Summary

In many respects, Soviet émigrés are less categorically unlike the Soviet population than has popularly been supposed. At the same time, there are selective differences between our sample and what we know or assume to be true of the Soviet population. The most obvious of these is, of course, their status as political refugees outside the Soviet environment. Associated with this are elements of possible bias such as origin in disfranchised classes, extensive experience of political arrest, and over-representation of the oppressed national minorities. These elements might be classified as "accidents" of the person's life history, determined by birth or chance. Even getting the chance to choose refugee status was something of an accident depending on whether or not you were swept out of Soviet territory by the tides of war. Such aspects of life history can be contrasted with other less special personal characteristics, such as "position" in the social structure as defined by occupation, education, or social class.

Our examination of the impact of the "accidents" of the life history on the individual's basic beliefs about the socio-economic order, and on his evaluation of the specific features of the Soviet system (as distinguished from its leadership), indicates they have only modest effect. By contrast the few glimpses we have had of the positional factors hints that they are extremely important. This is a point of major significance about our findings, and one of great importance in understanding the Soviet Union in its character as not only a totalitarian state but also a large-scale industrial society. This theme will therefore be a recurring one in our analysis.

At this point, however, we restrict ourselves to its implications for the generalizability of the conclusions we derive from our biased sample. We cannot match our sample to the parent population on most of the accidents of life history, since we do not know the distribution of such experiences in the Soviet Union. In any event, the relative saturation of our sample with regard to some of these experiences, such as arrest, could be a serious limitation on analysis of subgroup differences if proved to have a large independent influence on experience or attitude. Consequently, if these factors were major determinants of opinion and experience we would be in grave doubt as to how many still in the USSR could possibly be having similar opinions and experiences. Fortunately the factors which account for a person's becoming a refugee and entering our sample do not seem to be the ones which primarily determine his attitudes and his report of his experiences under Soviet conditions. These seem determined more by social characteristics, such as occupation, which the refugees share with groups still inside the USSR. We can therefore more easily relate the subgroups in our sample to subgroups inside the Soviet Union on the important "positional" factors of occupation, education and social class. We should do so, of course, only with caution and circumspection. Although our sample differs from the parent Soviet population much less than we might ordinarily expect, we cannot safely minimize the differences which do exist. Recognition of these differences and knowledge of their significance makes them a valuable tool for analysis, whereas if they are ignored they are a potential source of major un-controlled error.

III

Some Considerations of Method and Methodology

The problem of sample bias, discussed in the latter section of Chapter II, is one of whether or not we interviewed "the right people." The problem of response bias is one of whether or not our respondents (begging the question of whether or not they were "the right people") "told us the truth." The related problems of response and sample bias are largely separable, and for that reason we are treating them independently. As we shall see, however, they are also somewhat overlapping, and it will be necessary on occasion to refer back to some of the points made in the discussion of sample bias.

The Problem of Response Bias

Typical phrasings of the problem of response bias are: "How do you know they weren't telling you just what you wanted to hear?" "After all, they're against the system, how can you expect them to give you a true picture of it?" "Even if they tried their best, wouldn't you expect them to give you a distorted picture after all they went through?"

Like the question of sample bias, that of response bias is a real and meaningful one. Yet it tends also to become oversimplified when stated in its usual fashion. The myth of the "true answer" is one that is fairly well discarded by all sophisticated researchers. It is recognized that there is a multiplicity of determinants for what a person says in *any* situation. Even the most "factual" of information can be reported "unreliably." Suppose a market researcher wanted to find out what color neckties a random sample of men were wearing on a given day, and he were making a survey via telephone. His interviewer simply asks the man on the other end of the phone what color necktie he is wearing. In most instances the interviewer may accept the answer with confidence. The interviewer will be more confident if she asks the man to look at his necktie first. But, suppose he has just been arguing with his wife to the effect that he *did* put on his green necktie (actually it was the beige one that he wore). The chances are that he will repeat the error in answering the interviewer, since he now has an emotional commitment to the proposition that he put on a green tie, and is unlikely to check this judgment by taking a new look at it. Or, he may be color blind and not be able to answer the question. Or, he may use different color categories than the interviewer, calling the tie brown, tan, or dirty yellow, when it is actually beige. Perhaps he thinks the question is silly, or he resents the imposition on his time, and therefore he gives a deliberately false answer. Or, perhaps he thinks that there is a certain amount of prestige attached to a particular tie pattern, and his unconscious plays him tricks and he gives "false" information.

The above example may seem facetious. Yet it is a fair representation of the difficulties of eliciting the most obvious of information under the seemingly most simple of circumstances. The entire doctrine of social science interviewing and questioning is based on the explicit premise that the response which a person makes to a question *may* be consciously or unconsciously biased by virtue of the relationship of the person answering the question to the situation in which the question is asked. And, in making this assumption, the social scientist is adopting the same attitude toward his source of information that the historian does in evaluating a document, or the economist in his assessment of the statistics he uses. All this is no more than to say that the problems of acquiring information by interviewing émigrés may be somewhat distinctive and acute, but they are continuous with the problems of all interviewing, and in fact with all problems of data gathering and evaluation.[1]

However, to say that our problems are not distinctive does not argue them away. It is the purpose of this chapter to indicate the usual and unusual problems we faced, and the ways in which we dealt with them.

We have contended that the question of *sample* bias must be thought of from the point of view of the type of analysis being done, and the inferences made. The same is true of *response* bias. Just as we assumed that our sample was selectively weighted toward persons who by virtue of their life experience were strongly anti-Soviet, so we may for the moment assume that our respondents would put their most anti-Soviet foot forward because their interviewers were Americans. In other words, both sample and response bias would be reinforcingly anti-Soviet. Consequently, when we find that 78 per cent stressed the "harm" that Lenin did the Russian people as against 7 per cent who stressed the "good"[2] we certainly are not led to assume that any such ratio would exist among people inside the Soviet Union. On the other hand, when we find that a minimum of four out of five persons in each social group favors state ownership of heavy industry, an acknowledgment of these sources of bias only reinforce our assumption that such institutions find strong support in the Soviet populace. These examples illustrate the extent to which the problem of response bias must ultimately be handled in the process of analysis, and depends on a sufficient knowledge of the sample, of other of our findings, and of the interview situation. We cannot pass the last example, however, without pausing to tell the reader that he will note at many points that our respondents' answers lie in a direction counter to *American* values. This gives one general assurance that our respondents were not biasing their answers in the direction of what they thought Americans wanted to hear; or at least that they had no set fixed image of what Americans wanted, and therefore could not bias their answers systematically.

Before passing on to a more detailed consideration of our approach to these data, we may comment briefly on a particular problem that throws light on the notion of the "true answer." There was no reason whatsoever to doubt our respondents' sincerity in their expressions of anti-Soviet sentiment. In some areas we were quite surprised that expressions of anti-Soviet sentiment were not stronger. But in other areas it was obvious that we had to phrase questions in such a way as to make permissible and natural the expression of what might have seemed, from some points of view, to be pro-Soviet sentiments. This decision in itself brings into somewhat clearer focus the question of what is a "true answer." It was obvious that our respondents were "truly anti-Soviet." However, in the instances in question we were interested in the differentiations and distinctions which they would make within the framework of the generally anti-Soviet answers, and we were handicapped when certain words or phrases produced such global undifferentiated responses that it was not possible to detect shadings which might legitimately exist.

In one instance, we were interested in our respondents' attitudes toward child rearing in the Soviet Union. Informal conversations had revealed that Soviet émigrés had very definite ideas about how children should be raised, and that to some extent they felt that this was done successfully in the Soviet Union (this, despite the regime). Direct questioning brought a flood of statements about the negative aspects of child rearing in the Soviet Union — political interference via the school system, poor material conditions, etc. However, it was difficult to get at the positive aspects. Asked directly, the question was rejected flatly in the majority of instances. "There were no positive aspects." However, it was also known that Soviet émigrés had strong feelings against some of the ways in which Germans reared their children. Therefore, respondents were asked to evaluate the relative merits of raising children in Germany and in the Soviet Union. This form of the question produced answers which gave a more detailed picture of the aspects of Soviet child rearing which they favored.

In such instances it should be noticed that the problem with which we were faced was not that we would be misled by the "biased" answers of the respondents, since we were well aware of the strength of their sentiments on these issues. The difficulty was rather that the strength of their attitudes was such that differentiations within attitude areas was suppressed by their tendency to give all-or-none responses. Hence, the intent of rewording questions to offset response bias in these instances was to make possible analyses which could not otherwise be carried out.

Nevertheless, we could not at every point feel so confident of our ability to assess the relation between tendencies to distortion and our conclusions. We therefore made a major effort to identify those who might be guilty of one or both of two main types of response bias: (1) flattery, especially in the form of giving answers the Americans would especially like to hear, and (2) distortion, in the form of recasting one's actual attitudes or experiences so as to give the blackest possible picture of Soviet conditions. It was with these goals in mind that our associates from the Columbia University Project developed two instruments, labelled the indices of "flattery" and of "distortion," respectively.*

The index of flattery consisted of a series of 4 questions, certain answers to which made for exaggeratedly favorable statements about Americans.

1. Is it true that sometimes the Americans have acted unfairly against Europeans who have settled in the United States?
2. Some American newspapers reported that the Americans did not forcibly repatriate a single DP (Displaced Person) who did not want to return. Are these reports true?
3. Some people say that Americans are more intelligent than Europeans. Do you agree?
4. We have asked you many questions concerning Soviet life. Since we may be able to change some of the questions in the future, we would like to know whether you think we have asked the best possible questions to learn about the Soviet Union or whether the questions could be improved.

We assume that a person who answered a high proportion of these questions in the exaggeratedly favorable direction would do so only if he were consciously trying to flatter the American scholars involved in the Project.

The distortion index consisted of a number of factually correct statements about the Soviet Union with which most Soviet citizens would presumably be familiar, but which might in their minds reflect favorably on the Soviet system. We assumed that the respondent's objectivity

---

* The precise components of the index scores and their distribution in the sample are described in Appendices 14 and 11, respectively. We wish to express our particular indebtedness to Mr. Lee Wiggins of the staff of the Bureau of Applied Social Research at Columbia University for his aid in the development of these measures.

would be put to the test if he granted the correctness of these statements despite the fact that doing so put him in a position of acknowledging ostensibly favorable things about the Soviet Union.

1. Does the present day Soviet citizen have more opportunity to visit the theater and attend concerts than 30 years ago?
2. Was medical care more accessible when you left the Soviet Union than 25 years ago?
3. Was the production of agricultural machinery higher when you left the Soviet Union than 25 years ago?
4. Do you think that during the last 30 years the number of literate people in the USSR has increased significantly?

A statistical analysis of the answers to these two indices indicated that each did in fact touch some coherent attitude dimension, and that the two indices were relatively independent of each other. In other words, each measured "something," and they measured something different. Guttman reproducibility coefficients of .89 and .97 were obtained for the "flattery" and "distortion" indices respectively.

The number who gave "flattering" or "distorted" answers was generally gratifyingly low. Less than 4 per cent of the entire sample "distorted" on all four items on the distortion scale, and about half gave no distorting answers whatsoever. Since some of the "flattery" responses were highly plausible, the total number of "flattering" responses was somewhat higher. However, only 7 per cent of the entire sample gave the "flattering" responses on all four items, and 48 per cent gave only two or less. In fact, the great bulk of all flattering responses was given to one question, that on the treatment of Europeans who had settled in the United States. About two thirds "flattered," that is, disagreed with the statement. This disagreement may have been so common because the refugees, most of whom hoped to emigrate to the United States, were probably actively trying to persuade *themselves* that life would indeed be good when they got to the land of their dreams. By contrast, only 22 per cent of our respondents gave the flattering response by agreeing that our questions were the best possible.

If these two indices are taken at their face value, they indicate minimally that the tendency to "flatter" by *consistently* giving answers agreeable to Americans, or to "distort" by *consistently* presenting a consciously slanted image of the Soviet system, certainly did not characterize more than a very small part of our sample. Beyond this it is difficult to go in evaluating the proportion who received less than an extreme score on these indices, since almost everyone could rather understandably be expected to find something he could agree or disagree with among the statements we presented. The ultimate test of the indices lay in the expected association between the scores people received on them and their responses to questions which might be biased by a tendency to flatter or distort. Indeed, one of the basic motivations behind the construction of the two indices was our desire thus easily and quickly to separate the sheep from the goats. These indices were, therefore, run against dozens and dozens of other items in our questionnaire.

The results of our test of the flattery index were "disappointing," in the sense that no consistent, significant pattern of association emerged between a person's score on the index and a tendency to give seemingly biased answers on questions relating to the person's experience in or attitude toward the Soviet system (Table 7). Note, for example, that in this table in all five social groups, those high on "flattery" more often favor state control of light industry — an answer that is scarcely calculated to please "free enterprise" Americans. However, the "high flatterers" were less likely to favor state control of *heavy* industry. It is difficult to find a consistent pattern of "flattery" in these data. Close study of the associations between the index scores and the individual's answers on a variety of other questions led us to conclude that the "flattery" index was best regarded as measuring the genuine expression of a diffusely favorable attitude toward America and things American which did not, however, influence consistently the way in which a person described the Soviet system or his own life in it. A perusal of Table 7 will show some instances in which "high flatterers" gave answers that Americans presumably "like to hear," but at least an equal number of instances that point in the opposite direction.

Actually, we attempted a frontal assault on the issue of "flattery." We reasoned that if a person were attempting to "flatter" us, he ought to incline his answers in a direction which he thought would be agreeable to us. Therefore, we included in our questionnaire something we may refer to as an "index of expectation." It consisted of asking the respondents what they thought Americans wanted on issues on which they had previously expressed their own opinions: state ownership of transportation and communications, job security, and freedom of political expression. It would not be either surprising or disturbing if the group *as a whole* were highly inclined to see Americans and themselves as wanting the same things. It is a normal matter for a person in such a situation — if he lacks specific information about the other person — to assume that the other person is pretty much like himself. This is a phenomenon of simple projection.

Suppose, however, that two persons thought Americans did not want state ownership of heavy industry, and they themselves favored state ownership. Then the one of them who (judged by the independent instru-

TABLE 7 [2A]

EFFECT OF FLATTERY SCORE ON ATTITUDES AND EXPERIENCES
OF SOVIET LIFE: BY CLASS

(Per cent holding each attitude)

Attitudes and experiences	Intelligentsia		White-collar employees		Skilled workers		Ordinary workers		Collective farm peasants	
	H [a]	L [a]	H	L	H	L	H	L	H	L
Once in favor of regime	29%	28%	25%	24%	36%	30%	38%	22%	39%	39%
State to control heavy industry	82	86	70	89	87	94	83	86	87	88
State to control light industry	38	22	30	22	37	33	51	41	57	43
Lenin did much harm	66	75	73	84	70	81	74	67	73	66
Satisfied with job	74	84	63	73	61	78	29	47	24	23
Median number	98	305	159	236	75	80	160	87	146	52

a. "H" indicates high flattery; "L" indicates low flattery.

ment of the "flattery index") was more inclined to say things pleasing to Americans would also be more inclined to bend his own expressed opinion closer to that which he attributed to Americans. This would be essentially the sort of "response bias" we were trying to locate.

That is to say, if our "flattery index" measured what it purported to, *and* if our respondents did have a fixed image of what Americans wanted, then we should expect our "high flatterers" to exhibit a higher association between their own expressed opinions and their expectations of what Americans wanted. While, as we shall point out soon, the existence of such a pattern of association would not in itself be proof of flattery as a source of bias, it would certainly cause us to take the question quite seriously.

A convenient, clear presentation of the statistical data bearing on this question has defied us for several years.[3] The conclusion, however, is clear. *All* respondents see Americans as thinking pretty much like themselves. In every instance this is somewhat more true of the "high flatterers." It might be concluded therefore that the phenomenon of "flattery" has been demonstrated in principle. However, the magnitude of the relationships which might be attributed to "flattery" are proportionately so small (about one sixth), in comparison to the influence of other variables we studied that so-called "flattery" has no practical significance as a means of data control.

Furthermore, as we have suggested already, the fact that the higher flatterers are more likely to show concurrence between their own opinions and their anticipation of the wishes of Americans can not be taken as conclusive evidence that they are biasing their answers toward the American norm. They may, in fact merely be excessively pro-American, and therefore more likely to assume that Americans are like themselves. Certainly, as preceding data have shown, high and low "flatterers" give about the same view of the Soviet system and have about the same attitudes on social and political questions, and this presumably ought to be the final test. The result of our exploration of the "flattery index" was that we concluded that on most of the questions in which we were interested our respondents did not have a clear image of what Americans wanted, and therefore it was impossible for them to bias their answers in such a direction.

Assessment of the meaning of the "distortion index" was somewhat more difficult. With "flattery" we could ask whether high and low "flatterers" gave a different picture of Soviet life, or if they were conspicuously disposed to give what they conceived to be pro-American answers. For the "distortion index," however, we had less clear criteria against which to judge it.[4] Certain patterns in our data, however, led us to the belief that this "distortion index" did not tap a disposition consciously to falsify facts, but rather represented a measure of diffuse anti-Soviet hostility. The following is an example of the sort of analysis that brought us to this conclusion.

In every social group those who had themselves been arrested by the secret police or had experienced the political arrest of some member of their family were much more likely to have a high score on the distortion index. On the basis of this single relationship one might well reason that reporting an arrest to one's self or a member of one's family was a "typical anti-Soviet distortion." If this interpretation were accepted then it would be difficult to explain such additional findings as these: (1) Within any broad occupational category those persons who reported that they had jobs with administrative responsibility were twice as likely as their nonadministrative peers to report having been personally arrested. What sort of tendency to "distort" in an anti-Soviet direction would produce a systematic tendency for respondents to claim they had administrative responsibility, particularly when undertaking administrative responsibility tended to be a relatively pro-Soviet act? (2) Men were many times more likely to report having been arrested themselves, while women were more likely to report that members of their families were arrested. These answers would indicate reinforcingly that the men were more likely to get arrested. On the other hand, it would take a rather tortured set of assumptions concerning masculine and feminine psychology to explain these answers as "anti-Soviet distortions." Findings like these led us to the conclusion that it was more reasonable to regard the "distortion index" as a measure of generalized anti-Soviet sentiment; and to accept relationships such as we have been discussing as evidence for causation in the direction being-arrested-makes-one-hostile.

There were other "opportunities to distort" which re-enforced our impression that the "distortion index" was solely a measure of "true" anti-Soviet sentiment and did not identify persons who were systematically slanting their answers. One of these opportunities to "distort" came in connection with the question about one's early attitude toward the Soviet system. If those with high distortion scores were really going out of their way to avoid telling the truth we might reasonably expect them to deny ever having thought well of the regime. This proves not to be the case. Although those with high scores on distortion are somewhat less likely to declare themselves as having once been in favor of the regime (Table 8), the differences in every social group except the intelligentsia are very modest. To admit having once been in favor of the regime ran counter to the dominant mores of the refugee community, and presumably exposed the person to rejection by the Americans.

This question was, therefore, the chance *par excellence* for those with high distortion scores to "distort." If this interpretation is put on the differences in Table 8 then we have little of practical significance to fear from systematic "distortion." Even among the intelligentsia, where the effects of "distortion" might appear to be most strong, the percentage of "high distorters" is extremely small (66 out of 560) and would not significantly affect any of our conclusions. However, such relationships as are observed in the table are interpretable on the equally plausible basis that "distortion" is a reflection of hostility to the Soviet order, and that more "hostile" people might in fact have been (though by this evidence to a very slight degree) initially less pro-Soviet.

A further direct test of this last assertion is permitted by the series of questions dealing with government ownership and control of transportation and communication, and heavy and light industry. In every social

TABLE 8 [4A]

PERCENTAGE OF RESPONDENTS "ONCE IN FAVOR"
OF SOVIET REGIME: BY DISTORTION SCORE
AND SOCIAL GROUP

Social group	Distortion score					
	High		Medium		Low	
Intelligentsia	15%	(66) [a]	26%	(94)	30%	(400)
White-collar employees	22	(97)	16	(149)	28	(353)
Skilled workers	39	(46)	41	(64)	40	(127)
Ordinary workers	33	(133)	22	(99)	37	(169)
Collective farm peasants	33	(109)	43	(74)	37	(119)

a. Total number of respondents on the basis of which the percentage is computed.

group those with higher distortion scores were to some degree less likely to support government ownership (Table 9). But the outstanding fact with regard to the issue of honesty is that even among those with high distortion scores the overwhelming majority — ranging from 70 to 80 per cent in the several social groups — admitted that they favored government ownership of heavy industry.

Such relationships as exist between "distortion" and attitude may well express a legitimate linkage between anti-Soviet sentiment and attitudes toward institutions associated with the Soviet order.[5] No matter what interpretation is put on this relationship, however, the data in no way support the notion that there was some identifiable group of respondents who were deliberately "stacking the cards," to the extent that they should be isolated for separate analyses.

To sum up our experience with the measurement of flattery and distortion, we found our sample to contain gratifyingly small numbers of those who showed an exaggerated preference for answers which would "please" Americans or who seemed to distort more or less obvious facts about the Soviet Union. Further study of those who were more inclined to "flatter" indicated that this did not lead them to slant their answers about their own lives or the Soviet system. Consequently, we make little further use of this measure. Those with high "distortion" scores also seemed honest about themselves and their opinions. The association between the distortion scores and other questions, however, strongly suggests that the score can be used as a simple device for discriminating those most hostile to the Soviet system and Communist leadership. We have therefore used it repeatedly in our analysis, but under the name

TABLE 9 [5A]

EFFECT OF DISTORTION RATING ON ATTITUDES TOWARD
GOVERNMENT OWNERSHIP AND CONTROL: BY SOCIAL GROUP

(Per cent holding each attitude)

	Social group									
	Intelli-gentsia		White-collar employees		Skilled workers		Ordinary workers		Collective farm peasants	
Attitudes	H [a]	L [a]	H	L	H	L	H	L	H	L
State should control heavy industry	70%	89%	70%	86%	80%	94%	78%	89%	80%	84%
State should own and control light industry	26	25	25	27	48	36	40	48	53	46
State should own and control transportation and communication	77	91	80	88	85	92	82	93	85	90
Median number of respondents	65	398	95	351	46	127	131	165	106	119

a. "H" indicates high distortion; "L" indicates low distortion.

"hostility rating" which we feel much more accurately reflects what the score actually measures.

An additional bit of evidence on the meaning of the "flattery" and "distortion" scales came out of a comparison of responses of persons administered the written questionnaire in America with those persons who filled out this instrument in Europe.[6] It was found that both "flattery" and "distortion" were less in the sample interviewed in the United States. This suggested that exposure to the United States had given them a more realistic picture of America and lessened somewhat their tendency to project all their wishes and hopes onto America as a sort of promised land. At the same time, facing up to the actual problems of adjusting to life in a new country they also became more realistic about the country they had left, and tended less to see the Soviet system in black and white. This interpretation is given substance by the fact that these shifts in attitude were considerably more marked among the lower educated groups, who presumably had less factual knowledge about America, and who, on other questions, showed a strong disposition to see things Soviet in an undifferentiated fashion.

Our conclusion then is that our "flattery" and "distortion" indices were primarily measures of pro-American and anti-Soviet sentiment expressed in a tendency to see things American in a good light, and things Soviet in a bad light. This does not mean, of course, that there was no slanting of answers, whatsoever, on the part of our respondents. We are quite certain, for example, that there were tendencies to hide certain sorts of political affiliations and activities. An interview — and even filling out of a questionnaire — is to varying degrees a situation of interaction, and it must be assumed that each party to this situation will attempt by things he says and does to influence the other person. The expression of pro-American and anti-Soviet sentiments by our respondents was one of the devices open to our respondents.

Our staff studies indicate that such practices were not widespread or of major importance. This finding is, of course, consoling. However, this does not absolve one of the necessity for continued vigilance concerning such sources of response bias as *do* exist. As with so many other of our methodological problems, the final responsibility lies with the analyst, and the reader will have to decide whether or not the analyst did his job well.

The Quality of the Data

Many people are of the opinion that the "special" nature of the Soviet refugees and their situation at the time we reached them made it possible to get "reliable" information on a personal, face-to-face interview, but rendered it most unlikely that their answers to a written questionnaire would be of any value. Since we use data from both our oral interviews and written questionnaires, and indeed place greatest reliance on the latter, we deemed it wise to learn in detail the extent to which these two methods yielded comparable data. As we mentioned earlier, 46 of the persons who undertook the oral interview in the United States also filled out the written questionnaire about a month later. A comparison of the two sets of responses of course reflects both the lapse of a month's time, during which people can of course change their minds, and the difference in response between a free interview later coded and a pre-coded questionnaire. Nevertheless, a comparison of these cases on an *individual* basis revealed that respondents virtually never changed their report of demographic data such as age, sex, education, and occupation, after a month's interval, but there were occasionally appreciable differences in the reporting of attitudes. The latter of course made sense, since over a period of a month, in fact, even over a much shorter period of time, a person might shift in his judgment as to what should be done with the Soviet leaders or what was good or bad in the Soviet system. A certain amount of shift of this sort is to be expected in any individual.[7] The crucial question is whether or not the two instruments, applied to the same population, would yield the same *distribution* of answers. The analyst's summary of the results as they apply to the opinion of the group as a whole is as follows:

[On] 28 commensurate questions . . . the stability of response was very high, [variations] averaging less than 2 per cent for demographic data, and rising only to an average of less than 8 per cent on regime hostility. Only 5 questions of 26 (2 were eliminated because of slight variations of wording) showed more than 10 per cent variation, 10 showed less than 2 per cent variation, and 18 showed less than 6 per cent variation. Thus 70 per cent of the 26 commensurate questions showed a high stability of less than 6 per cent variation, and more than 80 per cent showed a good stability of less than 10 per cent [variation].

The greatest variations took place on questions of a hypothetical and emotive nature, such as attitudinal questions on [the] kind of government structure desired. All variations, however, were generally explained by the operation of three variables that were clearly the function of the interviewing context: [a] personal prestige variable, a pro-American bias, and an anti-Soviet bias. On questions which affect the respondent's personal prestige there is a consistent shift in the more personal interviewing context for the respondent to flatter himself. Similarly, on questions dealing with Soviet and American achievements, there is a consistent shift of some respondents who answer the same questions in the oral interviewing context to flatter the American interviewers by minimizing Soviet achievements and aggrandizing American achievements.[8]

Though the differences in the results obtained from the two instruments were not large in any event, those that occurred seemed to be a direct function of the differences between a person-to-person interview situation, and the more impersonal situation of a self-administered questionnaire. Because the number of cases (46) is so small, it is not safe to treat these differences as anything more than suggestive, yet they make such considerable sense as to warrant serious consideration. The respondents flattered both themselves and the interviewer more in the face-to-face situation of the personal interview. In the oral interview situation,[9] more respondents claimed to have tried "actively" to leave the Soviet Union (22 per cent to 8 per cent), even though the total claiming to have wanted to leave is about the same. More respondents claimed during the personal interview to have left the Soviet Union voluntarily (48 per cent to 37 per cent). Furthermore, there was a tendency for the results of the personal interview to yield somewhat more anti-Soviet answers on the distortion items: the differences on various questions ran from 0 per cent to 10 per cent.

For many kinds of questions, therefore, it could be argued that the written questionnaire was the more reliable instrument, since the content of a person's answers was visibly influenced by the more personal nature of the face-to-face interview. On the other hand, none of the 7 individuals (out of 46) who admitted Komsomol (Young Communist League) membership during the personal interview did so also on the questionnaire. It would appear that the superior rapport established in the oral interview gave respondents the courage to divulge confidential information that they were reluctant to commit to a piece of paper. The fact that this change occurred even though they had given such information to the same organization only a month earlier argues strongly that respondents had not remembered the answers they gave a month previously. Therefore, the degree of congruence on all the other questions is clearly an argument for the stability or validity of the opinions given. The answers on both occasions were the same not because people had good memories of what they had said the first time and took pains to be consistent, but because the second time around they still felt much as they did the first time.

While the consistency of response derived for a large proportion of the questions from the two methods is gratifying, the discrepancies which were obtained are also a substantial warning that no one approach is a perfect or completely reliable device for obtaining information. It would seem on the basis of this small experiment — and again we must indicate how tentatively such conclusions must be held — that the printed questionnaire minimizes the tendency of respondents to slant answers on which their own prestige or that of the interviewer may be involved. That is to say, the face-to-face situation is an invitation for the respondent to manipulate the interviewer. At the same time, the more personal nature of the interview makes possible a rapport between the subject and the investigator such that the interviewee is much more likely to give information of a confidential nature. As tentative as these conclusions are, they are well worth keeping in mind in assessing data derived from the two instruments. Ideally, these propositions should be tested with the total subsamples from the oral interview and the questionnaire. Unfortunately, we found the task of establishing sufficiently tight matching on the two subsamples so complicated as to make clear and unambiguous results beyond attainment. We rest our case on the assertion that on the vast majority of questions the two approaches yielded extremely close results.

Such differences as we find between the data garnered from the two types of instruments would be of maximum concern if we were interested mainly or exclusively in the distribution of isolated phenomena in our sample rather than in the relation between phenomena. Thus, while fewer Komsomol and party members reported their membership in this organization on the written questionnaire, a comparison of party and nonparty people ought to yield the same patterns on either instrument even though the nonparty group on one of the instruments was diluted with more "false negatives." Therefore, we have felt confident in using both instruments *for this sort of interrelation analysis,* even though each yields a somewhat different distribution in *some instances.* Part of our confidence in this use of the oral interview material for statistical rather than merely illustrative purposes lay in the high degree of reliability we attained in coding these qualitative answers.[10]

One difficulty in relying on the written questionnaire was that we could not check at first hand on the apparent sincerity and seriousness with which the respondent approached his task. The close similarity between the answers given on the forty-six written questionnaires later filled out by those who had taken oral interviews should serve as one important proof of the conscientious and thoughtful approach our respondents took to the questionnaire. Further, all the internal evidence available to us suggests that the questionnaires were filled out conscientiously and about as accurately as the conditions of the respondent and of administration of the questionnaire permitted.

One indication of the seriousness with which respondents took our interviews and questionnaires, is the low rate of failures to answer questions. For approximately half of all the questions, the rate of nonanswering was below 10 per cent. In only about one-quarter of the cases was the number of "no answers" high (over 20 per cent), and it is clear from the nature of these questions that it was their inherent difficulty rather than the indifference of the respondents that accounted for this fact. Such rates are comparable to those which one customarily gets with American respondents, particularly when asking difficult and conflictful questions. As it is reasonable to expect, the highest rates of "no answer" were among the lower educated groups and reflected the fact that these groups were having difficulties with the questions or having trouble in working fast enough to complete the entire questionnaire. The rate of not answering was not spread evenly over the questions by any means. On some questionnaires, failures to answer were almost entirely toward the end, indicating that the respondent had run out of time. It should not be forgotten that it required about six hours for an average person to complete the questionnaire. Of greater analytic value was the high rate of nonanswering that marked a few questions which obviously presented conflicts for the respondents. An especially acute instance of this occurred when we asked our respondents to evaluate a number of different occupations. The per cent who failed to evaluate each job on the list was quite low until the job of party secretary was reached. At this point the number leaving the question unanswered rose from an average of 7 per cent for the other jobs to 22 per cent for the party secretary. There is, of course, a good deal of additional evidence which indicates that our respondents were in genuine conflict in assessing the merits of this job.[11]

Another example of the seriousness which our respondents demonstrated in approaching their task is given by some checks on the consistency of their responses to certain issues which in modified form arose on more than one part of the questionnaire. For example, we asked at one point what the respondent would be sure to keep if the regime were eliminated but certain worthy features of the system could be kept. At another point we asked whether our respondents felt medical care to have become more accessible under Soviet conditions. Consistency would require that those who thought well enough of the medical care system to volunteer it as a feature to be kept should also vote in favor of it on the direct question. This is indeed overwhelmingly the case, with a range from 85 per cent among the peasants to 93 per cent among the employees showing this consistency. Similar consistency was shown with regard to opinions on the educational system, Soviet cultural achievements, and other items which permitted a similar check.

Quite a different check on consistency was provided by the questions dealing with rumor. At one point we asked whether or not our respondents heard rumors "frequently, seldom, or never," and later in the same question series asked whether they considered these rumors "more or less reliable than the official sources." Of those who said they were "never" exposed to such rumors, more than 90 per cent eschewed making the judgment about reliability. Since we placed no such restriction on them, their response indicates that they were carefully and conscientiously "policing" themselves in refusing to evaluate a form of communication with which they had had no firsthand contact.

Reference was made earlier to rumors that our questionnaires were filled out haphazardly and casually. The foregoing shows how unfounded this rumor was. There was, as we have previously indicated, an additional rumor (which apparently still has some currency) that large blocs of questionnaires were filled out by an "assembly line" consisting of a few individuals. In response to this allegation, which had some basis in fact, the entire block of questionnaires administered under circumstances making it possible for one person to fill out more than one questionnaire was set aside. Coders were instructed to watch this entire block for evidence of duplication of handwriting, and to watch all questionnaires for signs of a frivolous or consciously misleading approach to the questions. Of the 2718 written questionnaires, only 40 were removed from the sample prior to coding because more than one person had filled out two questionnaires, because two persons had filled out one jointly, because there were dis-

crepancies in handwriting, or on such fundamental facts as age or sex.*
Methodologically it is perhaps a moot point as to whether the exclusion
of such cases is preferable, in that their removal might be done on the
basis of criteria which prejudged the final conclusions. However, such
cases as were removed were quite clear-cut instances of some degree of
fraud. What is more important is the extremely small number of such
cases. It would have made no conceivable difference in our statistical conclusions if every one of them had remained in the sample.

Despite such isolated instances of deception, the overwhelming impression of team members in Europe and this country, as well as of other
persons who had contact with the émigré community at that time, was
that Soviet émigrés took our questionnaires and interviews with great
seriousness.

The Comparison of "Munich" and "New York" Cases[12]

As one of our efforts to establish control over potential sources of bias
in our data we interviewed and administered questionnaires to a number
of Soviet émigrés who had resided in the United States at least one year.
In Europe, 2080 questionnaires were administered, and we refer to this
set by the short title "Munich" sample. In the United States 638 questionnaires were completed, and these we refer to as the "New York" sample. We had no specific hypotheses in mind except the general one that
it might be instructive to compare the data from our large European
sample with data gathered from people interviewed in a different situation, and who had been exposed for a reasonable length of time to another
culture. It was hoped that this comparison would throw into perspective
any peculiarities of the European interviewing situation which might
affect seriously our conclusions. The method of comparison was to match
the New York sample on age, education, residence, and social class membership with persons from the much larger Munich sample. Comparisons
were then made of these two "matched samples."

The general conclusion of this comparative analysis is that none of the
conclusions we would have reached on the basis of the Munich sample
alone would be abandoned or reversed on the basis of the New York sample. Yet there were sufficient systematic differences between the data
gathered from the two groups that it is worth commenting on them.

A major finding that emerged from comparison of the Munich and
New York matched samples was that the differences in responses between
the two matched samples were much smaller for the upper classes than for
the lower classes.

* These were in addition to several dozen discarded in the field under conditions
described in Chapter I.

The responses of the social class subgroups in the matched samples were compared on 127 items. The intelligentsia group interviewed in Germany and that interviewed in the United States differed by less than 5 per cent on 47 per cent of the items, and by 9 per cent or less on 80 per cent of the items. In other words, using either sample as our main source would have made little difference in our estimate of the distribution experiences and attitudes of the intelligentsia. Much the same can be said for the employee group. By contrast, the manual classes interviewed in the United States often differed markedly from those in Germany. The proportions giving a particular answer differed by 10 per cent or more on well over half the 127 items, and by 20 per cent or more on more than a quarter of the items.

Because of the difficulty in obtaining large numbers of persons of lower class status among the émigrés in the United States, there was a considerable imbalance in the numbers of cases in each of the social class categories. The New York sample yielded only 32 peasants, 39 ordinary workers, and 37 skilled workers, in contrast to 173 employees and 209 members of the intelligentsia. As a result of this disparity in the numbers of cases in the manual groups and nonmanual groups, one might well raise the question of whether or not the differences of response between the Munich and New York manual groups were statistical accidents. However, the strength and consistency of the differences is such that in most instances they are statistically significant for the *combined* manual groups. In addition, the nature of the differences indicates strongly that we are dealing with a substantial and stable phenomenon. There was also a possibility that systematic response differences were a result of systematic differences in the samples extending beyond the variables on which we had matched them. This was explored with essentially negative results.[13]

All in all it has seemed to us that the fact that the lower status groups in our samples showed greater differences in their responses was a result of an effect that is met frequently in the literature on psychology of opinion change. People less informed and less interested in a topic initially are more subject to influence and change. Presumably our lower status (and thereby lower educated) respondents were, probably both in Europe and the United States, less interested in and informed about the political, economic, and social questions with which we were concerned. Accordingly, the experience of living in the United States for a year had more net impact upon such persons, than upon persons already better informed, more interested, and with more firmly formed opinions and impressions.

The manual classes in the United States differed from those in Munich mainly in that they took a less positive attitude toward America and things American, *less* often reported themselves as having been deprived while in the Soviet Union, and took a *more* positive view of Soviet achievements and accomplishments (Table 10). The focus and consistency of these differences incline us to treat them as real rather than due to chance or to peculiarities in the matched samples — which did, incidentally, exist.

The meaning of these differences is perhaps not too difficult to discern. The lower class groups based their judgments on less adequate information and thought than the better educated professional and white-collar groups. They also tended to adopt rather extreme positions. Both factors made them more vulnerable to the influence of later experience. This is especially understandable in the case of their image of the United States. Presumably, living in America proved not to be quite so carefree as some in Germany had dreamed. Accustomed to the securities of the welfare state, many found it hard to get along on their own as much as they were expected to in the United States. That they now came closer to reality in their assessment should be no great surprise.

These same facts probably contain the key to their less frequent report of having been deprived while in the Soviet Union, and their more positive image of certain Soviet achievements. For example, fewer of those in New York remembered themselves as having been dissatisfied with their Soviet jobs, and more felt the medical and educational systems in the Soviet Union worth saving. Now that they had at last reached their anticipated paradise they found that it, too, was a real world with problems. The effect seems to have been a drift in the opposite direction, a tendency to see the Soviet Union by comparison as not quite so bad after all. The interpretation is greatly strengthened by the fact that it was only the welfare state features of the Soviet Union which were seen in this better light. Attitudes toward the Communist leaders and the Soviet regime in general did not differ greatly in the two groups. Indeed, those questioned in the United States were more vigorously anti-Communist in formal political attitudes. For example, they more often charged Lenin with doing more harm and often blamed the Soviet leaders for faults of the system.

Whatever the explanation for the differences between the Munich and New York samples, there remained the question of what to do about them. Should the pattern of the Munich sample or the New York sample be accepted as closer to what was the actual experience of these people when they were still in the Soviet Union? The main reason the problem was so important was that the Munich sample revealed much sharper class differences in experience and attitude, whereas the New York sample moved the classes closer together, suggesting greater homogeneity in the life pattern of Soviet citizens. In most cases the effect was simply to reduce the magnitude of the class differences, without seriously affecting

TABLE 10 [13A]

COMPARISON OF ATTITUDES AND EXPERIENCES
OF THE MANUAL CLASSES IN THE NEW YORK
AND MUNICH MATCHED SAMPLES

Attitudes and Experiences	Munich		New York	
Least flattery of things American	25%	(59) [a]	51%	(74)
High occupational frustration	57	(108)	38	(108)
Denial of Soviet accomplishments	22	(79)	7	(92)
Weak support of civil liberties	52	(73)	64	(66)
Lenin did harm	71	(101)	88	(104)
Opposition because leaders were bad	2	(60)	16	(80)

a. Total number of respondents on the basis of which the percentage is computed.

the pattern (Table 11). Thus, in one of the more extreme cases, that of job satisfaction, the difference between the intelligentsia and the peasantry was reduced from 71 per cent to 45 per cent, but a significant class pattern still remained. In evaluations of the Soviet output of agricultural machinery and the comparison of the Bolsheviks and Nazis the clear class differences in the Munich sample "washed out" entirely in New York (Table 11), but this was true in very few other instances. Generally the class patterning remained, but it was often attenuated.

After long deliberation and many consultations with colleagues experienced in attitude study we concluded that we should have more confidence in the responses of the Munich sample and in the reality of the sharper class differences it indicated. We reached this conclusion on the following grounds: Whatever the size of the "original" difference in experience and opinion separating the social groups, that original difference presumably arose out of objective differences in the economic and social situation of the groups while they lived in the stratified social conditions of Soviet society. The further away they were from these objective factors which sustained the original differences in subjective evaluations, the smaller those subjective differences would become. In addition, the more new and *common* experiences the classes had, the more their old differences would be eroded. The Munich cases were still "closer" to their old home situation, living in camps which contained mainly Soviet people and had more of the old atmosphere. And the New York cases had shared new and, for them, rather unusual experiences in a year of life in the United States. Under the circumstances we would expect the New York cases to have become more homogeneous, as they were. It is important

TABLE 11 [13B]

DIFFERENCES IN ATTITUDES AND EXPERIENCES
IN NEW YORK AND MUNICH SAMPLES: BY CLASS

Attitudes and experiences	Intelli-gentsia	White-collar employees	Skilled workers	Ordinary workers	Collective farm peasants
Satisfied with job					
Munich	81%	73%	43%	26%	10%
New York	84	65	82	49	39
Agricultural machine production has risen					
Munich	95	91	82	76	69
New York	98	95	94	89	96
Read magazines and newspapers frequently in USSR					
Munich	62	58	35	22	4
New York	70	59	55	25	10
No news in Soviet press is reliable					
Munich	19	26	58	59	60
New York	21	28	33	48	19[a]
Had opportunity for a career					
Munich	34	20	17	5	7
New York	33	14	17	5	10
Had educational opportunity					
Munich	49	40	33	27	25
New York	40	27	38	17	33
Bolsheviks worse than Nazis					
Munich	74	62	55	42	28
New York	71	80	68	64	73
Median number of respondents					
Munich	201	162	33	36	27
New York	191	168	35	37	30

a. We are at a loss to explain the deviation of this figure. It may be due to sampling error or to some phenomenon we do not understand.

to note, in this connection, that although the greatest "contribution" to homogeneity came from the greater shift among the manual classes, the intelligentsia and employees also moved toward the middle, producing a general regression toward the norm of the group as a whole (Table 11).

Our general experience with such patterns suggests the greater original differences represent the more valid pattern.

Despite our conclusion that the European or Munich cases were probably closer to their counterparts in the Soviet Union, we decided to adopt the more conservative course of including the New York cases in our total sample for all analysis. We did this because we were eager not to reduce the number of cases available when we undertook more complex analysis. None of the basic conclusions we have reached are thereby altered, since the direction of the differences is the same in both samples. The inclusion of the New York cases, by making the class differences less sharp, therefore mainly has the effect of helping us to make a more conservative estimate of the otherwise strikingly sharp class differences our data reveals.

The Use of Statistics of Inference

The use of "statistics of inference" has become standard practice in many areas of the social sciences as a device for assessing whether quantitative findings may be attributed to the operation of more than mere chance. Such statistical tests are most useful when one is dealing with rather small numbers of cases and/or small effects or differences between larger samples. In the main, the important question to be raised about our data was seldom that of such "statistical significance." We ordinarily had a large number of cases, and have dealt mainly with differences of such magnitude that it would have been pretentious — and pointless — to employ such procedures. In addition, the employment of statistics of inference would in most instances be unwarranted since some of the basic assumptions of such tests would not hold. For example, in making such a test on a particular table which is employed in the text of this book we would properly have to take into account all of the related tables which had been run, but not used. Such data are not, and for practical reasons cannot be, available for a project employing dozens of analysts. Finally, the use of such tests, while at certain times unnecessary and at other times unwarranted, might actually — by virtue of the prestige associated with such "scientific procedures" — deflect attention away from the real problems of our data, namely what meaning could reasonably be read into them assuming that they represented something more than statistical artifacts.

This does not mean that we and other members of the Project have not used such tests of statistical significance when they seemed called for. The analysis of the clinical psychological data[14] where the number of cases was small required the consistent use of such tests. Furthermore, in the initial analysis of the data included in this volume, tests of statistical significance were applied for our own guidance in those special cases in which our analysis led us to deal with small numbers of cases. This is true, for instance, of some of the findings in the chapter on communications. It is also true of the comparisons made between the Munich and the New York cases. The reader will note that at these and other points we occasionally call attention to the small number of cases with which we are dealing, and couch our conclusions in appropriately tenuous terms. In practice we have tried to be more conservative than traditional tests of statistical significance would dictate, because of the other difficulties associated with our data. On the other hand, where the data suggest some possible interpretation which would be of very real interest *if* the data were statistically reliable, we have not hesitated to indicate these possibilities.[15]

Summary

No one, least of all the authors of this book or their colleagues on the Project, would claim for a moment that these data are without their difficulties. We have all spent many a week on particular problems where the data were complicated and their meaning obscure, in an effort to pierce some analytical fog. These efforts were, of course, not always successful. One of us, for example, was interested in the relative propensity of the members of the various social groups to flee the Soviet Union voluntarily, this offering some measure of the amount of active hostility within the various groups. Despite rather elaborate analyses it was never possible to make a satisfactory assessment of the differential *opportunity* of the various groups for voluntary emigration. The Nazis, for example, were more likely to recruit certain categories for forced labor, and thereby depress artificially the proportion of voluntary departures in such a group. Among the military, better educated men, being officers and therefore having a greater feeling of responsibility and loyalty *to the military*, might be less likely to surrender voluntarily even though "equally disaffected" (whatever that might mean according to various ways of looking at the problem). The number of such questions on which we could not satisfy our own doubts was considerable. We might easily write a volume, equal to this in size, devoted to "blind alleys of analysis" or "conclusions not reached." Such a volume would not be likely to attract a substantial number of discerning readers. However, we feel it important to call this circumstance to the readers' attention, since the present volume is necessarily devoted mainly to a presentation of our positive conclusions. As such it gives him little in the way of a picture of the conclusions we did *not* draw because of what we perceived to be the limitations of the data.

By their very nature these sorts of data are complex and difficult to deal with. Though they are manageable, those who use them are beset by many more potential sources of error than any social scientist ever hopes to find himself involved with. It is precisely for these reasons that we have devoted so much space to the methodological aspects of the Project, so that the reader might not only gather specific information, but have something of an introduction to how we think on these matters, how we habitually approach problems, and what sorts of interpretations we place on certain kinds of data. We have said several times, and repeat here, that a discussion of methodological procedures (and the reader has actually been burdened with only a portion of the side studies we made into the nature of our data) is not a complete answer to the quality of our data or of our conclusions. Particularly with data and problems such as we are working with, no rubric of procedure will solve all problems. In the substantive chapters which follow, the reader will have the opportunity to judge for himself, point for point, whether or not he accepts our conclusions.

PART TWO: THE ROUND OF DAILY LIVING

IV

Occupational Stratification and Mobility

Lenin's political philosophy was distinctively elitist. His work is permeated with references to the "torpor" of the masses, their lack of "consciousness," their "elemental, unthinking" quality, and their consequent need for a hard core of conscious, organized, professional, revolutionary leaders, to serve as "teacher, guide, and leader." At the same time there was also a strong current of equalitarianism in his writings. *The State and Revolution,* written at the height of revolutionary ardor in 1917, expressed an extreme, indeed utopian equalitarianism. In this mood Lenin asserted that in the new society every cook would help run the government, and managerial functions would be performed by any literate person. The national economy would be so organized that technicians, managers, and indeed all officials would receive salaries no higher than workmen's wages. This burst of enthusiasm was tempered in Lenin's practice by considerations of efficiency and the immediate requirements of the postrevolutionary situation. In fact, he himself argued the necessity of paying experts high salaries. To stimulate high output of good quality he was quite ready to accept differential rewards for the best workers. While still reaffirming equality of wages as an *ultimate* goal, at the Tenth Congress of the Communist Party in 1921 Lenin called upon the party to accept differential rewards as a device for increasing worker discipline and inducing higher productivity.[1]

Whatever reservations Lenin may have had about equalitarianism, the predominant belief in his party, and particularly in the leadership of the trade-unions, was that communism meant social and economic equality. Early Soviet policy therefore moved at rapid speed towards the elimination of social class differences in the Soviet population. Within about a month of the Bolshevik seizure of power a decree was promulgated abolishing "all the classes of society existing up to now in Russia, and all divisions of citizens, all class distinctions and privileges, class organizations and institutions. . . ." A month later another decree abolished "all titles and stations in the army," with the expressed purpose of effecting "the quickest and most decisive destruction of all remnants of former inequality. . . ." These decisions were in time given firm

standing as part of the basic law of the land, since the "Declaration of
the Rights of the Toiling and Exploited People," promulgated in January
1918, and later incorporated as part of the constitution adopted in July
1918, stated that the new society took "as its fundamental task the abolition of any exploitation of man by man [and] the complete elimination of
the division of society into classes." [2]

These formal legal moves to eliminate class differences were supplemented and complemented by a series of economic developments which
went far toward eliminating differences in material reward. The most
obvious of these were the formal measures for the expropriation of the
wealthy and the nationalization of the economy. Beyond this dramatic
leveling of the relatively small former upper classes, however, a much
broader equalization took place within the more numerous classes of the
population. The overwhelming majority were peasants, and in the rural
areas the poorer peasants, acting largely on their own initiative but with
the encouragement and legal support of the Bolshevik regime, seized and
redistributed millions of acres of land belonging to the large estates and
the richer individual peasants. Approximately one in every three acres of
land changed hands. The number of landless peasants was reduced by
half and the average holdings of the peasantry as a whole increased by
about 20 per cent.[3] As Hubbard summed up this development, he observed
that: "The most immediate and significant effect of the Revolution on
the peasant economy was the reversal of the process of differentiation.
Poor peasants who had previously had to earn a large part of their sub-
sistence by working for others found themselves again possessed of
land, and those who had raised themselves above the ruck were reduced
to the level of the ordinary peasant." [4]

In the cities a similar and no less drastic process went on. Although
formal wage differentials were maintained, with skills ranked on a scale
from one to twelve, wages were in fact equalized under pressure from
the more radical elements within the Communist Party and the trade-
unions. Wage differentiation was gradually whittled away, until in early
1921 the wages of the best paid were on the average a mere 2 per cent
greater than those of the least paid. Actually the money wage mattered
little, because by 1921 most payment was in kind, and under the rationing system the category of your ration card was more important than the
size of your pay. The ration card was used as a class weapon further to
decimate the unwanted class "remnants" of tsarist society. But in the
administration of the rationing system there was also a drift towards
equality in the distribution of rations within the working class.[5]

After 1921 the New Economic Policy or NEP slowed down this leveling, and brought about some return of economic differentiation. In the
rural areas, the hiring of land, implements, and individual labor was

resumed. This new freedom permitted the peasant who was more efficient or possessed of better resources once again to dominate the poor and ineffective, and slowly to absorb them. In the industrial realm the process of redifferentiation was much more controlled, but in the factory as well there was a return to less radical patterns. Rationing ended and wages again acquired real value. Although everyone from factory manager to unskilled worker was still placed on the same scale, there was now marked differentiation between top and bottom. The pay of the highest grade was eight times the lowest, and the most skilled worker earned three and a half times the unskilled.[6]

With the beginning of the forced industrialization in 1928 there was still another reversal. The system moved once again toward equalization of reward.[7] This arose in part from the restoration of rationing, in part from the general scarcity, and in part from the revolutionary ardor which the introduction of the First Five Year Plan again breathed into the Soviet system. The collectivization of agriculture, which followed in 1930, had an even more drastic effect. Initially it almost totally eliminated any differentiation among peasants, even though this was brought about by reducing all to the same state of relative poverty. The drift toward equalization, while not entirely a matter of conscious policy, seemed to have the support of most of the Communist Party and trade-union leaders. Just as the tide of equalitarian sentiment was at its height, however, Stalin threw an ideological bombshell which burst the dam of restraints on differentiation and started the whole stream of Soviet development on a new course of social and economic differentiation.

Stalin's surprise attack came in an address in June, 1931. There he launched a virulent attack on what he labelled the "evil," "leftist," and "bourgeois" practice of wage equalization or "equality mongering." By those labels he apparently meant the failure of pay scales adequately to distinguish between skilled and unskilled, and between heavy and light work. "We cannot tolerate a situation," he said, "where a rolling mill hand in steel mills earns no more than a sweeper . . . a railway locomotive driver earns only as much as a copying clerk." In every factory and enterprise, he affirmed, there is a "leading core" of workers who are the chief link in production. These should be treated to promotions, higher wages, and other benefits which would "give the worker his due according to his qualification." To do this would, in addition, provide those less skilled with both "the prospect and the stimulus of advancement." Not only the skilled workers, but the technical intelligentsia as well were to be given a new deal. An end was to be put to "expert-baiting." The old intelligentsia was to be shown new "solicitude," and a larger and highly rewarded new intelligentsia was to be recruited to join them.[8]

Following Stalin's pronouncement the regime put into effect a long series of measures which moved the society rapidly toward full-scale social class differentiation. This differentiation was of two major kinds. Within the laboring class — including therein, to some degree, the peasants — there was a sharpening of differentiation between the more skilled and more energetic and those not so endowed. This differentiation was effected largely through the systematic and rigorous use of a progressive piecework system of payment, even on the collective farms. The process of differentiation was given great impetus in the period beginning in 1935 when the Stakhanovite system was introduced. That system permitted unusually large rewards for those workers who succeeded in rationalizing their labor tasks, often through the organization of small teams of their fellow workers. This was done with encouragement and direct assistance by management under instruction from the regime. But the consequence was that Stakhanovites greatly increased their output and won large windfall payments under the progressive piece-rate system. Since the regime was intensely interested in the spread of the movement, it also rewarded the outstanding Stakhanovites by heaping social honors on them. More important, it gave them the best in housing, provided them with otherwise scarce or unobtainable goods such as radios and silk stockings, and sent them for vacations to the best resorts and rest homes. As a result, differentiation in style of life within the working class was increased. There emerged in Soviet society a manual group whose whole life pattern marked it off from the rank-and-file workers so definitely that it came to be known as the "workers' aristocracy." The acute awareness of these differences is well expressed in an anecdote related by an office worker in a trade cooperative:

> A big line of people is waiting to receive goods at a store. An old, half-deaf lady, comes up and asks "What are they giving out?" So a man in the lines says "A slap in the face." The old lady, not having heard precisely, responds "To everyone, or just Stakhanovites?"

Of course, the Stakhanovites were not a caste in the sense that entry into the group was sharply restricted on grounds of birth. Yet it seems that possession of the characteristics that gave one the chance to enter the group was not equally distributed in the population. Certain personality types and those from certain backgrounds were much more likely than others to win this position. Others implicitly or explicitly accepted the fact that they would not achieve the status. Consequently, the Stakhanovite group came to assume many of the characteristics of a fairly distinctive social class recognized as such by both those in the class and those outside. As one engineer put it:

> They chose for Stakhanovites people who are thirsting for a career, who did not achieve the high norms simply because they were pressed from above, but be-

cause they wanted to elbow their way up, to become members of the privileged group among the workers.

In the countryside there was a parallel economic differentiation within the collectivized peasantry. There were rich and poor peasants partly because of difference in individual productivity. Probably more important was the fact that the collective farms varied greatly in fertility, in closeness to market, and in the value the regime set on their crops, and therefore in the size of the shares they could pay their members. Nevertheless, the regime's policy was ultimately based on the impoverishment of the peasant as the means for securing those extreme forced savings in consumption which provided the capital for industrial expansion. Despite the differentiation among peasants, therefore, almost the whole of the peasantry came to be a vast, exploited lumpenproletariat of the Soviet system. It suffered extreme economic deprivation at the very time that the working-class aristocracy, at the other end of the manual scale, was winning its favored position. In addition, of course, the peasantry was a distinctive group by virtue of the way in which it earned its living, its rural residence, and its peasant culture patterns.

Along with differentiation *within* the working class, the second major consequence of Stalin's new line was the progressive separation *from* the working class of the nonmanual employees. In particular the "intelligentsia" progressively developed as a distinctive and generally superior and favored class in Soviet society.

During the early and mid-nineteenth century, Russia was a society essentially of the "estate" type. There were a limited number of legally recognized social classes, sharply defined and with relatively firm barriers governing movement between them. The old nobility, the country gentry and landowners, the clergy and the peasants made up the main class groups, with modest interstitial entrepreneurial trading and working classes in the cities. As long as the estate system persisted, without the presence of a major urban middle class the intelligentsia consisted largely of those members of the upper classes who had higher education and intellectual interests, particularly in the arts, philosophy, literature, and socio-political theory. It included, in addition, a small number of individuals from other class backgrounds who were then engaged predominantly in intellectual work. The estate system of Russia began to break up following the liberation of the peasantry. As the country became more industrialized and acquired a large urban middle class, the intelligentsia increased in size and changed significantly in composition and social origins. From being predominantly an intellectual segment of the dominant class, it came to be a more specifically defined occupational-class group, consisting mainly of members of the liberal professions of medicine, law, and education, and including growing numbers of engineers, technicians, and scientists. A very high proportion of this new intelligentsia still came from the same social groups as before, but its members were increasingly drawn from the growing urban middle classes, and the higher civil servants. In many respects, however, it preserved much of the cast of the old intelligentsia as a group interested in the arts, ideas, culture, and sociopolitical improvement.

Under the Soviet regime the intelligentsia was to undergo yet another and this time a more profound transformation. In the initial revolutionary period the intelligentsia met with extreme hostility. Defined as a class enemy of the revolution, it was to be utilized only insofar as necessary for its technical competence, but was to be distrusted, carefully watched, and stringently restricted in power and rewards. Industrialization and the collectivization of agriculture greatly expanded the need for trained personnel. As the regime realized its dependence on technical training, it changed its attitude toward the intelligentsia, especially after Stalin's new line was introduced in 1931. The material, social and legal status of the intelligentsia was gradually basically altered, so that by 1936 they were listed as one of three more or less "official" classes in the Soviet constitution.* The group grew tremendously in size, partly through direct promotion to its ranks and partly as a result of an elaborate and intense program of higher education and technical training. More than half a million graduated from universities and almost one million from technical and specialized secondary schools in the ten-year period of the first two five-year plans (1928–1937).

Meanwhile the regime, apparently taking the size of the intelligentsia as a symbol of accomplishment, expanded the meaning of the term to include practically all individuals with higher education, with specialized advanced training, or administrative responsibility. Thus the Soviet intelligentsia was defined by Molotov in 1939, apparently following the usage of the suppressed 1937 census, to include not only heads of large but also small enterprises such as cleaning establishments and restaurants. Junior as well as senior military officers, librarians, accountants, and statisticians, nurses and laboratory technicians were included along with those engaged in the arts and the traditional free professions of law, medicine, and education. As a result the officially designated group numbered about 9.5 million in 1937, and well over 10 million by 1940, the date to which our occupational data has main reference.

The intelligentsia was in turn differentiated from the ordinary white-collar employee. The Russian term *sluzhashchie* is often used in the Soviet Union to designate *all* white-collar personnel, including not only the intel-

---

* For reasons of technical Marxian purity they were dubbed a "stratum" and not a "class" as were the peasants and the workers.

ligentsia but also typists, clerks, shopkeepers, as distinguished from manual workers and peasants. In the 1939 census, for example, the published data on the social group composition of the population did not list the intelligentsia separately, but simply designated the proportion of individuals classified in a broad white-collar group (*sluzhashchie*). Our respondents, however, only occasionally had difficulty in distinguishing the two groups, and when asked to classify themselves only a small percentage placed themselves in both the intelligentsia *and* employee categories. In addition, the more specific term "intelligentsia" is regularly used in Soviet sources and in conversations of former Soviet citizens as distinct from the more general term "employee." These considerations, together with important differences in occupational and educational characteristics of the two groups, may be taken as justification for the distinction made between the intelligentsia and the rank-and-file white-collar workers.

The Soviet census of 1939 showed the population to be divided into essentially three classes — peasants, who, with their families, were about 49 per cent of the total, workers who accounted for 32 per cent, and "employees," including intelligentsia, who were somewhat more than 17 per cent of the total. In 1955 the pattern was not radically different, although the figures reflect the continuing effects of industrialization and urbanization. Including their families, peasants constituted 41 per cent, and workers and employees — including the intelligentsia — accounted for 58 per cent. The latter figure reflects an increment of 8 per cent over the combined figure for the two in 1939.[9] Since we felt this classification was too broad, we asked our respondents to place themselves on a six-level class hierarchy: party and government elite, intelligentsia, employee, skilled worker, ordinary worker, and collective farm peasant. In practice this reduced to a five level system, since only 12 individuals out of 2,718 placed themselves as party and government elite on the written questionnaire.

The terms we used were very close to those used by the Soviet government in the last census of 1939. With minor exceptions, they also were used to designate social class membership on Soviet internal passports carried by all Soviet citizens.* In addition, in Soviet official literature these designations are repeatedly used, and our experience with informal interviews made it clear that the terminology has a good deal of meaning for the average Soviet citizen. We found that the terms were regularly and spontaneously used in descriptions of individuals and groups in Soviet society. Most people were able without apparent diffi-

---

* The classification "intelligentsia" was not used as a formal category in the 1939 census on the social composition of the population, but it was used extensively in the articles and reports following the census. Internal passports give the precise occupation — doctor, engineer, professor — rather than the general designation "intelligentsia."

culty to place themselves in one of the six major social class categories. Less than 5 per cent failed to answer the question. Even if we include those who listed themselves as "student" and those whose answers did not fit the standard classification, the proportion who do not fit into these five categories is still only about 9 per cent.

It is one thing to check one's self as belonging to some class. It is quite another thing to do so "accurately" — in the sense that how one designates oneself will agree with either the judgment of others or with certain "objective" criteria of class membership. Obviously, we cannot assess our respondents' self-placement against the judgment of independent observers except to the extent that we ourselves become such "independent observers" through an examination of the relationship of this self-placement to the other criteria of class membership in the questionnaire data. Since no single criterion or correlate of social class membership can by itself serve as a definitive index, we can and should expect only that there be a high, rather than a perfect, correlation among such criteria. Judged by such standards, our respondents seem to have placed themselves very appropriately.

If *occupation* be used as a criterion of class membership, our respondents seem to have placed themselves accurately. Of those employed in the professions, 72 per cent listed themselves as members of the intelligentsia, and the remainder, without exception, as white-collar employees. Similarly those who were employed as manual farm and nonfarm positions, overwhelmingly listed themselves as members of the peasant, worker, or skilled worker classes. A mere 1 per cent upgraded themselves to the level of intelligentsia, a discrepancy small enough to be accounted for by mechanical errors in filling out the questionnaire. Education is another criterion frequently invoked for judging social class membership. Of those who completed higher education, 74 per cent described themselves as members of the intelligentsia, while this was true of only 3 per cent of those who had not gone beyond four years of schooling. Considering the volume of mobility in Soviet society and the amount of social dislocation following the revolution, the high interrelationship of these various criteria of social class warrants accepting our respondents' self-designation as a reliable index of their "objective" positions in Soviet society.

We do not mean to suggest that the six-level hierarchy on which we asked individuals to place themselves yields *the* class structure of Soviet society. In a modern industrial society which lacks formal legal class divisions, any formula for dividing the population into classes will be somewhat arbitrary as to the number of classes it designates. In addition, any one measure or index of class position will yield groups more homogeneous in some respects and less so in others. For example, the self-designated employee group includes a substantial range of education. Ten per cent had had four years or less, 31 per cent five to seven, 34 per cent regular secondary, and 21 per cent had some college training, were university graduates, or even had advanced degrees. If the sample were divided by level of education, therefore, many individuals who identified themselves as members of the employee class would be placed in different categories from others sharing the same self-identification. On the other hand, to take all those who had only some secondary school training is to get a mixture of occupational groups including peasants, workers, employees, and even some members of the intelligentsia.

For this reason we have reserved for ourselves the flexibility of using not only the person's class identification but also his education, occupation, and social origins, as indices of class position in Soviet society when the subject under discussion points to one of them as the most suitable. For example, it is obviously more appropriate to explore attitudes and experiences on the job with respondents classified by occupation rather than by social group identification, even though these measures are highly correlated with each other. Likewise, when exploring attitudes toward or access to education, it makes sense in some of our analyses to use our respondents' education as the major criterion.

Whatever the precise number of classes designated or the main indices used to determine a person's position in the social structure, the crucial point is that by the late thirties the Soviet Union had a social class structure which, in its broad outlines, was very much like that in the other major industrial countries of Europe and America. True, there were no landowning or industrialist upper classes and no nobility, but there was an analogous class in the distinctive political elite which lived on a relatively lavish scale, and shared its material abundance with a managerial, scientific, artistic and literary elite.* The lesser managerial and professional groups, shading off into semiprofessional and other less skilled or educated brain workers, the skilled workers, the white-collar workers, the semiskilled and unskilled workers, finally the peasants, and ultimately those half-starving in forced labor camps followed along in roughly that order of standing on the scales of income, education, authority, and prestige. As has been true with most class systems in modern times, these classes represented not totally distinctive, mutually exclusive categories. They are classes, however, in the sense that their "members" share "typical" or average conditions of life of sufficient importance to warrant the distinction. Although those in any one group often overlap in one or several respects they constitute sufficiently homogeneous sets of individuals to be meaningfully treated as members of a given class.

* The characteristics of the ruling elite are discussed in chapter 17 of our earlier book, *How the Soviet System Works*.

The class system thus established not only weathered the wartime experience of the Soviet system, but was greatly strengthened during the decade from 1940 to 1950.[10] In its broad outlines it apparently has become a standard structural feature of Soviet society as it is now constituted, and is likely to remain such for some time to come. This class structure constitutes the frame in which one must see the materials of this chapter on occupational mobility and stratification and that of the following chapter on making a living. Although we have, as occasion seemed to require, used other variables as an organizing principle for the presentation of our findings, it is mainly the variable of social class identification, or the more restricted criterion of the respondent's occupation which we have found most revealing as an ordering principle for our entire study.

Which Are the Desirable Jobs?

One could in the abstract imagine a complex, occupationally differentiated society in which all positions would nevertheless be equally "desirable." In practice, however, this is extremely unlikely to occur, especially when capable persons have to be recruited and motivated to take on key jobs involving much responsibility and long training. As we have seen, the Soviet regime long ago gave up any pretense of treating all jobs as equal. It seems that in popular judgments as well, there is in the Soviet Union, as elsewhere, clear-cut social differentiation in the evaluation of various occupations.

For each of thirteen occupations[11] we asked our respondents: "Taking everything into account, was the job of (*teacher*) in the Soviet Union: very desirable, desirable, so-so, undesirable, or very undesirable?" The answers were scored so that a vote of "very desirable" was given 100 points, a vote of "desirable" 75 points, "so-so" 50, and so on. Thus, if everyone in the sample had regarded a given occupation as "very desirable" it could have earned a score of 100, whereas if it were unanimously viewed as "very undesirable," it would have earned a score of zero. In Table 12 we have summarized the averaged ratings of overall desirability which our respondents assigned to these thirteen occupations, together with comparable ratings from a survey done in the United States on similar American occupations.[12]

Four Soviet occupations are bracketed and excluded from portions of the present discussion. There is no American data with which to compare the Soviet foreman. The brigadier, a kind of rural foreman on the Soviet collective farm, has no American opposite number. The jobs of party secretary and collective farm chairman, because of their association in one instance with the Soviet regime, and in the other with the despised institution of the collective farm, may have received artificially low ratings from our anti-Soviet refugee sample.[13] In general there was a striking

TABLE 12 [12A]

POPULAR EVALUATIONS OF COMPARABLE SOVIET
AND AMERICAN OCCUPATIONS

In the Soviet Union		In the United States	
Occupation	Rating	Occupation	Rating
Doctor	75	Physician	91
Scientific worker	73	Scientist	86
Engineer	73	Civil engineer	80
Factory manager	65	Member of corporation board	82
[Foreman]	[65] [a]	——	
Accountant	62	Accountant for a large business	77
Armed forces officer	58	Captain in regular army	76
Teacher	58	Teacher	73
Rank-and-file worker	48	Machine operator in factory	51
[Brigade leader (farm)]	[46]	——	
[Party secretary]	[41]	——	
[Collective farm chairman]	[38]	[Farm owner and operator]	[71]
Collective farmer	18	Farm hand	38
Median number of respondents	1989		2900

a. Occupations in brackets are ones for which there are either no comparable data or no comparable occupations in both countries.

degree of consensus in the ratings which our respondents gave to the set of thirteen occupations.[14] Not only were they rated virtually identically by all subsections of the sample (thus making it possible for us to use data for the total group without subgroup differentiation), but the average ratings for the sample as a whole correlated very highly with the evaluations of each occupation which were obtained from those respondents who had personally held such a job. When we compared the average ratings from the total sample with the ratings of former incumbents of such jobs the correlation on five different job dimensions ranged from .87 to .98.

Our refugee respondents appear to be reporting a stable set of images which apply to jobs in most large-scale industrial societies. Professional occupations — doctor, scientist, and engineer — involving high education, technical skill, and broad service to mankind rank highest. Other jobs involving skill, training, and administrative responsibility are found in middle positions. Manual labor, and particularly manual labor in a rural setting ranks lowest. If we forget the politically controversial job of party secretary, we find that the four lowest ranking jobs are manual and/or rural occupations. As one collective farm laborer put it: "The city intelligentsia looked down upon us and even joked about collective farmers. We were dirty and downtrodden."

In each case where there are comparable urban and rural jobs, the rural job is conspicuously more lowly regarded: factory manager ranked higher than collective farm chairman; foreman outranked brigadier; and rank-and-file worker stood higher than rank-and-file collective farmer. This may in part reflect a general tendency in countries which are rapidly being urbanized and industrialized. In any event, our interview material yields many specific complaints about the hardship, the isolation, and the deprivation of collective farm life at all levels. Particularly at the bottom, the ordinary collective farmer's life was viewed as materially deprived. As one peasant summed it up: "People in industry always earned more than people of the collective farm." The long work hours and the absence of autonomy were also major factors. A smith, for example, said: "A worker is higher than a *kolkhoznik* [collective farmer] . . . no matter how hard he works, he works eight hours and then he can rest. A *kolkhoznik* works from morning to late at night all the time." But rural jobs had no special attraction at any level. As one young Communist put it: "The best people left the collective farms if they could." And we know from frequent official complaints the regime's difficulty in getting trained people to leave the city and return to rural jobs.

The nine Soviet occupations not bracketed may be compared in Table 12 to their American opposite numbers. The American jobs have been arranged according to the rank ordering of the Soviet opposites, and there we find only one inversion. The "member of the board of a large corporation" is ranked slightly ahead of "civil engineer" by the American sample, whereas the Soviet sample puts the engineer ahead of the factory manager. Even if we include the questionable case of the collective farm chairman, the rank ordering of the ratings from the two samples yields a product moment correlation of .90, indicating statistically the extreme similarity of the popular evaluation of comparable occupations in the two countries. Similar comparisons between Soviet ratings and those for four additional countries on which data were available, yielded consistently high rank order correlations: with Germany .90, New Zealand .83, Great Britain .83, and Japan .74.[15]

We are aware, of course, that this similarity between the job ratings given by our respondents and by samples drawn from these other countries may be interpreted as indicating a "capitalistic bias" among our sample. We will let the reader judge for himself the extent of this "capitalistic bias" in the light of the social and political values and attitudes of our respondents as reported in Chapter X. We do believe that the anti-

Soviet (not antisocialist) bias of our respondents accounts for the low rating given to the job of party secretary, and possibly to that of collective farm chairman. As far as the other jobs are concerned, however, the ratings are congruent with the type of society the Soviet leaders have been trying to create. It seems that in modern industrial societies, "socialist" and "capitalist" alike, there is a general scheme or standard in the evaluation of occupations which is very similar from country to country.

All in all we feel that our respondents' rank ordering of the occupations, as well as the general magnitude of esteem accorded each job, corresponds quite closely to the ratings which would be gotten from a representative sample of Soviet citizens (party secretary, and possibly collective farm chairman, again being excepted). And there is nothing that we know about the official value scheme of Soviet society or the traditional values of the people who compose it, which would lead us to expect anything else. Having long ago given up stress on equality, the Soviet regime has over the years glorified the roles which involve scientific knowledge, including such applied sciences as engineering and medicine. This emphasis became so marked in the media of mass communication and in the curriculum of the schools that at one point the late president Kalinin was led to complain that the educational system was geared only to the training of intellectuals.[16] In recent years there have been repeated complaints in the press that every child wanted to become an academician or ballerina, but none wanted the "dirty, hot, and hard jobs" as steel smelters, rolling mill operators, and forge hands.

Our findings definitely corroborate Kalinin's complaint. To avoid doubts about the influence of prerevolutionary values and experience we have for the investigation of this topic constituted a special subsample which represents postrevolutionary, purely Soviet conditions and values as fully as possible, while still retaining a reasonable number of cases. In this analysis we therefore consider only those who were between twenty-one and forty in 1940. The oldest persons in this group were no more than seventeen years old at the time of the Revolution, and the youngest were born in 1919. This means that the majority grew up and were educated under Soviet conditions. With very few exceptions, even the oldest had their entire occupational experience under the Soviet regime.

We asked this group what sort of job they had hoped for when they were still adolescents. Half said they had hoped to go into the arts and professions, particularly medicine and engineering. Only a fifth of the choices were for manual work, and farming drew only 14 per cent, despite the fact that about a third of the respondents came from peasant families. Among sons of parents in professional or comparable occupations, 81 per cent opted for similar jobs. By contrast 62 per cent of the sons of peasants hoped to earn their living *some other way,* as did 62 per cent of the children of ordinary workers. Thus, one man of thirty-seven who had wanted to be an engineer but ended up as a teacher, spoke with more than usually strong feelings in declaring: "I did not want to remain in the *kolkhoz* [collective farm] forever. I saw my parents' material misery, heard their complaints. . . . During that time I never said 'It must be so, it must be so,' but rather I said 'I shall study in the university and get a good job.'"

From other analyses we have been led to believe that persons of lower social origins may, on the average, underreport their early ambitions.* Therefore, it is unlikely that these findings overstate the desire of the Soviet youth to move out of manual employment. This desire is a theme that runs through the pages of many chapters of this book, and we will return to discuss it in connection with our consideration of making a living, education, and family life.

Who Gets the Desirable Jobs? Patterns of Occupational Mobility

The reality of the occupational pyramid common to industrial societies unfortunately decrees that there are many fewer of the very desirable than of the undesirable jobs. Indeed, since the Soviet Union continues to be a heavily agricultural country, the largest single work group is engaged in the "undesirable" agricultural jobs which absorb the energies of about half of all those working.[17] Who then will get the desirable jobs? Will all have an *equal* chance to attain to positions of respect and comfort? Will those born into the more favored families have an undue edge, or will the Soviet regime produce a reversal of the usual pattern and give the children of workers, peasants, and other lowly origins an unduly favorable chance to win to the top? These are particularly pertinent questions for us to investigate since, having denounced equality of rewards the Soviet leaders nevertheless proclaim that Soviet society is still one of equality of opportunity.

Table 13 shows the occupational fate under Soviet conditions of sons born to fathers of various occupations. Since it is traditional to present such tables for males only, we have followed the custom even at the sacrifice of precious case numbers. But so high a proportion of women actually work in the Soviet Union that we have given the data for women in the notes for this chapter.[18] The gross mobility pattern of the two groups is similar, but women much less frequently attain to the professions and less often become workers, particularly skilled workers. Much more often they go into semiprofessional and white-collar work (at something like double the rate for their "brothers").

* Cf. pp. 90–91 below.

TABLE 13 [18A]

OCCUPATIONAL FATE OF SONS AGE 21–40 IN 1940:
BY FATHER'S OCCUPATION

	Father's occupation						
Respondent's occupation	Professional-administrative	Semiprofessional	White-collar	Skilled worker	Ordinary worker	Peasant	Percentage of 1940 labor force
Professional-administrative	65%	47%	40%	26%	9%	8%	2%
Semiprofessional	8	27	14	17	6	6	4
White-collar	9	17	30	9	11	10	11
Skilled worker	7	0	4	25	16	15	33[a]
Ordinary worker	7	9	10	23	55	29	
Collective farmer	4	0	2	0	3	32	50
Total number of respondents	76	41	70	76	159	343	

a. Skilled and ordinary workers are combined in this figure.

Regardless of regional policy toward social origin, young men apparently tended to remain on approximately the same occupational level as their fathers. This becomes clearer if we combine fathers' and respondents' occupations into categories simpler or broader than those employed in Table 13, (1) professional and semiprofessional, (2) white-collar, (3) workers (skilled, semi, and ordinary), and (4) peasant. Using these categories, we find that almost half (48 per cent, to be exact) of our respondents remained at the same occupational level as their fathers. It might be argued that while half of the sample did not "move" we should not lose sight of the half of the sample which did move. But such movement seldom amounted to change from one extreme of the occupational hierarchy to the other. More typically an individual would move from one category to an adjacent one. Using the more refined categories of Table 13, we note that of all the changes, 43 per cent were such one-step moves. For example, of the peasants who moved up, 43 per cent went up one step to become rank-and-file workers. Among skilled workers, 42 per cent of all shifts were either one step up into white-collar work or down to ordinary industrial work. There is much more movement up than down, particularly if one measures "up" and "down" in terms of crossing the manual/nonmanual line. The upward trend is most noticeable in the middle range of occupations. Some 52 per cent of children of skilled workers and artisans crossed the line into nonmanual occupations but only 16 per cent of the children of white-collar fathers left the nonmanual ranks to labor with their hands.

This greater upward mobility reflects mainly the tremendous expansion in professional, semiprofessional and white-collar positions which accompanied the development of industry and government under the five-year plans. But it also testifies to a most important characteristic of our sample, namely that it was an unusually successful group. They were by no means the depressed, unsuccessful, castoffs some assume them to have been.

To assess just how successful our group was we can apply a very simple test. Insofar as the Soviet Union has an occupational pyramid similar to that of other industrial countries, there can be only a little room at the top. Suppose we assume for a moment that fathers with professional and semiprofessional jobs had no children to fill their shoes, or that for some reason all these ended up in manual jobs. Under these circumstances all the nonmanual jobs would go to the sons of the workers and peasants. But, the fact that the sons of peasants and workers are so numerous would have limited the mobility rate into the white-collar jobs in the 1939 labor force to approximately 23 per cent for the Soviet male population.[19] In our sample the mobility rate* out of the manual classes was 29 per cent, actually higher than this maximum possible mobility for the population at large. Yet we know that in fact this maximum rate was not attained because all of the children of white-collar people did not move down into manual jobs. Consequently we must conclude that the rate of mobility in our sample was very high indeed, and, correspondingly, that our data by no means exaggerate the negative influence of one's origins on one's ultimate occupational fate and social status.

The sample certainly cannot be regarded as an unsuccessful, and therefore presumably occupationally disgruntled, group. On the contrary, the number of sons of workers and peasants who were mobile upward is apparently greater than was true for similar groups in the Soviet population at large. Yet to say that our young men, even the children of peasants and workers, were unusually successful does not tell us whether or not all had an *equal* chance for success. In fact, if we define success as the attainment of one of the desirable professional positions, then marked inequality of opportunity is actually the rule.

There is a simple way to measure absolute equality of opportunity even within the framework of the acknowledged pyramid of occupations.

---

* This rate based on all males in the sample, as reported with some adjustments by Robert Feldmesser, "The Persistence of Status Advantages in Soviet Russia," *American Journal of Sociology*, Vol. LIX, No. 1, July 1953. The rate for males 21–40 was very close; as shown in Table 13, it was 26 per cent.

Suppose all jobs were assigned by lot to young people at birth. The chance that any child would end up at any level of the hierarchy would be equal to the proportion which that job represented in the total distribution of occupations. Now we may very roughly estimate the total labor force of the Soviet Union as having been distributed in 1940, the year to which most of our occupational data has prime reference, as follows: Professional-administrative — 2 per cent; semiprofessional — 4 per cent; white-collar — 11 per cent; workers — 33 per cent; and peasants — 50 per cent.[20] These figures are repeated in the last column of Table 13. They enable us quickly to compare the mobility rate that absolute equality of opportunity would have yielded with that which actually occurred. Obviously for boys born into upper level families the actual rate at which they obtained professional positions vastly exceeded what their chances would have been if selection were at random. Instead of 2 per cent of the children of professionals and administrators becoming members of the intelligentsia 65 per cent do, and instead of 33 per cent becoming workers a mere 14 per cent moved down to that level. And, of course, very few indeed become peasants, whereas absolute "automatic" equality would have required that 50 per cent do so. By contrast the child of a peasant had a chance for ultimate placement at any given occupational level that was fairly close to what the random assignment of people to jobs would have decreed.

It is obvious that the ultimate occupational placement of a child, although not absolutely sealed at birth, was heavily determined by his father's position in the occupational structure. Two out of three male children born into a professional or administrator's home could count on attaining to the same level as their father did, whereas only one in twelve of the children of peasants could realistically have the hope of reaching the professional-administrative level. Less than one in five of the sons born into the favored homes was forced to toil with hands, whereas almost eight in ten of the peasant children earned their living in the "dirty, hot, and hard" jobs. We must repeat that this pattern developed in the face of an early social policy deliberately designed to turn the old social order upside down by selective encouragement of the mobility of the children of workers and peasants.

The mobility rates of Soviet groups revealed in Table 13 are very similar in broad outline to those reported for other industrial countries. Indeed, if we ignore refined differences the similarities are striking. For men of all ages and not just young men, in the United States, France, Germany and the Soviet sample, the proportions of workers' sons who hold white-collar jobs are, respectively, 35, 35, 30 and 39 per cent. Marked differences in the social and economic meaning of "farming" in the different countries make for more variation in the proportions of farmers' sons becoming white-collar workers. But here again the pattern is similar, the proportions being, respectively, 23, 16, 12, and 25. When we compare stability rather than mobility, the pattern remains unchanged. The proportion of sons born to white-collar fathers who themselves attained white-collar occupations were, United States — 71, France — 73, Germany — 80, and USSR — 85 per cent.[21]

In some respects the Soviet pattern is distinctive. In particular, mobility out of the worker and peasant category into white-collar work, and stability of status among those already in the white-collar milieu, are more evident in the Soviet data. This could be a product of some peculiarity of our sample, but we suspect it reflects more a peculiarity of recent Soviet history. The rate of Soviet industrial expansion was so rapid that it created rather unprecedented needs for trained technical personnel and associated managerial, professional and clerical employees. Not only did this provide unusual opportunities for those seeking to move up, but it put a premium on the advantages of literacy and general familiarity with office and technical work to which children of white-collar parents are more exposed. So great was the demand that even the less motivated and capable children of white-collar origin could find a niche in the white-collar jobs.

What Accounts for Differential Mobility Rates?

Since the mobility rates in our sample — and, so far as we can tell, in the Soviet Union itself — are so very much like those found in comparable large-scale industrial societies, it is likely that the underlying factors accounting for the mobility rates are also similar. We may delimit three major determinants of a person's chance to attain a desirable occupation in an open class society which places no formal legal restrictions in the path of a young person but leaves him free "to find his own level." The first and perhaps most obvious is his skill or ability to meet the demands of the more complicated and technical jobs. That ability depends, in turn, on a combination of inborn talents such as intelligence, and on the subsequent development or training of those aptitudes. The second determinant is the motivation of the individual to acquire necessary skills and training, and later to undertake the particular activities required by the high level jobs. The third is objective opportunity. In an expanding economy in which more and more technical positions are being created there is clearly more possibility for movement on the part of the talented and motivated. But even in an expanding economy there are fewer good jobs than ordinary and poor ones. The better jobs require more education, or skill, or motivation.

Individuals and groups may have differential opportunity to secure or develop such qualifications. All three of these factors tend to be closely associated with social status. Upper class families in virtually all societies are able to offer more objective assistance to their children in their pursuit of a career. In addition, they pass on to their children values which will motivate them to strive harder and, in most instances, provide a more stimulating intellectual environment. They may even transmit superior biological inheritance — at least as regards intelligence.

All in all, we would expect that if the Soviet population is like most others, children born into professional and other high status families are probably on the average more "intelligent," as measured by intelligence tests, than those born into working-class and peasant families. We have no direct data on the intelligence of our own respondents. However, we do know that in the Soviet Union for a number of years psychological tests consistently favored the children of upper-class families and gave them a preferential advantage. This was a matter of controversy in the schools, the Red Army, and in industry during the First Five Year Plan. At one point those who used psychological tests were instructed to take the class origin of those tested into consideration, so that the children of workers and peasants might have more nearly equal opportunities. Finally, psychological testing was outlawed altogether in 1936, at least in part because test results were apparently embarrassing the regime by consistently showing the children of worker and peasant families to be less talented despite the regime's proclamations to the contrary.[22]

But we know also that in the United States, and presumably in other countries, upper class children do not have a monopoly of ability, and large numbers of children of professional and other high status families manage to get the more desirable jobs despite only modest ability. By contrast, a large proportion of the highly able children of workers and other lower status families do *not* get jobs equal to their capacity.[23]

Soviet folklore, in common with that of many other countries, has featured "rags-to-riches" success stories of persons of poor origins and sparse education who climbed to high positions. But in all modern industrial societies education is clearly the prime determinant of occupational advancement. This is particularly true in the Soviet Union because ultimately almost every man is a government employee, and advancement in any bureaucracy is probably more dependent on education and/or the skills associated with education than is advancement in a more open, competitive situation. As Table 14 shows, becoming a college graduate virtually assured one of escaping manual labor, and indeed three fourths of the young men who were college graduates attained professional or high administrative jobs. On the other hand, only 5 per cent of those respondents who had five to seven years of schooling succeeded in attaining such desirable positions. Furthermore, among those who did not go beyond the basic four year school, 97 per cent ended up doing manual labor

portant on the alleged grounds that poor boys could not get ahead *even with* the advantage of education. On the contrary, as Table 15 shows, persons of peasant and worker origin who did acquire a better education than their peers *also* got better jobs for it. If they obtained ten or more years of schooling almost eight in ten of the worker and peasant origin boys and girls got out of the working class into white-collar work. Almost none who stopped with four years of schooling succeeded in making that advance.

TABLE 15 [25A]

OCCUPATIONAL FATE OF CHILDREN OF UNSKILLED WORKERS
AND PEASANTS ACCORDING TO RESPONDENT'S EDUCATION [a]

	Educational level of respondent		
Occupation attained	High (10 years)	Middle (5–9 years)	Low (0–4 years)
Intelligentsia	36%	4%	0
White-collar employee	43	28	3
Skilled worker	14	17	9
Unskilled worker	4	41	45
Collective farmer	3	10	43
Total number of respondents	102	190	291

a. Includes only respondents 21–40 in 1940.

The reasons for the educational advantage of the children of the professional and administrative classes are many and complex. For one thing, they may well be more intelligent. Whether they are or not, they do not suffer the disadvantage of the peasant boy, and often the worker's child, who often grow up in a community in which both the quality of the lower school and the limited availability of secondary schools place objective limits on one's opportunity to acquire an education. The children of those in the favored statuses were also given stronger parental support in their efforts to get an education. More than two thirds of the young men from white-collar homes stated that they were given complete support as against somewhat more than one third among those of manual origins.[26] There are still other things that getting an education requires. One must postpone for many years the gratifications of earning one's own money and of enjoying the autonomy and freedom from parental control which often go with being on one's own. It generally means putting off marriage. For children in less well-to-do homes, furthermore, it means making economic sacrifices or obliging one's parents to make them. All of this suggests that if a boy of humble origins is to get the training which occupational success so often requires he will need to be strongly motivated, indeed more so than the boy of more fortunate birth. Do the children of manual parents aim as high and have as strong a desire to get ahead as do those born into professional-administrative homes?

A large number of studies conducted in the United States *with adolescents* have shown that youngsters of more humble origins seem to set their occupational goals much lower than do those from better placed families.[27] For example, a study based on 1,000 New Jersey high school students drawn from middle-sized communities revealed that sons of professionals and owners and managers made about 80 per cent of their job choices at that same level, whereas only 54 per cent of the unskilled workers aimed so high. Manual jobs of any kind were chosen by less than 1 per cent of the sons of professionals, whereas 15 per cent of the sons of unskilled and semiskilled workers made such choices.[28] Much the same pattern seems to prevail in the Soviet Union.

As we will see more fully in a moment, one's actual attainments in the occupational realm are associated with one's report of adolescent ambition. To minimize as much as we can any ambiguity which might arise from this factor, we have chosen our very youngest respondents, those who were twenty or less in 1940, and who, therefore, in most cases, had little or no occupational experience in the Soviet Union. Despite the very small numbers this restriction yields, it is still unmistakably evident from Table 16 that boys from manual class backgrounds aim much lower than those from middle and upper class homes.

Ambition obviously far exceeds opportunity. For example, more than half the sons of workers chose jobs above the semiprofessional level, but only about 14 per cent were likely to make it. (See Table 13 above.) But even with so much unrealistic aspiration, the boys of manual origin obviously set their occupational sights much lower than did those from white-collar homes. Ninety-four per cent of boys of white-collar background were at the nonmanual level, whereas only 48 per cent of the boys from worker and peasant homes made such choices. By contrast, it almost never occurred to the children of the intelligentsia or even the ordinary white-collar level that a job as a peasant or even a worker was worth thinking about, whereas more than two fifths of the worker and almost two thirds of the peasant boys chose such manual jobs. Even here, however, it is interesting to note the avoidance of work as a collective farmer. Almost four times as many boys from peasant families wanted to become workers as were willing to stay on as collective farm peasants. Young women show the same class pattern, but they actually exceed their brothers in preference for the better jobs. This is especially evident among persons

TABLE 16 [28A]

OCCUPATIONAL ASPIRATIONS OF MALES UNDER 21 IN 1940:
BY SOCIAL ORIGIN

Occupation aspired to:	Social origin of respondent			
	Professional	Semiprofessional and white-collar	Worker	Peasant
Arts	20%[a]	18%	10%	4%
Applied science	38	42	26	6
Medicine	20	20	9	4
Military[a]	5	4	4	2
Other professional	10	7	4	6
Semiprofessional and white-collar	2	2	4	15
Worker	5	7	40	50
Farmer	0	0	3	13
Total number of respondents	40	45	77	68

a. Includes besides army, navy, aviation, and merchant marine.

of manual origins because of their choice of white-collar and semiprofessional rather than production jobs. In their choices at the upper levels, furthermore, they naturally favor the arts and medicine much more, engineering and science much less.

The difference in the drive to attain favored positions is also evident through a more direct question. Asked whether or not they "wanted a career" while in the Soviet Union, the proportion* who expressed *no* interest in a career rose from 20 per cent among the sons of the intelligentsia, to 34 for white-collar, 46 for worker, and to 59 per cent for peasant boys.** This seems to point unmistakably to a lower level of aspiration among the children from worker and peasant homes. More often they seem content to stay where they started out, or at least to

* Again we are here citing the report of the youngest group — 20 or under in 1940, because answers to this question were also influenced by the occupational level actually attained. This youngest group had almost no occupational experience in the Soviet Union, and therefore could not be influenced by such experience.

** It will be felt, perhaps, that the proportion expressing interest in a career is generally low. Unfortunately, this question seems not to have been asked of any other national population. Since the word "careerist" had pejorative meaning for Soviet refugees, connoting involvement with the regime, the level of reported interest in a career may have been depressed. We doubt, however, that this would have affected the *relative* proportions of respondents of different origins saying yes.

lack the drive to attempt upward mobility. The existence of such a low level of aspiration in people of low status background has been widely observed, and indeed has come to be accepted as a standard accompaniment of low status.[29]

However, we also know that many persons of lower origin do succeed in moving upward on the occupational ladder. It is then reasonable to assume that those persons who moved upward were more ambitious than the average person of comparable origins. From this we would predict that those among our respondents of lower class origins who "moved up" would be more likely to say they had "wanted a career." In Table 17 we have, therefore, organized the data so as to show the relationship of *both* social origin *and* occupational attainment to desire for a career. This requires that we shift again to a somewhat older age group than the adolescents we have just been considering. We return, therefore, to the group 21–40 in 1940, old enough to be at work but young enough to be predominantly Soviet products. Again only men are considered.

We still see here that on the average the higher one's social origin the greater the likelihood of his desiring a career. It is also true that the higher occupational level attained the higher the percentage who wanted a career. Furthermore, in any origin group those persons who advanced furthest are more likely to assert that they wanted a career than those persons of like origins who did not advance so far. This is seen most clearly if we compare the responses of those persons in the top row, who had attained professional-administrative jobs, with those in the third and fourth rows who were merely workers or peasants. It is also clearly evident in a comparison of the third row with the second.

The last table, in combination with number 16 on occupational aspira-

TABLE 17 [29A]

DESIRE FOR A CAREER IN MEN 21–40 IN 1940:
BY ORIGIN AND OCCUPATION

Respondent's occupation	Father's occupation					
	Professional and semiprofessional		Worker		Peasant	
Professional	62%	(93) [a]	56%	(34)	38%	(26)
Semiprofessional	48	(56)	57	(44)	34	(51)
Worker	26	(19)	32	(139)	27	(138)
Collective farm peasant	— [b]		— [b]		27	(85)

a. Total number of respondents on the basis of which the percentage is computed.
b. Less than ten cases in this category, a base too small to warrant percentaging.

tions, could be taken as presenting a clear, coherent picture of society in which social status is correlated with ambition in two ways. Those of lower status are likely to be less ambitious, but those with ambition are able to overcome the handicaps of low status. Unfortunately, Table 17 is equally susceptible to an alternative explanation based on a psychological mechanism memorialized in Western folklore as "sour grapes." It is quite possible that the tendency of adults who were not upwardly mobile or who moved down from a more favored origin to depict themselves as having been less ambitious in their youth is no more than a convenient face-saving device to explain their lack of success.

The fact that our subsample of very young adolescents, who at most had very limited occupational experience, acted just as adolescents do in the United States makes the "sour grapes" interpretation less compelling. In addition, we may call attention to the fact that the sour grapes mechanism hardly operates uniformly. If it did, no one now a worker or peasant would still admit to having earlier aspired to white-collar status. Yet of the young men who were workers and peasants by occupation, 67 per cent were still "able" to admit having earlier aspired to white-collar positions. Still the most prudent interpretation to put on our data is that while people of humble origin set their occupational sights lower, and those with more ambition are more likely to succeed, it is easier to admit having wanted to get ahead if you actually made it than if you remained behind in or fell down into the manual ranks. A man's report of his early ambition is only moderately trustworthy after the race is over and the prizes awarded.

Although our data do not cause us to challenge the common-sense observation that ambition and success are related to some degree, they do raise some question as to the differential effect of ambition in boys whose starting point is different. For this purpose we consider the extent to which people who aspired to more desirable jobs in fact succeed in winning such jobs. Table 18 shows that ambition was not enough. Lower status persons, even when they aspired to good positions, were less likely to achieve high status. Despite the very small numbers to which we are reduced by multiple controls, it is striking that we find such very regular patterns.* Holding constant the social origins of the respondents, we find that the higher their aspiration, the less likely that aspiration was to be satisfied. *In every origin group* the proportion who attained his aspiration goes down as we move from semiprofessional and ordinary white-collar jobs through the professional-administrative to the more esoteric arts. But more pertinent for this analysis, when we consider each category of

* The pattern shown in Table 18 is so striking we have departed from our usual rule of not giving a percentage for cells with a base smaller than ten cases. This table is again based on young men only. The pattern shown in a table for women was very similar.

job aspired to, persons of lower origins were less likely to achieve their aspiration. A peasant boy, even if he was unusual enough to aspire to a job in the arts, had only one chance in ten to make it, as compared to six in ten for the boy of favored background. Although the gap is reduced at the level of less outstanding jobs, it is true even for semiprofessional and white-collar positions that a boy of humble background has less chance of reaching his objective if such a job is his goal.

TABLE 18 [29B]

PER CENT WHO FULFILLED ASPIRATION TO WHITE-COLLAR JOBS AMONG MEN 21–40 IN 1940: BY FATHER'S OCCUPATION

Job aspired to:	Father's occupation							
	Arts and professional-administrative		Semiprofessional and white-collar		Worker		Peasant	
Arts	58%	(14) [a]	31%	(16)	20%	(20)	11%	(9)
Professional-administrative	82	(39)	45	(49)	29	(74)	29	(41)
Semiprofessional and white-collar	100	(4)	93	(14)	82	(16)	68	(19)

a. Total number of respondents on the basis of which the percentage is computed.

To sum up, we find that the mobility aspirations in Soviet Russia are much like those in the United States and many other industrial countries. Children of low origin, especially peasant and ordinary worker origin, set their occupational goals much lower than did the children of the more favored classes. Yet even in the lower classes high aspirations are plentiful. They are also important, since overcoming the disadvantages under which he starts out requires that a lower class boy have strong ambition or drive if he is to succeed. At the same time, such ambition increases the chances of disappointment, since the harsh realities allow only so much room at the top. Consequently the overwhelming majority of even the more ambitious young men and women of lowly origin were doomed to disappointment. This undoubtedly had an effect not only on those directly affected but also on those less ambitious around them who could see that even those boys of lowly origin with the necessary desire and drive so seldom fulfilled their ambition in life.

Some Consequences of Differential Mobility: Past and Future

Success is probably as much worshipped in the Soviet Union as it is in the United States, but as in the United States the chances for success are not equally distributed. One consequence of the differences in opportunity is lessened faith in the prospect of success among those of humble origins. A national sample of Americans was asked in 1946: "Do you think you have a good chance to get ahead in your present line of work?" The proportion who said "yes" fell from 87 among business men, large and small, down to 35 per cent among unskilled workers.[30] Similarly, when asked whether quite apart from their *desire*, they had a *chance* for a "career," the sons of Soviet professionals and administrators said "yes" more then twice as often as did those of skilled worker origin and more than four times as often as did those whose fathers had been peasants.

TABLE 19 [30A]

PER CENT WHO FELT CHANCE FOR A CAREER AMONG MEN 21–40
IN 1940: BY ORIGIN AND OCCUPATION

Respondent's occupation	Respondent's origin							
	Professional		Semiprofessional and white-collar		Worker		Peasant	
Professional	49%	(49) [a]	42%	(45)	36%	(31)	33%	(27)
Semiprofessional and white-collar	27	(11)	28	(47)	22	(46)	19	(53)
Worker	20	(10)	15	(13)	14	(145)	9	(145)
Collective farm peasant	— [b]		— [b]		— [b]		4	(106)

a. Total number of respondents on the basis of which the percentage is computed.
b. Less than 10 cases.

But manual class origins do not inherently compel one to deny that one had a chance. On the contrary, as Table 19 makes clear, the feeling of having had a chance for a career is also strongly dependent on one's success or failure in the occupational realm. Consequently, in every origin group the per cent who felt that they had a chance for a career rises fairly regularly as the attained occupational status of the respondent improves. At the same time, the tendency for people of manual origin to feel deprived of opportunity manifests itself to such a degree as to produce what seems an anomaly. Despite the fact that they have come so far along the road of success, the sons of workers and peasants who attained to professional and semiprofessional positions have no more marked a sense of opportunity than those whose origins were more advantageous but who reached no further. Indeed, they often have less sense of having had a chance for a career. Presumably they are therefore reacting not solely to their actual success, but also displaying their awareness of the obstacles they had to overcome to get there.

Since the feeling that one had a chance for a career is so much a product of one's occupational attainment, it seems as much a reflection of actual experience as it is a measure of sentiment. We cannot assume that those who remained behind in the working class and peasantry, and consequently report that they had "no chance" for a career, are necessarily expressing resentment or lack of faith in the general *possibility* of social mobility under Soviet conditions. To test the degree of faith in that possibility we must turn to the question: "Can any worker in the Soviet Union become a factory manager?" Those in the more favored occupations are prone to have substantially more faith in the prospects of a worker's advancement than do those in the manual occupations, the respective proportions being 46 per cent and 34 per cent saying "yes." *
This is in accord with the pattern of response in the United States, where people in business administration are also much more sanguine about the workers' opportunities for advancement than are the workers themselves.[31] The effect of social origins on the belief in mobility opportunities for the worker in the Soviet Union is similar, although less marked. Those of laboring class origins have less faith in the prospect of advancement for workers than do those born into more advantaged homes. The difference is, however, not sharp. Furthermore, this view is not fixed for life in early youth, since those of worker origin who were themselves successful in attaining to professional status were substantially more likely to affirm a belief in the possibility of mobility than were their less successful brothers in origin.

The less sanguine image of mobility opportunities among those of manual origins is also reflected in the reasons they give for occupational failure or success. In their explanations for the failure of the worker to become a manager they cite lack of capacity or competence less frequently than do those of nonmanual origin, and more often declare that workers would be too proud to do the bootlicking necessary to get ahead. Similarly, in describing the "sort of person who gets ahead in the Soviet Union" those of manual background cite *talent* and other positive personal attributes less than half as frequently as do those of nonmanual origin. Thus, one engineer said "it would be a mistake to think that only Communists can get ahead in the Soviet Union . . . people with good technical training and skill can also make rapid advancement." Sons of workers and peasants tend instead to give relatively more emphasis to

---

* In the chapter on education, we will see a comparable tendency for the more highly placed respondents to more likely say "yes" to the question: "Given ability, can one get as much education as he desires?"

political connections and to public avowal of support for the regime as explanations of success. The contrast between the view of those placed high and low is typified by the remark of a young man just under thirty who worked in collective farm administration after completing the ten-year school, and of an ordinary collective farm peasant of forty-five. The young man from administration identified as persons who succeed "those whose heads function, for one thing." The older rank-and-file peasant said: "People who lost their conscience, all their honesty, who are able to destroy other people in order that they themselves might live a good life, get ahead. . . . They are . . . willing tools of the Communist Party."

In order to minimize distracting side issues we have based our discussion up to this point almost exclusively on the mobility experiences and attitudes of the distinctively Soviet generation born or raised after the revolution. Dealing thus with a single generation we develop a somewhat static picture. A comparison of the age subgroups within our sample reveals important differences in their assessment of mobility.[32] Although we cannot be certain that these differences represent true generational differences or merely the effect of maturation and experience as people grow older, the trends deserve our attention.

The desire for a career is much greater among young people and in every social group the proportion reporting such desire rises steadily as one goes by ten-year age classes from the group over fifty to those under thirty. In addition, and in part corroboration of the career desire measure, the adolescent choices of job suggest a shifting emphasis. Among those in the younger age groups the high level intelligentsia jobs are, relatively speaking, more "over chosen" and the farm jobs relatively more "under chosen." The nature of such choices may be measured by an index, in which the per cent of an age group *actually* in an occupation is related to the per cent *desiring* to be in it. If these were equal the index is 1, if a larger percentage of people desired to be in it the index is above 1, if fewer desired it, below 1. Going from those over fifty to those under thirty the index for the intelligentsia jobs rose steadily from 1.80 among those over fifty to 2.26 among the youngest. By contrast the index for farm occupations fell drastically from 2.43 for those over fifty to a mere .26 for those under 30. This indicates again what we have already noted: the young people want to get off the farms.

Fortunately for the regime the sense of opportunity for a career is also greater among younger people. This is again true in every social group, with minor fluctuations, as one goes from those over fifty to those under thirty. But the crucial question arises: is the expanding sense of opportunity able to keep pace with the expanding hunger for careers? One way of measuring this relation is to compare the proportions in various age groups who wanted a career and felt they had the opportunity with those with the desire but no sense of opportunity.

TABLE 20 [32A]

CAREER DESIRE AND OPPORTUNITY AMONG MEN:
BY SOCIAL GROUP AND AGE

Desire career?	Have chance?	Intelli- gentsia	White- collar employees	Skilled workers	Ordinary workers	Collective farm peasants
under 31						
yes	yes	42%	22%	12%	11%	8%
yes	no	26	32	31	28	27
no	yes	7	8	6	2	2
no	no	25	38	51	59	63
Total number of respondents		166	129	126	178	126
31–40						
yes	yes	24%	8%	4%	4%	5%
yes	no	31	35	13	17	22
no	yes	10	8	8	3	0
no	no	35	49	75	76	73
Total number of respondents		85	87	52	76	56
over 40						
yes	yes	10%	4%	0%	2%	3%
yes	no	17	22	26	9	10
no	yes	16	8	5	0	0
no	no	47	66	69	89	87
Total number of respondents		82	130	19	46	31

The spreading hunger for a career has certainly not been matched completely by the rapid rise in the sense of opportunity. Indeed the portion whose ambitions were frustrated, that is, those who wanted a career but had no chance for one, increased substantially in most classes. Going from the older group, over forty, to those thirty or under, the number of the frustrated went from 17 to 26 per cent in the intelligentsia, from 10 to 27 per cent in the peasantry. But in the intelligentsia the rise in the percentage of those frustrated is greatly offset by a more dramatic rise in the per cent of those who were satisfied — wanting a career and having a chance. As a result, the ratio of satisfied to frustrated in the younger intelligentsia is almost 2:1, whereas in the peasantry the situation is sharply reversed, with the satisfied being outnumbered by the frustrated in the ratio of better than 1:3. There is, furthermore, marked change in these ratios over time for the intelligentsia, with the ratio of those satisfied to those frustrated changing from a balance of 10/17 among the older to the reverse 42/26 among the younger. By contrast in all age categories among the collective farm peasants the ratio of satisfied to frustrated remains on the negative side of 1:3. This strongly suggests that for the youngest people in the manual classes the sense of opportunity for a career has not so well kept pace with the expanding desire for a career, at least as contrasted with the situation of youths in the intelligentsia.

Thus, those of more humble origin emerge as substantially less impressed with the opportunities for mobility in Soviet society. The clearest and most striking manifestation is in the small percentage of those of humble origin who feel they themselves had a chance to succeed. But they also feel that any member of their class as a whole was less likely to succeed. And they are more inclined to believe that those who did succeed did so through acts, or because of the possession of qualities, which could hardly be unequivocally approved.

If our sample is at all representative of the occupational mobility experience of comparable origin groups in the Soviet Union it suggests some problems for the system. Of the younger men who are now members of the working class about one fourth reported that as adolescents they hoped to find positions in the arts or the professions. A greater portion may well have had such ambition, but found it too difficult to admit their failure or disappointment. The system has stimulated more desire for advancement than it can in fact provide even allowing for the great expansion in the number of more desirable positions. We do not assert that those who aimed high but could not rise are necessarily disgruntled with the system, although there is some evidence (see Chapter XI) that amongst manual-class people who did not achieve their career desires there is less support for the regime than among those of the same class who did not experience this frustration. Rather we feel that the existence of so large a corps of working-class people who would like to be something else and apparently *expected* or hoped to be better off is only the most acute manifestation of a more general and widely ramified problem.

It is a marked characteristic of Soviet society that belief in the importance of "success" or personal "advancement" is widespread. Success is most often defined to mean advancing along the occupational status ladder. The Soviet regime has indeed encouraged a cult of success similar to that often alleged to characterize the United States. In part this has derived spontaneously from Marxist and Leninist ideology. In good part, however, the cult of success has been consciously fostered by the regime as a way of solving some pressing practical problems in the realm of incentives. The rate of industrial expansion, and the associated growth of the apparatus of administration and service, required a tremendous increase in the number of well educated and trained persons. To fill this gap the regime felt it necessary to glorify the roles of engineer, doctor, manager, ballerina, in order to attract young people to make the effort required to win to such positions. Inevitably, any such program will have effects beyond those immediately intended and calculated. One such effect seems to have been the one we earlier noted: more people hope to advance than in fact do or can advance.

There is perhaps nothing unusual in this situation and certainly it does not necessarily presage a major crisis for the regime. At the same time it is obviously the basis for a genuine social problem with which Soviet leaders must deal. Several paths lie open as channels for relieving this pressure. The most obvious solution would be to reduce the appeal of superior positions, praising their importance less, paying them less, and so on. This solution is not only most obvious but also least acceptable. The regime is dependent on continuous recruitment of high level personnel, and the broader the base of those interested and motivated to attain high positions the better the candidates selected are likely to be. In addition, the regime is dependent on its specialists for the smooth working of the system, and is not likely to alienate them so grossly for any gain so modest as lessened competition for superior jobs. Consequently, although we may expect a periodic flurry of activity to cut the technical, scientific and managerial elite down a notch or two, we can hardly expect a serious and concerted effort to reduce their standing. Thus there was in 1956 a flurry of excitement about salary reductions and loss of car and chauffeur privileges for some. This was one of a series of measures designed to encourage the lower classes by seeming to deny the more favored. But nothing very much has come of it.

A quite different alternative is to maintain a high rate of mobility. This the regime has in fact done, aided by the tremendous increase in the number of favored positions which accompanied industrialization. Between 1928 and 1941 the number of specialists with higher and secondary specialized education increased almost fourfold, and between 1941 and 1946 it more than doubled again. This and the associated increase in routine white-collar jobs provided an opportunity for millions of the sons and daughters of workers and peasants to advance themselves.* Mobility opportunities should now be increased because of the great expansion in the availability of secondary education and the elimination of all tuition fees both for the three years of high school and all levels of college training. But impressive as these shifts in the occupational structure are, they

* For still further developments, see Chapter VI, on education, below.

cannot be expected to continue at the same rate indefinitely. In addition, the larger the size of the nonmanual white-collar force becomes, the greater is the pool of people of white-collar origin competing against those of manual labor origin for the favored positions.

Ultimately, therefore, the system must face the challenge of making manual labor more rewarding materially and psychologically. The substantial solution of this problem is often asserted to account for the pacific and nonradical quality of labor in the United States and Scandinavia as compared to France and Italy. Where mobility is limited, as it must of necessity be everywhere, yet where the working class has learned to expect rewards at least approximating those of the better educated and trained personnel, it is only through large increments in status backed by a solid and expanding standard of living that one can hope to avoid large-scale working-class resentment and consequent political unrest.

The post-Stalin loosening of the bonds of political control, while decreasing resentment, increased the freedom of communication and this facilitated the amplification of those grievances which still remain. After Stalin's death Soviet leaders adopted a series of new measures to improve the relative position of the working class. These included a new system of pensions, the sharp reduction in the salaries of those professors, inventors, writers and others whose earnings had been extraordinarily large, and the allocation of a large sum of additional monies in the budget to raise the minimum wages of low earners. At the same time, a large-scale program is under way in the factories to increase the qualifications of workers. After a long lapse following the demise of the Stakhanovite movement, the leading workers or "innovators" of Soviet factories and farms are again being glorified in the Soviet press as labor heroes. The challenge of improving the status and financial position of the peasant is more difficult, but here as well the regime has been moving to somewhat redress the balance.

These moves should serve to make the status of worker, and to a lesser degree of peasant, more acceptable, or at least less undesirable. But in an expanding economy social policy cannot stand still. The regime is therefore faced with a potential demand from its working class for ever increasing standards of living and increments of prestige. Whether it will be willing, or able even if willing, to divert resources to consumption at the scale such pressure may require is one of the major problems of future Soviet development. The alternative to meeting this demand would, however, be either ever increasing unrest and unruliness in the labor classes, or the reimposition of the Stalinist controls both on the workers' job rights and on their freedom as citizens. Although the last development is not to be ruled out, it seems the least likely.

If the current leadership is unwilling again to impose Stalinesque controls in order to keep the mass of workers in depressed conditions while highly rewarding a favored minority of the population, it may have to impose controls at the other end of the scale. Recent reports indicate the Soviet leaders may be considering such a new course, which while falling short of the stringency of Stalinist methods yet has as its objective to regain for the government leaders their control over mobility aspirations and individual career paths. Touched off by a "note" from Khrushchev which appeared on September 21, 1958, a full scale discussion of needed changes in the organization of Soviet education and technical training filled Soviet newspapers and journals in the fall of 1958. Khrushchev's note provided dramatic acknowledgment from the highest quarters of the condition which our data so sharply exposed. Manual labor is held in low esteem in the Soviet Union, and there is much more craving for white-collar positions than there are jobs available at that level. Khrushchev's comment echoed that made many years earlier by Kalinin, and expressed the same tone of disappointment:

Boys and girls who have graduated from secondary school as a rule consider that the only path acceptable to them is to continue their education in the higher, or in extreme cases, specialized secondary educational institute. Some of those who have finished the ten year school unwillingly go to work in factories and plants, on the kolkhozes and Sovkhozes, while some even consider this an insult to them. Such a haughtily scornful, incorrect attitude toward physical labor is to be seen in the home too.[33]

The measures proposed to meet this challenge would force youths to go to work after they had completed seven years of schooling. Education beyond this point would be permitted only after two or three years of such employment, and then only in conjunction with continuing "work in production." It is uncertain whether these measures will be adopted, and difficult to assess their effect if they are. Our estimate is that they would, perhaps unintentionally, act to increase the mobility differentials we have described. For one thing, a boy of working-class background, after two or three years in a factory, would be less likely to resume his education than one from a middle class home. Furthermore, there are indications that for a select group a different path to higher education will be left open through Khrushchev's favored boarding schools and other special channels. These opportunities would obviously fall disproportionately to the children of those presently in the ruling elite and the intelligentsia. Be that as it may, these latest developments provide striking evidence that the problems uncovered by our data continue to characterize the Soviet Union no less than they do other industrial societies which stress the ideals of mobility and equality of opportunity.

V

Making a Living

In modern industrial societies, a man's "job" tends to be the most important fact about him, since it determines how he spends his time, how he and his family live, how he will be treated by others, and his chances for pleasures and gratifications. The primacy of a man's occupational involvement is reflected in our tendency, when seeking information about a person, to ask, "What does he do?" rather than "Who is he?" or, "What kind of a person is he?" In human interest news stories, as in the hospital records on which they are based, the biologically determined facts of age and sex are almost always accompanied by a description of the socially determined fact of "occupation." In the Soviet Union the elimination of the traditional and hereditary classes, membership in which conferred a special status quite apart from occupation, has increased the central role which a man's occupation plays in determining his life conditions. The most important change, however, involved not the old nobility and the bourgeoisie, but the free peasant. The reduction of the peasantry to something roughly akin to hired labor of the state on collective farms has brought them fully within the realm of the labor force, in a fashion quite different from that in other peasant countries. In the Soviet Union, to a greater degree than in any other country in the world, there is no income except that earned by work. Furthermore, there is almost no way to earn income except by working in some enterprise in which the individual is an employee, even if only ultimately, of the state.

Soviet economic establishments are in many important aspects indistinguishable from similar enterprises in other countries. Hospitals, government offices, schools, and other noneconomic institutions are often also quite similar. The same range of techniques is employed, the same hierarchy of authority and responsibility is enforced, and the same goods or services are produced in a Soviet as in an American factory, department store, or hospital. Yet in several major respects, to have worked in the prewar years in the Soviet setting as against the American, or British, or French is to have lived in a different world. Although they were rocked by the depression, few fundamental changes occurred in the economies of the United States and Western Europe during the interwar years. In contrast the economic structure of Soviet society was undergoing an extraordinary revolution. Through the application of an extremely high rate of investment, based upon forced savings from consumption, Stalin sought through the five-year plans to transform "backward" Russia into an industrial power second only to the United States.

Although their claims were often exaggerated, there is no doubting that the men in the Kremlin successfully led an extraordinary economic movement which in ten years resulted in a fourfold increase in iron and steel capacity, while oil and coal increased by three and electrical output by seven times. A wide range of new industries was established. In other industries, earlier modest, the Soviet Union became first in the world — as in tractor and locomotive production. In agriculture, some twenty-five millions of individual farmsteads were combined into 250,000 large-scale, mechanized collective farms. Together these changes produced an extraordinarily rapid transformation in the composition of the population, as the number of wage and salary earners increased from one tenth to one third of the gainfully employed.[1]

The entire development was, however, carried out under the most extreme forced draft. Shortages were chronic, scarcities of the most basic items routine. Strict allocation of men and material was the rule. Everything was rationed and controlled. The regime, in a frenzy to achieve its objectives, applied force liberally to those who failed or were thought to lag behind. Every possible device to extract additional labor from the workers was resorted to, and as one engineer said of Stakhanovism, the foremost of these methods, "It was a terrible thing, to squeeze out of every worker the last drop of sweat and send him on the way to eternity."

This hurried forced pace of development, which came to be known as "the tempo," colored the experience of almost everyone engaged in the Soviet economy in the period before the war. The chronic shortages, the extreme pressure, the confusion and contradictions, the terrible crowding, the harsh labor discipline laws, the exercise of political terror, all contributed to make participation in Soviet economic life less rewarding and less romantically exciting than many in the West, impressed by the grandeur of the plans for economic development, imagined it to be.

Levels of Job Satisfaction

Fortunately, the sample of former Soviet citizens reached by the project was large enough to provide a group highly diversified in its occupational membership. Among those in the "arts," we had opera singers, ballet dancers, journalists, and painters; among the professional technicians there were more than seventy-five engineers representing many types of engineering, as well as agronomists and other agricultural scientists; in the liberal professional group there were many doctors and lawyers, with professors and scientific workers also strongly represented. Teachers predominated among the semiprofessionals, but the group ran the gamut from nurses to forestry technicians. Although the white-collar workers consisted largely of typists, secretaries, and bookkeepers, there were also draftsmen, cashiers, supply agents, and others having more unusual office work activities. The greatest variety, of course, was found among the workers, who represented dozens of different jobs, from watchmaker and locksmith, through crane operator and conductor, to sweeper and stoker.

Among those gainfully employed, women are strongly represented. They make up 25 per cent of those in the sample's urban labor force. If allowance is made for the fact that women were not half but only about one third of our total sample, it will be evident that the proportion of women in our sample's "labor force" compares quite favorably with the 38 per cent women represented in the Soviet work force in 1940.[2] Their distribution among the various occupations largely followed expectation. For example, more than twice as many of the women as men went into white-collar jobs; women who were at the higher levels held virtually no managerial posts, but were twice as likely as men to be attracted to the arts; and very few women qualified as skilled workers whereas a high proportion were laboratory technicians and similar white-collar equivalents of the skilled worker.

The basic question we asked with regard to occupational experience was: "Did you like the job you held (in 1940)?" The questionnaire item "do you like your job?" is now almost a tradition in surveys but we may still wonder how important and meaningful a response to it can be when it is given by politically disaffected refugees. Since about half of our respondents said they liked the job they held in 1940,* we can hardly assume that they were painting an all black picture. Still, is it not much blacker than need be? There are two dimensions of possible distortion to be considered. Either all are blackening the picture somewhat, or, some may be reporting truthfully and others are painting a very black picture indeed.

Fortunately, comparable questions have been asked of large representative samples in other countries. On the whole the general *pattern* of answers (Table 21), as distinguished from the particular levels of satisfaction reported, is about what we have come to expect from a European type population. Professionals and business administrators overwhelm-

---

* Throughout this chapter we have based our tables and analysis on the opinions of those who were gainfully employed while in the Soviet Union, rather than on the social class groups. Our assumption is, of course, that the opinions about work conditions offered by housewives and others not employed while in the USSR are likely to be mere hearsay even if relevant under certain circumstances. The correlation between occupation and social group identification is, of course, exceedingly high in our sample.

ingly report job satisfaction; the per cent satisfied generally decreases as we descend the occupational hierarchy; certain special groups stand out, like the skilled workers who are everywhere sharply separated from the ordinary workers and indeed often are more frequently satisfied than are the ordinary white-collar employees.

TABLE 21 [2A]

NATIONAL COMPARISONS OF JOB SATISFACTION: PER CENT SATISFIED: BY OCCUPATION AND COUNTRY

USSR		US		Germany		Sweden		Norway	
		Lg. business	100%						
Arts and profes-sional-ad-minis-trative	77%	Small business	91			Upper class	84%	Upper class	93%
		Profes-sional	82	Profes-sional	75%				
Semipro-fessional	70			Upper white-collar	65				
		White collar	82	Civil serv-ants (all)	51	Middle class	72	Middle class	88
				Lower white collar	33				
White-collar	60								
Skilled worker	62	Skilled manual	84	Skilled worker	47				
Semi-skilled	45	Semi-skilled	76	Semi-skilled	21	Work-ing class	69	Work-ing class	83
Unskilled	23	Un-skilled	72	Unskilled	11				
Peasant	12			Farm labor	23				

Although the class patterning of the answers given by the refugees seems to be relatively standard, the average degree of satisfaction and the per cent satisfied at any given occupational level clearly is subject to influences stemming from general cultural and economic differences between nations. Further difficulties of interpretation arise from differences in question wording and in methods for categorizing occupations. Consequently, the fact that the levels of job satisfaction in the Soviet groups are generally lower than in the United States and Norway, rather like those in Sweden, and as high or higher than those in Germany, certainly provides no grounds for rejecting the data and indeed gives some reason for accepting it.

Even if we do not challenge the general level of reported satisfaction, we cannot help but be struck by the extraordinarily low level of satisfaction among the peasants. The fact that so many of our peasant respondents had suffered from forced expropriation cannot explain this since, as we have seen (in Chapter II, Table 3), even the peasants who had not had this experience reported similarly low levels of satisfaction. But our suspicion of this response as possibly unrealistic and probably grossly exaggerated is reasonable only so long as we forget that these are collective farm peasants, and not the American farmer-businessman nor the independent, self-sustaining European peasant who operates his own small farmstead and markets his own produce. The *kolkhoznik*, or Russian peasant on the collective farm, can only meaningfully be compared to the depressed landless agricultural laborer, who works mainly for shares or wages on the farm of another and perhaps operates for himself — usually at an exorbitant rent — an extremely small farmstead little better or larger than the garden plot of the *kolkhoznik*. When such individuals are the standard of comparison, the refugee peasant in our sample is evidently reporting on his job satisfaction in much the same way as comparably depressed peasants elsewhere in Europe. In Germany, for example, 61 per cent of the regular farmers said that they would choose the same occupation if they had the opportunity to start over again, a level of job satisfaction close to that reported by the German upper white-collar groups. By contrast, among German farm laborers 77 per cent would choose a *different* job.[3] The extremely low level of satisfaction among the poor peasants of Germany which this registers, is very similar to the result obtained for the Soviet Union. Further supporting evidence is provided by an Italian study of satisfaction among manual workers. Of the four groups studied, the farm laborers were the group with the fewest satisfied, with a difference of 25 per cent between the proportion satisfied among skilled workers as against farm laborers.[4]

Women seemed consistently more gratified with their occupational experience than men. Of the eight occupations with sufficient women to permit comparisons, there were seven in which women liked their jobs more often than men, and often by a difference of 10 per cent or more. But women responded to their work experience predominantly according to occupational level and only incidentally according to their sex. Thus, men in the arts reported job satisfaction in 94 per cent of the cases, as against 11 per cent among the peasants, and for women we see a similar pattern with a drop from 100 per cent to 18 per cent. Occupational standing, not sex, is the prime determinant of job satisfaction. Consequently none of the conclusions stated in this section would have been basically different if the proportions of women in the group as a whole or in particular occupations had been very different. Much the same conclusion may be drawn with regard to the age composition of the various occupational groups. The significance of age and sex in occupational behavior will be discussed more fully in our conclusions to this chapter.

Before we proceed to use the pattern of response to a question on "liking your job" as a key to experiences in the occupational realm, we should satisfy ourselves that it is an important and meaningful response which is significantly related to Soviet conditions. It may be that "liking" the job has little to do with how *satisfied* or *gratified* you were in it. In particular, this might be true of the members of the intelligentsia, who may have "liked" being doctors, lawyers, and professors, but who were not "happy" in their work because they held these positions under Soviet conditions. Fortunately, we have available an independent measure of work satisfaction. In our life-history interviews we did not, as in the written questionnaire, simply ask each respondent to check off "yes" or "no," but rather spent an hour or more fully discussing each respondent's work experience. When each respondent was "coded" by us on the basis of this rich qualitative report, the resultant scores showed a pattern virtually identical with that obtained on the written questionnaire. For example, on the life-history interview 82 per cent of the intelligentsia and 24 per cent of the collective farmers were rated as apparently "enjoying" their work, whereas the comparable percentages of respondents who reported job satisfaction on the written questionnaire were respectively 77 and 12 per cent. These and other qualitative data leave little doubt but that the satisfaction obtained from one's total work experience varied markedly from the top to the bottom of the occupational ladder, and that liking or not liking one's job is a good general index to the degree of overall job satisfaction.

Since the members of the Soviet intelligentsia reported themselves satisfied at a rate similar to that of professionals elsewhere, and the low level of satisfaction among the peasants "makes sense" in view of the sentiments expressed by very depressed peasants in other countries, we incline to accept the report on job satisfaction as not disproportionately influenced by political sentiment. The systematic decline in the proportion satisfied as one descends the occupational ladder leaves little doubt that responses were determined primarily by the jobs individuals held rather than by their common status as political refugees. Nevertheless, we made a further test of the assumption that a person's political attitude induced him to respond to the job satisfaction question in a "political" way. If this were the case, a hostile person would presumably report himself dissatisfied with his job, in order to blacken the regime. This assumption was tested with the hostility, anti-Soviet sentiment, and flattery scales. Generally, but not consistently, those more hostile to the Soviets or favorable to Americans were somewhat less likely to report job satisfaction. To choose the most extreme example from what was in fact generally more inconclusive data, among the intelligentsia 82 per cent of those low in anti-Soviet sentiment were satisfied as against only 70 per cent of those who were strongly anti-Soviet. Among peasants the drop was from 22 to 11 per cent.[5] Even in this extreme example, it is evident the kind of job a man held and not his evaluation of the Soviet system mainly determined his report of job satisfaction. In the unlikely event that all peasants were among those favoring the regime, and all the members of the intelligentsia were most hostile to it, the proportion reporting job satisfaction among those holding professional-administrative jobs would still be three and a half times the proportion among peasants. It is therefore not very meaningful to ask "why did former Soviet citizens so dislike their jobs?" Rather we must ask why those placed in the occupational hierarchy were so highly satisfied and those in the manual occupations so relatively and absolutely dissatisfied.

Working Conditions

In the USSR the state is the overwhelmingly preponderant force in economic activity, and the Communist Party controls the state and infiltrates all spheres of economic life. We might, then, well expect the impact of the distinctive Soviet political system to be a major factor in the work experience of Soviet citizens and hence a prime determinant of the relative work satisfaction of various groups. Our data do reveal differences in the awareness of political interference and in resentment of it among the various social and occupational groups. Since it is mainly the upper level occupationally satisfied groups which are concerned with the problem, however, the political factor hardly explains the differential pattern of work satisfaction.

At several points in the life-history interviews, the awareness and concern of the upper occupational groups with the politicization of their work became manifest. For example, the proportion of the intelligentsia who spontaneously cited the effects of political interference in the work situation was more than three times that among the kolkhozniks. In discussing what aspects of the work situation made it difficult to do a good job in the Soviet Union, the intelligentsia cited political interference most frequently, and it was mentioned by almost three fourths of those who answered the question. In contrast, this category of complaint was mentioned by little more than one fourth of these collective farmers who cited some specific obstacle. The intelligentsia's sensitivity to the political coloration of their work was further exemplified by their propensity to attribute dissatisfaction with superiors to the latter's Communist Party affiliations. Of those in the intelligentsia who expressed any dissatisfaction with a superior, more than 60 per cent complained about his acting as a representative of the party, whereas this complaint was cited by only half as many peasants.[6] The strength of feeling concerning the intrusion of political factors into the work situation is well reflected in these comments by a former major in the Red Army:

> The commanding personnel was treated in a vulgar manner, particularly by the political personnel. All this chasing, this nervousness, it was on the basis of political work, because for all this work the political apparatus exerted the most pressure on the commanding personnel. . . . The political personnel created contempt against them . . . if something happened in a unit whose commander was not a Communist, they would say this is because he is not a party man.

Political interference on the job is probably only a mere irritation compared to the danger of political arrest, yet here again the arrest rates for specific occupations hardly help explain the greater job satisfaction of those occupationally well placed. Of those gainfully employed, about one fourth of each occupational level had themselves been arrested at one time or another, except for the professional group where the rate reached 37 per cent. At every occupational level, those who held responsible supervisory positions were more likely to have been arrested. Not only were the high level jobs factually at least as dangerous or more dangerous than the less responsible positions, but they were also judged to be more dangerous both by the incumbents and the general population.[7] A rating of above average exposure to arrest danger was assigned to factory manager by 79 per cent of the respondents, to engineers by 76 per cent, and to army officers by 62 per cent, whereas that dubious distinction was earned by bookkeeper in 43 per cent of the votes, teacher 37 per cent, and worker only 11 per cent.[8]

Professionals and white-collar employees saw their work environment as generally friendly, while the ordinary workers and peasants were definitely prone to see it as hostile or unpleasant. Apparently this does not result from different kinds of peer relations, since the proportions of those in each occupation who felt friendly toward their co-workers and believed that their co-workers felt friendly toward them were not significantly patterned. There is always the boss, however, and here we do indeed find some important differences. When encouraged to give spontaneous comments on their work superiors, the proportion of the intelligentsia, white-collar and skilled worker groups who had something positive to say about their boss was about equal to the proportion who had some dissatisfaction to express. Among the workers, however, the proportion of complaints to praise was about 3:2 and among the peasants

3:1. In relations with their superiors, then, the ordinary workers and peasants end up with a deficit of positive feeling.

Although it is not easy to trace a direct connection with the amount of job satisfaction, we should nevertheless not fail to note that there are major differences in the reasons offered by occupational groups for being either satisfied or dissatisfied with their superiors. The comments of professionals, administrators, and ordinary white-collar people concerning their boss focused about equally on his competence, his personal qualities, his political character, and his interest in the welfare of his subordinates. The peasants and workers distributed their comments in a markedly different way. Almost half of all their remarks dealt with the boss's concern, or lack of it, for their personal welfare. A mere 6 per cent of the comments were about his competence. Typical of the peasant's view was the response of a kolkhoznik of forty-four to the question "What do you mean by 'being a good boss'?" His response:

Save some fodder for the peasants, give them something for their own cow or sheep. One can always help in some little way. It's all only pennies, but you can save them or spend them, and that makes a difference.

The position of the two groups in the social structure of the work unit is of course very different. The peasant and worker are at the end of the chain of command performing jobs which on the whole are highly routinized. Their immediate superiors tend to be foremen and others fairly low in the chain of command. Under these conditions the competence of the superior is not so likely to be germane to the tasks performed or the sums earned by the worker and peasant. But the superior does have considerable power over the ordinary worker and peasant. He can be a screen and buffer between the great powers and those who work under him. Or, he can be rigid in his enforcement of the rules and exacting in transmitting orders from above, thus making the life of those under him less comfortable than it might be. Equally, he can aid those he liked. A stamp press operator of forty, had this to say of his supervisor:

The brigadier could place his friends where the work was easier; those whom he had little liking for were placed so that upon them would fall the hardest and most dirty type of work. The brigadier had this initiative because to him fell the responsibility of keeping track of the norm fulfilled.

Although the same sort of thing can happen in an office, in general the white-collar and particularly the professional worker is more likely to work in intimate collaboration with his superior and to share responsibility with him, a circumstance which makes that superior's technical competence a matter of greater importance. In addition, the work is not routinized and a proper evaluation of it requires technical competence.

Under the circumstances, we can well see how differences in one's location in the occupational structure would foster differences in the criteria applied in evaluating superiors. More typical for those holding managerial jobs was the comment of an accountant who said:

> The chief must be a person who is competent in all aspects of the enterprise whose head he is. He must be a specialist in his job, and not simply an administrator. He must be a man; he must be orderly . . . and he must demand fulfillment of his orders.

Similar differences emerged when we asked our respondents what specific factors made it difficult to do a good job in the Soviet Union. Poor working conditions and bad materials were cited much more often by the workers and peasants than they were by the intelligentsia and employees. Again we can see how their position in the occupation structure would account for the difference in response by the two groups. The peasant and worker is dependent on the tools and materials with which he works to a degree which substantially exceeds that of the white-collar or professional worker who is more dependent on the skills which he carries in himself.

In the Soviet Union piece rates predominate in industry, applying to about 65 per cent of all work. Further, the attempt to develop precise norms as a basis for payment, linked with penalties for underfulfillment and bonuses for overfulfillment, has probably been carried further in the Soviet Union than in any other country. The history of Soviet industry in the period of the five-year plans has been strongly colored by the regime's continuous efforts to increase labor productivity by constantly raising production norms. There is no such thing as a minimum wage for pieceworkers, and so one is driven to fulfill the norm. Indeed, it is difficult to convey adequately the malaise which the norm system seems to have developed. Gliksman[9] concludes that our respondents classified it as one of the worst evils of the entire Soviet system. He is supported in this conclusion by a profusion of statements from our interviews which labelled the norm system "inhuman," "a vicious thing," "beyond one's capacity," and "incredibly high." Indeed, one young engineer said: "I consider the work norms as the shrewdest invented means for the exploitation of mankind."

Here again, however, there are marked differences in perception and evaluation according to the person's position in the occupational structure. Norms cannot easily be applied to the type of work done by many employees and even less to the work of professionals, supervisors, administrators and others in the intelligentsia. It will be no great surprise, therefore, to learn that whereas well under half of the intelligentsia and employees felt that norms were excessive in the Soviet Union, this was the opinion of about two thirds of the workers and peasants. Furthermore, this opinion was based on marked differences in actual experience. Very few of the intelligentsia and employees who complained about work norms in general reported that they personally had any real difficulty with them, whereas a substantial proportion of the workers and peasants who felt the norms generally excessive reported this to have been true in their personal experience as well. Thus, the manual workers tended to complain about the norms with a sense of immediacy and bitterness, as in the comment of a Ukrainian who rose to be foreman, but in looking back on his days as a worker recalled:

We had to fulfill and overfulfill. . . . It was fear that made the workers work faster. If a worker gets 200 or 300 rubles, how can he live? If he has a family of six then it is life itself that makes him try harder to reach the minimum norm so that he won't starve to death.

In contrast, the members of the intelligentsia tended to be bland in their evaluation of the norm system. Indeed at times they reflected their role as management, and expressed criticism of the workers' attitude. Thus, one young engineer with wide experience in technical offices and factories who, as he put it, was "responsible for the worker's level of production," complained:

The workers don't understand our position. If they get high norms which they have to fulfill, or if they get low wages, they blame the administrators . . . they don't realize that these people have to do it because of the allocation of the budget. . . .

From these items in the life-history interview we conclude that the nonmanual groups are consistently more pleased with their working environment, both physical and human, and derive pleasure from it, whereas the manual workers and peasants find the working environment on balance unpleasant and uncongenial both in its personal and social aspects. Here again the skilled workers were in a rather special position, closer to the employees than to the ordinary workers. About a dozen of the items from the Sentence Completion Test — the only psychological test completed by all the life-history informants — also dealt with job and career situations. Such items were: #3 "When the work appeared very difficult to Michael . . ." and that which began, "When he was offered responsible work Pavel. . . ." Analysis of these items confirmed and enriched our impression of the adjustment of the several occupational strata to their work environment. For example, the elite, when faced with challenges such as competition or difficult work, responded by competing, persevering and showing more initiative than other groups (see Table 22). They seemed generally confident of their actual capacity to handle the normal exigencies of the work situation although they did seem rather anxious about threats to their status.[10] In contrast the general outlook of the workers towards most aspects of the work situation was negative, and there was much anxiety and insecurity evident. They seemed to lack confidence in their ability to cope with it in a flexible, easy way. The peasants were closest to the workers, although somewhat easier in their relations with superiors. Again the skilled workers showed distinctive qualities; they appeared much more persevering (see Table 22), and expressed more initiative and self-confidence than the ordinary workers.

TABLE 22 [10A]

RESPONSES TO A SENTENCE FRAGMENT: BY SOCIAL GROUP

"When the instruments he needed were not delivered in time . . ."

Response category	Intelligentsia	White-collar employees	Skilled workers	Ordinary workers	Collective farmers
Shows initiative or perseverance	44%	25%	22%	4%	9%
Indicates failure or stoppage	14	38	21	36	36
Becomes angry or distressed	41	36	55	60	57
Total number of respondents	91	55	32	47	34

Income and Satisfaction

Although occupational groups do differ in how rewarding or punishing they find their working conditions to be, the differences are not so massive as to account adequately for the differences in satisfaction. Indeed, it might be argued that complaints about work conditions are merely an alternative expression rather than a determinant of job dissatisfaction. Income is however quite another matter, since it can be reported more objectively and "independently" of satisfaction. Income is so markedly differentiated according to occupation (Table 23) that professionals and semiskilled workers in the Soviet Union seem to live in different economic worlds. Almost two thirds of the professional-administrative group earned more than 6600 rubles in 1940 against a mere 2 per cent of the unskilled workers. The median income of the professionals was more than twice the median income of the semiskilled worker. The fact that these median incomes in our sample follow very closely the official wage rates published in Soviet sources,[11] increases our confidence in the validity and reliability of the information our respondents gave with regard to their work experience.

TABLE 23 [13A]

INCOMES IN SOVIET OCCUPATIONAL GROUPS

Distribution according to annual income in rubles (1940)

Occupation	less than 3000	3000–4199	4200–5399	5400–6599	6600 and over	Total number of respondents
Professional-administrative	3%	5%	16%	13%	63%	(115)
Semiprofessional	27	16	22	15	20	(93)
White-collar	26	33	25	10	7	(130)
Skilled worker	21	31	21	11	15	(80)
Semiskilled worker	30	37	16	10	7	(195)
Unskilled worker	60	27	5	6	2	(64)

Unfortunately we do not have reliable income data on the peasants,[12] but the very close correlation between income and satisfaction with pay in the rest of the sample leads us to conclude that the earnings of the typical peasant were indeed exceedingly low. This assumption is supported by much of the available evidence from official sources. Indeed, only one conclusion can be drawn from the fact that the Soviet regime has kept detailed facts about peasant incomes almost as strict a secret as it does the most important defense data. Without doubt they have been extremely low. This conclusion is strongly supported by our qualitative data.

Those in the high level jobs, which we know to be generally well paid, are understandably more satisfied with their pay. The professional-administrative group regard their pay as equal to or better than that of people doing "other" kinds of jobs[13] twice as often as do semiskilled workers and more than five times more often than peasants (Table 24). It is worthy of note that the American and Soviet patterns are similar. In the United States, business and professional groups showed 66 and 58 per cent satisfied, respectively, as against 50 per cent for white-collar; skilled manual workers showed 61 per cent satisfied as against 33 per cent among the unskilled.[14] About the same percentage difference separates the professional-administrative and ordinary white-collar workers in both countries, and in both cases skilled workers seem twice as satisfied with their pay as unskilled workers. Indeed, high salaries seem to induce a diffuse glow of satisfaction. Those in the better paid jobs overwhelmingly regard their pay as commensurate with others doing similar work (Table 24), even though in fact many of them must of necessity have been earning less than the *average* for their occupational level, and therefore might well have complained. In contrast the peasants cast a cold objective eye on their income, and report what must have been closer to reality. Only half say their pay was commensurate with that of people doing similar work.

TABLE 24 [14A]

SATISFACTION WITH PAY COMPARED TO "OTHER" AND "SAME TYPE" JOB: BY OCCUPATIONAL GROUP

| | Per cent saying pay satisfactory: | | |
Occupation	compared to other jobs	compared to same type job	Total number of respondents
Professional-administrative	60%	86%	(379)
Semiprofessional	50	84	(213)
White-collar employee	46	77	(337)
Skilled worker	47	73	(177)
Semiskilled worker	27	70	(348)
Unskilled worker	23	67	(129)
Collective farm peasant	11	52	(317)

Since the middle rank occupational groups include a substantial range of income levels (Table 23), an evaluation of the relation between level of income and satisfaction with pay requires a more direct test. Although the progression is far from perfectly smooth, the amount of income is clearly related to the proportions who feel their pay to be commensurate with that received by those in "other types of job" (Table 25). Those in the highest income brackets are satisfied with their pay almost five times as often as those in the lowest.* In the intermediary categories, however, satisfaction with pay does not seem as responsive to income changes as we might expect. It may be that for those at the top, who can only look down, and those at the very bottom, who can only look up, it is unmistakably clear where one stands in relation to others. In contrast, those in the middle ranges, who can both look up to people earning more and down at those making less, find it not nearly so clear that they are

---

* This pattern of association between income and satisfaction with pay is similar to that reported in the Chicago Attitude Survey (1937). Using only four income categories, from under $1,000 to over $5,000, the Survey reported the proportions satisfied with their pay as 34, 35, 69, and 90 per cent, respectively. Not only is the income "spread" greater in the Soviet data, but the Chicago Survey did not include farm laborers who would have been the equivalent of the peasants. If these adjustments were made the two sets of data would probably be even more alike. See Arthur Kornhauser, "Analysis of 'Class' Structure of Contemporary American Society," in G. W. Hartmann and Theodore Newcomb, eds., Industrial Conflict (New York, 1939).

either better or worse off than those doing "other types of work." It may also be, of course, that there are income thresholds for misery and luxury. Those who cross the line at either extreme will be highly satisfied or dissatisfied with their pay, whereas all those in the middle range will not respond too definitely in one direction or the other. Unfortunately, the number of cases on which we had income data was too limited to explore these and other such plausible explanations of the observed pattern of pay satisfaction.

TABLE 25 [14B]

SATISFACTION WITH PAY AND JOB AT DIFFERENT
LEVELS OF INCOME

1940 income levels (in rubles)	Per cent stating:		Total number of respondents
	Satisfied with pay compared to other jobs	Liked job held in 1940	
Under 1800	16%	33%	(37)
1800–2999	29	38	(149)
3000–4199	40	53	(174)
4200–5399	41	68	(121)
5400–6599	40	73	(70)
6600–7799	40	71	(46)
7800–10199	73	74	(30)
10200 and over	73	88	(49)

In any event, our main interest here is in the relation of income to *general* job satisfaction. People with high incomes are not only more often satisfied with their pay, but also like their jobs better in general. More than twice as many people with incomes over 6,600 rubles liked their jobs as did those with earnings under 1,800 rubles (Table 25). But since the better paid jobs tend also to be the more attractive in other respects, perhaps the pay has little independent influence on the relative attractiveness of the job? We note, in this connection, that in the middle and upper range increases in income do not seem to bring about clear-cut changes in the proportions satisfied with their jobs (Table 25). Is this because the mixture of job types at a given income level obscures the relationship?

Controlling the level of income within occupations leaves us with too few cases in most categories for reliable judgment, but the data suggest that within any one occupational group there is a marked increase in the proportions who like their job as the income level rises. For example, among the semiskilled workers, the most numerous occupational group for whom we have income data, the proportion who liked their job rose

from 27 per cent of those with incomes under 3,000 rubles, to 54 per cent
of those earning 3,000–4,199, then to 66 per cent of those earning 4,200–
5,399, and finally to 73 per cent of those earning 5,400 or more. This
seems to be true, however, mainly at the lower and middle levels, that is,
for unskilled, semiskilled, skilled and white-collar workers. Perhaps because they are already concentrated in the highest pay brackets, perhaps
because their jobs are dominated by positive qualities other than pay,
those in higher status occupations seem less responsive to pay differentials
when evaluating the job satisfaction.*

This impression is confirmed when we consider the relation between
being satisfied with one's pay and liking one's job (Table 26). Liking one's
job is so characteristic of those in the professional and higher administrative posts as to be but little influenced by whether one's pay is regarded
as satisfactory or not. The lower we go in the occupational hierarchy the
more does satisfaction with pay seem to influence the attitude toward the
job. In sharp contrast to the situation among the professionals, peasants
who were satisfied with their pay were four times as likely to be reasonably content with their jobs.

It is perhaps obvious that we cannot properly understand the meaning
of a given amount of economic improvement unless we consider the relative level of the group experiencing the change. The same increment may
loom much larger to those on the bottom of the economic ladder than it
does to those higher up. But it is perhaps less obvious that we cannot understand the same *relative* degree of differentiation unless we consider
the *absolute* level at which those relatively poorly off find themselves.
The wage structure in the United States and the Soviet Union are sufficiently alike so that the position of the engineer and the unskilled or
semiskilled worker *relative to each other* is much the same in both countries. In each case professional and salaried administrative personnel earn,
on the average, between one and a half and two times what the average
semiskilled worker earns.[15] But in the United States the percentage who
are satisfied with their jobs falls only moderately from 82 per cent of the
professionals to 76 per cent among semiskilled workers, whereas in the
Soviet Union it falls from 77 to 45 per cent. If we consider the unskilled
worker the drop in the Soviet case is even more precipitous, satisfaction
falling to a mere 23 per cent, whereas in the United States there is a
modest additional decrease of 4 percentage points (Table 21). To understand this marked difference we must consider not only the *relative* disparity in income between those who earn more and those who earn less,
but rather the *absolute* meaning of being a low earner. This brings us
back to the thresholds of misery and luxury which we discussed earlier.

---

* As we shall see below, in evaluating jobs the intelligentsia gives great emphasis to
interesting work.

TABLE 26 [15A]

PER CENT LIKING JOB
AMONG THOSE SATISFIED AND DISSATISFIED WITH PAY:
BY OCCUPATION

Occupation	Persons satisfied with pay		Persons dissatisfied with pay	
Professional-administrative	82%	(221) [a]	76%	(155)
Semiprofessional	79	(105)	68	(101)
White-collar employee	74	(139)	55	(172)
Skilled worker	84	(81)	52	(85)
Semiskilled worker	66	(103)	41	(265)
Unskilled worker	38	(29)	19	(93)
Peasant	40	(38)	9	(276)

a. Total number of respondents on the basis of which the percentage is computed.

Even though he may earn half what an engineer gets, an American production line worker still can manage a comfortable minimal standard of living. He is almost certain to feel he has enough food and clothing, he is likely to regard his housing as adequate although subject to improvement, and he will very likely have at least some and perhaps all of the luxury items found in the engineer's home — such as radio, refrigerator, television, bicycles for the children, and probably a car. Thus, although we can well expect the American worker to hope for and claim the right to improvement, we also expect him to be relatively satisfied. In the Soviet Union the basic standard of living has been so much lower, the shortages of housing, food, and clothing so drastic, that the main struggle was somehow to fight oneself up to a *minimum* standard of living.[16] Those who failed to get above the minimum level were not merely relatively deprived, but suffered absolute deprivation — a sense of hunger, a feeling of having only rags to wear, and of living in dismally inadequate, tremendously crowded housing. Thus, it was a question of living, on the one hand, at a reasonably adequate level with your head above water or, on the other hand, living in poverty and misery at a definitely substandard level.

It is no wonder then that there is such a contrast with the United States, where low pay is mentioned as the reason for dissatisfaction by only one fifth of the complainants and actually is cited more often by white-collar than manual workers.[17] Among those dissatisfied in the Soviet Union, low pay was cited by more than two thirds of the workers and peasants and was mentioned by them much more often than by the

TABLE 27 [16A]

REASONS [a] FOR DISLIKING ONE'S JOB: BY OCCUPATION

Reason for dissatisfaction	Professional-administrative	Semi-professional	White-collar employee	Skilled worker	Semi-skilled worker	Unskilled worker	Collective farm peasant
Low pay	11%	18%	48%	64%	73%	67%	68%
Type of work	39	29	14	8	3	1	2
Boredom and frustration	23	20	31	4	15	8	3
Harsh discipline	11	17	18	34	30	36	37
Other reasons	34	40	21	4	8	5	12
Total number of respondents	62	45	91	53	133	78	217

a. Since respondents cited more than one reason, columns total over 100%.

ordinary white collars and six times more often than by the professional and administrative group (Table 27). The pattern of complaints suggests the greater relative importance to the manual worker of pay, and secondarily of working conditions (discipline), as contrasted with the nonmanual's concentration on the intrinsic qualities of the job. This impression was borne out, when we coded our life-history interviews to judge what a person *most* wanted in his job (Table 28). Pay emerged as overwhelmingly the most important element for the workers and peasants, whereas interesting work dominated the desires of the intelligentsia. The ratio between the proportion for whom pay was most important to that of those for whom interesting work was most important was about 6:1 among the peasants. It reversed to almost 1:8 among the intelligentsia. This does not, of course, mean that members of the intelligentsia were disinterested in salaries, but it does indicate strikingly the extent to which they took a decent standard of living for granted and concentrated on other aspects of the work situation. For the ordinary workers and peasants the intrinsic interest and related qualities of the job are a luxury which can be afforded by the well paid but which those with barely adequate pay must make very secondary to the struggle for existence.

Again the contrast with the United States is instructive. A national sample of Americans was asked to choose from among ten jobs, each described by one outstanding characteristic such as "where you could be a leader," or where you would be "very highly paid." [18] Following the pattern among the Soviet citizens, Americans in the higher status jobs were more likely than the manual groups to choose jobs which permitted "self-expression" and "interesting experience," in the ratio of roughly

TABLE 28 [17A]

QUALITY MOST DESIRED IN WORK SITUATION: BY OCCUPATION [a]

Quality desired	Intelligentsia	White-collar employee	Skilled worker	Ordinary worker	Collective farm peasant
Adequate pay	8%	23%	22%	48%	57%
Interesting work	62	31	27	20	9
Freedom from fear	6	13	15	13	17
Other reasons	24	33	36	19	17
Total number of respondents	95	58	33	56	35

a. From personal interviews.

three to one. Thus, although the sharpness of the contrast between occupations may vary, the interest and psychic reward of the job seems to play a very similar role for comparable occupational groups in both societies. But in sharp contrast to the Soviet refugees, *all* the occupational groups in the United States expressed relatively *little* interest in high pay as a *prime* consideration. A mere 3 to 8 per cent of any group made pay the basis of their *first* choice. Americans are, however, very sharply divided in the importance they attach to job security, even more sharply than the Russians on the pay question, since it was cited by only 2 per cent of the top group and by almost 30 per cent of the unskilled workers. The Russians were seldom worried about losing a job, but they rather strongly emphasized freedom from fear and threats to the security of their person.

It may be argued that our refugee sample would overemphasize concern over personal security in the job situation. However, the efforts of the post-Stalin leadership to reassure persons in responsible positions that they will no longer be subject to capricious arbitrary arrest is in itself sufficient evidence that concern over personal security has been a distinctive feature of earning a living in the Soviet Union. Of those in our interview sample who were employed, 28 per cent reported that the Soviet regime had a direct negative impact on their job or career situation. About one third of these were dekulakized farmers. That the proportion is in absolute terms so low may be taken as further evidence that our sample is not based overwhelmingly on disgruntled outcasts. But in more relative terms it suggests the widespread impact of social change on the conditions for making a living in the USSR.

In both societies those in higher level occupations apparently feel assured of adequate economic security and can afford to concentrate on the intrinsic qualities of the job. Americans in lower status jobs fear being without a job, but seem confident that if they can hold on to one they are assured of a decent standard of living. The Soviet citizens, in contrast, worry about personal security but seldom doubt that they will have work. Most outstanding is the extent to which the Soviet lower classes are concerned with the minimal adequacy of their standard of living. The pay of a job looms largest in their mind.

In summary, we have found incomes to vary with occupation, but only at the extremes of the skill hierarchy is there relative homogeneity of income. The middle occupational layers contain quite a range of incomes, and the middle income levels include a variety of occupations. Under the circumstances it is not surprising that income, although influencing job satisfaction, by no means predicts it with precision. A wide range of income groups report rather similar levels of job satisfaction. Within any given occupational group, however, increased income does seem to lead to increased satisfaction. This effect is most marked in those occupations in which low incomes are most characteristic. Increased income cannot alone act to eliminate differences in job satisfaction, because such satisfaction is influenced by a host of other factors such as the cleanliness of the job, the prestige it commands, the degree of autonomy it permits, and so on. But it seems evident that if the regime were to shift some of its resources in order to improve the economic return to the lowest occupational strata, it could derive markedly greater increments in job satisfaction than by comparable increases at the middle and upper levels. Indeed, it may well be that the announcement in 1956 of drastic reductions in the salaries of the highly paid artists, scientists, and factory managers is probably the initial move in that direction. The later improvement of retirement benefits, the raising of the minimum wage, the increased prices paid to farmers for their produce also point in the direction of more concentrated efforts to improve the financial position of the lower echelons.

Standards of Living

The importance of income does not lie mainly in its symbolic value, but in its power to command limited — and in the USSR generally scarce — goods and services. The average income available for each person in a household clearly exerts a marked influence on his perception of his standard of living. Less than a fifth of those in homes with less than 1,800 rubles per capita felt themselves better off than the majority, whereas in the higher income brackets the overwhelming majority took this view (Table 29). High per capita incomes are typical for the favored occupations, and low per capita incomes abound among the peasants and the lower worker echelons. It is no surprise, therefore, that those from professional-administrative households overwhelmingly recognize themselves

as better off, whereas a mere 10 per cent or less from the unskilled workers' and peasants' homes regarded themselves as so fortunate. The effect
of the greater earning power of the skilled as against the ordinary worker
is evident in the doubled rate at which the former report being materially
well off (Table 29).

TABLE 29 [18A]

MATERIAL WELFARE: BY PER CAPITA INCOME AND OCCUPATION

Per cent "better off" than majority among those:					
In families with per capita disposable income, in rubles, of:			In families where head of household's occupation was:		
7800 and over	85%	(46) [a]	Professional-administrative	72%	(399)
6600–7799	87	(24)	Semiprofessional	48	(163)
5400–6599	85	(34)	White-collar employee	42	(247)
4200–5399	50	(54)	Skilled worker	33	(189)
3000–4199	53	(123)	Semiskilled worker	16	(378)
1800–2999	25	(251)	Unskilled worker	10	(105)
900–1799	19	(290)	Peasant	8	(266)

a. Total number of respondents on the basis of which the percentage is computed.

When the general estimate of standard of living is broken down into
its components the contrast between reasonable comfort, on the one hand,
and a sense of marked deprivation, on the other, is no less sharp. About
half of the professionals reported food, clothing, and housing adequate,
but the proportions fall off steadily as we descend the social ladder until
we find virtually no one among the peasants satisfied with his supply of
food and clothing and very few reasonably content with their housing
(Table 30).

If one must suffer deprivation, most would agree that hunger is the
hardest to bear. Except for reports dealing with the famine years immediately after the revolution and then again following collectivization of the
peasants in the early thirties, most of the complaints about food dealt not
with absolute deficiency in the amount of food but rather with the extremely limited and monotonous nature of the diet and its high cost. Lack
of food is most likely to have the sharpest impact on one's estimated
material welfare and on reported satisfaction. It will be no surprise then
that the sharpest class differences in frequency of complaint arose in
regard to food, with the range extending from 34 to 97 per cent. The fact
that only 3 per cent were satisfied among the peasants may well occasion
some surprise. Surely the peasants, close to the supply of food, having

TABLE 30 [18B]

SOURCES OF MATERIAL SATISFACTION: BY SOCIAL GROUP

	Per cent reporting "adequate" supply of:			
Social group	Food	Clothing	Housing	Total number of respondents
Intelligentsia	66%	44%	56%	(95)
White-collar employees	43	22	49	(51)
Skilled workers	38	14	31	(28)
Workers	28	16	28	(56)
Collective farmers	3	6	23	(31)

a. From personal interviews.

their own gardens and often receiving food from the collective farm as payment in kind, cannot have been reporting objectively? Perhaps not. It certainly is true that the hostility the peasant felt to the collective farm system sharply colored his report of any subject close to the farm issue. In addition the peasant must have been influenced by his feelings about what his food supply *should* and *would rightfully* have been were he an individual free farmer rather than a poor laborer on what amounts to government-owned estates. Yet we would be naive to explain the peasant's image of his food supply mainly on these grounds. The regime's policy of commandeering the food of the countryside for use in the cities was very effective. In addition, there was extreme pressure on the peasant to sell on the market what little food he commanded from his garden plot and from pay in kind, in order to meet oppressive taxes and secure a little cash for the purchase of supplies. Consequently, large numbers of peasants did suffer from a real shortage of food. A by-no-means atypical complaint came from a kolkhoznik of thirty-two who said: "There was nothing to eat except potatoes. The state takes away all the grain, and what good are potatoes? We lived very badly."

With one slight exception, at every occupational level many fewer individuals were satisfied with their clothing supply than with either food or housing. A 32-year-old kolkhoznik spoke for many when he said "We lived in rags." Yet even in this area, where deprivation was so widespread, the significance of a professional's report that his clothing was less than adequate was often profoundly different from the same complaint made by a worker or peasant. Lower class respondents characteristically described their clothes as very old, threadbare, in need of repair and yet extremely difficult to replace because of the cost. One laborer charged that for his children schooling was in fact *not* compulsory because the children did not have enough clothes to wear, and a truck driver supported him in asserting that "in Russia in the wintertime you could see toes peeping out of children's shoes" while they walked to school. Similarly, a peasant reported that in his collective farm "no one had any shoes; they all wore sandals and leggings of cord bound in birch thongs or else they went barefoot. Only on holy days did the children wear shoes so as not to be ashamed."

Clearly for such people it meant something very different to enter a complaint about the shortage of clothing than it did for one of the favored, such as a journalist from the editorial board of a major regional newspaper, who said:

> In the Soviet Union the most difficult thing is to obtain clothing. I could buy a suit for 200 rubles, but it was poorly made and of very bad material. Such a suit is not appropriate for people doing my kind of work. So what I would do was to buy English or Japanese material and pay 1,600 rubles for a suit.*

These are perhaps extreme examples, but they help to emphasize the extent to which the contrast was not between being adequately taken care of as against being very well off, but rather between being comfortable or miserable. The situation with regard to housing was similar.[19] Housing competes directly with the needs for construction of heavy industry. As a result, housing construction has been extraordinarily neglected by the Soviet regime despite the vast influx into urban areas, which doubled in size in the intercensus period from 1926 to 1939. Despite a paper law which provides a so-called "sanitary living norm" of nine square meters per person, equivalent to a small room, the actual average space occupied per person is very often half that. The standard pattern has been to have an entire family in a single room, sharing the other facilities. The following description given by a woman dentist, married to an engineer, is characteristic of the period just before the war:

> We lived in Minsk . . . in a fairly new house built in 1936. . . . Because of the housing shortage they put one family in each room. Thus, in five rooms there were five families. All these families shared one kitchen and one toilet. There was a bathroom but it had not been finished. There was no bath in it and we had to go to the city bath house.

So severe was the housing shortage that even the middle classes often had very poor accommodations by common standards, which probably accounts for the consistently high level of complaint about housing in all classes. Even within this framework, however, occupational differences were often marked. Since the allocation of housing was controlled by

* Prices cited here of course apply to the prewar period. In the postwar period no suit could be had for 200 rubles, and suits of ordinary quality often cost 1,000 rubles or more.

official agencies, the power of money alone was limited, although connections in the right place could effect good results. Much more important was the fact that housing was largely either directly or indirectly controlled by the economic and governmental organizations by which people were employed. Consequently, the quality of the housing assigned varied largely according to one's importance to the organization. Thus a single apartment house might include a wide range of occupations, but the poorer working families were found mainly in the basements or on the upper floors. The basements were undesirable, among other reasons, because the ground water often seeped in, whereas the reverse evil afflicted the upper stories — if there were no pipes it was a tremendous distance to carry the water and if there were pipes the pressure was often insufficient to raise it up to that height.

Conclusions:

We are all aware that the Soviet Union is a totalitarian dictatorship, ruled until 1953 by a dictator perhaps more absolute and tyrannical than any in modern history. It is then no surprise that in describing their efforts at making a living our refugee informants referred frequently to aspects of the work situation which have no direct parallel in democratic Western societies. Outstanding among these were the extreme over-commitment of resources and the frenzied pace of development summed up in the expression "the tempo"; the extreme political coloration of the work experience, which meant constant irritating interference in technical matters; the system of terroristic arrests which produced a pervasive fear; the harshness of labor regulations both with regard to freedom of movement and such matters as lateness, excess breakage and similar matters; and the terrible "squeeze" exerted by the system of norms, piece rates, and rate-buster "Stakhanovites."

Despite such distinctive features of the Soviet occupational environment, we cannot but be struck by the degree to which its features resemble those of most Western industrial nations. The Soviet factory and large-scale farm have substantially the same structure of authority relations as a large factory or farm in Europe or America. The role of technical competence and the pattern of economic reward is very similar in both places. It follows then, as we have seen, that the relative evaluations of their work experience made by Soviet professionals and administrators, workers, and peasants should be similar in important respects to the relative evaluation of their experience by appropriate "opposite numbers" in Europe and the United States. In both settings the higher placed personnel are much more satisfied with their jobs, derive more pleasure from their work, have easier relations with their superiors, place greater emphasis on the intrinsic interest of the job rather than on the pay, and enjoy a better and generally more gracious style of living. Even the more subtle differences, such as the relatively better pay and greater job satisfaction of skilled as against ordinary white-collar workers, are evidently present in the Soviet environment as well as in the American.

Both the distinctive historical Soviet conditions and the general patterns of modern industrial society were intertwined in the system from the beginning. Yet if one had to choose one or the other element as his sole key to the life situation of participants in the Soviet occupational structure, an interpretation based on the *distinctive* Soviet conditions would probably have been much more realistic than one based mainly on the assumption that this is after all "just another industrial system." This was true for the past, but what of the future? It is our considered opinion that with the further progress of time the relative importance of the previously distinctive features of the Soviet occupational setting will decline, and the importance of the more general characteristics of modern industrial society will become more important. This may have major consequences for the whole tone of occupational life in the Soviet Union, and hence for the social system at large.

Our assumption about probable changes in the occupational environment and atmosphere is based on two main considerations: (1) that there has been a fundamental change in the conditions under which those gainfully employed must operate, and (2) that there have been important changes in the people who make up the labor force.

The change in the conditions under which the labor force must operate are perhaps self-evident. Soviet industry was developed by forced draft through the sudden imposition on the population of an extreme rate of obligatory savings effected through a drastic reduction in the standard of living. The regime had had little experience with the kinds of problems it faced and with the difficulties its program generated. It tended to meet those situations with a combination of excessive propaganda and extreme coercion.

By 1955 the economic situation, especially after the initial reconstruction of the wartime damage had been completed, was profoundly different. The industrial base of the country was well established, and in all the world it stood second only to that of the United States. In place of confusion and contradiction there is a relatively familiar and generally stable system of communication and command. Instead of an extreme shortage of skilled personnel there is a relatively broad base of competence and experience at all levels.[20] Dire scarcity and extreme rationing of materials has been replaced by a relatively adequate system of allocation. These and a host of other changes reflect the difference between a system which is just being started and one which is well established and quite successful.

The consequence is that work in Soviet industry occurs now in a quite changed atmosphere. The frenzied quality of the tempo, the frequency of arrest, the stringency of the labor discipline, the heavy emphasis on unusual devices like "Stakhanovism" to raise labor productivity are largely gone from the scene. There is less fear and more freedom for initiative, experiment and innovation. Technical competence and skill, and technological investment, are now viewed as the main road to increased productivity. These forces make for relatively greater efficiency, calm, and "normalcy."

The change in the personnel making up the labor force represents a similar historical transition. Although we found a man's level in the hierarchy of jobs to be the *prime* determinant of his occupational experience, we also found that at every level the younger group shows a markedly better adjustment to, and assessment of, the occupational side of life in the USSR.[21] There were few other general areas in which the young and old in our sample were so sharply differentiated as in the realm of occupational aspirations and, to some extent, experiences. It must be kept in mind, of course, that there are few areas in which the differences found are more likely to reflect primarily life-cycle rather than generational differences. The younger group, on the whole, had not yet entered upon or was still at an early stage in its occupational career, and many of the disillusioning experiences which come through time had not yet had a chance to manifest themselves. Nevertheless, we feel that in substantial measure the differences encountered here also reflect changes in the life experience of the generations. The older group worked throughout the period of confusion and turmoil while large-scale Soviet industry was being formed and developed, whereas the younger generation came to work in a more stable scene. They arrived at work with more familiarity with the system, and on the whole were better trained and equipped to handle the demands of the situation.

In any event, the younger group is distinguished by its greater tendency to express the *desire* to have a career under the Soviets, in feeling that an opportunity for such a career exists, and, if they had already been launched on it, in feeling that their early desires for a career had actually been *fulfilled* under Soviet conditions. On the job, they see the working atmosphere as friendlier; and despite their greater ambition, they are in general more satisfied with their jobs than are the old. Part of their positive view is reflected in the fact that they are more likely than the old to assume that if a person possesses positive characteristics he will indeed succeed. Furthermore, when they complain about the difficulties of their work situation, they tend to blame specific faulty aspects of the system, such as the poor quality or inadequate quantity of materials supplied them, rather than to blame the system of production itself. These are but a few of the illustrations of the greater tendency of the younger generation to take for granted the institutional features of Soviet society and to concentrate on how the institutions work rather than to question the institutions as such.

In the light of these changes our expectation is that a study comparable to this one conducted in 1965 would show a marked decrease in the frequency of complaints about tempo, arrest, harsh discipline, and other features historically linked to the forced draft stage of Soviet economic development. This assumes of course that peace prevails and the arms race is, if not reduced, at least not greatly intensified. We also expect that many of the more extreme complaints about the standard of living historically linked with the darkest period of rationing will become muted. By contrast, we assume that the general *pattern* of differentiation in occupational satisfaction between low and high placed occupations will continue to be manifested. Whether the sharpness of the gap between the strata will persist, along with the intensity and pervasiveness of complaints about the standard of living, will depend largely on what the regime does about the production of consumer's goods. If it moves in the direction of those "rather startling improvements in the standard of living" which economists say is possible,[22] then we would expect the Soviet pattern of satisfaction with occupational experience and living standards to move closer to the American pattern.

One major reservation might be made with regard to this estimate, however, and that involves the collective farm system. Although the worst phases of confusion and uncertainty are now merely part of history, the collective farm system is still a relatively unstable and only poorly integrated social and economic institution. We may assume that the regime would under no circumstances return to a system of private farming, although this is apparently what many peasants would like most. Failing this, satisfaction of the peasant can be obtained only by a drastic improvement in the size and steadiness of the economic reward he obtains through his work on the collective farm.

Although it is too early to judge the long-range prospects for such improvement, we should not overlook the striking increases in the prices paid by the government after 1955 for collective farm produce. This had the dramatic effect of doubling the income of the collective farms between 1950 and 1957. Much of this increase failed to reach the individual peasant, although in time its investment in the collective farm may be reflected in greater earnings for him. Enough of the increased income of the farms was distributed to the peasant, however, so that on the average he enjoyed perhaps as much as a 50 per cent rise in personal income. Although peasants still lag behind urban workers, these changes bring their standard of living much more in line. There is some reason to conclude that under Khrushchev's leadership the peasant will no longer be asked to bear so greatly disproportionate a share of the forced savings which the regime's economic plans have imposed on the people. Indeed, these adjustments may lead to a situation in which the burdens of financing the nation's growth will be borne equally by urban and rural workers. If there is such a fundamental change in policy, it may be expected to produce marked changes in the situation and attitude of the collective farm peasant, largely eliminating many of the striking differences in satisfaction which characterize him as compared with the urban worker.

Such changes in peasant satisfaction may in turn be reflected in much improved motivation and consequently in higher labor productivity. More energetic and enthusiastic effort on the part of the peasant cannot eliminate the limitations inherent in Russia's natural endowment of soil and climate. Nor can it, beyond a certain point, substitute for the long neglected program of capital investment which Soviet agriculture needs. But such increased motivation is certainly a major precondition for Khrushchev's sweeping plans to bring Soviet per capita production of milk, butter and meat up to the level in the United States in a matter of a few years. Such improvements may not come so easily as the promise of them. Indeed, in the case of meat so great an improvement in so short a time would be nearly miraculous. But if any substantial progress is made toward these goals it will mean that Soviet society has entered a new realm of consumption, which should yield even greater similarity in the patterns of satisfaction we have observed in our Soviet sample and those found in the United States.

VI

Getting an Education[1]

Both as a symbol and as a practical problem, education has occupied a particularly important place in the interests of the regime and the citizen throughout the history of Soviet society.

The regime's practical interest in education has become increasingly more sharply focused over the course of time. The period from 1918 to 1931 was one of high enthusiasm for progressive education. It was also marked, however, by a shortage of trained teachers, and most specifically by a shortage of teachers who were adequately acquainted with the philosophy and methods of progressive education. In the midst of the First Five Year Plan the leaders of the Soviet Union became acutely aware that the products of their lower and middle schools were adequately prepared neither for study in institutions of advanced learning, nor for work in the industrial system that was being rapidly developed. They were deficient in the basic skills of reading, writing, and computation, and they lacked discipline. Among the reasons to which these effects could legitimately be laid were the generally low level of competence in teachers, and the disruption of family life which lessened the parents' influence over the child. The regime, however, placed the responsibility almost exclusively on the philosophy and methods of progressive education. A more orthodox system, emphasizing the three R's and training in discipline, was introduced between the years 1931 and 1936. The older system was "child centered," insofar as at least lip service was paid to aiding the child to develop as a spontaneous, distinctive individual. The newer program is avowedly "system centered," organized around two goals: meeting the manpower needs of the society, and developing loyal, reliable citizens. These interests of the regime were by no means unexpressed in the earlier period, but they were not then nearly so sharply focused as they have been since 1931.

The basic organizational principles laid down in the early thirties continued to characterize the Soviet school system down through the period after World War II.[2] A series of ladders or steps is designed to carry the successful student more or less continuously from the early grades through college. At some points the student may step off, either permanently or onto a parallel ladder. The parallel ladder, however, may not go so far, and although theoretically the student can step back again to the main ladder, the crossing back is not easy and not many make it.

There are, of course, preschool programs in crêches and nursery schools, but the first section in this main ladder consists of the four-year, or primary school. It is currently begun at age seven, although through most of the earlier period of Soviet education the starting age was eight. Four years of schooling was declared compulsory in 1930, although for some time afterward in the rural and more distant nationality areas many did not attain even this modest standard. By the late thirties, however, almost every child was getting four years of schooling.[3] Indeed, many pupils of older age were held back. Consequently, in 1939, the number of children enrolled in the first four grades was 124 per cent of the total number of children ordinarily of primary school age!

The primary school is followed by the "incomplete secondary," or "seven-year" school, which encompasses grades five through seven, and in many ways is similar to the American junior high school. "Seven-year schooling" was decreed to be compulsory in major urban and industrial areas in 1943, and by 1949 Soviet authorities declared it to be compulsory everywhere. There is some doubt, however, as to whether in the rural areas it is really universally "required" or merely universally "available."

The next step is the complete secondary, or "ten-year" school. These are of two main types — regular and technical. Regular ten-year schools are the more important variety, and before the war had more than double the enrollment of the technical high school. They offer the standard European "gymnasium" curriculum, and are mainly preparatory for college training. The technical high school (*tekhnikum*) gives semiprofessional training in such fields as dentistry, medicine, engineering, and education. Although the *tekhnikum* graduation certificate fully qualifies one for further training, the *tekhnikum* is in fact terminal for all but a small proportion of its graduates. Only the top 5 per cent are permitted to apply for higher education immediately on graduation. The remainder must first hold a job for at least three years in a place assigned by the government.

Higher education is available in universities, institutes, and other institutions which are collectively designated by a set of initials yielding the word *vuzi*. There is nothing in Soviet higher education which approximates the general college education which can be secured in France, England, and particularly the United States. All Soviet higher schools are specialized and train people in some profession. Finally, beyond the four-to-six-year university level there is the usual range of advanced training.

Since 1940 there has been a program of State Labor Reserve Schools for youths between the ages of fourteen and seventeen, roughly equivalent to the ages of those in the incomplete secondary school. These schools train skilled and semiskilled labor for work in the metal, coal, railroading, and other industries, but they also provide some additional basic schooling beyond the four-year level. Once on the job the young person has available a system of special schools for working youths. Following the pattern of the so-called *rabfak*, or workers' schools, used for adult education in the early thirties, these schools are now established for working youths rather than adults. Those attending them work a shorter day, but even so must pursue a much more limited curriculum within the half of regular school time allotted. In urban areas they cover grades five through ten, and in rural areas generally only five through seven.

The attitude of the Soviet rulers toward education is exceedingly complicated. Marxism, being a rationalist school of thought, places a high value on education and learning *per se*. Education is "good." It would be a mistake, however, to believe that the Soviet leaders cherish the educated man in the classical sense of the intellectually curious, free-roving, skeptical inquirer. From the standpoint of the regime, education is, as we have noted, a means for training personnel to meet the manpower needs of an expanding industrial society, and for developing loyal, reliable citizens. A postwar textbook describes "communist education" as "the preparation of the younger generation for active participation in the building of communist society, and for the defense of the Soviet government which is building that society." [4] The development of loyal citizens, however, is dependent on more than the exposure of the child to political instruction in the school. It demands a reasonably literate and active reading public which can be reached via the communications network.

Beyond these immediate goals, however, education is positively valued in the official ideology. We are in no position to know to what extent the elite "believe" the ideology which they preach, but it is clear that the type of dictatorship they have established is based not on rote obedience, but rather on obedience through persuasion and indoctrination. In any event the regime realizes that the populace, too, values education highly. There has therefore been a good deal of exhaltation of the role of the teacher, constant advertising of the merits of Soviet "socialist" education, and stress on the expansion of the system of education as evidence of the regime's concern for the welfare of its subjects. The prerevolutionary education system is generally held up for baneful comparison, at least so far as the availability of education is concerned.

In stressing the advantages of Soviet education the regime strikes a resonant chord in the Soviet population, the majority of whom see schooling as very desirable. Among other things, occupational achievement is highly related to education, as it is in any industrialized society. There is some reason, in fact, to argue that education may be even more important for occupational achievement in the Soviet Union than in a country like the United States. In the Soviet Union there is no private business, which provides the major alternate route to success in most industrial societies. The only substantial opportunity for advancement is within the framework of the Soviet bureaucracy, which like all bureaucracies rewards skills which are ordinarily obtained through formal education. The Soviet citizen apparently recognizes that education is his channel to occupational success, to a good standard of living, and to "culture" and personal development. A persistent theme in our interviews is the necessity to get an education in order to acquire a "specialty." Without education, say our respondents, you cannot get a "specialty," and without a specialty you cannot advance and live well. As a young woman chemist said:

> People doomed to do only manual work have no possibility of doing "cultural work." There is a general looking down on manual work in Soviet Russia. Education is tremendously important not only from the material point of view. . . . The desire for education is widespread and extremely strong. For two reasons: to make one's future life somewhat easier, and then simply because they wanted to learn. Women knew even if they did get married they still would have to work. Education meant better working conditions on equal terms with men.

The popular involvement in education has been exploited to the utmost by the regime, but at the same time that this theme provided a potential source of support it also created expectations, the fulfillment of which were important factors in maintaining loyalty and support. The citizen's opportunities for an education thus became one of the most important aspects of his relations with the state.

Popular Evaluations of Soviet Education

No aspect of Soviet society received more warm and spontaneous support than did the system of Soviet education. Asked to list what they would be sure to keep and sure to change if the Soviet regime were overthrown, virtually no one selected the educational system as a prime target for rejection.* On the positive side, free education was cited as something which should definitely be kept more often than was any other feature of Soviet society. Only the system of free medical care came close to it in popularity. Indeed, leaving out the free medical system, the educational system (despite widespread complaints about the politicization of the schools) was listed as something to be kept about as often as all other specifically cited institutions combined! This was by and large true for both sexes in all age groups and in all social classes.

Approval of the regime's efforts in education is also reflected in the

---

* For further details see Tables 59 and 64 and discussion in Chapter X, below.

answers to questions directly focused on education. One of the educational accomplishments of which the regime boasts most is the increase in the rate of literacy. Asked if literacy had increased during the Soviet period, the overwhelming majority were willing to grant the regime this achievement. The peasants, as always, were the most grudging in giving any credit to the regime. But even among the peasants 83 per cent said that literacy had increased, as compared to 90 per cent of the workers, 96 per cent of the skilled workers, and 97 per cent of the intelligentsia and employees. Asked point blank whether they were in favor of the Soviet educational system, however, many fewer were willing to venture support, and the class differentiation was sharper. Only 80 per cent of the intelligentsia gave its approval, and only 45 per cent of the collective farm peasants did so.[5] In all these measures the younger generation contained a higher proportion giving support to the system.

The qualitative materials reveal that it is the idea of free, universal, compulsory education that was favored, but that our respondents held grave reservations about the way in which this policy is implemented in the Soviet Union. They complain, in particular, about the politicization of the Soviet schools. General approval for free education was expressed by people of all stations of life, as the following extracts indicate:

Leave free education, as it was until 1939, so everybody could get free education, all he wanted. That is the only thing I liked there, and it was good for the people. They had a very good policy in this respect (A young Azerbaidjan teacher).

In tsarist Russia, there was a fabulous amount of illiteracy. Thousands of schools were built up by the Soviets. There was a fierce battle against illiteracy. There has been a lot done in this field. And not only in the European part, every part of the Soviet Union (A young student whose father was of old intelligentsia).

It must be admitted that all children except from de-kulakized people or from White guards had the possibility of getting an education. If you studied hard you could even get a higher education. There was no charge for education. In the VUZ [university level] they also paid you a salary, and they would also pay for books. In this respect the policy of the Bolsheviks is very good. Some people would tell you this isn't so. But they are wrong. There are good and bad sides to everything. But if someone denies this fact, it means he is denying the truth (A young factory worker of peasant background).

Free education. This must always be. Everybody likes this (A young woman, collective farmer).

While these people represent the majority opinion about the Soviet efforts to expand education and literacy, there were a few dissenting voices from the older people on whom the regime put pressure to attend evening classes in order to learn to read and write. An older, illiterate peasant woman, although in fact revealing a yearning to study, nevertheless complained:

They punished you if you didn't go to school. They took away work days and everything. But all the same, people didn't learn. My cousin went for two years;

she was 23 years old. She went to evening school, but still couldn't read any more than the alphabet. If I felt good, if I had been in good health, I would have studied. But I had no food, and I had to get up at 4 A.M., so that I couldn't think about study under those conditions.

The main basis for complaint was the saturation of education with politics. This complaint was uniform for all classes, and was expressed by about three quarters of respondents from all social groups on the oral interviews. Many people who otherwise approved of Soviet education withheld approval on this score. An army officer said: "As for education, it isn't as monstrous as the rest. It is for all the people, but even here something should be changed. . . . Such things as Marxism-Leninism should be changed." And an ordinary worker, who had received a secondary school education before the revolution, made a bitter attack on the intrusion of politics into all fields of study: "All you get is the Bolshevik line and no matter where you study or what you study, all roads lead to Rome, or rather to Moscow. Probably everyone will agree about . . . getting rid of the political aspects of the educational system." On this point the political bias of our respondents may mislead us. Certainly, political education would be a source of annoyance for a person who was opposed to the content of the politics being taught. It is not safe to assume that this is equally a source of annoyance to people who agree with the regime. Frequent complaints in Soviet official sources, however, suggest that many inside the Soviet Union also find it somewhat boring. It is clear, nevertheless, that whether one likes it or not, one of the central characteristics of the Soviet system of education has been its politicization, and this certainly was perceived by our respondents. It is interesting to note that although this explicit political content was so heavily criticized, only about 10 per cent complained about the more general problem of totalitarian control of education or the more specific problem of extreme discipline and authority in the schools.

The approval of Soviet education, we noted, was based mainly on the extent to which it was free, universal, and accessible to everyone. The fact that so many peasants and workers withheld their approval indicates that by no means everyone was of a single mind as to the availability and accessibility of such formally free educational opportunities. For many the problem became acute in 1940 when the regime instituted tuition fees for high school and college training. In the personal interviews, the upper classes were much more likely than the lower classes to say that "all or many" could get as much education as they desired. The portions giving that response for the various social groups were: intelligentsia, 71 per cent; employees, 67 per cent; skilled workers, 50 per cent; workers, 39 per cent; and peasants, 27 per cent.[6] The image which our respondents had of educational opportunity for the Soviet population at large was apparently markedly influenced by their own life experience and educational attainment. They tended to think in terms of the experience of the groups with which they themselves were identified. Since approval of educational opportunity in the Soviet system at large was strongly correlated with the individual's satisfaction with the level of education he had attained for himself, we now turn to a consideration of the patterns of educational attainment in our sample.

Who Gets Educated?

The attainments of the Soviet educational system are substantial. Especially impressive were the gains made in the crowded years of most intensive development during the first two five-year plans. From 1927/28 to 1940/41 the enrollment of Soviet elementary and secondary schools increased from 12 million to almost 33 million, and in higher education from 169 thousand to 812 thousand.[7] The population increase over the same period was of course much smaller, being about 16 per cent by comparison with the almost threefold and fivefold increases in lower and higher education, respectively.

As a result of these educational efforts in the span from the 1926 to the 1939 census, the overall literacy rate was raised from 51 to 81 per cent among those over nine years of age. There were particularly dramatic changes in the nationality areas such as the Tadzhik and Uzbek republics, in which literacy increased from the extraordinarily low levels of 3.7 and 10.6 per cent to 71.7 and 67.8 per cent respectively.[8] The impact on the younger generation was especially marked. Of the 13 million people recorded in the 1939 census as having secondary education, 89 per cent were under forty and 73 per cent were under thirty years of age. Similarly, of the one million-odd who had higher education, about three fourths were under forty.[9]

The changing educational level of the Soviet population is dramatically evident in our sample. Table 31 compares the education attained by the Soviet generation which presumably had a chance to complete its education before the war, with that of their parents who were educated before the revolution. One must be careful not to place too much emphasis on anything but the cross-generational patterns shown in Table 31. As a sample of the parent Soviet population, our respondents were, of course, far above the education of the total population from which they were drawn.* This is because of the disproportionately large representation in our sample of individuals from the intelligentsia and white-collar groups. The systematic controls on the class composition of our sample which

---

* The 1939 census reported 89 per thousand among men and 68 per thousand among women as having completed secondary education; for *completed* higher education the rates per thousand were men, 9; women, 4.

we use are designed to meet this problem. In addition, it will be apparent that our subsample of women *as a whole* is also obviously skewed heavily in the direction of the better educated even as compared with male refugee groups. Peasant women in particular are underrepresented in our sample of women.

Keeping these cautions in mind we may nevertheless note the marked changes in the course of one generation. For both men and women educated during the Soviet era the proportion of those with only primary education is about half of what it was among their parents. At the other pole the proportion with some higher education almost doubled among the men and increased by four times among the women. The magnitude of the shift for the women in part reflects the sample's characteristic of having so many representatives from the middle educational level among the mothers ready to push their daughters over the line into college. But it also mirrors the striking work the Soviet regime did in drawing women into higher education. Before the revolution not more than 15 per cent[10] of the university students were women, but by 1927 it had risen to 31 per cent and by 1954 to 50 per cent.[11]

TABLE 31 [11A]

EDUCATION ATTAINED BY SOVIET GENERATION
AND BY THEIR PARENTS: BY SEX

(Respondents 21–40 in 1940)

Educational level	Men		Women	
	Soviet generation	Their fathers	Soviet generation	Their mothers
0–4 years	36%	65%	20%	43%
5–10 years	40	22	52	50
Higher	24	13	28	7
Total number of respondents	835	835	316	316

Impressive as these gains were, they were so inflated by Soviet propaganda, and so dazzling to friends and admirers of the Soviet Union, that a rather mythical image of the Soviet educational system developed. In this myth the Soviet Union emerges as a country in which education is equally accessible to all and all take as much as they possibly can. This is far from being the case. The Soviet educational system has actually been highly and rigorously selective. Thus, of every 1,000 students who entered the first grade in 1930, only about 50 graduated from the secondary school ten years later. In 1939 the enrollment in the five through seven-year school was 72 per cent of the eligible age group, but the complete secondary (eighth to tenth year) school contained only 20 per cent of the eligible age group.* Furthermore, attrition continued during the years of secondary school, so that only about 7 per cent of the eligible age group actually graduated from the regular high school.[12]

This is actually a very respectable success rate. It is lower than that of the United States, where selection is less rigorous, but is higher than that of England and many European countries. Yet if only 7 in 100 of eligible age were graduating from secondary school, this hardly suggests that young people in the Soviet Union were getting all the education they wanted and could absorb. On the contrary, the data show that in the Soviet Union even a mere high school diploma was still a relatively distinctive possession just before the war.**

From Soviet sources we can develop some gross impressions as to the degree to which different classes of Soviet citizens shared in the acquisition of the scarce good which better education represented. In the 1939 census 67 per cent of the population was defined as rural. By school level, however, the share of the rural regions in total enrollment got ever smaller as the higher reaches of the educational ladder were attained. In the primary school they accounted for 75 per cent, at the five-to-seven level 63 per cent, and in regular secondary school only 41 per cent of the total national enrollment.[13] Place of residence, however, is too gross a distinction, since it lumps together a range of occupational or status groups.[14] Fortunately Soviet sources did publish some information on the social composition of the student body as it applied to students in colleges and universities before the war.[15] In 1938, the last reported year, 42 per cent of university students were the children of professional, administrative or white-collar parents. This was almost two and a half times the representation of such groups in the population at large. By contrast, the children of peasants made up only 22 per cent of the students, even though their parents were more than 46 per cent of the population! Workers and peasants together accounted for 79 per cent of the population, but only 56 per cent of the university enrollments. This ratio is apparently not too dissimilar from that in the United States. Data for all college students are not available, but at a representative state university, Indiana, the sons of the manually employed were 31 per cent of all

* This does not count the students in secondary *technical* schools, who are usually not included in such tabulations. If they are included, the per cent of the eligible age group in school would be about 30 per cent.

** In the postwar period there were some changes in this situation, which we will discuss in the conclusions to this chapter. The bulk of the educational experiences of our respondents, however, relate mainly to the prewar period, which makes the 1939–40 situation the most relevant for us here.

students, whereas manual workers were 60 per cent of the state's labor force.[16]

Unfortunately, official Soviet data do not permit us to go much further than this. More refined estimates of the effects of the selection system and the unequal access to education among different residence and social classes have not been published. Indeed, no further information on the class background of students has been given at all since the 1938 data were published. Informal inquiries made by us of Soviet educational administrators in 1957 suggest, however, that the white-collar groups continue to constitute a disproportionately large percentage of the students in institutions of higher education. Our refugee materials are, however, rich in information on this subject. They permit us to trace the revolution's impact on the levels of education attained by different groups in the population, to explore some of the more subtle factors which influenced this outcome, and to learn something of the ways in which Soviet citizens evaluated the educational opportunities the system made available to them.

Education and social class identification are quite intimately linked throughout the Western industrial world. Using education as a measure of class, we may note that in the United States 100 per cent of the professionals and 57 per cent of those holding important positions in large business have some college training. Seventy-two per cent of unskilled workers and 65 per cent of farm laborers and tenants did not get beyond grade school.[17] In the Soviet Union as well, social classes tend to be relatively homogeneous with regard to education, with the classes higher in

TABLE 32 [17A]

EDUCATIONAL ATTAINMENTS OF SOCIAL CLASS GROUPS

Education attained	Intelli-gentsia	White-collar employees	Skilled workers	Ordinary workers	Collec-tive farm peas-ants
0–4 years	— a	7%	30%	56%	69%
5–7 years	7	26	43	33	22
8–10 years	22	40	24	11	9
Some college	28	12	3	— a	— a
College graduate	43	15	— a	— a	0
Total number of respondents	557	553	225	382	267

a. Less than 1 per cent.

social standing also being higher in average education (Table 32). At the one pole, those who identified themselves as collective farmers consisted almost entirely of individuals with only primary or secondary schooling. At the other pole, 71 per cent of the intelligentsia had attended college. Indeed, 43 per cent completed college, or had even done graduate work, a distinction understandably shared by not a single peasant in our sample. As one ascends the status ladder the modal educational group rises up the steps of the school ladder. In the middle range, however, the differences are not so sharp, and at the "common man" level (the ordinary, the skilled, and the white-collar workers) about one third of each group had the middling five-to-seven-year level of schooling. Many factors other than education, of course, enter into social class identity, and occupation in particular plays a role. We must note, therefore, that among those who identified themselves as members of the intelligentsia there were 7 per cent who had only seven years of school or less. The majority of these, of course, were those who started from humble backgrounds and worked their way up through administrative rather than technical professional channels.

These data tell only that there are very marked differences in the education of persons belonging to the several social groups. They do not tell us directly what social groups these people came from but only the groups they ended up in. However, our knowledge of the strong correlation between terminal status and social origins leads us to anticipate the findings of Table 33, in which are summarized the relations between our respondents' social origins and the levels of education they attained. Since there was an appreciable amount of dislocation of families during the early years of the Soviet regime, these data are assembled so that we may see simultaneously the influence of both the pre- and postrevolutionary standing of a boy's family on the level of education he attained. We restrict ourselves to those in school during the Soviet period, that is, those less than thirteen years old in 1917.

Both the pre- and postrevolutionary status of the individual's family evidently had a powerful effect on his chances to secure an education under Soviet conditions. Here we can clearly see the impact which the Soviet regime's denial of citizenship and other rights had on some families. Those in the prerevolutionary upper classes who were cast down by the new regime were much less able to provide their children with the sorts of educational opportunities which those who hung on to their relative status could manage. Thus, to have been "upper" class before and "lower" after, or to move from "middle" to "lower," meant that compared to someone who escaped this fall you had only about half the chance of attaining a given education. Yet such changes could not entirely offset the cultural values which the family presumably carried over from its previ-

TABLE 33 [17B]

PERCENTAGES WHO COMPLETED MORE THAN SEVEN AND MORE THAN TEN YEARS OF SCHOOLING: BY PARENTS' PREREVOLUTIONARY AND POSTREVOLUTIONARY SOCIAL STATUS

(Respondents under 13 in 1917)

Parents' postrevolutionary social status	Years of schooling completed	Parents' prerevolutionary social status			Total (postrevolutionary social status)
		Upper	Middle	Lower	
Upper	more than 7	82% (190) [a]	72% (21)	83% (12)	81% (223)
	more than 10	50	42	2	48
Middle	more than 7	74 (106)	65 (232)	46 (153)	61 (491)
	more than 10	41	28	14	26
Lower	more than 7	43 (26)	22 (45)	20 (677)	21 (748)
	more than 10	19	9	7	8
Total (prerevolutionary social status)	more than 7	76 (322)	59 (298)	25 (842)	
	more than 10	44	26	9	

a. Total number of respondents on the basis of which percentages are computed.

ous status. Thus, if a person came from a prerevolutionary "upper" class family that was moved downward after the revolution and ended up in the "middle" class, he stood a better chance (41 per cent) of getting beyond the ten-year school than if his family had originally been "middle" class and remained there after the revolution (28 per cent). Indeed, he had as good a chance as a boy whose family reversed the process and moved from the "middle" class before to the "upper" class after the revolution (42 per cent). Similarly a person whose family moved upward after the revolution, from "lower" to "middle" class, was less likely to go beyond the ten-year school than if the family were originally middle class, although more likely to get this level of education than if the family had not been mobile.

Although mobility under the impact of revolutionary conditions did affect educational chances, it is nonetheless evident that the overwhelming majority of the fathers of our respondents occupied approximately the same social status *after* as they did *before* the revolution. The most informative set of figures, therefore, is the summary of the educational level attained by respondents of upper, middle, and lower social origins regardless of their prerevolutionary status (the data summarized in the last column of the table). Those of "lower" postrevolutionary origins were only one fourth as likely to go beyond seven years of schooling as were persons of "upper" origin, and one third as likely as persons of "middle" origin. The ratios are even larger with respect to education beyond the ten-year school. The educational level of persons of "lower" origin were about 1 to 3.2 in comparison with the "middle" group, and 1 to 6 in comparison with the "upper" group.

To show more clearly the overwhelming impact of the father's occupation on his children's educational chances under Soviet conditions, we have in Table 34 used our more usual occupational designations. We have also restricted ourselves to those in the younger Soviet generation who were twelve or under at the time of the revolution, between twenty-one and thirty-five by 1940, and who therefore presumably had had a chance to get to college if they were going.

In this young generation the women of a given social origin do about as well as the men, except perhaps that those coming from manual class families less often get to college than their "brothers." Disregarding sex, then, we see that the great majority of the children of the intelligentsia got to college. Most of the rest got at least to high school, and very few "disgraced" their families by failing to get past the primary school. By contrast the overwhelming majority of the peasants got just this minimum although about one in ten did attain the exalted college level. Between these poles the proportions with only elementary schooling falls and with college training rises as one ascends the occupational ladder. The sharpest point of division comes, however, when we pass over the line from manual labor to white-collar jobs. The poor showing of the peasants cannot be attributed to the high proportion of the dekulakized among them, since they fared about as well as those not discriminated against by the government. It is interesting to note that these patterns closely parallel those which prevail in the United States. Thus Dael Wolfle has estimated the chances that a boy will get through college as 43 per cent if his father is professional or semiprofessional, 15 per cent if he is a salesman or clerk, and 8 per cent if blue collar.[18]

Impressive as is this evidence of differential access to education, it must be recognized as applying mainly to people who *completed* their education by 1940 or before. The data therefore fail to take full account of the leveling up which the continuous expansion of Soviet educational facilities was presumably fostering. Our materials fortunately do permit

TABLE 34 [18A]

SOCIAL ORIGINS AND EDUCATIONAL ATTAINMENT
OF RESPONDENTS 21–35 IN 1940

	Father's occupation				
Respondent's education	Profes-sional-ad-ministra-tive	Semipro-fessional and white collar	Skilled worker	Ordinary worker	Peasant
0–4 years	5%	4%	17%	30%	58%
5–7 years	8	17	28	47	25
8–10 years	20	35	30	13	9
Some college	24	15	6	4	3
College graduate	43	29	19	6	5
Total number of respondents	128	165	72	184	331

us to test the effects of these later developments, although we can deal only with the early stages of education and with only small numbers of cases. The first test consists in considering those of our respondents who were so young that they were still in the midst of their schooling before the war (Table 35). In this category we consider only those who were born between 1920 and 1929 and were therefore between eleven and twenty years of age in 1940. They made up the next younger school generation below those we have just considered, receiving their education exclusively during the period of greatest expansion of Soviet educational facilities.

Caution should be exercised in evaluating the absolute levels attained by this younger group because most had not yet completed their educations. But at the lower school levels, which even the youngest qualified for, this younger generation (ages eleven to twenty in 1940) did do better than the immediately preceding generation (ages twenty-one to thirty-five in 1940). This youngest group does then reveal the effect expanding facilities had in increasing the average educational attainment of younger Soviet citizens. This is especially evident in the disadvantaged classes. Whereas in the slightly older "generation" only 42 per cent of the peasants' children reached at least the fifth grade, 61 per cent in the next "generation" got that far. Indeed, the improvement would have been more marked had not the peasant group been held back by children of kulaks, who in *this* age bracket did show the effects of the dekulakization.[19] Similarly for the children of workers, the percentage getting at least as

TABLE 35 [18B]

SOCIAL ORIGINS AND EDUCATIONAL ATTAINMENT
OF RESPONDENTS 11–20 IN 1940

	Father's occupation				
Respondent's education	Professional-administrative	Semiprofessional and white collar	Skilled worker	Ordinary worker	Peasant
0–4 years	3%	2%	12%	17%	39%
5–7 years	25	28	30	43	40
8–10 years	39	50	43	33	17
Some college	33	20	15	7	4
Total number of respondents	95	117	33	141	152

far as the fifth grade in the younger group is 83 whereas, in the slightly older group it was only 70. But despite this "leveling up" of the lower classes, the basic pattern of differential class access to education has not been profoundly altered. The percentage who have *only* four-year schooling still rises steadily as we go down the class ladder, characterizing only 3 per cent of the children of the intelligentsia as against 39 per cent of the children of the peasants. And at the higher school levels, the proportion of the intelligentsia's children who attained the secondary school or went beyond it is three times the comparable proportion for the peasants' children.

A second test of the impact of late developments is provided by the comparison of the education attained not by our respondents, who perforce were mainly adults, but by the children of our respondents. We have data on 391 such children born between 1920 and 1929, and therefore between eleven and twenty in 1940.[20] In other words, they were of the same age range as our actual respondents described in Table 35, although not many had actually reached twenty. Evidently these children of respondents made out about as did those of our actual respondents who were in similar age brackets. Again we see that the youngest generation, those born after 1920 and attending school during the period of greatest expansion of Soviet education, were benefiting from that development. A greater percentage of them had attained the fifth grade than was typical for the somewhat older generation (compare with Table 34). Equally important, however, the class patterning in access to education remains clearly in evidence here too. Thus, among older children of the intelligentsia and white-collar families 20 per cent were in college, whereas among those of manual origin only 7 per cent were able to attain that level.

TABLE 36 [20A]

EDUCATIONAL ATTAINMENTS OF RESPONDENTS' CHILDREN

Respondents' social class and age of children in 1940	Years of schooling completed by respondents' children:				Total number of respondents
	0–4 years	5–9 years	10 years	higher	
Nonmanual					
Over 15 yrs. of age	17%	35%	28%	20%	(129)
11–15 yrs. of age	31	65	3	1	(118)
All age 11+	24	49	16	11	(247)
Manual					
Over 15 yrs. of age	32	45	16	7	(56)
11–15 yrs. of age	50	47	2	1	(88)
All age 11+	42	46	8	4	(144)

In sum, our data indicate: (1) Education is highly correlated with one's self-elected social group, and with one's occupation. (2) The explicit policy of the Soviet regime to favor with superior educational opportunities those in the laboring classes and to impede the opportunities of members of the "former exploiting classes" may have *inhibited* slightly the educational chances of this latter group. However, it did not offset to any *appreciable* degree the tendency of the children of the upper classes to secure superior access to higher education. Abolition of the regime's policy of discrimination during the mid-thirties has probably produced even stronger stratification. (3) The broad expansion of Soviet education has clearly had major results not only in upgrading the average, but also in putting a floor under the level of education received by the children of all social groups. For our respondents and their children this meant a certain equality with regard to at least the minimum level of education regardless of social origin. What still further postwar developments in education may mean for the current generation of Soviet youngsters we will consider after we have come to understand better the forces which seem to account for the differentiated patterns of educational attainment we observed.

Socio-Economic Factors Influencing Educational Opportunity

The opinion of various groups about their educational opportunities is perhaps most unambiguously measured by our oral interview code, which showed the per cent satisfied as follows: intelligentsia, 89; white-collar, 72; skilled worker, 67; ordinary worker, 46; and peasant, 50. Those more highly placed were obviously more satisfied with their educational opportunities. The same pattern prevailed when we turned to the children. Asked to compare their own opportunities with those of un-specified "others," the children of peasants revealed their sense of deprivation by checking "less than others" almost twice as often as did children from intelligentsia homes (Table 37). The absolute level of satisfaction with one's attained education cannot be safely judged from responses to this question because of the uncertainty as to the reference groups for those at each class level. Obviously those of intelligentsia background who felt they had less chance than "others" can hardly have had peasants in mind. But the question is revealing about the relative sense of deprivation and the results make sense in those terms, and they certainly can be accepted as further evidence that children of lower status parents are more likely to feel that their chances for an education were relatively poor.

TABLE 37 [20B]

CLAIMS OF INFERIOR EDUCATIONAL OPPORTUNITY
AND ITS ALLEGED CAUSES: BY SOCIAL ORIGIN

Social origin	Per cent claiming less opportunity than others	Total number of respondents	Per cent[a] citing reason for deprivation as:			Total number of respondents[b]
			Social origins	Political considerations	Lack of money	
Intelligentsia	42%	(169)	73%	35%	12%	(52)
White-collar employees	48	(227)	53	29	27	(85)
Skilled workers	57	(164)	37	25	54	(57)
Ordinary workers	69	(214)	39	28	39	(71)
Collective farm peasants	73	(408)	49	22	33	(180)

a. Percentages do not total to 100 because some gave more than one reason.
b. Includes only those citing reason for deprivation.

Economic factors played an important part in this outcome. Among those who gave reasons for their disadvantaged status, money was specifically mentioned by the children of peasants and workers about three times as often as it was cited by those of nonmanual origin (Table 37).

The personal interviews corroborate this finding. There the code emphasized the factors which *facilitated* getting an education, and 40 per cent of the reasons cited by workers and peasants, as against 20 per cent for the intelligentsia, had to do with being able to afford an education. The contrast is very apparent in the following comments:

A cleaning woman in the Soviet Union at that time [mid-thirties] got a salary of 90 rubles a month. On this it was impossible to send her child or children even to the middle school. It would not be bad if the child were in the Institute and got a stipend, but even then, after this stipend was cut out [a reference to the policy change in 1940 when free tuition was abolished and stipends limited to students with excellent grades] it was even worse.

It was difficult on the stipend . . . [cites long list of expenses, including 10 to 20 per cent contributed to state loans]. And so, if your parents did not have the money, you just couldn't go. My father did, and I was able to attend the Institute.

Far and away the outstanding obstacle to a superior education for those from upper class social backgrounds was not money, but rather the regime's treatment or evaluation of such backgrounds. Three fourths of all those of intelligentsia origins who had a complaint blamed their social origins for holding back their education. They cited this reason twice as often as political factors and six times as often as money. By contrast, among the manual classes little more than a third cited their social origin or position, and this reason carried only the same weight as economic factors. The peasants, perhaps because of the effects of dekulakization, somewhat alter this balance by giving greater weight to social origins than to family finances. Dekulakized peasants cited social origins twice as often as did those without this experience.

Respondents of "upper" social class origins who were of an age to receive their higher education in the years between 1920 and 1935 were acutely aware of regime policies which discriminated against them. They told many stories of their efforts to overcome the disadvantages of their social origins. Most frequently, however, they either disguised their origins or "won" status as workers by taking on manual jobs for a specified period of time. A young woman, whose father had been a well-to-do farmer, wanted to become a singer. But after her father's property was confiscated she found it difficult to get into school because of her class background. After a while she succeeded in being admitted to a musical technicum, but within four months she was expelled because of her class background. She then bought herself a passport on the black market, and worked for a while as a bookkeeper in a publishing house. Finally, in 1933 she was able, with the aid of the false passport, to enter a musical conservatory and she received a stipend which contributed to her support. Others earned "workers" status through more legal official channels. Thus one young man whose father had been a tsarist *gymnasium* teacher reported: "My elder brothers suffered because of my father's occupational status. Before entering the university they had to get a job in a factory so that they could qualify as workers and thus receive an easier admission to the university." Such stories are numerous. They almost indicate what we have already noted: that discrimination by the regime was on the whole not effective in preventing members of the "former exploiting classes" from attaining a higher education. The regime made that accomplishment more difficult and forced many to interrupt their education, but in the end most attained their goal despite their background.[21]

The perennial question raises its head: were the class differences in the *perception* of educational opportunities vanishing under the impact of Soviet developments? To answer this question we have differentiated three age groups, whose estimates of their educational opportunity we may compare. Since the question on educational opportunity referred specifically to Soviet conditions, it is meaningful to consider only those young enough to have secured at least some of their education in the Soviet schools. In the group between thirty-one and forty are those who completed their education either before the revolution or in the early Soviet years. Those who were between twenty-one and thirty in 1940 were between nine and eighteen in 1928. They would have received a Soviet education but a large proportion would have finished their education by the time the great expansion came along. The next age class would have been in schools during the great prewar expansion years.

At first glance at the differences between the three groups (Table 38) indicates that the younger groups generally rate their opportunities as having been better than those of the older groups. The percentage who felt they had as much or more opportunity than "others" rises steadily and markedly as we reach the younger age groups, although this is not clear-cut in the case of the workers.[22] It is possible to interpret the differences between the age groups either as "real" generational differences or as "illusory" life-cycle differences, that is, the younger people may answer as they do only because of the "optimism of youth." Since we know that the younger people did in fact have better opportunities because of the actual history of Soviet educational development, it seems more plausible to accept the differences as reflecting a real change in attitude between generations. If we accept these data as though they reflect actual changes through time in the preceived opportunity for education, they tell an interesting story.

The responses of the oldest group (31–40) are complicated by the early social policies which favored urban workers and discriminated against professional and white-collar groups. However, as we move more fully into the Soviet period with the two younger groups two changes are manifested. Education seems generally more accessible, in that each

TABLE 38 [22A]

RELATIONS OF SOCIAL ORIGIN AND AGE
TO PERCEIVED EDUCATIONAL OPPORTUNITY

(Per cent saying they had "equal" or "superior" opportunities)

Social origin	Age in 1940		
	Under 21	21–30	31–40
Professional	67% (103) [a]	55% (91)	32% (54)
Semiprofessional and white collar	61 (127)	48 (114)	20 (90)
Worker	37 (175)	38 (192)	40 (106)
Peasant	31 (141)	25 (202)	19 (178)

a. Total number of respondents on the basis of which the percentage is computed.

origin group now shows a higher proportion reporting educational opportunity than did so in the older group.[23] But in addition, there is more regular and clear differentiation between the social classes. The white-collar employees more often report educational opportunity than the workers, and the workers more often than the peasants. These patterns hold up as we move from the middle to the youngest group. But the pace at which gains are made is not evenly distributed. The intelligentsia shows far and away the most marked increase in optimism. In the oldest group only 13 per cent separated those from low manual and those from high white-collar homes. In the youngest group the gap is 36 per cent, and the percentage satisfied among children of professional-administrative background is more than twice the proportion satisfied among those of lower background. In part this has come about because the standard of what is an acceptable amount of education seems to have been changing. Among people over fifty with less than ten years of schooling the dissatisfied were only 18 per cent, whereas among those under forty more than 60 per cent were dissatisfied. Those who received more than ten years of schooling do not show similar generational differences.[24]

Thus, if we accept these data as reflecting real changes in values, it appears that the proportion who perceive educational opportunity is now greater, but the *differentiation* between social groups in their evaluation of their educational chances is actually also greater and more sharply graduated. This sharpened difference comes about in part because at one end of the status scale the people of humble origin have an increasingly high expectation or definition with regard to what is a satisfactory amount of schooling. At the other pole, the children of the intelligentsia and white-collar groups in the later Soviet period seem increasingly confident that they will have the educational opportunities they expect. This confidence is certainly reasonable in the light of their actual experience, which as we have seen does more frequently yield them higher education. It is, as we will see, also a reflection of their greater involvement in, and readiness to take advantage of, such educational opportunities as the system offers.

What Good Is Education?
Cultural Factors Influencing Opportunity

Although discrimination by the regime and economic pressures undoubtedly played a major role in determining who got educated, these factors alone cannot explain the great differences in educational attainment among those of different origins. On the one hand, we must note that despite the massive obstacles which the regime placed on their path to education, the children of those from the former "exploiting" and "possessing" classes nevertheless generally managed to get a substantially better education than the average. Along the same line we can show that whether or not there was a political arrest in the family, even when it led to a sentence to forced labor, the educational level attained by the children was substantially the same as in families which did not experience an arrest. We must acknowledge that there were fewer advanced schools in the countryside, which undoubtedly affected the educational opportunities of the rural youth. But we must also call attention to the fact that in the cities where presumably the higher facilities were equally accessible to the children of the intelligentsia and the workers, they were heavily used by the former and only sporadically taken advantage of by the latter. It is indeed interesting to note that whether workers' children lived in cities, which presumably had better facilities, or towns, which were inferior in this regard, the education they attained was substantially the same.

Such facts argue strongly what experience everywhere has taught us, namely that differences in opportunity and ability to pay for education will not alone explain differential educational attainment. There is a second important factor, namely differences in family atmospheres and in individual values, which strongly influences the chances that even equally free and available educational facilities will be taken advantage of.

The differences in orientations toward education in the several social groups is revealed on a general level by their willingness to support the educational aspirations of their children. Asked about their parents' attitudes toward their education, the great majority of our Soviet generation reported "they supported me completely." But the proportions giving this answer varied markedly according to the origins of the respondent.

Whereas almost three fourths of the sons of the intelligentsia reported complete support, only a third of workers' sons were able to give this favorable report on their parents (Table 39). While the peasants somewhat reverse the trend,[25] they nevertheless also report securing full support far less often than do those of white-collar origins. Furthermore, although the women in every class got less support than their brothers, the degree of support received was primarily determined not by sex but by class origin. Understandably, the proportion reporting parental support also rises with the degree of education attained quite apart from social origins. Working-class boys who secured a superior education are more likely to report parental support. Whether in fact their parents gave them more support than was given to other working-class boys we cannot tell. It seems reasonable to assume this was the case.

TABLE 39 [25A]

PER CENT RECEIVING "UTMOST" PARENTAL SUPPORT:
BY SOCIAL ORIGIN AND SEX

(Respondents 15–35 in 1940)

Social origin	Men	Women
Intelligentsia	73% (77) [a]	68% (94)
White-collar employee	63 (127)	53 (101)
Skilled worker	44 (125)	36 (39)
Ordinary worker	33 (139)	23 (69)
Peasant	45 (313)	31 (106)

a. Total number of respondents on the basis of which the percentage is computed.

"Support" can mean many things. Undoubtedly these answers in part refer to economic support, which we have already seen to be available in different degree depending on the class one is born into. But our personal interviews make it abundantly clear that the report of parental support referred also to the degree to which parents supported and encouraged the *idea* of education and its *value*. At one pole there was the pattern of complete support of education, typified by the comment of a twenty-nine-year-old sports instructor whose father had been an electrical engineer: "My father always told me: 'Study, study, study, that is the main thing. You cannot know what will come of it, but at least nothing bad can come from study.'" Such attitudes were certainly not common among those from more humble backgrounds. More typical, for them, was the report of a worker of forty, who said of his peasant father that "he wanted his children not to be illiterate; but he also wanted us to work, and he felt that four years of schooling were enough." The same quality emerges in the comment of the peasant woman born in 1904, who said: "In the villages we just don't think about such things. We don't think much about schooling. We had a good life when I was a child. It was alright, we didn't think about anything else. And we still don't in most of the villages."

Further confirmation of these patterns was provided in the coding of the personal interviews. Each individual was rated as coming, at the one extreme, from a family in which both the parents and the children valued education, and at the other extreme from a family in which neither valued it. The "plus-plus" proportions, that is, the percentage of cases in which both parents and children valued education, fell from 89 per cent of the intelligentsia down the class ladder to 81, 69, 72, and to 47 per cent in the peasant families.[26]

Not the parents, alone, of course, but also the children they reared and who became our respondents, reflect the differential evaluation of education. People of superior background were much more likely to report that they were among the better students, and that they enjoyed school. Their interest in school is further reflected in the fact that if their education was interrupted they were much more likely to resume it rather than merely to give up at whatever point they had reached.[27] In part the explanation for this superior adjustment to school must be seen as a reflection of differences in the underlying value systems of the several classes as they bore on the topic of education. Our data permit us to approach the attitudes of our respondents from two directions. Our qualitative coding of the history of each individual's educational experiences and the reasons he gave for pursuing his education give a clue to his more "public" attitudes toward his own education. An incomplete sentence fragment, "Education leads to . . . ," provides an expression of more subtle covert attitudes toward education in general.

The motives and orientation of our respondents toward their own educations are summarized in Table 40. One third of the peasants and one seventh of the ordinary workers who answered the question gave no reason for their getting an education other than the necessity to meet the legal minimum. Of course no one in the intelligentsia gave this reason. The failure of so many of the manual respondents to offer any more specific reason other than this indicates that they lack a clear picture of what education can in fact do for a person, which fits well with the impression of their orientation we draw from the qualitative materials. Obviously, then, upper social groups understand and value education more, but they also differ in the reasons *why* they value it. This is evident when we consider only the positive reasons (other than legal necessity) for getting an education.

In Table 40 we find several distinct relationships. (1) As we proceed

TABLE 40 [27A]

REASONS FOR SECURING AN EDUCATION:
BY SOCIAL GROUP [a]

Positive reason for securing education[b]	Intelligentsia	White-collar employees	Skilled workers	Ordinary workers	Collective farmers
Specific occupational interest	43%	39%	35%	27%	16%
Status, success	22	13	7	4	21
Material focus	15	35	42	52	47
Education for its own sake	20	6	7	2	5
Conform with peers and family tradition	5	13	14	17	11
Total citing positive reasons	110	54	29	48	19
Total citing legal requirement	0	3	3	8	11
Total answering question	110	57	32	56	30

a. From personal interviews.
b. Percentages equal more than 100 because more than one reason might be cited.

down the class ladder the proportion of persons in each group who valued education because it led to a specific occupation decreases; (2) with one exception[28] the proportion who saw their education as leading to material gain in general increases;* (3) the proportion who saw their education as producing advances in status and making them "successful" decreases (again with one exception); and (4) it was the intelligentsia alone which to any appreciable extent valued education for its own sake.

Equipped with superior knowledge, members of the intelligentsia are obviously better able to see the *specific* connection between education and success. This is reflected in their stress on the nexus between getting an education and training for a specific job. At the same time, they tend to take reasonable earnings more for granted. By contrast, it is this very factor which is dominant in lower class thinking about the reasons for securing education, just as economic factors were dominant in lower class evaluations of the factors which facilitate or hinder getting an education. The intelligentsia, understandably, could afford to be less concerned with

* It appears that over time, going from generation to generation, there is a general tendency to give more stress to material security as a reason for getting an education, and to do so at the expense of stressing family traditions. (Alice Rossi, "Generational Differences in the Soviet Union," unpublished report of the Harvard Project on the Soviet Social System, Russian Research Center, July 1954.)

whether they would succeed and more concerned with *how* they would succeed. The lower status respondents did not indulge in the luxury of valuing education in itself, but saw it mainly in instrumental terms, as leading to highly desired economic improvement.

Shifting from the evaluation of one's own education to attitudes toward education in general, as revealed in the completion of the sentence fragment, "Education leads to . . . ," we find many of the same trends repeated, but with interesting variations. The answers were divided into those which stressed (1) "instrumental-personal" results, such as "leads to a career," which represent benefits for an individual rather than for a group; (2) "humanistic-social" responses, such as "leads to the advancement of knowledge"; and (3) ambivalent or negative answers, such as "leads toward good, maybe toward evil."

TABLE 41 [28A]

VALUES REFLECTED IN ASSESSMENT OF
EDUCATION: BY SOCIAL GROUP

| Values | Social groups | | | | |
	Intelli-gentsia	White-collar employees	Skilled workers	Ordinary workers	Collective farmers
Personal, instrumental	43%	56%	70%	77%	87%
Humanistic, social and scientific	41	33	20	17	10
Ambivalent	16	9	10	6	3
Total number of respondents	85	45	30	46	31

The results summarized in Table 41 follow the established pattern. Seeing education mainly in terms of personal gain becomes more frequent as we descend the status scale. It is the overwhelming predominant response among the collective farmers, and is twice as common among them as it is in the intelligentsia (87 per cent — 43 per cent). Correspondingly, the category "humanistic, social and scientific," which includes all answers describing education as benefiting society or mankind in general, decreases in importance from intelligentsia to peasantry. The notion of service to the group is one that the Soviet regime has posed as a primary value, and it is therefore natural to find the intelligentsia and the employees — the most indoctrinated and most committed segments of the population — most accepting of this value. This acceptance, however, is more clearly exhibited in their evaluation of education in general than in their attitude toward their own education, where, by and large, the white-collar groups showed more concern with their own advantage and welfare. Finally, the intelligentsia exhibited the greatest ambivalence toward education, with 16 per cent seeing possible disadvantages in being educated. For example, one member of the intelligentsia completed the fragment by saying education leads to "happiness, but maybe to the just the contrary; the more you learn the more you react to all that happens in life, and there are so many bad events." The peasants were more firm in feeling that education is in general "good," with only 3 per cent recording ambivalence. The member of the intelligentsia had no doubt that he could and should be educated, and that it is personally worthwhile, but he apparently saw the possibility that he himself or the society might have to pay a high price for it.

Closer study of the first category of "personal-instrumental" responses reaffirmed the point that the lower classes have a less specific notion of the personally beneficial results which education can produce. When the answers in the "personal-instrumental" category are further divided* into those which include some reasonably concrete result, as opposed to amorphous, ambiguous answers such as "it advances one" or "is good," the proportion of ambiguous answers increases sharply as we descend the social ladder. More than half of *all* the peasants' answers to the sentence fragment, and almost two thirds of their "instrumental-personal" answers, were classified as "ambiguously hopeful." The percentage of such answers is very much lower for the intelligentsia; only 5 per cent of all their answers, and about one eighth of their "instrumental-personal" answers. The percentage increases in a relatively smooth progression for the employees, skilled workers and workers. Thus, in both their orientation toward their own education and their attitudes toward education in general, respondents in different social groups differ markedly in the immediacy of the relationships they see between education and the benefits it produces. There is no such variation in the proportion of ambiguous answers among the varied social groups in the American matched sample. It is unfortunate for the purposes of control that our American sample was somewhat better educated. Nevertheless, the results argue that a population in which education is taken more as a matter of course will develop a clearer image of the benefits of education.

Comparison of the Soviet with the matched American sample suggests that it is a distinctly Soviet characteristic to value education because it benefits the group, rather than to concentrate on benefits to the individual. Although not dominant in either sample, this response is many

* This further division is not shown in Table 41.

times more common for the Soviet group. The figures in Table 42 probably underestimate this difference, since the American group is somewhat better educated despite our attempt at matching the two groups exactly, and therefore would be weighted toward those elments of the population most likely to mention benefits to society. Whether this finding be attributed to Soviet propaganda or to the persistence of old Russian cultural values, the strength of such "socially conscious" tendencies among former Soviet citizens emerges not only in these data but in many other materials of the Project. Former Soviet citizens are more likely by far to think in terms of the group's purposes than are Americans, who almost inevitably identify and are mainly concerned with the welfare of the individual.

TABLE 42 [28B]

VALUES EXHIBITED IN RUSSIAN AND AMERICAN ASSESSMENTS
OF THE GOALS OF EDUCATION

Values	Russians	Americans
"Personal-instrumental"	66%	89%
Humanistic, scientific and social	23	5
Ambivalent	9	6
Total number of respondents	76	87

The evaluations of education revealed in our study undoubtedly reflect strongly the conditions of Soviet social development during the 1930's and the particular socio-cultural background of our respondents. In the period of the late twenties and early thirties Soviet society was just emerging from its "educational backwardness." A large part of the population, especially the peasants, had only mild interest in education. Access to schools was for these people often restricted to the bare minimum. The presence of many in our sample who came out of that earlier milieu undoubtedly helps account for the high proportion who thought education was "good" in some abstract, amorphous way, but had little concrete knowledge as to exactly how it would work these wonders. By contrast, the Americans, among whom there was almost universal clarity as to precise, *personal*, practical merits of education, grew up in a society in which universal education had long been established and taken for granted.

This is graphically illustrated by comparing some of the evaluations of education across the generations. Thus, a woman of fifty-six, herself a worker but from a peasant family, reported "my parents expected me to marry a well-to-do peasant and continue the same tradition as they." For *her* daughter, however, she wanted a higher education. Again, a forty-three-year-old male farm mechanic whose father had been a peasant, said of him: "My father wanted me to be peasant like himself." For his own children, however, he set different goals: "In the Soviet Union I wanted my children to get an education. I would have liked them to study some kind of profession or specialization, so as to assure themselves a good income."

The youngest people were most firm on this score. Thus, a male collective farmer who was only twenty-six said: "I would give my last strength to raise and teach my children and educate them, because to be a peasant is no good. I would try to get my children to go to school and enter into production or some such thing." And a young woman of twenty-seven, of peasant origin and herself an office worker on a collective farm, said that if she had had a son: "I absolutely would not want him to be a peasant; I would want him to study and have educational and other opportunities."

Future Prospects

The young peasants we have just quoted may still be a minority among Soviet peasants, but they certainly indicate the trend. The Soviet system has obviously unleashed the floodgates of ambition and desire for advancement through education. This raises serious questions as to whether or not the educational channels are sufficiently large and the control points open wide enough to contain and channel the flow.

Despite major wartime attrition, the Soviet school system grew rapidly after World War II.[29] In 1949 seven-year schooling was declared compulsory everywhere, and during the period from 1952 to 1954 there was considerable discussion in the Soviet press about making ten years of schooling compulsory. Although not much has been heard since on this score, Soviet authorities do claim that ten-year schools are "universally available." Enrollment figures are misleading unless they can be related to the size of the eligible age groups. Success rates, however, reflect the trend quite well. As against a survival rate of 50 per 1,000 among those who started in 1929, of those who started in 1945, 250 per 1,000 completed the ten-year school in 1955. This is a tremendous increase, and speaks unequivocally of expanding opportunity to attain secondary school education.

Oddly enough, however, the opportunity of the 1955 secondary school graduates *to continue on to college* was less than that of those who graduated fifteen years before. The simple fact is that higher education was not expanding as rapidly as was secondary education. Up to 1940 the number of "vacancies" or admissions open in higher education actually exceeded the size of the graduating classes coming from the secondary schools. This meant that virtually every graduate of the ten-year school could go directly on to college and there was even room for some who had earlier been shunted off the main track. By 1956 the graduating class coming out of the tenth year had risen to one and a half million. Only one in three of this army could gain admission to higher educational institutions. This means that three out of four must now go to work or switch back to a vocational, technical, or semiprofessional school which is essentially at the secondary level. Having learned to value education and what it leads to, not many are willing to do this. We should not then be surprised that in the mid-fifties Soviet officials began to complain more often about "white hands" among Soviet youths.[30] In the summer of 1956 one high educational official listed as her prime difficulty the fact that too many children wanted to go to college.[31] Another expressed interest in the reintroduction of intelligence testing.[32] The attitudes of these officials suggested that the idea of higher education for all who were qualified was not likely to be encouraged. Finally, in September 1958 Khrushchev spoke out against the widespread desire and expectation of boys and girls who completed the secondary school to go on more or less automatically to higher education, and presented his unusual proposal to oblige all students to go to work after seven years of schooling.*

Although Soviet educational progress continues, it certainly cannot be assumed that the obviously rising *average* level of education necessarily means that class differences in access to superior education will disappear. Indeed, if they had, we may be sure the regime would proudly have announced this consequence of the expansion of their educational facilities. Their silence on this question suggests that the facts are quite to the contrary. Certainly we can see this ourselves if we consider that in 1956 only 250 in 1,000 were completing secondary school, of these only one in four entered college, and of those only three out of four would complete it. This means that only about 40 of the original 1,000, or one in twenty-five, would finish college.[33] College degrees obviously will remain in limited supply, to be had only through fierce competition. And in this competitive race we have seen how the lower class boy starts off with a substantial handicap and faces higher hurdles all along the way. The revocation of the tuition payments in secondary school and college and the restitution of a full program of stipends certainly gives him a better chance than he had in 1940. But it is undoubtedly the case that the probability of attaining a higher education which society "awards" at

* For a fuller account of these proposals, see the concluding section of Chapter IV.

VII

Keeping Up with the News[1]

Contrary to popular belief, the Soviet regime is by no means uninterested in the state of public opinion. Lenin early introduced the principle that the Soviet state must be based on a balance of coercion *and* persuasion. But the interest of the Soviet rulers is not in adjusting its policies to the wishes of the people. The regime is concerned with molding public opinion to the support of policies established by the Communist Party. In order to effect its goals of mass persuasion, the party has established a special Department of Propaganda and Agitation directly under its main policy-determining organ, formerly the Politburo and currently the Presidium of the Central Committee. While the party and its agencies set policy in the field of communications, operations are in the hands of a series of special government agencies within the Ministry of Culture.[2]

The common goal of the party and the government is to have the most effective network of mass communications, fully geared in structure with the policies of the party. This goal is reflected in the size and structure of the official media and the nature of the controls exercised over them. The official media include not only the pointed sources (newspapers, magazines, and journals), and the radio and a developing television network, but also the theater, movies, the arts, and a system of oral agitation. Through the system of oral agitation the regime attempts to capitalize on captive audiences. Two million agitators — and as many as three million in times of special campaigns — regularly carry the message of the party to their fellows at work, play, and even in workers' dormitories and apartments. They gather together their fellow citizens in small groups to hear an article read from the press, to describe some recent policy decision, to lead a "critical" discussion of the work performance of the group, or to enlist their support in some drive or campaign. Oral agitation is but one manifestation of the official policy of tying communications as closely as possible to the characteristics of the various subgroups to which the party and the government address themselves. There are, for example, about 150 newspapers for the youth of the country, and special newspapers and journals for various occupational and other groups, such as the railroad man, the peasant, and the member of the navy. Not only are there regional and local newspapers, but even a very large factory will have its own regular newspaper, and each office, school, and shop has its own "wall newspaper" with a regularly appointed editor and staff.

The seriousness with which the regime takes the job of getting its message to the public is seen in the efforts made to expand the facilities of communications. In 1939 there were 8,769 newspapers with single issue circulation of under forty million. As a result of postwar consolidations only about 7,200 were operating, but the single issue circulation had risen to forty-nine million.[3] In very broad terms this network compares reasonably well with that in the United States. In 1952 the United States had 229 metropolitan dailies, 1,551 small city dailies, and about 10,000 weekly, semiweekly and biweekly newspapers.[4] At the top of the Soviet hierarchy there were 25 "central" or "All-Union" papers, and about 460 republican and regional papers which are the equivalent of American metropolitan newspapers. The great majority of these are dailies. Smaller cities have about 1,000 dailies. The remainder of under 6,000 small city, district, and local newspapers are published less frequently.

The radio network is not nearly so impressive. In 1952 there were only 125 broadcasting stations in the country, and there were well under 100 receivers per 1,000, 80 per cent of which were not actually radio sets but wired speakers connected with a master receiver. This compared quite poorly with the rate of over 200 receivers per 1,000 in many European countries and was far below the United States rate of 500 per 1,000 of population. As late as 1955, there were only 26 million receivers,[5] still well below Western Europe on a per capita basis. The theater and movies are only partially media of information and will not be considered systematically here. They are generally quite readily accessible in the cities and often inaccessible in the rural areas, with constant shadings and gradations of availability in the towns and cities of intermediate size.

Accessibility to the press is fairly uniform for most citizens except those in the more isolated rural areas. Two thousand newspapers are printed in languages other than Russian in order to reach the national minorities. For most citizens the availability of newspapers is conditioned mainly by their own interest in obtaining them. Radio is fully accessible mainly in urban areas, but has become increasingly available in the countryside through electrification. Television cannot be taken seriously yet as a mass medium, since it is restricted to large cities. Accessibility to the movies and theater parallels closely that of the radio. Of the system of agitation, probably the most pertinent statement that can be made is that there is more difficulty in avoiding it than in making contact with it. In general, the regime has fashioned a technically adequate network of official media for getting its message to the people. Its dimensions, except for the system of agitation, are not as great as those of the United States, but considering the limitations of resources under which the regime operates the magnitude of this system is impressive and is a testimonial to the regime's concern with molding public opinion.

In order to understand the communications behavior which our respondents report, we must know something also of official communications policy. The major premise of Soviet communications policy has been the monopoly of the media of communications. Only the official point of view of the regime may be expressed in the formal media. Very recently we may have observed some breaks in this monopoly. After the "de-Stalinization" at the Twentieth Party Congress in 1956, opposition viewpoints — notably criticism of Soviet policy made by foreign communists — were in some instances reported in such a way as to define these views as legitimate points for discussion. If this should continue, we will be confronted with a fundamental change of policy. As of 1957, however, the loosening up process was itself still under very tight control, and by 1958 there was evidence of a return to the more stringent pattern typical of the period before the 1956 "thaw."

The system of controls extends to all the media and from central areas out into the remotest regions on the periphery. Because the regime tries to use the media as efficiently as possible to convey its messages, the media, especially the press, are dull, heavy, densely packed, lacking in human interest. In the overwhelming proportion of the press and magazines the tedium of dryly presented news is broken only by occasional satirical pieces. Those of our respondents who worked within the communications system and claim to be in a position to know, say that the regime is fully aware that the media are exactly what the bulk of our respondents, and any foreigner who has read Soviet sources for a time, report them to be — dull, tedious, tendentious, boring. Soviet propaganda operates on a principle of frontal assault by a mass of heavily weighted arguments, rather than by subtle indirection. It believes in presenting one side, the official side, vigorously and repetitively, not in discussing both sides of the question in a detached fashion. These characteristics of official communications policy have a strong influence on the communications behavior of the Soviet citizen.

The Sources of Information

While the regime regards the communications network which it has set up as a means of getting its message across to the citizen, the citizen often regards his own communications behavior primarily as a way of informing himself as to what is going on in the world about him. Even if he is a completely loyal supporter of the regime he is frequently aware of a disparity between its policies and his own sense of curiosity or his need for certain sorts of information. As a result he tries to get information through unofficial channels, which exist despite official attempts at suppression. He also applies certain interpretive principles to the content of the official media in the hope of discovering that which the regime hopes to conceal. "When I read about an event in the paper, by the logic of the question I see what is missing. Then I know what is needed in order to fill the gap," said a postwar refugee. We must therefore think of the system of communications in the Soviet Union as actually two parallel systems, one the official system, and the other a series of devices and media whereby the citizen seeks to supplement, correct, and replace the official media.

In our individual interviews we asked each person: "While you were in the Soviet Union, from what sources did you draw most of your information about what was happening?" This was followed by the probe: "Which of these sources was most important for you? And then?" A medium was scored as a "source" for a person if he seemed to make any meaningful use of it, even if it did not seem particularly important to him, or even if he did not use it frequently.

In dealing with the entire group, as we do for the moment, we tend to overestimate the rate of exposure to all media because of the disproportionate number of highly educated persons in the oral interview sample. In any event, rating a medium as a "source" has a rather ambiguous meaning since it does not indicate any absolute rate of exposure. We therefore restrict ourselves to only the relative frequency with which the various media were cited. The newspaper is the medium our respondents most often report using, and it is cited as a source of information by nine out of ten (Table 43). Next in frequency of mention are radio and word of mouth, each of which is cited by half our sample. "Meetings," which include all agitation activities, were mentioned by only one out of five persons, while personal observation is mentioned by about one in seven. If we use as our baseline the source least often mentioned, namely magazines, the relative importance of each medium is expressed in the ratios: magazines, 1; personal observation, 1.2; meetings, 1.6; radio, 4.2; word of mouth, 4.2; and newspapers, 7.4.[6]

In some respects this pattern is very much what we have come to expect in industrial and "industrializing" countries, but in other respects it may reflect the special nature of Soviet society or of our sample. The most notable similarity between the Soviet pattern and that found in other countries is the widespread use of the newspaper. A national sample of adults in the United States revealed that 82 per cent looked at one or more newspapers each day.[7] Similar rates of newspaper reading have been reported for the United Kingdom, Germany, and Scandinavia, although in France and Italy substantially lower rates prevailed.[8]

TABLE 43 [5A]

MEDIA CITED AS ORDINARY AND AS
MOST IMPORTANT SOURCES OF INFORMATION [a]

Media	(1) Per cent citing as source[b]	(2) Per cent citing as most important	(3) Stability of salience[c]
Newspapers	89	44	.49
Word of mouth	50	35	.70
Radio	50	13	.26
Meetings	19	2	.11
Personal observation	14	5	.36
Magazines	12	1	.08
Total number of respondents	312	275	

a. From personal interviews.
b. Percentages total more than 100 because more than one source could be cited.
c. Column 3 figures are derived by dividing the per cent in column 2 by that in column 1.

The relative standing of the radio as a major source of news is perhaps lower in our sample than for the United States, and this may reflect the lesser availability of radios in the Soviet Union.[9] It is obvious, however, that the radio is a major source of information. The spontaneous citation of the newspaper by almost everyone, the high number who remembered to cite the radio, and the fact that almost 20 per cent cited agitation and similar meetings to be news sources suggests that our respondents were quite extensively exposed to the official media of communications. They can hardly be thought to be "deviants" or "alien" citizens in this respect.

The relatively low emphasis which these people place on meetings as a source of "information" may be interpreted as an expression of the disparity between the points of view of the government and the people — at least the kind of people we have in our sample. The accounts which people give as to how they learned about specific events or specific policies leads us to suspect that meetings were a more important source of information than this table would indicate. In addition, the "time budget" questionnaire showed that the median for time spent in meetings was an average of one fourth of an hour daily. What this suggests is that the citizen — or at least the refugee ex-citizen — is likely to regard "information" as that which *he* wants to learn, not that which the regime wants him to know. We should perhaps assume that our respondents underestimate the importance of oral agitation as a source of information. Certainly, their attention to it as a source of information underestimates its importance to the regime. We must note, however, that frequent complaints in the Soviet press offer evidence that the agitation meetings generate boredom on a national scale and are not often attended willingly or with genuine interest.

What will most occasion special notice in Table 43 is the fact that half cited word-of-mouth sources (other than official meetings), and that this source was as frequently mentioned as was the radio.[10] The significance of word-of-mouth communication is further accentuated when we consider the proportions of people who cited the various media as their "most important" source of information (second column of Table 43). Newspapers *and word of mouth* are outstandingly the most frequently cited — 44 and 35 per cent. Furthermore, they have the most stable saliency (see third column). That is, when they are mentioned as a "regular" source of information the probability is most high for these two media that they will *also* be mentioned as the "most important" source. Word-of-mouth communication has far and away the most stable salience. Two out of three persons who mentioned word of mouth as a regular source also cited it as "most important," whereas this is true of only one tenth of those who mentioned meetings.

The absolute importance of word-of mouth sources and their relative salience may be mainly a reflection of the special nature of our sample. Since they were alienated people they perhaps more often went *outside* the official channels and relied on informal communications from personally trusted informants. Although this conclusion seems very plausible, we should not jump at it too quickly. Indeed the matter is much more complex than appears on the surface. In general, the less hostile to the Soviet system our respondents were, the *more* likely they were to report exposure to rumor. In the large written questionnaire sample, only 37 per cent of the most anti-Soviet group said they got information through rumors, whereas 64 per cent of the least anti-Soviet subgroup gave this answer.[11] Therefore, to the extent that our sample is anti-Soviet, it ought in general to give us an *underestimation,* not an overestimation, of the use of informal communications.

Of course we do not assert that the nature of our sample in no way colors the picture of Soviet communications with which we emerge. We mean only to caution against treating the picture which develops as if it can all be automatically explained by the nature of our sample. It is obvious that the real conditions of Soviet society encourage the use of informal unofficial sources of information. The absolute monopoly of communications maintained by the regime almost obliges the citizen to look elsewhere to supplement the limited information the regime makes available. The existence of an extensive network of word-of-mouth communications is attested to by the regime itself in its attacks on "rumor mongering" and its attempts over many years to isolate persons — such as those who had contact with the West — who might be the originators of unpalatable opinions and information that would circulate through unofficial channels. Foreign observers confirm the ubiquity of rumor in the Soviet Union, and our informants talk about it in many contexts. It is the citizen's device for keeping himself informed in a system of controlled communications.

The two systems of communications, the official and the unofficial, exist side by side and at various points shade off one into the other to the extent that it is difficult to say where one begins and the other ends. For some people the unofficial media serve as a substitute for the official sources and they withdraw almost completely from the use of the latter. Others use the official channels almost exclusively. Most persons, however, use both the official and informal media in a complementary relationship, each utilized as a check on, and as a basis for the interpretation of, the other. The nature of the Soviet Union is such that the communications behavior of the citizen must be regarded as one of the dimensions of his relations with the regime itself.

The Class Patterning of Communications Behavior

Study of communications patterns in European countries has consistently revealed that major subgroups of the population differ markedly in their communications behavior. This seems true for the Soviet Union as well. The main bases for these variations are: (1) a combination of educational and occupational factors which affect interest in what is going on, shape reading and listening habits, determine access to information and the media, and generate situational pressures which put a premium on being well informed; (2) residence, which primarily affects accessibility to sources of information, but must also be presumed to present environments, which vary in degree of intellectual stimulation; and (3) attitudes toward the regime, which are reflected in turn in attitudes toward the media of communication. Obviously, differences on these various dimensions are highly correlated with social class, and the various classes are therefore characterized by marked differences in communications behavior. Except for a few instances, sex and age differences affect communications behavior surprisingly little.* Variations in the age and sex composition of the class groups in our sample, therefore, do not significantly affect the class differences which we will discuss in this section.

On the written questionnaire we named eleven different sources of information, and asked our respondents to indicate for each whether they had frequently, seldom, or never utilized the particular source. The re-

* The statement is *generally* true, but has interesting exceptions. Movie attendance, for example, drops off rapidly in the older groups — as it does in the United States.

sultant pattern of answers produced a series of "exposure types." These types were not deduced on *a priori* logical grounds, but rather were empirically derived. They reflect the natural or "operative" clustering of communications behavior in our sample. Thus, we found that those who frequently read newspapers and magazines also tended to report frequently reading books, *and* frequently listening to the Soviet radio. It did not automatically follow, however, that such a person would be a frequent listener to the foreign radio or would often attend lectures. Those particular habits of communication were in fact associated with other modes in different distinctive clusters.[12] The clusters which emerged from our sorting out of the actual patterns of communications, and the names we assigned them, were as follows:

1. Mass Official: Newspapers and magazines, books and Soviet radio.
2. Aesthetic Official: Movies and theater.
3. Personalized Official: Lectures, agitation meetings, and other official sources.
4. Covert: Discussion with friends, rumor, and foreign radio.

Table 44 shows the percentage of each social group which received a particular exposure score for each type of media. No matter what type of media is involved, there is an extremely sharp drop in the frequency of exposure as we proceed from the intelligentsia down through the collective farmers.

Thus, 52 per cent of the intelligentsia, but only 3 per cent of the peasantry, reported frequent exposure on all three sources included in the "official mass media" category (Table 44). Even in the case of newspapers, the most widely used individual medium, only 17 per cent of the peasants were "frequent" users — as against 84 per cent of the intelligentsia. Aesthetic media also show a very sharp decline in exposure as we descend the status scale. In the case of both these sets of media, cost, availability, and education probably exert their largest effects. But even in the case of the personal and the covert media, universally available, free of cost and setting no educational qualifications, the peasants are noticeably inactive. Indeed, the intelligentsia is actively exposed to all media, while at the other pole the peasants are markedly withdrawn from participation in the communications network.

Differences in the frequency of exposure are of course not the only measure of the importance of any specific source of news. On the basis of our oral interviews we rated each informant's report to assess which source was *most* important for him regardless of the frequency of his exposure to it (Table 45). Although the number of cases is small, the general pattern seems quite clear and makes good sense. For the better edu-

TABLE 44 [12A]

SOCIAL CLASS PATTERNS OF EXPOSURE
TO COMMUNICATIONS MEDIA

Type of media	Intelligentsia	White-collar employees	Skilled workers	Ordinary workers	Collective farm peasants
Official Mass Media Exposure					
High	52%	38%	22%	7%	3%
Medium	45	47	38	32	21
Low	3	15	40	61	76
Personalized Media Exposure					
High	14	7	6	3	2
Medium	33	18	9	6	6
Low	53	75	85	91	92
Aesthetic Media Exposure					
High and Medium	63	44	35	18	8
Low	37	56	65	82	92
Covert Media Exposure					
High	20	11	7	2	1
Medium	26	25	16	10	12
Low	54	64	77	88	87
Total number of respondents	642	679	282	494	387

cated intelligentsia and white-collar groups, the printed word carried by the official newspaper was far and away the most important source. Limits on reading ability pull down the importance of the newspaper for the manual classes to a point where it is not much more important than the radio, even though the latter is often inaccessible in the countryside. Most interesting, however, is the shift in the relative importance of word-of-mouth communication. Not only does its relative importance rise as we go from the better placed to the less advantaged, but among the peasants, and to a lesser degree among ordinary workers, it emerges as outstandingly the most important source of information. Thus it appears that as total communications activity decreases, going from intelligentsia to peasant, the relative importance of informal, word-of-mouth communication progressively increases at the expense of the more official, formal, printed sources.

TABLE 45 [12B]

INFORMATION SOURCES MOST IMPORTANT
FOR VARIOUS SOCIAL GROUPS [a]

Media	Intelligentsia	White-collar employees	Skilled workers	Ordinary workers	Collective farm peasants
Newspapers	47%	59%	30%	35%	18%
Word of mouth	34	23	26	43	60
Radio	9	9	22	14	18
Meetings	2	4	0	2	0
Other	8	5	22	6	4
Total number of respondents	100	56	27	49	27

a. From personal interviews.

Although status attributes such as education, occupation, or social class membership seem to be the major determinant of the communications patterns, there are individual differences within the classes which seem to exert some independent influence. In particular, the extent to which an individual was politically "involved" played such a role, with those more deeply committed to the system and more actively participating in its development reporting greater exposure. Thus, former members of the Communist Party and Young Communist League, even though closely matched on age, sex, and occupation with nonmembers, scored substantially higher in exposure to official media, including mass, personalized, and "aesthetic" media.

The persistent effect of political sentiment is further strikingly evident when we compare individuals within the same broad occupational categories but differing in their anti-Soviet feeling. In Table 46 there are 55 pairs of figures, and in 45 cases the comparison within each pair reveals that those who were less *hostile* to the Soviet system were the more active "communicators." All of the reversals of the pattern are evidently minor in scale. For the official media the relationship holds cleanly and firmly within each of the several social identification groups. In each instance — press, radio, and books — the less anti-Soviet group gives evidence of higher exposure than does the more anti-Soviet. The relationship is strongest in the intermediate groups, the employees, the skilled workers, and workers, than for the peasants and the intelligentsia. Evidently membership in one of the polar groups puts something of a floor or ceiling on one's communications behavior. There is a limit to how infrequently a member of the intelligentsia will read newspapers no matter how much he may be opposed to the regime and distrust the press. There is similarly a limit to how often a peasant will read them regardless of how favorably inclined he may be toward both the regime and the press. These limitations are clearly more or less imposed by their life situations.

TABLE 46 [12c]

PER CENT FREQUENTLY USING VARIOUS COMMUNICATIONS MEDIA: BY SOCIAL GROUP AND ANTI-SOVIET SENTIMENT SCORE

Communications media	Social group and anti-Soviet sentiment score									
	Intelligentsia		White-collar employees		Skilled workers		Ordinary workers		Collective farmers	
	Low	High	Low	High	Low	High	Low	High	Low	High
Soviet radio	68%	57%	59%	48%	43%	33%	25%	21%	15%	6%
Foreign radio	14	13	12	8	5	7	2	1	1	1
Newspapers and magazines	87	77	77	64	55	37	32	18	27	13
Books	94	90	79	74	54	47	40	23	23	17
Movies	57	50	45	37	38	38	31	14	14	6
Theater	49	43	27	22	19	15	10	5	3	2
Agitation meetings	22	29	19	13	21	9	9	7	13	9
Lectures	43	38	23	17	19	11	11	7	7	6
Rumor	30	30	21	19	16	13	9	6	7	10
Discussion with friends	33	22	24	19	13	14	10	7	5	7
Other	11	10	5	3	5	3	2	2	3	1
Median number of respondents	422	177	370	263	110	133	139	265	93	215

Much the same effect is observed when we compare those who wanted a career with those who did not. To indicate a desire for a career is to suggest that one is ambitious, possibly more alert to opportunity, more in need of the information requisite to success. Under Soviet conditions it also indicates willingness to participate in "the system," from which many in our sample claimed to have held back. In every occupational

TABLE 47 [12D]

CAREER DESIRE AND TYPE OF EXPOSURE TO COMMUNICATIONS MEDIA: BY OCCUPATION

Occupation and career desire	Per cent frequently using:					Median number of respondents
	News- papers & magazines	Soviet radio	Movies	Agitation meetings	Rumor	
Professional						
Wanted a career	92%	71%	65%	31%	40%	(175)
Did not want career	84	61	35	26	35	(191)
Semiprofessional						
Wanted a career	76	69	60	14	25	(183)
Did not want career	76	51	37	21	16	(326)
Skilled workers						
Wanted a career	66	44	49	16	23	(45)
Did not want career	48	36	24	14	15	(102)
Ordinary workers						
Wanted a career	30	32	35	18	12	(123)
Did not want career	26	26	21	9	9	(274)
Collective farmer						
Wanted a career	21	15	12	9	7	(66)
Did not want career	11	5	4	6	7	(177)

group those who wanted a career are more active in exposing themselves to the communications network. This holds, furthermore, not only for the more formal official sources such as the newspaper and radio, but also applies to "aesthetic" media like the movies, "personalized" official media like agitation meetings, and even to covert sources like rumor.

Our general theme that communications behavior is independently influenced by the degree of the individual's involvement in the system, seems borne out. The more ambitious and the less anti-Soviet members of our sample consistently report more frequent communications exposure, and in particular exposure to the formal, official media. Such differences, however, work mainly within the class framework and do not override its influence. In most cases, those one class "up," even though more anti-Soviet, still have higher exposure scores than those in the class below, and those far separated by class are far different in communications pattern even when more alike in anti-Soviet sentiment or career desire.

The constellation of factors which affect and accompany these patterns of communications activity can perhaps be grasped more easily from profiles of the two contrasting communications types, the intelligentsia and the peasants. We hope the reader will keep in mind that the phenomena we discuss here are essentially continuous in distribution. The fact that we are discussing polar types should not create the impression of discontinuity between the groups at the poles.

The Peasant: Any description of the communications behavior of the peasant must necessarily be something of a stereotype. There are marked variations in the life conditions of the Soviet peasantry depending upon the prosperity of their region, its distance from established urban centers, the type of crop raised, and other factors. In general, however, the life of the Soviet peasant is characterized by isolation from the city, low living standards, long and difficult work days, low levels of education, and poor communications facilities. His environment does little to stimulate intellectual activity, and he has little time or energy for reading. In fact, many of the older peasants exhibited retrogressive illiteracy: they have *forgotten* how to read. Radios are few in the countryside, numbering 650,000 in 1936, and 1,300,000 in 1947. Sixty per cent and more of the population there shared something like 20 per cent of the already modest supply of radios. Newspapers are less accessible as well as less in demand than in the city. Furthermore, the peasant has little need to be well informed in order to carry out his daily work. Finally, the peasantry is outstandingly the most disaffected group in the Soviet system, and, as we have seen, disaffection is directly related to withdrawal from the official media of communication.

By and large, the communications behavior of the Soviet peasant has been similar to that of the peasant in nonindustrialized countries, in his limited access to and slight use of the formal media. A typical description by a tractor driver who left the Ukraine in the summer of 1950 revealed that in a village of a thousand households there were a few regular radios and 80 wired loudspeakers. Yet, his farm was in a prosperous area and must be assumed to be better supplied with radios than was the average kolkhoz. His collective farm subscribed to a newspaper, but only a few members of the farm subscribed individually "and this was mainly for rolling cigarettes." They all liked the well-worn story about the man who goes up to a kiosk to buy a copy of a major newspaper. The woman asks him "Which will you have?" and he answers, "The one with the thinnest paper."

The regime is neither unaware of nor indifferent to the fact that the peasant's voluntary involvement in the system of official communication is remarkably low. The Soviet regime wants no group isolated from its system of propaganda and agitation. But the peasantry is not a key target group, and in fact seems to be quite low on the priority scheme of propaganda effort. Nevertheless, the regime has made appreciable efforts to bring this group into the official network of communications. Advances have been made in extending the facilities of the press and radio, and the regime has tried to stimulate the interest and involvement of the rural groups by oral agitation. Morover, the educational level of the younger generation has been raised. Despite these measures young and relatively well-educated peasants, as well as the old peasants, remain comparatively untouched by the mass media and express little interest in what is going on in the world around them.

When it is necessary, from the regime's point of view, that the peasants be informed of some event or policy, an official representative conveys the information to them directly. For example, one young woman collective farmer who never read a newspaper or listened to the radio on her collective farm learned about the beginning of the war when the village Soviet convened the field hands in the evening after work and a spokesman told them of this event. Another collective farmer, when asked how he had learned about new laws and regulations, gave the typical answer that the brigadier or the head of the collective farm told him about such things. In addition, the regime has an organized corps of official opinion leaders on the collective farms, largely in the person of members of the party and Komsomol, who serve as spokesmen for the regime in their informal day-to-day personal contacts. Not only do they convey specific information but they shape the peasants' attitudes and opinions on larger issues. The young woman mentioned above, when asked what her impressions of the Germans were before her farm was overrun, could answer only in terms of what the "party people" on the kolkhoz had told her about them. The task of being such an opinion leader is part of the regular assigned work of many of the white-collar personnel in these rural areas. Teachers, for example, may have to go into the fields during the lunch periods and read to the field hands while they eat their lunch. As one respondent reports, "Teachers used to tell us about things, but they usually said just what they saw in the newspaper. They would read the newspapers at night and then tell us about it in the morning."

The importance of such word-of-mouth communication in American society has been carefully noted by communications specialists in recent years.[13] Increasingly we have come to realize that certain members of society play a major role as intermediaries between the formal media and the great bulk of the people. In the Soviet Union this role has been formalized, and the members of the agitation network are the chief contact that the peasant and many other persons in comparable situations in Soviet society have with the official media. But even though the regime reaches out to the peasant with the "agit-prop" system, he does not necessarily respond actively. When official meetings are called, many of the peasants attend them with reluctance. One peasant reported: "Usually one member of our family went to such a meeting and told the others what was said, not in detail, just a little. . . ." Many other peasants indicated in the personal interviews that they were almost completely indifferent to meetings and other official oral communications.

The most important source of information for the peasant is word of mouth. For him the secondary, *unofficial* network of communications is actually primary. It is this which explains his claim to rely so heavily on word-of-mouth communication, despite his indifference to the official agitation. To a great extent he acquires his information, that is otherwise readily available in the press, via conversations with friends, co-workers, and kin who read and listen to official media or who have heard it from someone who did. One field hand, for example, heard of the Stalin-Hitler pact in a casual conversation with his brigade leader. Additionally, the peasant acquires a good deal of illicit and unofficial news in this manner. Yet, except for information about local events, his sources are very poor. He is very far from the big cities in which most really important events are occurring. The transmission of such information is dependent on someone's physical mobility, and much of the illicit information which the peasant gets about what is happening throughout the country or in the world at large comes from people who are traveling about. One respondent reports:

In the course of conversation with people who came to the kolkhoz to recruit industrial workers you learned something about how people were living in various areas. . . . There were also collective farmers who did seasonal work elsewhere . . . these people have seen living conditions themselves in various areas and were acquainted with them at firsthand.

Other sources of information for the peasant are fellow collective farmers who have gone to city markets, and truck drivers, who are referred to by one respondent as "a genuine rumor factory." But the rank-and-file peasant seems to be quite passive with respect to the information that comes to him by word of mouth. Thus, we have seen above that he describes this activity as "discussing with friends," rather than hearing "rumors." He takes what comes, but displays little initiative in seeking it out. For the more highly placed rural personnel, however, the geographical isolation of the countryside is a real source of frustration, and the rural-technical and administrative personnel describe themselves as quizzing and cross examining anyone who might have juicy gossip or the inside story on some current event. A rural technician says:

We were always trying to get information from people who had come from Moscow. The local party secretary always asked me to tell him what I heard in Moscow when I went there. Everybody returning from Moscow used to tell about the rumors he heard there.

As a further result of the geographical isolation of the countryside the peasant is flooded by rumors of a low order of plausibility. In very few instances does he have access to competent, informed sources of information. One respondent reports, for example, that in the summer of 1950 a collective farm in the Ukraine was swept several times by a rumor that the United States had attacked the Soviet Union. As we will see shortly, the low "quality" or plausibility of the rumors he hears is connected with the degree of confidence he has in this source of information.

The Urban Intelligentsia: In marked contrast to the peasants, the urban intelligentsia is very active with respect to all the communications media. Whereas 76 per cent of the collective farmers reported "frequent" exposure to *none* of the three official mass media, only 3 per cent of the urban intelligentsia did so, and more than half reported "frequent" exposure to all three (Table 44). But this high exposure to official mass media is not at the expense of exposure to unofficial sources. While the *relative importance* of unofficial media is equally high for the peasants, the *absolute rate of exposure* to these media is higher for the intelligentsia. The typical member of the urban intelligentsia reads newspapers regularly and probably has a subscription to at least one newspaper, reads books and magazines very often, maybe several of each a month, has a radio, which in a fair proportion of instances can receive foreign broadcasts, and in addition picks up from friends and acquaintances a considerable amount of reliable supplementary information that never appears in official sources.

His attitude towards the official media is more differentiated and discriminating than is that of the peasant or worker. The members of the less educated groups seem either to accept what they read and hear in a rather blanket fashion, or to reject it in an equally categorical manner. The member of the intelligentsia, whether he likes or dislikes the regime, is more likely to assume that what he reads and hears is reliable and complete to varying degrees. Even the loyal member of the urban intelligentsia acknowledges that "policy" dictates the withholding of certain categories of information. Insofar as he believes that there are gaps or direct falsehoods in the information which is given to the public, he seeks to supplement the formal channels via his own resources. He will apply his own interpretation of the official release, reading "between the lines." The intelligentsia uses the official and unofficial networks in a complex and complementary fashion. His attitude toward the relationship of his various sources of information is best exemplified in the fact that he uses word-of-mouth communications as a corrective device for understanding the newspapers. Intelligentsia informants frequently said: "Rumors made it possible to read the newspapers intelligently," or "We read the Soviet newspapers constantly, but here it is necessary to make certain automatic corrections, so our next source was from conversation with people."

Whereas for the peasants the most important source of information is by word of mouth, for the intelligentsia it is invariably the official media which play this role. Virtually never do they rely on word of mouth to learn something that is readily available in the press. The nature of their work generally made it imperative that they keep in touch with official sources. Indeed our informants sometimes describe going to great efforts to assure themselves of subscriptions to the Moscow papers, as the following comments indicate:

> Most important for me was *Pravda* and then the technical journals, because I needed to know the correct approach to problems, and I also needed to know which author was being criticized so as to get his books off the shelves and the cards out of the catalogue quickly (A librarian).
>
> I applied for the Moscow *Pravda* on the grounds that in my work I must be informed of all government decrees that might affect my specific field. As long as my work was considered important I was permitted to•subscribe (An engineer).

We do not mean to disregard the fact that 31 per cent of the intelligentsia group said in the personal interview that word-of-mouth sources were "most important." They did not seem to mean, however, that these sources were primary in giving them the greatest *volume* of information, but rather that they were important in the sense of being reliable and furnishing the crucial bits of knowledge without which they could not fill in the mosaic. Word-of-mouth information for the intelligentsia is, in other words, qualitatively quite distinct from its role for the peasant. For the peasant it is a substitute for the official media. For the intelligentsia it is a supplement and corrective. They use the official media avidly but they also use the unofficial in conjunction with the official. For the intelligentsia rumor is likely to come directly from reliable sources. Members of the intelligentsia report much more often than members of the lower classes that their word-of-mouth information came from people with special competence. Most frequently these sources are persons inside the party who themselves had legitimate access to esoteric information, or who at least hear the rumors which circulate in such circles. The following quotation from an interview with a nonparty member gives some idea of the range of information which could be obtained from such sources:

> I had good relations with the director of the Institute. He explained many questions to me which had been discussed in the party organs. And in talking to party members you could hear very interesting things. In Leningrad, the chief of the planning department . . . informed me about conditions inside the party after the assassination of Kirov. Also, through the members of the party you could learn the party's attitude towards you. For example, in 1938 a general conversation started up on Soviet policy between me and several other plant employees. One very pro-Soviet person expressed herself violently against religion. I pointed out to her that she was not completely right. . . . She attacked me very violently.

The next day the director called me and told me that she had asked that I be turned over to the NKVD. He warned me about the impending danger. But finally he exerted influence on this woman, who was his subordinate, and he saved me from the NKVD. . . .

Reliance on word-of-mouth communications as a corrective and supplement for the official media implies a high degree of confidence in one's sources. Throughout their discussions, our intelligentsia respondents refer to the greater reliability of word-of-mouth sources in general, but most especially with reference to news of political import. More striking, however, is the response on our written questionnaire to a question on the reliability of rumor compared with newspapers and magazines. Referring to the bottom row of Table 48 we see that the majority of each class cited rumor as more reliable — which might be expected if we assume the anti-Soviet bias of the sample to be demonstrating itself.[14] But there are vast class differences. Whereas somewhat more than half of the peasants considered rumor as more reliable, 90 per cent of the intelligentsia placed greater reliance on the reliability of rumor. Whatever reservations we may have about the absolute levels of attitude described in these data, it is striking that the urban elite gave so much more credence to rumor than did the considerably more disaffected peasantry. We presumably see here the consequences of the nature of the rumors heard by the two groups. The peasant generally hears low level rumors of little plausibility, whereas the superiority of the sources on which he drew for rumors apparently enabled the member of the intelligentsia to give them relatively greater credence.

TABLE 48 [14A]

RELIABILITY OF RUMOR:[a] BY CLASS
AND ANTI-SOVIET SENTIMENT

Anti-Soviet sentiment	Per cent stating rumor more reliable than newspapers among:										
	Intelligentsia		White-collar employees		Skilled workers		Ordinary workers		Collective farm peasants		All classes	
None	90%	(147) [b]	86%	(114)	63%	(30)	73%	(22)	70%	(10)	84%	(323)
Low	91	(149)	95	(129)	73	(33)	64	(44)	64	(25)	86	(380)
Medium	90	(82)	89	(95)	83	(35)	63	(53)	49	(35)	80	(300)
High	82	(43)	85	(65)	82	(45)	74	(83)	58	(50)	76	(286)
All levels	90	(421)	90	(403)	76	(143)	68	(202)	57	(120)		

a. This question was asked only of those who reported obtaining some information by rumor.
b. Total number of respondents on the basis of which the percentage is computed.

A further note along this line is provided in the main body of Table 48, which indicates that within each class there is no consistent pattern of association between anti-Soviet sentiment[15] and assessments of the reliability of rumor. The most and least anti-Soviet are about equally likely to impute greater reliability to the unofficial media. In contrast, as we will see below in Table 49, the more anti-Soviet of each class are much more likely to say that nothing in the official media was reliable. In other words, one's assessment of the reliability of *official* media is clearly related to one's political attitudes, but one's assessment of the relative reliability of *unofficial* media seems to bear no such relationship to political attitudes. Rather, the evaluation of the unofficial media follows mainly from one's class position and remains relatively the same whatever one's political opinion. This also argues that assessment of the unofficial media is a direct reflection of the quality of the word-of-mouth information that circulates within the social environment of the rater. The lower classes, whose sources are of poorer quality than those of the upper classes, reflect this fact by proportionately less often acknowledging the rumors they hear to be reliable.

The communications behavior of the peasant and those in the intelligentsia is a reflection of their different life situations. In most instances a member of the intelligentsia comes from a family with an established cultural tradition of intellectual activity, with a relatively broad horizon which stimulates curiosity in what is going on in the world. He can afford the radio and newspapers, and his urban residence makes them more available. His job places pressure on him to be well informed. He must know about changes in policy and politics, about new and crucial developments in the nation as well as technical problems in his own special area. He uses the official media avidly, but he also uses the unofficial media in conjunction with the official. It is his very involvement in the system, his proximity to people in the know, his active curiosity, the necessity for keeping abreast of developments that make it both possible and necessary for him to get good, reliable information by word of mouth to supplement the official media. The official and unofficial media are used in conjunction with each other. For the peasant this is not so. He uses the word-of-mouth network because he is a rather inert "communicator" who also distrusts the official media and does not want to have too much traffic with them. Word of mouth is for him a substitute for the newspaper, the Soviet radio and magazine. As he withdraws from them he turns to rumor, and more and more uses word-of-mouth communication.

The Impact of the Official Media

Disaffected Soviet citizens are no doubt far from ideal subjects to use in assessing the impact of Soviet propaganda. Their very status as political refugees makes them living proof mainly for the failures rather than the successes of the system. In addition, they all had a period of extended residence in a society outside their original home, and thus acquired other information against which to assess what had been said in the Soviet media. The matter is further complicated because much of their resentment against the Soviet system was channeled toward the propaganda apparatus of the Communist government. Yet even here, in the very process of condemning the media for lying, our respondents reveal the obvious fact that there are many Soviet citizens who believe the press and other official media without major reservations. A typical instance is this statement by a former Red Army officer, who reports:

In the summer of 1940 a *Tass* report said that the Japanese press had false reports that Soviet troops were being transferred to the Polish front. But we saw these troops traveling over the railroad with our own eyes. We were right next to the railroad. That was the first time I began to doubt what I read in the papers.

Although our interviews are replete with similar, and even more frank, acknowledgments of once held faith, the nature of our sample does not permit us to go very far in assessing those effects of Soviet propaganda which, from the regime's point of view, would be "positive." It is our impression that the greatest success was attained in shaping the Soviet citizen's image of the outside world. This applies especially to the foreign policy of "capitalist" countries and the international role of the Soviet Union.[16] Soviet propaganda also apparently had substantial success in selling its version of conditions of life abroad. The relative wealth and affluence of the United States was an image hard to dislodge and one which indeed the Soviet propagandists often inadvertently fostered. But they seem, nevertheless, to have had substantial success in creating the impression that misery and starvation were so much the lot of the European worker that the Soviet Union was almost a worker's paradise by comparison.

The propaganda system also succeeded somewhat in inculcating a series of standard images of the outstanding features of Soviet society — to wit, that it was "democratic," "progressive," "classless," "without conflict," and so on. These images were apparently maintained by people in the face of evident contradictions provided by their own life experience. For example, a twenty-seven-year-old worker who himself had been unable to go on to further education because there was great need for the income he could bring into the household by going to work, nevertheless said: "In the Soviet Union education, even higher education, is equally available to all people, to workers, peasants, and intelligentsia. There are no classes there, you see!"

But beyond these direct and obvious propaganda successes, the most important effect, was the subtle shaping of the whole pattern of human thought which Soviet "agit-prop" attempts. These results, of course, were achieved not by the mass media alone, but also notably by the school. It is probable that the most difficult material to unlearn or to challenge is that which is implicit. Both the interviewers and persons who have read the interviews were struck by the peculiarly Soviet style of thinking, and of formulating problems that the respondents exhibited. By its very nature, this phenomenon is difficult to illustrate. It is almost a matter of flavor. Yet it emerges in the discussion of many topics. One violently anti-Soviet doctor amused the interviewer by referring to the first and second world wars as the First Imperialist War and the Second Imperialist War. Another highly educated man, who claimed to have been highly skeptical of the Soviet press gave a version of the Shakhty trials, in which prominent engineers were in 1928 accused of a "counterrevolutionary plot," which showed that although he himself was an engineer he implicitly accepted the official version of the story. Other respondents exhibited such confusion about events in Soviet history as to suggest that the rewriting of history which took place under Stalin had many of the effects that were intended. Furthermore, the attitudes toward the welfare state, civil liberties, and other issues we take up in later chapters all reveal major influences on basic thought processes arising from the propaganda efforts of the regime.

In addition, Soviet citizens seem to absorb a good deal of the "metaphysics" of Marxism. We do not mean so much that they used the language of Marxism, although they did that, too, but that they couched many of their comments and descriptions in a mold we have come to recognize as distinctive in Soviet Marxist writing. A special study of our personal interviews from this perspective[17] revealed that the concept of the "dialectic" and the idea that "existence determines consciousness" were the two most frequently mentioned. Asked whether religion and atheism should coexist in society, one respondent replied: "Yes, it should be this way. The Marxists are right, probably, in this respect. There should be contradictions and something new developed out of them." Another revealed his indoctrination when, in response to the question as to who believes in the regime, he replied: "The fanatic who doesn't realize the contradiction. They think they can hold them back by force. This can be done, but only up to a certain point. Because man does not make history. History makes man."

It is impossible to be exposed to a system of propaganda as all pervasive and monopolistic as that of the Soviet regime and escape without some influence. The areas where greatest influence was exerted were precisely those our knowledge of human learning points to, namely the basic values of the individual and the implicit dimensions of his thought. These elements of the mental processes are those which are most often affected by outside forces quite independently of the individual's wishes, and what is acquired is most difficult to unlearn. Here the influence of Soviet media,

Soviet education, Soviet culture is most pervasive. This influence becomes more spotty as we move out into areas of more explicit content. It is difficult to say who in the populace is most subject to this influence, since it is virtually impossible to set up a yardstick with the spotty data which we have on this question. We hazard the guess that the influence of the Soviet media in shaping implicit thought patterns is probably most strong on the intelligentsia. They are, after all, the most highly indoctrinated, highly exposed portion of the population, and are forced in their daily life to learn the proper forms of expression and argumentation if only to use them in a *pro forma* fashion.

In any event, the members of the intelligentsia were very much more likely to grant that some (or even most) of the news in the Soviet press was reliable. About 80 per cent of the intelligentsia granted this point, but its acknowledgment falls off sharply until among the peasants we find two thirds asserting that *none* of the news was reliable (Table 49). These data should not be interpreted as indicating the greater gullibility of the intelligentsia, or the greater skepticism of the manual classes, but mainly the characteristic way the different classes handled questions requiring evaluations on a continuum. The more highly educated groups are considerably less likely to give undifferentiated answers to any such question, and obviously regarded a statement that "nothing" in the Soviet press was truthful as an extreme assertion that was *prima facie* nonsense. It is our impression that among the more highly educated groups there are fewer categorical reactions either of acceptance or rejection of the mass media. There is much differentiation and selection of what to believe or disbelieve. Among the lower classes — and again this is an impression based on a variety of scattered bits of evidence — it would seem that there is less differentiation and one tends more either to accept or reject *all* of what he hears and reads from official sources.

Beyond the influence of his class position, however, a man's attitude

TABLE 49 [17A]

RELIABILITY OF THE SOVIET PRESS:
BY CLASS AND HOSTILITY TO SOVIETS

Hostility to Soviets	Per cent stating "nothing reliable" among:					
	Intelligentsia	White-collar employees	Skilled workers	Ordinary workers	Collective farm peasants	All classes
High	52% (27)[a]	60% (60)	45% (22)	73% (77)	73% (59)	65% (245)
Medium	23 (125)	30 (176)	50 (78)	67 (123)	68 (92)	45 (594)
Low	16 (392)	24 (347)	39 (121)	51 (153)	56 (105)	30 (1118)
All levels of hostility	20 (544)	30 (583)	43 (221)	58 (353)	64 (256)	39 (1957)

a. Total number of respondents on the basis of which the percentage is computed.

toward the reliability of the Soviet press was obviously intimately related to his attitude toward the Soviet system at large. In the intelligentsia the percentage who deny that there is anything reliable in the Soviet press increases more than threefold, and among employees it doubles as we go from those who were least to those who were most hostile (Table 49). Among the workers and peasants the impact is also evident, although the effect of hostility is attenuated. The influence of political orientations is strong; sufficiently strong so as to water down the influence of class *per se*, and to bring closer together in their assessment of the press people who are quite widely separated by class. In the intelligentsia as a whole, the typical pattern was to allow some reliability to the Soviet press, but those very hostile to the system acted more like the average worker in denying the reliability of the press. To some degree, obviously, the valuation of the press became a target for expressing hostility to the regime in general. The relation was sufficiently strong, in fact, to warrant inclusion of this item on reliability of the press in our "Index of Anti-Soviet Sentiment." *

Interpreting the News

Even though the intelligentsia makes the most use of the official media, it nevertheless also most *frequently* utilizes rumor, and has most *confidence* in it. The intelligentsia is also the group which shows the least tendency to distort Soviet reality, the greatest willingness to praise Soviet achievements, the least hostility to the leaders and the system. We feel it not unreasonable to argue on this basis that even those most committed to the Soviet system were aware of the distortions which crept into official Soviet communications, and felt a need to develop informal ways of learning about events and of interpreting the news for themselves. One obvious method was through the use of rumor. Quite another was through the development of subtle interpretative principles whereby the citizen attempted to discern what was *really* going on. Like all peoples whose news sources are censored and controlled, the Soviet citizen tries by inference to detect that which was withheld, or the truth that lies behind what he considers to be an untrustworthy statement.[18] Respondents asserted frequently and spontaneously, "You had to read between the lines." The techniques they cite for reading between the lines are based on a combination of the degree of distrust for the official media and a series of implied assumptions about the nature of the Soviet system, particularly as regards its communications policy. The technique favored by a particular individual, and the degree and literalness of its application, was of course a matter of the individual's personality, his life experience and his social position.

The most drastic device suggested was that one should believe exactly

* For a description of this index, see Appendix 5.

the opposite of what the Soviet press said. Obviously, in such a categorical form this is more an expression of hostile sentiment than a serious suggestion of how to read the newspapers. Some respondents went so far as to insist that the Soviet populace initially gave the invading German troops such a warm reception during World War II because the people automatically assumed that any government which had been attacked in the Soviet press was a good one.[19] Certainly there is extensive evidence that even Soviet Jews did not believe stories about the Nazis that later turned out to be quite true. This circumstance demonstrates at the very least that there are a considerable number of Soviet citizens who disbelieve much of what they read in the press, and disbelieve it to the extent of being willing to act on this basis in matters that affect their very lives. As one of Calas' informants says, ". . . it is obvious that the crudest mistakes were made by this method of simply assuming that the reverse of any official statement was necessarily true — to wit, the disbelief in German atrocities." [20]

One relatively sophisticated assumption which leads at times to the acceptance of the opposite of what is found in the Soviet press is that the Soviet government projects its own motives onto foreign governments. Thus, a middle-aged bookkeeper says, "The Soviet press interprets events in Korea as American aggression, when in actual fact the contrary is true and it is really Soviet aggression." Another, a Ukrainian dairy technician, says, "If they wrote that our enemies abroad were arming for war, I knew that the Soviet Union was arming."

Another assumption about Soviet news policy made by our respondents was that the Soviet government would always attempt to prepare the populace in advance to accept unpleasant developments. "If there were going to be a famine in the Ukraine, we always used to hear that there was hunger in Germany and Austria, and that children were picking food out of garbage cans. When I saw such examples I knew that soon we would have a famine." A Ukrainian carpenter says that when he saw a series of newspaper articles deploring the effects of abortion he inferred that legislation controlling abortion was forthcoming. He proved to be right. A cooper of fifty says he always regarded news about social improvements as intended to divert attention from a forthcoming unpleasant event. Some readers will see the parallel between this assumption and the popular belief, common in wartime even in the Western democracies, that the population was always "prepared" for the announcement of a defeat by prior publication of news about some little "victory."

The refugees claim that they learned much from official sources that was quite different from what the regime wanted people to learn. Thus, a middle-aged engineer and former party member stated that if he read in the Soviet press that workers were striking for higher wages in New York

City, the main conclusion he would draw would not be that there was industrial unrest, but that American workers could afford to strike *and that they had the right to strike.* A former professor who wrote for the film industry says: "I taught myself to translate the lies of the press into my language of relative truth." He gave these examples:

1. There is a report of a demonstration of dissatisfied workers in Paris. His translation is: "What would Stalin's Chekists do with a similar demonstration in Moscow?"
2. There are reports of the daring and open deeds of Communists in America. Translation: He is surprised at the "childlike naivete of Americans who permitted the most deadly enemies of their country to do whatever they wanted to do."

One story which had wide general circulation in the Soviet emigration suggests the strange mixture of acceptance and rejection of the content of Soviet communications which was typical of the attempts to "interpret" those events the censor permitted to come before the Soviet audience. It concerns a newsreel of race riots in Detroit, shown in the Soviet theaters to demonstrate the degree of racial discrimination in the United States. In one scene a Negro is shown being hurled through the air. There is a pan shot of his shoes as his feet pass the camera. The Soviet audiences, the story goes, noticed the quality of the shoes. *Accepting the official image of the plight of the Negro in America,* they concluded that no *American* Negro would be wearing shoes of the quality shown in this shot. Therefore, they reasoned, the Negro must have been a professional Soviet actor, and the film the propaganda effort of a Soviet studio. The story may be apocryphal, but it is nevertheless revealing.

Obviously, attempts to "interpret" the news as it appears in official media can backfire. Assuming that everything in the media is false can lead to grotesque errors. The skillful interpreter of the news must have some criteria of what to accept and what to question. In many instances he must use *ad hoc* criteria — the internal coherence of the particular story, or its congruence with other information in which he has a considerable degree of trust. Certain general criteria were advanced, however, by some respondents. Some said that you could believe the "facts" but not the interpretation that the official media put on them. "I must take the facts in an article and assimilate them critically, and I would come to conclusions quite different from the ones written in the article," said a schoolteacher who had served also as an army engineer. Other respondents said they believed stories on topics where the Soviet government had a neutral interest. Still others said they believed only what was unfavorable.

Say there is an article describing a plant; there is disorder, nonfulfillment, spoilage of production. This I believed. But if the article writes about success, for example, that the Astrakhan Fish Trust has overfulfilled by 125 per cent the catching of such and such a fish, and by 130 per cent of some other fish. . . . How can I believe that when I see that there are no fish products in the stores for 2 or 3 months?

This story reflects what was probably the most outstanding difficulty faced by the Soviet propagandist — the glaring contrast between the regime's claim that "life is getting ever easier," on the one hand, and on the other the harsh and grinding poverty of daily life in city and farm. The Soviet worker and peasant could not judge for himself the intentions of a Roosevelt or a Hitler; he could not for himself assess the conditions of life of workers in Detroit or farmers in Australia; but he could count the number of families living in his apartment, the number of pants he owned, his wife's dresses, and his children's shoes. He did not have to count very high — one was generally enough — and for the child zero might do, for some items like shoes. Yet the Soviet press continued to picture the workers' paradise. It is not hard to believe that so many Soviet citizens came to distrust the official media.

None of the interpretative devices employed is surprisingly original, nor is the attempt at interpretation *per se* something distinctive of the Soviet system. Even where the media of communication are little subject to political control, there is always a substantial amount of guessing as to what lies behind certain news stories. A prominent public official is sick, but the disease is not mentioned. Is it cancer? The president affirms his faith in a political boss who has been charged with corruption. Does he believe the man is honest, or is this political expediency? The examples could be multiplied. What is distinctive about the Soviet system is the great extent to which these practices were developed and the high degree to which the Soviet citizen was dependent on inference and on interpolation and extrapolation to satisfy his information needs. Some foreign observers have extolled the ability of the Soviet citizen to read between the lines of the official media. It is quite obvious, however, that even though this practice may be productive and worthwhile, it can also produce errors of inference and be quite misleading. With all his reading between the lines, however, the Soviet citizen could not develop the most valuable instrument which he could possibly have for interpreting the news — a good background of reliable information.

Summary and Future Prospects

Under Stalin the Soviet regime, urgently concerned with molding public opinion to the support of the party's policies, developed an elaborate system of official communications media. The system is designed, with respect to structure and controls, to reach a maximum proportion of the population and carry the regime's message in such forms as to convince and exhort the populace to implement the party's wishes. The communications policy of the regime, however, was such as to make even its supporters dissatisfied with the coverage of news and the reliability of the information they got via overt means. As a result, there grew up parallel to the official system of communications an unofficial one including word-of-mouth communication, personal observation, and a pattern of interpretative inferences applied to the official media. In one sense, this unofficial system was not different from that which develops in any society. Any social order feels the necessity, and develops the devices with which to withhold certain types of information. The special characteristics of Soviet communications policy, including monopoly over the media and a militant and one-sided presentation of the official point of view, particularly fosters the development of this unofficial system and it has reached distinctive proportions.

The official media, indeed all media, are most extensively used by those higher in education and/or occupational status. Those who are active users of one medium are more likely to be active in the use of others. Distrust of the official media is a function of attitude toward the regime in general. However, some degree of distrust of the official media does not, *per se,* necessarily mean that one is disaffected from the system. Among the intelligentsia a person is quite capable of being a firm supporter of the regime and simultaneously of feeling that the official media cannot be relied on completely. He tends to accept the idea that reasons of "security" and "state interest" make censorship imperative. This does not keep him from seeking out supplemental, covert sources of information such as rumor and word of mouth. Quite to the contrary, his position in society makes this both possible and necessary. He needs such information to survive and advance; he has access to it because he is in contact with people in the know. Members of the lower classes are more categorical in their reaction. The evidence, sparse as it is, suggests that they are more likely either totally to accept or totally to reject what they read and hear from official sources. Acceptance of the regime, involvement in the system, and attention to official media are positively related to the exploitation of the unofficial media among the upper classes. By contrast, the anti-Soviet member of the lower classes withdraws from the system, avoids the official media, and relies primarily on rumor, word of mouth, and other unofficial sources to find out what is going on.

Faced with this picture of the communications process in the Soviet Union, one naturally raises the question of influence: Quite apart from what they *say* they believe, how much of what they read and hear do they believe *implicitly?"* Obviously, our sample has gross limitations as a source of information for answering that question. It is clear, however, from even our presumably anti-Soviet sample that there are people in all ranks of life who believe implicitly what they read and hear. We have no means of ascertaining what proportion of the population, or of any one group, falls in this category. Our sample may be a limiting case of extreme doubters, and we know our respondents had access to non-Soviet communications for several years. Yet despite this it is striking how the more implicit aspects of Soviet official communications, the mode of thought and the categories in which events are grouped, are reflected in the thought patterns and expression of our informants. This may be most true among the intelligentsia, who, whether they accept or reject the regime must, by virtue of their place in society, learn and repeat the official line to the point where it becomes second nature. There is also evidence of the more direct influence of the official media at a number of particular points. For example, the images of life in the West, and of the policy and intentions of other governments, seem to have been greatly influenced by the official media.

Even the loyal citizen was often frustrated and displeased by the official communications policy. While he may have approved of it in the whole, he chafed at it in detail. The secondary system of unofficial communications served him with information which he might need for the conduct of his job, to save his skin, to satisfy his curiosity; at the least it gave him a little bit of a flesh and blood view of the big shots.

The regime obviously believes in its policy of restricted information or it would not pursue it so vigorously. The unofficial network is a source of irritation to the leaders. But the regime also adapts and accommodates somewhat to the inevitable. Many of our respondents, including some who were in a position to know authoritatively, report that the regime exploits the existing system of word-of-mouth communications in two ways. It plants rumors that it wants circulated, and it taps the rumor network as a method of assessing public opinion.

There is a strong possibility, however, that the system of unofficial communications has certain latent functions of which the regime may not be sufficiently aware. Certainly it effects a modicum of tension reduction by supplying people with information which they desire. Beyond that, the additional information that they acquire may help them to do their jobs better. Like any overly bureaucratized society, the Soviet system tends to be hyper-cautious in the circulation of information that is required for the operation of the system itself. By supplementing these sources *unofficially* people are often better able to perform their official duties.

Very few areas of Soviet life were as totally and distinctively shaped by the impact of Stalin's rule as was the realm of communication. Under his guidance, the Soviet propaganda apparatus was enormously expanded, and the size of the lies and distortions in which it dealt expanded proportionately. Not only current news but history was rewritten to order. Since his death there has been some easing of the controls over mass and private communication. The marked decline in the rate of political arrest will, if the process is not reversed, undoubtedly do much to foster the circulation of critical opinions which earlier no one dared to utter or even to think. The reverberations of such opinions will be important in setting up currents which in time may give rise to the beginnings of genuine, and perhaps mildly influential, public opinion within Soviet society. The chances for the development of such currents seem best in scientific and intellectual circles.

At the same time it would be unduly optimistic to assume that the Soviet leadership is to any major degree moving toward the establishment of free discussion, and least of all that it will permit the use of the official media of communications for the wide dissemination of "private," or "minority," that is, of nonofficial, opinion. The adjustments being made at the moment probably are not an attack on the *principles* of the Leninist and Stalinist methods of thought control. Rather, they are best understood as efforts to remove some of the worst abuses and rigidities which had crept into the system, and were actually interfering with the effectiveness of the propaganda effort as a whole.

What we may, therefore, expect is a continuation, with modifications, of the general patterns sketched in this chapter, rather than a sharp shift in practice. The increasing education of the population and the increasing availability of electric power, and hence radios, in the countryside, will undoubtedly increase the communications activity of the ordinary workers and peasants. Although this should somewhat narrow the gap between the intelligentsia and the manual classes, it can hardly be expected to eliminate it. Neither widespread education nor ready availability of the mass media has had that effect in England or the United States. The better educated, the occupationally more highly placed, the politically more involved, will undoubtedly continue to be much more active "communicators" than will those of lower standing in these regards.

As to the quality of communications activities, it is more difficult to say. We anticipate that continued control and censorship of the Soviet press will foster the kind of reading between the lines in the official media, and the reliance on rumor to supplement them, which we have noted. But, this may decrease over time in certain areas. For a short period at least the startling admissions which the regime made after Stalin's death about the distortions of news and history which characterized *his* realm may tend to increase disbelief in and suspicion of the official media. But in the long haul, assuming there is no major retrenchment, the acknowledgment of *former* distortions should increase confidence in the reliability of the *current* communications. In addition, the

regime now has less need to lie, and as it lies less the contradiction between propaganda and reality will become less. More than anything else,
this should serve to increase confidence in the reliability of the official
media.

Furthermore, as the pressures put on managers and others in responsible positions become more reasonable, the need to seek "inside" information to increase one's security will probably decrease. On the other hand,
the sharp controls which continue to exist on free access to information,
symbolized by the jamming of foreign radio broadcasts, the uneven pace
of Soviet economic development, and the great curiosity and hunger of
the Soviet people for information about the outside world, should support
extensive use of informal, nonofficial sources of information and widespread
tendencies to continue to "read between the lines" in the official media.

It is difficult for us to imagine conditions under which Soviet communications policy and the reaction of the citizen to it could be more
extreme than it was under Stalin. Therefore, almost any change must
be for the better. How much improvement there will be will depend on
(or be reflected in) the factors noted immediately above.

VIII

Patterns of Family Life: Getting Under Way[1]

Marx and Engels centered their attention on the history of capitalist development and fully explored the specific conditions of its collapse, but they did very little to blueprint in detail the institutional pattern of the communist society which was to replace capitalism. They regarded the family and the church as sufficiently important, however, to single them out from all other capitalist institutions and to mark them for eventual destruction. Indeed, so important was the family that Engels used it as the central focus of his analysis in one of the fundamental classics of Marxism under the imposing title of *The Origin of the Family, Private Property and the State.* His marked hostility to the "bourgeois" family was absorbed by almost all conscientious Communists including the leaders of the Soviet revolution.

It was to Engels quite obvious that "the modern individual family is founded on the open and unconcealed domestic slavery of the wife." In the bourgeois family the husband was the equivalent of the exploiting capitalist and the wife the oppressed proletariat. There could be only one cure for this condition: to take the entire female sex out of the home setting and put it back into productive industrial life, which "in turn demands the abolition of the monogamous family as the economic unit of society." Instead of the family as an economic unit, said Engels, it would be necessary to make housekeeping a "social industry." Under socialism, as he imagined it, the "care and education of children becomes a public affair; society looks after all children alike, whether they are legitimate or not.[2]

In the early period of the revolution many of the prominent Bolshevik leaders took Engels' pronouncements on the family seriously and indeed quite literally. The chief spokesman in such matters was the famous Madame Alexandra Kollontai, a member of the Central Committee of the Communist Party and the head of its Women's Department, who was the intellectual and practicing leader of a "free love" movement. In a basic policy pamphlet she published in 1919 on *The Family and the Communist Government* she asserted that "the family is ceasing to be a necessity for its members as well as for the state." In that document Kollontai expressed the regime's intention to proceed as rapidly as possible to take over responsibility for the care, upbringing and instruction of children.[3] Lenin did not look with favor on some of the more radical trends such as the free love movement, but he nevertheless followed the general Marxist line in regard to the family, and was often quoted as saying: "it is impossible to be a democrat and a socialist without immediately demanding complete freedom of divorce." [4]

In their hostility to the family Soviet leaders were motivated not only by general social radicalism and their desire to carry out the mandate of Marxist theory, but by quite practical considerations as well. When it came to power the Communist Party had only a very narrow base of social support, and as its rule was prolonged it lost even some of that. Much of the resistance to the party's program was attributed by its leaders to what they called "remnants of outmoded bourgeois ideology," and they looked to the youth being raised under Soviet control for a main base of future social support. But the children were being raised by parents who were the products of the old regime and in home atmospheres often hostile to the new order. Bukharin, one of the ruling figures in the party, expressed the feelings of the Communist leaders when he said at the Thirteenth Congress of the party in 1924 that the family was "a formidable stronghold of all the turpitudes of the old regime." [5] Indeed the family was conceived as a battleground in which, as one Soviet handbook on education put it, "the old is fighting for its existence and for young recruits." [6]

Acting on these premises, the Communist regime from its very early days adopted a series of laws which, while admittedly improving the legal status of women, also were designed to undermine the strength of the family as an independent social institution. For example, women were granted full equality with men under the law in all matters and freed from the obligation to follow their husbands; unregistered marriages were given the same legal status as those registered with the civil authorities; children born out of wedlock were granted full rights equal to those born in registered marriages; abortions were legalized; and divorces were granted on the basis of petition to the registry by either one of the partners. This last came to be known as "divorce by post card." As one of the leading Soviet jurists summed up the general intent of this series of laws, *"a dissoluble marriage* and not a lifelong union was the first principle of the new legislation." [7]

The regime did not limit its attack on the family to formal legislation. It invaded the confines of the home, and sought through appropriate indoctrination to make the youth impervious to parental influence. Indeed, the regime trained and expected the youth to propagandize their parents in an effort to win them over to the side of the regime. There is in Soviet law no provision to free persons from the necessity to give testimony against close relatives, and in the hard and insecure days of the early industrialization program and the forced collectivization of agriculture the regime actively and vigorously encouraged youngsters to spy and report on their parents. They went so far as to launch an extremely intensive propaganda campaign to make a hero of the boy Pavlik Morozov who was murdered by his uncle for having denounced his father to the Soviet secret police.

In the mid-thirties the Soviet regime gradually began to abandon its more radical social program and moved in the direction of a more conservative and traditional orientation toward institutions such as the family. Indeed, the years from the mid-thirties down to the Second World War have been termed the Soviet period of the stabilization of social relations. One of the earliest signs of a change in family policy came with the adoption in 1935 of legislation which made parents legally responsible for the misbehavior of their children. This legislation was accompanied by propaganda warning parents to live up to their "parental" responsibilities. In 1936, a further change of profound importance occurred when abortion was declared illegal and heavy penal sentences provided for those performing it.* At the same time, as a harbinger of things to come, the 1936 law introduced some minor changes in the divorce law, such as the requirements that both husband and wife had to appear at the registry bureau, that the fact of divorce be entered in a person's identification papers, and that modest graduated fees be paid for each successive divorce. As part of the same law, mothers of large families were granted subsidies which began with the birth of the seventh child. All in all it was apparent from the discussions in the official press at the time that a basic shift in the official position was in process, and that the new theme was one of "strengthening the family." [8]

This early promise was fulfilled by a series of decrees and administrative decisions adopted toward the end of World War II. Despite Lenin's argument against divorce, and the earlier assertions by Soviet legal experts that divorce proceedings such as existed in Western society would be unthinkable in the Soviet Union, the 1954 law provided for just that. Indeed, the court procedure adopted was complex and involved. Judges were to grant divorces only where it was "impossible to restore or preserve [the marriage] by any measure whatsoever," [9] and otherwise to

---

* The strict legal penalties for performing abortions were suddenly lifted in November 1955. It was evident from the preface to the decree, however, that this reflected no return to earlier views about the family and the freedom of women. Rather it was largely to prevent the more dire consequences which were following from the fact that many desperate women were suffering grave harm from abortions they underwent outside the hospital. See Mark Field, "The Re-legalization of Abortion in Soviet Russia," *New England Journal of Medicine,* 255:421–427 (1956).

concentrate on reconciling the parties. Furthermore, the cost of securing a divorce was raised to levels which for ordinary workers was very nearly prohibitive. Other measures adopted provided that only legally registered marriages would be regarded as having the force of law, and that suits seeking to establish the paternity of a child were no longer to be permitted — thus creating a factual state of illegitimacy. Finally, payments to mothers were increased and made more widely available since they were to begin with the birth of the third rather than the seventh child.

With this legislation the family was restored to its former status as a central social institution. Instead of talk about marriage as a "dissoluble union" the legal commentators now assert that the government "supports it with all the force of its authority, favors it, and places it under its care and protection." The family is now declared to be the very basis of society, such that the stronger it becomes "the stronger will be society as a whole." Normal family life is expected to lead to many children, and their upbringing is declared to be a sacred duty of the parents in which they act as "partners" of the state in inculcating "those qualities and traits which should form the norms of behavior of every citizen of the Soviet Union." [10]

This great swing in Soviet policy from an extremely radical to a very conservative orientation toward marriage and family life has understandably attracted much attention. The dramatic quality of this shift has however deflected attention away from some of the less striking influences of Soviet developments on family life, although these may have been of greater magnitude and more lasting significance than the changes in official policy. Indeed, dramatic as the shifts in formal policy have been, there is very little evidence that official policy as such directly produced many important changes in the pattern of Soviet family life.

The Russians and Ukrainians are a modest, indeed somewhat prudish, people, and the "free love" practices of the early twenties were evident mainly in the urban centers which contained a minority of the population, and even within those centers the movement affected only a fringe of the population among the more avant-garde in the Communist Party and intellectual circles. Since the Soviet regime is very remiss about publishing social statistics we cannot adequately assess the effects of the easy abortion and divorce laws. It is very likely that they did act to increase the frequency of divorce and especially of abortions. But it should not be forgotten that in countries in which abortion is illegal it is nevertheless exceedingly common, and Soviet sources suggest that those who took advantage of the provisions for legal and free abortions were largely women who might otherwise have had illegal abortions — namely young unmarried girls and older women who already had many children and wanted no more. Similarly with regard to divorce, the absence of published Soviet divorce rates precludes exact comparison, but divorce rates have been rising in the United States despite the stringent laws in many states. Nor should we overlook the fact that many of the divorces in the Soviet Union which were legally registered might have occurred *de facto* through separation and desertion had not the law made it simple to legalize the factual break up of the marriage.

Our data strongly suggest that most Soviet families were relatively unaffected in any direct way by the swing of Soviet family legislation. At least insofar as the *law* was concerned, marriage and family life went on pretty much as before. This should not be taken to mean, however, that our data suggest that the family was unaffected by the developments which accompanied the revolution and the subsequent process of massive social change. On the contrary, our materials indicate that the revolution and the subsequent course of Soviet social development had profound effects on marriage and the family in the Soviet Union. These effects were not, however, the direct result of official family policy but rather the indirect result of the broader processes of social change which the regime set in motion.

The most profound cause of change in family patterns resulted from the combined influence of the mutually linked processes of industrialization and the collectivization of agriculture. Before the revolution the patterns of family life had, of course, been determined by the culture of the traditional village community in which about 80 per cent of the population lived. The collectivization of agriculture broke up the old village commune and profoundly altered the economic significance of the old family unit. At the same time it fostered or forced the movement into the urban areas of millions of peasant individuals and often entire families. The size of the industrial labor force more than doubled during the First Five Year Plan, and it continued its rapid growth thereafter. As a consequence many millions were exposed to new patterns of family living in crowded urban areas. Extraordinary opportunities for social mobility were opened up to those willing to go along with the regime or able to acquire more specialized skills. The spread of mass education, and the associated development of mass communication by press and radio diffused new ideas, values, and goals to all parts of the country. The regime's war on religion closed most of the churches and otherwise limited the ability of religion to influence the young, and in its place "scientific propaganda" was disseminated. The allegiances of youth were assiduously sought after by the Young Communist League Movement. As the expansion continued the size and relative importance of the white-collar occupations increased, and through the medium of sons and daughters who became teachers and clerks the tastes and aspirations of those in the manual classes were much influenced. Thus, the Soviet Union was experiencing a revolution of "modernization" not too dissimilar in important respects from that which had affected other major countries in Europe and Asia somewhat earlier.

Not Soviet family policy, but rather the more general decision to collectivize agriculture and build up heavy industry, were the root causes of the changes in Soviet family life. Such forces as mechanization and urbanization which have everywhere acted to change the patterns of family living, were given special impetus and produced distinctive effects in the Soviet Union because of the forced pace at which they were carried out and because the full power of the totalitarian state was placed behind their operation. At the same time it must be recognized that the family is not infinitely malleable, and that it often has great power of resistance to social change. Indeed, it has often been this very resistance which has most irritated the regime and most often forced it to compromise. In this and the following chapter we plan to explore the relations between the larger processes of social change in Soviet society and three aspects of marriage and family living — demographic patterns in marriage and family growth, the solidarity or cohesiveness of the family unit, and child rearing values and practices.

Selecting a Marriage Partner

Our everyday experience informs us that people tend to marry individuals whose background is very similar to their own. This impression of our senses is confirmed by the tables of the social scientist which indicate that in a variety of different social environments individuals marry persons of similar social background much more frequently than they marry individuals of different background. Indeed, if a broad division such as manual worker or nonmanual worker is used, two thirds or more of all marriages will be between individuals of the same background in countries as widely separated as England and the United States. Furthermore, a great many of the marriages which seem to cross class lines do not really involve much real line crossing, since they take place between persons whose origins may differ but who, as a result of social mobility on the part of one or both mates, have a similar social class or occupational position at the time of marriage.

This sort of "endogamy" along class lines is, of course, easily understood. Intimate social contact between individuals of different background is infrequent, and, therefore, the opportunities for courtship across class lines are correspondingly limited. There are, of course, many contacts in office or shop between persons on different class levels, but these are more likely to lead to affairs than to marriages which breech the class barriers. In addition to the limits on contact, of course the differences in the values, attitudes, and habits of life of individuals from different backgrounds decrease the chances that when thrown in contact such persons will fall in love and marry. Finally, the culture norms and the folklore, although they give support to the ideal of romantic love, also are full of wisdom about the dangers of marriage between those of different background, and in the upper classes at least this wisdom is often backed by action which pulls an erring child out of harm's way by a sudden change of venue.

All of this applies, of course, mainly to unreformed and unregenerate capitalist society. What about Soviet society? Has the end of capitalism and the announced arrival of socialism in the Soviet Union led to the development of a new Soviet generation untainted by capitalist attitudes toward marriage as essentially a "contractual" relation? Has it brought about that new set of marriage practices which Engels prophesied? Soviet vital statistics on this subject, assuming they are gathered, have not been published. In our questionnaires, however, we did inquire into the social background of the wives and husbands of our respondents. With these data we are able to determine not only the frequency with which marriage took place across class lines, but also to trace this development through time so as to ascertain whether or not the Soviet Union is moving noticeably in the direction Engels set for it. Although there are substantial risks in using a sample such as ours for making any kind of population estimate, we feel that in the absence of any other data our findings are at least worthy of cautious consideration.

In Table 50 we have grouped our respondents according to whether their fathers were in manual or nonmanual occupations, and then have indicated the proportion who married persons from the same side of the line. It will be immediately apparent that there is a striking stability in the proportions who crossed over the line in each of the three periods — the prerevolutionary, the postrevolutionary, and the more recent Soviet years. In each period only 25 per cent or less of all marriages in our sample represented a crossing of the manual/nonmanual line, and both the manual and white-collar classes have shown very high rates of class endogamy. We are forced to conclude that the patterns of interclass marriage are largely fixed by cultural traditions and by the facts of life in a stratified society. In such a society the class of the family into which he is born largely predetermines where the child will end up and with whom he will associate when he gets there. Despite the official fanfare of the regime, no longer so often heard these days, the patterns of marriage across class lines in recent times are very much what they were before the revolution and during the earlier years of the Soviet regime. It is a simple fact of life then, that in the Soviet Union as in other industrial societies with roughly comparable class structure, marriage is largely class endogamous. It is *particularly* interesting that this should remain true even for the group married in the years 1931 to 1945. In this period, because of the rapid industrial expansion, there was a mass up-grading of a large portion of the Soviet population which maximized the possibility of contact for persons of different class origins. Nevertheless the proportion of class endogamous marriages remained about constant.

TABLE 50 [10A]

HOMOGENEITY OF CLASS AND NATIONALITY
IN MARRIAGES: 1900–1945

Respondent's social class origin	Date of marriage							
	1900–1920		1921–1930		1931–1945		Totals	
	Per cent of respondents whose spouse is of the same class origin							
Nonmanual	82%	(77) [a]	74%	(121)	79%	(158)	77%	(356)
Manual	72	(98)	76	(168)	81	(156)	77	(422)
All classes	76	(175)	75	(289)	80	(314)	77	(778)
Respondent's nationality	Per cent of respondents whose spouse is of the same nationality							
Russian	89%	(83)	88%	(137)	85%	(137)	87%	(137)
Ukrainian	87	(61)	85	(107)	85	(108)	85	(276)
Both nationalities	88	(144)	87	(244)	85	(245)	86	(633)

a. Total number of respondents on the basis of which the percentage is computed.

Class endogamy is largely matched by endogamy on national or ethnic grounds. In this instance we need not rely solely on our refugee data, since the regime has published a few scattered figures on the rates of marriage across nationality lines. In connection with the publication of results from the 1939 census the regime reported that in the period from 1927 to 1937 the proportion of marriages between persons of different nationality had risen from 7.5 to 19 per cent in the Ukrainian Republic and from 1 to 7.4 per cent in the Armenian Republic. These figures were published, of course, only because in the eyes of the regime they could be cited as support for the assertion that social differences between nationalities were being eliminated under Soviet conditions. They were obviously care-fully selected to give the proper impression. We cannot be at all sure that the same picture would emerge and the same conclusion be justified if the regime were to reveal the rates for the nation at large. Indeed, the arbitrariness of the selection is reflected in the fact that a third set of figures given was not for the same decade span used for the first two sets, but which rather arbitrarily compared 1936 with 1937 as showing an increase in marriage across nationality lines from 3.4 to 7 per cent of all marriages in the Kazakh Republic.[11] This suggests that the figures cited are not representative, but rather were selected from a larger array as those presenting the "best" picture.

Even if we accept these figures at their face value, however, they indicate that twenty years after the Bolshevik revolution the number of marriages which crossed national lines was modest, and almost certainly did not exceed 15 per cent of all marriages taking place in the Soviet Union. Furthermore, although the carefully selected figures published by the regime indicate that this rate may have been increasing, if the cited figures are the most outstanding examples of cross-national marriage we must conclude that the increase is also very modest.

Our own data, which includes information as to the nationality of husband and wife, support this conclusion. The proportion of marriages across nationality lines in our sample as reported in the lower half of Table 50 is roughly congruent with what one would expect from a fairly representative sample, since about 15 per cent of those married in the more recent Soviet period were married to a person of different nationality.* There probably was a modest rise in the proportion of cross national marriages. The rate of increase was too slight, however, to conclude that the conditions of the Soviet life, or the regime's presumed policy of national equality and its associated propaganda, have had a marked effect. The cultural and religious differences which tend to limit opportunities for cross national marriage and to decrease the chances that such marriages will take place even where opportunities for contact exist, seem to have continued to operate. Indeed, the influence of nationality membership was so pervasive and uniform that within nationality groups the class membership of the respondent had only a minor influence on the chances that he would marry outside his national group, although white-collar persons appear to do so noticeably more often than others. As the process of Sovietization continues, of course, and as urbanization increases, the rate of cross-national marriages may also be expected to increase, perhaps sharply. But at least until the Second World War there is evidence that the old cultural forces were still powerful influences in the choice of a marriage partner.

Similar persistence of old patterns is evident when we assess a woman's chances of finding a husband. It has been widely observed that the daughters of fathers in the upper occupational groups seem more likely to become spinsters. In the United States there is reliable statistical evidence that this pattern prevails. Since there is a strong cultural prescription

* This figure is indeed slightly inflated because the frequent presence of both husband and wife in our sample made for double counting on this dimension.

against woman marrying "down," the women of advantage and background start with a narrower field of choice. Girls from upper and middle class backgrounds are also more likely to get a superior education, and education seems to play an independent role in depressing marriage chances. In any event, whatever the initial cause, once the pattern is established it produces a kind of self-fulfilling prophecy. If the culture pattern permits men to marry *down* as well as up, but frowns on women doing so, it follows automatically that every man of better status or education who marries down leaves a potential spinster at his own level. And since the upper classes are so less numerous compared to the rest of the population, the effects should show more noticeably in the rates of spinsterhood. Naturally, we are tempted to inquire as to whether or not the greater equalitarianism and the "freeing" of women which the Soviet regime purports to encourage has had any influence on this pattern in Russia.

Our data also *strongly* suggest that as is true in the United States and elsewhere, in the Soviet Union the daughter of a professional or semi-professional father is somewhat more likely to become a spinster than is the daughter of a manual laborer. If we assume that most women who are going to get married will have done so by age forty-five, then we can see the disadvantage at which the girl of white-collar parentage is placed, because among female respondents between fifteen and forty-five only 66 per cent of the daughters of professional and white-collar fathers were married whereas 69 per cent of the workers' daughters and 77 per cent of the peasants' daughters had found husbands. Viewed through time this appears to be a rather stable expectation, since the same pattern was evident in each specific age group.

Furthermore, as in the United States, Sweden and elsewhere,[12] the better educated a woman is in the Soviet Union the greater is the likelihood that she will fail to find a husband. This holds for all women ages twenty-five to fifty-five taken together and for particular age classes. If, for example, we consider the women in our sample who were between thirty-five and forty-five, by which time it is likely they would have found their husbands if they were going to get one, we find a smooth progression downward in the percentage ever married as we go up the educational ladder, with 83 per cent of the women with only primary schooling married, 74 per cent among those who went to junior high school, 69 per cent among the women with secondary school training, and 65 per cent of those with some college training or better having ever been married. Thus, it appears that the revolution and the development of the Soviet system have rather failed to negate the influence of the culture pattern common to Western Europe, which tends through a variety of means to reduce the chances that a well-educated woman will find a husband.

Finding a Friend

Although they are not strictly part of the family, friends are close enough to justify considering them in this chapter, especially since the class endogamy in marriage is paralleled in friendship patterns. To learn about the friends of our respondents we asked them: "Please recall your closest friends in 1940 and give the following information about them — what brought you together; what was his (her) class origin; what was his (her) occupation in 1940; how much education did he (she) have; was he (she) a member of the party or Komsomol; what did you do together most frequently?" This is an imposing question when asked about three friends, and it will be no surprise that a large number of our respondents, representing more than a quarter of the total, simply failed to answer the question entirely. This was more marked among the less well educated, lower status groups, 40 to 50 per cent of whom failed to answer the question at all. Of those who did answer the question, each respondent was classified as falling in one of four groups, ranging from those who answered only to the extent of *asserting* that they had no friends through those who gave details about one, two, or three friends. For simple presentation we have in Table 51 grouped those who described one or two friends into a category of "limited friendship," and have polarized the others into a category of "isolates" who assert they had no friends and a category of "active friendship" for those who described three friends.

TABLE 51 [12A]

FRIENDSHIP PATTERNS OF THE SOCIAL GROUPS

Friendship pattern (number of friends)	Intelligentsia	White-collar employees	Skilled workers	Ordinary workers	Collective farmers	All groups combined
"Isolates" (no friends)	13%	17%	15%	23%	37%	19%
"Limited friendship" (1–2) friends)	34	36	36	41	32	36
"Active friendship" (3 friends)	53	47	49	36	31	45
Total number of respondents	581	539	182	296	233	1831

The proportion of respondents who described three friends falls fairly markedly as one descends the status scale among the identification groups, from over half of the intelligentsia to under one third of the peasants.

Since we did not ask how *many* friends our respondents had, but only asked them to describe three, these differences cannot necessarily be taken as indications that among those who had any friends at all peasants had fewer friends than those in the intelligentsia. The differences could be due to the fact that those in the lower groups did not finish their answers to the question, finding it rather difficult to give full information on as many as three friends.

The proportions of the identification groups who stated specifically that they had *no* friends may, however, be taken more at their face value since they represent a direct assertion about the *number* of friends each individual had. It is quite noticeable that the proportion stating they had *no* friends rises sharply as we descend the status scale from the intelligentsia to the peasantry, with peasants giving this response almost three times as often as the members of the intelligentsia. Parallel findings are reported for the United States. In Middletown the business class women had only 3 per cent with "no friend" and 3 per cent with "no intimate friend." In the working class the comparable proportions were 13 and 34 per cent, respectively.[13]

We should perhaps not be surprised to find that the peasantry more often, indeed in more than a third of the cases, reports having no friends. The peasant lives much more in the limited circle of his rural community with fewer opportunities for extending his contacts to new individuals who might become his friends. More of his life is lived within the close circle of his family, which even under the collective farm system remains an important economic producing unit, and, therefore, tends to exhaust more of the possible range of individual involvements. The extended family is better preserved in the villages and provides a wider range of choice of associates among one's relatives. Further, traditional culture is stronger in the village and it pushes the Russian peasant to a more nearly total identification with his family unit. Finally, the peasant may treat friendship less casually than his urban brothers, especially those in non-manual work, and will not consider a man as really a "friend" simply on the basis of short or casual acquaintance.

Although all of these characteristics of the peasant to a large extent explain his greater propensity to *state* he had no friends, the apparent uneven distribution of friendship must be regarded as being of structural significance for the respondents and for the system. It appears that our worker and peasant respondents lived in a more closed life circle which made them less accessible to the influences which permeate the society and particularly those which the regime wished to set in motion. Under these circumstances such individuals tended to be more constricted and narrow in their thinking, yet internally consistent and coherent, no matter how rigid. Most of the peasant's close contacts were with relatives who shared his views and way of life. Unlike individuals with more and wider contacts, he was not subject to the modification or softening of his ideas. This throws light on what we have already often noted that, among the peasants more than in any other group, there are many individuals with relatively extreme ideas, rather rigidly held even in the face of that conflicting social reality which an observer living in a wider circle of contacts can see and be influenced by.

Not only the number of his friends but also their homogeneity or diversity will influence their impact on a man's thinking. If we approach the occupational characteristics of friends in terms of the manual/nonmanual line it will be apparent, as is true in so many other respects, that individuals tend to be involved in personal relations primarily with others who have essentially the same broad social characteristics (Table 52).

TABLE 52 [13A]

OCCUPATIONS OF THREE FRIENDS: BY SOCIAL GROUP

Friends' occupations	Respondents' social group					
	Intelligentsia	White-collar employees	Skilled workers	Ordinary workers	Collective farm peasants	All groups combined
Professional	59%	26%	8%	1%	0	30%
White-collar	31	53	19	10	8	32
Worker	9	18	70	77	23	27
Peasant	2	3	3	12	69	10
Total number of friends	731	721	225	278	191	2146

Again the peasants stand out as the group living within the most sharply circumscribed social circle, with about 9 out of 10 peasant respondents drawing their friends from the manual groups. This is approximated at the other pole by the intelligentsia which draws its friends overwhelmingly from those in nonmanual occupations.[14] The employees and skilled workers present a less sharply defined picture, with about one quarter of their friends coming from across the manual/nonmanual line. This, of course, reflects an important aspect of social reality, since the social status, the income and life style, and the marriage patterns of these two groups tend, in important respects, to throw them together as a kind of middle stratum in a society which otherwise shows strong polarization at the extremes of the socio-economic status scale. The skilled workers do not fall neatly into the manual group, but rather have important connections with those in the semiprofessional and white-collar groups more than twice as often as do the ordinary workers. The skilled worker who has semiprofessional and white-collar friends is looking "up" the status scale to his friends. As we have often noted, his attitudes and opinions do indeed often lie close to those in these classes.

How Many Children?

It is sometimes assumed that either the turmoil of Soviet life, or the growing industrialization and urbanization, or both have led people to marry later and to wait longer before starting a family. Our data were not well suited to testing this assumption, but they yielded no clear evidence of such trends.[15] Nevertheless, we did find striking confirmation of a strong trend toward smaller families.

Restriction of family size over time could not be adequately measured by a study of the number of children which respondents in our sample had themselves, because those in the younger age brackets had not completed their families. But by grouping the respondents into age categories, and then considering the number of *siblings* each had, we could obtain a rough but adequate measure of family size through time. We found strikingly large, steady, and consistent reductions in family size over the years. To choose but one example, among respondents from working-class families, 80 per cent of those born between 1895 and 1904 had two or more siblings, but among those born in the next decade only 73 per cent, in the next decade 63, and in the youngest group, who were twenty-five or under in 1950, only 51 per cent had two or more brothers and sisters. A similar pattern was manifested in the families at each level of the social class hierarchy. It is apparent then that a long term trend toward the reduction of family size has existed in Russia since well before the Revolution, and this has rather steadily and smoothly carried forward into the Soviet period.

Until the mid-thirties, of course, the policy of the regime was hardly one which would have led to a reversal of this trend. On the contrary, the regime's policy was more likely to lend impetus to it. After 1936, however, the regime became interested in fostering large families. The family subsidy benefits it offered, at first on the birth of the seventh and later on the third child, and the medals for mothers of larger families, were part of a conscious campaign to reverse the trend toward smaller families. The effect of this campaign cannot be assessed until families begun just before or after that year have been completed. Such a study is not possible with our sample. To judge from the impression our sample gives of the propensities of Soviet citizens to restrict family size, however, we would not estimate the regime's chances of carrying this campaign to a successful issue to be too high. The recent break of a long information blackout has for the first time in twenty years given us an official birthrate. Its quite small magnitude (31.7 in 1940 and about 25 from 1950 to 1955)[16] leaves little room for assuming that the small family will soon be replaced by larger ones.

Although the trend toward smaller families was unmistakably evident in all the social classes, it was apparently not equally strong at all levels of the class hierarchy. The rate of decline in the proportion of large families has been most marked in the families of professional and white-collar workers. This is reflected in the size of families raised in the different social groups. Considering only the respondents over forty in 1950, who may be assumed to have nearly completed their families, we find that in the intelligentsia the modal family size is one child, with over half of the families falling in that category, whereas among those in the manual classes less than 10 per cent of the families had only one child. At the other pole, 67 per cent of the families in the manual classes had three or more children as compared to a mere 18 per cent of the non-manual families. It is apparent then that the white-collar family tends to be much smaller than the family in the manual classes, and this, of course, may be expected to have important effects on the patterns of interpersonal relations in the family. The regime, moreover, appears in the light of this difference to have very poor chances for having its hopes for large families fulfilled, because the concommitant of its development of big industry and big government is an increase in the proportion of all families which are white-collar. The increased proportion of such families, with their characteristically low birth rate, may be expected to accelerate still further the movement toward small families in the population at large.

Working Wives and Mothers

Engels asserted it to be plain that "the first condition for the liberation of the wife is to bring the whole female sex back into public industry." [17] This mandate from the ideological founder of Marxism happened to fit very nicely into the practical need of the Soviet system for an expanding labor force, and as a result the regime has fairly consistently urged and induced women to enter the labor force. In this drive they were not beginning entirely new, since the proportion of women in industry in tsarist Russia had been rapidly rising after the turn of the century. Nevertheless, the movement of women into the nonagricultural labor force was given tremendous impetus during the years of industrial expansion under the five-year plans, and from 1929 to 1938 the proportion of women in the nonagricultural labor force rose from 27 to 38 per cent. The war years further intensified this movement, and by 1942 women made up 54 per cent of the labor force. Although there was some decrease with the postwar return of the men, it was still true in 1949 that 50 per cent of the workers and employees in the Soviet Union were women.[18]

The fact that women represented an even larger proportion of the rural labor force suggests that a larger proportion of all women are working. For various technical reasons bearing on the composition of the Soviet population and labor force, however, this cannot safely be assumed.[19] But beyond getting some idea of whether women were proportionately more often employed under the Soviets we want particularly to know the proportions of working women among those from different social backgrounds, and among the single as against the married, and those with children as against those without.

If the standard pattern in Soviet life was for able-bodied women to work, our respondents were probably not unrepresentative, since about three fourths of those beyond school age reported that they had been gainfully employed. But one important question which this proportion of the sparse official statistics leaves unanswered is whether the probable increase in the number of working women came about through increased participation by women of all ages and backgrounds, or whether it was a more selective process in which, for example, the younger generation or women from certain backgrounds contributed disproportionately. The answer to this question is important both in assessing the strength and effectiveness of the regime's appeals and in gauging the probability that in the future the regime can continue to count on extensive female participation in the labor force.

Unfortunately, this question cannot be firmly answered except with data very carefully collected over a long period of time. Simply to inquire into the proportions of various age groups who were employed would not answer the question, since the older women, assuming they worked less often, might be doing so primarily for reasons having to do not with their generation but rather with the stage of the life cycle. Our concern here is with changing patterns through time. In other words, we wish to know whether in the current Soviet *generation* more women are working than was the case for the older generation when that older generation was at the same stage of the life cycle and facing roughly equivalent family problems. We asked each respondent whether or not his *mother* had been employed. By dividing our respondents into four age groups and then assigning their mothers to a "generation" on that basis, we obtain groups of women (in Table 53) who were bearing and raising their children in different, although somewhat overlapping, periods of Russian and Soviet history. The question asked was not whether the mother worked when the respondent was a child, but whether or not she had ever worked. It is therefore possible that a higher proportion of the young people would have reported their mothers as working even though they did not do so

TABLE 53 [19A]

PER CENT WHOSE MOTHER HAD WORKED:
BY AGE AND FATHER'S OCCUPATION

Occupation of respondent's father	Age in 1940			
	Per cent whose mother had worked among respondents whose 1940 age was:			
	under 26	26–35	36–45	over 45
Professional	62% (42) [a]	70% (121)	50% (69)	26% (97)
Semiprofessional	64 (56)	62 (161)	49 (117)	25 (183)
Worker	53 (49)	45 (204)	42 (137)	28 (117)
Peasant	48 (31)	35 (251)	27 (203)	25 (266)

a. Total number of respondents on the basis of which the percentage is computed.

regularly, whereas older people would say yes only if aided by memory of a steadily working mother. Allowing for this, it still seems strikingly evident that there has been a marked generational trend in the likelihood that at some point in their lives women would work. Among the women who were of child bearing age in the tsarist era only about a quarter in each social group worked outside the home at any time, whereas among the women who were bearing children in the later Soviet years the range was from about one half to almost two thirds depending on the social group. Thus, the conclusion must be reached that the Soviet regime secured the increased participation of women in the labor force not by more or less equal contributions from all groups, but rather by a disproportionately heavy participation on the part of those in the younger generation, who greatly outdid their mothers' generation in the frequency of participation in what the Soviets call "productive life." Furthermore, although increased participation was marked in all groups in the younger generation, it was notably women in the white-collar classes who poured into the labor force.

On the debit side, from the regime's point of view, this suggests that it was hardly uniformly successful in inducing women to leave the home and enter the labor force. On the contrary, among the women of the older generations, many of whom were nevertheless young enough to work during the Soviet era, there appears to have been much more resistance to either the inducements or pressures to leave home and take a job. On the positive side from the regime's point of view, however, the evidence of a clearcut trend toward higher participation in the labor force on the part of women in the younger generations suggests that there has been a real change in practice and probably in values, and that at comparable ages and stages of the life cycle women of the more distinctively "Soviet" generations are much more likely to participate freely in gainful employment.

Although the Soviet regime seems to have registered a success in that the generations of women raised under Soviet conditions are more likely to participate in gainful employment, this is hardly all that the regime hope to accomplish. Ideally, the regime would prefer that women continue to work after marriage, and indeed after they have children, at the same rate as before those events. To legitimate this expectation the regime claims that the maternity leave and other benefits which it allows the pregnant woman, and the crèche which it provides for the young child, have eliminated the strain elsewhere attendant upon being both a mother and a gainfully employed worker. The network of maternity and crèche facilities is, however, hardly adequate to the demand, and in addition many people apparently look askance at those facilities because of their poor quality and the resultant inferior care.

But one powerful force, economic necessity, was on the regime's side. To maintain the family standard of living under Soviet conditions it was generally necessary to have two earners where one had sufficed before. Dire necessity, therefore, drove hundreds of thousands of women to work after marriage, and to a surprising degree it kept them on the job after they had children. Consequently, withdrawals from the labor force on account of marriage and childbearing were much more modest than might otherwise have been expected. For example, among the women who were between thirty-one and forty in 1940, 71 per cent of the married women as against 80 per cent of the unmarried reported themselves as having a steady occupation. These differences increase somewhat as older age groups are compared, but they are still modest. The arrival of children was, of course, more important in forcing withdrawal from work. Among women between thirty-one and forty, married women with children were more likely to be at home than those without, but the drop was only from 84 per cent of those without children working to 68 per cent working among those with children. A similar pattern was shown by the other age groups.

In part this result may have been an artifact of the measures we used.[20] Some effect might also be attributed to an emergency law, promulgated in June 1940, which denied a woman the right to leave a job merely because she married or had children. The date of the law is such, however, that it could have had only a slight effect on the outcome of our investigation which relates mainly to earlier periods. Allowing for all other considerations it still seems necessary to conclude that the regime has been rather successful in inducing or obliging women to continue working after they enter on marriage and even after they have children. By contrast with the prerevolutionary period, furthermore, the tendency for women to go on working under Soviet conditions seems to apply more or less equally for those in white-collar as for those from the manual classes.

Although economic necessity alone may well explain the persistence of women from the manual classes, it does not do full justice to the facts in the case of women from white-collar and professional families. Strong interest in a career and in independence and freedom from the confines of the home were very prominent factors in the occupational involvement of women from that environment. A woman economist of forty-four whose husband was an engineer asserted that she pursued her career after marriage "because I did not want to be dependent upon a man and I did not want to sit in the kitchen and take care of children." This is not to say, of course, that economic pressures did not contribute in motivating women from upper class and semiprofessional homes to work. On the contrary, such pressures were widely prevalent. But the tone of the comments suggests that the economic considerations were not really urgent. The income was not needed for food and basic necessities. In contrast, in the case of the lower class women it is exceedingly rare that there is any reference to the pursuit of a job or "career" for its own sake, and it was not often that the women talked of escaping from the monotony of the home. Rather the tone of the comments makes it very clear that lower class women found it more of a strain to work. One woman employed as an ordinary worker protested against the theory that men and women were equal and that women could do anything, "But women *should be* different. A woman can't be equal because when a mother works it's bound to weaken the family." Thus, in the lower class it was mainly direct and often dire economic need that forced the women to work to supplement the family income, and were it not for that pressure these women would have much preferred to stay at home.

If this interpretation be correct, and if our women be not too unrepresentative of women still in the USSR, we venture to predict that an improvement of the standard of living, in particular an increase in the value of real wages, might lead to a much greater withdrawal from the labor force of women from manual class families. If such an improvement took place under conditions of rising labor productivity and of a less intense pace of industrial expansion, then the regime might be indifferent and perhaps even pleased to have women withdraw voluntarily from the labor force. If, on the other hand, a rise in living standards took place concurrently with continuing heavy rates of capital expansion, then the regime might find it necessary to resort once again to some form of special incentive or compulsion to keep sufficient numbers of lower class women in the labor force.

Summary and Conclusions

Our brief survey of some of the demographic indices of stability and change in Soviet family patterns has revealed a more complex picture than might have been predicted either on the basis of a simple assumption that there was widespread resistance to change among our disaffected respondents, or on the basis of the equally simple assumption that the force of regime policy and the pace of social change in Soviet Russia would sweep all the old patterns aside. In some respects marriage and family patterns, as measured by our demographic indices, have remained surprisingly constant despite regime policy and the processes of social change. These are the patterns which most directly express cultural values or are connected with enduring structural features of modern society. Thus, marriage (and friendship) across class and ethnic lines apparently occurred at a very modest rate, with surprising constancy over a period of more than forty-five years. This reflects both the continuation of differential opportunity for marriage across these lines and the strength of the cultural values which emphasize patterns of group endogamy. In addition, these rates and those for marriage among women of superior status point to the existence of many elements in Soviet social life which are common to the large-scale industrial societies of Western culture, shared by the USSR and countries of similar structure and background such as the United States.

In contrast with this stability is the marked change in the chances that women will work — even after marriage and childbirth — which apparently greatly increased under Soviet conditions. In part, especially in the manual classes, this appears to be largely a product of the increased necessity to work which faced families under Soviet conditions. The decrease in the standard of living and the value of real wages attendant on the years of collectivization and industrialization forced many women to go to work to supplement the husband's income in order to maintain their family's standard of living at its earlier level. To maintain the same standard of living it now often required two earners where before one had sufficed. In the case of women from the white-collar classes, however, our materials suggest there has also been a real change in values. Women with white-collar backgrounds indicate broad acceptance of the values espoused by the regime to the effect that women should and must work in order to be free of that "slavery" of the household which Engels pictured so darkly. Finally, we have seen evidence of *continuity*, rather than fixed stability *or* change, in the steady decrease in family size which began in the families of individuals whose parents were having their children long before the revolution and which apparently continued steadily in time down into the Soviet period. Only by assessing *both* the relative strength of the forces of change in the system on the one hand, and of continuity in the cultural traditions and personal values of the people on the other, can we make reliable statements about the "impact" of Soviet conditions or of Russian tradition on family patterns in the USSR.

Patterns of Family Life: The Inner Family

It has become commonplace to assert that the family is being "weakened" under the conditions of modern life, particularly because of the rapidity of social change experienced in so many countries. It has, however, proved exceedingly difficult to devise satisfactory measures of the weakness and strength of family ties other than by resort to such gross measures as rates of divorce, separation, and desertion, and these are often more indicative of legal and other *opportunities* for separation than measures of the actual strength of family ties.[1] Our task was all the more difficult because we did not have access to Soviet families in action, where we could directly observe the interaction of family members and the functioning of the family as a unit. To explore family cohesiveness and disruption under Soviet conditions we were therefore obliged to resort to the less desirable procedure of putting direct questions to our respondents.

The Solidarity of the Family

Each was asked to indicate which of three family types, briefly characterized by us, came closest to describing the situation in his own family: In the first case the family members became alienated after the revolution, were afraid to speak frankly with each other, and as a result of the Soviet regime's interference in family affairs the children drew apart from the parents; in the second the members of the family drew closer together, spoke freely with each other and felt most secure at home; and the third family was not greatly influenced and its life went on much as before. We do not, of course, assume that because a person says his family grew closer together under the conditions of the Soviet system that this necessarily reflects the "real facts" as some outside observer might judge them. Neither do we assume that there is any necessary connection between the proportion of refugees giving a particular answer to this question and that which might be secured if such a question could be asked and honestly answered by those still in the Soviet Union. Nevertheless, the answers to such a question do reflect a feeling or attitude, and feelings are real facts too. Furthermore, as we shall see, an examination of the pattern of answers can prove quite interesting because it tells us something about the differential impact of Soviet conditions on the family as perceived by people in different social groups.

With the exception of the peasants, at least one third of the respondents in each social group reported that their family had been relatively unaffected by Soviet conditions, in the sense that life had gone on about as before the revolution (Table 54). It was characteristic of those who gave this response that since no change was perceived no explanation was offered. Typical was the statement by a young student, whose father had been an engineer, that in his family people continued "to live in accordance with the old tradition, and relations among the members of our family were as close as they would probably have been under any circumstances."

TABLE 54 [1A]

THE COHESIVENESS OF THE FAMILY UNDER SOVIET CONDITIONS

Condition of family ("Under Soviets my family . . .")	Social group				
	Intelligentsia	White-collar employees	Skilled workers	Ordinary workers	Collective farm peasants
Grew apart	7%	12%	20%	22%	30%
Grew closer	58	54	43	42	45
Was unchanged	35	34	37	36	25
Total number of respondents	224	323	87	162	189

The fact that as many as one third of our respondents, and rather consistently from class to class, reported their families unchanged certainly suggests that the family policies of the regime had rather less direct effect on family life than many might have expected. This is particularly the case since both the "grew apart" and the "grew together" responses offered our respondents an opportunity to express antagonism to the regime, through the former by showing how evil were the consequences of the Soviet system and through the latter by demonstrating how much solidarity there was in resistance to Communist influence. It should be noted, for example, that in each social class those more hostile to the regime were more likely to assert that their family drew apart.[2]

The most frequent response in each social group is that under Soviet conditions the family drew closer together. The significance of the modal position of this response is not, however, easily assessed. The "true" facts might have been otherwise, yet people may have found it difficult to admit to themselves and to the world that relations at home had been strained. But even if we could assume that the answers given were not influenced by such considerations and reflected the "true" state of affairs, the significance of the observed frequency of "grew together" responses would not be unmistakable. Is it more common for families living under conditions of social change and subjected to various crises to draw closer together or to be pulled apart? Reports on families under stress in other countries produce conflicting and indeed often contradictory interpretations.[3] Where social change is general and does not seem to be directed against the particular family, and where the agent causing the difficulty is not easily identified — as in a family suffering economic deprivation during depression — then family tensions are apparently more likely to increase than decrease. On the other hand, where the change is felt to be brought on by a specific *external* agent, and especially where the members feel that their particular family has been singled out for persecution, then the chances are apparently much greater that the family members will rally to each other's support and strengthen the ties of mutual solidarity.

In our sample the regime appeared to many respondents to be the definitely responsible agent for all aspects of the social upheaval through which the society went in the postrevolutionary period. Of course, the regime's policy of making large-scale political arrests contributed to the sense of persecution and the need to draw closer together for mutual support. Among our respondents this was understandably often graphically described. A teacher of thirty-seven whose father had been a middle peasant in moderately good circumstances described the reasons for his family's cohesion as follows:

My father lost his property and was persecuted. Before the revolution, he was master on his fields. He worked when he wanted. Under the Soviet regime we became slaves. *And it was only natural that at home, we felt secure and safe. At home, we wept, we smiled, we criticized or cursed those who made us poor and hungry.*

Of course, it was not only the sense of persecution, but also the restriction on the activities of many of our respondents which increased family cohesion, as in the case described by a former student, who reported that although her father had many friends before the revolution the friends became estranged after it and "as a result of this the family came closer together." In still other cases, family solidarity increased because people felt more need for warm personal support under the conditions of disruption and change caused by the revolution. One engineer of thirty-nine, whose father had been a teacher, reported:

We lived separately before, but after the revolution we all came together and talked on political subjects. We talked freely only in our own family. In difficult times we came closer together.

By comparison with the nonmanual groups, workers and peasants are noticeably more likely to assert that their family was rent asunder by the events experienced under the Soviet regime. There is a steady and marked increase in the frequency of this response as one descends the class ladder, so that it is about four times more common in the peasantry than in the intelligentsia (Table 54). Among families in the intelligentsia, for every one reported to have grown apart there were eight which came closer together, whereas in the peasantry the ratio was a mere 1:1.5. Here we seem to have a major difference which requires explanation and which may lead us to understand better the effect of the Soviet regime on the family.

Individuals from families in which some member had been arrested by the secret police tended more often to report their families drew together. But the frequency with which such arrests were experienced was rather too similar in the various social groups to account for the differences in response to questions on family cohesion. On the other hand, families with low incomes were much more likely than those with good incomes to report their family had drawn apart. Since income and social class are so highly correlated we checked this association *within* class groups. We found that in the ordinary worker and skilled worker families the proportion reported as drawing apart rose regularly and sharply as per capita income fell. For example, among those in the ordinary worker group, the portion who reported the family to have drawn apart increased from 6 per cent to 18, 19, and 35 per cent as per capita income fell from 4,200 rubles and more to 1,800 or less. But this relationship was not very sharp in the employee group, and was not at all evident in the professional and administrative category.* It would seem then, that the white-collar families were in some way more "protected" from the tensions which often accompany financial strains, whereas the situation of the manual classes made them more easily "unbalanced" by this source of strain. To understand this pattern we must consider the differential impact of Soviet social developments on the various levels of the population.

In the early years of the regime the old intelligentsia was under great suspicion from both the officials and the major segments of the rank and file. Many suffered substantial indignities, and a significant number were arrested on purely political grounds. Yet the new regime's

* Budgets had been collected from peasant families, as well, but technical difficulties posed by the fact that income "in kind," is so important for peasants, led us to abandon efforts to code the data.

need for technical personnel was pressing and it could not quickly and easily train proletarian replacements. To a surprising degree, therefore, the members of the old intelligentsia managed to survive and indeed to continue to hold the same jobs they had held before the revolution. For example, among the fathers of our respondents more than two thirds of those who were in the intelligentsia *before* the revolution continued in that occupational group *after* the revolution.

Although their old style of life was often replaced by one much more shabby, threadbare, and less gracious, most of the families of the intelligentsia managed to maintain a great deal of continuity. In many cases, the adversity faced by the family only led it to rally more firmly around its basic values, because the members held either the process of change or the regime, rather than the head of the household, responsible for its deteriorated condition. By the mid-thirties, furthermore, the policy of the regime was substantially revised and the intelligentsia was restored to a position of relative honor and respect, accompanied by high material rewards. It became more and more differentiated from the rank and file of workers and peasants.

Quite a different pattern prevailed at the other end of the class hierarchy. In the early years of the regime the social structure of rural Russia remained much as it had been before the revolution. The landlord had been eliminated, but the pattern of peasant landholding and tillage, based on the "household" or extended family unit, continued essentially unchanged. In 1928, however, the regime began its program of rapid industrialization, which drew hundreds of thousands of peasants to the new industrial plants being built or just beginning to operate. Then, in 1930, there began the incredibly rapid program of forced collectivization which completely revamped the structure of rural life in Russia. Under the collective farm system the family lost much of its economic function and power, since all the land except for modest garden plots was held by the collective farm and worked collectively. Furthermore, the individual, not the family, became the basic work unit. Payment went to the individual not the family, and most of it was in money rather than in kind. The collectivization was effected by force, and at least one million peasant families encompassing perhaps five million souls among the so-called *kulaks* or rich peasants, were expropriated and obliged to leave the areas in which they had lived. Many of these families drifted to the cities to work in the newly established industries. They were accompanied by millions of others who were unwilling to work in the harsh conditions of the collectives or whose labor had been made surplus by the mechanization of the farms.

At the same time, the collectivization of agriculture and the growth of industry and cities were accompanied by mass education and mass communication which spread the new values and attitudes fostered by the regime as competitors to older traditional peasant values. This process was intensified by the mobility opportunities both in the more bureaucratic and mechanized collective farms and in the expanded industries, thus exposing the younger generation to influences and values different from those earlier experienced by their parents in the villages.

In these conditions lie the explanation for the greater sense of family disruption which characterizes the peasants and to a lesser degree the workers, many of whom were but recently drawn from a peasant background. Our qualitative materials indicate that it was the physical separation and geographical dispersion of the peasant families which most accounted for their feeling that the regime had pulled them apart. Often this was a direct result of action of the regime, as in the family of a fifty-six-year-old collective farmer who reported on the dispersion of his family of four brothers and six sisters as follows:

My youngest brother had been killed during the revolution . . . (later) a very heavy tax was levied on my father, so heavy that he was not able to pay it. So a younger brother went to Central Asia. My mother and four sisters went to Tiflis, and we all split up in that way, fleeing to different places. . . .

Of course, the impact of the changed conditions was clear not only in the case of families which suffered, but was evident even in the case of those families which apparently benefitted from the course of revolutionary change. Thus, a forty-year-old journalist, whose father had been a poor peasant, effectively communicated the sweep of events as it affected his family when he reported:

In the First World War, one of my brothers went into the war and returned just before the revolution. Three others were killed. One brother, who was a veteran, lost both his hands in the war, became chairman of the Soviet. My brother, who distinguished himself in the Red Army during the revolution, was called to Moscow to receive formal education. From there he called me to join him. My brother by this time was sent to a post in Turkestan. Another brother joined the army and became a commander of a division in Mongolia.

It is no accident that both of these quotations describe peasant families. Of course we know that the revolution also brought about the physical separation of many families in the intelligentsia. But such separation had quite different meaning for those in the intelligentsia. As compared to the manual classes, the intelligentsia had quite different traditional patterns of family living and expectations concerning family cohesion. The traditional pattern of peasant life led to the expectation, in the past often fulfilled, that the children would settle down on land in the same village or very close by. In contrast, parents in intelligentsia and middle class families assumed and accepted the idea that as their children became educated and took up professional or business posts they would likely be obliged to work in a different city from that in which their parents lived. Although the actual degree of physical dispersion in peasant families may indeed have been greater, the attitudes and expectations of those in such families gave special meaning to this separation which made it seem far more important than it was for those from the intelligentsia.

Other differences in the attitudes and behavior of the parents and children in the nonmanual as against the manual families apparently also contributed to the greater sense of disruption of family life felt by those in the worker and peasant groups. This was particularly evident with regard to political and religious disagreements. The concerted influence of the school, the youth organizations, and the mass media was to push the child to be antireligious and proregime. To the extent that his parents were proreligious and antiregime, the chances for conflict with them increased. To a striking degree parents in intelligentsia and other white-collar families were less likely to hold views which might lead them into conflict with their children and thus create a sense of the family being pulled apart. Thus in one small group which we studied more intensively we discovered that parents who were *both* overtly antiregime and strongly religious made up 56 per cent of the manual group but 15 per cent the nonmanual parents.[4]

In the light of these figures we can understand why conflicts over religion and political belief permeated the reports on family life given by those from peasant and worker backgrounds. From the parents' point of view it seemed that their children were being torn away from them and won over to or at least significantly influenced to be irreligious and to support the Communist regime. The children, in turn, often felt their parents to be backward or ignorant, and thus were alienated from them. This was especially evident when the children were advancing themselves and thus coming ever more under the influence of values which ran counter to those of the parents. A Komsomol member, who was a student at the time the war began, reported that when he came home from school he demanded that the ikon which his peasant mother kept in plain sight be removed from the home. "When younger," he said, "I had been afraid to discuss the matter with them, but growing older *and being away from home* I found the courage to do this." He hid the ikon, but his mother found it, and after a scene he agreed not to remove it again. Thus, a resolution was achieved, but it is clear that the residue must have been a sense of alienation between parent and child. Another respondent, also a young man but one who worked on the *kolkhoz*, described a visit by his brother who had gone away from the farm to Moscow and joined the Communist Party. At first, the joy of reunion predominated. There were three days of eating and drinking, and many friends from the village were invited into the parents' peasant hut. But on the third day, perhaps feeling the effects of the festivities, the father began a political discussion and spoke critically of the regime for its conduct of the great purges. "The next morning very early," our respondent concluded, "my brother left without saying goodbye. For six months he did not write even so much as a letter." Still another respondent, son of a worker but himself a student, said rather scornfully of his father's failure to adapt to the Soviet regime: "He was an ignorant person. He didn't know anything about politics."

The likelihood of disagreement among family members was determined not only by the greater frequency of strong religious and anti-regime sentiments in the manual class families, but also by major differences in the patterns of interpersonal relations and the ways of handling problems in the two types of family. Even when they were strongly religious and opposed to the regime, parents in the nonmanual classes were very likely to suppress these facts in order not to raise painful problems and expose their children to embarrassing experiences. Thus, an NKVD official reported he knew his intelligentsia father to be religious. Indeed when he was young they had ikons at home. Yet his parents did not try to influence him because, as he put it, "if they fought the school they would be fighting the Soviet power." The willingness to accommodate to reality and to forego resisting the influence of the regime on the children was very apparent in the intelligentsia. They recognized that in the future the children must accept the system if they were successfully to pursue the careers their parents planned for them. Consider, for example, the case of a quite successful woman biologist of fifty-nine, who asserted that she and her husband had been religious "in our souls" although outwardly professing atheism while in the Soviet Union. She claimed to have had her daughter secretly baptized in the Soviet Union and now as a refugee sang in the church choir. Nevertheless, she reported that while in the Soviet Union her attitude was that:

Inasmuch as we were living in the Soviet Union we knew that our children would have to continue to live there even after we are gone, and so we tried to introduce Communist ideas for them. What can I say about the education of our children? It was of a different sort than I would have preferred, but I didn't object. I considered that my children were grown up and that they should be able to judge and decide for themselves.

Such a permissive or liberal approach was quite rare in worker and peasant families. Parents at the manual level were much more likely to express their political feelings to their children frankly, indeed bluntly. Apparently, they were much less appalled at the thought of fighting against the awesome "Soviet power," and were less worried about hurting either their children's feelings or their future career prospects. For example, a Komsomol member who had attended military school, two of whose brothers were in the Komsomol and another in the Communist Party, reported that despite the children's obvious involvement with the system his parents "cursed the regime freely in front of us." Another military student from a worker's home reported that his mother "cursed the regime; she could express herself more freely, and she was not afraid of anything that she said, because she thought 'we will die anyway.' "

Thus, we have seen how the disruption of traditional patterns and the introduction of new values and lifeways must have created in the manual classes a strong sense of the dissolution of the highly valued tradition of family strength, stability, and continuity. Undoubtedly it was both the strong expectation of family stability and solidarity as well as the actual changes in the patterns of rural life, which contributed to the greater tendency of peasants and workers to report that their families had grown further apart.

We should not forget, however, that even in the peasantry to describe the family as drawn apart was a minority report. In addition, we should keep in mind that in all classes the tendency to report family disruption was higher among the old than among the young. Most likely the different standards of family solidarity held by the peasants, and particularly the older generation, led them to feel more strongly that under Soviet conditions the family deviated from the idealized norm. The younger people, with milder expectations about family solidarity and its importance, seem to have more often felt that things were proceeding normally. It is to be expected, furthermore, that as these new and less rigorous patterns of expectation concerning family life become thoroughly institutionalized in Soviet society, the problem of family cohesion will become less central. We may anticipate a shift in emphasis to problem areas more nearly like those which constitute the central family problems in the United States. This, in turn, may be expected to have important consequences for the future stability of the Soviet regime. As people become less conscious of the regime as a source of forced change and consequently of family disruption, so there will presumably be less projection onto it of blame or responsibility for the tensions engendered by modern urban family living. Furthermore, if the regime comes less often to be perceived as an external force imposing its will upon, and as an alien institution injecting its influence into, the confines of the family, to that degree its actual impact and influence, although more subtle, will nevertheless likely become even more substantial. This can be strikingly demonstrated in the study of child rearing values to which we now turn.

Child Rearing Values[5]

The most important effects of the Soviet regime on the family need not, of course, have been so immediately evident that our respondents could report on them as directly as they did with regard to family cohesiveness. More subtle processes may well have been at work, which, although relatively unnoticed, were effecting a fundamental transformation. As the regime so clearly recognized, the most important battle was fought not with post card divorce or through the "abortatoriums," but in the school and indeed earlier in the nursery and the play room. For it was here the child acquired the values and motives which would guide his future adult behavior. We rightly think of the family as conservative and resistant to change and innovation, preserving and transmitting intact the basic values of the folk culture. In the case of our respondents, who were so frequently disaffected from the regime and hostile to its values and goals, we would particularly expect them to report that the old values had been preserved in their families and strong resistance shown to the newer values espoused by the regime. If it develops, therefore, that important changes in family values occurred within our sample, and these go in the direction the regime desired, this must be taken as all the more indicative of the vigor with which such changes probably occurred in the larger population still at home.

During the course of the life-history interview each informant was invited to speak at length about the way in which he had been brought up and had brought up *his* children, or intended to when they came along. These materials were then coded to indicate the values or the areas of concern which appeared to be most important to the parent in raising his child. Since we asked about child rearing as practiced by our respondents' parents, and by the respondents themselves acting in the role of parent, we are in the fortunate position of being able to survey child rearing practices in Russia and the Soviet Union over a span of sixty years — in the tsarist period, in the postrevolutionary era, and in the current Soviet situation.*

Six major themes emerged as prominent value orientations guiding child rearing as our respondents experienced it when they were children, or practiced it as parents. The value of "tradition" was coded mainly for emphasis on religious upbringing, but included as well references to maintenance of strong family ties, respect for elders, and carrying on family traditions; "adjustment" reflects emphasis on "getting along," staying out of trouble, and keeping an eye on one's security and safety;

---

* Some of the methodological problems involved in this effort to use our material to judge child rearing over a three generation span are discussed in the note 5A to this chapter.

"achievement" was coded when parents stressed attainment, industrious-
ness, mobility, material rewards, and similar goals; "personalistic" values
were checked when the parent showed concern with such qualities as
honesty, sincerity, justice and mercy; "intellectuality," where the emphasis was on learning and knowledge as ends in themselves; and "political" when the focus was on attitudes, values, and beliefs dealing with
government and particularly with the Soviet regime.

The Soviet regime was, of course, fairly specific about what it wanted.
It sought to wipe out the importance of religion and religious training
as a central value in family living, and in its place to institute a secular
morality which put political considerations above traditional loyalties to
the family. It further sought to weaken traditional family ties, especially
the authority of the father and mother. The Soviet leaders wished to insure themselves of a large supply of energetic, active, and mobile labor by
stressing opportunities for social advancement and achievement. Closely
linked to this program was the great emphasis placed on expanding education and learning, and the publicity given to the new educational opportunities. In addition, the regime hoped to make everyone politically
"conscious," that is, to make the political realm, and in particular the
leaders of the Communist Party, a central focus for personal identification
by the young. Some of these general objectives were made the basis of
policies directed specifically at altering the patterns of family life. The
regime conducted antireligious propaganda. Through the school and the
Communist youth movements it attempted to weaken the authority of
the parents, whom it defined as "holdovers" from the old regime, and
to spread its own values instead. But the regime had even greater allies
in forces which were generated for quite different reasons — forces such
as mass communication, urbanization, and the increasing physical and
social mobility which broke in upon the isolation of the old family.

Arrayed against the regime and these forces which it had set in motion were the forces of tradition, the influence of the old folk ways, and
the desire of parents to bring children up in "the right way." Indeed,
in many of our respondents there was a conscious intention to resist
the influence of the regime upon the children, and the following remark
of a sixty-six-year-old grain elevator worker is not unusual.

We tried to see that our children knew of religion when still young. We also
wanted them to know what Soviet rule was really like, although we were very
careful to warn them of the danger of repeating elsewhere what we told them. We
were proud that our children were anti-Bolshevik while still in the Soviet Union.

In Table 55 we have indicated the distribution of emphasis on the
various child training values in the three periods — prerevolutionary,
postrevolutionary, and contemporary Soviet — and have in each case
given separate data for the manual and the nonmanual classes. There

is substantial continuity in the pattern manifested in all three periods. In the manual classes tradition is the most important category, and achievement is consistently second in rank order, in all three periods. Similarly for the nonmanual classes, the achievement value has persisted as a central focus, holding rank order number one for the first two sets of parents and second place in the third period.

TABLE 55 [5A]

VALUES EMPHASIZED IN CHILD REARING BY THREE
GENERATIONS OF PARENTS: BY CLASS

	Period of child rearing					
	Prerevolutionary (1880–1915)		Postrevolutionary (1916–1940)		Current Soviet (1941–)	
Values	Non-manual	Manual	Non-manual	Manual	Non-manual	Manual
Traditional	31%	40%	15%	29%	12%	25%
Achievement	34	28	27	26	23	23
Adjustment	5	12	14	9	14	15
Personal	18	11	22	23	25	17
Political	4	7	8	9	12	11
Intellectual	8	2	14	4	14	9
Total number of respondents[a]	161	85	120	93	147	119

a. From personal interviews.

The observed continuity may in part have been an artifact of our method. Substantially the same set of individuals provided the information on the prerevolutionary and postrevolutionary period, with regard to the former describing how they had been raised, and with regard to the latter how they raised their own children.[6] Rather than stability through time, therefore, we may have here mainly a reflection of consistency in individual values. There is, however, much more continuity between the postrevolutionary and the current period, based on the report of *different* sets of individuals, than between the first two periods despite the fact that the *same* individuals provided the information for those first two periods. We feel that the general continuity of emphasis in child rearing patterns reflected in Table 55 is quite reasonable when one considers that after all the individuals throughout represent substantially the same Russian and Ukrainian culture, and indeed the same broad European civilization. In fact, the general stability of the overall pattern may be taken as support for the validity of the report as a whole, and as therefore giving particular significance to those instances in which there *were* shifts. It is to these we now turn our attention.

Most striking is the decline in the importance of traditional values, predominantly of emphasis on training in religion, as we move from parents in the prerevolutionary period to those who are today raising their children. In the old days religion and traditional values were apparently the central interest in child rearing activities, accounting for the exceedingly high total of 40 per cent of all references among the manual groups. Typical of this emphasis on religion, respect, propriety, and the other now "old-fashioned" values is the description by a forty-four-year-old woodcutter, son of a station master, as to how his parents had raised him in the years before the revolution:

> They reared me to respect religion and my elders, and people of my own age as well. They also taught me to love work of every kind. . . . Our parents never permitted anyone in the home to sit down and eat without saying a prayer before eating. Yes, we all respected and still respect religion.

Although emphasis on religion and the traditional virtues of respect for elders and loyalty to the family continued to be stressed, they suffered a sharp decline in importance during the main postrevolutionary period. Indeed in the nonmanual classes they were reduced to much less than half their former weight. Furthermore, despite much talk about religious revival, there is little evidence that the youngest generation of parents, those of an age equivalent to that of parents currently rearing their children in the Soviet Union, are giving any more emphasis to religious training than did their parents before them. On the contrary, interest in religious training for children among the younger Soviet parents has become but one among many themes. In the white-collar classes it has become of definitely minor importance, accounting for fewer responses than any other category!

Training children in religion and in the old-fashioned traditional values was, of course, not training in a single value but a system of values. When the strength of such training was weakened, the traditional virtues which people earlier sought to inculcate in children did not completely disappear, but rather came to be expressed in more secularized form. This is reflected in the increased stress on good personal adjustment, on positive personal qualities, and on learning — not as the path to God but as an end itself. Indeed, in the white-collar classes good personal qualities came to be the most often mentioned area of concern for the parents in the current Soviet period.

The gradual shift in emphasis from religious upbringing to stress on personal qualities and good adjustment was rather strikingly illustrated by a perceptive young technologist, whose father had been an architect.

In describing how his parents had been educated in the tsarist period, he said of them: "Like all people who have been educated in the old time, they were more religious than we are today. They fasted and went to church. They followed the rules given to them by my grandparents." But in describing how those very parents had reared him in the postrevolutionary period, he asserted that his father and mother did not force religion or the old values on him. On the contrary, "like all parents they tried to educate a person if not to be ideal at least to be decent and to correspond to all of the social requirements made on him." This young man, furthermore, was apparently going to carry this new approach into the next generation. When asked what he wanted for his son, he said that above all else, "I should have educated him to be a decent man." Thus, the traditional religiously based image of the "good" man was replaced by that of secularly validated "perfect man." When we asked a young sports instructor what his father, a Soviet engineer, had meant by telling his son that he should become a "perfect man" he responded:

First, he must be educated; secondly he must be cultured (*kul'turny*); thirdly, he must have an honest character, and not be a coward. (What do you mean by an honest character?) Well, the ability to keep one's word, to have an honest attitude towards the problems of life and towards one's surroundings.

We have as yet not commented on two of the value areas, achievement and politics. Emphasis on achievement dimensions, such as social mobility and social distinction, attainment of high economic rewards, and similar goals continued of major importance in all three periods. Indeed, it maintained a surprisingly stable position as either the first or second most important emphasis in child rearing for both manual and nonmanual groups in all three periods. This is so striking because, as our respondents often realized, it was very difficult to pursue achievement goals within the framework of Soviet society without participating in, and implicitly supporting, the regime's effort to rebuild the society along Communist lines.

Our materials are permeated with references to the hopes and aspirations of parents for their children's success in occupational, cultural, and scientific endeavors. Often the parent would enter a reservation, indicating that he wanted his child to select an occupation which would give least support to the goals of the regime. Witness the case of the engineer who wanted his son to avoid the humanities and become an engineer because "technical jobs are not connected with Marxist philosophy, but history, literature and art must be interpreted exclusively according to dialectical materialism." Yet, it is a testimonial to the strength of the emphasis on achievement that parents managed to see virtually every career in which they personally were interested for their *own* children as one not too supportive of the regime. Furthermore, it was not rare for parents to say that after all the child had to make his own way, and if the road to attainment led to involvement with the regime, then it would just have to be that way.

Yet, in the light of the opportunities for mobility and "service" which the Soviet system opened up, and the emphasis which the regime placed on them as appropriate social goals, one is led to wonder why achievement did not increase in absolute importance in the Soviet period. It may be, of course, that our informants, including a disproportionately large number of disaffected persons, were less inclined than others to stress achievement because they felt that the more a person became involved in an active career the more he became implicated in the regime. There is some evidence for this in our interviews, as for example, in the peasant who sent his boy into a stable rather than a factory, saying, "In my simple head I understood that the Communists will perish sooner or later, and I did not want my family to be soiled with Communism."

On the whole, however, our interview materials do not indicate that the desire to avoid involvement with the regime was the prime reason for the failure of achievement values to be stressed more and more by successive generations of parents. Rather it appears that a more subtle process was in operation. Apparently a change in the value scheme was occurring, with ever increasing importance assigned to social and psychological adjustment and to positive personal qualities. In the earlier period achievement was generally seen as an end in itself. But in the more contemporary period it was seen more instrumentally, as the *means* whereby a person could secure the levels of prestige and pay which would assure him that sense of positive adjustment and personal well-being which became relatively so important. Although we cannot firmly substantiate this hypothesis, it seems congruent with the facts of Soviet social development, in particular with the movement towards a stable social system possessing many institutional features in common with other large-scale industrial nations. Thus, not only are religious values transformed into secularized morality, but secular values such as achievement are also transformed and "revalued" in the hedonistic calculus of the contemporary era.

Concern for the child's proper orientation to the political realm increased in importance among parents in the postrevolutionary and current Soviet periods as expected. There were, of course, some parents who sought to bring up their children as loyal Communist-style Soviet citizens. Most comments in the political area, however, reflected the desire that the child not grow up to be a Soviet sympathizer. Considering the disaffected character of our sample, we were surprised to find the increase in attention to politics so relatively modest. This area was not raised to the level of a major concern in child rearing for either the postrevolutionary or the current Soviet generation of parents. This is all the more noticeable since in our coding the political category was checked when the parent showed any concern with it at all, even if the "concern" consisted merely in mentioning that the parent did not interfere to push the child to be either pro- or anti-Soviet. Thus, the main impression created by our materials is that despite the considerable malaise which surrounded the problems of politics, it did not become a dominant factor in child rearing. The other more subtle and even more pervasive forces of social change set in motion by the regime, rather than its direct political program, seem to have been most influential in penetrating the home and influencing the patterns for raising children.

Since we have focused on the change or stability of particular values, it may have escaped notice that the manual and nonmanual classes differ markedly in the extent to which their child rearing values were stable or shifted over time. In the nonmanual classes, the differences between the prerevolutionary and the current Soviet generation are consistently statistically significant, one at the .0001 level, two at .01 level, and two at the .05 level. Only one, the "intellectual" fails to attain this level of statistical significance. All the changes in the manual class were in the same direction as those for the nonmanual, but by contrast only two of the changes were significant at the .05 level.* It is evident, therefore, that the revolution and the subsequent processes of social change produced a much more profound effect on the child rearing values of white-collar groups. Furthermore, the change was largely what the regime would have wanted — less traditionalism, controlled achievement drive, more emphasis on politics and getting along. We may well recall the earlier comments from the family solidarity section, where we noted and illustrated the greater readiness of white-collar parents to accept the Soviet reality and to bring their children up so as to fit in with it. The upper status family, precisely because it is better educated, informed about what is going on, interested in "keeping up" or in advancement, seems just to that degree more "permeable," more open, to the influence of the processes of social change which the Soviet regime set in motion.

The changed conditions of social life also influenced the parents' approach to more specific problems such as securing an education or selecting an occupation. Table 56, following the pattern used earlier, shows the distribution of emphasis among four basic values which influenced the way in which three generations of parents shaped or planned to shape the occupational aspirations of their children. The presence of these values was not deduced from the specific occupation the parent chose for his child, but rather was derived from the *reasons* the parent gave for

* For details concerning these tests see note 5A to this chapter.

feeling that any particular occupation would be desirable. Thus, a collective farm parent who wanted his son to remain a peasant and a doctor who wanted his son to become a doctor would have been scored the same way if both made their individual decisions on the same ground of family tradition. They would have been scored differently if the one stressed avoidance of political involvement and the other emphasized "service to the people." The number of cases from which we had information on this topic is unfortunately small, but the gross pattern is so much like that manifested in the study of general child rearing values, and the size of the shifts so marked, that we may have considerable confidence in the data.*

TABLE 56 [6A]

VALUES EMPHASIZED IN GUIDING THE CHILD'S OCCUPATIONAL
ASPIRATIONS: BY CLASS AND PERIOD OF CHILD REARING

| | Period of child rearing | | | | | |
| | Prerevolutionary (1880–1915) | | Postrevolutionary (1916–1940) | | Current Soviet (1941–   ) | |
Values	Non-manual	Manual	Non-manual	Manual	Non-manual	Manual
Tradition	30%	60%	5%	27%	6%	6%
Rewards	38	24	21	31	25	29
Self-expression	28	13	52	19	48	44
Political	4	3	22	23	21	21
Total number of respondents[a]	50	30	37	26	48	48

a. From personal interviews.

In the tsarist period the extremely high figure of 60 per cent of the worker and peasant parents selected an occupation for their children on grounds of family tradition. Typical of the concern for continuity among the parents of the tsarist generation is this report by a forty-three-year-old rural mechanic who said: "My father wanted me to be a peasant, like himself, and this is what I wanted to be. He hoped I would inherit the results of his hard labors. My father wanted me to get as much education as possible, so that I would become an intelligent farmer." It is of

* The chi-square for the total table equals 65.94 with 15 degrees of freedom. The probability of obtaining such a value or a higer one is .001. For details on tests of significance for particular comparisons with the Table, see note 6A to this chapter.

special interest, in this case, that although the respondent's parents wanted him to have education, they wanted it mainly not as an end in itself but as something instrumental to the better maintenance of the family tradition. A similar emphasis on tradition could, of course, be found outside the farm family in both worker and white-collar families.

In the postrevolutionary period, family tradition, although still of some importance, suffered a precipitous decline, and was mentioned less than half as often by the manual classes and hardly at all by the non-manual classes. Instead, the emphasis shifted to permitting the child free choice, and particularly to allowing him to find that level to which he would feel "best suited," where he would be "happiest" and most "at ease." Thus, one young student whose father had been an engineer, knew that his father was disappointed because his son's interests were in the cultural field. His parents were concerned that in becoming an artist he ran large risks of failure and of leading a below-standard existence. Yet, he reports: "neither of my parents ever talked about my changing my chosen profession. I think the attitude of my parents was that I had to decide for myself and try to be successful and happy through my own endeavors, without help from outside."

Of course, not all the parents who stressed self-expression and self-determination in the choice of occupational careers for their children were actually so permissive. In many cases they were willing to leave the choice of a specific occupation to the child, but it was clear that they assumed that the occupation would be one based on the acquisition of some education and would have good pay and high prestige. The degree of indefiniteness about the child's occupational level, seemed to be associated with the age of the children. As the children became older the parents tended, presumably on the basis of fuller knowledge of the child's character and potentialities, to think more in terms of definite occupations. It was probably this factor, in addition to changing parental values, which made for the extremely heavy emphasis which the group of current Soviet parents placed on self-expression.

Psychological rewards such as prestige and the inner satisfaction of public service, and material rewards made possible by high earnings, were of major importance in guiding the child's occupational choices in all three periods. But as was the case with "achievement" among the general child rearing values, the expected *increase* in emphasis did not materialize. The rewards of the job cover a wide variety of gratifications, and there may well have been some shift in relative emphasis within this broad category, but our data are insufficient to support any firm conclusions. The increased stress on political factors is, however, marked, and the point of increase clearly evident. From an almost insignificant factor in the training of children in the tsarist period, political considerations came to be an important element in guiding the child's occupational choices during the postrevolutionary era.

The shift in values guiding the child's occupational choices is an important example of a general tendency which these child rearing materials expose to view. Parents seem to make an intelligent assessment of the changing conditions in their social environment, and then purposefully adapt the way in which they rear their children to insure that the children will be better adjusted to the adult world as they will know it when they are grown up.[7] One of our rural mechanics, for example, stressed that he wanted his children to have a good income and concluded that some kind of specialization or profession was the only possible route to that goal "since under Soviet conditions private property was prohibited." Similarly, a skilled worker of forty-nine, who had striven to give his children a higher technical education reported:

> I felt that under existing conditions, technical training offered the possibility of a better life, and at the same time was more secure and further removed from politics. There was a general conviction that technical work provided a better existence, and that such a job, well done, gave some protection against the NKVD.

Summary and Conclusions

In many important respects the struggle between the conservative culture values and the forces of the Communist regime apparently ended in a victory for the regime, although the surrender of the old family system was far from unconditional. Indeed, our impression is that it was not primarily the direct impact of the conscious family policy of the regime, but rather the other social processes which it initiated — such as mass education and communication, occupational mobility, and employment for women — which carried the day. But wherever the credit or the blame may lie, the values governing child rearing in the Soviet Union seem to have changed, and the change is in many respects in tune with the desires of the regime and the needs of the new social system which it has created. The most striking and most consistent trend, equally evident in general child rearing ethics and in the occupational and educational guidance given the child, is the decline in the importance of traditional values of religion, respect for custom, and carrying on the family heritage. The training of children has come instead to reflect a more secular morality which emphasizes personal qualities such as kindness and justice, and the contemporaneously important mass-culture values of good personal adjustment, security, and "happiness."[8] Political considerations, which used to be of extremely minor significance have risen to the level of an important factor guiding the parents' training of their children. The emphasis on achievement, on pursuit of the rewards of status, security, and income in occupational and educational activity, while not increasing sharply, have continued to be major value areas in rearing children.

Clearly, we cannot assume that these trends exactly mirror the pattern of change in the larger population still in the Soviet Union. Nevertheless, the nature of the change is such that, with the exception of the political factor, we must assume that those elements of the Soviet population who are not disaffected would, if accessible to study, reveal at least an equally marked shift in values. It is of critical importance, furthermore, that from the point of view of the regime most of these trends would be looked on favorably. They promise the raising of young people who will be responsive to the kind of incentive and stimulus the regime provides, and who will fulfill the needs the system has for an energetic, highly motivated, mobile people easily moved from one objective to another. The emphasis on good adjustment, on getting along and staying out of trouble, may be expected to lead to the development of young people who are not too strongly principled, willing to accept the leadership of the regime so long as it seems to provide for the personal needs which they have or will develop. Without the principles and scruples which were part of traditional religious upbringing to provide a foundation for their values and belief, the young must, of course, be expected to be more open to influence by the official idea and belief system disseminated by the schools, the mass media, and the political organizations for the youth.

Although the influence on child rearing practices is probably the most important and critical, this is hardly the only area in which we have seen the effects of changed Soviet conditions on patterns of family living. More and more women have been drawn into the labor force and thus have become participants in the process of so-called "socialist construction," inevitably thereby advancing the goals of the regime and its leaders. Wives have put pressure on their husbands to increase their skills and thereby their earnings,[9] which again has given the men incentives to act in ways tending to further the purposes of the regime. In many instances, these developments were, of course, not products of the regime's conscious family policy, and indeed were not directly planned to occur as they did. Rather they arose from the large-scale forces which the regime set in motion as part of its general program, forces such as the expansion of industry, the collectivization of agriculture, the spread of mass education and mass communication. Indeed, at some points, these very forces which the regime created seem to have encouraged behavior which the regime frowns upon and would like to prevent. The outstanding example would, of course, be the restriction of family size which appears to be associated with increased urbanization, increased emphasis on having women work, and the general shift towards middle class values and the middle class style of life as an idealized or "model" way of life. In this way the family reveals itself as not merely a passive object of change, but shows itself a vital institution which independently adjusts and adapts, and sometimes itself shapes, the process of social change.

On the whole, however, we conclude that the pattern of family life has changed in directions congruent with the needs and demands of the regime. We have the strong impression that Soviet parents are bringing up their children pretty much as the regime wants them to. This then is an area in which the regime has won a major victory, even though it was not the direct assault but rather the influence of more subtle and indirect forces which carried the battle. We often hear these days the complacent assertion that the strength of the family is proved by the fact that the Soviet regime was finally forced to compromise with it, as it did with religion. Reassuring as this may sound, it can be very misleading. For it is not with the traditional family as it earlier existed that the regime has compromised, and which it has restored to its former standing as a pillar on which the state rests. On the contrary, only the changes in the family that came about over the years, and the fact that in many ways the old family and its value system were transformed and no longer threatened the regime, made the compromise and present truce possible. The regime is no longer fighting the family, it is true, but not because it has been forced to a truce. Rather, the fighting is at an end because in large measure the Soviet family has been captured, and captured from within, by the regime.

PART THREE: THE INDIVIDUAL AND THE STATE

X

The Sources of Support: Popular Values and Aspirations

Even a totalitarian system cannot operate effectively unless there is considerable congruence between its institutions and objectives and the prevailing ideological orientations of the people. In the Soviet Union there is probably more congruence than many like to think. Complaints and conflict are more easily perceived than are satisfaction and congruence. One is therefore more likely to be aware of the strains than the strength of the system.

We have often been tempted to state that the alienated Soviet citizen accepts "the system" and rejects "the regime." By this we mean that hostility and alienation focus selectively on the men who run the society, rather than on the institutional forms of the system. This statement — while generally true — is not sufficiently precise. Certain institutional features of Soviet society, especially the collective farm and the secret police, are virtually unanimously rejected by Soviet refugees. Those institutions generate doubt and questioning even in the most pro-Soviet citizens. Furthermore, many Soviet émigrés automatically define "the system" as embracing the Communist Party and also the secret police. Since those organizations are the object of so much hostility, many reject the notion that there is *anything* desirable in "the Soviet system." When questioned about the system in a general way these are the persons who say they would "keep nothing." Yet they actually favor many of the institutional features that we ordinarily associate with the Soviet system.

In Table 57 are found some striking illustrations of the tendency of former Soviet citizens to approve in principle some of the specific institutional features, while simultaneously saying that "nothing" should be kept of the present system. Attitudes about state ownership and control of basic industries are not markedly different among those who said "keep nothing" and those who said there were things worth keeping. There are a few minor differences, not all, in the expected direction. For example, "only" 86 per cent of those who said "keep nothing" favor state ownership of transport and communications in comparison with

TABLE 57 A

PER CENT VOTING FOR GOVERNMENT OWNERSHIP AND CON-
TROL OF VARIOUS BRANCHES OF ECONOMY: BY SOCIAL GROUP
AND ATTITUDE TOWARD SOVIET SYSTEM

Social group	Attitude to Soviet system	Branch of economy			Median number of respondents
		Trans-port	Heavy industry	Light industry	
Intelligentsia	keep some things	91%	87%	23%	(427)
	"keep nothing"	80	79	23	(119)
White-collar employees	keep some things	90	85	24	(394)
	"keep nothing"	82	75	23	(155)
Skilled workers	keep some things	88	92	35	(127)
	"keep nothing"	94	92	42	(76)
Ordinary workers	keep some things	88	89	42	(164)
	"keep nothing"	82	75	30	(155)
Collective farmers	keep some things	93	90	53	(127)
	"keep nothing"	93	82	50	(119)

90 per cent of those who specified something to keep. This difference is, however, unimportant in the face of the fact that both groups are virtually unanimous in their approval of this characteristic Soviet institution. On the basis of such evidence we regard the assertion that "nothing" of the present system should be kept more as an expression of generalized hostility toward things Soviet than as evidence of literally complete rejection of the entire Soviet institutional apparatus.

Alienation is clearly a selective process. Even the refugee group was by no means antagonistic to all aspects of the Soviet order. Indeed they were very enthusiastic about some of its features. In this chapter we review the evidence of the refugee project to see what light it sheds on such questions as: What does the Soviet citizen accept and reject of the Soviet system? What type of society would he like to live in? Despite their general alienation from the Soviet system, the testimony of our refugee respondents was very valuable in suggesting answers to these questions. An exploration of the underlying social and political values of the Soviet citizen gives us further insight into the sources of allegiance and the process of alienation.

In making this analysis we have several series of questions on which to draw: 1. Respondents were asked which things in the "present system" — in the event that the Bolshevik regime were removed — they would be sure to keep, and which they would be sure to change. In response to these questions they were free to specify any aspects of the system they chose. 2. On another series of questions they were asked directly how they felt about the Soviet leadership and various features of Soviet life. 3. Finally, there were a number of inquiries into basic social and political attitudes, such as government ownership, social insurance, and civil liberties. In these latter instances the issue was posed in general terms not linked to the Soviet system. Each set of questions gives us a distinctive perspective on the social and political attitudes of our respondents. Taken together, they present a definite picture of the type of society our refugee respondents would like to live in.

TABLE 58 [B]

EVALUATIONS OF THE SOVIET SYSTEM: BY SOCIAL GROUP

Social group	Per cent globally rejecting the Soviet system, saying:		Total number of respondents
	Keep nothing	Change everything	
Intelligentsia	19%	20%	(642)
White-collar employees	23	22	(679)
Skilled workers	29	30	(282)
Ordinary workers	33	34	(494)
Collective farm peasants	32	31	(387)

In response to the question of what they would keep and change of the present system many, though far from a majority of the respondents, rejected categorically the notion that there was anything good about "the system." They replied, "keep nothing" and/or "change everything" (see Table 58). This global rejection, however, characterized only a minority of the sample, with the proportions varying from social group to social group. Only one fifth of the intelligentsia exhibited such categorical hostility to "the system," while such global rejection was much more typical of the peasants, almost one third of whom said "keep nothing" or "change everything." As we have suggested above, such answers stem largely from the particular meaning which is attached to the concept of "the system." A separate analysis of this response[1] indicated that it cannot be taken literally, but rather that it largely reflects a generalized feeling of hostility toward the regime and "the system" identified with it. These people are reacting more to the words "Soviet system" than to the substance of the question. They do not reject all or even most Soviet institutions which a Westerner would regard as part of the Soviet system (see Table 57).

The Welfare State

There appears to be a deep-rooted expectation among Soviet citizens that their government and society will provide extensive social welfare benefits, including job security, universal education, medical care, and other securities and guarantees. This attitude is found in virtually all individuals with almost no variation from social group to social group.

TABLE 59 [1A]

PER CENT[a] SPONTANEOUSLY CITING CERTAIN FEATURES
OF SOVIET SYSTEM TO BE KEPT IF BOLSHEVIK
REGIME IS REPLACED: BY SOCIAL GROUP

Features to be kept	Intelli-gentsia	White-collar employees	Skilled workers	Ordinary workers	Collective farm peasants
Welfare features					
Education	66%	55%	52%	60%	53%
Public health	57	58	51	56	50
Workers' benefits	39	32	25	17	12
Institutional forms					
State ownership	22	13	13	8	12
Social equality	21	20	13	11	12
General accomplishments					
Technical development	20	6	11	13	11
Arts and science	11	10	6	8	4
Other	7	7	8	10	8
Total number of respondents	425	381	119	127	96

a. Because more than one feature could be cited, percentages total to more than 100.

In response to the question of what should be kept in the event the Bolshevik regime were replaced, our respondents gave far and away their strongest support to the system of public education and the socialized health services, with the special benefits for workers running a poor third (see Table 59). It is evident both from the quantitative data and the qualitative impressions gathered from the personal interviews that the refugees most favor those aspects of the Soviet system which cater to their desire for welfare benefits. Such institutions form the cornerstone of the type of society they would like to live in. Indeed, if we pool all the "votes" cast for any institution, three fourths were citations of welfare state features. The distinctive economic institutions, such as state ownership of the means of production, were cited much less often in all the social groups. Table 59 should, of course, not be taken to mean that only a small percentage of the former Soviet citizens support the idea of state ownership. On the contrary, we know from other questions (see Table 57) that the former Soviet citizen overwhelmingly supports government ownership and control of industry. The special role of Table 59, therefore, is not to suggest the absolute level of support for any institution, but rather its relative salience or importance in the spontaneous evaluation of Soviet institutions. The question was "open-ended" and people were left free to mention any institution they wished. In that sense, the welfare features of the state are clearly the most salient and perhaps important to the people.

TABLE 60 [1B]

MUNICH-NEW YORK DIFFERENCES IN OPINION CONCERNING
WHAT SOCIAL PROGRAMS SHOULD BE KEPT
IF THE BOLSHEVIKS WERE OVERTHROWN

Social group and place of interview	Per cent of respondents mentioning:			Total number of respondents
	Education	Health program	Workers' benefits	
Intelligentsia				
Munich	57%	49%	19%	(145)
New York	66%	60%	43%	(150)
White-collar employees				
Munich	50	44	29	(97)
New York	57	62	39	(117)
Skilled workers				
Munich	50	36	29	(14)
New York	52	61	35	(23)
Ordinary workers				
Munich	47	41	18	(17)
New York	70	78	39	(23)
Peasants				
Munich	25	25	13	(8)
New York	53	70	24	(17)
Total sample				
Munich	53%	45%	23%	(281)
New York	61%	63%	40%	(330)

As a capstone to our argument that Soviet refugees, and presumably the Soviet population as a whole, favor a welfare state, we present Table 60 in which responses of our larger European (Munich) sample are compared with those who had the experience of a year of life in the United States. We see here that refugees of all social groups respond to contact with American society with a renewed desire for the welfare provisions of Soviet society. In response to the query as to what should be kept of the present system in the Soviet Union, *every social group* among those interviewed in the United States (New York) was more favorably inclined than the "matched" Munich group toward *all three* social welfare features of Soviet society — the system of education, the health program and workers' benefits. Despite the small number of cases this trend persists in all nine of the comparisons in the manual groups, as well as in the nonmanual groups — where the case base is larger. If these welfare features were salient in the minds of our respondents when they discussed the Soviet system, they were virtually unanimously approved of when evaluated *in principle*. Table 61 shows the almost universal support given by persons from all social groups for a cradle-to-grave welfare program and government guarantee of work for all in an ideal society.

TABLE 61 [10]

ATTITUDES TOWARD THE GOVERNMENT'S ROLE IN WELFARE
ACTIVITIES IN AN IDEAL STATE: BY SOCIAL GROUP

Social group	Favors cradle-to-grave welfare program[a]		Favors government guarantee of work to all [b]	
			40 and under	41 and over
Intelligentsia	87%	(90) [c]	89% (319)	80% (264)
White-collar employees	90	(52)	92 (264)	82 (346)
Skilled workers	94	(30)	86 (154)	76 (91)
Ordinary workers	94	(52)	93 (253)	87 (176)
Collective farmers	90	(30)	85 (211)	83 (110)

a. From personal interviews.
b. From written questionnaires.
c. Total number of respondents on the basis of which the percentage is computed.

It is not enough for many respondents that the government works for the material well-being of its citizens. They believe that the government must also work for their cultural and even spiritual well-being. As one young woman, a student, put it: "The state must look after its citizens. It must give them opportunity. It is not enough merely to provide material security, it must secure the person. After all a person has a soul. It must make it possible for a person to live in cultural surroundings." Where the Soviet regime meets such expectations, its activities are approved. Probably no three accomplishments of the Soviet regime are so freely acknowledged as those in the field of education and literacy, cultural advancement, and access to medical facilities. The following quotations illustrate the nature of the feeling toward these features of Soviet life:

"The accessibility of education was the great 'plus' in the Soviet Union." "I value the Russian system of education very highly." "Medical assistance should be free. That is one of the few measures of the Soviet government that was extremely popular." "You must admit . . . the peasant reads better than before . . . There was no sanitorium in the old days. There was no medical assistance for the poor people at all . . . There is a great difference in the peasantry. Culture has really come to the village."

Even the peasants, the group most hostile in their attitude toward the Soviet order and the group which in fact was most deprived under the Soviets, show a surprising tendency to acknowledge the achievements of the regime in these areas (Table 62). Two thirds of the peasants said that access to medical facilities improved under the Soviets; 83 per cent said literacy was raised, and almost half (43 per cent) said that access to the theatre had improved — a rather impressive concession considering the fact that such improvements were very slow in reaching the countryside. As might be expected, going up the social ladder the percentages of members of other social groups granting these achievements of the regime increased. Nine out of ten of the intelligentsia said access to medical facilities had increased, 97 per cent said that literacy had improved, and 72 per cent said that there was better access to the theater under Bolshevik rule.

TABLE 62 [1D]

ACKNOWLEDGMENT OF SOVIET WELFARE ACHIEVEMENTS:
BY SOCIAL GROUP

Social group	Percentage acknowledging improvement under Soviet conditions in availability of:				Median number of respondents
	Medical care	Theatre and concerts	Agricultural machinery	Literacy	
Intelligentsia	90%	72%	96%	97%	(583)
White-collar employees	85	60	91	96	(612)
Skilled workers	82	53	87	96	(245)
Ordinary workers	69	42	78	90	(425)
Collective farmers	68	43	80	83	(315)

Our respondents indicated very strongly that in principle they favor a welfare society. Furthermore, they favored the welfare features of Soviet society relative to other aspects of Soviet life. But this does not imply by any means that they were enthusiastic about the way in which welfare policies were carried out in practice in the Soviet Union. The hollowness of the promises which the regime made in such areas was the source of much bitter complaint. In particular, the shortages of food, clothing, and housing, described in the chapter "Making a Living," made it difficult to accept the Soviet Union as an effective welfare state. On the contrary, it often seemed the home of want and deprivation. And even education and other welfare measures were more accessible "in principle" than in reality, as many a Soviet citizen found to his dismay.

In Germany, respondents were asked whether they preferred the Soviet system of medicine over the German one, or vice versa.[2] The response was two to one in favor of the German system of medicine. The German system was one of socialized medicine, very similar to that in the Soviet Union, except that the German facilities in doctors, medicine, and clinic and hospital accommodations were much better. Just to make it clear that this was not merely anti-Soviet feeling coming out we should point out that in the United States a comparable group of refugees were asked for their preference this time between the American and Soviet systems of medicine. The group chose two to one in favor of the *Soviet* medical system. Soviet refugees prefer socialized medicine, but they insist that it be fully implemented and carried out. They expect their government to provide this for them free of charge. As one engineer interviewed in New York said: "Between a doctor and a lawyer an average person in America is always broke. In the Soviet Union it is quite different. The poorest and the richest receive the same medical care."

We have already mentioned the extent to which the Soviet system of education was approved. Free, universal education was cited by 60 per cent of the persons who mentioned any aspect of the Soviet system that they would like to see kept. The oral interviews produced a considerable amount of approval for the Soviet schools. However, this approval was firmly tempered by disapproval of the intrusion of politics into education. When we questioned respondents on their attitudes toward Soviet education, we attempted to dissociate their dislike of the politicization of the Soviet schools from their feelings toward the way Soviet education was organized. We asked if they were in favor of the Soviet system of education, not what is taught, but the system itself; for example, the investment in school buildings, "Are you in favor of this or against this?"

Despite our efforts to focus their attention at this point on the organization of Soviet education rather than on its content, the inclusion of specific reference to the "Soviet" system of education apparently caused many persons to generalize their basic anti-Soviet sentiments to the Soviet school system. Yet fully 70 per cent approved of the Soviet system of education, with the reservations built into the question. Even this degree of verbal support seems low in light of the variety of evidence we have for our respondents' general approval of the Soviet system of free, universal education, and the relative support given for other institutions. Experience in pretesting our questions showed that the inclusion of the phrase "like in the Soviet Union" would reduce markedly the proportion of persons who approved of a given type of social institution or policy. Such institutions or policies might be favored in principle, but not as they were carried out by *Soviet* authority.

There is further support for our contention that there are many things about the Soviet "system" which would be approved in principle if they were not linked in our respondents' minds with other disagreeable features of Soviet life. Early in this chapter we showed that those persons who said "keep nothing" of the present system and those who said "keep something" were about equally likely to favor state control and ownership of many parts of the economy. We suggested, largely on the basis of staff studies of the meaning of the "keep nothing" response, that it represented more a generalized statement of hostility toward things Soviet than a genuine rejection of many of the institutional features which *we* would associate with the Soviet system. Therefore, it should not surprise us that when the wording of our question facilitated our respondents' association of a particular institution with the Soviet order, those persons who were most anti-Soviet would therefore be more likely to reject this institution. We find this to be true of reactions to the "Soviet" system of education. Those who said "keep nothing" of the present system were markedly more likely to disapprove the "Soviet" system of education. Among the intelligentsia, 39 per cent of those who said "keep nothing" were opposed to the Soviet system of education, as compared to only 9 per cent of those who cited some things as worth keeping. Comparable figures for the peasantry were 70 and 52 per cent, and the same pattern held among the other social groups.

Unsatisfactory experience with the Soviet welfare state seems then to have lowered the appeal of Soviet administration of such institutions, but has not much lowered the desire of the Soviet refugees for a welfare state society *in principle*. The high degree of support for welfare features of Soviet life, and approval of many other features when not identified specifically as "Soviet," should in itself be sufficient indication of this. What is conclusive demonstration, however, is that such attitudes seem to be equally characteristic of those portions of our sample which on a wide variety of criteria measure up as among the "most disaffected." One might have expected, for example, that the most "hostile" among our respondents would show considerably less enthusiasm for the welfare state. In practice this turns out not to be true, or to be true only to an insignificant extent. Even among those who said that "nothing" should be kept of the Soviet order, 85 per cent approved of a government which guaranteed job security. No important relation was found between support of the welfare state institutions and such strong correlates of hostility and disaffection as having been arrested or having fled the Soviet Union voluntarily.[3] *Those who experienced arrest and those who had no contact with it, those who were forcibly evacuated and those who fled the Soviet authority of their own volition were alike in high support for the principles of the welfare state.*

A variety of such findings convinced us that the desire to live in a welfare state is rooted in deep values of the Soviet citizen. We were also convinced that a welfare system which did not fulfill its promises would generate resentment. In establishing a society which purported to be based on welfare principles, the Soviet regime appealed to fundamental attitudes of the Soviet citizenry. In doing so, however, they also raised expectations which were frustrated by the failure of the Soviet regime to implement these promises effectively. One might therefore expect disillusionment with the principle of the welfare state. But strange as it may seem, the Soviet leadership seems to have strengthened belief in the principle's desirability even while engendering hostility toward itself for not carrying it out. Continued frustration of these expectations will produce continued resentment among the populace. However, it must be recognized that if the regime is able to deliver such welfare benefits as the people expect they will tap a strong reservoir of favorable popular sentiment.

Economic Institutions and Policies

To say that the Soviet citizen prefers a society that offers him extensive social welfare benefits is to open up as many questions as it answers. If this is what he wants, then what sorts of economic and political institutions does he consider as necessary for attaining this goal? What other considerations make up his image of an ideal society? What is his priority of goals, or — in other words — what price is he willing to pay in order to have a welfare state?

Apparently Soviet refugees are convinced that the welfare state which they desire cannot be achieved under a free enterprise capitalist economy. Approximately two thirds of each social group favored under "ideal conditions" state planning as well as ownership of the economy. In the course of the personal interviews 191 respondents outlined the form of economic system which they preferred. Of these only 14 per cent favored an essentially "capitalist" system. Four out of five indicated a preference for some sort of socialized economy, although only a small portion of this group (4 per cent) wanted state control as all pervasive as that in the Soviet Union. The opinions of the members of the various social groups are summarized in Table 63. Despite the small number of persons in some of the groups, they show rather strong agreement on this question.

TABLE 63 [3A]

PREFERRED MODE OF ECONOMIC ORGANIZATION:
BY SOCIAL GROUP

Mode of economic organization	Intelligentsia	White-collar employees	Skilled workers	Ordinary workers	Collective farm peasants
Soviet Communism	7%	2%	0%	0%	0%
Basic socialist economy as in the NEP period	75	86	81	69	80
Capitalism	12	5	19	28	20
Other	6	7	0	3	0
Total number of respondents[a]	77	41	21	35	10

a. From personal interviews.

Support of state ownership was strongest in the basic areas of the economy, such as heavy industry and the system of transport and communication. In response to a direct question, state ownership and control of transportation and communications was favored by 87 per cent of those who had an opinion on this topic. The percentages were virtually identical in each social group. State control of heavy industry such as coal and steel was favored by an equally high number, 85 per cent, and the various social classes were again in complete agreement. This virtual unanimity in support of state ownership and control of the basic economy is made more impressive in the light of two additional facts. This was not a question on which our respondents seem to have had any appreciable doubts, since fewer than five per cent of the total sample failed to offer an opinion on any of the direct questions bearing on this issue. Furthermore, a year's experience of living in a free enterprise society did not alter their opinions. Those respondents interviewed in the United States and those interviewed in Europe gave replies to these questions which were almost identical.

However, it does not seem that state ownership and control is regarded as a goal in itself. It is more likely that our refugee respondents thought of it as a way to achieve the welfare state which they desired. There are two things which point in that direction. The first is the fact that economic institutions were considerably less salient as features "to be kept" of the present system. A glance back at Table 59 shows that on this more indirect "write-in" question, economic institutions received conspicuously fewer votes than did the welfare features of the system. The second indication that economic forms are not considered goals in themselves is revealed in the attitudes of our respondents toward the collective farm system and toward light industry.

The collective farm is one instance of a government controlled economic institution that consistently violated rather than helped the welfare of the citizenry. As a result, nothing approaches the directness, simplicity, and pervasiveness of hostility toward the collective farm system. Only 2 per cent of the sample had no opinion on this subject. All groups without distinction and virtually unanimously wanted it eliminated. On a direct question, nine tenths of the entire sample said flatly that the *kolkhoz* should be abolished and all the land distributed.* Some small groups suggested variations on this policy, including the distribution of part of the land, or leaving the decision in the hands of the peasants. Less than 2 per cent thought the present system of agriculture should be maintained, and they added the qualification that this should be done only if the collective farms were administered for the benefit of the people who work on them.

It is no surprise, therefore, to find in Table 64 that among the features of the system to be changed the collective farm was cited first by four classes and ran a strong second in the intelligentsia.** This opposition to the collective farm system stems not only from the abuses experienced in connection with the operation of the collective farms in the Soviet Union, but equally from a general feeling that this institution constitutes an unwarranted intrusion upon the personal freedom of the peasant. It would be erroneous to infer that our respondents were unconcerned with the problem of personal initiative in the economic sphere merely because they advocated a *basically* socialist economy. The peasants were vigorous in complaining that they were not able to dispose of their time as they wished, that the entire work of the *kolkhoz* was dictated from above, and that they were not rewarded in proportion to their efforts. On the oral interview the overwhelmingly predominant reason for opposing the col-

* This did not, however, equally apply to agricultural machinery. Our coded interview data revealed that either government, or more often cooperative, ownership of farm machinery was favored by twice as many as favored private, individual ownership.

** Again we must caution against use of this type of table for any purpose other than assessing the relative salience of particular institutions as against the absolute levels of support or opposition to them. As we have already noted, the proportion voting against the collective farms on a direct question was much higher than the proportion *spontaneously* citing it as an institution to be changed. Similarly it is obvious that more than 50 to 60 per cent of our respondents were against terror and the absolutist acts of the Soviet state.

lectives was that they conflicted with man's natural inclination to work better and be happier on his own land, and the other major reason given was the stringency and harshness of collective farm life. It is interesting to note that demands for improvement in labor conditions account consistently for half or less the number of demands for a change in the collective farm system, even among the workers. This both suggests the pervasiveness of the opposition to the collective farms and the comparatively easier situation of the workers.

TABLE 64 [3B]

PER CENT [a] SPONTANEOUSLY CITING CERTAIN FEATURES TO BE CHANGED IF BOLSHEVIK REGIME REPLACED: BY SOCIAL GROUP

Features to be changed	Intelligentsia	White-collar employees	Skilled workers	Ordinary workers	Collective farm peasants
Collective farm system	58%	55%	50%	56%	60%
"Absolutist" state organization	47	41	39	30	25
Terror and injustice	67	52	33	26	27
Absence of private initiative	28	22	12	11	13
Labor conditions	25	22	20	12	9
"Communism" and Bolshevik ideology	18	15	12	24	33
Total number of respondents	312	311	119	178	121

a. Because more than one feature could be cited, percentages total to more than 100.

Our respondents' attitudes toward state ownership of light industry reflected the desire for a certain amount of personal initiative in economic activities. On this issue there were marked class differences in opinion, a pattern which is quite contrary to that found in attitudes on most social welfare issues. The number favoring government ownership and control fell from 52 per cent among the peasants to a mere 24 per cent in the intelligentsia. The interpretation we place on this is that the prospect of individual ownership of light industry, such as the manufacture of shoes and textiles, had more immediate meaning for the upper classes. It was realistic for them to think of running such industry privately themselves, and therefore the possibility of exercising initiative in such an area had greater attraction for them.

An interesting feature of our respondents' attitudes toward state ownership of light industry is that this is the one opinion on economic matters that was markedly influenced by life in the United States. Among the respondents interviewed in this country there was about a 25 per cent shift toward greater opposition to state ownership of light industry. The shift was least among the intelligentsia who were already most opposed to state ownership; the number opposing state ownership was by 12 per cent greater among those interviewed in this country. The gain in opposition sentiment was greatest in the peasant group, the difference in the two figures being 36 per cent. Obviously, contact with our economic system showed that privately owned light industry can provide a high standard of living. This wiped out many of the remaining doubts about liberating this sector of the economy from state control. We must remember, however, that contact with the American economy did not shake their faith in a basically socialized economic system, nor in social welfare plans such as socialized medicine.

The economic system to which Soviet citizens appear to aspire can best be described as "NEPism" (see Table 63). Only about one in ten of our respondents indicated in the personal interview that they regarded the period of the NEP as anything but good. The period of the NEP or New Economic Policy, from 1921 to 1928, not only seems to furnish the model for the type of economy our respondents wanted, but was itself looked back on as a kind of golden age of Soviet development, as will be evident from the following remarks made by people in all walks of life:

"The standard of living of the workers and peasants at that time, that is during the period of the NEP, was higher than in any other country of the world at that time." "People nowhere suffer as much as in Soviet Russia. We lived poorly before the revolution; only under the NEP was it easier." "It was good under the NEP." "It was the period of the NEP, and things were good." "During the NEP, therefore, life was better than even under the tsarist regime. You could buy everything you wanted, and there was no unemployment." "Yes, life under the NEP was free. It could be compared with the old times. . . ."

Political Institutions and Policies

The Soviet citizen's desire for a welfare state as reflected in the refugee data is modified by his personal desire for greater autonomy. We faced them with the rather stark question as to whether they would prefer a government which guarantees freedom but does not assure them of a job, or one which guaranteed a decent standard of living but not personal rights. Between 80 and 90 per cent in each social group chose the government which guarantees personal rights. If we were to state in a single sentence the political forms and policies which the Soviet citizen, as represented by our refugee respondents, would favor, it would be this: A paternalistic state, with extremely wide powers which it vigorously exercised to guide and control the nation's destiny, but which yet served the interests of the citizen benignly, which respected his personal dignity and left him with a certain amount of individual freedom of desire and a feeling of security from *arbitrary* interference and punishment.

In Table 64 we see that "absolutist" state organization and "terror and injustice" are rather consistently second and third among the worse features of the system in the opinion of our respondents. Indeed, absolutism and terror blend into each other and can best be summed up in the term "absolutist terror." This "absolutist terror" is the focal point of hostility toward political features of the Soviet system. Which aspect of absolutism in the system was more resented varied with the individual. Some gave more stress to the political terrorism represented in arrests and other activities of the secret police. Others gave primary emphasis to the absolute hegemony of the Communist Party, and the arbitrary way in which decisions were arrived at. In these comments there was less emphasis on the importance of strict legality and political freedom *per se,* more on the absence of moral justice and personal freedom, and on violation of the public welfare. Taken together these two categories accounted for almost 45 per cent of the total number of "votes" cast against particular Soviet institutions, and on this basis we can say that the "absolutist terror" was far and away the prime institutional feature of Soviet society which its citizens wanted eliminated.

Former Soviet citizens showed a fairly marked and uniform propensity to declare themselves in principle in favor of civil liberties, such as freedom of the press, assembly and religion. However, when they were faced with specific conditions or concrete situations, a good deal of the support for civil liberties melted away in favor of varying degrees of government control and intervention. Less than half the respondents felt that the government had no right to intervene in an assembly if the purpose of the assembly is to "attack" the government. Only about a third believed people should be permitted to say things against the government. Sentiment in favor of civil liberties was weakest among the lower classes. Of course, former Soviet citizens are not unique in this respect. Indeed, studies in the United States show quite comparable proportions of the American public voting for restrictions on civil liberties. A Roper survey before World War II revealed that 44 per cent of the American public advocated restrictions on the freedom of speech with respect to time, subject, and group. In 1954, only 58 per cent would have allowed a man to make a speech in their community advocating government ownership of railroads and big industry, and only 37 per cent would have permitted it if the talk was against churches and religion.[4]

The data in Table 65 might be subject to serious questioning because of imperfections in the wording of certain of the questions,[5] but the

TABLE 65 [4A]

VIEWS OF FREEDOM OF SPEECH, ASSEMBLY, AND PRESS:
BY SOCIAL GROUP

Social group	Per cent favoring various limitations on freedom of:					
	Speech		Assembly		Press[a]	
Intelligentsia	57%	(624) [b]	49%	(608)	57%	(92)
White-collar employees	67	(668)	52	(644)	57	(51)
Skilled workers	63	(268)	57	(261)	59	(32)
Ordinary workers	64	(465)	62	(438)	44	(50)
Collective farmers	60	(351)	63	(328)	58	(24)

a. From personal interviews.
b. Total number of respondents on the basis of which the percentage is computed.

general direction of sentiment which they indicate is also supported by the qualitative data of the life history interviews. It is characteristic of our respondents that after insisting that the press be free, they would qualify their remarks in a manner similar to this statement by a lawyer and former officer in the White armies:

> The government must make an effort to raise the level of the press so that the press will educate the people of the state. If the press, for example, publishes nothing but humorous stories, it will not be good for the people . . . the state should publish literature which would accomplish its aims. For example, if there are many thieves in the country, the state must publish literature which will re-educate them, show them that they are harming the state. Or if the people are amoral, the state must publish literature to raise the morals of the citizens.

Soviet refugees and presumably Soviet citizens do not, of course, value government control as an end in itself, but mainly because they see it as the natural way to facilitate both group and private interest. In general they seem not to have the reputed American tendency to see "government interference" as bad *per se*. Again, the Soviet refugees' reaction to life in the United States gives a clue to the strength of this feeling. After a year or more of residence in the United States they were delighted with their *personal* freedom, their ability to move about unimpeded, to shift jobs at will, to feel secure from arrest or arbitrary government action. However, the freedom of dissident groups in America to criticize the government disturbed many of them. Contact with refugees in this country quickly brings to attention the persistent difficulty many of them have in accepting naturally the rather sweeping nature of our traditional rights of freedom of press and assembly. A good indication of the depth of this feeling is the fact that, in comparison with respondents interviewed in Europe, 18 per cent *more* of the respondents interviewed in this country were opposed to unlimited free speech.

Not only did Soviet refugees react negatively to our tolerance for expression of deviant opinions, but they were disturbed that the American government does not do more to direct the activities of its citizens *for their own good*. They objected to the laxity of American authorities in not exercising more control over the routine behavior of the public. Typical was this complaint about the lack of regulation in a New York hospital in which a refugee's wife had been confined:

Another thing, I came to visit my wife after a long ride through dirt and grime of the New York subways. Nevertheless, I was shown to my wife's bedside just as I was, in my overcoat. In the USSR I would have changed my outer clothing for a hospital gown. Also, there is no control whatsoever as to what visitors might bring to the patient.

Other respondents, while complaining about the interference of the Soviet government in the reading material available to Soviet children, thought that Americans went too far in the other direction. Thus, a fifty-nine-year-old professor of engineering said: "On the other hand, when I arrived in America, I thanked God that we did not have the demoralizing comic strips, the cheap vulgar literature that is available to children here." And an engineer-mechanic of thirty-nine complained: "In America youth is allowed to attend all kinds of films which make it sexually premature." Similar remarks are, of course, made by many Americans. It is our impression, however, that the strength and frequency of such remarks was greater among Soviet refugees. But, it is perhaps more germane to the main issue that contact with the Soviet totalitarian government did not produce an extreme counterswing toward espousal of a completely liberal or individualistic orientation.

When Soviet refugees complain about lack of freedom in the Soviet Union, they are mainly referring to personal freedom to talk openly with one's friends, to be able to move about and conduct one's own affairs as he will, not having to fear arbitrary action from the government. When opinions were volunteered on this subject, there was almost complete unanimity among our subjects in espousing freedom of job choice and freedom of movement from place to place. The Soviet citizen feels that the government should stay out of what is essentially a man's "private" affairs, particularly his home, his friendship and family relations, his church, his clubs and cliques, and such organizations as unions and professional societies. The government is expected to help in such areas, but not to control.

There is an obvious conflict in simultaneously wanting the government to "help" but not to "interfere." But the Soviet citizen does not seem to seek the resolution of this conflict in a formalized system of checks and balances, or in constitutional limitations on the powers of the government so much as in the good intentions and wisdom of the men who run it. This is reflected not only in his attitudes toward the Soviet leadership, but in his general approach to questions of legality and morality.[6] He is more concerned with seeing that justice is done and good relations maintained than with strict observance of legal procedure of the enforcement of legal norms. Moral considerations not infrequently take precedence over legal distinctions. As one young man, a student, put it: "One stealing from a hundred wealthy can do no harm, if by this he helps starving persons. It is not wrong in the usual sense of the word." And an electrical technician said: "We have to make some compromise between the law and reality." When respondents were presented with the legend of St. Krispin, who stole from the rich in order to help the poor, only one person in five condemned this action as "illegal." Many disapproved of the action, but the majority of them did so on other than "legal" grounds; they did not condemn it because "stealing is wrong" *per se.*

The same conceptions apparently apply to the government. By implication — and in contrast to at least the formal values of Anglo-Saxon society — the government may do almost anything, and be approved for doing it, *so long as the action is in the public interest.* It makes little difference if in this process the government may exceed its formal legal or constitutional powers. In the political sphere, the basic expectation of the Soviet citizen is an analogue of that in the economic realm. A strong central government is assumed as giving the nation direction and purpose, as providing the stimulus for improvement and advancement, and as facilitating the economic features of the welfare state which are so strongly desired. Such a government must have the characteristics of a just and benevolent father. It may be autocratic, indeed it is almost expected to be, but it should not be sternly authoritarian and certainly not totalitarian. This idea was rather strikingly expressed by a young chauffeur who had been a Komsomol member: "The state can do anything. Without a government you cannot exist. On the contrary if you love the government you will do as it wishes."

The government must look after the needs of the people and nurture them, but it must also see to it that basic values are preserved, that morality is maintained, and malfactors, "enemies" of the common good, are punished. From our qualitative materials we judge that in the view of our respondents, if the government has these characteristics, it should be honored, obeyed, loved and respected. The test of the right to govern lies in the interest of the people as they themselves define their interest. Such a government is "good," and by definition a "legal and just" government, and one need not bother too much about fine points of law, or the observance of fixed rules and regulations. On the other hand, if the government is harsh, arbitrary, disinterested in public welfare, then it loses its right to govern *no matter how legal its position,* and no matter how close its observance of the letter of the law.

The former Soviet citizens felt that government should, of course, be representative (and preferably elective) but largely in the sense indicated above. For the majority, if the government was "good," that is, paternal, nurturant, friendly and helpful, then political parties and factions were felt to have little special place or meaning. This despite the fact that the majority also felt that the government's right to govern should be periodically affirmed by the ballot. But even such an approved government was expected to operate within limits, to restrict itself to fostering the welfare of the citizen and to punishing only those who transgress against the morality of the people in such areas as religion or the press. It may not invade the privacy of the home, it should not restrict a man's movement from job to job, and place to place, or his right to associate freely with others and express normal free opinion and disagreement. If it does so, it is perceived as having broken the bond which ties citizen and regime, and the citizen feels legitimately free to adopt an attitude of noncooperation and to treat his government as alien or illegitimate.

Attitudes Toward the Regime

It was perhaps reasonable to extrapolate from our sample to the Soviet population when we found strong support of the welfare state and of a basic socialist economy, since in these instances our refugee sample — presumably anti-Soviet in its bias — was strongly in favor of these aspects of the system. Hatred of the collective farm system was so universal and so intense, and conforms so closely with what can be readily inferred from official Soviet statements, that again we could be confident that such feelings were also strong in the Soviet population. These attitudes appear to be very firmly anchored in basic values which probably characterize the Soviet population as a whole. When we talk about the attitudes of our respondents toward the Soviet leadership, however, we must be especially aware of the fact that we are dealing with a relatively disaffected, predominantly anti-Soviet group, and must exercise more caution before extrapolating from our refugee data to the parent population. Nevertheless, these refugee data permit us to make some important inferences to the attitudes of the Soviet population itself.

Among the refugees, attitudes toward the leaders and their agents are not only generally unfavorable but also are relatively more unselective and undiscriminating than is the case with attitudes toward particular

Soviet institutions. Even Lenin, who is associated with the generally well regarded NEP period, was regarded by about three fourths in each of the social groups as having been basically harmful to the Soviet people (see Table 66). Between one and two thirds in each social group advocated death for the Soviet leaders if they were overthrown. This figure is even more impressive than it seems at first glance. A sizeable group of respondents, particularly those who had experienced political arrest, announced that "death is too good" for the leaders. They advocated imprisonment because they regarded it as *worse* than death. Similarly, when the harmfulness of various social groups is assessed, about 90 per cent of all respondents, regardless of their own position, say it was the Communist Party members who did the most harm to other groups in Soviet society.

TABLE 66 [6A]

PER CENT OF SOCIAL GROUPS EXPRESSING
VARIOUS HOSTILE ATTITUDES TOWARD THE REGIME

Social group	Lenin did much harm	Bolshevik leaders should be put to death	Bolsheviks worse than Nazis	Median number of respondents
Intelligentsia	74%	39%	70%	(622)
White-collar employees	78	46	68	(665)
Skilled workers	70	47	60	(268)
Ordinary workers	73	54	51	(458)
Collective farmers	72	60	44	(348)

These figures may have little meaning by themselves. They are "about what you'd expect of a group of hostile refugees." However, it must be remembered that many of the responses from this same group of refugees presented earlier in this chapter were *not* what would be expected of a refugee group. Hence, we must conclude that the hostility of the refugees is focused predominantly on the leadership and their agents, such as party officials, rather than on the whole system of social institutions which the Bolsheviks introduced — strongly excepting, of course, particular institutions such as the terror and the collective farm. As one respondent put it: "The *system* would not have been so bad. It depends on how the system is carried out. It depends on who 'is in control.' " Hostility is directed against the regime primarily as it is symbolized by its formal leaders, by the top men of the Communist Party and the secret police, and only to a much lesser degree as it is symbolized by the rank-and-file membership of those bodies.*

It is little wonder that the party regime should become the focus of both loyalty and alienation since it is so persistent in defining itself as the prime mover of everything that happens in Soviet society. The impression that for good or ill the leadership was responsible for all that happened was created by such slogans as "the leading role in the party," and the excessive adulation of Stalin, in his time, with such phrases as "genius" and "inspiring leader." While our data show only that a disaffected group places the blame for the failures of the system predominantly on the men who run it, we may perhaps assume that the converse is also true, namely that those who *approve* of the existing state of affairs give the *leadership,* and not merely the system, credit for what has been done.

As always, having made these statements, we must qualify them. It is only in a special sense that it is correct to say that disaffection is from the regime, not from the system. It will be remembered that a sizeable proportion of our sample said they would keep nothing and would change everything of the present *system.* Particularly among the lower classes there was a tendency to project general hostility onto everything to which the term "Soviet" was attached. The proportion of persons in the lower classes who said "keep nothing" or "change everything" was almost twice that in the upper (Table 58 above). Yet, with respect to particular features of the system, the lower classes were no more, in fact were somewhat less, anti-Soviet than the upper classes. They were, for example, more in favor of state ownership of light industry and less critical of governmental forms in Soviet society.

There is additional evidence in the life history interviews in support of our view that "alienation is from the regime rather than from the system." When respondents were asked if they thought conditions in the Soviet Union would have become better or worse if someone other than Stalin had come to power, 42 per cent replied that things would have been *better.* A smaller group, 34 per cent, said they would have been the same. A still smaller number, 24 per cent, gave qualified answers to the effect that things might have been better in some periods of time or in certain ways, but by and large would have been the same. Thus, at least 40 per cent viewed the unfortunate state of affairs in the Soviet Union as the responsibility of a particular leader or type of leadership. When we consider that many who thought conditions would have remained the same concluded this because they felt *all* the available leaders

* In contrast to their reaction toward party *officials,* our respondents were careful to make precise distinctions with regard to the relative capability of different kinds of ordinary party members. See the section of Chapter XIV, "The People, The Party and Political Cleavage."

were bad, and take into account the 24 per cent who have qualified answers, it would seem that a substantial majority of our respondents thought the blame for things lay more with the leadership than with the system. Again we must note that people meant different things by "the system." But allowing for the sliding definition of the system, it still seems the case that they were less alienated from it than from the leaders.

It is of crucial importance that the trends and patterns we have been describing are increasing in strength over time. In general, the picture we have been painting in this chapter is a conservative one as concerns the potential strength of the system. The younger people react more affirmatively to the "positive" aspects and less violently to the negative aspects. Alice Rossi, in her study of the generational differences among our respondents, found that the younger people were more inclined to favor the institutional structure of Soviet society — state ownership, control, and planning and welfare institutions. Even though they are overwhelmingly opposed to the collective farms, they are not as firmly and unanimously against the kolkhoz system as in the older generation.[7] Furthermore, they are more likely to say that things would have been better if the leadership had been different. The figures presented in Table 67 are from the oral interviews. Since the number of cases is rather small, it is impressive to note the strength of the trends, particularly among those in the manual classes.

TABLE 67 [7A]

PERCENTAGE SAYING SOVIET UNION WOULD HAVE BEEN BETTER
IF THERE HAD BEEN DIFFERENT LEADERSHIP:[a]
BY SOCIAL GROUP AND AGE

| | Social group | | | |
Age in 1950	Intelligentsia and white-collar		Workers and collective farmers	
Under 36	49%	(43) [b]	55%	(44)
36–45	35	(46)	44	(25)
Over 45	32	(54)	27	(26)

a. From personal interviews.
b. Total number of respondents on the basis of which the percentage is computed.

All in all, the evidence available shows not only that discontent and alienation are focused selectively on the leadership rather than on the full range of Soviet institutions, but that this pattern is becoming progressively stronger in the younger generation.

XI

Sources of Hostility and Disaffection[1]

The underlying theme of many previous chapters has been the struggle between the interests and intent of the regime and the interests and intent of the individual citizen. Even in the finest and most democratic of societies there is some conflict between personal interest and the requirements of the government. But these conflicts take on a peculiar intensity and become much more prevailing in a totalitarian society in which the leaders are attempting to direct the efforts of all the citizens toward goals many of which are not accepted by the rank and file, yet can be pursued only through great sacrifice on their part. The role of the individual in Soviet society, and the nature of the relationship of the citizen to the system, therefore, takes as its point of departure certain essential and distinctive aspects of the Soviet system. Other totalitarian societies have discriminated against subgroups, but the Soviet Union is distinguished by the extreme demands which the regime places on even its loyal supporters. As one young woman, an office worker, succinctly put it: "Though Hitler was bad to other people, he was good to his own people. The Germans say they liked living under Hitler. Our government was bad, not only to other people, but to its own." No society, no ruling clique, cherishes discontent and disaffection for its own sake. The persistence of such sentiments over a period of time implies incapacity to relieve sources of dissatisfaction, a priority of goals which prevents an end to certain dissatisfaction, or operating conceptions of social control which favor measures other than the release of tension. Throughout most of Soviet history the Stalinist program and code for social and economic change created discontent and prevented its reduction.

The forced draft expansion of heavy industry and armaments production which the program demanded, was effected directly at the expense of the standard of living, the peace and personal security of the Soviet citizen. The Stalinist notion of how to effect social change was based on a direct assault on goals with only a secondary consideration of cost and consequences. It involved running roughshod over individuals and groups which stood in the way, and exacted a maximum of exertion out of the Soviet citizen. This produced many of the special deprivations of Soviet life which we have already met: a frenzied pace of life, which was called the "tempo"; extreme physical exertion and hardship; scarcity of food and shortage of clothing; deterioration and frightful overcrowding of housing; forced population movements and disruption of family life. These developments in their turn produced the alienation of groups injured in the process of social change; deprivation and discontent among loyal citizens who paid the cost (along with those discriminated against) of rapid social change and economic expansion; and pressure toward illicit behavior, such as theft of state property to alleviate low living standards and illegal procedures for meeting one's responsibilities.

Such policies could, of course, be continued only in a totalitarian state in which the leaders had the disposition to use ruthlessly the instruments of coercion available to them. The methods of a totalitarian society for the control of disaffection in turn increase discontent and disloyalty. Direct control over all major institutions of society makes it possible to subordinate the interests of the citizen to those of the state and this lies behind the difficult life conditions which the regime imposes on its subjects. The citizen's effort to defend his interest by "cheating" the system is met by intensified controls and punishments from the regime. These very methods used to control disaffection — arrests, intense spying, an all-pervasive distrust, bombardment with propaganda — then become additional irritants to those who are not loyal, and on occasion turn the loyal citizen from the regime.

Beginning with the First Five Year Plan the interests of the individual citizen were made clearly and unequivocally secondary to the overall goal of industrial and military development. But to say that the interests of the individual in Soviet society are placed second to and far below the interests of the state should not lead us to assume that the regime is not "concerned" about the individual. The very nature of the Soviet system makes this body of citizens, collectively, the key resource of the regime, and thereby a matter of great concern. Under the conditions of overcommitment of resources which characterized Soviet policy for many decades, the mass of its subjects was treated by the regime as the most flexible of its resources. Economy and efficiency in the handling of physical resources such as coal, machine tools, or agricultural produce, can be effected only up to a certain point; there is some clear physical limitation on the extent to which such resources can be stretched. There is, however, no clearly known limitation on the degree to which the human contribution to the social effort can be stretched, either by evoking greater exertion from the citizen, or by bringing about an increase in his skills and abilities. It can be said with only slight exaggeration that the tendency of the regime has been to treat people as *the* flexible resource in the system. To maximize the yield from this resource the regime worked from both ends at once — using the classic carrot and stick technique. On the one hand through propaganda, education, and lavish rewards it sought to *enlist* the enthusiastic *support* of the population. At the same time through violence and threats of violence it has sought to *compel* the *obedience* of those it could not entice or enlist.

While seeking to enlist voluntary and enthusiastic support when possible, the Soviet regime has recognized that at the price it was asking people to pay for Soviet development, the maximum yield from most people could be exacted only by strict control and strong pressure. If anything had to give, it was to be the citizen, not the system. Rather consistently the regime refused to reduce commitments, to cut back its goals except under extreme pressure (such perhaps as existed following the death of Stalin), or basically to alter the institutions it had established. The regime held that all goals were attainable, that existing institutions were adequate, and it therefore was up to individuals to attain the prescribed goals within the framework of existing institutions. Goals and institutions were revised only after every effort had been made to accomplish a given task by exerting greater pressure on the individual citizen. One of the salient features of the operation of all Soviet institutions is the extent of the demands and responsibility placed on the individual — the extent to which, with a minimum of assistances, resources, authority, and information, he is expected to accomplish a task without fail. While he is in general expected to follow correct procedures, his failure to deliver the goods is almost invariably considered to be a worse offense than violation of correct procedures.

The official formulation of the relationship of the individual to the state has been given an appearance of spurious continuity by adroit verbal manipulation. Throughout the history of the Soviet Union the regime stressed the harmony, in a socialist society, between the needs of the individual and the needs of the state. In the early period, for approximately the first decade after the revolution, the meaning of this statement was that a social order would be developed to serve the needs and interests of the individual citizen. Since the inauguration of the First Five Year Plan, however, it has come to mean that a type of citizen will be developed who serves the needs and interests of the state.[2] This goal is achieved, or at least pursued, through elaborate concern for character training and social control. The regime is not *indifferent* to the welfare of its citizens. In fact it makes a great show of concern for their welfare. But this concern has been dictated almost exclusively by the relevance of their welfare to the functioning of the system and the accomplishment of the long-range goals of the regime. The leaders have gone as far as they can in pressing armament programs, industrialization, the collectivization of agriculture. These things come first and goals are not cut back out of consideration of the welfare of the citizen so long as the morale of the people does not become so low as to threaten these programs.

It has been characteristic of the regime's policy that very little margin of safety is allowed in calculating the allocation of any resource, since such a margin of safety represents a potential increase in productivity. The natural result is that quite regularly resources are overcommitted. This happens with the individual citizen as surely as it does with physical resources. Consequently, in many sectors of Soviet society and at regular intervals the strain on the citizen exceeds the "optimum" point (from the regime's viewpoint), and morale drops to such an extent that other objectives must be curtailed in order to restore morale. Such a condition apparently obtained in the post-Stalin period. But it should be reaffirmed that — unless there has been a far more drastic shift of general attitude than we have any reason to believe — concessions to the populace are intended to increase the individual's effectiveness as a contributor to the state, not to maximize his freedom or well-being as an individual. In the foreseeable future, concessions for that purpose will not be made, at least insofar as such concessions conflict with the program of maximal industrial expansion.

Our findings on political loyalty have prime reference to the conditions of Soviet life under Stalin. At least some features of that period, particularly the mass terror, seem greatly muted in the post-Stalin era. Others, such as the tendency to overcommit resources and to hold the individual responsible for failings which really inhere in the system, seem to continue. In the conclusions to this part of our book,* and again in the concluding chapter we will seek to assess the significance of the post-Stalin developments for the problem of loyalty. But if any projection into the future is to rest on a solid foundation, it must be based on a fuller understanding of the political meaning of daily life experience as it was lived in the era of Stalin's rule out of which the future will grow. To that end we present in this chapter an analysis of some of the consequences of Soviet reality under Stalin as it impinged on the citizen and generated hostility and even disaffection.

Hostility and Conditions of Daily Life

The difficult living conditions in Soviet society not only produced momentary situational dissatisfaction, but also affect the degree of hostility which individuals feel toward the Soviet order in general. Our respondents indicated dissatisfaction with many of the conditions of life which we discussed in preceding chapters. Our knowledge of Soviet so-

* See the last section of Chapter XII, "The New Line."

ciety makes it clear that these complaints are based not on imaginary but rather on very real and pervasive deficiencies in the working of the Soviet system. A reasonable, but not inescapable conclusion is that dissatisfaction would be generalized to the society in which it was experienced. To test whether this was in fact true, we studied the interrelationship of the various conditions of life experienced by our respondents and the extent of hostility they felt toward the Soviet system. The establishment of such interrelationships does not, of course, automatically demonstrate the direction or even the existence of causation. For the moment, however, we shall describe some illustrative correlations *as though* the attitudes of our respondents toward the Soviet order were determined by their life conditions, rather than assume that cause operated in the opposite direction, or that both are a result of some third condition. As we go along we shall indicate our reasons for this assumption.

There were in our data several criteria of hostility toward the Soviet system. To begin, a number of direct expressions of attitude toward the Soviet system, its leaders, and some of its institutions were elicited. These are summarized in an index of "Anti-Soviet Sentiment." Another direct measure of the individual's attitude toward the Soviet order which can be used is his statement of whether or not he was sufficiently dissatisfied to want to leave the Soviet Union in the years immediately preceding his actual departure. The presence of hostility could also be assessed through the more indirect measure provided by the "distortion" index, discussed in some detail in Chapter III in connection with problems of methods and methodology. The use of any one of the measures of hostility which assess its degree largely by what the person says he felt about the regime rather than by what he *did* about it leads to the same conclusions. Our main concern here is not with the subtle differences in the sensitivity of one or another measure of hostility, but rather in the effect of different kinds of experience on hostility. We have therefore decided to simplify our analysis by concentrating on only one of the "verbal" measures of hostility, namely, the "distortion" index. We feel this procedure to be justified because the pattern of association between the distortion index and the important variables dealt with in this chapter was basically the same as that obtained when other measures of hostility were used.[3] We chose it rather than any other because for various technical reasons it proved to be the least ambiguous and most reliable of our measures of verbal hostility.[4]

On the basis of this index we may identify three gorups: approximately half whose pattern of response suggests that for all practical purposes they showed no active hostility to the Soviet system; an intermediate group who distorted on one of the items deemed especially sensitive to distortion; and a third group of those most hostile, including approximately one fifth of the sample who distorted on two or more items.* For most of the analysis in this chapter we used an even simpler division by combining the "intermediate" and "most" hostile into a single category of the "hostile," and contrasting them with those showing least hostility on the index. Obviously all of our respondents, even those who distorted on not a single item, must be assumed to have some hostility to the Soviet order, as evidenced by their status as refugees. And there is apparently a substantial difference in the *intensity* of hostility felt by those who distorted only one as against those who distorted all four items of information. Because the number of cases we have is limited, and our analysis often complex, however, we adopt the simple dichotomy of those showing "some hostility" and "no hostility." It will be seen that even this crude measure can be quite revealing.

When measured on the index of distortion, hostility, as might be expected, is closely related to the individual's life experience. The most hostile people come from social groups having the most disadvantaged life situation. Table 68 shows that hostility is strongly correlated with social group membership. For example, the proportion of persons who express more marked hostility rises from 12 per cent among the intelligentsia to 36 per cent among the peasants. Hostility is also independently related to age. The relationship is not strong, especially if class is held constant, but at each class level there is somewhat more hostility among those over forty than among those who were younger. In the following analysis of hostility we have therefore controlled throughout for class but generally not for age.

TABLE 68 [4A]

DEGREE OF HOSTILITY TO THE SOVIET SYSTEM:
ACCORDING TO SOCIAL GROUP

Degree of hostility	Intelligentsia	White-collar employees	Skilled workers	Ordinary workers	Collective farm peasants
Least	71%	59%	54%	42%	40%
Medium	17	25	26	24	24
Most	12	16	20	34	36
Total number of respondents	567	607	243	410	312

The differences in levels of day-to-day satisfaction which we described

* For details see Appendix 11.

at various points in this book seem to be reflected in the close correlation between hostility toward the Soviet system and social group membership. This indicates that the differences in life satisfactions associated with membership in the various social, and to a lesser degree age, groups do, in fact, generalize to influence attitudes toward the system as a whole. Such a conclusion is bolstered by the fact that all the various criteria of hostility which we mentioned at the outset are also highly correlated with social group membership, *and* with the various measures of life satisfaction, such as the standard of living which a person reports, the extent to which he was satisfied with his job, and his opportunities for an education and for social mobility.

So much of the satisfaction or dissatisfaction that the Soviet citizen experiences is associated with his job situation that it is no surprise that hostility is closely related to job satisfaction both within and among social groups. Using the index of occupational satisfaction, in which were included a number of attitudinal items and which gives a cumulative picture of the various dimensions of the individual's satisfaction in the job world, we have in Table 69 summarized the relationship between the degree of hostility expressed by representatives of the several social groups, and the degree of occupational satisfaction which they expressed. The degree of occupational satisfaction is linked to one's social group membership, as we already know. The modal rating for members of the

TABLE 69 [4B]

PERCENTAGES OF SOCIAL GROUPS EXPRESSING
SOME HOSTILITY TO SOVIET SYSTEM: BY LEVEL
OF OCCUPATIONAL SATISFACTION

Occupa-tional satisfac-tion	Social groups				
	Intelli-gentsia	White-collar em-ployees	Skilled workers	Ordinary workers	Collective farm peasants
High	20% (288) [a]	33% (173)	40% (58)	35% (46)	32% (22)
So-so	34 (214)	44 (273)	42 (116)	57 (140)	52 (64)
Low	45 (67)	45 (164)	59 (68)	63 (225)	65 (227)

a. Total number of respondents on the basis of which the percentage is computed.

intelligentsia is that of "high" satisfaction. For the workers and peasants, the mode is "low" satisfaction. But, as we see in Table 69, hostility toward the system is also related to job satisfaction about as strongly as to social group membership. *Within* each class, differences in occupational satisfaction are associated with large differences in level of hostility.

Indeed, in any given group there are likely to be people hostile to the regime almost twice as often among those who are occupationally dissatisfied as among those who are satisfied. Workers and peasants as a whole were much more hostile than those in the intelligentsia, but workers and peasants who were occupationally well satisfied were actually hostile less often than members of the intelligentsia who were occupationally dissatisfied. It is clear, therefore, that the individual's experiences in the occupational realm exert a marked independent influence on his evaluation of the Soviet system. Less satisfaction in the occupational realm makes for more hostility to the system. The concentration of people with less job satisfaction in the manual classes must, therefore, be seen as one of the important facts accounting for the greater hostility to the Soviet system manifested by those classes.

Similarly, Table 70 indicates that the degree of hostility which the members of the various social groups expressed is also correlated closely with their recollection of their standard of living in the Soviet Union. On the average, the members of the nonmanual groups report their standard of living as "better than the majority" (this is the modal answer for both the employees and the intelligentsia), while members of the manual groups tend to say their standard of living was worse than that of the rest of the population. The hostility which respondents expressed on the distortion index parallels the standard of living they reported. Within each social group, those who said their standard of living was worse were also more hostile. However, hostility also increases with each successive step down the social ladder.

TABLE 70 [4C]

PERCENTAGES IN VARIOUS SOCIAL GROUPS EXPRESSING
SOME HOSTILITY TO THE SOVIET SYSTEM:
ACCORDING TO THEIR STANDARD OF LIVING

Standard of living in relation to to the majority	Intelligentsia		White-collar employees		Skilled workers		Ordinary workers		Collective farmers	
Better off	28%	(326) [a]	39%	(260)	39%	(76)	41%	(39)	45%	(31)
Worse off	37	(136)	52	(213)	58	(106)	67	(282)	63	(204)

a. Total number of respondents on the basis of which the percentage is computed.

On a number of other measures, such as feeling one had a chance for an education, the same pattern is manifested. Within each social group, those who felt they had less chance for an education are more likely to show hostility. Thus, there seems a clearcut pattern of association between reporting one's life conditions to have been difficult and expressing hostility to the Soviet system.

It certainly can be argued that we are dealing here with a relatively coherent attitude cluster, in which causation could be running in either or both directions. In other words, we might assume people who were generally "hostile" personalities would report everything negatively, or that people who were hostile to the regime would give a selectively distorted picture of their life experience in the Soviet Union. Our data do not permit us to rule out this possibility completely, and we must assume from what we know of psychological processes in general that some such effect as this takes place to some extent. Yet, the pattern of our results still suggests strongly that the life experiences reported are more the determinants of hostility than vice versa.

The most important reason for assuming that the direction of causation is from frustration in daily life to hostility against the regime is, of course, the logic of the connection as we know it in political life in all industrial societies. We may note, in addition, that there is substantial independent evidence in our data in support of the objectivity of the various measures of life experience we used. For example, reported job satisfaction is correlated with income, and the evaluation of one's "chance" for an education with the level actually attained. To the degree that these are objectively verifiable conditions, therefore, to that extent we must assume they more likely caused the observed hostility rather than the reverse.

In addition, if the correlations we have observed between reported life conditions and hostility were no more than a reflection of a general attitude of hostility toward the regime, then this habit of viewing one's status in the Soviet order in gloomy terms should express itself in certain other areas where, in fact, it does not. For example, the more hostile members of our sample are not particularly more likely to report that they were always opposed to the Soviet system than are the less hostile. About 30 per cent of all our respondents admit having once been supporters of the regime regardless of the degree of hostility expressed on the distortion scale. When this relationship is examined within each of the social groups (Table 71) the picture is more complex, but it does not alter our interpretation. Among the peasants and the skilled workers virtually identical proportions admit having once favored the regime, regardless of the degree of their hostility. There is some tendency for the white-collar respondents to report having earlier opposed the regime if they are more hostile. However, our data indicate that on almost all questions it is the lower status respondents who are more likely to contaminate their answers on a given question by projecting onto it their attitudes on related topics. Therefore, if retrospective falsification were at work we should expect a pattern opposite to that which we find: namely, "hostility" should be negatively correlated with admitting onetime support of the regime among the manual groups, but not necessary among the non-manuals.

TABLE 71 [4D]

PERCENTAGES OF SOCIAL GROUPS ONCE IN FAVOR
OF REGIME: BY HOSTILITY

Hostility	Intelligentsia		White-collar employees		Skilled workers		Ordinary workers		Collective farm peasants	
"Some hostility"	22%	(161) [a]	18%	(249)	40%	(109)	28%	(232)	38%	(184)
"No hostility"	29	(400)	28	(352)	40	(127)	37	(169)	37	(119)

a. Total number of respondents on the basis of which the percentage is computed.

There is one additional finding (in Table 72) which supports our assumption that hostility was generated by life conditions, as against the argument that hostile personalities simply blackened the description of their experience. The data show that hostility is related not only to a person's final status in the Soviet system, but also to the point of origin and the direction of his movement in the system. Those persons who moved down (for example, skilled workers, ordinary workers and peasants who had nonmanual origins) are more hostile than their fellows who had not taken such a downward route. Perhaps this could be attributed to retrospective distortion — that "hostile" persons would paint a more gloomy picture of their own fate in the Soviet system. But, another pattern that is exhibited in this table could not conceivably be explained in these terms. Members of the higher status groups (intelligentsia, employees, skilled workers), who were of *peasant origin* but moved up to the higher status, were, nevertheless, considerably more hostile than were those who had not been upward mobile. There may be a number of explanations for this, such as that persons of peasant origin, coming from the most anti-Soviet segment of Soviet society, carried their class-based hostility along with them, or that they experienced greater dislocation on moving into the cities and advancing upward in urban circles.* The crucial fact for us here, however, is that the more hostile groups nevertheless found it possible to admit their good fortune in having moved up. Clearly if hostility were mainly a personality measure and hostile people always blackened

* In the chapter on the nationality problem (XV), we report evidence that those who were forced to move from the countryside to the city were more violently anti-Russian than either the regular rural or urban dwellers.

the description of their life condition the cells of Table 72 representing the upward mobile groups should have a lower, not a higher, proportion of the hostile than the cells representing those who were not upward mobile.

TABLE 72 [4E]

PERCENTAGES EXPRESSING
SOME HOSTILITY TO THE SOVIET SYSTEM:
BY OWN SOCIAL GROUP AND SOCIAL ORIGIN

Respondent's origins	Respondent's own social group								
	Intelli-gentsia		White-collar employee		Skilled worker		Ordinary worker		Collective farm peasant
Nonmanual	25%	(348) [a]	36%	(260)	40%	(20)	68%	(22)	60%	(10)
Peasant	30	(56)	51	(109)	54	(78)	62	(167)	60	(240)

a. Total number of respondents on the basis of which the percentage is computed.

Because of these and other findings previously mentioned we are convinced that the hostility which our respondents expressed toward the Soviet regime or system was in good part determined by the opportunities and rewards they experienced in routine daily life in the Soviet Union. If we contrast the extremes — those who had the most satisfying experiences in the occupational realm with those most frustrated and those whose standard of living made them better off than the majority with those worse off than the average — in each case the proportion in the category of those "most hostile" to the system increases by as much as two or three times. Even when we control for the influence of social class, with which these life experience variables are highly correlated, they continue to exert an independent effect. The greater hostility evident in the manual classes must, therefore, be in part attributed to the greater concentration in those classes of less gratifying or more frustrating conditions of daily life.

Nationality and Arrest as Sources of Hostility

The personal characteristics or experiences which might lead one to feel hostile to the Soviet system should perhaps not be assumed to be limited to those highly correlated with social class membership. Many observers on the Soviet scene would certainly expect the individual's nationality to affect the degree of his hostility toward the system, and most would expect contact with the secret police to play an important role. It will come as a surprise to many that merely being a member of one of the national minorities, does *not* seem to have affected hostility *as measured on our index.** In Table 73 it will be evident that members of the national minorities express no more hostility on the distortion index than do those of Great Russian nationality. Indeed on the average the minor nationalities emerge as less hostile. These data show clearly that hostility as measured on the distortion index is highly related to social group membership, but within any one social class does not appear to be markedly affected by nationality membership. The number of cases on which some of the percentages are based is very small. It is, therefore, all the more striking that the pattern of relationships is relatively so clear and stable.

TABLE 73 [4F]

PERCENTAGE OF EACH NATIONALITY
WHO EXPRESS SOME HOSTILITY TO SOVIET SYSTEM:
BY SOCIAL GROUP

Nationality	Intelli-gentsia		White-collar employees		Skilled workers		Ordinary workers		Collective farmers	
Russian	28%	(348) [a]	42%	(335)	48%	(125)	57%	(184)	67%	(87)
Ukrainian	29	(154)	43	(195)	47	(89)	63	(177)	60	(124)
Other	27	(63)	33	(79)	36	(28)	47	(49)	55	(101)

a. Total number of respondents on the basis of which the percentage is computed.

However, one common occurrence in Soviet life which does have a marked effect on hostility is the experience of arrest by the secret police of oneself or a member of one's family. In Table 74 we see the effect which such an arrest has on the hostility of members of the various social groups. The percentages in the body of the table represent the proportions in each of the combined class and arrest experience categories who were "hostile," that is, whose scores were "intermediate" or "most" hostile on the index of distortion. In some social groups the presence of an arrest in the family approximately doubles the probability of a person's expressing hostility to the Soviet system.

Being arrested or having a member of one's family arrested is quite a different order of experience from having a poor standard of living, or being dissatisfied with one's job. For this reason it is interesting to consider the relative impact of these different determinants of hostility. It will be recalled from our earlier discussion, that with some variation from

* In the chapter on the nationality question (XV), additional evidence will be presented to indicate that most of the features of the Soviet system are evaluated in much the same way by people of the same social class but different nationality. *This does not hold, however, for issues which touch directly on the nationality problem.*

class to class, the proportion giving a more hostile response as much as doubled among those more frustrated by daily life conditions. A glance back at Tables 69 or 70 will reveal a very similar pattern to that shown in Table 74. Both arrest experience and disadvantaged life conditions produce much the same range of impact on hostility. But these comparisons are confounded by the fact that the two rather different determinants of hostility are not controlled or screened out.

TABLE 74 [4G]

PERCENTAGE OF PEOPLE IN THE VARIOUS SOCIAL GROUPS
WHO EXPRESS SOME HOSTILITY: BY THEIR ARREST EXPERIENCE

Arrest experience	Intelli-gentsia		White-collar employees		Skilled workers		Ordinary workers		Collective farmers	
Self or family arrest	35%	(398) [a]	43%	(422)	51%	(161)	68%	(245)	67%	(173)
No arrest	12	(65)	24	(71)	33	(27)	30	(49)	49	(41)

a. Total number of respondents on the basis of which the percentage is computed.

To attain that objective we present in Table 75 the percentages who showed hostility to the system in such a way as to permit a more precise assessment of the separate effect of arrest and life conditions. We take job satisfaction as the representative of the latter set of variables, using a simple dichotomy of "satisfied" vs. "dissatisfied" on the index of occupational satisfaction. We find that both arrest and occupational satisfaction produce an independent effect. Arrest experience seems slightly the more powerful influence producing an average percentage change of 19.5 points as against 16.5 points accounted for by job satisfaction.[5] The differences, however, are not great. Both job satisfaction and arrest seem important. More striking in Table 75 is the evidence of the marked effect produced on individuals who experience *both* occupational dissatisfaction and arrest, as against those who experienced neither. In Table 75 we see that in the former category the percentage who are hostile is two and a half times what it is among those who experienced neither arrest nor occupational frustration.

Since we know social class to have so strong an association with occupational satisfaction, we should note that, broadly speaking, the same patterns are manifested within the separate classes. Arrest raises the percentage of the more hostile among the occupational satisfaction groups, as does occupational dissatisfaction in the arrest categories. Throughout, the greatest impact by far comes from experiencing *both* arrest and occupational frustration simultaneously. For example, among

TABLE 75 [5A]

PER CENT SHOWING SOME HOSTILITY TO SOVIET SYSTEM: BY ARREST EXPERIENCE AND JOB SATISFACTION

	No arrest experience		Self or family member arrested	
Occupationally satisfied	23%	(141) [a]	36%	(561)
Occupationally dissatisfied	33	(114)	59	(637)

a. Total number of respondents on the basis of which the percentage is computed.

the employees going from those who had neither negative experience to those with double exposure raises the proportion of the "most hostile" from 2 to 21 per cent, and among the ordinary workers from 12 to 42 per cent.

The relations revealed in Table 75 in which hostility was measured by the distortion index are also evident when other measures of verbal hostility are used. For example, we may consider the impact of occupational frustration and arrest experience on the expression of a "desire to leave" the Soviet Union. In Table 76 we follow the model of the preceding table, but use as our measure of hostility the proportion who claimed to have had some desire to leave the Soviet Union in the last prewar year (1940). To take account of the known correlation of class and occupational satisfaction, we have this time given not the simple "raw" per cent in each category, but one which gives equal weight to the manual and nonmanual classes.[6]

Using this new measure of verbal hostility we see much the same

TABLE 76 [6A]

PER CENT [a] WITH SOME DESIRE TO LEAVE USSR: BY OCCUPATIONAL SATISFACTION AND ARREST EXPERIENCE

	No arrest experience		Family member or self arrested	
Occupationally satisfied	48%	(113) [b]	66%	(475)
Occupationally dissatisfied	60	(104)	77	(541)

a. Weighted to give equal representation to manual and nonmanual classes.
b. Total number of respondents on the basis of which the percentage is computed.

pattern we saw earlier. Within each occupational satisfaction category, the experience of arrest produces a marked increase in the proportion who were hostile. Within each arrest category the experience of occupational frustration has a similar but less marked effect. Far and away the greatest impact is felt by those who experienced both arrest and frustration. We see from Table 76 that the proportion who showed some desire to leave was almost twice as large among those with this "double exposure." Furthermore, when we consider only the "most hostile," that is, those who wanted to leave *and tried to,* we find they were 30 per cent among those with double exposure as against a mere 5 per cent so classified among those who experienced neither arrest nor occupational frustration.

It would appear that so long as we concern ourselves with verbal statements of hostility to the regime there is little difference in the effect of the several sources of hostility which we have discussed. It is true that there are other actual or potential sources of hostility such as ideological opposition to the regime, with which we have not dealt in this context largely because of the absence of a convenient criterion. The purpose of our analysis here, however, was not to identify the full range of sources of hostility. We sought, rather, to establish the fact that day-to-day conditions of life such as outlined in the preceding chapters do indeed produce a certain level of hostility. This in turn permits us to inquire further into the significance of the hostility so generated. In particular we wish to know whether the hostility generated by the frustrations of daily life are sufficient to produce disaffection and alienation from the Soviet system, and if not where we must look further for such causes.

"Hostility" vs. "Alienation"

As long as we employed as our yardstick a verbal criterion of hostility, we found little difference in the effect of such disparate determinants as standard of living or arrest. The picture is quite different, however, if we invoke a more stringent criterion of hostility, measuring it not by what a person says he felt about the system, but rather by what he *did* about it. The measure of such action is whether a person left the Soviet Union under conditions beyond his control, as in the case of prisoners of war and forced labor, or instead left of his own volition. We would regard the latter as clearly having gone beyond mere hostility to active alienation or disaffection from the regime.

Obviously, it is a moot question as to the point at which a person ceases to be simply "hostile" and becomes "disaffected" or "alienated." Furthermore, whether or not a person takes a specific action such as fleeing his country voluntarily is a function of a complicated concommitance of circumstances, including differential opportunity, relative risks, and offsetting sentiments and involvements. We only contend that *on the average* those persons who claimed to have fled voluntarily come closer to meeting some criterion of alienation than do those who claim they were initially removed from Soviet control involuntarily, as prisoners or forced laborers. It is further clear that the benchmark of alienation or disaffection may be placed at many points on a continuum. Again, our claim is minimal. We merely argue that on an *a priori* basis voluntary flight indicates greater "disaffection" or "alienation," regardless of where the benchmark is placed, than does the mere utterance of hostile sentiments.

The best test of such an *a priori* assumption is to see where it leads us. Suppose we reproduce our last table, in which we tested the relative impact of job satisfaction and arrest history as determinants of hostility. This time we will substitute voluntary departure in place of the mere expression of desire to leave the Soviet Union as our criterion of alienation. Again we have an "inbuilt" control for the correlation of class and job satisfaction, since the per cents have been averaged to give equal weight to the manual and nonmanual classes. We find in Table 77 that when we employ this more stringent criterion, arrest continues to have a considerable impact, but job satisfaction, which was a good determinant of hostility as long as we were concerned only with the verbal expression of it — has virtually no effect on mode of departure from the Soviet Union. Of those who reported an arrest to themselves or a member of the family about 45 per cent said they fled voluntarily whether they were occupationally satisfied or not. Among those who reported no arrest, about 28 per cent said they departed voluntarily, again with almost identical proportions in both the occupationally satisfied and dissatisfied groups. The pattern and magnitude of the differences say clearly that while day-to-day life conditions may well increase the kind of hostility a man expresses mainly in words, they have little or no effect in producing alienation of the sort that is required before one flees his country voluntarily. Such an action depends on more drastic instigations such as an arrest in the family, which does apparently have greater alienative force or power.

Relatively direct confirmation of our contention that the standard of living is ineffective in producing alienation whereas arrest experience does have such an impact is also found in the reasons respondents gave for "turning against the Soviet regime." We asked our respondents whether they had ever favored the Soviet system or had always been opposed to it. Following this question, they were asked their *reasons* for having turned against the system. It is clear from Table 78 that the system of police terror and arrests loomed very large, whereas standard of living played a minor role in precipitating disaffection from the Soviet system. The "terror" was cited first in each social group, while "standard of liv-

TABLE 77 [6B]

PER CENT [a] WHO LEFT USSR VOLUNTARILY:
BY ARREST EXPERIENCE AND JOB SATISFACTION

	No arrest experienced		Family member or self arrested	
Occupationally satisfied	29%	(146) [b]	45%	(566)
Occupationally dissatisfied	27	(118)	44	(675)

a. Weighted to give equal representation to manual and nonmanual classes.
b. Total number of respondents on the basis of which the percentage is computed.

ing" ordinarily fell in seventh position among ten categories. Depending
on the social group, our respondents cited "the terror" from one and a
half to almost five times as frequently as they did standard of living as
their chief reason for "turning against" the Soviet regime. The results
hold up quite well when an age control is applied. Thus we see exposure
to the deprivations imposed by the secret police, experienced either directly or through the arrest of a family member, emerges as the prime
cause of disaffection from the Soviet system. The conditions of daily life
make for expressions of hostility, for grumbling, if you like. But it apparently required the extra push of police terror impinging on the individual to convert hostility into alienation or disaffection from the system.

Political loyalty and disloyalty, affection and disaffection, allegiance
and alienation, result from a complex of positive and negative attitudes
and of inhibiting and facilitating circumstances. The preceding analysis
has indicated strongly that mere hostility to the regime or the Soviet system is not quite the same thing as alienation, measured by voluntary departure from the Soviet order. If the distinctiveness of hostility and
alienation, or attitude and action, needs further demonstration, Table 79
should provide this conclusively, since it shows the relation between hostility and voluntary departure. Within each age group there is only a
slight relation between verbal hostility and mode of departure from the
Soviet system. Among the younger respondents, 5 per cent more of the
hostile respondents said they left voluntarily. Among the older group, the
difference was 4 per cent. The relation is obviously weak compared to
others we have been observing. As can be seen from Table 79, age had
more effect on voluntary departure than did verbal hostility. Older people were much more likely to leave voluntarily regardless of how hostile
they were. The role of age in affecting voluntary departure, substantially

TABLE 78 [6C]

REASONS FOR TURNING AGAINST SOVIET REGIME
GIVEN BY THOSE WHO "ONCE FAVORED" IT: BY SOCIAL GROUP

Reasons cited [a]	Social group				
	Intelligentsia	White-collar employee	Skilled worker	Ordinary worker	Collective farmer
Political reasons					
Terror, brutal, inhuman	38%	43%	43%	35%	37%
No freedom	13	13	14	14	15
Regime vs. people	8	5	5	2	2
Anti-regime principles	3	4	6	3	3
Socio-economic reasons					
Agricultural policy	15	20	29	17	26
Other economic policy	2	3	4	11	5
Living standard	9	12	19	8	10
Other reasons					
Exposure to the West	18	19	15	19	8
Empty promises	16	13	7	8	5
Other	11	12	18	11	8
Total number of respondents	170	156	106	145	130

a. Reasons cited total to more than 100 per cent because more than one reason was cited by some respondents.

greater in effect than hostility, raises issues which are important in understanding the problems of loyalty and disaffection in Soviet society, and we therefore now turn our attention to this factor.

TABLE 79 [6D]

EFFECT OF HOSTILITY TO SOVIET SYSTEM
ON MODE OF DEPARTURE FROM USSR: BY AGE

Mode of departure	45 and under in 1950		46 and over in 1950	
	Hostile	Nonhostile	Hostile	Nonhostile
Voluntary	38%	33%	56%	52%
Involuntary	62	67	44	48
Total number of respondents	517	817	351	328

Some Contrasts Between Generations

The distinctiveness of hostility and alienation was suggested by a number of findings. The notion probably arose first from our close acquaintance with a number of cases of young persons who had fled voluntarily. One young woman technician seemed to have been anti-Soviet throughout all her life. She lived in a city which was occupied by the Germans, and had many opportunities to flee from Soviet territory. But, she was held there by love of homeland, her native culture, and her family and friends. It was not until the Germans evacuated her city that she decided to flee. She believed her family and friends to be in German territory and, furthermore, feared that she might be viewed with suspicion by virtue of the fact that she had lived under German occupation (although she apparently strongly resisted collaborating). If it had not been for these considerations she would have remained in the Soviet Union. An intellectual escaped from a prison camp, and during the unsettled conditions of the war rose to a responsible administrative post, having disguised his past record. He fled only when it appeared that a general checking of credentials would reveal his false papers. An officer, in German territory after the war, was informed on the eve of his return home, by a friend in the secret police, that he was under suspicion. He chose not to return. A junior officer, captured by the Germans, returned after the war and attempted to resume a normal life. Eventually the strain of suspicion, which he felt himself to be under, proved too much for him, and he deserted to the American forces in Germany. The sentiments of these refugees ranged from strongly anti-Soviet to strongly pro-Soviet, but in each instance the circumstance which motivated their fleeing was relatively independent of their attitudes toward the system.

By thus concentrating on the act of fleeing in extreme cases, we can see clearly the separability of attitude and action. However, to stress the distinction in any absolute sense, considerably over-simplifies the process of alienation. While we assert that attitude and action are separable, we certainly do not maintain that they are unrelated. For the prerevolutionary generation in particular, it would appear that deep-seated hostility toward the Soviet system was often sufficiently intense to produce alienation, as judged either by the more subjective data of our life history interviews or the criterion of voluntary departure measured statistically on the written questionnaire. However, since the difference between attitude and action seems to be more distinct in the younger generation than the older, this line of inquiry has particular importance for the future of the Soviet system. The remainder of this chapter will be concerned with various age groups and the differences in the way in which their experiences were responded to by hostile feelings or active alienation. We hope thereby not only to strengthen and further clarify our argument, but also to gain increased understanding of the important current Soviet generation.

We are able to deal statistically only with the prerevolutionary generation and the *immediately* postrevolutionary one, but not with the youngest or current generation. With a very few exceptions, no one born after 1930 is included in our statistical analysis. However, those things which we have to say about the younger people in our sample appear to be even more true of the current Soviet youth. Our oral interviews with young postwar refugees combined with other sources of information on postwar conditions in the USSR make us confident that the trends which we observed may be extrapolated to the youngest portions of the Soviet population.

Each successive age group in the population seems to take the Soviet order more for granted, beginning its adult life in an acceptance of the Soviet system. Among the members of our sample who were born before 1900, those who were adults at the time of the revolution, 82 per cent said they were always opposed to the Soviet system; whereas 45 per cent of those born after 1920 say they had once been in favor of the system. Each successively younger age group in the sample contained a greater proportion who initially accepted the Soviet order. There are, furthermore, rather obvious reasons for believing that these figures underestimate the support of the regime which we would find present in comparable groups of the Soviet population: for example, the situational pressures on our respondents to report that they had been consistent opponents of the Soviet order; the fact that they were in all probability more anti-Soviet than comparable segments of the Soviet population; and finally the fact that our sample did not include the youngest age groups in the population. Consequently, we cannot help but conclude that the overwhelming majority of Soviet youth initially are supporters of the regime.

As previously stated, from our qualitative interviews we got the impression that the sources of alienation, and the qualitative nature of alienation, were quite different in the older and young generations. Those of the older generation, when alienated, were saturated with complaints arising from recollections of a prerevolutionary life in which they had often fared relatively better. They felt many conflicts of value with the new order. They had experienced the impact of a long series of upsetting historical events — the revolution itself, the Civil War, the raised hopes of the period of the New Economic Policy, the violence of the collectivization of agriculture and the effort and sacrifice of the First Five Year Plan, the years of the "Great Purges." These frequently had meant personal hardships and difficulties. For the older generation there were often sufficient accumulated grievances and disagreements to produce alienation without any single event standing out as a clear precipitating cause.

Among those in the younger generation, however, the picture appeared to be rather different. More often their alienation seemed to stem from specific situational factors, rather than from intense hostility caused by disagreements of principle and accumulated grievances. Quite a number of findings in the quantitative data support these impressions. We discovered that the younger people in each social group were much more likely to indicate that their turning against the regime was linked with *some event that impinged directly on themselves.* The proportion of young people citing such a personal event as precipitating their defection was close to two to one over that in the older generation. When social group was held constant by the device of assigning equal weight to each group, direct personal experience was mentioned by 45 per cent of the younger group and by only 26 per cent of the older one.

If our impressions from the qualitative interviews were correct, and if the data just cited can be interpreted as meaning that those in the younger generation are less likely than the older generation to turn against the regime on grounds of general principle or because of an accumulation of grievances, then we ought to expect that the impact of arrest on the incidence of voluntary departure would be greater in the younger generation than in the older one. This assumption is to some extent borne out by the fact that the older people, regardless of social group membership or any other background factor, are considerably more likely to say they fled the Soviet Union voluntarily than are the younger people. But our prediction bears more specifically on the *differential* impact of an event like the arrest of oneself or some member of the family. The hypothesis says that because of the relatively high level of endemic disaffection in the older generation the effect of a single additional factor such as arrest should be less in that group.

TABLE 80 [6E]

EFFECT OF ARREST HISTORY
ON VOLUNTARY DEPARTURE FROM USSR: BY AGE

	Per cent who voluntarily departed, among those	
Arrest history	45 and under in 1950	46 and over in 1950
Self arrested	49% (138) [a]	58% (260)
Family member arrested	38 (731)	54 (380)
No arrest experienced	26 (211)	46 (50)

a. Total number of respondents on the basis of which the percentage is computed.

Table 80 shows that this prediction is borne out. Arrest experience had a marked capacity to generate voluntary departure among the young. Of the younger respondents who were themselves arrested, 49 per cent said they fled voluntarily, while this was true of only 26 per cent of those who were neither themselves arrested nor had members of their immediate family arrested. The older group, however, seemed to be sufficiently saturated with sources of alienation so that the impact of arrest was considerably less. Of those who personally had been arrested, 58 per cent said they fled voluntarily, but so did 46 per cent of those who reported no arrests either of self or family. If we contrast the impact of family arrest and self arrest we find the same pattern. The difference in the impact of these two types of arrest is greater in the younger group.

TABLE 81 [6F]

EFFECT OF ARREST EXPERIENCE
ON HOSTILITY TO SOVIET SYSTEM: BY AGE

	Per cent expressing some hostility, among those	
Arrest experience	45 and under in 1950	46 and over in 1950
Self arrested	43% (136) [a]	56% (237)
Family member arrested	43 (644)	53 (275)
Self and family member arrested	43 (780)	55 (512)
No arrest experienced	23 (204)	34 (48)

a. Total number of respondents on the basis of which the percentage is computed.

Another interesting aspect of the impact of arrest on alienation is that while it increases the rate of voluntary departure markedly more in the younger group than in the older group, it does not have a corresponding *differential* effect on the verbal hostility expressed by the two groups (compare Table 80 with 81). An interesting feature of Table 81 is the fact that in neither age group does it make any difference whether the respondent was himself arrested or if a member of the family was arrested. It will be remembered, however, that particularly among the young group, those who were themselves arrested were considerably more likely to depart the USSR of their own volition, than were those who had had a family member arrested. Truly, hostility and alienation appear to be separable if not separate phenomena, with their separability being more marked among the young.

For one in the younger generation of Soviet citizens, being arrested or having a member of his family arrested meant rejection by, and disillusionment with, the society with which he identified himself. To some extent it prejudiced his chances for future advancement. The persons in our sample who reported an arrest to themselves or a member of their family were more likely to have moved downward in Soviet society in comparison with those persons who reported no arrests (cf. Table 82).

TABLE 82 [6G]

RELATIONSHIP OF ARREST EXPERIENCE TO OCCUPATIONAL MOBILITY

Arrest experience	Respondent's occupation, in relation to father's occupation, was:			Total number of respondents
	Higher	Similar	Lower	
No arrest experienced	32%	50%	18%	(199)
Self and/or family member arrested	31	39	30	(1007)

However, even if an arrest in the family has no such direct, immediate consequences for him, he feels the necessity to "prove himself" to the regime. And he lives in apprehension that his past, and the past of his family and associates, will be held against him. Furthermore, he resents being cast into the role of a second-class citizen. It seems to us doubtful that the majority of the younger members of our sample who fled voluntarily did so because they *had* to, because they were exposed to some specific concrete threat. Rather they resented acutely living in a chronically deprived status and feared the continued disadvantage of their tainted origin.

On the basis of our qualitative data we concluded that the younger generation's allegiance is not only far more influenced by arrest than that of the older generation, but its allegiance also is influenced more by its perception of the strength of the regime. This showed itself in the reactions of the younger people to the early defeats of the Red Army under the Nazi attacks, and also in the feelings of disillusionment which they expressed as a result of their contacts with the superior material culture of Western Europe. The youngest group in our sample gave a good deal of weight to this experience as a reason for turning against the regime. The idea that the regime was strong, in fact almost omnipotent and omniscient, facilitated inhibiting or suppressing doubts and negative feelings toward it. As long as they felt the regime was strong they did not dare think such subversive thoughts. As soon as they thought it was weak, their doubts came readily to the surface. It is of course extremely difficult to find direct confirmation for such propositions. However, we found indirect supporting evidence in the responses to a question in a special questionnaire completed by those who had lived under the German occupation. The question asked whether or not the respondent had thought, in the first two years of the war, that the Germans would win over the Bolsheviks. Table 83 indicates that belief in a German victory considerably enhanced the probability of voluntary departure among the younger respondents, while it had little effect on the older ones. Such data are scarcely direct proof of our contention, but they are certainly consistent with the notion that the allegiance of the younger generation is dependent on their image of the strength of the system.

TABLE 83 [6H]

EFFECT OF ESTIMATES OF GERMAN VICTORY ON VOLUNTARY
DEPARTURE FROM USSR: BY AGE

Estimates of German victory	Per cent who voluntarily departed, among those	
	45 and under in 1950	46 and over in 1950
Thought at beginning that Germans would win war	46% (309) [a]	52% (197)
Did not think at beginning that Germans would win	19 (119)	51 (65)

a. Total number of respondents on the basis of which the percentage is computed.

Some of the statistical relations we have observed in our analysis of generational differences are not overwhelming. For example, the data of Table 80 show that arrest had *more* of an impact on alienation in the younger generation. But it also had a considerable impact on the older generation. One might argue that the similarities are more important than the differences. However, there are two points to enter in rejoinder. The first is that we have been analyzing a trend phenomenon, and any differences which we observe between the prerevolutionary and the postrevolutionary generations ought to be magnified in the current Soviet generation which did not fall in our sample. Secondly, as always in this study, we are operating with crude indices of the phenomena in which we are interested. Report of voluntary departure, for example, cannot by any means be considered a perfect criterion of alienation. Accordingly, we must consider the relationships which we have observed as understatements of those which we would obtain with more refined criteria. In general, however, the weight of the evidence is that alienation is in certain respects a phenomenon qualitatively distinct from verbal hostility. The difference might be considered analogous to that between the griping which takes place among a group of soldiers and the act of going A.W.O.L. Griping reflects the day-to-day complaints of the soldier, but may never result in anything beyond the expression of complaint. Going A.W.O.L. is quite a different matter, and the A.W.O.L. soldier is not necessarily the one who has been doing the most griping. Alienation, in addition to involving a certain amount of hostility toward the society in which one lives, is more specifically a feeling of not being part of that society. Among the older generation, the distinction between alienation and hostility is less easily established. To some extent, they were defined as not part of the new system. Much of their hostility stemmed from their identification and familiarity with the older society. The difficulties of Soviet life were both objectively and subjectively greater for them. Since they had the pre-revolutionary society as a standard of comparison these difficulties were perceived more intensely and associated more directly with the Soviet system. The younger generation begins life with more of a sense of "belonging." As a result, rejection by the system (represented in our analysis by the phenomenon of arrest), and/or disillusionment with the system (in the form of contact with the West, or belief that the Germans were going to win the war) had a correspondingly greater differential impact on the younger generation.

Once dumped out of the system by the fortunes of war, they were of course influenced to remain behind by fear of the consequences on their return or the hope of benefiting from the higher standard of living they found in Europe outside the Soviet Union. These, at least, were overwhelmingly the most important reasons expressed for not returning, generally given in the ratio of two to one. But barring such an unusual crisis and opportunity for outside experience as World War II provided, the truly disaffected may be expected to emerge disproportionately, and perhaps predominantly, among those who suffered arrest experience as the final straw on top of the accumulation of grievances of the sort which were most common and intense among those from the prerevolutionary generation.

We have talked little about the role of ideological factors as a source of alienation. We have a very strong impression from our reading of the life history interviews that "ideological" reasons in the strict sense played a very small role in the alienation of Soviet refugees. The coding of the answers on the questions "Why did you turn against the regime?" (see Table 78) and "Why did you not return?" also gives little reason to hold ideological factors a prime determinant of alienation from the Soviet system, unless you consider fear of the terror and opposition to the collective farms a form of "ideological" complaint. The absence of freedom, and the conflict of interests between regime and people were generally

XII

The Problem of Loyalty in Soviet Society

Deeply alienated or merely very hostile Soviet citizens still in their homeland in peaceful conditions have had precious few opportunities to express feelings of alienation and hostility. Only the unusual conditions of the war gave those who were alienated the opportunity to flee voluntarily. Many others, although removed from Soviet territory on other than their own initiative, had accumulated sufficient grievances or fears to be unwilling to return. But unless we grossly overestimate the extent of the conditions met in our sample — especially the experience of arrest — there must have been at least many millions of Soviet citizens with such deep grievances. Yet on the surface Soviet society did not seem to most observers to be a bubbling cauldron about to explode into political revolution. And despite the great personal sacrifices they made, Soviet citizens obviously worked productively and effectively in raising the USSR to its position as the second greatest industrial power in the world. It is, therefore, a necessary sequel to our exploration of the sources of hostility and alienation to explain how the system acted to contain and control these sentiments and how the individual responded to the simultaneous pressure of personal feelings and political and social reality.

Our discussion is couched in the past tense, but we do not mean thereby to be too quick in prejudging the degree of the break between the post-Stalin situation and the long era of his rule. Indeed, we feel that there is more continuity than otherwise. Yet we also feel there have been certain crucial changes introduced by Stalin's successors. But we postpone until the end of this chapter the more systematic consideration of the significance of those changes for the problem of loyalty and disloyalty in Soviet society. We need to see those changes against the model of Stalinist control which we present first. We mean thereby to do justice to the past, the remembrance of which is still quite real to most Soviet citizens, and an influence on their current expectations and behavior. This model also is the pattern from which future developments must start. It is the material with which the present leaders work. And it may well be the model to which they will yet return.

The Stalin Formula for Social Control

Rather than striving to reduce discontent, the Soviet regime's policy has been primarily to isolate it and to suppress open disloyalty. As we said in the previous chapter, it would be erroneous to say that the regime is completely unconcerned with the political sentiments of its people. But, Soviet leaders seemed to accept the fact that the programs to which they were committed were inherently bound to create a substantial amount of hostile sentiment, and they therefore focused their attention not on sentiments but on *behavior*. Every effort was made to structure the life situation of the Soviet citizen so that he would do what was expected of him *regardless* of his feelings toward the regime and the system. This, again, is not to say that there are not and have not been many loyal citizens who were willing and eager to do what the regime desired. What we are saying, however, is that regime policy for social control was designed to make the loyal and disloyal citizen behaviorally indistinguishable. This may seem to be an overstatement at first glance. But the recent revelations by Soviet leaders about their powerlessness in the face of Stalin suggest that this may have been true on all levels of Soviet society. While this picture of their relations to the dead leader may be an expedient fabrication, it would seem at the very least to be a fabrication couched in terms that made sense to the rank-and-file citizen in terms of his own life experience.

The basic principle for the control of loyalty in the Soviet Union was to offer the citizen no viable alternative except to conform. Strong negative sanctions for nonconformity were complemented by a carefully structured system of rewards for conformity. The regime's insistence upon suppressing manifestations of discontent and disloyalty was no more striking than its policy of demanding positive affirmations of loyalty. The populace receives a thorough political education in how to think, talk, and act "correctly," and it is expected on appropriate occasions to indicate its acceptance and support of the system by politically "correct" behavior and pronouncements. The frequency of these appropriate occasions is outstanding, particularly for members of the intelligentsia. This necessity of affirming regime policy as one's own belief is often a source of acute irritation and conflict for citizens of marginal loyalty. At the same time it probably effects a certain amount of self-persuasion. In any event, it serves to re-enforce the façade of monolithic proregime sentiment which the leaders seem to cherish.

The fact that a person was suspect as potentially disloyal did not mean that the regime could not use him, nor did the fact that he might actually have an attitude of, at best, mixed loyalty mean that he would not work for the regime. Indeed, some people did an effective job precisely because they did *not* like the regime. Their work was their refuge *from* the regime, because it brought them a reasonable measure of security and a chance to enjoy their personal lives through "the inner emigration."

In general, the capacity of such a system to absorb deviants must not be underestimated. Essentially, every person was regarded as potentially disloyal. The regime tried to control the life situation of each individual, to insure the reliability of his behavior, regardless of his underlying political sentiments. In some instances — notably spying for the secret police — suspicion of disloyalty has often been the very basis of recruitment. Such individuals were told that they would have to "prove themselves" by this type of work. These police jobs are ordinarily not very important. However, persons of dubious loyalty have regularly been employed on rather high-level assignments. When paranoiac suspicion has been pushed to the extreme, there is no longer any real differentiation between the "trusted" and the "mistrusted." Consequently, a totalitarian society such as the USSR may have a surprising ability to absorb and use potential deviants. Yet, the society also loses valuable people because of unwarranted political suspicions.

Perhaps the best summary statement that can be made about this policy was its main objective: to assure reliable *behavior* regardless of how the citizen might *feel* about the regime. Stalin was obviously aware that he had created an enormous amount of hatred in very large groups which suffered directly from regime policies and actions. The regime further realized that it had not done a satisfactory job of meeting the "normal, loyal citizen's" needs. Until recently Soviet leaders refused to make substantial concessions in that direction. Accordingly, Stalin could not rely on the great mass to support him out of sentimental allegiance, and primary reliance was therefore placed on external coercion to enforce behavioral conformity. *Abstractly,* loyalty is tested in a situation of free choice, when a citizen opts to support or not support a given group. Actually, such a situation of free choice seldom occurs in any society. In the Soviet Union, it is a cardinal point of policy to structure the individual's life situation so that such choice situations occur as seldom as possible. A middle-aged army officer, rather strongly pro-Soviet in most respects, stated this attitude eloquently:

During collectivization, political considerations were quite important. At present [the late forties] the basic criterion is one's attitude toward the task assigned him. You are permitted to criticize, to criticize yourself, to criticize your superiors, to let off steam about everything and everybody concerned. Perhaps even high officials, but you may not criticize the "general line." If you are conscientious and stick to your job, it will be easy to get ahead. You may once in a while laugh or smile about even Kaganovich, but never about Stalin. Whether you are sincere or not doesn't interest anybody. You have to do your job. Stalin knows that a good many of his subjects laugh about him. But the job must be done.

Regardless of the limitations of this formula for social control, it achieved its main objective of ensuring political and social conformity, at least during periods of stability. Our refugee respondents, despite their anti-Soviet bias, reported virtually no disloyal *behavior* on their own part during their life under the Soviet regime, at least during periods of social and political stability, if not in such times as the Civil War or the years of German occupation. But, we could have concluded the same general conclusion equally readily by virtue of the simple fact of the relative success of the regime in its operation of the system.

We can understand the success of this system of controls only if we view it explicitly from the citizen's point of view. The preceding statement of official policy merely sets the stage; the main purpose of this section is to consider those aspects of the citizen's reaction to his life situation which will best help us to understand the effectiveness of official policy for the control of disloyalty. The net effect of our temporary concentration on the exclusively negative aspects of the citizen's relation to the system will probably be to create in the minds of some readers the impression that we regard *all* Soviet citizens as disloyal or as actively doubting the system. This is far from our position. Indeed, our concern here is not so much with disaffection as with the mechanisms whereby *loyalty* is maintained, whereby doubts are *kept out* of consciousness, whereby the individual not only *controls* his behavior but his thoughts as he pursues his life goals in the context of the Soviet system.

Despite the high incidence of dissatisfying experiences in the life of Soviet citizens, their usual response was one of accommodation, or even positive loyalty. Only occasionally under the normal conditions of Soviet life did someone "turn against the system." Our present purpose is to make psychological sense out of this pattern by spelling out the processes and modes of accommodation that characterized various groups in Soviet society. Here we must rely on more qualitative data, case studies, and inference. We will deal here with the psychological mechanisms underlying political loyalty and disloyalty. In touching on such problems we must invoke certain cautions: in any state, no matter how polarized it may be, the issue of loyalty is at any moment a matter of salience to only a very small proportion of the citizenry. Most persons take their life in a given society pretty much for granted, and very seldom do they pose for themselves the question of where their allegiance lies. However, we assume that no person in any society is absolutely and unexceptionally loyal or disloyal. Each citizen, whether predominantly loyal or predominantly disloyal, has moments of patriotism and moments of disaffection. Whether consciously or unconsciously, the same processes are at work in the minds of all, even though the balance of forces may be different. Hence, when we talk about mechanisms for controlling doubts or disloyalty in a person, it is not assumed that in every case the person is conscious of these doubts, or that he is close to disloyalty; these mechanisms may be the very devices whereby *unquestioned* loyalty is maintained. We assume, therefore, that we are dealing with mechanisms and modes of accommodation that are present in *both* loyal and disloyal persons. Again we note that our analysis has reference mainly to the conditions which prevailed under Stalin, although we feel that many of the same problems persist today and are met by many of the same mechanisms of accommodation.

The basic life problems of the Soviet citizen are: (1) to attain those values which he cherishes — making a living, receiving acceptance and recognition, having a feeling of accomplishment and self-fulfillment, gaining the affection and love of others; (2) to maintain his psychological self intact; (3) to avoid undue conflict with the control machinery of the state. These problems are faced in one form or another by the citizens of all states. In the Soviet system they are more likely to place conflicting demands on him. The Soviet system has been designed to maximize the probability that the citizen will strive to attain his personal goals within the framework of existing institutions and the existing framework of social control. But the person who assumed a responsible post in order to attain material success ran an increased risk of arrest. Furthermore, he faced moral conflict; he became identified with the system and had to execute policies about which he often had doubts. To the extent that he attempted to pursue his values without conflict with the control machinery of the state, the problem of maintaining his psychological self intact became accentuated.

If one takes into consideration the absence of a viable alternative, and the state's monopoly of employment, one can understand the extent to which the Soviet citizen must accommodate to the negative aspects of the more responsible or "involved" positions. Assuming that the forces working for disloyalty are in some measure present in everyone, these two factors aid in preventing these forces from becoming consciously active. Many persons who would otherwise have had conscious doubts about the Soviet order repressed or suppressed those doubts because they saw no viable alternative except to live within the Soviet system on its own terms. Thus, one said: "But all our attempts to leave our country are unsuccessful. Mother finally made her peace with this. She did not talk against the Soviet power, but she quietly did her own work."

We have stated our conclusion that the loyalty of the younger Soviet generation is anchored in its image of the strength of the system (or perhaps more accurately, of the regime) and introduced statistical evidence to support this contention. However, even among the older generation, and even among the most disaffected, belief in the strength of the regime inhibits disloyal *behavior*. Our refugee respondents, travelers' accounts, and many statements in the Soviet press attest to the existence in Soviet society of behavior that is something other than what the regime ideally desires. There is juvenile delinquency,[1] ordinary theft, crime, and "hooliganism" to use the Soviet term, and there are occasional short outbursts of hostile feeling on which a genuine political interpretation might be put. There is — under stable conditions — little or no concerted, politically oriented disloyal activity. Our assertion that inhibition of disloyal behavior is dependent on the absence of any viable alternative except to accommodate is supported by the fact that there have actually been manifestations of disloyal behavior in times when the regime *is* unstable — note the defections during the early years of World War II, overt rejoicing among Soviet troops after the death of Stalin, reports of riots in Soviet labor camps in the same period, and the injunction of the new leadership against "panic." [2] In the satellite countries, "de-Stalinization" and concessions to the populace had more the effect of releasing discontent than of placating it.

The direct inhibition of disloyal behavior is obvious and readily understandable in such a state as the Soviet Union in conditions of political stability. There are other processes which are less obvious. The fact that the citizen looks to the state for employment, which in turn is contingent on his being judged loyal, combined with the absence of any possibility of effective disloyal behavior produces a situation in which the individual develops within himself mechanisms for suppressing both disloyal deeds *and thoughts*. Accepting the impossibility of any action except conformity, even the essentially disloyal — that is, those who in a situation of free choice would reject or act against the regime — adopt mechanisms of accommodation to facilitate their adjustment.[3] These self-induced mechanisms include: (1) generation of reenforcing images of society; (2) control over own communication; (3) control of own behavior; (4) control of own impulses; (5) psychological devices for the resolution of moral conflict. These mechanisms help the citizen adjust to a situation regarded as inevitable. They may in fact, keep his doubts completely out of consciousness, and thus insure his unquestioning loyalty. But they do not necessarily succeed completely in reducing underlying tension. His doubts, fears, and compromises may continue to act corrosively on his inner, deeper self. A young artist who fled in the postwar period (1950) was able to describe his own psychological defenses with unusual sensitivity:

This is an interesting psychological process. The process of disbelief developed unconsciously. Externally I remained a loyal Pioneer, but inwardly I felt differently. I continued to argue and tried to convince other people. I was looking for external support. I think that this process, this split state of mind, is characteristic of the vast majority of people of that age in the Soviet Union.

One of the mechanisms of adjustment which the Soviet citizen adopted was to accept unquestioningly, and possibly to exaggerate, certain images that the regime tried to create, such as the image of the strength and durability of the system and the infallibility and relentless cruelty of the secret police. We are not arguing that the Soviet system has been anything other than strong and durable, nor do we imply that the secret police have been unvigilant or tolerant of political deviation. Yet, there is reason to believe that the Soviet citizen retained and, to a measure, created in his own mind an extreme image of the system's strength as a control over his own behavior and impulses. He kept telling himself how omniscient and omnipotent the secret police were, so that he would not be tempted to stray from the path of conformity. He told himself how strong the state was, thereby simultaneously strengthening his pride in it, and warning himself — even though it might be unconsciously — of the danger of being disloyal to so stong a power. The destruction of this image of a strong system re-enforced by an infallible, punishing police is the event most calculated to release repressed feelings of resentment and hatred toward the regime. Thus, as we have seen, the loyalty of the younger generation was markedly affected by the anticipation of a German victory.

In order to avoid trouble both for himself and for people around him, the Soviet citizen voluntarily controls the content of his communications. Again this does not mean that he never says anything improper, but the flow of information and opinions contrary to the regime's interests is considerably reduced by his own *voluntary* actions. In this way, he cooperates spontaneously with the regime's policy of suppressing and isolating manifestations of disloyalty. A young postwar deserter, who had been an officer, gave a typical account of a parent who voluntarily restrained himself from expressing his own feelings to his son who supported the regime:

(Question). After your father returned from prison, how did he feel about your attitude toward the regime? (Answer). He didn't talk about it. He didn't tell me I had to be against the regime. He figured that I had to live under the regime and I should learn to get along with it.

H. K. Geiger's study of the Soviet urban family, and several others,[4] indicates that this pattern of suppressing deviant political opinions in the family became a dominant pattern in the newer generation of Soviet parents.

An obvious point, but one necessary for completeness, is the fact that the citizen controls his own behavior within safe limits. He learns what is "correct" and adheres closely to the formula of correct and safe behavior. One of the most dangerous elements of the Soviet citizen is his own feelings. Control over his own behavior is endangered by feelings of antagonism toward the regime, since these feelings may burst forth at any moment and prompt some impulsive act insuring disaster. One of the dramatic mechanisms of self-constraint that characterizes the Soviet citizen's adjustive pattern is the process of self-indoctrination, of repressing and denying hostile feelings, and reaffirming loyalty. Since most such processes are largely unconscious, it is somewhat surprising that a considerable number of respondents described them so articulately. One reported that while he was in the occupation army he deliberately spent his free time sleeping in order to avoid drinking bouts. His fear was that under the influence of liquor he might say or do something that would get him into trouble. Yet the very event he feared actually occurred. After he had been drinking he had to attend a speech given by a political officer. He made a side comment on the officer's speech which the officer overheard. Being called to task, he struck the officer in the face. As a result, he was arrested. After escaping and being recaptured twice, he finally succeeded in fleeing to the American zone. Another young man, of peasant origin, commented: "Conditions of life aboard ship were dangerous as well as substandard; you fear that you might say something against the regime while asleep. I remember one of our sailors disappeared for this reason."

The young officer who escaped after the war and who has been quoted above on the silence of his father was asked why he did not return to the Soviet Union. His partial answer was that, having seen conditions of life in Western Europe, he would find it harder to refrain from making dangerous statements even though his own life conditions would not be worse than average. He said: "Well, I could work as a chauffeur. My life would be about average, but it would be harder for me to keep quiet." Still another, former member of the Komsomol and the secret police, said:

I saw how people lived and how much they got. I could not always think about this, but could only say it to myself. One could not tell this to anyone. If you keep these things in your head they might come out some day. You are afraid that you might tell somebody. Therefore, very few people in the Soviet Union think about these things. There is no time to think about them. One thinks only about his fate and how he can get along.

Those of the younger generation are probably not faced with genuine moral conflicts so often as the older generation. But, faced with a moral conflict, the individual must either withdraw from the situation, adopting the course of internal emigration, as did the older generation, suffer under this conflict if it is bearable, or find some psychological defense even if an unconscious one against it. Our estimate is that the overwhelming majority of the younger generation follows the last of these courses.

Failure to exhibit loyalty and/or reliability jeopardized one's job. The greater a man's ambition and the more involved the posts to which he aspired, the more strongly he inclined to trim his political thinking and behavior to that pattern best facilitating his advancement. There are, of course, persons who deliberately curtail their ambitions and bypass this adjustment, but they are a small minority in the younger group. In the younger group, both the citizen and the regime probably take loyalty and reliability for granted. However, even the "loyal" citizen, one without any severe conscious doubts, adopts certain mechanisms of defense. Realizing that any expression of doubt, disloyalty or unreliability would prejudice his occupational chances, he shuns thinking of political and other dangerous matters, learns the correct forms, and adheres to them. The state's effective control over employment is in effect a most ingenious device for ensuring conformity and conscious loyalty. A large number of respondents reported that even though their families were strongly anti-Soviet, all members of the family were united in the desire that the children should have successful careers.[5] The tendency to link political behavior with occupational aspirations is stated lucidly in the description of a factory meeting, given by a middle-aged engineer.

Most workers tried to avoid these meetings, and at the meetings they were sitting and sleeping. Some people did speak up, indeed, but not because they had illusions of participating in making the plans, but only because it offered a possibility of advance. Especially among the young people. Young people spoke up, especially those who wanted to make a career.

To a great extent, this involvement of the Soviet citizenry, and in particular the younger generation, in occupational success and advancement results in a form of depoliticization. The individual becomes only secondarily concerned with the content of his political utterances. Primarily, he is concerned with their effect upon his career. Often, he develops a detached instrumental attitude to his own political professions, much like the attitude the leaders themselves hold toward their own statements. One respondent said that the fact that he was politically suspect for having been captured by the Germans prompted him to join the Young Communists League for protective coloration. A former Soviet soldier said: "Well, that was in 1946. You know that I had been repatriated and I had to cover up a little so I joined the Komsomol." And a young engineer commented:

To advance on the job, one needs to be energetic and persistent and he must be able to keep his mouth shut and to wear a "thick mask," because of the deplorable conditions one has to live in, such as lack of food, living in unheated quarters, lack of clothing and of practically all of the necessities of life. If one can shout: "Da, zdravstvuyet Stalin!" (Long live Stalin) . . . and, "I know of no other country in which a man breathes so freely" (from a Soviet song), then he will succeed.

The citizen's involvement in his job seems to produce, indirectly, a certain degree of identification with the regime and its goals. Especially when the individual is in a responsible position, he must from day to day deal with solving tasks related to the regime's goals. He is to a greater or lesser degree solving the regime's own problems. To do his job adequately (even from the point of view of his own self-interest) he must address these problems in their own terms. From what we know of psychological processes in general, it seems inevitable that as the individual deals with these problems, he must come to accept as legitimate the goals at which they are directed. In effect he thereby comes to identify himself with the regime and its objectives. Again, it is necessary to repeat that none of these processes need ever rise to the individual's consciousness. While many challenges to his loyalty may actually operate on him, the factors offsetting his doubts may be sufficiently powerful to keep *all* crises in the unconscious. It is important, however, to be aware of these processes, because their suppression is dependent upon the stability of the Soviet system: they may at some time assert themselves.

Whereas the stability of a liberal society is based on the loyalty of its citizens, it is probably correct to say that the loyalty of the Soviet citizen has been based on the stability of the system. It is not sufficient to say that for many Soviet citizens the basis of loyalty evaporates as the system becomes unstable. In addition, under conditions of stability their loyalty is secured by psychological mechanisms for containing the sources of doubt and disaffection. Under conditions of social instability, these doubts become conscious, active sources of disloyalty. They then act in concert with the dissolution of those positive motivations heretofore holding the citizen to the regime. In a sense, this is true of any social system. It is particularly relevant in the Soviet case, however, where all forces are so intense. The result of disillusion is dramatic and violent. The dividing line between rigidly correct and reliable behavior and violently disloyal behavior may be a very fine one, dependent entirely on the citizen's estimate of the regime's strength. A small, critical shift in this estimate can produce a major reversal of behavior.

The Stalinist formula for handling disloyalty produced an exaggerated picture of actual loyalty. This, in turn, effected a further containment of disloyal expressions, since each person must inevitably underestimate the potential disloyalty in those around him. Any break in such a monolithic image of loyalty will tend to snowball. It is essential, therefore, in discussing political loyalty, its strength or weakness, to specify whether a given proposition pertains to a situation of system stability or instability.[6]

Obviously, there are various degrees of instability. To some extent even a "stable" system — one which shows little prospect of fundamental change — contains some small areas of instability. Thus, the fragile image of the omnipotent regime and system is a chronic source of instability in the Soviet mind, a potential source for disaffection. A political crisis, such as that following the death of Stalin, is a more drastic instance of instability. A series of military defeats, like those during the first year of the German invasion, produces even more "instability." "Stability" and "instability" are reciprocal states, operating on a sliding scale: more properly, we should talk of relative degrees of stability and instability. The less stable the system, the greater the potential for disloyalty among the populace. Yet, instability, by itself, is not a sufficient condition for disloyalty, since disloyalty will be a resultant of various forces. If instability is coupled with events that evoke reenforcing loyalty to the system, then the system has a good chance of regaining its equilibrium. The German invasion, for example, stimulated the patriotic feelings of the populace, and induced intense resentment against the behavior of the Nazis. Although the evident weakness of the regime in meeting the first onslaughts had initially caused loyalty to ebb away at an alarming rate, after the first few months of war the strength of feeling against the invaders combined with increased evidence of firmness and competence in the regime to restore loyalty.

The New Line

Popular values do not clash with most of the values *implied* in the Soviet system itself. On the contrary, there is in general marked congruence between popular values and the goals the system purports to pursue. But the failure of the Soviet regime to implement these implied values has been a source of real conflict. The welfare features of the system are widely approved, but there has been much resentment over the inadequate implementation of the program. State ownership and direction of economic activities are favored both as a means of achieving the desired welfare benefits, and as a natural function of the strong government which the Soviet people seem to expect and demand. It was only where government owned and controlled economic institutions failed to provide the expected benefits or intruded drastically in the personal freedom of the citizen, as is especially true of the collective farm system, that private ownership was favored.

In some respects the institutions of government in Soviet society are also congruent with or do not violate the values of the people. They expect, and apparently favor a strong paternalistic government. But they want it to be a benevolent rather than a punishing and depriving "father," and in this respect the Soviet regime has alienated the affection of many citizens. Soviet citizens — or at least the Great Russians among them — cherish their role in the collectivity more highly, we believe, than most people. They like to think of themselves as "full valued citizens," making a contribution to the general welfare. This disposition could be and to some extent actually is a source of strength to the system. But it is also a source of acute friction in that sizable portion of the population who find themselves treated as second-class citizens because of the regime's suspicions of them. Typical was this complaint of a young man, who had loyally served as an army officer and party man until he was dismissed upon the discovery that his father had been shot as an enemy of the regime: "Why was I a class enemy of the Soviet regime, so that they had to follow me; so that I had no right to study or participate in production or to be an engineer?"

The regime exploits as fully as possible all motives not systematically thwarted. Indeed the policy of the regime may be defined as the maximization of certain motives. Many of the youth derive strong psychic satisfaction from identification with it. One of the most potent advantages it has in enlisting such support lies in the dynamic element in the Soviet system. The regime can point to impressive specific achievements in industrial and military development, and to future, long-run social goals. The real gains which have been made, combined with the pronounced trend in either Russian culture or Russian "national character," toward identification with the group and toward valuing service to the group, taps the romanticism of many Soviet youths. The regime deliberately exploits these advantages. The following quotations demonstrate how intense this tendency for identification with the "collective" can be.

It's interesting how we were brought up in the Soviet Union, because in the books and the movies we saw pictures like that of a boy who went to the NKVD and said that his father was a spy. I thought that he must be a hero. And I wanted to be one too. Yes, it's hard, but maybe you can understand how young people are in Russia, not all of them, but most of them were like me (young woman, piano student).

I liked my work because of my character, as I explained to you before. It was live work. I felt that I was doing important work for the state, of the people, and on a great scale, covering the whole Soviet Union (male, government employee, postwar refugee).

The Komsomol was a cooperative of young people sympathetic to the ideas of Communism. To be torn away from this cooperative, to remain isolated from this collective, from this monolith, this was unbearable for me (young army officer).

The strong effect of the psychic satisfaction which a person can derive from success in the Soviet system is reflected in the account of another young army officer whose father had been arrested. When asked how it felt to be an officer, he replied:

Yes, I was enthusiastic. I was very young to have had such a high rank. Naturally, I was very proud. Maybe this kind of pride is of rather low quality, but still I felt it. Just imagine. Say there was an old peasant in the army and I, so young a man, was so high above him, and he had to esteem me. When I thought about my father, my heart hurt me, but I was now a full valued Soviet citizen.

It is obvious, of course, that this policy of maximizing the motivation of the individual citizen was in Soviet society to be reconciled with another closely related policy, that of *minimizing* the economic product turned over to the consumer. This does not mean, however, that economic incentives are not a very important part of the system of social control devised by the Soviet regime. The policy employed in the use of economic incentives has been to force Soviet citizens to compete among themselves for scarce goods via such devices as a graduated piece work system in factories. The result is to increase individual exertion in the scramble for the meager portion of the total product that the Soviet regime allots to the citizen. Auxiliary "social" motives and other forms of recognition for achievement are also employed, and it is not uncommon for individuals to work particularly hard in order — as the refugees say — "to get their picture in the paper." [7]

A substantial amount of control and direction of their lives is expected by Soviet citizens, but of course they do not want this to extend in a totalitarian fashion to their everyday private affairs. The liberties that are desired are personal rather than political. There certainly is a strong desire for some checks on the exercise of arbitrary authority, but there is much less concern over formal or "constitutional" guarantees and procedures than is found in countries of the West such as England, France, or the United States.

Certain features of Soviet life are wholeheartedly disliked, the low standard of living, the collective farms, and most especially the police terror. But to a large extent, as with other sources of discontent, the deficiencies and the "bad" institutions are attributed to the leadership rather than to the broad form of government or economy. As one man put it: "I did not comprehend the whole system, yet I thought the system was good and that only the people in it were bad."

In the preceding chapter we learned that the frustration of daily life produced hostility against Soviet leaders and the "Soviet system," but were not sufficient to produce the kind of alienation or disaffection which leads one voluntarily to break away from his native society. Only the earlier experience of arrest at the hands of the secret police or the latter expectation of terroristic reprisals seemed sufficient to drive people out, and to keep away those who initially were involuntarily removed from Soviet control. The findings on popular values in Chapter X, however, enable us better to understand that pattern, because they reveal the broad range of congruence between so many of the basic values and sociopolitical expectations of Soviet citizens, on the one hand, and on the other many of the features of Soviet society.

On the basis of these findings, we concluded quite early in the course of our investigation that Soviet leaders had the possibility of enlisting a vast reservoir of popular support if they would seriously implement promises of greater welfare benefits and particularly if they combined this with a marked reduction in the activities of the secret police and the general operation of the political terror. When we first put forth these ideas[8] Stalin was not only alive but was intensely pursuing the round of repressive measures which made the last years of his life a nightmare for millions of Soviet citizens. Under the circumstances our suggestions seemed to many to be farfetched and unrealistic. But after Stalin's death first Malenkov and then Khrushchev startled the world by their sweeping promises to the Soviet citizen of more consumers' goods, better housing and, in general, a fuller share of the nation's output. More important, the secret police was so reduced in importance, and the terror so greatly reined in, as to produce a great change in the life situation of the average citizen.

Even though the improvement in living standards has been modest, the prime fact of the reduction of the terror seems to have effected a profound transformation in the political atmosphere. Reports from journalists and the firsthand experience of numerous scholars, including the authors, who were able to visit the Soviet Union after 1955, testify to this fact. With this change the *main* basis for active disaffection or alienation from the Soviet system has been radically reduced in importance. There remain other sources of alienation, of course, such as the nationality policy and the collective farms, but our data certainly indicate that neither of these really competed with the terror for pervasiveness. It was only the terror which cut across all lines, national, geographic, social and economic. The weapon of the secret police of course remains in existence and in operation, but on so reduced a scale as to produce not merely a quantitative but a qualitative change.

At the same time that the reduction of the terror has largely removed the chief source of alienation, the gradually improving standard of living has greatly reduced the main force acting to inhibit the generation of spontaneous popular support for the regime and the Soviet system. It is true, of course, that the improvements have been quite modest. But our investigation leads us to conclude that it is not so much the size of the increments as their steadiness, which is crucial to Soviet citizens. This is perhaps the more important dimension because the improvements are valued not in themselves alone, but also as evidence of the interest of the regime in improving living standards and its sincerity in implementing its alleged good intentions.

In the face of this rather rosy picture, many may wonder why it is that we never heard of anything like the riots in the slave labor camps, the disturbances among the students, and the challenges tossed out to representatives of the Central Committee at gatherings of workers in the main factories which have been persistently reported since Stalin's death. There is, of course, the possibility that such things *did* happen under Stalin, and that the main difference in the present situation is that they are reported. On the contrary, we feel that there *are* more surface manifestations now of disturbances, difficulties, and doubts among the Soviet citizens. For one thing, decades of accumulated grievances are not to be siphoned off in a matter of days or even years. In particular, the relaxation of the terror now obviously tempts the more hostile or the more daring to express the accumulated grievances stored up and suppressed, sometimes over decades. In addition, we call attention again to our analysis of the control of disloyalty and our conclusion that in important respects the loyalty of the Soviet citizen depends on his impression of the regime's strength and stability at any given moment. Both the fact of uncertain transition of power from Stalin to the group or individual who may become his successor, and in its special way the reduction of the terror, undoubtedly gave many Soviet citizens an impression of the current leaders as vacillating and even weak. This is especially marked by contrast with the behavior of Stalin in his last years.

The Soviet regime in the very process of going over to a potentially much wider base of broad spontaneous popular support *at the very moment of transition* exposes itself to the greatest expression of accumulated hostility and to manifestations of civil disobedience. This period of transition is therefore one in which the whole system is in a state of delicate balance between the forces which, on the one hand, pull the leaders back toward the Stalinist patterns as the obvious answer to these manifestations of popular independence, and those forces which, on the other hand, urge them to press forward to place the regime on a new and wider base of social support. The outcome we feel is not so uncertain as many believe. But before we attempt our predictions for the future, which will be the concern of our last chapter, we should consider one additional and highly relevant theme: namely, the sources of cleavage within the population as such. This is the subject of the next part of our study.

PART FOUR: SOURCES OF CLEAVAGE

XIII

Social Class Cleavage[1]

In 1936 Stalin made a series of bold, and to many startling, assertions about relations between the social and economic classes in Soviet society. So profoundly had the revolution changed the character of those classes, he asserted, that the usual political and economic class "contradictions" were "declining and being obliterated." As a result of these economic and political changes, furthermore, the "dividing lines" between the working class and the peasantry, on the one hand, and the intelligentsia on the other, were also being "obliterated." "The old class exclusiveness is disappearing," he affirmed, "and the distance between these social groups is steadily diminishing." [2]

We have in this study presented abundant evidence that the social strata in Soviet society are markedly differentiated in economic reward, and often have profoundly different views on basic social and political issues. But Stalin was not asserting that there was "equality" or absence of differentiation in Soviet society. Indeed he had long before made it clear that he was opposed to what he scornfully and rather foolishly termed "bourgeois equality-mongering." [3] Clearly what Stalin meant was that in the Soviet Union differences in economic welfare and political experience were not converted into class consciousness, particularly into feelings of solidarity with one's own class and hostility toward other classes further removed in the social hierarchy. It would indeed be remarkable if Stalin were correct in assuming that in a modern society as definitely stratified as the Soviet Union there would not be substantial class consciousness and class antagonism. Yet Stalin has strange bedfellows here, since many émigrés and numerous Western observers of the Soviet scene have affirmed that the Soviet people are so united in their *political* opposition to the regime that all class antagonism has been swept aside. If this were the case it would be of substantial importance in our assessment of Soviet society. This chapter, therefore, inquires into the degree and content of class antagonism in the Soviet Union and assesses its implications for the functioning of the social system.

Although a variety of items in our questionnaire dealt with the situation of the several Soviet classes, we will give our attention here mainly to a set of three questions which dealt explicitly with the problem of class cleavage and which form a coherent unit. The questions deal with the issue of "fair shares" — whether the classes received disproportionate amounts of the goods offered by society; with the problem of coincidence and conflict of interest between strata; and with the perceived "harmfulness" of one class to another. The four classes whose situation was evaluated were the "intelligentsia," "employees" or ordinary white-collar personnel, "workers," and "peasants."

There was also a fifth category which we did not regard as a social class in the same sense, namely Communist "party personnel." As we shall see in the following chapter, both in their spontaneous references to the subject of class differentiation and when specifically asked to designate the major social groups in Soviet society, our respondents in overwhelming degree suggested a distinction — although not always a well defined one — between "the party" or "party people" and the "nonparty people." We believe that this probably reflects, although in greatly exaggerated form, one of the massive structural features of Soviet society. In the mind of the population the distinction between party and nonparty is apparently one of the most meaningful and significant bases of social differentiation (although not of political cleavage) and one which looms as large as any other. But the uniformity of emphasis on the distinction between party and nonparty tends to obscure certain other important differences between the social classes in Soviet society.

Before proceeding to the substance of our discussion of social class cleavage, we must anticipate in a measure the findings of the following chapter, so that those of this chapter will be seen in proper perspective. It is true, as we have already said, and will continue to say in this chapter, that our respondents were inclined to mention spontaneously the distinction between party and nonparty people with such frequency that it tended at times to obscure other possible points of cleavage in the Soviet social structure. As we shall see in the next chapter, there are various reasons why the party, nonparty distinction should have high salience among the refugees. However, this salience tells us little about the depth or qualitative nature of party and nonparty cleavage.

Fair Shares

To ascertain the views of our respondents as to the legitimacy of the rewards received by the major social classes in Soviet society we put the following question in our written questionnaire.

In every society each social class* has a definite investment in the well-being

---

* Unfortunately, the social strata being assessed and those doing the evaluation have the same formal designations. To avoid confusion we have adopted the convention in this chapter of calling the sets of respondents "rating groups" or "opinion groups" and

of society, and in its turn receives a definite reward from society. Certain classes get more out of society than they deserve; some classes less, and others just what they deserve. Below is cited a list of classes in Soviet society. We would like you to indicate which of these you think receive more, which less, and which receive what they deserve. Check the line which you think correct for each.

In contrast with the opinion about the party people, concerning whom there was virtual unanimity that they received *more* than they deserved, the overwhelming majority of our respondents felt that those in all other classes were receiving less than they deserved (Table 84). The central tendency in our sample, which cuts across class lines, is to say that the Communists in Soviet society were in a category by themselves, receiving more than they deserved, whereas the rest, the ordinary nonparty people regardless of class differences, received less than they deserved.* A forty-four-year-old industrial engineer and administrator, who was, in fact, quite well off, expressed this sentiment precisely when he said:

Yes, some people lived well in the Soviet Union, like Ilya Ehrenburg and others who toady to the regime, let alone the *Politburo* people. But for the rest, for me, the directors, the factory workers, and worst of all, the farmers — there is only poverty.

TABLE 84 [3A]

PER CENT STATING SELECTED SOCIAL CLASSES RECEIVED
"LESS THAN DESERVED": BY RATING GROUP

Social class whose situation is judged	Rating group				Average for all groups
	Intelligentsia	White-collar employees	Workers	Collective farm peasants	
Intelligentsia	74%	72%	51%	50%	62%
White-collar employees	83	88	66	59	74
Workers	93	93	93	94	93
Peasants	99	99	98	97	98
Total number of respondents	623	659	727	338	2347

A further glance at Table 84 however, makes it perfectly evident that below this general level of agreement and mutual compassion there is sub-

the strata being judged "social classes." In the original question the word "group" was used, but the wording has been changed here in accord with the convention adopted for this chapter.

* Unless placed in perspective, this finding would lead one to exaggerate the significance of the party-nonparty cleavage. In the next chapter we shall see that although our respondents did see party people as having material advantages, they were also seen as suffering disadvantages in other respects.

stantial difference of opinion as to how far various classes were from receiving a fair share of the rewards offered by Soviet society. Opinions
are divided, however, only in regard to the situation of the nonmanual
classes, and the break of unanimity comes mainly in the ratings by
workers[4] and collective farmers. Thus, virtually everyone in each rating
group is willing to acknowledge that the peasant received less than he
deserved, and on the average 93 per cent of all respondents, regardless
of their own identification, were willing to allow the same in regard to
the workers. There is no such unanimity of opinion regarding the situation of the intelligentsia and the employees. Indeed there are differences
of 24 and 23 percentage points, respectively, between the rating groups
which most and least frequently acknowledged these classes to receive
less than they deserved.

The employees and the intelligentsia were not nearly so likely to see
themselves as suffering deprivation as they were to see the deprivation
suffered by workers and peasants. To this extent they appear to be willing
to admit and to be influenced by the objective reality of a differential
in the rewards received by them as against those which fell to the peasant and worker class. For example, an industrial administrator, over
fifty, reported:

I had a good job. I belonged to a very small number of the well off. . . . But
imagine now if only one member of a family works, and if he should have three
children, how they live no one knows. Before the war, there was plenty to eat
if you had the money. I had the money, but the poor workers had little.

The crucial point, however, is that workers and peasants appear to
be more strongly affected in their "subjective" reaction to this "objective"
differential reward. For the individual who identified himself with the
worker or peasant group it was about equally likely that he would look
upon the members of the intelligentsia as receiving about as much as they
deserved, or even more than they deserved, as it was that he would acknowledge them to receive less than a full share. Further, although the
feeling was somewhat less strong, workers and peasants apparently take
much the same view of the rewards of the employees as they do of those
received by the intelligentsia. There is, then, a fairly sharp split along
the line of manual vs. nonmanual groups on the question of the legitimacy
of rewards, but the doubts are expressed mainly *in* and *from* one direction. The nonmanual groups grant the relative deprivation of their
compatriots engaged in physical labor, but the manuals fail to recipro-
cate to the same degree, workers and peasants expressing substantial
doubt as to the relative deprivation of the employees and the intelligentsia. Thus, a forty-three-year-old smith, responded to a question on the
material conditions of workers and peasants by saying: "They are alike;

neither has anything. People live from day to day." But he went on, without prompting, to add: "I don't count the employees . . . They are better off."

Another important dimension of this problem only implicitly treated in our discussion up to this point, involves the degree of differentiation manifested in the opinion expressed by each of the rating groups. This degree of differentiation is most simply expressed by the spread from the lowest to the highest percentage of each group which acknowledged the deprivation of the classes on which it was asked to vote. A glance at Table 84 will reveal that although in *each* rating group the smallest percentage rated the intelligentsia as deprived, and the largest number rated the peasant as deprived, the difference between the two percentages varies substantially from one rating group to another. The nonmanual groups show much less "spread" in the perceived levels of deprivation than do the manuals. In one sense, therefore, the opinions of members of the intelligentsia and the employee rating groups about the deprivation of their own and other classes are relatively less differentiated than are the opinions of the ordinary workers and the peasants.

There are various interpretations which can be put on this difference. One explanation might be that the workers and peasants are more discriminating and less prone to generalization than are the employees and the intelligentsia. This must be rejected, however, since our extensive experience with the questionnaire shows that to an overwhelming degree the tendency to give more discriminating answers is greater among the intelligentsia and employee groups. It seems reasonable to assert, therefore, that to some extent the nonmanual group members are repressing, or at least glossing over a distinction which it is painful to admit. It is as if some members of the intelligentsia were saying in effect, "Well, we were all so relatively deprived that one should not make too much of any slight differences between us." As one young construction engineer and inventor put it: "The workers may say that the directors lived well and get well paid, but this is not so. The director has his fill of troubles." By contrast the workers were in effect saying, "Yes, indeed, we were very badly off, but the other fellows, those in the position of intelligentsia or employee, did not fare so badly after all."

It is understandable that being themselves better off the intelligentsia and the employees were more easily able to feel and express their sympathy for groups other than their own, in contrast to a less empathetic orientation among the workers and peasants. It might also be that there were stronger feelings of guilt about their position in Soviet society among those in the intelligentsia and employee groups. The workers and peasants had little enough to feel guilty for. Or it might be that there was a higher level of aggression toward other social classes, or at least a lesser inhibition on its expression, among the workers and peasants. As we shall see, the remainder of our evidence gives some support to each of these interpretations, which are indeed relatively congruent.

Coincidence of Interests

Although the salient social cleavage in Soviet society is between the party and nonparty segments, our respondents' images of who gets his "fair share" suggests that there are points of appreciable tension within the nonparty portion of the populace. Some classes are seen as doing proportionately better than others, and those who did least well were most conscious of the inequities. It does not necessarily follow, however, that these inequities are perceived consciously as a consequence of incompatibility of interests between the various nonparty social classes. Each person was, therefore, asked a question directed at his perception of conflicts and congruence of interest between the social classes of Soviet society. The question was: "Below is given a paired list of classes in Soviet society. We would like to know for each of these pairs . . . do their interests coincide with or contradict each other? Check the condition you think correct for each group." Six pairs of classes were listed: workers-peasants, workers-intelligentsia, peasants-intelligentsia, [white-collar] employees-workers, [white-collar] employees-intelligentsia, and party-nonparty people.[5]

Once more our respondents saw the basic cleavage of interests in Soviet society to be between party and nonparty persons, since about 95 per cent in each rating group said that the interests of party and nonparty people were in conflict. On the other hand, our respondents predominantly saw the interests of nonparty groups as coinciding. If we look at Table 85, in which the rating for the nonparty groups are summarized, we see that there are only two instances out of twenty-four in which a majority of any rating group felt that the interests of two paired classes were in conflict. The rating group was in both instances the peasants, and they most often saw their *own* interests to be in basic conflict with those of the intelligentsia and employees.[6]

However, within this general picture of harmony of interest among the nonparty portion of Soviet society there are substantial variations. The greatest conflict of interest is seen as occurring between the intelligentsia and the peasant, over half our respondents saw a conflict of interest between the two groups (row 3). The least conflict is seen between neighboring groups at either end of the social ladder — between workers and peasants (row 6), and between intelligentsia and employees (row 1). Again, the basic cleavage point within the nonparty populace is seen to lie between the manual and nonmanual groups. White-collar employees

TABLE 85 [6A]

PER CENT OF RATING GROUPS WHO SEE COINCIDENCE OF
INTERESTS BETWEEN SELECTED PAIRS OF SOCIAL CLASSES

Pairs of classes judged	Rating group				Average for all groups
	Intelli- gentsia	White- collar employees	Workers	Collective farm peasants	
Intelligentsia — White-collar employees	89%	80%	76%	67%	78%
Intelligentsia — Workers	72	59	56	51	60
Intelligentsia — Peasants	69	55	52	44	55
White-collar employees — Workers	77	72	67	55	68
White-collar employees — Peasants	72	70	60	48	63
Workers — Peasants	83	74	88	80	81
Total number of respondents	519	545	470	249	1783

and workers (row 4) — neighbors across the manual-nonmanual boundary
— are seen as having somewhat less concurrence of interest than either
of the other paired *adjacent* groups, namely, the intelligentsia-employee
pair and the worker-peasant pair. All groups in the sample share this
pattern of perception. We feel it not unlikely that all segments of Soviet
society share an image of class relations in which: the greatest conflict of
interests is seen between the classes at the opposite ends of the social
scale; the greatest congruence is felt to exist between strictly adjacent
groups; and the manual-nonmanual distinction is more important than
class differences *within* each of these two larger social categories.

While a majority among the members of all social groups would see
group relations according to these patterns, there are interesting variations in the ratings made by particular social strata, variations which are
evidence of some measure of cleavage in the society. In virtually every
instance the members of the higher strata saw more harmony in the
society as a whole than did those lower in standing. If one looks at the
rows in Table 85 he sees that in every instance but one, the proportion

who saw congruence in the interests of any pair of social classes drops regularly with each step down the social ladder. The trend is perhaps best exemplified by row 3, in which 69 per cent of the intelligentsia see their interests and those of the peasants as coincident, whereas a majority of 56 per cent of the peasants reject this notion. The exception to this trend involves the worker-peasant pair (row 6). Here we see that the two manual groups see somewhat more harmony in this relationship involving themselves, than do the members of the intelligentsia and the employees who rate them.

This strong contrast in the views which the intelligentsia and the peasantry hold with respect to their mutual relations suggests that it would be of interest to look more closely at such reciprocal images. Table 86 presents some figures which give us a picture of the tendency of each rating group either to overestimate or underestimate the degree of harmony between itself and other groups. Consider, for example, the previously cited disagreement about the peasant-intelligentsia relationship, with regard to which 69 per cent of the intelligentsia but only 44 per cent of the peasants saw a coincidence of interest (row 3 of Table 85). The intelligentsia may be scored as overestimating the coincidence of interest, and the peasants as underestimating it. Furthermore, the *amount* of over and underestimation may be given as the difference between the two percentages. In this case 69 minus 44 yields 25. Such a comparison was made for each such paired groups, and we know that each group rated itself *vis à vis* the three other groups. In the first two columns of Table 86 we have recorded the number of times members of a given rating group over or underestimated the degree of coincidence of its interest with that of the other group making the same rating. In the third and fourth columns we have recorded the direction and the sum of the magnitudes of such over and underestimations. And in the last column the net error, with a plus for net over and a minus for net underestimation.

The final column of Table 86 shows more clearly what we saw above in Table 85, namely that the manual groups more regularly and more often see conflict of interest between the classes of Soviet society than do the nonmanual groups. The peasants never "overestimate" the amount of harmony between themselves and any other group. Rather in all three instances they "underestimate" it. The exact opposite is true of the intelligentsia. The employees and workers, standing at neither extreme of the social scale, had to rate themselves in relation to adjacent groups, both directly above and directly below them, and for this reason show a mixed pattern. In all the ratings made, there is no case in which a group higher in the social hierarchy did not see more harmony in its relationship with a lower status group than did the lower status group rating that same relationship.

TABLE 86

RECIPROCAL JUDGMENTS OF COINCIDENCE OF INTERESTS AMONG SOCIAL CLASS GROUPS

Rating group	Instances of		Sum of		
	"over-estima-tion"	"under-estima-tion"	"over-estima-tion"	"under-estima-tion"	Net[a]
Intelligentsia	3	0	50	0	+50
White-collar employees	2	1	27	9	+18
Workers	1	2	8	21	−13
Collective farm peasants	0	3	0	55	−55

a. + equals net overestimation; − equals net underestimation.

As we found in comparing the rating groups' estimates of how the several social classes fared in getting what they "deserved," we now see again that the lower classes take a less sanguine view about the absence of conflict within the nonparty segment of Soviet society. In particular, the workers and peasants quite often see themselves as sharing common interests *in opposition* to the nonmanual classes. We make no inferences at this point as to the strength of the social cleavage which is reflected here, but the pattern is clear. One factor which may have exerted a dampening effect on the tendency to see conflict *between* classes comes from the fact that there were important strains within classes. The conflict between the party and nonparty member, especially within the intelligentsia, is an outstanding example. There were similar strains within the manual classes. The Stakhanovites, or super-workers, were notable sources of within-class conflict. As one tractor driver put it, "they made money *at the expense of the other workers.*" Yet despite such targets internal to one's class, and despite the availability of the super-enemy in the form of the Communist Party, many of those in the manual classes showed a marked sense of conflict with the intelligentsia. One kolkhoznik of fifty-five, expressed such sentiment clearly when he said:

The city intelligentsia looked down upon us and they even joked about collective farmers. We were dirty and downtrodden. A person who had any pity or sympathy would ask himself why certain people were created to do such heavy and unpaid work. . . . They [the workers] were more sympathetic to the extent that they themselves had originally come from agriculture.

Harm Inflicted by and on Various Classes

Respondents to our written questionnaires were asked: "Which of the following classes has done the most harm to the (*workers*) under the

Soviet regime? The workers themselves, the peasants, the employees, the intelligentsia, the party cadres?" They were then asked: "Which of these groups is second in this respect (of harmfulness)?" These questions were repeated for all four social classes: intelligentsia, employees, workers, and peasants.

It will not surprise the reader to learn that 95 per cent of our respondents chose the party cadre as *most* harmful to each other social class. The salience of the basic party-nonparty cleavages was reflected in the fact that about one quarter of our respondents also nominated the party cadres as the *second* source of harm. Our interest here being confined to cleavages other than the one between party and nonparty people, our analysis is restricted to those respondents who cited classes other than the party as sources of harm. In other words, we are dealing only with data describing which classes were seen as *second* in harmfulness, since the party was almost always mentioned as first in harmfulness. While this procedure is legitimate in view of our specific objectives, we must be more cautious than usual in interpreting the absolute figures yielded by the responses to this question. Our respondents' answers are not spontaneous assertions that one class harmed another, but represent

TABLE 87 [6B]

PERCEIVED SOURCES OF HARM TO FOUR SOCIAL CLASSES:

BY RATING GROUP

Rating group	A Per cent of rating groups asserting harm done to intelligentsia by					B Per cent of rating groups asserting harm done to w.c. employees by				
	Intel.	Empl.	Wrks.	Psnts.	Total resp.	Intel.	Empl.	Wrks.	Psnts.	Total resp.
Intelligentsia	[56][a]	12	30	2	(361)	12	[56]	31	1	(341)
White-collar employees	[55]	10	31	4	(347)	17	[47]	34	2	(334)
Workers	[63]	21	12	4	(304)	37	[45]	13	5	(327)
Collective farm peasants	[62]	24	8	6	(151)	44	[38]	11	7	(154)

Rating group	C Per cent of rating groups asserting harm done to workers by					D Per cent of rating groups asserting harm done to peasants by				
	Intel.	Empl.	Wrks.	Psnts.	Total resp.	Intel.	Empl.	Wrks.	Psnts.	Total resp.
Intelligentsia	13	17	[66]	4	(394)	11	18	30	[41]	(378)
White-collar employees	20	16	[61]	3	(373)	20	16	32	[32]	(366)
Workers	40	23	[33]	4	(365)	40	28	11	[21]	(358)
Collective farm peasants	38	29	[28]	5	(157)	39	35	14	[12]	(164)

a. Numbers in brackets indicate the per cent who asserted that the group rated harmed itself.

choices which we forced them to make. Even in this situation of forced choice, they appeared to be reluctant to admit that anyone other than party cadres did harm.

The basic data pertaining to our analysis are summarized in Tables 87 and 88. It will be noted that the answers to this question can be organized around either the recipient or the originator of the harm. Table 87 focuses on the recipient, and shows us who was seen as harming each of the four social classes. Table 88, on the other hand, tells us to whom each of the classes was seen as doing harm. Each table contains, of course, the same data, but organized so as to bear on a different problem focus.

The main impact of the data in these tables is to reinforce the evidence that our respondents were extremely reluctant to claim that any non-party class was a source of harm to any other. Part A of Table 87, for example, may be regarded as an answer to the question: "What non-party class did most harm to the intelligentsia?" We see that the members of each rating group agree that the intelligentsia were most harmed by *themselves*, that is, by members of the intelligentsia. The modal response that each social class was most harmed by itself (the numbers that are bracketed in each table) was given in eleven out of sixteen instances.

TABLE 88 [6c]

ASSESSMENTS OF HARM DONE BY FOUR SOCIAL CLASSES:

BY RATING GROUP

Rating group	A Per cent of rating groups asserting harm done by intelligentsia to				B Per cent of rating groups asserting harm done by w.c. employees to			
	Intel.	Empl.	Wrks.	Psnts.	Intel.	Empl.	Wrks.	Psnts.
Intelligentsia	[56][a]	12	13	11	12	[56]	17	18
White-collar employees	[55]	17	20	20	10	[47]	16	16
Workers	[63]	37	40	40	21	[45]	23	28
Collective farmers	[62]	44	38	39	24	[38]	29	35

Rating group	C Per cent of rating groups asserting harm done by workers to				D Per cent of rating groups asserting harm done by peasants to			
	Intel.	Empl.	Wrks.	Psnts.	Intel.	Empl.	Wrks.	Psnts.
Intelligentsia	30	31	[66]	30	2	1	4	[41]
White-collar employees	31	34	[61]	32	4	2	3	[32]
Workers	12	13	[33]	11	4	5	4	[21]
Collective farmers	8	11	[28]	14	6	7	5	[12]

a. Numbers in brackets indicate the per cent who held that the group harmed itself.

The exceptions to this general pattern occur where we have by now learned to expect them — the manual groups more often feel that they were harmed by the intelligentsia and less often see the harm as coming from their own manual class ranks.

Table 88 is organized so as to answer the question: "To whom did each nonparty class do most harm?" In this instance, the unanimous opinion of our respondents is: "They harmed themselves more than they harmed anyone else." Thus in part A of Table 88 the representatives of each social group give as their most frequent response the opinion that the intelligentsia harmed themselves more than they harmed any other class group. The relevant percentages are bracketed. The same agreement is expressed in each of the other divisions of Table 88. Again, looked at in this perspective, the data show that this refugee group was reluctant to state that any class *except the party* was harmful to any other non-party stratum.

Accepting this basic fact, we may now turn to the exceptions, and other variations in these data. We have noted already that in Table 87 the workers and the peasants were not consistently in agreement with the prevailing opinion that all nonparty groups were harmed most by themselves. There are indeed a number of sharp divergences in the interpretations of the source from which the harm experienced by any class emanated. In some cases, this involves a fairly smooth progression, as in evaluations of harm done to the peasants by peasants (bracketed column of part D in Table 87). In other instances there is a sharp break at the dividing line between manual and nonmanual occupations, as in evaluations of harm done to employees by the workers (third column in part B, Table 87). Whichever the pattern, the end result is a marked disagreement between those at the bottom and those at the top of the occupational hierarchy. For example, in assessing the harm done by the workers to the intelligentsia (column 1, part C, Table 88), the employees cite the workers as having harmed the intelligentsia four times as often as the peasants make that charge (30 per cent vs. 8 per cent). Although this is the most extreme case, the opinion groups repeatedly differ in the ratio of 2:1 in the proportions citing one class as the source of harm to another.

In Table 89 we have summarized the "harmfulness" of each class as it is perceived by the members of the various rating groups in our sample. Each figure in the body of the table is an average of three different percentages, or "votes," on the harmfulness of a group as measured against three social class targets. The bottom row sums up further to give an average of nine "votes," three by each rating group for three different situations. This should, therefore, give us a clear impression of the overall attitude about each social class's harmfulness. We can see, from the bottom row of Table 89, that the intelligentsia is rated by the others as far and away the most harmful, and the peasants as least harmful to other social classes. The percentages are in the extraordinary ratio of eleven to one. No more than 4 per cent of any other group ever sees the peasants as harming another social group. For all practical purposes everyone agrees that the peasantry is harmless to other social classes.

TABLE 89 [6D]

AVERAGE HARMFULNESS TO OTHER GROUPS ATTRIBUTED
TO FOUR SOCIAL CLASSES

Rating groups	Social classes judged			
	Intelli-gentsia	Employ-ees	Workers	Peasants
Intelligentsia	[12]%	16 %	30 %	3 %
White-collar employees	19	[14]	33	3
Workers	39	24	[12]	4
Collective farm peasants	40	29	11	[6]
Average opinion of all groups[a]	33	23	24	3

a. The figures in this row average those in the columns, exclusive of the bracketed numbers.

While the intelligentsia, the employees, and the workers are all in complete agreement as to the harmlessness of the peasants, we find that there is less agreement when our respondents rate the other classes. The intelligentsia, for example, get their "bad reputation" primarily from the ratings given them by the workers and peasants, the employees having a much kinder opinion of their fellow nonmanual group. Essentially the same pattern holds for the ratings given the employees and the workers. The nonmanual groups see the workers as proportionately more harmful, and the manual groups see the employees as such. Thus, with the exception of the unanimity expressed on the harmlessness of the peasantry, the basic manual-nonmanual cleavage reveals itself once more in these data.

To this point we have not referred to the ratings which each rating group gave to itself, presented in the figure on the descending diagonal of Table 89. We notice that no group sees itself as particularly harmful to others. But, what is more interesting is that the opinion which each group has of itself is very close to that held by its partner on the same side of the manual-nonmanual line. The self-images of the intelligentsia and the employees are similar to the images they have of each other, and comparatively dissimilar to the images which the workers and peasants hold of the two nonmanual groups. The same pattern holds — in reverse of course — for the self images of the workers and peasants. This suggests that not only is the manual-nonmanual distinction a point of cleavage, but also that on this question the groups on either side of the line exhibit a good deal of class solidarity.

We may now summarize the images which our respondents have of the harmfulness of the various classes. Major harmfulness is attributed to the party, and all groups show a reluctance to attribute harmfulness to any nonparty group. In a situation of forced choice our respondents tend to say essentially: "If the nonparty people harmed anyone, they harmed themselves, but not anyone else." The manual groups, and the peasants in particular, do not however, agree entirely with this. Indeed, the manual-nonmanual distinction appears to be of more salience on the issue of "social harm" than on other questions. When the members of the several social groups do see a nonparty group as being harmful to others, it is predominantly a group on the other side of the manual-nonmanual line which is seen as doing the harm. Workers and peasants show a quite noticeable tendency to see the nonmanual classes, and particularly the intelligentsia, as harmful to the manual classes. The strength of feeling they sometimes showed may be seen in the following comment by a forty-five-year-old woman Ukrainian collective farmer, who identified those who got ahead in the world as:

People who lost their conscience, all their honesty, who are able to destroy other people in order that they themselves live a good life. . . . They are cruel, they are willing tools of the Communist Party. They are the dirtiest element in the Soviet Union.

Additional Indices of Class Antagonism

The questions we have just examined all have in common a rather explicit focus on the issue of class relations, and their very wording might have aroused or excessively stimulated class consciousness. As a result, those questions may give an exaggerated impression of the intensity of class sentiment. This would by no means invalidate the answers, but it does oblige us to ask whether the same patterns would emerge, and with comparable intensity, in the answers to questions not so explicitly focused on themes like sharing, conflict, and harm. Fortunately, there were several other questions in our schedules which in rather different contexts led our respondents to evaluate the relative situation of the several social classes.

On the whole the same pattern we have noted emerged from the answers. For example, when we asked how various elements of the population had fared under the German occupation, a question in some respects similar to that on fair shares, the manual and nonmanual rating groups certainly did not agree on the condition of the peasants and the intelligentsia (Table 90). Indeed the members of the intelligentsia rate themselves to have been worse off four times as often as the peasants were willing to grant them that honor. There was a similar disagreement concerning who was most friendly toward the occupying Germans. In this particular context to say a group was "friendly to the Germans" was more complimentary than not, since in this context it was equivalent to being "hostile to the Bolsheviks." Again then, to the manual groups the reputation of the intelligentsia is not nearly so shining as it appears to the nonmanuals, and indeed members of the intelligentsia rated the intelligentsia as "friendly" six times more often than did the peasants.

TABLE 90 [6E]

DIFFERENTIAL PERCEPTION OF CLASS ADJUSTMENT TO GERMAN OCCUPATION

Rating group	Per cent stating:			
	Peasants fared best	Intelligentsia fared worst	Intelligentsia most friendly	Total number of respondents
Intelligentsia	47%	41%	30%	(184)
White-collar employees	39	27	26	(211)
Workers	24	14	10	(281)
Collective farmers	22	10	5	(118)

The disagreement as to the qualities of the various classes extended to the area of manners and social deportment. When asked who would offer an old lady a seat in a streetcar the intelligentsia overwhelmingly (87 per cent) nominated their own class, and a mere 9 per cent thought that a peasant would be so courteous. Again the workers and peasants hardly agreed unequivocally with this picture of the gallantry of the intelligentsia and their own lack of manners. Only 54 per cent of the workers acknowledged the courteousness of the intelligentsia, and they named themselves as the gallant ones three times as often as the white-collar people admitted that possibility.

Further evidence of the meaningfulness to our respondents of their class identification and of their sense of distinctness from other classes distant in the social hierarchy, comes from our qualitative interviews. An independent analysis of class images spontaneously presented by our informants during those interviews led to the conclusion that both peasants and workers tend rather persistently to think of themselves as belonging to a distinctive social group, defined largely in terms of its powerlessness and its relatively depressed economic state compared to the more favored strata of society.[7] As compensation they seemed to regard themselves as having certain special qualities which by implication or directly they denied to the "others" who were in more favored statuses. Among these qualities were hospitality and the ability to get along with people. At the same time it was evident that many of the workers and peasants also looked up to the intelligentsia and admired their attainments.

People who did not regard themselves as definitely one of "the plain ordinary people," were generally not very specific as to what their appropriate designation should be. Their self-conception apparently was defined largely by what they were not: neither one of the common people, nor one of the elite. Skilled workers often viewed themselves in this light, but mainly the group contained the range of white-collar personnel from clerks and bookkeepers through the professional and administrative ranks. Although in this group too there was evident concern with the material conditions of life, such problems were clearly not the essential criterion of their self-defined class position. Indeed, their being better off than the "plain workers and ordinary peasants," was not perceived as just and proper, but rather was tinged with guilt and a quality of compassion for those "less well favored." At the same time they certainly did not look up to these "plain" people. On the contrary they often viewed the lower classes as lower not merely in income and status, but also as lower in development, accomplishment, sensitivity, culture, and other desirable personal qualities associated with the higher status.

Conclusions

In marked contrast to their hostile reaction to Communist Party members *taken as a class,* these former Soviet citizens feel that on the whole the other four classes all got less than they deserved, had interests in harmony with those of the others, and did relatively little harm to each other. Half of each social group agreed that the peasants were most friendly to the Germans and very few in any class asserted the contrary. Half or more of each group nominated the intelligentsia as the most polite of all, and less than 5 per cent of each class claimed they were impolite. This suggests that our sample showed only a modest degree of class hostility or conflict, and insofar as this is an index of class cleavage, we might conclude that such cleavage does not run very deep in the Soviet Union.

Against this impression, however, we must weigh the evidence of disagreement in the mutual images the classes have of each other. There

is evidence of conflict and hostility below the surface of general agreement and harmony. We found substantial and consistent differences in
the assessment of the situation of the nonmanual as against the manual
classes, which was most sharp when the poles of the class hierarchy
were contrasted. Workers and peasants are seen as more deprived, as
sharing common interests, and as being less frequently the cause of harm
to other classes, and there is good agreement about this from rating group
to rating group. The nonmanual classes are seen as not quite so deprived,
as having interests in common with other classes less frequently, and as
more often being the source of the harm done to others. In part these
trends are a reflection of interesting differences in the class patterning of
perceptions of the whole structure of interclass relations. In general the
upper classes were less sure of their virture than the lower groups, and the
lower classes indeed often failed to allow the uppers the benefit of the
doubt. Thus, the intelligentsia see everyone as rather deprived, but
the workers and peasants felt that the nonmanual classes were not always
so badly off; the nonmanuals more often saw coincidence of interest
where the lower classes saw conflict; and the nonmanuals more often
saw themselves as harming, whereas the manuals more often saw themselves as harmed by others. Furthermore, these differences in perception become really outstanding when the situations evaluated involved
relations across the manual-nonmanual line, over which most of the
tension seemed to be expressed. Indeed, there is much evidence that solidarity is felt on a class basis, with an important cleavage line separating
the manual from the nonmanual classes. When half the workers and
peasants feel the interests of the intelligentsia and the laboring classes
do not coincide, this must be recognized as far from inconsequential. It
indicates a degree of class antagonism which must be given careful consideration.

The ultimate significance of those sentiments, of course, depends on
the action consequences which follow from them. One may well ask
whether the degree of hostility and resentment apparently felt by the
manuals toward the nonmanuals, and the lesser respect which the white-
collar people have for the manuals, has any significant influence on the
political sentiments of our respondents; and whether this in turn has
implications for future political developments inside the Soviet Union.

The influence of class cleavage on political judgment is clearly evident
in Table 91. Members of the intelligentsia give the leading role in a
future state to the professional and technical intelligentsia as against
the workers and peasants in the ratio of more than 2:1, whereas the ratio
is only 1:1 among the manual groups. Further evidence of hostile feeling
is reflected in the high proportion of the intelligentsia (56 per cent), and

to a lesser extent of the employees, who voted for *exclusion* of the workers from the leading role in politics, even though the question made available the easy target of the vaguely defined "Politicians" as a group against whom to cast their vote.

TABLE 91 [7A]

PER CENT[a] CITING VARIOUS TYPES AS MOST AND LEAST DESIRED LEADERS IN A FUTURE STATE: BY RATING GROUP

	Rating group			
	Intelli-gentsia	White-collar employees	Worker	Collective farm peasants
Type of person *most* wanted as leader				
Intelligentsia	66%	63%	48%	42%
Workers and Peasants	25	34	49	41
Politicians	40	41	31	30
Total number of respondents	(493)	(501)	(504)	(229)
Type of person *least* wanted as leader				
Intelligentsia	12%	15%	19%	17%
Workers and Peasants	56	40	26	26
Politicians	51	54	54	58
Total number of respondents	(485)	(472)	(497)	(224)

a. Per cents may total to more than 100 since some respondents named more than one group as "most" or "least" wanted.

To balance this impression, we should keep it in mind that the question asked not for an opinion as to the *extent* of any group's political role, but rather for an absolute judgment as to which group was *most* wanted and which *least* wanted. Considering the stringency of this "most-least" test, it is perhaps striking that almost half of the manual groups voted *for* the technical and professional intelligentsia as the group they wanted *most* to lead. Further, less than a fifth of the manual groups would specifically assign the intelligentsia the least important role, and it is particularly notable that the manuals assigned their own group this lesser role at least as frequently as they assigned it to the intelligentsia. Thus, we have evidence that class antagonism does convert to political antagonism, producing a significant cleavage between the classes, but it hardly takes on the dimensions of an unbridgeable chasm.

Since some of the class antagonism felt with regard to economic and social matters seems to convert rather readily into political sentiment, we are obliged to consider its probable significance on the level of practical politics. To do this meaningfully we need to estimate the level of such politically tinged class antagonism inside the Soviet Union. The level there might be considerably lower, in which case, of course, there would be no consequent problem for the system. It seems to us, however, that this assumption does not merit great confidence. There is nothing in the composition of our sample which would reasonably lead us to expect it to express *more* interclass hostility than comparable groups in the Soviet Union. On the contrary, we feel that the individuals in our sample were on the average consciously or unconsciously motivated to play down the amount of class hostility they actually felt in order to give a stronger impression of the solidarity among the Soviet people, regardless of class, in opposition to the Communist Party and the Soviet totalitarian regime.[8] If this is the case, it might well be that among those in the Soviet Union the levels of class antagonism would be higher than in our sample.

Assuming that the level of class hostility is as high in the USSR as in our sample, or even higher, would this be a critical problem for the system? Our answer is, in general, "no." To begin, it seems unlikely that such sentiment could find a political channel for expression. In the nature of the case, the one-party system in the Soviet Union does not allow the significant political expression of class feeling through the organization of a distinctive class based party functioning in opposition to other parties. Furthermore, the sharp restrictions on free discussion and on the development of factions or other formal divisions within the one legal party largely preclude the effective expression of this sentiment within the Communist Party as it is now organized. There was never any doubt about this in the Soviet Union, but now that they have available the horrible example of Djilas' book, *The New Class,* the possibility is more remote than ever.

If class feeling can find no formal political outlets, will it not then become a potentially explosive force within the larger system, or at least a consistent major drag on organized, unified efforts in pursuit of the common political goals of the society? We think not. We note again that the amount of hostility we have uncovered is hardly at an absolutely high level. Although class feeling may be a force in Soviet society, we feel it to be much less intense than political sentiment, and much less likely to produce cleavage than the Communist vs. non-Communist dichotomy. Our confidence in this conclusion is strengthened by such comparative material as we have. Two of the questions in our set on class relations have been reasonably matched in opinion studies in the United

States. One closely matched the question on "fair shares," since it asked a representative sample of Americans whether they thought the pay of unskilled workers and laborers, office clerks and stenographers, and business leaders and executives was "too much, not enough, or about right." Table 92 compares the results in the United States with those obtained

TABLE 92 [8A]

SOVIET AND AMERICAN VIEWS ON FAIR SHARES: BY CLASS

(Per cent saying groups judged received less than fair share)

Groups judged	Occupation of person judging			
	Professional-administrative	White collar	Skilled worker	Ordinary worker
1. American — "business leaders"	33%	33%	19%	16%
2. Soviet — "intelligentsia"	74	72	55	48
3. American — "office workers, clerical"	63	71	68	61
4. Soviet — "white-collar employees"	83	88	70	63
5. American — "unskilled workers, laborers"	70	67	81	85
6. Soviet — "workers"	93	93	96	93

from Soviet refugees. A broadly similar pattern emerges, in that the majority of the more favored white-collar classes acknowledge the deprived condition of the ordinary worker, while the manual laborer finds it more difficult to acknowledge business executives as underpriviliged than the white-collar workers, businessmen, and professionals do. Indeed, the data might be interpreted as suggesting that if anything the extent of class antagonism in the United States is greater, although this might be explained by the fact that the question was asked during the late depression year of 1938.

The similarity of the popular image of class relation in the United States and in our sample is further indicated by responses to a question on coincidence of interests. In February of 1940, a national sample of Americans was asked "Do you think interests of employers and employees are, by their very nature, opposed or are they basically the same?" Among executives 80 per cent, white-collar workers 70 per cent, and factory labor 41 per cent, said they were basically the same.[9] The comparable figures for the question on coincidence of interest asked of the refugees are: (from row 2 of Table 85) 72 per cent, 59 per cent, and 56 per cent, respectively. These figures indicate quite remarkable agreement on this issue in the two national groups.

These impressions drawn from comparative poll data are further supported by our own firsthand observation and that of our colleagues during our travels in the USSR in 1956 and 1957. Several of our colleagues concluded independently of each other that although the Soviet citizen seemed well aware of the class differences in his society these differences did not seem to be the basis of deep resentment or burning antagonism. On the contrary, they seemed quite calmly accepted, were not treated as deserving special attention, and seemed far less important than strictly political issues. Several observers were spontaneously struck with the fact that Soviet attitudes on this issue reminded them of popular sentiments on that same issue in the other great open class society, the United States. We were, in particular, struck by the tendency in the Soviet Union to follow the pattern of the American social structure in encouraging the discharge of feelings focused around the class issue through approved, politically neutral, channels. These include feeling morally superior, engaging in increased economic and social competition, and striving for still more mobility. In the light of these considerations and observations, we no more expect the Soviet Union to cleave asunder along this "fault plane" than the United States.

Nevertheless, it is clear that just as some of the hostility felt toward the regime "rubs off" on the intelligentsia, which is identified with the powers that be, just so some of the hostility against those who are better off and higher up "rubs off" on the regime in which the intelligentsia is seen to participate. We do not know how consciously it was done, but it seems that the regime's policy of periodically throwing the mighty down from their high places, and its more regular program of public criticism of "bureaucrats," have in part been efforts to placate some of the hostility which the lower classes apparently feel for those who are economically more favored. The latest manifestation of this tendency to occasionally cut down the advantages of the elite came in 1956 with the announcement that the extremely high earnings and special privileges of some categories of writers, artists and others would be cut down. There are, of course, sharp limits on how far the regime can go on this course without in turn unduly alienating the elite on which it rests so heavily. In the long run only a marked rise in the standard of living and the general life conditions of the lower classes can be expected to effect much reduction in their resentment of that small Soviet middle and upper class which derives so many more economic benefits and has so much larger a share in power. It is our impression, however, that the level of interclass antagonism which will exist until that time comes will not go beyond the levels easily managed by the system. Indeed the moderate existing class hostility may be manipulated by the regime to its own advantage by always keeping the "haves" slightly insecure, and the "have nots" always slightly hopeful.

XIV

Political Cleavage in the Soviet Union: Popular Images of the Party and the Secret Police*

Political cleavage can be defined in many ways. But crucial to any definition is the notion that one or more groups within a society feels itself to be a "We" against which is opposed a "They." Between the two there is felt to exist a deep and enduring conflict of interests and values as they pertain to the political community. There are many "We's" and corresponding "They's" upon which we might focus. In the other chapters of this part of our book we examine the relations among the various social class and nationality groups in the population to assess the extent of "We vs. They" feeling which develops around those foci of group allegiance. In this chapter we take the ordinary citizen as the "We" and inquire about the role of the party and the secret police as the "They." The questions we shall ask are: (1) To what extent and in what way are each of these organs of state power viewed by the people as a "They" against whose interests and values the people are opposed; (2) Who falls within the bounds of this group, and who does not; and (3) What is the significance of these inclusions and exclusions?

It is obvious that our formulation of the problem assumes that the "people" can be viewed as a whole without regard to the various ways in which we know them to be differentiated. There are, as we see in the preceding and following chapters, some social class, age, nationality and other differences relevant to our discussion of political cleavage. We shall ignore most of these differences and stress instead the areas of consensus. This is not so arbitrary as it might sound since feelings about the party and the secret police are largely shared by all segments in our sample.[1] Consensus far outweighs disagreement on this issue. Where various group differences are most relevant, however, they will be cited.

* This chapter was contributed by David B. Gleicher. We have condensed and somewhat altered the longer document of the same title written by him which appeared originally in the collaborative report by David Gleicher, Arthur E. Adams, Elisha Greifer, and Anna Weintraub, "Political Activism and Social Cleavage in the USSR," Harvard Project on the Soviet Social System, Russian Research Center, October 1954. We take full responsibility for any distortion which may have crept in as a result of our efforts.

The People and the Party

In 1917, Russia was a country which, after some twenty or thirty years of fairly rapid economic and social development, had been plunged into war and consequent economic and social breakdown. Its population was composed overwhelmingly of illiterate peasants. Only a small proportion of the population was in the industrial labor force or the technical intelligentsia. After the seizure and consolidation of power by the Bolsheviks the country was transformed into a powerful industrial giant, ruled by a vast bureaucratic network. In the process, every organized activity was controlled and directed from the center. Thus the single factory, the isolated collective farm, the youth club, the great trust, the regiments in the field and the boats on the ocean, even the theater company — all of these work structures were integrated directly in the bureaucratic machinery. In short, not only does *political* power reside in the state, but all power.

But the state itself is controlled by the Communist Party. This organization, just before its seizure of political power in 1917, had some 24,000 members. At that time it was a revolutionary organization whose members had that ideological elan which provided the zeal and self-sacrifice required for the fulfillment of revolutionary functions. The ordinary party member generally had a sense of full participation in the making of history. The contrast with his situation today was aptly summed up by a forty-six-year-old engineer: "The early communist considered himself a creator of the revolution; he felt its master, he was full of revolutionary romanticism. Now he is only an instrument of the leadership of the party."

From this organization of 24,000 the party now has grown to one of about seven million, and this figure does not include membership in the Komsomol or Young Communist League, whose membership comprises fully 50 per cent of all those in the age bracket roughly fifteen to twenty-five. The overwhelming bulk of the party members, at least 90 per cent, are not professional party functionaries, but rather are the people who staff the vast Soviet bureaucracy on all levels and in all its activities.

From the time of the First Five Year Plan the Soviet Union has experienced a severe shortage of technical, professional, and supervisory personnel on all levels. The regime made use of the technical and professional personnel inherited from the tsar, but there were not enough of them and their political reliability was in question. The regime tried to use party personnel as political guardians of these skilled people, but this did not work — how was the unqualified layman to assess the difference between technical need and sabotage, much less get the work done? The problem was to get reliability and skill in the *same* person. The skilled person had to be trained and disciplined, but so did the reliable person require training and discipline of another sort. For the politically reliable, formal technical education was required; for the technician, Komsomol and party membership. Hence the more than five-fold increase in the size of the party between the start of the First Five Year Plan and the present.

Today the party members are not only the political elite. They also comprise the bulk of the elite among personnel in all other segments of society — cultural, medical, academic, worker and peasant, military and police, and so on *ad infinitum*. In sum, the Soviet regime, through the party members acting in their various roles, controls all organized activities, not from the outside, but from the inside. These facts are crucial. For this common and nominal political identity of all elites in the Soviet Union, this near total identity between elitehood and party membership, is a crucial consideration with respect to political cleavage.

The elite composition of the party reflects two of the three major functions which it serves for the regime, namely the administration of Soviet life, and related to this, the provision of cadres from which the administrative personnel can be chosen. In addition, there is, of course, the more manifestly political function, whereby the regime seeks simul-taneously to assert its identification with the Soviet masses and to have agents of political agitation and propaganda among them. It is in the pursuit of this function that the party membership is assigned its mass character by the regime. Yet this is a highly variable function as the history of the party membership attests. When the regime is concerned about improving or "deepening" its contacts among the masses, the party's size increases rapidly — witness, for example, the wartime increase in party membership. The working and peasant class component of the party membership is quite modest, and it certainly represents an excep-tionally small fraction of the working and peasant classes themselves. Even after a tremendous postwar recruitment campaign, estimates for 1956 placed the proportion of party members who were junior foremen and rank-and-file workers at 18 per cent, and at 10 per cent for junior foremen and ordinary peasants on the collective farms. The 1,300,000 worker members were about 1 in 10 among their fellow workers, and the 750,000 peasant members a much smaller proportion of all collective farmers. On the other hand, among the intelligentsia and especially among supervisory personnel of all levels, the proportion of party mem-bers is very much greater. Despite minority status in the population they make up at least 50 to 60 per cent of the membership of the party. The proportion of members in various professions is generally at least 30 per cent and ranges as high as 80 or 90 per cent.[2] Membership is particularly expected of those with responsibility. Thus, in our refugee sample, males whose occupation gave them supervisory responsibilities, reported being party or Komsomol members twice as frequently as did those in similar occupations, but without such responsibility. It is these latter groups which, in the party as well as outside of it, wield the greater influence, carry the greater prestige and are socially more visible. And finally, it should be noted that the party is committed in its own words to enlisting only "the very best sons and daughters" of the nation. In short, the inherent dynamics of the party in Soviet society press for an elite membership, even on the worker and peasant level.

The Typical Party Member
Differentiated from the Nonmember

Our average respondent seems to have a pretty sharp sense of his separation from the party membership. Asked a direct question as to whether the interests of party members and other social groups "coincide," at least 95 per cent said they did not.[3] A less marked but nevertheless strong reaction was evident in the personal interviews, where 75 per cent cited important differences between the typical party member and everyone else.* The differences cited dealt with the following issues: opportunities for a good job and living standard; opportunities for self-expression, leisure and happiness in general; opportunity to participate meaningfully and responsibly in the life and destiny of the nation; differences of personal character and behavior; and finally, differences of a direct political nature involving belief and activity. Not all of these distinctions stressed the advantages of party membership. Indeed, a substantial number stressed the disadvantages. And no *one* distinction was cited by more than a minority of our respondents, indicating they held no clearcut, simplified stereotype of the party member.

With respect to opportunities for a good life, the general notion was that party members live better than nonmembers. It is notable that the people whose social class position is that of worker or peasant are about twice as likely (28 vs. 15 per cent) as the nonmanuals to cite this difference. The views of a fifty-year-old kolkhoznik are representative of the former. He says:

Now take the time of the famine; who lived and who didn't live? The party people lived because when everybody else had nothing to eat, the party people could go to special stores and get good food. [Then he says of the current situation] "Suppose I am a Communist and you are not. I will live well and you will live poorly. If I am a nonparty man and I have three children, they cannot get

* Except where otherwise indicated, the material in this chapter is based on the personal interviews. The written questionnaire provided only a few opportunities for commenting on the party personnel.

the education they need and they cannot get the food they need. If I am a party man, we will have plenty of money and we will get along well. Our kids can go to school.

This is the kind of statement which in other countries we have come to expect about social class rather than political membership differences. In the Soviet case, the nominal identity of political and economic elites is such that the political elite is to a marked degree seen in economic terms. We shall return to this subject shortly but we might note, meanwhile, that even among the economically most disadvantaged, only 28 per cent stress this economic aspect of political elite membership.

In the matter of opportunities for leisure, security and expressive behavior in general, party membership is associated with *disadvantage even more than with advantages*. This area, moreover, is stressed about twice as much by persons of nonmanual as by those with manual occupations. With regard to leisure, the view proposed is that the party member is committed to attending meetings, to reading the party press and to being examined on the adequacy of his reading, to participating in agitation efforts, to being the first to "volunteer" for the various special activities initiated by the party, and so forth. He is viewed as having less time in which to enjoy the pleasures of home life. This is considered a sacrifice because our informants so highly valued spending time with family and friends.

Along the same lines, the party member is seen as sacrificing his sense of individuality; as having to play the role of a convinced and energetic party member even though he does not believe in it at all. This is the element of "two-facedness," the notion of a party mask, the wearing of which is obligatory and prevents the party member from being himself. Clearly, this pertains mainly to the members who are "nonbelievers" and who, unlike the "careerists," * do not easily accept living a lie.

But if the party member sacrifices his leisure and his opportunity to be himself, he is assumed to gain nevertheless in his sense of security and confidence; he is on the side of the Soviet power. This means not only that he has fewer worries about making ends meet, but also that he can look upon his future with more confidence. In the popular image, he is seen as having less need to anticipate being sacrificed during the regime's pursuit of its various goals. The nonmember assumes that even if ultimately the member shares the popular fear of the secret police, he nevertheless is more secure against police action for petty infringements of the rules. Even though it is recognized that he too is limited in his power to manipulate his life situation, he nevertheless is felt to be in a better position than the nonmember to get scarce goods, to get a

* These and other types of party members are defined and discussed in the next section of this chapter.

job reassignment, to place his children in choice schools and jobs. In all these respects, it is assumed, the party member can feel more secure in his control of his life situation.

The person who seeks responsible and leading roles in the development of the Soviet nation, in the initiation of new and desirable techniques in industry, science, housing and architecture, or social services, is viewed as more likely to accomplish his aim with than without party membership. To a certain extent — for it certainly is possible to do so without the party card — party membership provides a kind of union card, permitting access to various types of work. And although it is possible for the nonparty man to achieve positions of trust and responsibility, it is much more probable that the party man will be found in such positions. Manifestly, this is not a problem for the mass of Soviet citizens, although it becomes a problem for ever larger numbers as the size of the technical and administration labor force increases. It is worthy of note that the greater mobility or advancement of the party person is cited especially, albeit not generally, by the intelligentsia. It seemed to reflect not so much a feeling of frustration in the nonmember, but rather suggested he was stimulated himself from time to time to join in order to get ahead faster.

Let us turn now to the differences in the personal qualities which our informants felt distinguished the party from the nonparty person. No one of these differences is cited by anything approaching a majority, and we cannot, therefore, assume that there is any common image of the party member's personality. We can, however, identify those characteristics which are most often attributed to party members. Some 25 per cent of the sample, nonmanuals and manuals alike, describe party members as overbearing, adopting a "herrenvolk" stance with respect to the nonmembers. One man put it this way:

Party people behave themselves more or less insolently. They are too proud and they want to show that they are the bosses. . . . They like too much to put forward their own self, to show that they know everything, that they understand everything. [And as a thirty-eight-year-old carpenter says]:
The party man, particularly in the small localities, is vulgar. They behave very haughtily because they feel that they are strong. They always talk in convinced tones and they never say "maybe it should be. . . ." They always say, "Things are like this and that's the way it should be." They don't even argue.

This is the picture of the party member that we might have expected to follow from the image of him either as having political elite status, or as a believer in the Bolshevik mission. Since only one person in four made such a reference, however, we cannot assume that the great majority view the party members as far removed from the people, as emphasizing their differences from the superiority over the people. In fact the great majority of our respondents tend to emphasize the opposite in their references to those party members in their actual ken.

The overbearing member is the one called the "activitist." He is the person who makes all the appropriate noises, who gets the line from his party superiors and who attempts by every gesture to prove his enthusiastic support of it. He is noisy, strident, self-assured, and brooks no opposition because, after all, the line has been set by the party center and "this is the way it must be." The fact that only 25 per cent of our respondents cite such a person as a typical party member suggests in the popular image the great majority of party members are believed not to be activists, but, on the contrary, people who participate only minimally. In fact, Malenkov, at the Nineteenth Party Congress, gave a hint that this is true of the membership, since he decried the frequency of merely nominal membership. Further support from our data is provided by the failure of our respondents to cite items in the category "political beliefs and activity" as areas in which the party members are differentiated from the nonmembers.

Although references are frequently made to the careerist in the party and to his cruelty, cynicism and dishonesty, and although many held that the party literally demanded such behavior from its members by the logic of its practice, it is striking that less than 10 per cent of the sample cited such characteristics as applying to the typical members. We might note here, that this is far different from the case of the secret police or the NKVD'ist. At any rate, the failure of more people to make such citations emphasizes further the lack of a clear stereotype of the party member as an object of popular hostility.

Lastly, there are the differences associated with political belief and activity. Again, we find less than 10 per cent of our sample saying that what distinguishes the typical party member are his undying political beliefs and activity. Ninety per cent of these former Soviet citizens fail to "see" the party member in manifestly political terms.

Perhaps most important, with respect to these images of how the people in the party differ from those outside it, is the fact that no one difference is cited by more than one quarter of our respondents, much less by a majority. In short, so far as our respondents are concerned, there is no typical party member. As they said with regard to the treatment a party member deserves: "It depends." There is nothing approaching a stereotyped image of the party members, but there are conceptions of the differences among party members.

Popular Images of the Party Member

Only 16 per cent of those who were personally interviewed at length about their Soviet experience, failed to distinguish between different

kinds of party members. This minority lumped the party members all
together, big and little, under the category, "People's Enemies." They
put it this way: "They are wicked people. Those who get there (into the
party) accidentally will not last long," or, "All members of the party
should get a bullet. They all stood for the same program." But this
tendency for a wholesale lumping and rejection of party membership is,
in all social groups, a small minority response. The remaining 84 per
cent saw differences between and differentiated among party members.
The distinction made by these people were of three sorts, and most
people made more than one distinction: 78 per cent distinguished between
those who joined because they believed in the Communist dogma and
mission from those who joined for reasons other than belief; about 60 per
cent made contrasts on grounds of action and motivation, classifying some
as cruel, evil or bad, and others not; and 51 per cent made distinctions
according to the amount of power different party members had.

Believers vs. Nonbelievers: On the matter of belief, it is striking that
the great majority of party members are seen as nonbelievers. A frequently quoted estimate was that only 10 per cent, and these largely young
people, believed in the party ideology. In general, the notion is that the
believers left the party in the persons of the old Bolsheviks who are
viewed also as the victims of Stalin. The rest of the party members were
seen mainly as observers of ritual so far as political beliefs are concerned.
The top party leadership itself acknowledges the lack of political commitment among its membership, although the leaders are less inclined to
describe it as so widespread.

The residual mass of the nonbelievers is further differentiated in the
popular image, according to the reasons for their membership. In the first
place, there is a distinction made between voluntary and forced membership. As one young woman, a typist, put it, "It is not easy in the Soviet
Union to avoid going into the party if you are asked. If a person refuses,
he may be punished, or his wife and children may suffer." We might call
this type of member the "draftee." A second type is thought to have been
"forced" into membership by different pressures, such as the desire to fulfill their responsibilities toward themselves and their families, that is,
to achieve or maintain a decent standard of living. We might call him
the "compelled" member. This view was expressed most cogently by a
young kolkhoznik who said:

The *capable* person is invited to the party office and he is told that a man with
his ability and his talent could be a Communist and could have a good life and
a good job. And a lot of people went, of course. . . . Some people get tired of
having nothing, of the lack of everything, of being naked and hungry. And then
a man *decides,* maybe I will live a little better, and then he goes in. But not because he really wants to. And if you get into the party maybe you can be sent

to take a course. Maybe you can be a brigadier* or a leader, a man who gets more money, and really works less.

The idea of the "draftee" member is found only infrequently in its pure form. It is much more common to think of him as a man "compelled" to make an adjustment to the fact that the power and prestige of party membership lead to the avenues of successful participation in the various social, economic and cultural activities of the nation. This is the nature of the compulsion. To the extent that a person aspires to success — variously defined — he must to some degree feel pressured to join the party. This is not to say that party membership is viewed as the "open sesame" to Soviet success — some achieve it without the party, and many who are in the party fail to exploit their advantage. But for the man who combines ability, ambition and energy *with* party membership, the latter plays a significant role. Nonparty people appreciate this fact and the result is that the legitimacy of party membership, in the people's minds, comes increasingly to depend on the legitimacy they attach to the urge for successful participation in Soviet occupational life. It is in this sense that the meaning of party membership is increasingly. seen in nonpolitical terms.

Among those felt to have joined for reasons other than belief, there is a third type which is singled out for the most acrimonious criticism — this is the "careerist." As a type the careerist seems clearly delineated to most of our respondents, but on closer inspection this apparent clarity proves to be spurious. The "careerist" is the person who, in his own self-interest and self-seeking, sacrifices others to his own needs. It is not that he manipulates the party and mouths hypocrisies in its simulated support — this is accepted as *à la mode* — nor is it the fact that he wants a good life, for this too is accepted. It is rather the fact that he *willfully* sacrifices good people, and especially nonparty people, to the pursuit of his own ends which makes him a reprehensible character. We should here recall the previous observation that the legitimacy of party membership comes increasingly to depend on the legitimacy of social and economic rather than political motivation. The careerist represents those social and economic motivations whose legitimacy is *denied* by the people. As one young man put it, there are those among the party people "who have no morals and who want to make big careers." It is the lack of morals that defines the careerist.

But the careerist is much more easily defined in the abstract than he is in the case of a specific person. This is so because it is not so much *what* he does as *why* he does it. What this requires, of course, is that each case be examined in detail and by people who know the case best. As a young kolkhoznik said:

* The brigadier is a kind of foreman on the collective farm.

Some party people are themselves against the power and they have to live, and they have not hurt *many* people. Others desire a career and they want power and they have sent hundreds of people to prison. These people must be severely punished. Those who are *less* bad should receive less punishment. *You must ask people. You must find out what they have done.*

This quotation draws attention to the fact that by virtue of party membership people are expected to have done perhaps more, perhaps less, but certainly *some* bad things, and for more or less bad reasons. Thus, the careerist cannot be identified simply by the degree of success he has achieved, nor solely by the various party actions in which he was implicated, but rather by *how he himself viewed his own participation.* Similar considerations are applied in evaluating the "draftee" and the "compelled" member. Crucial in determining the extent of his guilt is his motivation, whether or not he himself hated what evil he had to do, and tried to avoid doing it.

It is apparent that in the popular view the meaning of party membership lies largely in its provision of an effective means of adapting to Soviet reality. Yet there are frequent references not only to what people "get out" of party membership, but also to what they have "to give" to it, what they are obliged to do for it. It becomes clear that despite all the empathy and understanding with which nonparty people view the individual members' reasons for joining, many, nevertheless, tend to regard the party group as a whole with distrust and suspicion. They feel this way largely because of their image of what happens to a member once he is in the party. It "forces" him to be a bad actor.

Good vs. Bad Actors: Party members are generally viewed as bereft of power to make policy. They are viewed as having an option, however, to behave decently *within* the range set by party policies. Accompanying the general notion that the party member is *supposed* to do evil things to people, is a majority viewpoint which holds that the party member *can,* in many ways, show that "he has a party card, but not a party heart." Within the limits set by his official responsibilities the party man is believed to have the option to be a "good or bad actor." Some of the illustrations which follow might appear to involve petty details. As such they emphasize perhaps the narrowness of the limits for action set for the member by party policy. Nevertheless, these actions were important to the people in our sample, and presumably also to the Soviet people themselves. As one young house painter put it, when asked about the differences between party and nonparty people:

It all depends. You cannot indicate any overall distinctions here. One of them, a party member, was a wonderful fellow; he lived very poorly, he helped his old mother, and he worked very hard. There are some wonderful people among the members. There are people who are in the party and are still a hell of a lot better than nonparty people. It is not as simple as that.

In other cases, we find references to party members who, in carrying out policies which they knew were generally disliked, indicated their helplessness or attempted reasonably to point out why they were good policies. Others are cited as accessible sources of friendly influence and advice. We find frequent references to party members in whose presence the most antiregime statement could be made without fear of this being reported. On the other hand, we find also, but *less* frequently, statements about party members who informed, who carried out party policies ruthlessly and with no apparent regard for the people involved. But more important than the relative infrequency with which such actual "bad actors" are cited, is the implicit assumption, and frequently explicit statement, that this is the way in which party members *are supposed* to behave.

The refugee view is that *if* all party members behaved as the regime would have them behave, then they would indeed all be "bad actors," whatever their motivation. Short of proof to the contrary, a party member is presumed to be a bad actor in effect, if not in intent. But those party members known at first hand are generally sympathetically understood and often excused. The same does not hold for the vast membership outside the individual's personal ken. Although he knows that it is possible for party members to avoid or attempt to avoid doing harm to others, and although he apparently believes that a large number of the rank and file do succeed in keeping their hands clean, he is not so sure that he would count on it being the case in any given instance. Hence the general tendency is to avoid either the blanket exemption or blanket inclusion of the rank-and-file member in the category of "bad actors."

In response to the question of what to do with the party members, therefore, the most common answer was: "It depends." Each case must be referred to the people with whom the member was associated, for, "the people will know." The upshot of this view is not the assumption that every party member is guilty, but rather that "some" *are bound* to be guilty, and can be located only by subjecting all the members to the people's scrutiny. Thus, the pervasive suspicion attached to membership in the party coexists with an empathic and sophisticated view of the origin of party membership.

The Rulers vs. the Ruled: The clearest set of images which the people have of the party member involves the dimension of power. On the one hand, there is, or rather was, Stalin and around him the Politburo and, on the other hand, the vast rank and file of the party. The former rules and the latter is ruled. One of our respondents puts the matter succinctly and in representative fashion when he said:

As to the party people, all they can do is to be obedient, like the nonparty people. They have no political influence. Only the Politburo can issue orders. None of the Communists could do anything. Everyone must obey the orders of the Politburo. They can do anything.

It is important to keep in mind that what is involved here is the power of the party member to determine party policy, and not his power to affect the way in which it is carried out. It is in this latter area that the party member is seen as having some, albeit limited, option. This difference is, of course, a crucial one. The vast party membership is not viewed as the source of the party policies which the people either accept or reject. Instead, the members are viewed as instruments of the power which is seen as residing in the party center. The fact that here reality and image coincide as much as they do, means that the responsibility for what the party has done to the people is clearly assigned mainly to the party center. The guilt of the party membership is defined with reference to how they permitted themselves to be used by the "party center." And, as we have seen, this is admitted to be a very complex assessment. Party members are all so "different": some believe in the Bolshevik mission, but more do not; some were forced into membership, but others were not; some wanted merely to get a little more bread, whereas others wanted to extract more party advantages; some maintained their humanity, their concern and sympathy for others, whereas some threw this overboard as excess baggage hindering their progress toward success. Such refined distinctions among party members, and such widespread acceptance of the variation in motivation and behavior, is in marked contrast to the image of the secret police.

The People and the Secret Police[4]

As compared with their view of the party membership, our informants showed little empathy or understanding, and much more hostility and stereotypy, in their description of the NKVD'ist.* The terror and its agents — this was the prime meaning to them of the secret police. Other police functions, including border patrol, passport and civil record functions, received but scant mention from our interviewees.

Whereas only 10 per cent of our respondents said that all or most party members can be held *personally* responsible and accountable for what the party has done, about 54 per cent held this view as regards the NKVD'ists. And about 50 per cent, nearly twice as many as in the case of the party members, spontaneously declared that all or most NKVD'ists

---

* The secret police have had various names, most recently MVD, for Ministry of Internal Affairs. During most of the period we mainly deal with, it was NKVD, for People's Commissariat of Internal Affairs, and we therefore use that designation as the one which meant most to our respondents.

would be on the regime's side in the event of popular uprising or foreign invasion. In both of these respects it is apparent that the NKVD'ists are much more likely to be included in the "They" than was true for the party member. This is evident in the frequency with which our respondents point to the NKVD'ists as being by nature a "different" sort of people, with different interests and values. Often they are pictured as cruel and sadistic people who found in secret police work the ideal job for the expression of warped personalities. They are seen, too, as people who have no regard for the rights of individuals, much less concern for them. And especially important to our respondents, the NKVD'ists are viewed as alienated from and not identifying themselves with the people. Along the same lines, the NKVD'ists frequently are seen as rejecting such values as loyalty, honesty, truth, the family, friendship, and spontaneity. They are excluded from the popular notion of what "the real Russian people," or the "real" Ukrainian or Georgian, are *really* like. In short, our informants describe the NKVD'ists as the "Enemies of the People."

Particularly interesting, and relevant to the contrasting image of the party people, was the almost universal belief that no one, explicitly including the party people, was free from the threat of the NKVD and its personnel. This was a potent factor in the degree of empathy and understanding popularly shown to the party members. They, too, shared the status of the "victim." The party card is seen as exercising little or no influence once its holder is suspected by the NKVD, and people were not at all sure that the party card served even as a deflector of such suspicion. But interestingly enough, even the NKVD'ist was recognized as not immune to the terror. Our respondents saw so clear a centralization of initiative residing in the party center that they assumed it to exert massive and determining force on its various instruments, to use and even consume them as it saw fit. The fact that purges also hit the NKVD personnel, even the leading ones, and the frequency with which they were deposed or disappeared, was taken by the people as evidence of the universal vulnerability of all to destruction by the party bosses.

The People, the Party and Political Cleavage

The absence of a stereotype of the rank-and-file party member, and the lack of any definitive emphasis on either their inherent goodness or badness suggest the improbability that the vast rank-and-file party membership could serve as an unambiguous object of popular hostility or as a scapegoat for the harsher features of Soviet life. Indeed in our sample we found an unqualified and universal belief that the ordinary party member, whatever else he might be, does not in any meaningful way share the power that resides in the party as such. In the popular view, he is at best an unwilling pawn, and at worst, a willing one. That he derives personal benefit from his party membership is generally acknowledged, but this is viewed more as a common sense adaptation to Soviet reality than as *prima facie* evidence of the party member's cupidity and culpability.

The important thing, in the popular view, is what membership demands of a person and what a person gives to the party. He may be the kind of member who gives freely to the party what it demands, one who treats people as instruments of party policy, barrages them with strident and repetitious harangues, informs and spies on them. Or, he may behave like a frightened mouse or a routinized bureaucrat, without making use of whatever influence and authority he has for the good of the people around him. When a party member acts in either of these fashions it is taken to indicate that he has placed himself unalterably on the wrong side of the line drawn by the party center, and he becomes an object of popular hostility. For then he has demonstrated his own personal and positive identification with the party center. But the people believe that there is a different course of action open to him. He may give only reluctantly to the party what it demands. He can treat individuals with respect and concern. He does not have to mouth the party line at every opportunity, inform and spy. To some extent he can stand up for intelligence and humanity in the performance of his work. If in these and numerous other available ways he sides with the people, then he does not become an object of popular hostility for he is not then identified with the party center.

The importance of such an identification stems from the fact that it is the party center and not the party membership as such, which is seen as the fountainhead of power in the Soviet Union. The party membership is seen as the group closest to the source of power and as serving as its conductor, but it is also recognized as unable to command the direction of the current or turn it on or off. It is the party center which bears responsibility, in the popular view, for initiating what the party has done, the good as well as the bad. Since the rank-and-file party member is seen as playing little or no role in the determination of party policy, and in fact is generally seen as coming to the party for nonpolitical reasons, the clue to the "side" he has chosen, the people's or the party center's, is given by the way he performs his party role, the way he "conducts" the party's power. The mere fact of party membership by itself does not indicate his choice. Perhaps the most striking aspect of these popular images is this failure of the party card to serve as a "fair-traded" label which indicates the content of the product it marks. It is as if the party membership were the cast of a masquerade in which all are clothed in the one party costume — leading devils and their willing pawns, angels, and fallible humans alike. Watching this masquerade, the people know that the cast is mixed, but they cannot tell by the costume itself who is who.

Were it the case that people believed in the greater frequency, within this cast, of leading devils and willing pawns, then they might be disposed to risk castigation and punishment of the innocent few so that the evil ones might receive their due. Yet, when we asked about the party members' personal accountability for what the party has done, only 10 per cent say that all or most members should be held accountable. On the other hand, were it the case that the overwhelming majority were believed to be angels or simply fallible human beings, then our informants might be expected to risk the escape of a few guilty ones so that the overwhelming majority might be free of onus and punishment. Yet, in answer to the same question, almost no one said that "none" or "few" of the party members should be held personally accountable for what the party has done. Furthermore, no more than about 20 per cent said that *only* the Politburo members and the top party echelons in general should be held accountable. In short, 70 per cent of our sample refuse either to assume or deny, *a priori,* the probable guilt of the rank-and-file party membership. Ten per cent assume this guilt, and 20 per cent deny it, but the overwhelming majority say in effect: "It depends on the individual." Thus, in the popular image the party member receives neither a whitewashing nor a tar brushing. The popular notion is that when the power of the party is broken, then each party member will be treated separately: the presumption is not that he is guilty, but that he might be, and therefore must be judged by the nonparty people who know him and his work.

For most of the refugees the Soviet regime meant Stalin and his immediate henchmen. He and "his" had the power, made the decisions, pulled the strings which controlled the instruments of power — the political, administrative, police, military, economic elites on various levels. The people knew where power lay, who it was that controlled their fate and was accountable for whatever has been done to them, good or bad. When one mentioned such terms as "regime," "government," "state," to former Soviet citizens, they understood them to refer to the party center. This is what we mean when we say they really understood the operation of Bolshevik totalitarianism. And this knowledge is, of course, crucial to the way in which the people experience cleavage between themselves and the Soviet political system. Even when they are profoundly alienated from the regime, from the party center, they do not necessarily generalize their hostility to the entire party membership. This is due, among other things, to the following aspects of the people's knowledge of how the system works.

First, there is the knowledge that in matters of policy making, the average party member is simply the instrument of the center and shares the powerlessness of the people. Hence the fact of party membership does not automatically signify personal identification with the center's policies.

Second, there is the knowledge that among the motivations of party members are the desire for comfort, security, and interesting and responsible work, motivations which the people themselves share. In the popular view, the party members pay a price for the fulfillment of these motivations, because to fulfill them they must subordinate themselves and participate in the demands of the party center. But then, the very omnipresence and omnipotence of these demands, make this the "going" price.

Third, people realize that the realities of power being what they are, it is crucial for the party people, more so than for anybody else, to make the gestures and wear the mask of conformity. This pertains to those personally identified with the regime as well as to those who do not so identify. But in the popular view, there are "good" people among these human instruments of the party center, people who are only nominal rather than real or "bad" members. The people know and expect that the "good" member can distinguish himself from the "bad" one. And this leads to a universal sensitivity to the clues of goodness, the indicators that a member's motivation accords with the people's various needs, interests and values. To the extent that the people feel powerless to change the situation, it is important to them that they locate good people in positions of immediate authority; these are the only signs of better things to come.

But this search for clues to goodness is not the sort of operation which can be done by any individual with respect to the total party membership; he can do it only with reference to those members in his ken. For the rest, he can only anticipate their masks of conformity, he cannot judge what lies beneath them. Hence, his power to construct a clear image of, and adopt a fixed and summary stance with regard to, the party member is checked and inhibited. This, we submit, is the reason why the people do not include the party members in the "They."

One of the striking strengths of totalitarianism is that it co-opts into its ranks precisely those individuals who under other circumstances would be the natural leaders of "the people." Co-opted into the party, they become the various high and low level elites of the Soviet system. In the process they become the objects of a significant measure of popular suspicion which is directed toward them as agents of the center, and this then prevents them from realizing their independent leadership potential. Yet there exists sufficient popular empathy and understanding with respect to the party members so that the suspiciousness of the people is inhibited and contained. In addition, many members of the party are people of quality, natural leaders, and they thus bring a measure of legitimacy and prestige to the entire membership. This further inhibits the development and spread of a global bad reputation for all party members.

The people are thus "denied" the opportunity to crystallize a pure and sharp "We vs. They" feeling with regard to the party. As far as the party center is concerned, this is the form which political cleavage seems to take in the Soviet case. Asked the direct question: "Do you think there are good men left in the Bolshevist leadership, 59 per cent of our informants said flatly "none." Only 4 per cent checked "many," and the remainder said "very few." Even this is far from total rejection of the leadership, since 41 per cent allowed *some* good men were still there, but it suggests most of the top leaders were seen quite negatively. But the party membership as such is less the subject of hostility than might be the case, because so many of its members are exempted from identification with the party's role as symbolized by the party center.

If the average individual party member were uniformly hated, if he were seen as personally causing and personally accountable for the sufferings inflicted on the Soviet people, then we could consider the line separating the "nonparty masses" from the party membership as one of the main lines of potential cleavage in the Soviet Union. In fact the line is not so sharply drawn, the gap separating these two groups is not such a gulf. On the contrary, the line runs an uncertain zigzag. The people see themselves as sharply separated only from the party *elite*, at the very center of power. The ordinary members are seen in part with the leaders, but in part with the people, in part oppressors, but in part fellow victims and co-sufferers. Some are bad, but some are good. Some are exploiters and opportunists, but some are felt to be working for ideals or for the people. The image of a party member brings no automatic, clearcut, repugnant stereotype to the mind of the average person. It is the beginning, not the end, a part, not the whole, of the characterization of a man. The party vs. nonparty division, therefore, does not seem to be one of the crucial fault planes, one of those cracks, in which some well-driven wedge might find a vital flaw to split the system.

Since Stalin's death, the regime has been ruled by a group of ever-changing composition. In addition, many of the worst grievances generated by Stalin's rule have been either eliminated or softened in their impact. If the course of improvement continues, the party member may lose in power, but he may also gain in respect. If the current of liberalization is turned back, and one man emerges again as supreme ruler and acts as ruthlessly as did Stalin, the party member will again be obliged to act as an unpopular agent of the center. But he will probably also again seem to the victim, the simulator and conformer, or the opportunist, which he was felt to be under Stalin. Either way, the line which divides the people from the party membership (as distinguished from the party' center) does not seem to be the line along which Soviet society is likely to split.

XV

The Nationality Problem[1]

The expansion of the Russian empire, particularly during the nine-teenth century, brought many non-Russian and indeed non-Slavic groups under the tsar's rule, and the Russian empire became a vast conglomerate of nationalities ranging from small primitive tribes to exceedingly large and culturally "advanced" populations which had been and could again easily become independent political entities. So numerous and great were the national enclaves engulfed by this expansion that the census of 1897 revealed the Russians to be a minority of about 45 per cent in their own empire. In taking over political power within the Russian empire the Bolsheviks became the warden of this "prison of nations," as it is often called by émigré leaders of the national groups. The new warden might well have thrown open the gates to freedom, but was restrained by power considerations and by an ideologically based unwillingness to surrender to heathen capitalism any souls captured for the socialist paradise. In-stead a relatively restrictive policy was adopted. Indeed, in areas as widely separated as Georgia and the Ukraine armed force was used to prevent the political separation of the former tsarist territories from the new Communist polity.[2]

The partly willing and partly forced surrender of control over Poland, Finland, and the Baltic States somewhat redressed the balance of num-bers, however, and the 1926 census showed the Great Russians holding a slim majority in the nation. In addition, the regime adopted a new na-tionality policy giving relatively greater recognition to popular interest in native languages, folklore, art, and other cultural forms which tsarist autocracy and Russian Orthodoxy had often sought to suppress. The political gains from this policy of cultural tolerance were, however, often outweighed by resentment aroused by the tight economic control and firm political integration of these people into the larger structure of Soviet society under the hegemony of the Communist Party centered in Mos-cow. Consequently, Soviet history has been witness to many massive campaigns directed against the so-called "bourgeois-nationalist" attempts to detach segments of the Soviet federation and return them to "capitalist, anti-Soviet" rule.[3]

It should then be no surprise that in the development of political strategy vis à vis the Soviet Union much attention has been given to the nationality problem as perhaps the weakest link in the chain of Soviet armor. Interest in the question has been intensified because exiled representatives of the national minorities have been extremely vocal in calling attention to the nationality question and its potentialities as a focus for psychological warfare. Indeed some of those leaders have gone so far as to insist that they can, if given sufficient resources, foment internal revolutions and successful independence movements among those of their own nationality inside the Soviet Union. Quite apart from this political issue, however, we cannot assume to have understood Soviet society without having explored the nationality problem. National or ethnic membership constitutes a basis for loyalties and identifications which cut across the lines of class, political affiliation, and generation. Nationality could, therefore, easily be a major determinant of the attitudes and life experiences of the individual, and consequently a central element in the functioning of Soviet society.

In view of the political and sociological importance of the nationality problem, our study was from its inception designed to yield a large body of material bearing on the issue. Yet the diversity of the national groups composing the Soviet Union presented a major obstacle to a really definitive study. Not only were our financial resources limited, but so were our capabilities for devising questionnaires and conducting interviews in such languages as Armenian, Georgian, Mongolian and others more exotic. Because many national refugee groups were very small or highly scattered, it was not possible to develop study samples economically, and indeed in many cases it was impossible to compose samples comparable to those drawn from other national groups. In the face of these and a host of other difficulties, we decided to concentrate our resources in a large-scale and highly focused study of *one* national group, rather than in several smaller but individually less adequate efforts.

The Ukrainian national group was clearly the outstanding candidate for this purpose. At the time of the last published census (1939) the Ukrainians numbered almost thirty million, or more than 16 per cent of the total population. They were outnumbered only by Russians, and indeed are five times more numerous than the Byelorussians, the next largest group. In addition, the Ukrainians are culturally a highly developed people, with their own language and literature, and they inhabit an economically rich territory which is fully developed agriculturally and industrially. Indeed at the time of the 1917 Revolution an independent Ukrainian government was set up, and for a short while ruled the Ukraine and conducted an armed struggle against both German and Soviet invading forces.[4] The Ukrainian people now inhabit the second largest republic of

the Soviet Union, which bears the title Ukrainian Soviet Socialist Republic, and which has a representative with voting power in the Assembly of
the United Nations. It is clear, therefore, that the Ukraine is a national
symbol with which one can quite meaningfully identify, and that such
identification can be expected to have some influence on the pattern of an
individual's attitudes and life experiences. Indeed, the leaders of the
Ukrainians in the refugee community are among the most tightly organized and vociferous in arguing the cause of political independence for their
people.

We collected three main types of material for our exploration of
Ukrainian attitudes and patterns of life experience. To compare the attitudes and daily life experience of the Ukrainians with the Russians we
sought to have a strong representation of Ukrainians among those who
took the detailed life-history interview or completed the written questionnaire, both of which dealt with matters applicable to any Soviet citizen.
About one fourth of those who undertook the personal interview, and
more than a third of those who completed either the general written questionnaire or that on the wartime German occupation, gave their nationality as Ukrainian. In each case these people formed a core of respondents
sufficient to permit meaningful comparison with the responses given by
Russians.

On the whole, however, neither the personal interview nor the questionnaires dealt directly with the nationality problems as such, although
they provided several opportunities for the respondent to bring it up spontaneously. As second source of information, therefore, we constructed and
administered exclusively to Ukrainians a special questionnaire which dealt
explicitly with various dimensions of the nationality problem or with
matters highly germane to it. Through this questionnaire we sought to
assess the degree of knowledge individuals had of Ukrainian history and
national leaders, the strength of their identification with the Ukrainian
nationality, the nature of their attitudes toward Russians, and the sources
of their information and values with regard to the regime's nationality
policy. This questionnaire was completed by 459 former Soviet citizens
of Ukrainian nationality who had lived in the pre-1939 borders of the
Soviet Union.[5] As a third source of information, we conducted a series of
interviews with several dozen Ukrainian intellectual, cultural, and political leaders. These have influenced the conclusions drawn here, but do not
enter directly into the analysis because they were focused mainly on
the historical development of Soviet policy with regard to the Ukraine.[6]

Many assertions are made about the role of nationality in determining
the individual's attitudes and experiences in Soviet society. Most frequently it is assumed that the national minority member is exposed to
discrimination in access to the advantages, limited as they may be, offered

by Soviet society. It is further assumed that as a result of this discrimination and the frustration of their legitimate desires for autonomy and political independence, the members of the national minorities are more hostile to the institutions of Soviet society and to the group which makes up the government or "regime." In addition, it is sometimes affirmed that quite apart from the effects of discrimination, Ukrainians (or other minorities) are less accepting of totalitarian governmental authority and the Communist type of system than are the Russians. These and other factors, so the argument runs, tend to make the national minority member, as against the Russian, more restive under Communist rule and more active in his opposition to the regime. Finally it is asserted that this rejection of Soviet rule is intimately tied in with a consciousness of nationality membership. The resented Soviet system is seen as primarily a *Russian* form of government imposed by an alien ruler, and the only perceived and acceptable solution is therefore national political independence from the Russian dominated state.[7]

Virtually all of these propositions can to some degree be tested with materials collected by the interviewing project. The answers provided are by no means absolutely definite, but our materials do permit an assessment, or better a reassessment, of the nature and importance of the nationality problem which goes far beyond anything which has previously been possible. For the first time we can examine this question not merely on the level of political assertion and counterassertion, but by utilizing the reports of hundreds of former Soviet citizens who lived as members of a national minority while in the Soviet Union. In addition to checking the adequacy of some of the common political assertions, we may through these materials come to a better understanding of a sociologically interesting question: What is the relative influence of ethnic or national as against other types of group membership on the attitudes and life experiences of the individual in a large scale industrial society?

Life Chances of Ukrainians vs. Russians

The Ukrainian people have borne their share of the social and human costs of the Bolshevik revolution and the subsequent development of Soviet society. Much of the fighting of the Civil War period was in the Ukraine, and its towns and fields were often ravaged under the heels and wheels of advancing and retreating armies and guerrilla groups. When Stalin launched his momentous campaign of forced collectivization, it was the black earth of the Ukraine and its wheat raising potential that was the prime initial target, and it was in this same Ukraine that the subsequent famine was at its worst.[8] Somewhat later in the thirties, when policy was reversed and development of the local national cultural heritage no longer so encouraged, the attack on the "bourgeois nationalists" of the Ukraine was most intense, and the Ukrainian national elite in the cultural as well as the political sphere was largely decimated.

With reference to these and other developments, however, some will say that comparable, indeed equal, sufferings were undergone by those of Russian as well as Ukrainian origin. It is argued that the regime did not discriminate on grounds of nationality in meting out punishment and reward, but rather did so mainly on grounds of presumed loyalty or disloyalty to its goals and purposes. Is there then any evidence in our interviews and questionnaires which indicates a systematic policy of individual, personal discrimination against the national minority member? Does a boy born into a Ukrainian home have less chance to receive a higher education and to advance himself to a position of power and responsibility, or is his chance more or less equal to that of the boy born into a home which is similar in other respects but which is Russian in nationality? To answer these questions without having the outcome unduly influenced by pre-Soviet conditions we selected a special subsample of our respondents, all born in 1905–1925, and who therefore grew up, went to school, and achieved the status of adolescent or young adult predominately under Soviet conditions. In other words, this group constitutes a more or less pure Soviet generation. Dividing the group into Russians

TABLE 93 [8A]

EDUCATION RECEIVED BY YOUTHS OF DIFFERENT NATIONALITY BUT EQUAL SOCIAL STATUS

Social origin and nationality	Educational level attained				Total number of respondents
	0–4 years	5–7 years	8–10 years	more than 10 years	
White-collar					
Russian	1%	12%	38%	49%	(242)
Ukrainian	0	18	35	47	(117)
Worker					
Russian	24	42	20	14	(194)
Ukrainian	26	39	26	9	(147)
Peasant					
Russian	49	30	14	7	(155)
Ukrainian	50	33	10	7	(172)

and Ukrainians we can, by comparing those of comparable social origins, learn whether or not a youth's nationality had much influence on his chance to attain various goals in Soviet society.

In Table 93 we compare the educational levels attained by these youngsters up to the time of their departure from the Soviet Union, and reproduce the table in full because it is characteristic of the general pattern we find when we explore this problem. It is clear that as compared to social class background, nationality is not to any significant degree a determinant of one's chances for an education. Youths born into a white-collar home apparently reached college level (represented by the last column) with pretty much the same frequency regardless of whether their fathers were Russian or Ukrainian. At the other pole of the status hierarchy the children of peasants characteristically failed to get beyond the seven-year school, again almost entirely without reference to their nationality. Thus, as judged by their "chances" of acquiring a higher education, the son of the Ukrainian intelligentsia and of the Russian intelligentsia have more in common than either has with his compatriot born into a worker or peasant home. If one wished to predict the educational fate of a boy at his birth, it could clearly be done with considerable accuracy on the basis of his father's occupation even if nothing were known about his nationality, whereas only a very poor prediction (if in fact any) could be made if one had knowledge of the boy's nationality but did not know his social class origins.

Not only did boys and girls of the same social background but different nationality have the same objective chance to attain given educational levels, but their subjective evaluation of their opportunity for an education was also determined mainly by class position rather than national membership. Thus when asked whether their chances for an education had been equal to or better than those of "others," almost two thirds of the children from the intelligentsia families, Russian and Ukrainian alike, stated that their chances had been better or at least equal to those of others. In contrast, among the children of peasant origin only about one fourth felt that they had a chance equal to or better than that of other youths, and again the proportion giving this answer was roughly the same for both Russians and Ukrainians. Once more social origin emerges as a more significant determinant of life chances than does nationality. Those of the same class but different nationality have much in common, whereas those of the same nationality but different social standing are more likely to have widely divergent life chances.

We found this pattern consistently manifested when we explored a diverse set of additional measures of possible discrimination against the younger generation on grounds of national membership. Thus, we looked into the occupational fate of boys born into families at different levels of the social hierarchy, their feeling about their chances to make a career under Soviet conditions, the standard of living they enjoyed when they were children, and the degree of cohesiveness of their family of origin under the impact of revolutionary social change. These and a number of other measures failed to produce significant differences in the early life experience of young Russians and Ukrainians sufficient to constitute evidence of systematic discrimination based primarily on their nationality as against their social origins. This is not to say that there were absolutely no differences. For example, it may be that Ukrainian youths were slightly disadvantaged in the occupational realm. The proportion of those whose father was in the intelligentsia and who themselves attained that status was 7 per cent greater among the Russians than among Ukrainians. At the other end of the occupational hierarchy, more of the Ukrainian peasant youths remained peasants. It was a characteristic of such findings, however, that they did not present a consistent pattern. Thus, in the case in hand, children of employees who were Ukrainian by nationality actually fared somewhat better occupationally than Russian children of the same origins. In most cases such differences appear to reflect normal sampling error. There is very little basis here to challenge the overriding importance of social origin over nationality membership as a determinant of the pattern of life chances among the youth.

It might be, of course, that the regime does not discriminate in a noticeable way against the youth, but nevertheless restricts the life chances of the national minority member by progressively narrowing his opportunities as he matures and becomes more consciously and effectively identified with his national group. To assess this possibility we can no longer concentrate on the very young but must rather study the life situation of the more adult population. Since many of the more mature respondents grew up, were educated, and began to work before the revolution, our data will reflect influences which go back to tsarist times rather than being exclusively Soviet. Nevertheless, in its main outlines our data reflect the general influence of Soviet conditions.

One major possibility, particularly crucial in an industrial society such as the Soviet Union, is that members of the minor nationalities are discriminated against in their efforts to gain access to the more desirable and important jobs. In Table 94 we have therefore presented in full the data describing the occupational levels achieved by Russians and Ukrainians of comparable educational qualification. Again the basic pattern noted earlier emerges. A Russian and a Ukrainian have very much the same chance of attaining a white-collar or professional post if they have acquired secondary schooling or some college training. However, Ukrainians with low education, that is with seven years of schooling or less, were definitely less likely than Russians to become workers or to reach white-collar status. What this means, in effect, is that they were more likely to remain peasants. The lower rate in attaining white-collar positions for Ukrainians with little schooling might be connected with language barriers. Most white-collar jobs required a knowledge of Russian, which is the chief language of administration even in the Ukraine. If two men

were equal in education, the Russian might have a greater chance of winning a white-collar job than the Ukrainian. But this explanation can
hardly hold for the less frequent acquisition of worker status among the
Ukrainians. There appears to be a much stronger tendency for Ukrainian
than for Russian peasants to continue to live on the collective farms
rather than move to a city job. A detailed examination of relevant factors,[9]
furthermore, strongly suggests that this was less a matter of differential opportunity than of cultural differences in attitude. Ukrainian peasants
seemed less frequently to accept the *value* of social mobility and tended to
cling to the peasant style of life more strongly. Whatever the factor which
accounts for the apparent lesser mobility of the less educated Ukrainians,
the basic general fact reflected in Table 94 is that those with more
advanced education have very similar chances of entering the favored
white-collar and professional posts regardless of nationality. Although nationality does appear to play a slight role in occupational mobility, those
of similar education have much more in common than those of the same
nationality.

TABLE 94 [9A]

OCCUPATIONAL LEVEL ATTAINED BY THOSE
OF EQUAL FORMAL EDUCATION BUT DIFFERENT NATIONALITY

Formal education	Nation-ality	Occupation attained					Total number of respondents
		Profes-sional	White-collar em-ployee	Skilled worker	Worker	Collec-tive farmer	
Over 10 years	Russian	68%	31%	—[a]	1%	0%	(246)
	Ukrainian	68	29	2	1	0	(138)
8–10 years	Russian	22	52	12	13	1	(196)
	Ukrainian	15	58	11	11	5	(133)
5–7 years	Russian	9	39	10	37	5	(245)
	Ukrainian	2	28	15	39	16	(179)
0–4 years	Russian	2	7	11	53	27	(276)
	Ukrainian	1	3	9	41	46	(243)

a. Represents less than 1 per cent.

Since the data on occupational attainment suggests that quite frequently Ukrainians fare less well than Russians with the same educational qualifications, we expect that Ukrainians will be somewhat less
satisfied with their occupational experience. This is indeed the case with
a variety of measures of occupational satisfaction, although the pattern
is not consistent. For example, at each educational level the proportion of

Ukrainians who felt they had an opportunity for a career was somewhat less than the proportion of satisfied Russians. Similarly, holding occupation constant, Ukrainians are more likely than Russians to feel that their pay was not commensurate with the pay received by others doing similar work and those doing different types of work. The differences may be expressed in summary fashion in a composite "occupational satisfaction" score which shows the combined influence of these and other measures. It is evident from Table 95 that Ukrainians are more likely to be dissatisfied with their job experience than are Russians working at comparable jobs, although this is more noticeable in the older generation and really marked mainly in the case of the peasants. Despite the nationality difference, however, it remains the case that nationality is of much less importance than the occupation itself as a determinant of job satisfaction. A Ukrainian professional is much more like a Russian professional than he is like a Ukrainian peasant in the satisfaction he derives from his job. Overwhelmingly, it is his job and not his nationality that determines his occupational satisfaction or dissatisfaction.

TABLE 95 [9B]

PERCENTAGES OF OCCUPATIONALLY DISSATISFIED RUSSIANS
AND UKRAINIANS: BY OCCUPATION AND AGE

Occupation of respondent	40 and under		41 and over	
	Russian	Ukrainian	Russian	Ukrainian
Professional	7% (58) [a]	10% (30)	12% (142)	15% (83)
White-collar employee	28 (123)	35 (85)	29 (188)	35 (83)
Worker	43 (202)	48 (139)	34 (128)	46 (107)
Collective farmer	73 (40)	79 (75)	66 (32)	83 (59)

a. Total number of respondents on the basis of which the percentage is computed.

In four of our basic social groups, that is in all except the collective farmers, the proportion of individuals who were themselves arrested or experienced an arrest in the family is greater among the Ukrainians by between 6 to 11 per cent. In assessing these differences it is important to keep in mind that Ukrainians were subject to arrest on one important ground which did not apply to the Russians, namely "bourgeois nationalism." The consequences of arrest, as measured either by the proportion receiving sentence of more than five years or of those forced downward in the occupational realm, however, were not more severe in the case of the Ukrainians than the Russians. The observed differences between the

Ukrainians and the Russians in arrest rates, while by no means insignificant, are modest when measured against the extremely high rate contact with the secret police which characterized this group as a whole regardless of nationality. Thus, the Ukrainians might point to the fact that 88 per cent of their intelligentsia among our sample were *either* themselves arrested *or* had contact with the terror because of the arrest of a family member, but the Russians could hardly be regarded as favored in this respect since 82 per cent of them fell in the same category.

To sum up, we found little evidence of gross discrimination in the life chances which the Soviet regime provides to youths of Ukrainian as against Russian origin *when the background of the two was* otherwise comparable. Russians and Ukrainians did differ somewhat in the occupational levels they attained and the material and psychic rewards they derived from the job later in life, with more restricted opportunity and lesser rewards being the apparent lot of the Ukrainians. These differences, however, are exceedingly small compared to the differences in reward which come to the individual according to whether he holds a post high or low in the occupational realm. Thus, one's occupation, or in the case of arrest, one's Soviet citizenship, rather than one's nationality appears to be the prime determinant of one's life chances in the Soviet system. This, of course, should not be taken to mean that the relevant nationalities taken as a whole have equal chances. On the contrary, in many nationality areas the availability of schools and other facilities is much less than in others, and this means that the national group as a whole may suffer. Under such conditions it may be true that a native boy whose father is a lawyer or doctor has as good a chance as a Russian boy of the same background. But taken as a whole the nationality may have few doctors and lawyers, and if most of the given nationality are peasants their lower mobility rate will be reflected in the lower mobility rate of the nationality as a whole. In addition, the chances for mobility of any given boy should not be confused with the share in power possessed by the nationality as a group. From 1938 on the Politburo, the fountainhead of power in the Soviet system, did not include a single representative of the Ukrainian nationality. But such discrimination, if such it was, affects the life chances of only a very small part of the population, whereas most are more concerned about discrimination in the school and on the job.

Basic Attitudes and Evaluation of the Regime

The regime may not discriminate too noticeably in distributing opportunities and rewards among the Ukrainians and Russians, yet the Ukrainians may for other reasons be more vigorous in their opposition to the system and the regime. It has often been suggested in émigré circles, and sometimes by Western observers, that the Russians have much more of a propensity to accept a communal, socialist, welfare type of society and indeed have a need to subordinate themselves to strong centralized authority.

Our data provide scant basis for arguing that there are clear-cut differences between Russians and Ukrainians of comparable social background in their attitudes toward the welfare state and the proper limits on government authority and responsibility. Table 96 summarizes the evidence on four economic aspects of the welfare state, and with regard to each aspect — and others not presented here such as government planning — Russians and Ukrainians show a very similar orientation. Indeed, in so far as there is any substantial and regular variation, as in the case of attitudes towards government control of light industry, the determining factor is the social class rather than the nationality of the respondent. A similar pattern was revealed in the attitudes of our respondents toward libertarian issues such as the government's right to forbid the open expression of opinion. Scores obtained by Ukrainians and Russians on the political rights index — summarizing opinions with regard to four civil liberties issues — were very close, although the Ukrainians more consistently favored personal rights against the rights of the government to restrict individual freedom.[10]

Since all of the questions on the economic and political aspects of the state dealt with "government" in general rather than specifically with the Soviet system we may assume that we here tapped general and basic sentiments of our respondents rather than their more limited reactions to concrete experiences in the USSR. Considering the range of issues involved, from the ownership of light industry to the freedom of assembly, the similarities between Russians and Ukrainians are striking. Both nationalities emerge as strong supporters of the general features of the welfare state, and both show a strong tendency to qualify their support of personal freedom and civil liberties by affirming the rights of the government to protect its interests and its prestige, to preserve order and propriety or public morality. Further, the relative absence of strong class-linked variation suggests that these attitudes toward the ideal government and social and economic organization of society are a general culture trait shared by both Russians and Ukrainians.

The sharing of *ideals* and *values* in regard to government and social organization does not guarantee that Russians and Ukrainians will have the same evaluation of the concrete reality of Soviet society and its leadership. Indeed, since the Soviet system is outstanding for the contrast between official promises and actual attainments, crucial differences might have been expected in assessments of the regime's accomplishment as made by Ukrainians as against Russians. On the whole, this area again failed to yield significant differences. Ukrainians and Russians equally acknowl-

TABLE 96 [10A]

PER CENT WHO SUPPORT VARIOUS WELFARE STATE PRINCIPLES:
BY NATIONALITY AND SOCIAL GROUP

Welfare principle	Nationality	Intelli- gentsia	White- collar em- ployees	Skilled workers	Ordinary workers	Collec- tive farm- ers
Government should guarantee employment	Russian	83%	87%	83%	91%	82%
	Ukrainian	84	84	82	88	84
Government should own heavy industry	Russian	86	80	89	64	82
	Ukrainian	87	86	92	83	83
Government should own light industry	Russian	23	24	40	43	53
	Ukrainian	24	24	43	46	51
Government should prevent economic inequality	Russian	37	35	48	34	41
	Ukrainian	45	43	33	34	26
Total number of respondents	Russian	371	357	138	211	101
	Ukrainian	175	206	93	193	143

edged certain Soviet achievements in increasing the production of agricultural machinery, the accessibility of medical care, and the availability
of theaters and concerts. They were equally favorable to the Soviet school
system, and acknowledged the same degree of reliability in Soviet official
communications. When asked what they would keep or change in the
Soviet system if the Bolsheviks were driven out, similar proportions of
Russians and Ukrainians said they would "keep nothing" or "change
everything." Furthermore, in selecting specific features of the system for
retention or discard the Russians and Ukrainians spontaneously chose
much the same range of elements with much the same frequency. There
was a slight tendency for Ukrainians to be more sensitive to political issues and slightly less interested in the welfare aspects of the state, but
the differences which emerged were neither strong nor consistent, and
appear minor in the face of the massive agreement between the groups.

An exception must be made, however, for the "institution" represented by the nationality policy of the regime which was more often cited by Ukrainians as requiring to be changed. The point is discussed in detail below.

Despite the apparent absence of fundamental differences between Russians and Ukrainians in their assessment of the positive and negative institutional features of the Soviet system there was still the possibility that they would differ in their evaluation of the regime, that is, the group of men who run Soviet society. Indeed, we had some reason to expect such differences because it is often asserted that members of the national minorities see the Soviet regime not merely as a *Communist* but essentially as a *Russian* creation. This expectation was, however, not borne out. In the younger generation, Ukrainian youths joined the Komsomol about as often as did the Russians. Roughly equal proportions of Russians and Ukrainians in each social class felt that Lenin did much harm, and the two national groups were also very much alike in the percentage urging that in case the present regime were overthrown the Bolshevik leaders should be put to death.

Stronger Ukrainian opposition to the regime is suggested by the fact that in four of the five social classes Ukrainians more often than Russians asserted that they had always been opposed to the regime rather than having once favored it and then turned against it. The differences were modest, but should be noted. Further, Ukrainians more often declared that in 1940 they had "wanted to leave" the Soviet Union. Ukrainians gave this response more frequently than Russians, in four of the five class groups, and did so with the appreciable difference of 15 per cent in the case of the peasantry. This remains a fairly isolated set of statistics, however, and other indications that Ukrainians played a more active role in disaffecting from the Soviet regime failed to emerge. Thus, when we examined the *actual* mode of departure from the USSR we did not find the same "active" pattern characterizing the Ukrainians. In three of the five social classes the proportion of Ukrainians who left Soviet control *voluntarily* (as against going under German orders) was actually smaller than the proportion of Russians who acted that way. Indeed, if we define as the "activist" defectors those who *wanted* to leave in 1940 *and* then did leave *voluntarily* when the opportunity came along during the war, we find that among both Russians and Ukrainians in the manual and nonmanual classes the proportion of such activists was virtually identical.* This finding is furthermore congruent with that on other meas-

---

* There is a potential difficulty with these data in that *on the average* Ukrainians were more likely to have lived under German occupation and to have lived longer under the Germans. Therefore, there may have been a greater possibility of being forcibly evacuated by the Germans, and hence less actual "opportunity" to leave voluntarily.

ures of active opposition. Listening to the foreign radio, for example, is often cited as an expression of alienation from the regime, and indeed it exposed the listener to some risk if the secret police were aware of it. We found no differences in the proportions of Ukrainians and Russians who engaged in such clandestine listening, nor indeed in the proportions who claimed to have engaged in other forms of disapproved communication such as discussing political developments with their friends or acquiring information through rumors.

The numerous items which we have examined — and many others not cited here — fail to reveal a marked and consistent pattern of difference in the life experience and attitudes of Russians and Ukrainians who held comparable positions in the social class system. A variety of items show some difference between the groups. For example, Ukrainian peasants apparently are more bound to the farm and are less likely to be able or to want to move into urban jobs; Ukrainian nonmanual groups have a slightly higher proportion of those who favor personal freedoms; the Ukrainian worker and peasant are somewhat more distrustful of the news that they read in the press; and Ukrainians of all classes were more likely to reply that in 1940 they hoped they could depart from the Soviet Union. The differences are, however, rather minor compared to the relative uniformity of opinion and experience that characterize the two groups with regard to most issues and areas of life experience.

Furthermore, the same pattern is manifested when national groups other than the Ukrainians are studied. Because the number of such non-Slavic nationals was small, and the total group exceedingly heterogeneous, we felt that it would be inappropriate to present statistical tables based on the responses of these other national minorities. To an extraordinary degree, however, the statistical material on those groups reveals the same pattern exposed by the comparison of Ukrainians and Russians. Our data suggest most strongly, therefore, that ethnic identity is of comparatively minor importance relative to social class membership as a predictor of the individual's life chances, his attitude toward the regime, and many of his general socio-political values.

The Salience of the Nationality Problem

To say that nationality is not too firm a base for the prediction of many, or even most, socio-political values is not to assert that it is of little relevance for *all* such questions. It is characteristic of the numerous items we have so far examined that they do not deal explicitly or even implicitly with nationality as an issue. What then happens when questions are raised which in some way permit the respondent to show awareness of his ethnic identity or which offer him an opportunity to reply in a way that actively affirms his sense of national membership?

Several items on the written questionnaire to which the nationality problem was potentially relevant were "open-ended," that is, the respondent was not presented with fixed alternative answers but was invited freely to write in answers of his choice. The questions inquired into who gets ahead in the Soviet Union, what should be kept and what changed if the present regime were overthrown, and the reasons for always opposing or for turning against the regime. If the nationality problem were very salient for Ukrainians, if it were much in their consciousness, we would expect that in response to these questions Ukrainians would have frequently mentioned the nationality policy of the regime as holding people back from mobility or as something badly in need of change. It is a surprising fact that not one of these questions elicited enough mentions of nationality problem to warrant making a separate code category for the answers of that type.

On the question "What would you be sure to change?" all of the miscellaneous answers given in the oral interviews had been recorded. When we scanned them we found 10 of the 49 miscellaneous comments touched on the nationality problem. These ten citations are modest indeed compared to the 239 votes cast against the collective farm system, and the 132 demands for elimination of the police terror system. Perhaps more important, however, is the question of who made these comments and where? Two were contributed by Russians, and one by a Byelorussian. The remaining seven were contributed by Ukrainians. Thus, of 76 Ukrainians who were given a personal interview, only 1 in 10 spontaneously cited the nationality policy as requiring change. All 7, furthermore, were among the group of 16 interviewed in New York, where a politically oriented Ukrainian national independence movement has been strongly developed and conducts extensive propaganda among the refugees.[11]

These data argue strongly that the nationality problem is not very salient for Ukrainians, and that they do not spontaneously bring it up if they are not directly stimulated by the mention of some symbol of nationality. Nevertheless, when such symbols *are* directly introduced, *then* Ukrainians do respond in a fairly distinctive way, as is apparent from Table 97. The influence of the nationality symbol is most directly evident in a simple and straightforward way in responses to a check list on factors making for a happy marriage. One of the items on the list was "nationality." Clearly nationality is for neither group the most important factor, both groups having assigned that role to "common interest." Nevertheless, in each social group Ukrainians were about twice as likely as Russians to designate "nationality" as the most important factor in a happy marriage, and these differences hold up quite well with both age and sex controls applied. This suggests that the Ukrainians feel their national membership to be more important than do the Russians, and are more concerned with the exclusion of other nationalities from their family units.

TABLE 97 [11A]

RUSSIAN AND UKRAINIAN VIEWS ON QUESTIONNAIRE ITEMS
INVOLVING NATIONALITY DIMENSION: BY SOCIAL GROUP

Social group	Consider nationality most important in marriage		Favor A-bombing Moscow		Total number of respondents	
	Russian	Ukrainian	Russian	Ukrainian	Russian	Ukrainian
Intelligentsia	5%	15%	12%	25%	(372)	(176)
White-collar	6	10	15	33	(353)	(199)
Skilled workers	7	19	27	38	(123)	(80)
Ordinary workers	10	20	27	39	(180)	(175)
Collective farmers	17	22	24	50	(89)	(113)

The other item in Table 97 poses a somewhat more complex problem. On the surface the question as to whether or not it would be a good idea to drop an atom bomb on Moscow seems to be mainly a measure of strength of hostile feeling against the regime. As we have already seen, Ukrainians on all other available measures of hostility seem no more intensely antagonistic than Russians of comparable social status. Yet on the question of bombing Moscow Ukrainians are roughly twice as often in favor of doing so now. Indeed a direct check on the role of hostility in this outcome shows that for people of equal hostility to the regime it is still the case that Ukrainians about twice as often recommend dropping a bomb on Moscow. Neither is the factor of residence an adequate explanation of the differences, since even among those who resided in large cities Ukrainians were much more likely than Russians to favor dropping the bomb. It is an almost inescapable conclusion, therefore, that the word *Moscow* elicits a quite different response from large numbers of Ukrainians (and indeed those of other nationalities) as compared to Russians. It hardly seems to be stretching the point to suggest that more Ukrainians were willing to see the bomb dropped on Moscow because they regarded it not merely as the center of the Communist regime, but also as a *Russian* city which was the capital of a government alien to them. This feeling was expressed with intensity by a former Ukrainian school teacher who said:

Russian imperialism systematically oppresses and colonially exploits other nations subjugated and controlled by *Moscow*. . . . Russia is a ruling, dominant nation. . . . Great Russians are the only ones who want to preserve the Russian empire.

A third illustration of the importance of the nationality issue as an influence on attitudes and perceptions comes from the investigation into experiences under the German wartime occupation of the USSR. Those who had lived under the occupation were asked both to evaluate the strength of the independence or self-determination movement in their national republic, and to report the attitude of the German occupying authorities toward the movement if there was one. Unfortunately, the number who answered both questions is extremely small, partly because many of the respondents lived outside one of the national republics such as the Ukraine and partly because so many said that they knew nothing about the strength of the independence movement nor of the German attitude towards it. Nevertheless, the number who answered in full is large enough to justify an examination of their responses.

TABLE 98 [11B]

RUSSIAN AND UKRAINIAN VIEWS
ON THE NATIONAL INDEPENDENCE MOVEMENT

	Russians	Ukrainians
Independence movement was *strong* and:		
Germans supported it	29%	15%
Germans hostile to it	18	60
Independence movement was *weak* and:		
Germans supported it	46	21
Germans hostile to it	7	4
Total number of respondents	55	78

The results provide striking evidence of the influence which the respondent's ethnic origin can exert on his perception of what might otherwise be termed an "objective" fact. In reporting on the "strength" of the independence movement, for example, Russians found it "strong" not much more often than weak, the ratio of weak to strong being practically 1:1, whereas the comparable ratio among Ukrainians was 1:3. Russians and Ukrainians also differed sharply in their estimates of the attitude of the German occupying authorities toward the movement. More than twice as many Ukrainians as Russians stated that the Germans had actively discouraged the independence movement. Further, when we pair the responses of the "strength" and "German attitude" dimensions

(Table 98) we find that for Ukrainians the overwhelmingly dominant modal response, given by them three times as often as by Russians, asserts in effect: "The independence movement was strong despite the discouragement by the Germans." In contrast, the dominant mode among the Russians is in effect to assert: "The Ukrainian independence movement was weak despite the fact that it was encouraged by the Germans."

It is apparent from these three items that once we dip into the reservoir of feeling which springs from the well of ethnic identity, important differences emerge in the attitudes and perceptions of former Soviet citizens which are apparently accounted for mainly by the nationality of the respondent.

Patterns of Nationalism Among Ukrainians

Can we then ascertain just how much national feeling there is? Who are the "nationalists," that is those most strongly identified with their national group, what is the precise content of their nationalist feeling, and what implications does this have for the future stability of Soviet society? To answer these questions we must turn to our special written questionnaire on the nationality problem completed by the 459 Ukrainians earlier described in this chapter.

In the light of the low salience of the nationality issue noted above, special caution is required in our approach to the responses given to this questionnaire. The questionnaire was administered in the Ukrainian language, and was plainly focused on the nationality problem. It raised many issues which the respondents might otherwise not have thought about or which they might have thought about in a different way had the context been changed. The impact of the questionnaire was apparently to maximize the display of national feeling by calling up haloed national symbols and by more or less directly obliging the respondent to take a stand on issues involving expressions of loyalty and solidarity with one's nationality group.

Striking evidence of the tendency of the nationality questionnaire to heighten the sense of national identity is found when we compare the responses evoked by our query as to the most important factor in a happy marriage as given on the general written questionnaire and on the special nationality questionnaire. Precisely the same question was asked and exactly the same check list of alternative answers offered to those who completed each questionnaire. The responses on the different questionnaires are presented in Table 99. The contrast is marked, and is rendered all the more striking because the answers were given not merely by generally comparable Ukrainian class groups, but in the majority of cases by the very same individuals. On the nationality questionnaire, the number who chose common nationality as the most important factor in a happy marriage is generally twice as large as it is in the case of the general questionnaire. Although there were no other questions of this type asked on both questionnaires, it seems clear that the general effect of the nationality questionnaire was to induce people to show relatively stronger national sentiment than was the case with our other instruments.

TABLE 99 [11c]

UKRAINIAN OPINIONS ON ROLE
OF NATIONALITY IN A HAPPY MARRIAGE
AS TESTED BY TWO DIFFERENT QUESTIONNAIRES:
BY SOCIAL GROUP

	A Percentage citing nationality as most important on:		B Percentage citing nationality as least important on:	
Social group	General questionnaire	Nationality questionnaire	General questionnaire	Nationality questionnaire
White-collar employees	13% (275) [a]	30% (72)	59% (264)	28% (67)
Workers	18 (218)	29 (134)	46 (204)	29 (129)
Collective farmers	15 (112)	31 (118)	27 (97)	20 (116)

a. Total number of respondents on the basis of which the percentage is computed.

While allowing for the special stimulus provided by the nationality questionnaire, we may nevertheless ask how strong is the national consciousness and sensitivity to the nationality issue among the former Soviet citizens who identified themselves as Ukrainians? If for the moment we disregard internal or subgroup differences and take our sample as a whole, we find substantial ill feeling directed against the Great Russians and against Soviet nationality policy and its effects on the Ukraine and the Ukrainian people. On most questions, however, the proportions who gave such hostile or negative answers were far smaller than the assertions of political leaders in the Ukrainian emigration had led many to believe would be the case. This is especially so if you allow for the tendency of the nationality questionnaire to heighten national consciousness. On a wide range of items, varying of course with the particular question, a minimum of one third and a maximum of about two thirds of the Ukrainians give answers indicating dissatisfaction, resentment, or disagreement with Soviet nationality policy or with the Russians. At the opposite pole, between one third and perhaps one half of the respondents showed little or no hostility and indeed often commended the nationality policy and praised the Russian people. In addition, there was often a middle group of approximately one third of the respondents whose answers could not clearly be placed at one pole or another.

Understandably, the questions which elicited the most vigorous expression of ethnic solidarity were those which played on the more general symbols such as the Ukrainian "people" or the Ukrainian "land." Thus, when asked whether Soviet nationality policy improved the position of the Ukrainian people, 91 per cent said "no." [12] This degree of unanimity is unusual in the sample, and undoubtedly is related to the wording of the question. Thus, if we had asked if the Soviet nationality policy had *harmed* (instead of "improved") the position of the Ukrainian people, it does not follow that 91 per cent would have said "yes." Still, the drawing power of ethnic symbols is substantial, as indicated by the fact that 66 per cent felt that there were relatively more arrests of the intelligentsia among the Ukrainians than in other nationalities, 50 per cent held the Ukraine to have been more exploited than other areas, and 72 per cent that Ukrainians benefited less from the nationality policy than did other groups.* The following are typical of the comments of those who "voted" this way:

The Soviets decided to destroy the idea of the Ukrainian nation; they killed and deported. Now three fourths of the population of the Ukrainian cities are not Ukrainians (Ukrainian, a painter and railway worker, age 29).

The Ukraine was a colony in tsarist times, and is one now (Ukrainian teacher and sometime collective farmer, age 49).

The Ukrainian language is dying out because those who use it are suspected as nationalists. . . . National feeling in the Ukraine is of the strongest, imbibed with the mother's milk, reinforced by everything the Bolsheviks have done, and still do, to destroy it (a Ukrainian lawyer, age 74).

In response to these same questions, however, the remainder of the sample did not merely acquiesce through silence. On the contrary, 44 per cent named non-Ukrainians as more arrested or asserted that arrests hit all nationalities with equal force[13] and 38 per cent said that all areas were equally exploited. Furthermore, when asked whether Soviet conditions encouraged the speaking of Ukrainian, almost as many gave an unqualified "yes" (34 per cent) as did those who gave an unqualified "no" (39 per cent). Often the same person acknowledged discrimination in one area, but denied its existence in another. For example, the passionate old lawyer quoted above did also assert: "There is no discrimination in employment." Other typical comments, reporting fair treatment to Ukrainians were as follows:

* On this last item, the other groups offered on the checklist for a comparison were, in order of presentation: Byelorussians, Ukrainians, Volga Tartars, Georgians, Turkmen, and Kalmyks.

Lines between nationalities have been almost entirely wiped out. Politically all are absolutely equal (Ukrainian journalist, age 50).

A characteristic of the Soviet Union is that there is no difference in nationality; no privileges for any nationality (Ukrainian government supply agent, age 51).

One important feature of the Soviet state is that there is absolutely no nationality prejudice (Ukrainian school teacher, age 46).

Identification with and compassion for the motherland, the folk and the culture is perhaps the most positive form of national patriotism, but it seldom is restricted to those forms of expression. A good deal of the national feeling in our sample of Ukrainians took the form of hostility toward the Russians and the Jews. Thus, 32 per cent charged that the Russians were the group most responsible for the fact that the Bolsheviks came to power, and 20 per cent named the Jews. Fifty-seven per cent implied that Russians had given more support to the Bolshevik regime,[14] 41 per cent said directly they had presented less opposition to the collectivization than did the Ukrainians, and 30 per cent felt that there was a "clash of interests" between the Ukrainian and the Russian people. The following remarks are representative expressions of such sentiments:

Great Russians supported the revolution more, Ukrainians less (Ukrainian engineer, age 45).

Great Russians brought the kolkhozes into the Ukraine, and would fight to preserve the regime (a 53-year-old Ukrainian dressmaker and washerwoman).

Russian nationalists and patriots will fight for the regime, because every Russian admires those who make Russia bigger (a postwar escapee, formerly a movie projection operator, age 29).

Here again, however, the remainder of the sample did not acquiesce by silence, but on the contrary many of our respondents disagreed with these judgments. "Members of the party" rather than the Russians or Jews as national groups were singled out by 59 per cent as the cause of the Bolshevik rise to power.[15] Thirty-one per cent felt that the Ukrainians gave as much or even more support to the Soviet regime than did the Russians, 35 per cent credited the Russians with being as much opposed to collectivization as were the Ukrainians, an additional 18 per cent actually credited them with more opposition, and 32 per cent affirmed that there was a community of interests between the Ukrainian and the Russian people.

This pattern of response hardly lends credence to the oft drawn image of the Soviet Union as a seething cauldron fired by nationality sentiment and generating such uniform pressure of resentment and resistance that the regime can barely hold the lid on even when applying the most repressive measures. Certainly there is evidence here of strong nationality feeling and widespread identification with nationality symbols, but the degree of such identification and the intensity of feeling associated with it hardly seems remarkably high. Wherever ethnic groups are thrown together, and particularly where they have free contact and compete socially and economically, there is, even in the freest society in the West, an appreciable amount of tension and hostility generated. Furthermore, although our Ukrainian respondents tend on the whole to reject the Soviet nationality policy, it hardly seems to be uniformly regarded as a bad policy. On the contrary, on most dimensions at least a third are unwilling to go along with condemnation of it. Indeed, in some respects the nationality policy comes in for surprisingly strong approval. For example, when asked whether or not members of the party and Komsomol sought to "root out" cases in which people were offended on grounds of their nationality, 82 per cent said yes, and all but a few of those felt those efforts to have been successful.

In the light of such marked approval for the race relations component of the nationality policy we should perhaps re-examine the responses of the 91 per cent who asserted that the position of the Ukrainian people was not improved under the Soviet regime, this time considering the *reasons* each respondent gave for his answer. Of the reasons given for assuming the Ukrainians to be less well off, a larger number (150) blamed this on the *general* economic policy of the regime — including such factors as the forced collectivization — than the group (135) who blamed it on suppression of the nationality as such. We may conclude that even in so far as the nationality problem is presented as a target for criticism, the criticism directed against it derives as much from the more general complaints shared by Ukrainians with all other people in the Soviet Union, as it does from the distinctive features and consequences of the Soviet nationality policy, *per se.*

Our Ukrainian respondents as a whole showed a definite but by no means extreme amount of identification with national symbols and a considerable but by no means rabid resentment of the Russians. We could not take it for granted, however, that if we were to meet the "average" Ukrainian refugee he would resemble the group at large. It was possible that most strong identification with Ukrainian national symbols and resentment against the Russians would be found concentrated in a particular segment of the population. Or it might be that some would emerge as strongly identified with national symbols although not particularly hostile to the Russians, whereas others would show the reverse pattern. We needed to know, therefore, what were the patterns and the frequencies in which nationalist sentiments were distributed among the individuals in our sample, and what were the identifying characteristics of those who might fairly be termed some kind of Ukrainian nationalist. It should go without saying that the term nationalist is not used here in a pejorative sense, nor is it meant as praise. It is used merely to designate a person distinguished from others in the degree and intensity of his identification with his own nationality group and his conscious rejection of other nationalities.

One characteristic emerged as the outstanding indicator of the nationalist, namely membership in the Ukrainian Autocephalous Church as against the Synodal Church. In Table 100 we present a comparison of the responses of these two groups on a variety of items which tap three main dimensions of nationalism — identification with national and folk symbols, hostility to the Russian "outgroup," and denial of the value and accomplishments of the official nationality policy. The association of church membership and degree of nationalist sentiment is obviously quite strong. It is manifested clearly in each of the three areas tested, although the differences are most dramatic on items dealing with Russian-Ukrainian relations. On item after item the proportion who give a more nationalistic response is once, twice, and even three times greater among those in the Autocephalous Church. Furthermore, there is not a single instance of a reversal of the relationship either in the items listed here or in many additional items tested but for which there was no room in the table. Indeed, of the dozens of items which measure different forms of nationalism there is only one type on which those in the Autocephalous Church do not far exceed the Synodal Church members, namely on extent of knowledge about or familiarity with figures important in Ukrainian history and culture including the Ukrainian independence movement. The amount of information about such figures is determined overwhelmingly by the respondent's educational level, and at comparable educational levels the Autocephalous do not have a significantly higher score than those in the Synodal Church.

The consistent difference in the proportions giving nationalistic responses cannot be assumed to be due to differences in the social composition of the two religious groups, since they are extraordinarily similar in age, sex, occupation, and place of residence.* We will at a later point discuss the effects of occupation and other factors more systematically, and note here only that in general the application of appropriate controls serves mainly not to diminish but to highlight the importance of church membership as an indicator of nationalist sentiment in the Ukrainian group.

Since membersip in the Autocephalous Church is so strongly associated with nationalism we need to consider at least briefly the history and nature of that church. Christianity came to Russia largely through Kiev and until quite late in the seventeenth century the Orthodox faith, which

---

* This similarity was not the product of an effort on our part to match the two groups on any of these variables when we drew our sample.

TABLE 100 [15A]

VIEWS ON THE NATIONALITY PROBLEM AMONG UKRAINIAN AUTO-
CEPHALOUS AND SYNODAL CHURCH MEMBERS

Nationality views	Per cent of church members with nationality view:	
	Synodal	Autocephalous
On symbols of national life		
Ukrainian language not encouraged	30%	55%
Ukrainian intelligentsia arrested more	48	79
Ukrainian territory most exploited	44	59
Nationality most important in marriage	15	40
On behavior of Russians		
Russians responsible for Bolsheviks' rise	15	38
Russians offered less opposition to collectivization	33	46
Russians' interests clash with those of Ukrainians	21	64
Russian-Ukrainian relations in factory were bad	16	69
Russian-Ukrainian relations in school were bad	17	62
On nationality policy		
Nationality policy did not bring harmony between peoples	54	81
Nationality policy caused career discrimination against respondent	16	31
Nationality policy cause of Ukrainians being badly off	24	39
Nationality policy did not lead to elimination of offenses	13	17
Total number of respondents	140	253

was dominant, was tied to Constantinople. As the Muscovite tsar extended his political control over the area, the Ukrainian Orthodox were simultaneously brought under the religious control of Moscow and integrated into the Russian Orthodox Church. They remained so until the Bolshevik revolution and subsequent Civil War. One element in the movement for political independence of the Ukraine from Russia, which was at its height at that time, was an upsurge of interest in the development of an independent Ukrainian Church. Such a church was established by a decree of the Ukrainian Rada in January of 1919, and held services on May 9, 1919, which is counted as the church's Foundation Day. The outstanding characteristic of this church lay in the use of Ukrainian rather than Old Church Slavonic as the language for sermons, prayers, hymns, and even liturgy. In addition, its independence from the Patriarch in Moscow insured the dominance of those of Ukrainian extraction in the priesthood and the hierarchy. In many ways, therefore, the church was an expression of Ukrainian national aspirations and to a degree of anti-Russian sentiment.

Following the defeat and dispersal of the Ukrainian independence forces, and the establishment of Soviet control over the Ukraine, this church became one of the strange beneficiaries of the new regime's policy twists. The Bolsheviks felt that the greatest threat to them from organized religion stemmed from the centralized Russian Orthodox Church under the Patriarch in Moscow. Consequently, in addition to direct onslaught against religion the regime used the principle of divide and conquer. Thus, in competition with the Orthodox Church the Soviet regime fostered the so-called "Living Church" which had earlier been a schismatic movement within the parent body. It was this Living Church which overruled the earlier refusal of the Patriarch Tikhon to grant the autonomy of the Ukrainian Church.

As frequently happens with such satellite organizations, however, the Autocephalous Church showed unusual vigor and independently added its own resistance to the antireligious measures of the regime. As a result, it was not spared in the general war on religion in the late twenties and early thirties. In 1930, under the pressure of the secret police, the Ukrainian (Autocephalous) Church Council "confessed" to having engaged in counterrevolutionary and nationalist activities, and the Soviet government thereupon "dissolved" the central church organizations. Although parish priests were apparently permitted to continue functioning it is hard to estimate how effective a force this religious movement remained after dissolution of the Council. During the German occupation in World War II the church was reconstituted with German support under Bishop Polycarp, only to be eliminated again when the Soviets reoccupied the Ukraine. The Ukrainian Church is active in the emigration, and it has a wide following, although the distribution of such membership among émigré and refugee Ukrainians is not known.

In the light of this history it is apparent that members of the Ukrainian Church would be more likely to develop a strong sense of national identification, and the fate of the church under the Soviets could be expected to intensify the feeling. At the same time, it is reasonable to assume that causation worked in the opposite direction, and that those who were most nationalistic preferred to be members of the Ukrainian rather than the Synodal Russian Orthodox Church. Indeed, membership in the church is probably only the most evident part of a complex of factors which differentiate the more from the less nationalistic Ukrainians. For example, members of the Ukrainian Autocephalous Church were much more likely to report that they learned about the Ukraine, its history and aspirations *at home from their parents*. This learning at home was cited by 64 per cent of the Autocephalous against 44 per cent of the members of the Synodal Church. Typical of the comments testifying to the role of the home in transmitting national sentiment is one from a young Ukrainian school teacher who reported "my first outlook (on the Ukrainian question) was formulated exclusively in my family," and a collective farmer who reported that her mother told her about Petluria, the Ukrainian national independence leader, when she was still quite young, and taught her secretly to sing the Ukrainian national anthem. This last quotation also illustrates still another characteristic of those in the Ukrainian Church; namely, their tendency to feel that the training they received about Ukrainian history and culture was illegal, a position they took three times as often as did those in the Synodal Church, the respective percentages being 37 as against 12. Thus, those in the Ukrainian Church generally experienced a complex of influences which together generated strong national identification. Of the elements in this set, however, no other taken alone distinguishes between the more and the less nationalistic as sharply as does church membership.

Since membership in the Autocephalous Church is so highly associated with nationalist sentiments, information on the extent and distribution of such affiliation within the Ukraine would enable us to make a relatively informed guess as to the extent of more intense Ukrainian nationalism in the USSR and as to the regions and social groups in which it might be strongest. Unfortunately, information on church membership in the USSR is exceedingly scarce. The available estimates suggest that at about the time the Autocephalous Church was broken up in 1930–31, as many as one third of the Ukrainians were members.[16] In addition, the church appears to have been strongest in rural areas, in which the number of Russians was very slight. In the cities of the Ukraine the Russians figured prominently, the influence of Russian culture was widespread, and major segments of the Ukrainians were much Russified. Beyond this, however, the published record tells very little about the geographical and social distribution of the membership. We must, therefore, fall back on our sample, since it is the only source of data we have, acknowledging that at best this is an extremely risky procedure.

There was no special plan or design in the collection of cases to complete the Ukrainian questionnaire, except that budgetary restrictions set an upper limit of about five hundred on the number we could collect. The questionnaire was largely administered on a mass basis, as were our other written questionnaires, with all the individuals in a given camp who regarded themselves as Ukrainian invited to appear on a specified day to fill out a questionnaire about the Ukraine and life there. Thus, al-

though the method of administration might have attracted a disproportionately large share of Ukrainian nationalists, and hence of Ukrainian
Orthodox Church members,[17] there is no reason to assume that *within*
each of these two religious groups any special distortion in the social
composition of the sample should have arisen. We must, therefore, be
struck by the extremely close demographic composition of the two religious groups. Those in the Autocephalous and in the Synodal Church
show an extraordinarily similar distribution by age, and sex, occupation,
region of birth, and region of residence. The sole differences of any substance were that 10 per cent more of the members of the Autocephalous
Church lived in the village rather than in the city, and 10 per cent more
lived in the east and northeast Ukraine. This argues very strongly that
members of the Autocephalous Church are not distinctively drawn from
any particular area, or social group, but rather they are to be found in
all places and all walks of life. It suggests therefore that the associated
nationalist sentiments may be found equally commonly in all spheres of
Ukrainian society.

No other social characteristic approximates the significance of church
membership as a correlate of attitudes on the nationality question. Nevertheless, place of residence, occupation, education and age are all to some
degree associated with the kind and extent of nationalism manifested
by our respondents. Some of these factors are of course closely inter-
related, and our sample was not sufficiently large to permit the isolation
of the independent effects of each characteristic through simultaneous
controls on several dimensions. By examining the influence of these factors
within the two major church groups, however, we may hope to develop a
fairly reliable estimate of their effect on Ukrainian nationalism.

Within the context of the major and crucial division by church membership, the sharpest and most consistent differences between subgroups
of the population emerged when they were further divided along occupational lines. In general those in the white-collar jobs (professional, semiprofessional, and clerical) were much more hostile to the Russians than
were the workers or the peasants.* This difference was extreme in the case
of those in the Autocephalous Church, within which the white-collar
personnel were markedly more anti-Russian on all available measures.
Probably this difference is associated with the more frequent and intimate
contact between Ukrainian and Russian white-collar workers and the
greater degree of direct competition between them for the more favored
positions. Very often Ukrainian white-collar personnel worked mainly
under Russian supervisors. In contrast the worker, and particularly the
peasant, lived in a more homogeneous community, often had no direct

---

* This contrasts, of course, with hostility against the leaders and the regime, which
generally was much *less* marked among the more advantaged classes.

contact at all with Russians, and hence was not in obvious competition with them. Although the differences were less consistent and generally less marked, those in professional and white-collar jobs also were more strongly identified with the fate of the Ukrainian language, and were much better informed about Ukrainian culture heroes. On the other hand, the upper occupational groups spoke more favorably than the lower about the official nationality policy, and more frequently acknowledged it to have led to harmony between groups. Among those who were more identified with these national symbols, the white-collar groups placed the blame for the condition of the Soviet Ukraine about equally on the Russians as a nationality and on the Kremlin leadership. The people in manual occupations placed much more of the blame on the regime, less often cited the Russians.

Since education is highly correlated with occupation, it will be no surprise that education showed much the same pattern of association with nationalism as that which emerged from study of the influence of occupation on nationalism. Rural versus urban residence did not have a marked effect on nationalism, except in so far as place of residence reflected the influence of occupation and education which are associated with it. We have one set of striking findings, however, which reveal that those who were raised in a rural setting but then moved from the countryside to the city were very often more nationalistic than *either* the city dwellers amongst whom they have come to live or the country residents among whom they formerly dwelt. The influence of this experience is strikingly consistent, manifesting itself within both church groups — although much more sharply among the Autocephalous — and within groups sorted by occupation, education, and age.

A large segment of those who moved from the countryside to the city did so under the impact of the forced collectivization of agriculture. It is also likely that a significant proportion were in the category of "dekulakized" peasants whose families were deported from the villages after forceful and often bloody expropriation of their property. Once in the city, such peasants were subject to continuing discrimination. Even among those who were not kulaks, the impact of collectivization was probably felt even more intensely when it was accompanied by a shift in residence and the associated strains of adjustment to new ways of life in the city. In addition, in the cities the Russians were much more in evidence than in the countryside, and it was much more apparent that they were the main formulators of policy and the chief authority in its execution. Nationalism is often expressed mainly by showing hostility to another group, and prejudice often increases as frustration increases. Under the circumstances, we might well expect those who experienced the shift from rural to urban residence to be the most nationalistic and to express this mainly in hostility towards the Russians, who were perceived as the designers and executors of the collectivization.

On the whole, age alone does not discriminate between degrees of nationalism, but on those issues on which there were differences the young were as a rule less nationalistic. In particular, the young were noticeably less hostile to the Russians than were the older age groups, a difference really marked in the category of the well educated. These young people had benefited from advantages provided by the Soviet regime and spent much of their time in the relatively Russified atmosphere of university and administrative life, but had not yet met many real frustrations in their career pursuits. They were therefore markedly more prone than the older generation to speak positively of the nationality policy and of relations between the Russians and Ukrainians. The older people with higher education had presumably obtained their education under pre-Soviet auspices. Many had experienced the national awakening of the independence movement after the revolution and during the early Soviet years when the regime more strongly encouraged the flowering of local national culture. Whether the younger generation or the well educated will in its turn be disillusioned by the reality of Soviet life and become less well disposed toward the Russians and Soviet nationality policy cannot be directly deduced from our data. We suspect, however, that the quite different historical conditions in which they live will influence them to continue to mute their identification with their nationality.

The Issue of Ukrainian Independence

From a political point of view the content of nationalist sentiment, and indeed even its distribution, are of less interest than the potential for *action* which inheres in it. The crucial question is whether, and to what degree, their nationalism leads those with more intense national identification to desire the political independence of the Ukraine. The independence issue was so highly charged in émigré circles that we found it impossible to phrase a direct question that might not be interpreted as biased in one direction or the other.

We did approach the question indirectly, however, by posing the issue of independence and separatism in a historical context. Phrasing the question in this way probably yielded a substantially smaller vote for separatism than we would have obtained by a direct inquiry. But since our interest was not so much in establishing the frequency of separatist sentiment as in discovering what kinds of people chose the more separatist answer, the failure to ask the direct question may not be too serious a drawback.

The question we did use asked which of three alternative descriptions "conforms most closely to the existence of the Ukrainian nation," listing the following choices:

1. The existence of the Ukrainian nation from ancient times to the present cannot be separated from the existence of the Russian nation.

2. The existence of the Ukrainian nation, from ancient times to the present, was separate from the Russian nation.

3. In former times the Ukrainian nation had its own separate existence, but beginning with the time of Catherine the Great to the present, its existence was tied to the existence of the Russian nation except for the period 1917 to 1920.

The last of these is probably the more accurate statement of history, and is relatively neutral in its emotional and political tone. The other two answers are more extreme. We assumed that in so far as our respondents reacted strongly to the idea of separatism they would reveal their sensitivity to the issue by passing over the obvious third alternative in favor of one of the two more extreme positions.

TABLE 101[17A]

UKRAINIAN VIEWS ON SEPARATISM AND HISTORY:
BY OCCUPATION AND CHURCH MEMBERSHIP

Views	Professional & white-collar		Worker		Collective farmer	
	Synodal church	Auto-cephalous	Synodal church	Auto-cephalous	Synodal church	Auto-cephalous
Ukraine cannot be separated	56%	4%	46%	7%	40%	11%
Ukraine always was separate	4	20	3	16	10	11
Ukraine was separate until Catherine	40	76	51	77	50	78
Total number of respondents	25	46	39	57	30	54

The response to this question does indeed vary markedly according to church membership (Table 101). The contrast is most evident in connection with the idea that the existence of the Ukrainian nation from ancient times cannot be separated from that of the Russian nation. This idea has a great deal of appeal to those in the Russian (Synodal) Church, and is indeed about as popular as the historically more accurate third alternative. But those in the Autocephalous Church shun this answer, and in so far as they depart from the historically more accurate statement tend instead to assert that the existence of the Ukrainian nation was *always* separate. The contrast is most marked in the professional group, in which we have earlier noted the greatest contrasts, with 56 per cent of the Synodal as against a mere 4 per cent of the Autocephalous Church members allowing that the history of the two people cannot be separated. Those who can acknowledge some degree of separation in the existence of the two people (alternatives 2 and 3) as against those who deny the idea altogether (alternative 1) are found in radically different proportions in the two church groups. Among members of the Synodal Church those who see some degree of separateness in this history of the two peoples are in the ratio of roughly 1:1 with those who see none. Among those in the Autocephalous Church the ratio is about 10:1. Occupation has but little effect on these patterns, which are remarkably stable considering the small number of cases available for Table 101. It is important to note, however, that age does bear a strong relation to this question, even when occupation or education is held constant. For example, among the well educated more than twice as many of the younger respondents as of the older (36 per cent versus 17 per cent) choose the first alternative which asserted that the history of the Ukraine could not be separated from that of Russia.

The conclusion is inescapable that amongst the more nationalistic, as measured by church membership, there is a much greater propensity to see Ukrainian history as involving at least some degree of separation from Russian history, and indeed a rather greater tendency to adopt the extreme position that the existence of the two nations has always been "separate." We learn as well that those in the Synodal Church also react strongly to the stimulus of separatism, but do so in the opposite direction by asserting that the existence of the two people *cannot* be separated. Thus, it appears that both among those who are extremely nationalistic and those who are relatively lacking in nationalist sentiment the issue of separatism is salient. The more nationalistic tend strongly to favor it, the less nationalistic tend on the whole to be strongly opposed to it.

A further check on our conclusions is provided by the materials from the life-history interview materials. Here again the approach was indirect, in this case even more so. In the course of the personal interview each respondent was asked to comment on the distinguishing "national characteristics" of the Great Russians, Ukrainians, Georgians, Jews, and other Soviet national groups. He was not restricted to answering the question precisely as asked, however, and those who were so inclined could drift into a discussion of related topics such as the nationality problem.

There were 76 Ukrainians who took the life-history interview. Twenty-six made comments which marked them as overtly hostile to or prejudiced toward the Russians.[18] Of those who showed such prejudice, half also spontaneously expressed their interest in and support of the idea of Ukrainian separatism and no one explicitly criticized the idea. In contrast, among the 50 Ukrainians who were *not* overtly anti-Russian a much lower proportion, only 22 per cent, spontaneously supported the cause of Ukrainian separatism. Further, all five of the Ukrainians who spontaneously criticized the idea of separatism fell in the category of those who did not manifest any anti-Russian feeling. Again, it is apparent that political separatism is much more likely to be associated with hostility to the Russian people, and opposition to separatism will be more frequent among those without strong resentment of the Russians.

The total amount of support for the idea of a politically separate and independent Ukraine was certainly not negligible. Considering that we did not ask a direct question and the opinions were volunteered, the fact that almost one in three Ukrainians spoke for separatism suggests the existence of widespread sentiment for this idea. In assessing this finding we should probably make allowance for the effects of exposure to émigré politics, in which the idea of separatism is almost an article of faith, in developing the degree of observed sentiment in favor of an independent Ukraine.[19] Projection to the parent population of Ukrainians in the Soviet Union must therefore be approached with considerable caution. The most our data permit us to say is that the idea of Ukrainian separatism could be expected to win neither overwhelming support nor rejection from Soviet Ukrainians. Rather the idea would tend to meet both significant amounts of support and opposition on all levels of the society with the lines of cleavage being by religion, degree of anti-Russian sentiment, and age.

Summary and Conclusions

The first part of our exploration of the nationality problem led inescapably to the conclusion that a Ukrainian's life chances in the Soviet system and his reactions to it are determined first and foremost by his status as a Soviet citizen of a given occupation or social class, and only very secondarily by his nationality. Unless the subject of nationality is brought up by the questionnaire or interviewer, the Ukrainian will very rarely explain his life conditions on the basis of his nationality, and will seldom spontaneously make any reference to the nationality policy as something that particularly should be changed. Indeed, even those we know, on the basis of other evidence, to be strongly nationalistic do not think first of their nationality or of the nationality policy of the regime when invited to explain or complain about life in Soviet society. Regardless of degree of nationalism or church membership, Ukrainians as a whole hold very similar views of the good and the bad society, have essentially the same complaints to make about the Soviet regime and the institutions it has established, and show the same amount of loyalty toward and disaffection from the system as do the Russians. There is little evidence for assuming that any but a very few of the Ukrainians left the Soviet Union mainly because of dissatisfaction with the nationality policy of the regime or with the treatment they personally had received as members of a national minority.

Nevertheless, their national group membership is by no means irrelevant in understanding the attitudes, values and adjustment patterns of Soviet citizens of Ukrainian nationality. When faced with questions which invited them to express identification with their national group and its symbols and when asked *directly* to evaluate the Soviet nationality policy, a substantial proportion of the Ukrainians revealed that they felt that their national group had been exploited, the use of their language discouraged, and their national leadership subjected to a disproportionately high rate of political arrest. There was also a widespread feeling that the nationality policy had led neither to benefit for the Ukrainian people nor harmony between the Ukrainians and other nationalities. Many felt that the Russians were more implicated in the Soviet regime, were more supportive of its policies, and had generally bad relations with the Ukrainians. On the whole, however, such views were held by only half or fewer of the Ukrainians we interviewed despite the fact that the form of the questions and the special context in which they were asked tended to encourage the expression of the latent nationalism which was present in the group.

Furthermore, it is clear that the total amount of nationalism in our sample at large was by no means evenly distributed. On the contrary, it was concentrated predominantly in members of the Autocephalous (Independent) Ukrainian Church, and secondarily in the group most uprooted by Soviet developments during the thirties — in particular by the forced collectivization of agriculture. They have the strongest feeling that the Ukraine and its people have been ill used, that the nationality policy has brought nothing but bad feeling, that Russians and Ukrainians cannot get along, and they feel that they were personally discriminated against on nationality grounds. The only measure of nationalism with regard to which they are not particularly distinguished is in knowledge about the organizations and leaders important in Ukrainian history and in the independence movement, with regard to which the level of education of a respondent is definitive.

Our findings cannot be generalized to other nationalities except on a frankly speculative basis, yet we must at least consider the implications of our Ukrainian study for such groups. The Ukrainian national group has a long history of independence movements, and indeed there was briefly an independent Ukrainian government. The Ukraine has a national literature and a nationally conscious intelligentsia, and is advanced economically and socially. The people have felt with full force the impact of Soviet policy with regard to collectivization and the crackdown on "bourgeois nationalism." Furthermore, all of our respondents had for some time been exposed not only to anti-Soviet German Nazi influence, but subsequently to strong nationalist propaganda emanating from the political parties in the emigration. Those parties were overwhelmingly nationalist and separatist, and they generally controlled the émigré Ukrainian language press. It seems not unreasonable, therefore, to assume that the level of nationalism and independence sentiment revealed by our Ukrainian respondents would not be greatly exceeded in the relatively advanced national groups such as the Byelorussians, Georgians, or Armenians. Indeed on the general written questionnaire there was a sufficient number of respondents from each of these groups to support the assertion that on the whole their life chances in, and pattern of response to, the Soviet system is very much like that of Ukrainians and the Russians so long as the comparison is of individuals in the same social class. We do not know how Georgians, Armenians and others among the more privileged national groups would respond to a questionnaire specifically on the nationality problem, but we venture to guess that in that respect as well they would behave in a fashion generally comparable to the Ukrainians, at least in the sense that neither nationalism nor separatism would be overwhelmingly high. This applies, of course, only to the older Soviet areas. We make no assertions with regard to more advanced nationalities more recently incorporated into the USSR, such as the Lithuanians, Estonians, and Latvians.

It is even more difficult to assess the significance of our findings on the Ukrainians for the attitudes of the minor nationalities and peoples who come from what might be classified as the "underdeveloped" parts of the Soviet Union. Many of them have no history of existence as an independent nation, and sometimes even their alphabet was not acquired until one was developed for them by Soviet authorities. Under the circumstances, nationalism and particularly separatism cannot be assumed to be highly developed. On the other hand, in many of these areas there are few ties of religion, or culture to bind these people to the Christian, Slavic Russians. In addition, many still remember with anger the harsh measures of the collectivization, which to them seemed mainly a *Russian* attack on their tribe, their culture, and their religion. The arbitrary dissolution of the local national government and the dispersion of the peoples of the Kalmyck, Chechen-Ingush, and Crimean Tatar regions during World War II indicate that the regime certainly finds many of the minor nationalities unreliable and indeed dangerously so. Yet we have no basis for knowing how extensive the disaffection was in those areas. The Stalinist regime did not hesitate to disperse a whole nationality as a reprisal for the acts of a few, although the subsequent acknowledgment of these acts as among Stalin's mistakes may presage better treatment for, and less consequent resentment among, such nationalities.

In the light of our findings and our assumption as to their generality, we find ourselves unable to assert that the nationality composition of the Soviet Union is an outstandingly critical feature of its social structure, or that it will play a decisive role in determining the system's long range stability *under normal conditions*. By comparison with socio-economic class, the effect of nationality on life experience and attitude is both extremely limited and much more a latent or potential than an active factor. We have seen that even where the national problem is attacked by our respondents, the most important reason for criticizing it lies in the economic hardships imposed by the Soviet regime. This suggests that the nationality problem is more a channel for expressing grievances shared by the population at large rather than a distinctive cause of discontent in and of itself. Since it is such a channel, it is certainly a force to be reckoned with. Were it not for the nationality problem there would be less strain in the system. But the locus of the strongest national sentiment lies, at least in the case of Ukrainians, in groups whose weight in the population will be decreasing as time advances. The Autocephalous Church is not organized and effectively operative. Of course the home often serves as a source for the transmission of strong national sentiments, but we have in our chapter on the family shown how permeable the home is to the influence of the forces emanating from the larger society. The collectivization, which did much to stir up nationalist feeling, was an event of a nonrecurrent type. Finally, as the younger generation, raised in the Soviet schools and less subject to "deviant" church and home influence, replaces the older generation, the frequency of nationalist sentiment and of rejection of the nationality policy will undergo still further reductions.

The strength of nationalistic feeling among members of the Soviet national minorities could perhaps be increased and the feelings of the nationalities intensified by heavy propaganda designed to arouse national feeling and hostility toward the Russians. But it is very doubtful that the levels attained could be brought to the point where the issue became that powder keg, the national republics that tinder box, which so many have asserted them to be. On the contrary, if we assume that the post-Stalin leaders will not markedly reverse current policy by instituting large-scale persecution and discrimination, then time appears to be on the side of the Soviet regime in the probable future development of the nationality problem. This by no means implies that the problem has been "solved" or that it will likely be solved in the near future. The anxiety of Moscow about national defection, reflected in the passing references to the issue in the charges against Beria, and the continuing presence of excessive local patriotism and independence sentiment in the minority republics, will keep the nationality problem alive and important for some time to come. Indeed, if the evident tendencies toward the expression of Great Russian nationalism develop unchecked, the amount of alienation based primarily on grounds of ethnic patriotism may even increase temporarily. The problem is therefore perhaps chronic, but generally not acute. In any event, it remains the case that on all matters not bearing directly on the nationality problem or closely associated with it, one can over a wider range and more accurately predict a man's attitudes, values, and life experiences if one knows only his social class than if one knows only his ethnic group.

PART FIVE: CONCLUSIONS

XVI

The Future of Soviet Society[1]

Well before Stalin's death we were already launched on one of the great debates of our time. Could the Soviet system survive the death of the supreme dictator, and if it did, what would be the nature of its future development? At least five years after Stalin's death the Soviet system still seems very much with us. There are those who still see in it only the seeds of a soon forthcoming paroxysm of political fratricide and consequent dissolution. Most students of Soviet affairs, however, accept the idea that the system will not soon collapse from internal pressures. A war of "liberation" and total destruction now also seems rather unlikely. Assuming then that neither an internal explosion nor an external attack materializes, what seems the most likely course of Soviet development in the next two or three decades?

Two major and rather polarized positions have come to dominate the discussion. At the one pole there are those who assert that what Stalin wrought was a kind of modern oriental despotism, even more effective than the earlier absolute states, such as traditional China, because the modern instruments of force, communication, and education facilitate even greater mobilization of the population in the service of the dictator. This group holds modern totalitarianism as developed in the Soviet Union to be unchanged and unchanging. Nothing, except the complete destruction of the system, can stop the drive toward dictatorship and nothing can sway the dictator from the absolute exercise of power, from the total mobilization of the population for the ends of the state. In this system there is no such thing as a "concession" to popular will. The dictator acts as he sees fit, now playing soft, now hard, but always according to his own plan — "from above." Classes are made, and when they grow too powerful, unmade. Institutions are created, and when they have served their purpose dissolved. Police controls, censorship, terror, a dark struggle for power at the higher reaches are inherent qualities of the system. Indeed even the leaders are powerless to change the system. They must preserve all its essential features as a total unity. To compromise is to risk destruction, to lose the power which is presumably the main motive force for the leaders.

By extension to the realm of foreign affairs these theorists hold that Soviet policy is undeviatingly committed to the destruction of the free world, and that it is premised on this destruction being ultimately effected by force of arms. All treaties, agreements, arrangements and understandings are purely tactical manoeuvres to gain time or other advantage. The Soviet word cannot be trusted, the very idea of good intentions is alien to them, and negotiation with them can have no other useful purpose than to demonstrate *our* gullibility or our good intentions.

This rather grim picture, perhaps stated most fully by Bertram Wolfe, must be set opposite a much more cheerful political landscape as sketched by Isaac Deutscher and others. They see the gradual democratization of Soviet society as inevitable, and indeed claim to have substantial evidence that the process is already far advanced. They maintain that Stalin's system was developed largely to meet the unusual conditions of forced draft industrialization and the threat of war. But in this process the country became industrialized, the farms mechanized. A large urban population was assembled and trained in the "higher" culture of the cities. Education became very widespread. Most important, a large technically trained, responsible, educated middle class arose which had aspirations for a more sane and rational pattern of life. At the same time, the leadership itself was changing as more men whose experience lay in this new middle class themselves attained positions of power and responsibility. Thus, the needs felt by the leaders for rational, orderly, efficient, processes, for higher labor productivity, for more spontaneous and intelligent compliance, joined forces with desires for a better life on the part of the population. Together they set in motion a retreat from Stalinist extremism, towards reform and liberalization of the system. These changes are assumed to be irreversible, and therefore are taken to promise the gradual democratization of the Soviet system.

By extension to the realm of foreign affairs those who hold this position claim that the present Soviet leaders are genuinely interested in a peaceful, stable world order, within the framework of which they can engage in friendly competition with our democratic capitalist system for world leadership. It is assumed that they seek a reduction of international tension and a consequent reduction in the arms burden, in order to free them for more effective action in this competition. The exchange programs they have undertaken are assumed to be a genuine expression of their intentions in this direction. The Soviet leaders are taken to be reasonable men amenable to reasonable argument.

As is so often true with such theories, one can find substantial evidence in support of both. The release of thousands from forced labor camps; the tremendous reduction of political arrests to the point where they affect only a small proportion of the population; the cessation of obligatory deliveries from the private plots of the peasants; the opening of the Soviet Union to foreign tourists and the permission for Soviet citizens to travel abroad; the numerous programs for the exchange of scholars and students — these and a host of other measures taken by the government all argue that a new style of governing has come to the fore after Stalin's death. In contrast to Stalin's time the system is more "liberal," and the process shows some signs of further development.

On the other hand, those who argue for the unchanging nature of the system can point to the fact that people are still arbitrarily arrested by the secret police — even if they are fewer in number — and sentenced without open trial. The dark struggle at the top continues — as Beria and his associates were first to discover, and Molotov and company not so long after. The use of force on a mass scale against a whole population was amply demonstrated in Hungary to the horror of the entire world. Hence, in essence, they would argue, the system remains unchanged.

Both of these positions suffer from a certain degree of rigidity which makes them inadequate for an assessment of future Soviet development. They are rigid in that both assume that totalitarianism is an "either-or" proposition rather than a matter of degree. In our opinion each of these contrasting views depicts one of the two sets of forces at work in the Soviet Union, one stemming from the nature of the totalitarian system established under Stalin, the other from the nature of the industrial society which has grown up beneath the totalitarian structure. The two sets of forces have already demonstrated a certain measure of compatibility, and the pertinent question is not which one will triumph, but what the concrete resolution will be.

It seems highly unlikely that the Soviet system, any more than any other modern industrial society, can be, or indeed has been, unchanging. It may be true, for example, that the shift from mass terror to political arrest limited to a small group at the top is not a change in principle, but merely in degree. Yet for the hundreds of thousands of Soviet citizens who now sleep more securely, without the continuous fear of the early morning knock at the door, the change is real enough. They would think us mad to argue that this was not a "real" change. Yet such changes do not add up to democratization. Although few are arrested, no man is granted a true immunity from arbitrary arrest, and none can assume they will be protected by proper safeguards of due process if they are arrested. There is very little evidence of any deliberate move by the Communist Party to share power, or even to observe democratic processes within its own organization. The term "liberalization" of the system may be granting too much if we insist on giving the word liberal an even moderately strict limitation. In any event there certainly seems nothing inevitable about the process.

Indeed, inevitability is a rock on which most theories of history founder, Marx's theory being not the least example. We can assume neither the inevitable stability nor the inevitable democratization of the system. In any event, either designation is largely a label we apply to a social process. Rather than argue about the labels we might do better to go directly to the social processes which the labels presume to describe. The following pertinent conclusions emerge from our study.

1. Stalinist rule created a deep and long lasting impression in the Soviet people, and left a residue of bitterness and resentment against arbitrary, violent, and despotic patterns of governing with which all subsequent governments must reckon. There is a widespread feeling that this was a terrible aberration, and a general determination that it must not happen again.

2. The prolonged depression in the standard of living associated with collectivization of the farms and the years of forced industrialization was a source of resentment second only to the terror, and a widespread basis for questioning the legitimacy of the regime. The same deprivations (unless the people genuinely saw them as necessitated by external threat) would not again be accepted without large scale passive resistance and the generation of tensions which would threaten to become explosive.

3. While consciously resenting the deprivations which Stalinist rule introduced into their lives, most Soviet citizens were nevertheless strongly, albeit more subtly and unconsciously, influenced by the processes of social change which Stalin set in motion. These changes are to be measured not merely in terms of the usual census categories of increasing education and urbanization, but more in terms of changed attitudes, values, and life patterns. The values of the peasant family rooted in the local community, devoted to the soil, and consecrated to the continuance of religious and social tradition have suffered enormous attrition. We believe these patterns, though they still exist, now characterize only a minority of the population. In their place the culture of the cities, the values of the rapidly changing industrial order, have now been ensconced. The job he holds in the economic realm has become the prime determinant of a man's life chances, his opportunities for earnings, the pleasure he will derive from his job, the success of his children, the assessment he makes of his life situation.

Under these circumstances, the idea of following traditional family pursuits has been replaced with the value of success, or of security where success is not possible. Religion has much less of a hold on the population, and much of the religious sentiment that remains has become more secularized and is expressed in the form of social ethics. The parents' chief concern is that the child be "happy" and well adjusted, which generally means being financially comfortable and personally well liked. The "consumption ethic" has come to Russia as it has to other industrialized countries. Indeed, it is our impression that this quality is almost as strong in the Soviet Union as it is in the United States. It is obvious that to manipulate the Soviet population the regime will be less effective if it uses force or coercion than if it juggles opportunities and rewards in the form of occupational advancement and other tangible and intangible goods.

4. Despite great hostility to the Stalinist rule of terror, and profound resentment against the depressed standard of living, the great majority of Soviet citizens seem to find much that is acceptable in the system. This applies particularly to the idea of government ownership and operation of industry, transportation, and most trade, and to the concept of the welfare state exemplified in government guarantees of work, medical care, and education. Opportunities for social mobility are sensed and appreciated, probably beyond what the actual situation warrants. There is great pride in the industrial attainments of the society, and in the apparent "cultural" development of the country, as represented in the theatrical arts, music, literature, painting, sculpture and, to a lesser degree, architecture. The performance of both the government and the people during the war and the period of reconstruction is a source of admiration and pride, tinged with a sense of wonder. By extension, the central position of the Soviet Union in world affairs is a source of gratification. "The Soviet power" is a big thing, which no one takes lightly.

5. Resentment of the oppressive features of the Soviet system took, in *some* instances, violent and explosive form — a total or global rejection of everything "Communist" and Soviet. However, for most people grievances tended to be highly concrete and specific. The main themes were "end the terror," "slow up the pace of economic life," "improve the standard of living," and so on. The execution of the program, rather than the conception itself, was deemed bad. Even though the essential disparity between the Soviet system as idea and as reality was grasped, there was still a woeful failure to generate alternatives which commanded respect or attention. The Soviet refugees often left us with the impression that there was not only little understanding, but relatively little need felt for the *strictly constitutional* apparatus of guarantees, rights and safeguards which characterize the democracy of Western Europe. Good rulers, kind, considerate, and compassionate, who "cared" for people, and did not terrorize them or push them too hard, would be quite acceptable, especially if they provided an increasing standard of living and opportunities for personal advancement.

6. Most Soviet citizens seem to have accepted the main outlines of the official image of foreign affairs disseminated by the official media. They see the United States government as dominated by powerful groups who seem committed to waging a war of destruction against the Soviet Union and other countries. They imagine a vast conspiracy by the West to prevent colonial and underdeveloped areas from attaining their independence and achieving their rightful national aspirations for peaceful economic development. They take substantial pride in Soviet strength and the image they have of the USSR as a leading world force. They believe the Soviet government to be a champion of peace and a defender of the small and weak. They are eager for peace and the smaller burden of arms a stable world order would yield. But they do not assume they understand the complexities of world politics, and incline overwhelmingly to leave these issues to the leaders "who understand these things, and know best."

After Stalin's death his successors acted with intelligence and forcefulness to eliminate or reduce most of the prime sources of popular resentment and discontent which Stalin left them as part of their political heritage. They did this by drastically reducing the application of terror, taking measures tangibly to improve living standards, and giving more meaning to the welfare state guarantees of free education, medical care and old age security. They also reduced the intensity of the pressures put on intellectuals and the enormity of the controls placed on administrators and economic managers, and made substantial concessions to the peasants. No one of these concessions and grants to the people is necessarily "permanent." Neither do they represent "permanent" solutions of the several social problems to which they were a response. Their significance lay mainly in the evidence they offered that the leaders were aware of the greatest sources of tension and the worst grievances in the system, and were willing and able to take effective measures to deal with the situation. This suggests, therefore, that even within the structure of the perhaps unstable Soviet oligarchy, there are greater capacities for change and adjustment than many have been willing to allow.

The leaders' capacity to make such adjustments argues well for the short-run stability of the system. It does not, however, insure its long-range stability, nor does it give us any sure guide lines as to what that long-range stability will be like. It is one thing to make some concessions to the collective farm peasant by excusing him from obligatory deliveries to the state from his home garden plot. It is quite another matter to develop a stable and adequate motivation in the peasant to work productively on the collective farm, so long as it continues to be the segment of the economy which is milked to permit the economic advances of heavy industry.* It is one thing to accuse Beria and others of resisting the legitimate aspirations of the national minorities. But it is quite another thing to yield to those aspirations while still maintaining necessary integration of the system and controlling centrifugal tendencies towards national independence. And one may threaten reprobate students with expulsion, but this will not give young people the belief in ideology or the faith in the system which their truculent questions show them to lack. It is one thing to decentralize industrial management. But it is quite another problem both to permit meaningful local autonomy and simultaneously preserve the general integrity of centralized planning and its associated economic controls.

These comments point to some of the special and enduring problems of Soviet society. They are certainly not exactly the same as the problems of any other society. Indeed, they are quite distinctive, arising from the specific conditions of Soviet history and the particular institutional complex which constitutes the Soviet system. In the United States, for example, there is not even a remote equivalent of the problem posed by the organization of the collective farm or the motivation of the peasant. There is a race problem in the United States. But it bears only the remotest similarity to the nationality problem in the Soviet Union, which concerns not so much ethnic discrimination as national movements based on distinctive cultures, languages, and political histories. Although the problem of industrial monopoly may be a crucial one in American society, it is so because it seems to challenge certain values implicit in the idea of the free-enterprise economy, whereas in the Soviet Union the principle of monopoly is of course taken for granted, and only the issue of efficiency is an adequate basis for challenging any particular degree of centralized planning and control.

Yet to stress the distinctiveness of Soviet problems is perhaps to misplace the emphasis. The distinctive features of Soviet totalitarianism have for so long commanded our attention that we have lost our awareness of an equally basic fact. The substratum on which the distinctive Soviet features are built is after all a large-scale industrial order which shares many features in common with the large-scale industrial order in other national states of Europe and indeed Asia. It is just this fact that we regard as the single most important conclusion to emerge from our study. Trying to read the future of Soviet development solely on the basis of the distinctive characteristics of Soviet totalitarianism without taking ac-

---

* It is fresh testimony to the dynamism of the Soviet system and the vitality of its leadership that in 1957 and 1958 measures were adopted which have very substantially reduced the disadvantaged status of the collective farm peasant relative to the city worker. In the course of a very few years the personal incomes of peasants have increased 50 per cent.

count of the changes in the Soviet industrial social structure and in the Soviet people is like trying to understand a story when the pages have been torn in half, lengthwise, and you have only the left halves to read. This story is obscure enough when we have both halves of the text. It will defy understanding if we attempt to read it from either half alone.

The basic question, then, comes down to this: in what degree are the distinctive features of Soviet totalitarianism compatible with the rest of the social structure we associate with large-scale industrial society? The question could, perhaps, have been put the other way around. But we take it that history has already given us a partial answer. A totalitarian government of the Soviet type obviously does constitute an adequate, if not ideal, basis for transforming a somewhat backward subcontinent into an overpowering industrial giant in the course of some twenty or thirty years. We also put the question as we did as a way of making clear our assumption that the Soviet Union, no matter what its form of government, will never revert to being the predominantly rural, agricultural, peasant based society which existed before 1917. For better or for worse, geography, resources, population, and later development under the stimulus of Stalinist totalitarianism have produced a highly advanced and extremely capable industrial base in the Soviet Union. It is completely unreasonable to assume that it would be done away with no matter who ruled in Russia. The system which must look to its survival, therefore, is not the industrial but the socio-political structure of Soviet society.

To answer our question, we must perhaps specify more fully what we mean by "Soviet totalitarianism" and "the industrial social order." The former is perhaps the easier to define, since this is ground which has been much worked over of late, and there seems good agreement on the issue. The Soviet system has been characterized by certain features which it shares with other modern totalitarian states, most notably Germany.[2] These include, first and foremost, a system of absolute, autocratic and essentially unconstitutional "above the law" rule, exercized by a single party holding a monopoly of power and organized on the principles of an army under the leadership of an all-wise supreme commander assisted by a general staff largely of his own selection. The leader, his staff and his army, are armed by an essentially eschatological ideology which preaches the necessity of violence in the destruction of certain essentially "evil" features of the old social order, which are to be replaced by a new, planned, and in some sense holy or sanctified form of social organization, the precise shape of which is, however, only vaguely specified. To effect this objective the totalitarian party uses the instrument of the state, which grows enormously in scope, size, and power. Other than the party and the state, which is the instrument of its program, no independent or quasi-autonomous associations or organizations which might become foci for alternate loyalty or bases for secure opposition, are permitted. There is, therefore, a war against the church, and either the destruction or subversion of unions, professional associations and fraternal societies of all kinds. In their place concensus is manufactured and thought controlled through centralized manipulation of the means of mass communication and dictation of the form and content of art, literature, and drama. To increase the probability that the "learning" of consensus will be effective, to liquidate the remnants of the evil past, and to deal with the discord produced by the forced changes being made, extensive use is made of the monopolized instruments of force in a program of repression and, when necessary, police terror directed against individuals and whole strata of the population both outside and within the ruling party. An effort is made in this way to secure the total mobilization of all resources, and above all personal human resources, in the assault on the goals set for the society by its ruling elite. It is this absence of pluralism, and the denial of the validity of a private sphere of life as against the complete or *total* subordination of the individual and institutions to the purpose of the state, which lends its special name to totalitarianism.

The foregoing is, of course, a schematized view of totalitarianism. It is a model which the Soviet leaders strove to approximate, and which they approximated more closely than has been done in any large scale society in modern history. A few words of explication are perhaps necessary to suit these rather general features of totalitarianism to the concreteness of Soviet reality. In the Soviet case the ruling ideology has, of course, been Marxist-Leninist communism, and the eschatological belief has posited the "final" combat between dying capitalism and communism aborning. The growth of the state has particularly involved government control of the productive apparatus and its operation on principles of strict planning. And in the Soviet case there has been, in addition, the generally high value placed on technology and a distinctive, if not unique, worship of science, especially the biological and physical sciences.

The modern industrial social order is perhaps more difficult to define, and certainly we can expect less agreement for our formulation — if only because our readers live in such a society and will be appropriately aware of the limitations of such generalizations. Nevertheless, we suggest that the following are important characteristics of that social order as it has emerged in large scale industrial societies such as the United States, Germany, and the Soviet Union.* Obviously, we cannot hope to be exhaustive in this description, but rather must select certain salient features which

---

* We have not included England here, despite the fact that it was probably the first great industrial country and for a long time the leading industrial power. In our opinion England represents the model of the *early* industrial nation, but does not fit the model of the *modern* industrial order described here. It will probably move in the direction sketched here, and to some extent has already done so.

have the greatest relevance for the functioning of the socio-political order.

We take the central feature of the modern industrial order to be the large corporation, or super-firm, one integrated, coordinated, and highly ramified organization which controls a very large portion of the production of a crucial section of the economy. Production is, of course, *mass* production. The assembly line method is used whenever feasible, and there is some degree of automation. The situation in the American automobile, steel, or chemical industry would be typical, since in each case a small number of very complex firms control between them all but a relatively unimportant segment of the market. Certain characteristics tend to be associated with this pattern. Management becomes divorced from ownership, and is relatively specialized as a profession. More and more these super-firms acquire the character of enormously elaborate bureaucratic structures, which have complex patterns of recruitment, in-service training, "staff colleges," and so on. Long-range planning and centralized funding or allocation of resources become pervasive. Because of the rapid accumulation of capital relative to labor, advanced industrial countries need worry less about the conservation of capital than of labor. As a result of the tendency of labor to become scarce relative to capital, special efforts are made to maximize the yield from it. This takes the form, amongst other things, of stress on fringe benefits and other inducements to good labor relations. There is, finally, general emphasis on rationalization of production, and an associated emphasis on scientific research for the development of new products and processes. The market is less problematical and tyrannical. The super-firm acts assured of its market, within limits, and indeed often counts on "making" or shaping the market to suit itself.

Associated with the super-firm is the development of the super-community, the vast, generally sprawling, massive urban conglomerates which we often speak of as metropolitan centers. In these super-cities individuals are much less atomized than is commonly supposed. Nevertheless, there certainly is a tremendous attenuation of all sorts of *extended* primary group ties. The village community, the clan, tribe, or region, the extended family all atrophy, if they do not disappear. This means in the first place, that the differentiation between subgroups in the population is greatly reduced. This applies both to ethnic and class differences. There is an extensive homogenization of values and life styles, often expressed in the United States in the comments: "We're all Americans now," and more recently "We're all middle class now." This process of homogenization, which has its roots in the common status and experience of most as employees of super-firms, is reenforced in this group and extended to the rest of the population through the influence of uniform schooling, uniform exposure to certain communications emanating from the ubiquitous mass media, and a highly developed transportation network which greatly facilitates physical mobility. A second consequence of the atrophying of extended primary ties is the transfer to other agencies of the prime role in developing and sustaining values, standards of behavior, and styles of life. This further contributes to homogenization, since more and more the standards derive from an external and uniform norm, including "what other people are doing." At the same time, it greatly increases the susceptibility of people to manipulation by increasing their dependence on external authority.

Since there are rather generally accepted notions about industrial society with which we do not agree entirely, it is necessary at this point to make explicit what we are *not* saying. As we indicated earlier in this chapter, we do not believe that the citizen of an industrial society is as "atomized" as some writers assert. Certain primary group relationships have unquestionably atrophied or disappeared. For example, the individual no longer is a member of an extended family on whose implicit support he can count. On the other hand, there are new primary group relationships, such as the factory work group, which has been subject of so much discussion by industrial sociologists. The importance of such new primary groups has been noted by us for even the most extreme periods of Stalinism in the USSR. Furthermore, "reference groups" have recently been demonstrated to play a crucial role in response to communications on the part of citizens of industrial societies. There are, however, crucial qualitative differences between reference groups, the newer primary groups, and the older extended primary groups. Reference groups are often groups of which the individual is not personally a member. They are, rather, broadly extended groups which the individual uses as "benchmarks" for his own opinions and behavior. Only in a marginal sense can he count on such groups for personal support (for instance, when he receives vicariously their approval for his actions). The newer primary groups, such as the factory work group, lie intermediate between the nonmembership reference groups and the extended primary groups of a nonindustrial society. They are membership groups which offer at least minimal support. However, they are not such multipurpose, long standing, all supportive groups as the extended primary groups of a European agricultural society. While we reject the idea that the citizen of an industrial society is devoid of group membership and identification, we do affirm the qualitative difference in the influence of primary groups.

Assuming that the features we have described are generally associated with the modern industrial order, is there any necessary or even probable contradiction between them and what we have described as the defining characteristics of Soviet totalitarianism? If by Soviet totalitarianism we assume its more extreme forms, especially as practiced in the last years of Stalin's life, the answer would perhaps be yes. But as the system has been shaped and operated by Stalin's successors, we see no inevitable or necessary clash of really fundamental nature. On the contrary, many of the general features of the modern industrial order are remarkably close to the special features of the Soviet system.

The principle of the super-firm is very strong in the Soviet Union, as represented at least in the government economic ministries — say the Ministry for Heavy Machine Building. Indeed it might be said that in the Soviet Union the principle has been carried almost to its ultimate conclusion, with the state being the super super-firm, a single employer who employs everyone. Management is completely divorced from ownership, and is a highly specialized profession, working in an elaborate bureaucracy. Long-range planning and centralized allocation of resources are, of course, the essence of the Soviet economy. The market is assured, under the plan, for those who serve government and other industries, and for industries supplying the consumer it is relatively unimportant. Only in labor policy has there traditionally been a major departure from our model, with capital more scarce than labor and the latter greatly exploited. But even here, the combination of continued economic growth and population decline aggravated by war has brought a shift towards pacifying and conserving labor and pursuing a more considerable personnel policy in general.

Furthermore, by its disruption of the extended primary groupings the modern industrial social order weakens the chief institutional units in which the individual might learn values running counter to those disseminated by the totalitarian party-state or which might serve him as a base of support in case of conflict with that authority. At the same time, the weakening of the extended primary institutions eliminates them as a source of values and a focus of allegiance. Individuals then tend to turn even more to the state and party to acquire their values and focus their loyalties. Thus in the totalitarian society everyone may in time become an "organization man." The escape from freedom is complete.

If anything, the Soviet formula has carried the industrial society to its most exaggerated manifestation. If we are to look for sources of change in the Soviet order, we are *not* most likely to find them in an incompatibility between totalitarianism and industrialism. We will do better to seek the dynamics of change within the fabric of the industrial order *per se*. If we take as a point of departure the achievement of maximal industrial efficiency, and we take the American experience as our guide, then it seems that the super-firm, and particularly the super super-firm as exemplified in the Soviet instance, have carried the characteristic features of industrial society beyond the point of maximal efficiency. As we shall indicate later, totalitarianism may be *too* compatible with the characteristic features of industrial society for the optimal realization of the benefits of mass industry.

The most crucial argument posed against the compatibility of the Soviet political system and its newly-developed modern industrial order is that the very development of Soviet industry and the modernization of Soviet society — with its emphasis on rationality, its dependence on science and research, its ever increasing corps of well-educated and well-trained engineers, managers and other professionals — has made the usual Soviet pattern of operation unsuited to the needs of Soviet society and unacceptable to the new managerial class, which some believe to hold the balance of power in Soviet affairs.

There is in this argument more assertion, or perhaps faith, than hard substance. To begin, there is hardly much evidence to support the assertion that education by itself generates a love of freedom. It was, after all, a country with one of the best educated populations, and one with the largest numbers of industrialists, engineers, scientists and other educated men, which treated us to the experience of Hitlerite Germany. And there are few who will deny the widespread, indeed pervasive, support he received among the educated classes in the military, business, industry, education, and other realms. In the second place, and perhaps more important, there is good reason to believe that the underlying principles of Soviet political control over the *ends* of economic and administrative behavior are accepted by most Soviet engineers and managers, indeed are willingly supported by them. They accept these as "political" decisions to be decided by political specialists. They are, in other words, largely withdrawn from politics, "organization men" similar to their counterparts in the United States. Their main complaint in the past was not over the principle of directing the economy, but rather over arbitrary political interference in predominantly technical decisions, the unreasonably high goals often set in the face of insufficient resources to meet them, and the treatment of failures in judgment or performance by management as if they were acts of political defiance or criminal negligence. Since Stalin's death such abuse has been tremendously reduced. Soviet managers seem, on the whole, quite satisfied with the situation.

We have been talking about Soviet managerial personnel. But in this context the general question of the relationship of education to desire for political change and freedom inevitably arises. In recent years there has been indisputable evidence of some degree of restlessness, perhaps rebelliousness, following from the increased open discussion of political matters by Soviet students. We have no reason to doubt that some "demonstrations" have in fact taken place. But, what interpretation is to be put on all this? Our own data indicated quite clearly that Soviet youth — as other youth — passed through a period of political doubt and crisis

even during the most stringent years of Stalinism. Our conservative interpretation of the recent phenomena is that they may represent only
greater freedom to express these feelings, rather than an increase in
political thinking and political doubts *per se*. While we may be proven
wrong by history, our best guess is that we are dealing with a life-cycle
phenomenon rather than with a generational change. Or, to put it more
directly, we assume that these very same "rebellious youths" will become
not so rebellious adults.

Of course, there is always the risk that the political leaders will over-
reach themselves, and in seeking to maintain their own initiative will violate the rights of the managerial class so flagrantly as to provoke retalia-
tion. The facts of recent experience indicate such a sense of outrage is
not easily aroused. The top political leadership has been able to effect
massive changes in the formal structure of economic administration in
the Soviet Union without any sign of major resistance or even disturbance.
Indeed, even the outstanding military leader of the country, Zhukov, has
been dismissed summarily without apparent serious repercussions. While
these very events were in progress the Soviet Union successfully launched
no less than two earth satellites, which hardly argues that it is having
great difficulty either in motivating its scientists and engineers or in
organizing their efforts effectively around important governmental programs.

Far from running counter to the evidence of our studies with Soviet
refugees, these developments are completely consistent with our earlier
conclusions. Thus, in the final report of our Project, produced in October
1954, and again in our published essay *How the Soviet System Works*,
we challenged the theory that political domination within the Soviet
system was threatened by a "managerial-revolution" and asserted:

> Our data indicate rather that the technical and managerial personnel, having a
> stake in the existing system, have developed an interest in maintaining it in pre-
> dominantly its present form. They are concerned *mainly* with reducing interference
> and extreme pressure from the center, and beyond that in improving the sys-
> tem, and making it work more smoothly.[3]

We argue then, that there is no necessary, or even compelling, force in
the modern industrial social order which clearly makes it incompatible
with totalitarianism. On the other hand, we do not mean to suggest that
there is an inherent tendency in the modern industrial social order which
drives it *toward* totalitarianism. Our position is rather that the modern
industrial order appears to be compatible with either democratic or totalitarian political and social forms. Either arrangement requires some,
but not necessarily fundamental, adjustments in the systems combined.
Either arrangement has distinctive strengths and weaknesses. Early in

1959 no one can with confidence say which arrangement, however evaluated in moral terms, has the greater efficiency and probability of surviving in the "competition of systems."

But in arguing that there is nothing inherent in its economic system which would prevent the Soviet Union from going on for some time in substantially its present form, we have perhaps permitted the main object of our attention, the Soviet citizen, to drop out of sight. The chief burden of our argument has been that we do not look for change to come from the striving of Soviet citizens for new political and economic forms or from the *inherent* incompatibility of totalitarianism and industrialism. However, we believe that change is inevitable in all societies, including Soviet society, and under the conditions of modern industrialism social change is simply unavoidable. Therefore, we propose to look concretely at those responses of the Soviet citizens and of the Soviet leaders that will produce the sorts of change which we anticipate.

The response of the Soviet citizen to the Soviet system must be divided into two parts. One element is distinctive, and is a response to the distinctive totalitarian features of Soviet society. It is this dimension which has received the most attention in Western commentary on the Soviet system. We have also dealt with it at length. But perhaps the most important general conclusion which emerges from our study is that in large measure the response of Soviet citizens to their social system is to an extraordinary degree comparable to the response of citizens in *other* large-scale industrial societies, notably the United States, to their industrial system. Thus we have observed that the *patterning* of values about the occupational structure, of opportunities for mobility, of the evaluation of education, of ideas about child rearing, of communications behavior, and many other realms of experience is broadly similar in the Soviet Union and other large scale industrial societies. This seems a finding of substantial general significance for social science, since it so strongly suggests that the industrial social order carries with it certain inherent propensities which influence individual values and experience relatively, if not completely, *independently* of the political setting. We must, of course, be cautious in drawing *political* implications from this striking sociological fact. It is certainly of great interest that people in the Soviet Union and the United States react to their status in the occupational hierarchy in a similar way despite the profound differences in the larger socio-political setting in which they live. We cannot help but be struck to find that both American and Soviet workers like a boss who is a good guy, and both Soviet and American professionals prefer a boss who is first and foremost technically competent. But we must initially assume that these similarly patterned responses are limited to the realms of common experience in a modern industrial setting. We cannot safely expect that the Soviet and American worker will also be alike in their reaction to their, in this case *different*, socio-political systems.

The crucial difference between the citizen of the Soviet Union and that of the United States, England, France, or West Germany would lie predominantly in the realm of political and cultural freedom and responsibility. The Soviet citizen will continue to have little direct say about the general policy of his country, particularly the share of national income which goes to investment as against consumption. He will not be free to speak his political mind if he has one. He will have available to him only the most restricted contact with the thought, the art and literature of the free world, and the domestic product will be almost entirely thinly disguised propaganda of low aesthetic value. If he finds these conditions unacceptable and seeks at all vigorously to change them he will find that the secret police still know how to deprive a man of his freedom without recourse to strictly legal means.

As we read history, it hardly seems to argue that the main drive of men is towards ever-increasing freedom. The peculiar cultural tradition and historical development which yielded the free democratic political systems exemplified in the Anglo-Saxon countries and on the continent of Western Europe may have been a very special development not easy to borrow or emulate, nor likely to be again spontaneously generated. To say that we doubt that the main drive of men has been invariably toward increased freedom is not to say that men do not desire or will not on occasion fight for freedom. Nor, is it to say that mankind as a whole desires bondage. But in the pursuit of his varied goals man requires a stable societal framework which in turn inevitably requires some restriction of freedom. This restriction generally is accepted readily and naturally. If the societal framework affords the opportunity to satisfy well a wide range of goals, men may readily accept a considerable degree of political bondage and not *feel* bound so long as their wants are met.

In any event, the totalitarian political system in the Soviet Union is well entrenched, and the question is whether there is sufficient cause for the mass of citizens to move them to the forcible action that would be required to change it. We think not. We found that even the refugees were broadly accepting of many of the salient features of the Soviet Union. They accepted and supported the idea of government ownership and control of the economy, and they seemed basically disposed as well to accept the idea of centralized and essentially autocratic determination of national policy. Their grievances were highly specific and focused — end the terror, ease the pace, improve the impoverished standard of living, make the welfare state principles more effective, pay a decent return for farm labor. Their demands were quite simple — decent treatment from leaders who took some interest in their welfare. Very few could see beyond these concrete demands to the very nature of the system which lay at the root of the matter. And a distressingly small number based their rejection of the system predominantly on general ideological grounds, on matters of principle. With the terror vastly reduced, with the tempo eased, the standard of living rising modestly but steadily, with the peasant getting much better returns for his work on the kolkhoz, and with many measures taken to implement the social welfare program, the most important specific grievances of Soviet citizens have been substantially met by ameliorative action. The more general absence of freedom, particularly of intellectual freedom remains, but we judge its influence to be intensely felt only by a limited segment of the vast intelligentsia. Most seem to be willing to leave the big decisions to the leaders, "who know best." And the prestige of those leaders has been greatly enhanced by Soviet accomplishments in science and in the conduct of foreign affairs.

Lovers of freedom can, unfortunately, take little cheer from this account. For good or ill, we must recognize that Stalin, evil genius though he was, wrought a miraculous transformation of Russia. Although the human cost was extraordinarily, perhaps unimaginably high, he forged in Russia a new social order, a new form of social organization. Oddly enough the vessel seems to run much better without the designer and builder at the helm. Once the extremities of his personal rule were eliminated, the substantial coherence, the great vitality, and the probably long-range viability of the system emerged with new clarity. Of course the system has serious defects. Every system does. It also has extraordinary advantages in the struggle between systems, some of which have recently become painfully apparent. For example, it is much easier in the Soviet Union than in the United States to increase the proportion of national income allocated to scientific training and research. It is also easier in a nondemocratic society to *exclude* from high schools and colleges the inferior students who hold back the average performance. It is even easier to employ scientists who are security risks in a police state, where everyone is already suspect and under surveillance anyhow, and in any event is not allowed dangerous contacts with the outside world. It is much easier to do these and many other things when the leaders need not consult the people, nor respond directly to their will, but need merely act effectively to attain national goals.

Yet, it is in this very social organization and in the acceptance of it by the broad mass of Soviet citizens that we may look for sources of change in Soviet society. If we are to grant a grudging accolade to Stalin it is that he was *effective* in establishing a new social order. But this effectiveness was purchased at the cost of gross inefficiency, particularly in the brutal toll exacted from the citizens of the Soviet state. It is characteristic of newly formed organizations that they pass from a first stage in which effectiveness is the major criterion of action, into a more mature phase in which efficiency becomes the main criterion. In this we find an explanation for many of the changes which are taking place in the Soviet Union.

We will beg for the moment the question of the long-range implication of changes which are taking place and which will take place in the Soviet Union in the immediate future. We will only contend that the *intention* of such changes is not and will not be to alter the major institutional features of the Soviet society, but rather to make them work better. Factory managers have pressed for more autonomy in operating their firms so that they may do a better job of getting out production; and the Soviet leaders have granted some decentralization of the economy for the same purpose. This is not to say that *all pressures* for change will have the intention of improving the existing system. Certainly this is not true of the desire of writers for greater freedom of expression, or of the peasants' passive resistance to the collective farm. We would say, however, that in the immediate future all *effective* pressure will be couched in terms of the improvement of the existing system. Or, to put the matter in reverse, the Soviet leaders will permit changes to the extent that they see such changes as improving the efficiency of the existing system; and, the majority of changes which the Soviet people will press for will be such changes.

Let us consider a limiting case. At the time of writing of this manuscript, Khrushchev has announced the impending dissolution of the Machine Tractor Stations, and the handing over of tractors and other machines to the collective farms. Our best guess is that Khrushchev's ultimate intention is to convert the collective farms into *Sovkhozi*, state farms operating pretty much on the model of a factory. But let us suppose, for the sake of argument, that the greater autonomy which the collective farms will experience in the next few years — the years before the transition to state farming — will spur collective farmers to work more energetically on the collective farms. This could result in the collective farms being more productive than the state farms. In that event, we would anticipate that Khrushchev and/or his successors would choose to settle for this increased efficiency rather than push through to a dogmatic goal of converting agriculture to the model of industry. In this, we would see the present leadership as deviating from Stalin's operating code. Furthermore, we would expect such a resolution to make the peasant less resistant to, perhaps even accepting of, the collective farm system.

We do not forsee the possibility that the Soviet leaders would deliberately relinquish any significant measure of political power. We do, how-

ever, believe that the present leadership is more concerned with questions
of efficiency than was Stalin, and we do not rule out the possibility that
certain decisions made in the interest of efficiency will have the effect of
limiting political power. Again turning the coin over, we expect the bulk
of the pressures exerted by the Soviet population will be for the improvement of the existing system, rather than for fundamental changes in the
system. Once more, such "improvements" may well lead to fundamental
changes, but we think it by no means so likely as many assume that the
consequence of such changes will be an inevitable movement or even
"drift" of Soviet society toward democracy and constitutional government.

There are three main sources from whence a fundamental change in
the pattern of Soviet development may spring, especially as it affects the
Soviet impact on the rest of the world. One possibility is that the problem
of the succession crisis will never be solved; eventually one of the strug-
gles for power at the top will break out in the open, and in the process
of resultant conflict the old order will be destroyed. Although we regard
such an event as being of a rather low order of probability it certainly
cannot be discounted. But we believe it an error to assume that the inevitable outcome of such a struggle would be a democratic Russia. On
the contrary, we believe it highly likely that whoever would be the victor
in such a struggle would in his turn impose the standard pattern of totalitarian rule, and probably with renewed vigor.

A second possibility is that a future breakup of the Soviet satellite
empire, as exemplified by the revolt in Hungary, and the relative defection of Poland, might have sufficiently serious repercussions within the
Soviet Union to change materially the path of Soviet development. Although there are major sources of instability in the Soviet empire, or
coalition, we do not believe that it is markedly unstable. But even if
there were serious defections from Soviet control, there is no absolute
reason to assume the response within the Soviet Union would be in the
direction of democracy. On the contrary, there is greater likelihood that
under such circumstances there would be increased totalitarianism in an
effort to recapture lost or ebbing control over the satellites.

A third prospect is that the industrial maturation of Soviet Russia,
the mellowing of its social structure, will progressively "erode" the dictatorship and set in motion important processes of social change which will
lead to a transformation of Soviet society and perhaps of its foreign
policy as well. As we have already indicated we feel this possibility must
be taken quite seriously. Indeed we feel that Soviet society has already
changed substantially in the years after Stalin's death. But change is
inevitable. If the Soviet system did not change at all it might indeed be

more prone to breakup and much less a threat than a dynamic, changing Soviet Union. The crucial problem then is to ascertain what is eroding, and what is not, and to specify the direction of change.

Certain of the salient features of Stalin's Russia seem to have been dropped out of the Soviet picture. The terror is not likely to be applied again on a mass scale, at least not at home. The "tempo," or pace of development, has been slowed, or at least is not so grim and overriding as it was. The leaders seem to accept the fact that people want a few pleasures and are even entitled to a little easier life. There is more acceptance, although it is not too much admitted publicly, that people are entitled to a small sphere of life that is in some sense private and not the ultimate property of the state. Economic efficiency, the challenge of producing quality and getting high yields, is given more weight as against the old drive for volume production at any price. People are more recognized and valued as a national resource. They are now trusted, and this permits more decentralization of decision making and relatively more autonomy for the responsible and capable in all spheres.

All this, and more, can be and should be cited as reflecting the maturation, the mellowing, even to some extent, the "liberalization" of Soviet society. The Soviet system is in some important degree less "total" than it was under Stalin. But we submit that it is a serious error to assume that departure from the Stalinist model means movement *toward* the democratic constitutional model. Many observers seem to conclude that many amnesties make for an honored bill of rights. But of course the contrary is probably the case. Historically, regimes which have featured mass amnesties have been regimes which have violated rights *en masse*. It is the old problem of how many swallows make a summer, with the added complication that some believe that since summer is finally here there will be no more winters.

In our opinion the formidable challenge which faces the world rises not from the unchanging character of the Soviet Union, but precisely from the fact that its present leaders have been able to make adjustments in the structure which have adapted it to take account of the earlier development of the society. The crucial point is that they have done so without sacrificing the basic features of the system — the monopoly of power in the elite of the one-party state, the absolute dominance of the state in the control and direction of economic life, the limitation of freedom of opinion and expression to those few cases and to that degree which the regime regards as politically harmless, and the use of force or extralegal measures, however selective, to impose the will of the leaders in such a way as to make an ultimate mockery of the law and constitution.

But what of the features of Stalin's Russia which have been dropped? We see the significance of those features as having lain in the absence of popular consensus in support of the Soviet system. So long as Stalin was trying to impose on the people a whole set of new institutions which were not of their own choosing, indeed were often alien to their hopes and traditions, then the whole grim apparatus of Stalin's totalitarian rule was inevitable. It was the only way to get most people to do a job and to contain the resentment thus generated. The crucial change in Soviet society is that now the main outlines of the system seem to enjoy the support of popular consensus.

If this is so, it is a change of utmost importance. It can explain why the leaders who followed Stalin were able to give up some of the most unpopular aspects of Stalin's method of rule without giving up most of the undemocratic features of the Soviet system. Such a society is perhaps less totalitarian, less absolutist, even less dictatorial. It is no less auto-cratic and certainly not *more* democratic, in the sense of acknowledging the supremacy of law and individual rights. But such a society is more, not less, a challenge to the free world. The leadership may have lost some of its freedom of manoeuvre, so that it can no longer so readily commit the whole nation to an assault on objectives the people do not support. But the regime is so far compensated by the vastly increased popular support for the objectives to which it has committed the nation. And it presents an immeasurably improved facade to the world.

Related to, but not entirely identical with the foregoing issues, is that of whether or not the Soviet leaders will be more or less cooperative in international affairs. On both sides of the Iron Curtain people seem to assume that if the two systems — capitalism and Soviet communism — were more like each other there would be less international tension. Certainly we found this belief to be widely held by Soviet citizens with whom we have talked. Unquestionably present international tensions are in some measure a result of the fact that Soviet and Western societies are organized on different premises. However, in the past similar so-cieties have engaged in violent conflict, and dissimilar societies have lived together in relative peace. Even if we believed that Soviet society and ours were rapidly becoming alike, we would not expect international tensions to melt automatically as a result of this circumstance. Nor would we despair entirely of some temporarily stable modus vivendi with the existing Soviet order. This is a problem that may indeed be related to the future development of Soviet society, but it is one which must be approached without the comforting assumption that evolving events in the USSR will make the problem either easier or nonexistent.

In the balance hangs the decision as to what the dominant cultural and political forms of human endeavor will be for the remainder of this century and perhaps beyond. It is perhaps only a little thing that sepa-rates the Soviet world from the West — freedom. Inside the Soviet Union there are some who ultimately are on our side. But they are a minority, perhaps a small one. Their ranks were first decimated by Stalin and later thinned by the refugee exodus. We had therefore better turn our face elsewhere, rest our hopes on other foundations than on the belief that the Soviet system will mellow and abandon its long-range goals of world domination. We must look for our defense to the capacity of our own social order to yield fuller, richer, more dignified life *under freedom* not only for ourselves, but for the uncommitted, the half committed, the neutralists, and even those who have already cast their lot with the Soviet Union. If we are not equal to the task, we will leave it to the Soviet Union to set the pattern of human existence for the next half-century. Many of the distinctive features of Soviet life we have sketched in our book may then come to characterize not merely the Soviet citizen, but the citizens of the world.

APPENDICES

NOTES

INDEX

Appendix I

The Written Questionnaires

(English Translation from the Russian)

The written questionnaire presented here has three parts. The basic or "core" questionnaire is divided into sections by topic, each identified by a Roman numeral. The questions are numbered separately within each section. The second part contains a set of questions dealing with social stratification issues, and the third concerns the occupational realm. They are identified respectively, as "Stratification" and "Job" questionnaires. Questions, in arabic numerals, are numbered separately within each.

There were several other written questionnaires administered by the Project which for lack of space are not reproduced here. These include questionnaires on wartime experiences under the German occupation, the nationality problem, medical services in the USSR, the urban Slavic family, and one on family budgets. When items from those questionnaires are used as the basis of tables or other important citations, the notes generally give the wording of the relevant questions.

WRITTEN QUESTIONS OF THE HARVARD UNIVERSITY EXPEDITION

As you know, the Harvard University Expedition is studying the conditions of life in the Soviet Union. Our group consists of American scientific workers who are interested in the study of daily life in the USSR in order to obtain a correct impression of the life of the people in the USSR and of their interrelations with the Soviet regime.

You, people who have lived in the Soviet Union, are the best source for the information that interests us.

Our approach to questions of life in the USSR is purely scientific. We are not interested in anyone personally, nor are we interested in Christian or family names. You are interesting to us only as one of the former Soviet citizens. Therefore we do not need your exact name. Of course, it is important for us to obtain as many facts as we can about how people live in the Soviet Union and we will appreciate it if you will try to answer all the questions.

The staff members of the Harvard Expedition have conducted oral interviews with various people and groups of people who are here in the emigration during the past several months. Unfortunately, due to lack of time, we have not been able to talk with everyone. Therefore we have worked out this questionnaire which contains most of the questions of interest to us. By distributing this questionnaire we hope to reach a great number of people.

We hope that you will help us in our work by giving us these facts.

INSTRUCTIONS

We would like to explain to you the manner in which this questionnaire should be filled out. The questions are divided into several types. One example of each type of question is cited below.

Let us consider the most general type, we ask a question and you answer it freely. Do not forget to read the question carefully so that your answer covers the question asked. For example, we might ask you: "How did you feel about the abolition of coeducation in the Soviet schools?" In such a case you should write your answer in the space provided below the text; for example: "I paid no attention to this change because all my children had already finished school."

Most of all we ask a question and request you to put an "X" in front of one of two or several of the answers given below:

Example:

Were you aware of the abolition of coeducation in the Soviet schools? (Check one)

___ I was not aware of this change

X I was aware of this change

Here you mark the second answer, since you knew about the change. If you did not know about it at the time, then you should check the first answer.

X I was not aware of this change

___ I was aware of this change

Let us suppose that you checked the answer which states that you were aware of this. Then read further and you will find the following question:

If you knew of this change, were you for it or against it? (Check one)

___ I was in favor of it

___ I was against it

If you had indicated above that you did not know about this, then, of course, you should not check off either answer. Just omit this question — do not put an "X" before "for" or "against." If you were aware of this change, and were in favor of it, then check the appropriate answer.

Correct example:

X I was in favor of it

___ I was against it

Always be sure that you have made your "X" directly in front of the answer you have chosen; then we will know what answer you intended for the given question. The following example serves to show you how not to put your "X."

Incorrect example:

X   —— I was in favor of it
      —— I was against it

Always put it exactly on the line in front of the answer. It will also be wrong if you mark both answers at the same time. For example:

Incorrect example:

<u>X</u> I was in favor of it
<u>X</u> I was against it

There is still another type of question in which you are asked to check one of several items suggested as answers. Thus, for example:

Who wears the best clothes? (Check one)
—— Party workers
—— Sluzhashchiye (Employees)
—— Workers
—— Peasants
<u>X</u> Intelligentsia

Mark *only one* item. In this case we have marked the intelligentsia as an example. Frequently you will find that we are also interested in your second choice.

Who was next best dressed? (Check one)
<u>X</u> Party workers
—— Employees
—— Workers
—— Peasants
—— Intelligentsia

If you think that the second best dressed group are the party workers, then you would make a cross in front of "Party workers." Again, make *only one* cross.

For this type of question we will also ask who was worst off. Thus, for example, you will see below the following question:

Now, who was worst dressed? (Check one)
—— Party workers
—— Employees
—— Workers
<u>X</u> Peasants
—— Intelligentsia

If you think that the peasants were dressed worse than the others, you should put your "X" in front of the word "Peasants."

Sometimes you will find the word "Remarks" (Zamechaniye) beneath the answers.

Example:

Did you have an automobile in the Soviet Union? (Check one)
—— Yes —— No

Remarks:

This is to give you an opportunity to make whatever comments you want to make. *But do not forget to check off one of the answers as well.*

Always remember that you must answer all parts of the question. Often we ask whether you did something or other. For example, "Did you ever write a letter to Stalin when you were in trouble?"

___ Yes ___ No

And then we ask:

(If yes) Why?

(If no) Why not?

Be sure you do not omit the second part. Tell us why you did or did not act in this way. This second part of the question is just as important as the first part. Sometimes it is even more important.

In filling out the questionnaire, please follow all these rules:

1. Read the question carefully and be sure you are answering what it asks.

2. Answer every question.

3. Answer all parts of every question.

4. Make your crosses and write your answers carefully so that subsequently we will know what you meant.

Core I

I. First we would like to obtain some data about you and your family.

    1. Your sex? (Check one)

___ Male ___ Female

    2. In what year were you born?

    3. To what national group do you belong? (Check one)

___ Russian

___ Ukrainian

___ Byelorussian

___ Armenian

___ Other (indicate which?) ___

    4. Are you married at the present time? (Check one)

___ Yes ___ No

When did you marry?

    4A. His (her) nationality?

___ Russian

___ Ukrainian

___ Byelorussian

___ Armenian

___ German

___ Other (which?) ___

    4B. His (her) class origin?

    5. Were you in the Soviet Army? (Check one)

___ Yes . . . What was your rank and title? ___

___ No

6. What kind of place did you spend most of you life in, in the USSR? (Check one)
___ Large city
___ Town
___ Village or the country

7. To what social group did you belong in the last years of your life in the Soviet Union? (Check one)
___ Party-Soviet apparatus
___ Intelligentsia
___ Employees (sluzhashchiye)
___ Skilled workers
___ Ordinary workers
___ Collective farmers (kolkhozniki)

Perhaps none of these groups applies to you, then indicate the social group of which you consider yourself a representative.

Now several questions concerning your status here in the emigration, because it is important for us to know the desires of the people who answer our questions, and also the milieu in which they are living.

8. Have you had steady work here in the emigration since the end of the war, or (if you came to Germany after the war) since your arrival here?
___ Yes ___ No

9. Are you working now?
___ Yes ___ No

10. Do you want to leave Germany?
___ Yes ___ No

11. What do you think are chances for leaving?
___ Excellent
___ Good
___ Poor
___ None at all

12. Which of the following emigrant political groups do you consider the most satisfactory? (Check one)
___ ABN — Anticommunist Block of Nations
___ The Bandera movement
___ VMS — The Higher Monarchists' Council
___ Hetmanovtsy
___ Cossack Union of Glazkov
___ Cossack Union of Bavaria (P. N. Donskov)
___ KOV — Committee of United Vlasovites
___ League for the Fight for Peoples' Freedom (New York)
___ NOKRE — National Committee of Russian Emigration
___ NTS — National Workers' Union (Solidarists)
___ Society for Fighting Communism
___ RONDD — Russian People's Might Movement
___ SBONR — Union for the Struggle for the Liberation of the Peoples of Russia
___ Union for the Fight for Russia's Freedom (S. P. Melgunov)

___ SAF — Union of the Flag of St. Andrew
___ SVOD — Union of Warriors of the Liberation Movement
___ URDP — Ukrainian Workers' Democratic Party
___ TsPRE — Central Representation of the Russian Emigration

Core II

II. Now we would like to know something about your work in the USSR.

1. What was your steady occupation in the USSR? (Please be exact in explaining the nature of the work you did.)

2. What other types of work did you do in the Soviet Union? (Please try to explain the exact nature of the work you did and the dates when you held one job or another.)

3. Did you like the job you held in 1940? (Check one)
___ Yes ___ No
If not, then why not?

4. Was your pay commensurate with the pay of people who held other types of jobs in the USSR?
___ Yes ___ No
Remarks:

5. Was your pay commensurate with the pay of people who held the same kind of job that you did in the USSR?
___ Yes ___ No

6. While you were in the Soviet Union, if you had had a free choice of jobs, what job would you have chosen for yourself?

7. Why would you have chosen this particular job? (Check one)
___ I feel suited to it
___ According to family tradition
___ Because it is politically less dangerous
___ Because it is not very responsible (work)
___ Because this is work that needs to be done for the people
___ For the material reward for this work
___ Other reasons (Specify)

8. Do you think you had a chance to make a career for yourself while you were in the Soviet Union before the war?
___ Yes ___ No

9. Regardless of whether you had an opportunity to forge a career for yourself or not, tell us if you wanted to have one. (Check one)
___ I wanted very much to have a career
___ I wanted to have a career, but not as much as some other people
___ I wanted to have a career, but in general it didn't make much difference if I had one or not
___ I did not want a career
___ Under no circumstances did I want a career

Core III

III. 1. Which of the following statements most accurately characterizes your relation to the Soviet regime? (Check one)

A. ___ I was once favorably inclined toward the regime, but turned against it in _____ (year) before I left the USSR, because (insert appropriate reason in detail)

B. ___ I was always opposed to the regime because (give detailed reason)

C. ___ I have always been in favor of the Soviet regime, and still am because (insert detailed reason)

D. ___ I was in favor of the Soviet regime even at the time when I had to leave the USSR but did not return because (insert detailed reason)

    2. When did you leave the USSR?

___ Before June 1941

___ Between June 1941 and June 1945

___ After June 1945

    Depending on when you left the USSR choose the appropriate answer:

(1) If you left the USSR during the war

A. How did you leave the USSR? (Choose one)

___ Taken prisoner by the Germans

___ Deserted (escaped) to the Germans

___ Evacuated forcibly by the Germans

___ Voluntarily escaped with the Germans when the Soviet troops approached

___ Other . . . (Specify)

B. Why didn't you want to return to the USSR?

___ Feared repression

___ Desire to live under better material and cultural conditions

___ Other reasons. . . . Which?

(2) If you left the USSR after 1945

A. How did you do this?

___ Deserted (escaped) from the occupation army

___ Deserted (escaped) from a civil occupation organization

___ Other . . . (Specify)

B. Why did you decide to leave?

(3) If you left the USSR before 1941

Please tell us how and why you left the USSR

    3. In 1940 how strong was your desire to leave the USSR? (Check one)

___ At that time I didn't want to leave the USSR

___ I wanted to leave the USSR for several reasons, but for other reasons I didn't want to leave

___ I wanted to leave the USSR but didn't try to do this

___ I wanted to leave the USSR very much and tried to do it

    4. Were you or any member of your family ever arrested?

(If yes) Who? When?

On what grounds?

What were the consequences? (Freed or arrested)

    4A. (If sentenced)

For what term?

When did you (or they) leave the camp or prison?

    5. Were you ever called up by the authorities and not arrested, but only interrogated? (Check one)

___ Yes ___ No

5A. (If yes) Please describe this case in detail

6. Were you ever a member of the Komsomol? (Check one)

___ Yes ___ No

7. Were you ever a member of the party? (Check one)

___ Yes ___ No

Core IV

IV. In this section we are interested in your personal opinion on the following questions:

1. What chance do you think there is that Russia and the United States will be at war within a year? (Check one)

___ No chance

___ Slight chance

___ Even chance

___ Very good chance

___ Certain

2. In every society, each social group has a definite investment in the well-being of society, and in its turn receives a definite reward from society. Certain groups may get more out of society than they deserve; some less, and others just what they deserve. Below is cited a list of groups in Soviet society. We would like you to indicate which of these groups you think receive more, which less and which just what they deserve. Check the line which you think corect for each group.

A. Soviet workers receive (Check one)

___ More than they deserve

___ Approximately what they deserve

___ Less than they deserve

B. Soviet peasants receive (Check one)

___ More than they deserve

___ Approximately what they deserve

___ Less than they deserve

C. Soviet employees receive (Check one)

___ More than they deserve

___ Approximately what they deserve

___ Less than they deserve

D. Soviet intelligentsia receive (Check one)

___ More than they deserve

___ Approximately what they deserve

___ Less than they deserve

E. Party workers receive (Check one)

___ More than they deserve

___ Approximately what they deserve

___ Less than they deserve

3. We would like to know more about the conceptions that former Soviet citizens have of the Americans. If you do not have a definite opinion, then answer to the best of your ability.

A. Do you think that the majority of Americans feel that transport and communication should be under state government and control? (Check one)

___ Yes, Americans are in favor of this

___ No, Americans are against this

B. What kind of job do you think that most Americans prefer? (Check one)

___ A job which pays comparatively well and is secure, but has little chance for advancement?

___ A job which pays less and is not secure but has good chance for advancement?

C. Do you think that Americans feel that people should be permitted to express their opinions freely and say anything they want to, or do the Americans feel that the government should forbid certain things from being said? (Check one)

___ Americans think that people should be forbidden to say things which are detrimental to the government.

___ Americans think that people should be permitted to say anything they want to even if these are directed against the government.

4. Below is given a paired list of groups in Soviet society. We would like to know for each of these pairs — do their interests coincide with or contradict each other? Check the condition you think correct for each group.

	Interests Coincide	Interests Do Not Coincide
A. Workers & peasants	___	___
B. Workers & intelligentsia	___	___
C. Peasants & intelligentsia	___	___
D. Employees & workers	___	___
E. Employees & intelligentsia	___	___
F. Party & nonparty people	___	___

5. Is it true that sometimes the Americans have acted unfairly against Europeans who have settled in the United States? (Check one)

___ Yes, this is true

___ No, this is not true

6. What kind of government do you prefer? (Check one)

___ A government which guarantees personal freedom, such as the rights to criticize the government, worship freely, etc., but does not assure you of a job?

___ A government which guarantees a decent standard of living but does not assure you of these personal rights?

7. Should a government permit some people to be rich and some to be poor, or should it forbid such inequality?

8. Some American newspapers reported that the Americans did not forcibly repatriate a single DP who did not want to return. Are these reports true? (Check one)

___ Yes, not one single Russian DP was forcibly repatriated

___ No, a small number of DP's were forcibly repatriated

___ No, there were many DP's who were forcibly repatriated

9. Do you think Lenin did good or harm for the Russian people? (Check one)

___ He did much good

___ He did a little good

___ He did some good and some harm

___ He did a little harm

___ He did much harm

10. If the Bolshevist regime were overthrown, what should be done with the kolkhozes? (Check one)

___ They should be abolished and all the land distributed

___ Part of the land should be distributed and part should remain collectivized

___ The kolkhoz system should be kept but administered for the benefit of the people who work on it

___ Any other suggestions? (Specify)

11. Some people say that Americans are more intelligent (sposobny) than Europeans. Do you agree? (Check one)

___ I agree with this

___ I do not agree with this

12. In some countries of the world today the transportation and communications systems are owned and controlled by the government. Are you in favor of this or against it? (Check one)

___ For ___ Against

13. What kind of person gets ahead in the Soviet Union?

14. Two 18-year-old schoolboys were returning home one night after having been to a party where they had a good deal to drink. One of them talked the other one into climbing onto a statue of Lenin and putting his cap on Lenin's head. Just as the schoolboy was climbing the statue, a militia man came along. The first boy managed to run away, but the second one was caught.

What does the militia man do with him?

A. Does it matter in this case who his father is? (Check one)

___ Yes, it matters who his father is

___ No, it doesn't matter who his father is

B. (If yes, then what significance does it have who his father is?)

15. In general what kind of a job do you prefer? (Check one)

___ A job that pays fairly well and is secure, but offers little opportunity for advancement

___ A job that pays less and is not secure but offers good opportunities for advancement

16. During the war an American soldier was working in a supply depot which he wanted to leave in order to get to the front and take part in battle. His superior officer did not let him go explaining that soldiers are also necessary for this kind of work. Nevertheless, the soldier quit his job and left for the front. What do you think, was the soldier right in leaving his job and going to the front? (Please explain your answer).

17. What should be done with the Bolshevist leaders if the Soviet regime were overthrown?

18. Do you think the Bolshevist regime is better or worse than the Nazi regime in Germany was? (Check one)

___ The Bolshevist regime is not as bad as was the Hitler-Nazi regime

___ The Bolshevist and the Hitlerist regimes are about the same

___ The Bolshevist regime is worse

19. Do you think that all people should have full freedom to organize political parties without interference by the government? (Check one)

___ Yes

___ No

A. How strongly do you feel about this?

___ Not at all strongly

___ Not so strongly

___ Fairly strongly

___ Very strongly

20. Suppose that the Bolshevist regime were removed and a new government came to power.

A. What things in the present system would you want to keep in the new one?

B. What things would you be sure to change?

21. Was the production of agricultural machinery higher when you left the Soviet Union than 25 years ago? (Check one)

___ Yes ___ No

22. Was medical care more accessible when you left the Soviet Union than 25 years ago? (Check one)

___ Yes ___ No

23. How dangerous are Soviet agents in Western Germany? (Check one)

___ Extremely dangerous

___ Moderately dangerous

___ Not at all dangerous

24. Do you think that people should be permitted to express their opinions openly and say anything that they want, or should the government forbid certain things from being said? (Check one)

___ People should be forbidden to say things detrimental to the state

___ People should be permitted to say anything they want even if it is against the government

A. How strongly do you feel about this?

___ Not at all strongly

___ Not so strongly

___ Fairly strongly

___ Very strongly

25. Who do you think sacrificed more in the last war — the Americans or the British? (Check one)

___ The English

___ The Americans

26. Which broadcast do you think is better, "The Voice of America," or the B.B.C.? (Check one)

__ Voice of America

__ B.B.C.

27. Do you agree with the following statement: The Soviet press and radio *never* tell the truth? (Check one)

__ I agree

__ I do not agree

28. Do you favor dropping an atomic bomb on Moscow right now in order to destroy the Bolshevist leaders, even though it means killing thousands of innocent men, women and children? (Check one)

__ Yes, a bomb should be dropped on Moscow now

__ A bomb should be dropped only as a last resort after everything else has failed

__ No, a bomb should not be dropped on Moscow

A. How strongly do you feel about this?

__ Not at all strongly

__ Not so strongly

__ Fairly strongly

__ Very strongly

29. In some countries of the world today the state owns and controls light industry, for example, furniture and clothing manufacture. Are you in favor of this or against it? (Check one)

__ For this __ Against this

30. Does the present day Soviet citizen have more opportunity to visit the theatre and attend concerts than 30 years ago? (Check one)

__ Yes __ No

31. In many countries the state controls heavy industry (such as coal and steel industry). Are you in favor of this or against it? (Check one)

__ In favor __ Against

32. What is your opinion of the organization of the system of Soviet education (not about what is taught, but the system itself, for example, the number of school buildings, etc.)? Are you in favor of this or against it?

__ In favor __ Against

33. Do you think that America has contributed more to the fields of art, music and literature than Europe? (Check one)

__ Yes __ No

34. Do you think that during the last 30 years the number of literate people in the USSR has increased significantly (Check one)

__ Yes __ No

35. What should be the relations between the church and state? (Check one)

__ The church should be completely independent of the state

__ The church should be independent of the state but should receive legal and material support

__ The church should be independent of the state but should receive only legal support

___ The church should be completely dependent on the state

36. Is it true that the American government is so well set up that there has never been any political corruption in the United States? (Check one)
___ Yes, it is true
___ No, it is not true

37. The state has the right to prevent people from participating in meetings if the purpose of the meeting is to attack the government. (Check one)
___ I agree ___ I disagree
A. How strongly do you feel about this? (Check one)
___ Not at all strongly
___ Not so strongly
___ Fairly strongly
___ Very strongly

38. In some countries the government guarantees work for everyone. Are you in favor of this or against it? (Check one)
___ For ___ Against

Core V

V. Now several questions about your family.

1. To what social group did your parents belong before the revolution? (Check one)

Father	*Mother*
Nobility	Nobility
Intelligentsia	Intelligentsia
Landowners	Landowners
Officialdom	Officialdom
Merchants	Merchants
Craftsmen (artisans)	Craftsmen (artisans)
Workers	Workers
Peasantry	Peasantry
Middle class	Middle class
Clergy	Clergy
Military	Military

Perhaps your parents did not belong to any of these groups, then please indicate to what population group they belonged before the revolution?

2. To what social group did your parents belong after the revolution? (Check one)

Father	*Mother*
Party-Soviet apparatus	Party-Soviet apparatus
Intelligentsia	Intelligentsia
Civil servants	Civil servants
Skilled workers	Skilled workers
Ordinary workers	Ordinary workers
Artisans	Artisans
Kolkhozniks — dekulakized	Kolkhozniks — dekulakized
Kolkhozniks — not dekulakized	Kolkhozniks — not dekulakized

Perhaps your parents did not belong to any of these groups, then please indicate to what population group they belonged in Soviet society?

3. What was your father's regular job? (Be concrete in explaining the exact nature of this work he did. If your father worked both before and after the revolution, then please tell his job in both cases and indicate how long he spent at each job.)

4. What school did your father finish?

5. What school did your mother finish?

6. Did your mother ever have a job (not counting housework at home)?
___ Yes ___ No
A. If yes, what did she do?

7. Did all the members of your family have the same attitude to religion or did any of them differ from the rest? (Check one)
___ All felt the same and were in favor of religion
___ All felt the same and were against religion
___ Some differed from the others (Please explain the difference)

8. What was your parents' attitude toward your education? (Check one)
___ Tried to prevent it
___ Only encouraged my ambition
___ Helped me
___ Supported me completely

9. What sort of work did you want for yourself?
A. What sort of work did your parents want you to do?

10. What was your family's material condition when you were a child? In comparison with the majority, were you better or worse off? (Check one)
___ Better ___ Worse
Remarks:

11. Did any of your relatives or dear ones remain in the Soviet Union? (Check one)
___ Yes, many remained
___ Yes, some remained
___ No, none remained

12. In the Soviet Union there were three families: (1) The first family's members became alienated after the revolution. They were afraid to speak frankly with each other and the Soviet regime interfered in family affairs to such an extent that the children were torn away from their parents.

(2) The members of the second family drew closer during the Soviet regime. They spoke freely among themselves about such things that they could not talk about with other people, and the children drew closer to their parents since they only felt secure at home.

(3) The third family was not much influenced by the Soviet regime and their life went on much as before.
A. Which of these three families most closely describes the typical Soviet family? (Check one)
1. The family which grew apart
2. The family which grew together
3. The family which was not influenced

B. Which comes most close to describing your own family? (Check one)
1. The family which grew apart
2. The family which grew together
3. The family which was not influenced
13. What was your marital status when you left the USSR? (Check one)
___ Single   ___ Married
___ Other (divorced or widowed)
14. If you were married at the time you left the Soviet Union, what was your wife's (husband's) job at the time? (Please describe the work in detail).
15. If you were married: When did you marry? Please show the exact year of the marriage. (a) If you were married more than once, please give the year of each marriage
16. What was the class origin of your spouse?
17. What were your material conditions during the last years of your life in the USSR? In comparison with the majority, were you better or worse off?
___ Better   ___ Worse
Remarks:
18. Which of the factors cited below do you consider the most important for a happy marriage between two people in the Soviet Union? (Check one)
___ That they both have the same interests
___ That they both have the same nationality
___ That they both belong to the same social group
___ That they both have the same political views
___ Anything else? What?
A. What do you think comes second in importance for a happy marriage? (Check one)
___ That they both have the same interests
___ That they both have the same nationality;   ___ Both belong to same social group
___ That they both have the same political views
___ Anything else? What?
B. Now, what do you think is least important? (Check one)
___ That they both have the same interests
___ That they both have the same nationality
___ That they both have the same political views
___ That they both belong to the same social group
19. What was your wife's (husband's) attitude toward the Soviet regime?
20. Did her (his) opinion change in time, and if so, how?

Core VI

VI. Now, please remember your three closest friends in 1940 and please give the following information about them:
A. First friend:
What brought you close to each other?
His (her) class origin?

His (her) profession in 1940?

How many years did he (she) study?

Was he (she) a member of the party or the Komsomol?

What did you do together most of the time?

B. Second friend: (Same questions)

C. Third friend: (Same questions)

Core VII

VII. This section concerns your education.

1. What formal education did you receive in the Soviet Union?
(Please indicate exactly the highest class you attended, how many years you attended school and did you finish your school. Please do not forget to include all special schools and courses that you may have attended: for example, rabfak, tekhminimum, evening courses, etc. Indicate exactly how long you attended and exactly what you studied there.)

2. What kind of a student were you?

__ Very good   __ Good

__ Average   __ Weak   __ Poor

3. While you were in the Soviet Union did you have the same opportunity as everyone else to receive an education? (Check one)

__ I had the same opportunity as others

__ Some people had more opportunity to receive education than I

__ I had more opportunity to receive an education than others

If you chose the second or third answer, then please explain your answer.

Core VIII

VIII. 1. When you were in the Soviet Union how often did you do the following?

	Frequently	Seldom	Never
1. Listen to the Soviet radio?	__	__	__
2. Listen to foreign radio?	__	__	__
3. Read newspapers & magazines?	__	__	__
4. Read books?	__	__	__
5. Go to the movies?	__	__	__
6. Go to the theatre?	__	__	__
7. Go to agitation meetings?	__	__	__
8. Go to lectures?	__	__	__
9. Get news & information from some other official sources (not given above)	__	__	__

2. How much of the information you received from the newspapers and magazines did you consider reliable? (Check one)

__ Most of the information

__ Some of the information

__ None of the information

3. What information reported by Soviet sources did you consider most reliable?

A. Which least reliable?

4. While you were living in the Soviet Union how often did you discuss with your friends about what was happening? (Check one)

__ Never __ Seldom __ Often

5. Where did you usually talk with them? (Check one)

__ At work

__ In a restaurant or club

__ At home

__ Someplace else (where?)

6. While you were living in the Soviet Union, did you get any information by rumor? (Check one)

__ Often __ Seldom __ Never

a. If yes, then what kind of rumors?

b. Where did you hear these rumors?

c. Did you consider these rumors more or less reliable than the official sources? (Check one)

__ More reliable

__ Less reliable

7. We have asked you many questions concerning Soviet life. Since we may be able to change some of the questions in the future, we would like to know whether you think we have asked the best possible questions to learn about the Soviet Union, or whether the questions could be improved. (Check one)

__ The questions are the best possible.

__ Some of the questions are good, some are not so good.

__ Most of the questions are not good.

WRITTEN QUESTIONNAIRE ON STRATIFICATION

Since we are interested in a large number of complicated subjects, we are unable to give every one of you all the questions that we would like to.

The questions below concern a series of special problems, and also seek more detailed elaboration of some subjects on which we have already touched in the preceding questions.

We are grateful to you for the service which you have already rendered to us by answering the preceding questions, and we will be still more grateful if you can devote a little more time to giving us some further information.

First, we would like your opinion on the following questions.

1. Some Soviet refugees have said: "Every worker in the Soviet Union can become a factory manager."

What is your opinion about this? (Answer one)

__ I agree with this. Every worker who has the necessary capabilities can join the party and eventually become a factory manager.

__ I do not agree with this.

(If you do not agree, choose from among the reasons given below the one which you think is most important. Answer only one).

____ Workers do not have the opportunity to receive the necessary education.

____ Workers do not have the necessary connections.

____ Workers do not want to engage in the boot-licking which is necessary for promotion.

____ Workers are not accepted into the party.

____ Workers could not handle the job of manager.

2. Which of the following groups has done the *most* harm to the *workers* under the Soviet regime? (Answer one)

____ The workers themselves

____ The peasants

____ The employees

____ The intelligentsia

____ The party cadres

A. Which of these groups is *second* in this respect? (Answer one)

____ The workers themselves

____ The peasants

____ The employees

____ The intelligentsia

____ The party cadres

3. Which of the following groups has done the *most* harm to the *peasants* under the Soviet regime? (Answer one)

____ The workers

____ The peasants themselves

____ The employees

____ The intelligentsia

____ The party cadres

A. Which of these groups is *second* in this respect? (Answer one)

____ The workers

____ The peasants themselves

____ The employees

____ The intelligentsia

____ The party cadres

4. Which of the following groups has done the *most* harm to the *employees* under the Soviet regime? (Answer one)

____ The workers

____ The peasants

____ The employees themselves

____ The intelligentsia

____ The party cadres

A. Which of these groups is *second* in this respect? (Answer one)

____ The workers

____ The peasants

____ The employees themselves

___ The intelligentsia
___ The party cadres

5. Which of the following groups has done the *most* harm to the *intelligentsia* under the Soviet regime? (Answer one)
___ The workers
___ The peasants
___ The employees
___ The intelligentsia themselves
___ The party cadres

A. Which of these groups is *second* in this respect? (Answer one)
___ The workers
___ The peasants
___ The employees
___ The intelligentsia themselves
___ The party cadres

6. An old lady gets on a crowded street-car in a Soviet town. Do you think someone should offer her a seat?
___ Someone should offer her a seat
___ No one has to offer her a seat

A. Whatever your answer was, which of the following people probably would offer her a seat?
___ A member of the intelligentsia
___ An employee
___ A worker
___ A peasant
___ A party official

B. And now, who probably would not offer her a seat?
___ A member of the intelligentsia
___ An employee
___ A worker
___ A peasant
___ A party official

7. In the state which you would like to see in the future, which of the following groups should, in your opinion, play the *leading* role? (Answer one)
___ The workers
___ The peasants
___ The technical intelligentsia
___ The professors
___ The politicians

A. Which of these groups would you *least* like to see in the leading role?
___ The workers
___ The peasants
___ The technical intelligentsia
___ The professors
___ The politicians

Now we would like you to give us some additional information about you yourself.

8. How many members were there in the family in which you grew up (*not counting yourself*)?

A. Parents ___

B. Brothers ___

C. Sisters ___

D. Step-brothers and sisters ___

E. Grandparents ___

F. Others ___   Who? ___

G. Were any of them members of the Komsomol?

___ No ___ Yes

If yes, which ones were they? ___

H. Were any of them members of the party?

___ No ___ Yes

If yes, which ones were they? ___

9. How many children did you have during the time you were in the Soviet Union? Please tell us not the number of children you had at the moment you left the Soviet Union, but the number of all the children you had during *your entire life* in the Soviet Union.

A. During my entire life in the Soviet Union I had ___ children

Now please give us the following information about your *first* child:

B. My first child was born in ___ (year).

C. This child was a:

___ Boy ___ Girl

D. Up to the beginning of the war with Germany, how many years of education had he (she) had? ___

E. At the outbreak of the war with Germany, what job did he (she) have? ___

F. Was he (she) a member of the Komsomol?

___ Yes ___ No

G. Was he (she) a member of the party?

___ Yes ___ No

H. If he (she) died before you left the Soviet Union, what was the cause of death? _____

10. Now please give us the same information about your last child: (Same questions as above)

11. We are interested in how Soviet citizens spend their time. Please tell what you did on an ordinary working day in *1940*. (For example, if you read, listened to the radio, and went to the theater and movies about four hours a *week*, then for *one day* you should write down one-half hour. The total sum of hours spent by you in all activities should, of course, be 24.)

How much time did you spend in a day in 1940 in each of the following activities?

Write the number of hours on the space left for this at the end of each statement:

1. I worked (studied) .... ____ hours
2. In going to and from work (school) I spent .... ____ "
3. I went shopping and stood in lines .... ____ "
4. I prepared meals .... ____ "
5. I ate .... ____ "
6. I slept .... ____ "
7. I attended meetings .... ____ "
8. I read, listened to the radio, went to the theater and movies ____ "
9. In conversation with my family, or in other activities at home, I spent .... ____ "
10. In conversation or other activities with my friends or relatives, at their house or mine, I spent .... ____ "
11. In other activities (specify what), I spent .... ____ "

                                    Total: 24 hours

JOB QUESTIONNAIRE

We are interested in finding out what people think of different kinds of jobs in the Soviet Union.

Suppose that you had the chance of an absolutely free choice of job (trade) during your last years in the Soviet Union, and that any job (position) was equally available to you, regardless of your past, your education, etc.

We are going to present you with thirteen different kinds of jobs which are common in the Soviet Union. First we want to know how desirable, taking *everything* into consideration, it was to have the given job in the Soviet Union. Then we would like to know how satisfactory was the material position of a person who had this job; how dangerous this job was, from the point of view of being arrested; how high was the personal satisfaction of a person at this kind of work; and finally, how the population in general regarded people who were doing this job.

For example, let's take the job of commissar. Taking *everything* into account, how desirable was it to have this job in the Soviet Union? If you think that this job was undesirable, but still not *very* undesirable, then put a cross "X" in the appropriate space, as shown in this example:

____ Very desirable
____ Desirable
____ So-so
 X Undesirable
____ Very undesirable

Now the next question. How satisfactory was the material position of a commissar? If you think that the material position of a commissar was excellent, then put a cross "X" in the appropriate space, as shown in the example below:

 X Excellent

___ Good
___ Average
___ Poor
___ Very poor

Please do the same thing for all the questions and kinds of jobs given here, making a cross "X" before that statement which most closely agrees with your personal opinion in each case.

1. *Teacher*

a) Taking *everything* into consideration, how desirable was it to have the job of teacher in the Soviet Union?
___ Very desirable
___ Desirable
___ So-so
___ Undesirable
___ Very undesirable

b) How satisfactory was the material position of a teacher?
___ Excellent
___ Good
___ Average
___ Poor
___ Very poor

c) How high was the personal satisfaction of a teacher with his work?
___ Very high
___ High
___ Average
___ Low
___ Very low

d) In comparison with other kinds of jobs, how dangerous was the job of teacher, from the point of view of being arrested?
___ One of the safest
___ Safer than some
___ So-so
___ More dangerous than some
___ One of the most dangerous

e) How did the population regard teachers in general?
___ With great respect
___ With respect
___ With indifference
___ With contempt
___ With great contempt

The same questions are asked for each of the following jobs:
Kolkhoz chairman
Rank-and-file worker
Doctor
Foreman
Scientific worker

Officer (in armed forces)
Rank-and-file kolkhoznik
Engineer
Bookkeeper
Secretary of a party organization
Factory manager
Brigadier

Appendix 2:

The Personal Interview: Questions and Probes

W 1. Will you tell me about the jobs you worked at when you were in the Soviet Union? Start with the first one and enumerate all of them in order.

W 2. Please tell me about the establishment (enterprise, factory, farm) in which you worked in . . . . ; what was its chief product?

A. Was it a large, small or medium organization for its type of work?

B. What did your work consist in?

W 3. How was this work, pretty good?

G 1. Now we would like to find out the means which the average Soviet citizen can use to protect his personal interests under the present regime. I will give you three situations in which a Soviet citizen might find himself and ask you to think what he could have done.

(Situations: select 3; give one at a time, that applying to him *first*)

1. It is 1940. He has just been graduated from an engineering institute in Moscow. He has been ordered to take a position as engineer in Komsomolsk but prefers to remain in Moscow.
2. It is 1940. He is employed as a bookkeeper in the offices of the Narkomat of Foreign Trade in Odessa, the city in which he was born. He has just received an order transferring him to the offices of the Narkomat in Leningrad, but he does not want to go.
3. It is 1940. He is a lathe operator in an aircraft factory in Chelyabinsk. He cannot support his family on his wages. His apartment is miserably inadequate. His wife is sick, and the doctor says that the climate in Chelyabinsk is bad for her. The lathe operator wants to secure a better paying job in another city.
4. He is a Red Army officer and has just received an order transferring him from a comfortable staff assignment in Leningrad to a line outfit in Uzbekistan. He wants to get the order rescinded.
5. He is a kolkhoznik. His chairman does not leave him enough time during the sawing season to work on his private lot. He wants to get the situation corrected.

   (Probes: ask after presenting each situation, where applicable)

A. What could he have done in such a situation?

B. Could he have taken his problem to a government official? To a party official? To a trade union official? To an influential friend? To the local

newspaper? Would he have gone in person or would he have written? Would a bribe or a deal have helped his case?
(Only for the situation that applies to him)
C. Now suppose that this had happened to you. Which of these things could you personally have done if you found yourself in such a situation?

G 2. Two schoolboys, about 18 years old, are returning home at night after being to a party where they had a good deal to drink. One dares the other to climb up on a statue of Lenin and put his cap on Lenin's head. While he is doing this a militia man comes along. The first boy runs away but the other is caught.
What does the militia man do with him?

A. Does it make any difference who the boy's father is?

G 3. While you were in the Soviet Union did you or any of your close relatives or friends have any trouble with the secret police (NKVD, MGB)? Were you or they ever arrested?

A. (If answer to either of above questions is *Yes:*)
Tell me about the case that produced the greatest impression on you.
B. (After completion of account:)
Please give me a list of all such incidents which happened to your family and close friends. We do not need the details, just a simple list.

G 4. If you had to advise some young person in the Soviet Union on how to steer clear of trouble with the secret police, what would you tell him?
(*Optional:*)
A. Are there any safe jobs?
B. Does it help to be active in the party or Komsomol?
C. Does a connection with the NKVD bring safety?
D. Does a good class background help? Is it possible to conceal an unfavorable class background?
E. If one knows how to keep his mouth shut, is he likely to escape trouble?
F. Do the members of some nationalities have less trouble with the secret police than members of other nationalities?
G. Does protektsiya help?
H. Does it help to have money?

G 5. Did you ever have an opportunity to join the Komsomol?
(Ask question and use the probes for the Komsomol; then ask question again for the party.)
Did you have an opportunity to join the party?
(If the answer is *Yes:*)

A. Did you feel any pressure to join?
B. What did you do?
(If the respondent joined:)
C. Under what conditions were you accepted?

D. What were your duties and what positions did you hold?
E. What advantages and disadvantages did membership bring?
   (If the respondent had an opportunity to join, but did not:)
F. What explanation did you give for not joining?
G. How did your action affect your later life?
   (If the answer is *No*, respondent had no opportunity to join:)
H. Why?
I. How did you feel about the lack of opportunity?
J. How did this lack of opportunity affect your life?
   (Ask everyone:)
K. Does the rank-and-file party member have influence on party policy?
   (If *Yes* to K:)
L. In what ways?
   (If *No* to K:)
M. Who does?

G 6. (Dropped)
F 1. What was the class origin of your family?

A. What was your father's occupation?
B. What did your mother do?
C. What advantages and disadvantages did the fact that your parents were
   _____ (peasant, intelligentsia, etc.) have for you?
D. How did you feel about it?

F 2. When you were young, what sort of person did your parents want you to be?

A. Did they want you to follow any particular line of work?
B. How much did this affect your formal education?
C. Did you ever want to do something else? What was it?

F 3. How did your family feel about religion?
F 4. Did you have children in the Soviet Union? (If the respondent had no children, ask the question and probes hypothetically, i.e., If you had had . . . . . etc.)

A. What kind of character did you try to impart to your child?
B. What kind of a career would have liked (each) to have?

F 5. We have talked about children in the Soviet Union somewhat. But you have lived now for several years in Germany. I wonder if you could tell me in what ways it is better or worse to rear a child in Germany in comparison with the Soviet Union.

A. What could the child have here that he could not have in the Soviet Union?
B. What could the child have in the Soviet Union that he could not have here?

F 6. Now I would like to know something about material conditions of your family life in the Soviet Union. How did your family get along financially in the last years of your life in the Soviet Union?

A. Did you have enough food?
B. How about clothing?
C. What about housing?
D. Which of the difficulties you had bothered you most?

F 7. Please recall a family among your acquaintances that was worse off than anyone you knew.

A. Why do you think this particular family was in such dire straits?

F 8. Now please recall that family among your acquaintances that was better off than anyone else you knew. Describe how they lived.

A. Why do you think they were able to live this way?

F 9. I will tell you of three families that lived in the Soviet Union, and I would like you to tell me which of these three comes closest to describing the typical Soviet family.

The members of one family grew apart after the revolution. They were afraid to talk freely among themselves, and the Soviet regime interferred in the family until the children became drawn away from the parents.

Another family grew closer together under the Soviet regime. They talked freely about what they could not talk to other people and the children grew closer to the parents because there was no other place they felt safe.

The third family was not much influenced by the Soviet regime, and life went on much as before.

Which of these families comes closest to describing the typical Soviet family?

A. Which comes closest to describing your family?

F 10. Now I have one more question, which concerns methods of handling infants in the Soviet Union. It is said that in the past in some parts of the Soviet Union there existed the custom of swaddling infants. To what extent is the swaddling of infants customary at the present time?

A. Are infants swaddled in hospitals and crêches?
B. Were you or other members of your family swaddled?
C. Can you describe the swaddling — were the arms tied in, was it tight, etc.?
D. Until what age were infants swaddled?
E. For what reasons are infants swaddled?

C 1. While you were in the Soviet Union, from what sources did you draw most of your information about what was happening?

A. Which of these sources was the most important for you? And then?
B. (Dropped)

C 2. What sort of news did you get by word of mouth?
A. From what sort of people did you get this news?
B. Was this news more or less reliable than the other sources?

C 3. Please think of a typical month when you lived in the Soviet Union in 1940. Then tell me what you did during that month, concerning each of the following:

A. (Radio) Did you listen to a radio or reproducer? (If "Yes," ask the following:)
  1. What programs did you listen to?
  2. Approximately how many hours a month did you listen?
  3. How reliable did you consider the information you received?
  4. What kind(s) of receiver(s) did you listen to? Where — at home, friends, etc.?
  5. (If illegal receivers were used, ask the following:)
     How difficult or dangerous was this listening?
B. (Newspapers and Magazines) Did you read any newspapers or magazines? (If "Yes," ask the following:)
  1. Which did you read?
  2. How frequently?
  3. What sections did you read?
  4. How reliable did you consider the information you received?
C. (Movies) Did you attend any movies? (If "Yes," ask the following:)
  1. What sort of movies did you attend? (Domestic or foreign)
  2. How many in a typical month?
  3. Did you think that they showed things in a true light?
D. (Meetings) Did you attend any meetings? (If "Yes," ask the following:)
  1. Which did you attend?
  2. How many in a typical month?
  3. What subjects were discussed?
  4. How reliable did you consider the information you received?
E. (Books) Think of the entire year 1940 instead of one month. Did you read any books? (If "Yes," ask the following:)
  1. What titles?
  2. How many during the entire year?
  3. Did you think that they showed things in a true light?

P 1. Let us suppose that the Bolshevik regime were removed and a new government came into power. What things in the present system would you allow to remain?

A. What things would you be sure to change?

P 2. Suppose we had a government that would work only for the welfare of the people and would want to organize agriculture in a way most desirable

to everybody. Which do you think would be better. Collectivized agriculture
or individual farming?
(Ask only if reply to question is "individual farming.")

A. Suppose the collective were voluntary, and people could join or leave as
   they chose?
   (Ask only if reply to main question is "individual farming.")
B. Would it be desirable to be able to use collectively owned machinery,
   such as tractors hired from the M.T.S.?
   (Ask in every case:)
C. What do you think is better — sovkhozes or kolkhozes?

   P 3. (Dropped)
   P 4. If there were a people's uprising in the Soviet Union, what groups
of the population would fight to preserve the Soviet regime? Who would
fight against it?

A. Suppose there were a war and the people were sure that the powers fighting the Soviet power would not behave like the Germans. Who would
   fight to preserve the Soviet regime? Who would fight against it?

   P 5. If the Soviet regime were overthrown, what should be done with
party members?

A. Should they all be treated the same?
B. How about the MGB (NKVD) and the militia?
C. What other people should get special attention?

   P 6. Everybody seems to agree that the N.E.P. was a rather good period
under the Bolsheviks. Suppose that someone other than Stalin had come to
power at this time. From what you know of Soviet history, would conditions
have become better or worse?
   P 7. What should the government do for its people?

A. What should the government do about education?
B. What should the government do about the press?
C. What should the government do about social insurance?
D. In what areas of human life should the government not interfere?
E. What duties does a man have to his government?

   P 8. What do you think the relation between church and state should be?

A. Do you think that the state should ever interfere in matters of religion?
B. For example, how about people who hold beliefs which are incorrect:
   should they be permitted to teach them?
C. (Select appropriate probe:)
   Should the state support or help the church in any way?
   (Or:) — Should the state take any active role in combating religion?
D. What role do you think the church should have in the state?

P 9. A group of English students were walking through a public park singing songs. They approached a place where a Communist orator was addressing a crowd. A policeman stopped them and asked them not to sing while passing the crowd since this would disturb the speaker.
Do you think the English policeman was right in protecting the Communist orator from being disturbed?

P 10. We have been talking a good deal about the Soviet system and the Bolshevik regime. Now I would like your opinion of the people who live under this system. What traits of character and behavior distinguish Soviet citizens in general from the people of other countries, let's say the Germans?

A. Have these traits changed since the 1917 Revolution?
B. Are there differences of character and behavior between workers, peasants, and white-collar workers?
C. Are there differences between party and nonparty people?
D. (Dropped)
E. Are there traits distinguishing the following nationalities: Great Russians, Ukrainians, Jews, Georgians, Armenians, Tartars?

P 12. What sort of person gets ahead in the Soviet Union?

P 13. Saint Krispin stole hide from rich shoemakers and gave it to poor people. What do you think of this action?

P 14. There is a Russian proverb that says: "Without God you can't even get to the rapids, but with God you will reach the sea." Another proverb says: "God is God, but you are responsible for your own behavior."
What, in your opinion, is the role God plays in life, and what is the role man plays?

P 15. A man brought another man into court and explained to the judge that they owned a small shop together and that the second man had taken things from the shop unfairly. The judge listened carefully to the story and agreed that the second man had been unfair to the first one, but said that unfortunately there was no law by which he could make the second man give the things back.
What should be done about this man?

A. An American soldier was working in a supply station during the war, but he wanted to get into combat. His commanding officer explained to him that soldiers were needed for this kind of work too. He deserted and went to the front to fight. At the front he was arrested and brought to trial for deserting.
What should be done with this soldier?

Appendix 3:

Alienness of Origin Code

This code is an index of the *probable* attitude of the Soviet regime toward the respondent's social origin in terms of Marxist-Leninist ideology. Males born before 1900 were classified by their own prerevolutionary occupation where possible; females born before 1900 were classified as uncertain. In all other cases, classification was made on the basis of father's prerevolutionary social group or occupation. The composition of the categories is as follows:

Munich	Marginals New York	Total	
276	146	422	*Alien:* nobility, landowners, businessmen, clergy, lawyers, judges, tsarist governmental officials or police or army officers, members of the White armies, and those whose fathers were specifically reported as "disfranchised."
474	69	543	*Proletarian:* wage-workers of all skill grades, and non-dekulakized peasants.
67	39	106	*Nonpoliticized:* Students, white-collar employees, and professionals and semiprofessionals other than those classified as alien (e.g., doctors, teachers, engineers, artists); these are people to whom the ideology failed in general to give a clear-cut definition.
1263	384	1647	*Uncertain:* those for whom the PPQ data are not sufficient to define origin; this category includes in particular those peasant fathers reported as "dekulakized" on the assumption that the respondents in many cases extended the meaning of this term to include fathers who were merely "collectivized" without actual prejudice to their children's ideological standing.

The roughness of this index is to be emphasized. The regime never translated the ideology into precise legal definitions of the varieties of "social origin," and frequently postrevolutionary activities were also taken into account, as well as such highly individual factors as attitude toward the regime itself.

(A code summarizing V, 1 and V, 2 has been developed to indicate the respondent's social background in terms of parents' prerevolutionary and postrevolutionary group membership. In terms of the prerevolutionary social group, "upper" includes the nobility, intelligentsia and landowners; "middle" the civil servants, merchants, artisans, middle class, clergy and military; "lower" the workers and peasantry. In the case of postrevolutionary social group, "upper" includes the party-Soviet apparatus and the intelligentsia; "middle" the employees, skilled workers and artisans; "lower" the rank-and-file workers and kulakized and non-dekulakized kolkhozniks. If the father was dead, the mother's social group was used.)

Munich	*Marginals* New York	Total	Pre	— Post
231	141	372	Upper	— Upper
20	11	31	Middle	— Upper
96	66	162	Upper	— Middle
339	173	512	Middle	— Middle
182	37	219	Lower	— Higher (i.e., middle or upper)
35	13	48	Upper	— Lower
76	23	99	Middle	— Lower
99	12	111	Peasant — Worker	
979	159	1138	Lower	— Lower

Editorials

Munich	New York	Total	
329	48	377	Worker origin
832	148	980	Peasant origin
272	127	399	Prerevolutionary only
21	5	26	Postrevolutionary only
22	3	25	No information on social background

Appendix 4:

Anti-Leadership Sentiment Score

This index is based on answers to the following two questions:

1. What should be done with the Bolshevik leaders if the Soviet regime were overthrown? (IV, 17 open-ended). Responses to this question were divided into those which specified death to the leaders as opposed to all other responses *and* nonresponses.
2. Do you favor dropping an atomic bomb on Moscow right now in order to destroy the Bolshevist leaders, even though it means killing thousands of innocent men, women and children? (IV, 28 check-list). Responses to this question were divided into those who said, "Yes, now," those who said "Only as a last resort," and those who said, "No." See below re treatment of No Answers.

The response on the bomb question, "Yes, now" was given the score 2 on the grounds that it expressed the ready willingness to pay the highest price to "get the leaders" and also, because with respect to other measures of hostility toward the regime, this response was the most highly discriminating.

The responses "Bomb as last resort" and "Death to leaders," were both scored 1 on grounds similar to those just indicated.

The response "Don't bomb" was scored 0, as was the failure to respond on "Death to leaders."

These scoring procedures permitted a high score of three and a low score of 0.

With respect to no answers; on the "bomb question"; people making this nonresponse were given a score *only* under the condition that they had made a positive response to the other question. It was felt that the response "Death to leaders" indicated the presence of a degree of hostility which should be indicated. The distribution of the scores is shown below:

			Marginals
Munich	*New York*	*Total*	*Anti-Leadership Sentiment Score*
379	65	444	Score 3
609	170	770	" 2
702	236	938	" 1
328	147	475	" 0
63	20	83	Not ascertainable

Appendix 5:

Anti-Soviet Sentiment Score

A. The following questions were used to form the index:

IV, 17. What should be done with the Bolshevist leaders if the Soviet regime were overthrown? (Respondents who said "Violent death" were scored +)

IV, 20B. If the Bolshevist regime were overthrown and a new regime came to power what things would you be sure to change? (Respondents who answered "Everything" were scored +)

IV, 28. Do you favor dropping an atomic bomb on Moscow right now in order to destroy the Bolshevist leaders, even though it means killing thousands of innocent men, women and children? (Respondents who answered "Yes" were scored +)

IV, 32. What is your opinion of the organization of the system of Soviet education? Are you in favor of this or against it? (Respondents who answered "Against" were scored +)

VIII, 2. How much of the information you received from the newspapers and magazines did you consider reliable? (Respondents who answered "None" were scored +)

Marginals Munich	New York	Total	Anti-Soviet Sentiment Score
381	186	567	0
559	229	788	1
483	142	625	2
370	57	427	3
182	12	194	4
45	5	50	5
500	158	658	No answer to one of the items
152	23	175	No answer to two of the items
60	7	67	No answer to three or more of the items

Appendix 6:

Arrest Experience of Respondent and Family

The purpose of this summary code is to separate out those respondents who have themselves experienced arrest *with a sentence or injurious* effect and those who have not, also those respondents from immediate families with such experience from those whose families were relatively unscathed. Therefore, each respondent was assigned to one of the following eleven categories:

Munich	Marginals New York	Total	
			Respondent himself not arrested, or if arrested, then acquitted or pardoned
448	164	612	Member of immediate family arrested and sentenced.
466	179	645	No member of immediate family arrested, or if arrested, then acquitted.
58	60	118	Family member arrested and sentenced, but some ambiguity as to whether reference to immediate or extended family.
155	52	207	Insufficient information to determine seriousness of consequences of arrest in R's family.
			Respondent himself arrested and sentenced
56	20	76	Member of immediate family arrested and sentenced.
125	39	164	No one in family arrested, or if arrested, then acquitted.
184	18	202	Insufficient information on family's arrest history.
			Insufficient information to determine seriousness of consequences of respondent's own arrest history
21	13	34	No one in family arrested, or if arrested, then acquitted.
22	2	24	Member of immediate family arrested and sentenced.

8	6	14	Insufficient information on family's own arrest history.
713	96	809	NA to entire question.

Appendix 7:

Arrest Profiles: A. Family Arrest Profile
B. Personal Arrest Profile

A. Family arrest profile:

The purpose of this profile is to indicate the arrest experience of the respondent's family in terms of its likelihood of affecting the respondent's subsequent life chances and attitudes. Consequently this profile involves:

1. The closeness of the family member: immediate (parents, spouses, siblings, and children) vs. the others;
2. the age of the respondent at the time of this arrest;
3. the severity of the arrest to the family member involved.

The construction of this profile involves a number of ambiguities, none of which, it is hoped, destroy its usefulness as a general measure of close contact with "terror."

1. The coded data does not permit specification of the immediate family member involved. Those whose family arrest took place in their childhood or adolescence are not likely to be referring to their spouses or children whereas, for those who were adults at the time of this arrest, it is unclear whether they are referring to their family of orientation or of procreation. At any rate, a close family member is involved.
2. In the case of multiple citations of family arrest (36% of the cases), we cannot pair up the appropriate date of arrest with the appropriate family member, with the appropriate consequences of arrest. The procedure followed here was to use the earliest date of arrest and the severest consequence *as if they were* appropriately paired for the arrest of the member of the immediate family. To check on the legitimacy of this procedure, a 10% sample was taken of the 412 cases involving multiple arrests of immediate family members. In some 91% of the cases, there was no distortion resulting from the use of this procedure. That is, the severest arrest consequences referred to the earliest arrest of an immediate family member. The major reason for this is that the great majority of the multiple arrest cases involved the entire family, or a large part of it, at the same time.
3. In relating the age of the respondent to the date of the earliest family arrest, we have to deal with five-year periods whereas the life cycle

stages of childhood, adolescence, and adulthood are defined by a unit year. The procedure followed here was to compare the mid-points of the five-year periods of both the respondent's age and the date of family arrest. Thus, an arrest occurring in the period 1930–35 was treated as if it occurred in 1933, and a person who was 30–35 at the time of interview was treated as if he were 33. The life cycles stages at the time of arrest were defined this way: Childhood (less than 11 years old). Adolescence (11–20 years old). Adulthood (more than 20 years old).

To obtain maximum differentiation, severe experiences were defined as those which involved a sentence of 5 years or more. They include those people who, although sentenced to less than 5 years, in fact disappeared or died subsequent to arrest. All other cases, including the No Answers to "consequences" were treated as not severe.

	Marginals		
Munich	*New York*	*Total*	*Family Arrest Profile*
			Immediate family arrest
451	141	592	No family arrest
72	23	95	Childhood experience : severe
58	25	83	" " : not severe
127	64	191	Adolescent experience: severe
108	34	142	" " : not severe
187	95	282	Adult experience : severe
106	76	182	" " : not severe
64	14	78	No specification : severe
69	16	85	" " : not severe
			Nonimmediate family arrest
81	37	118	Severe consequences
45	17	62	Not severe consequences
			Other
295	186	481	More than one family member arrested
711	95	806	No data

B. Personal arrest profile:

This profile is based on the time of the respondent's first and/or only arrest with respect to his age at that time — whether or not the arrest occurred before or after the age of 20 — and it involves also the severity of the consequences — whether or not the consequences were more or less severe than an imprisonment of 5 years. Those who were never arrested are divided into two groups and appropriately identified; those whose family members were arrested and those whose family members as well as themselves were never arrested. Following are the categories and marginals:

Munich	*Marginals* New York	Total	*Personal Arrest Profile*
			Self not arrested
246	60	306	Neither self nor family arrested
803	347	1150	Not self but family arrested
			Self arrested
21	12	33	Acquitted: pre-adult
54	35	89	" : adult
25	8	33	Under 5 years: pre-adult
60	31	91	" " " : adult
26	5	31	Five years or more: pre-adult
63	17	80	" " " " : adult
69	27	96	Unspecifiable
712	96	808	NA to arrest question

Appendix 8:

Aspirations Index

The index is a comprehensive measure of relative aspirations drives. It has been combined from the response patterns on four pairs of items. These response patterns were scored independently for each separate pair of items on a 5-point scale (from *"1" low* aspiration to *"5" high* aspiration). The separate scores were then summed and averaged for each respondent to give a mean score. The overall index was constructed from the distribution of these mean scores. Only those respondents who could be scored on at least three of the four pairs of sub-items enter the final index.

The four response patterns which were used follow. Each set of items was scored separately, and the scoring system is entered in the cells on the right. *Note that the same scoring schema is used for items 2–4.* The derivation of the final score will be illustrated below.

ITEMS		*SCORING*				
		Preferred job attribute				
		Opportunity	Security			
1. Career Desire x Job Preference	*Career* +	5	4			
	Desire 0	4	3			
	—	2	1			
			Categories equivalent to:			
		TO: *Elite*	*Empl*	*SkWrkr*	*Psnt*	*Wrkr*
2. Respondent's Current Occupation	FROM: Elite	4	3	2	1	1
x Free Job Choice						
3. Father's Social Group (in Respondent's adolescence)	Empl	4	3	2	1	1
x Respondent's Adolescent Job Aspiration	SkWrker	5	4	3	2	1
4. Parents' Job Aspiration for Respondent (in Respondent's adolescence)	Wrkr	5	5	3	2	1
x Respondent's Adolescent Job Aspiration	Psnt	5	5	4	2	2

On Item 1 — Somebody who wanted a career (+) and preferred a job with security to one with opportunity received a score of 4 points. A combination of no career desire (−) with preference for opportunity was worth 2 points.

On Items 2–4 — A standard scoring schema was devised to evaluate the relative amount of "positional span" expressed. And the common point system was applied to the three items. The point values abstract clusters of span which are assumed to be fairly homogeneous in the relative amount of aspiration drives which they reveal. Thus, for example, we assume that a Kolkhoznik who wants to be a Skilled Worker is actually asserting as much ambition-drive as the Intelligentsia member who wants to remain a member of the Intelligentsia. Or an Employee who just wants to remain an Employee is revealing about as much ambition as the Ordinary Worker who wants to become a Skilled Worker.

In the scoring table, the "positional" categories have been standardized for all questions. The classification of the rows refers to the first variable in each pair: Respondent's Occupation, Father's Social Group, and Parental Job Aspirations for Respondent on items 2–4, respectively. The classification of the columns refers to the second variable in each pair: Free Job Choice, and Respondent's Adolescent Job Aspirations (for the last two items). Thus, the value of a Skilled Worker who aspires to be a member of the Elite can be found in the cell of the Skilled Worker row and the Elite column (worth 5 points). Aspiration points are graded from the lowest (1) to the highest (5).

To illustrate the derivation of a final mean score for a respondent, let us assume the following data: a Kolkhoznik who is the son of a Kolkhoznik wants to be a Skilled Worker and indicates no career desire, but wants opportunity on a job. As an adolescent, he had wanted modestly enough to be only a Kolkhoznik although his father had wanted him to get some kind of Employee job. To score this case, the procedure is as follows:

On Item 1: No career desire X preference for opportunity   2
   Item 2: Kolkhoznik who wants to be a Skilled Worker   4
   Item 3: Father a Kolkhoznik and as adolescent respondent
             only wanted to be a Kolkhoznik   2
   Item 4: Father wanted R to be an Employee while R wanted
             to be a Kolkhoznik   1
                                                                              9

A total of 9 aspiration points yields a mean score on the 4 items of 2.25 (or 2.3).

This composite index requires some clarification prior to its use in analysis. As a comprehensive measure, the index consists mainly of "sociometric"-type expressions about "class-position span." Therefore, it tends to order people largely according to the relative *quantity* or "reach" of their aspiration drives. Note, however, that this makes no assumptions about the quality of these aspirations — about motivational categories or subjective meaning of these expressed ambitions. We have not systematically built in any *value* commitments to chosen positions, such as positive identification with life types class values, etc. These may be present, but are not systematically ordered and must not be assumed on a priori grounds. In other words, *our aspiration types are not exhaustive social types*. The explicit continuum of ordering is purely that of aspirational strength.

This may be noted, secondly, in one artifact of the scoring system. This is the limitation on the possible expression of strong ambition by high class groups and the limitation of expremely weak or negative ambition by the lowest class group. For example, the absolute maximum possible score of highly ambitious upper class people of upper class background would average out to 4.3 — which barely qualifies for the most ambitious class interval in the scale below. Consequently, people of this type who achieved almost, but not quite, the maximum score possible for them appear in the second highest group on the scale. Conversely, at the low end of the class structure, peasants who doggedly have no desire whatever to change their station in life, would have to get the absolute minimum score possible *for them* (7 points, or an average of 1.8) in order to appear in the lowest aspiration level. In other words, all groups except the non-manuals can score 5 upward-aspiration points on Items 2–4, but the non-manuals can only achieve 4. Conversely, all groups except the peasants can be scored 1 on these Items, but the peasants cannot be scored lower than 2. This, of course, permits Item 1, where all groups have a full scoring range open to them, *to discriminate the most highly-ambitious upper class groups and negatively-ambitious peasants for inclusion in the extreme classes on the scale.* Characteristically, however, because of these restricted class opportunities for the full scoring range on all items, the extreme groups will not be predominantly drawn from the highest and lowest social groups, but rather from those who potentially can express the greatest upward or downward mobility spans. The polar aspirations groups do contain the most ambitious Intelligentsia and least ambitious Peasants. While the extreme aspiration groups are not "class" homogeneous, they do isolate the extreme aspirant types. In general, the aspiration scale will function best when used as a trichotomy or a dichotomy (or with the polar groups alone).

Certain very gross reference points may be taken as guides. If we take the prototype "stable" responses of people in various class positions — viz., peasants, or peasant background always having wanted to be peasants, etc. — the respective average scores of such "stable" class aspirations would be as follows: Peasants and Ordinary Workers, 2.0; Skilled Workers and Employees, 3.0; Intelligentsia, 4.0.

In the following index, then, scores range from an average of 1 (low aspirations) to 5 (high aspirations).

Marginals			
Munich	New York	Total	Aspirations Index
			Average score
233	32	265	1.0–1.8 (Lowest aspirations)
221	66	287	2.0–2.8
227	142	369	3.0–3.3
221	88	309	3.5–3.8
141	60	201	4.0
207	68	275	4.3–5.0 (Highest aspirations)
830	182	1012	Reject: No index rating
434	183	637	Index based on only 3 scores

Appendix 9:

Communications Typologies

Munich	Marginals New York	Total	Communications Typologies
			I. Exposure to mass media (newspapers, magazines, Soviet radio and books). Score = number of mass media exposed to.
			Score
489	269	758	3
407	200	607	2
359	93	452	1
826	76	902	0
			II. Exposure to legitimate non-mass media (agitation meetings, lectures, other official sources). Score = number of media exposed to.
			Score
12	6	18	3
116	61	177	2
281	157	438	1
1671	414	2085	0
			III. Exposure to primarily entertainment media (movies and theatre). Score = number of media exposed to.
			Score
277	148	425	2
425	158	583	1
1378	332	1710	0
			IV. Exposure to non-legitimate media (foreign radio, rumor, discussion with friends). Score = number of media exposed to.
			Score
24	22	46	3
118	89	207	2
360	159	519	1
1578	368	1946	0

V. Exposure to party and Komsomol members (self, friends, relatives). Score = number of members exposed to.

			Score
36	3	39	3
126	30	156	2
270	107	377	1
1524	490	2014	0
124	8	132	No answer

Note: The series given above are based on positive mention of each of the media. A "no answer" is counted as a negative mention and does not appear separately except for Index V.

Appendix 10:

Cultural Level of Family of Orientation Index

This index is based on the educational levels of one's parents. Its purpose is to indicate the cultural context in which the respondent matured in terms of its homogeneity or heterogeneity as well as its level or levels.

Prime importance is given to the educational level of the father; the mother's educational level is related to the latter in terms of its being the same and/or higher, or lower.

Munich	*Marginals* New York	Total	Cultural Level of Family of Orientation Index
			Father: College
69	30	99	Mother: college
182	142	324	Mother: no college (92% of these had 10 yrs. of school)
			Father: 10 years of school
205	119	324	Mother: same or more (only 20 had more)
91	52	143	Mother: less than 10 years (the modal category here is 1–4 years)
			Father: 5–9 years
46	15	61	Mother: same or more
62	6	68	Mother: less
			Father: 1–4 years
31	7	38	Mother: more
526	106	632	Mother: same
108	17	125	Mother: illiterate
99	15	114	Mother: no formal education
			Others
109	9	118	Father illiterate (93% mothers in same category)
173	26	199	Father had no formal education (74% of mothers in same category and 17% more were illiterate)

Appendix II:

Distortion Scale

A. Questions used to form the scale:

Does the present day Soviet citizen have more opportunity to visit the theatre and attend concerts than 30 years ago?

Was medical care more accessible when you left the Soviet Union than 25 years ago?

Was the production of agricultural machinery higher when you left the Soviet Union than 25 years ago?

Do you think that during the last 30 years the number of literate people in the USSR has increased significantly?

B. Scoring the responses:

"Yes" responses were scored −

"No" responses were scored +

The following patterns of "Yes" and "No" responses were rated as follows:

Theatre	Medical	Machinery	Literacy	Rating
+	+	+	+	4
+	+	+	−	3
+	+	−	+	4
+	+	−	−	2
+	−	+	+	4
+	−	+	−	3
+	−	−	+	4
+	−	−	−	1
−	+	+	+	4
−	+	+	−	3
−	+	−	+	4
−	+	−	−	0
−	−	+	+	4
−	−	+	−	0
−	−	−	+	0
−	−	−	−	0

As the reader will see all items were not assigned equal weight. The assignment of weight was based on the relative frequency of the various "distorting" answers. A rare answer was given more weight than a usual one.

C. The ratings are as follows:

Munich	Marginals New York	Total	Ratings
143	9	152	4
148	18	166	3
144	42	186	2
410	110	520	1
935	373	1308	0
297	86	383	No answer on any one or more items

Appendix 12:

Family Cohesion Response Pattern

(This code summarizes the responses given to the two sections of question V, 12.)

Marginals			
Munich	New York	Total	
478	199	677	Soviet family grew together; respondent's family grew together
288	110	398	Soviet family grew apart; respondent's family grew together
330	43	373	Soviet family grew apart; respondent's family grew apart
236	90	326	Soviet family grew apart; respondent's family not influenced
212	80	292	Soviet family not influenced; respondent's family not influenced
91	24	115	Soviet family grew together; respondent's family grew apart — OR Soviet family grew together; respondent's family not influenced — OR Soviet family not influenced; respondent's family grew apart — OR No answer on Soviet family; respondent's family grew apart
83	31	114	Soviet family not influenced; respondent's family grew together — OR No answer on Soviet family; respondent's family grew together
108	14	122	Soviet family grew apart; no answer on respondent's family
171	23	194	No answer to both sections
38	17	55	No answer on Soviet family; respondent's family not influenced
45	7	52	Soviet family grew together; no answer on respondent's family — OR Soviet family not influenced; no answer on respondent's family

Summary Code for Family Disruption

819	331	1150	Any respondent who reported himself divorced or widowed (37/X), arrested and sentenced (17/2–5), or members of his immediate family arrested and sentenced (18/2, 19/2–5, 0, 80/X, Y) received a 53/7 on the family deck.

Summary Code: Occupational Group of Head of Household referred to in the Family Cohesion Question, V, 12.

17	11	28	High military, government, party, high managerial
312	221	533	Intelligentsia
97	60	157	Semiprofessional
284	157	441	White-collar
141	41	182	Skilled workers and artisans
534	65	599	Semiskilled and unskilled workers
646	67	713	Peasants
1205	444	1649	Occupational group of head of household ambiguous
291	43	334	Rural occupation, non-Slavic

Appendix 13:

Financial Responsibility Scale

This expresses the ratio of the Respondent's Total Net Disposable Income to the Per Capita Net Disposable Income of the Total Household. The scale states precisely the number of people who are supported directly by the Respondent's income. The people who are coded "1," "4," "7," or "0" below are cases of complete dependents with no earnings (1), self-supporting individuals living alone (4), or sole breadwinners of a family (7, 0, or X). All other coded cases are families with more than one member employed.

Notes:

The data were drawn from the Budget Questionnaire administered only to people in the Munich sample. Some editorial revisions were made, as follows:

Fifty-six Munich cases originally "Y" were recoded "1" as complete dependents. These consisted of 47 lower school children and 9 housewives.

Eighty-two cases originally "4" were re-coded "5." These were all single-person households (i.e., people living alone and self-supporting) who contributed *more than 25 rubles per year* to someone else's support.

Included in the Munich "No Budgets" group are 65 cases who were given the Budget Questionnaire, but who returned it blank.

Marginals			Code	Number of people whom respondent
Munich	New York	Total	number	supports
163		163	1.	0
22		22	2.	.001– .499
67		67	3.	.5 – .999
304		304	4.	1
184		184	5.	1.001–1.499
45		45	6.	1.5 –1.999
74		74	7.	2
24		24	8.	2.001–2.499
14		14	9.	2.5 –2.999
60		60	0.	3
89		89	X.	Over 3
373		373	Y.	Defective Budget: Uncoded (including kolkhoznik households)
661	638	1299		No Budgets.

Appendix 14:

Flattery Scale

A. Questions used to form the scale:

Is it true that sometimes the Americans have acted unfairly against Europeans who have settled in the United States?

"Yes" responses scored −
"No" responses scored +

Some American newspapers reported that the Americans did not forcibly repatriate a single DP who did not want to return. Are these reports true?

"Yes," not one single Russian DP was forcibly repatriated" scored +
"No, a small number of DP's were forcibly repatriated" scored +
"No, there were many DP's who were forcibly repatriated" scored −

Some people say that Americans are more intelligent than Europeans. Do you agree?

"Yes" responses scored +
"No" responses scored −

We have asked you many questions concerning Soviet life. Since we may be able to change some of the questions in the future, we would like to know whether you think we have asked the best possible questions to learn about the Soviet Union or whether the questions could be improved.

"The questions are the best possible" scored +
"Some of the questions are good, some not so good" scored −
"Most of the questions are not so good" scored −

B. Scoring the responses:

American treatment of immigrants	American treatment of DP's	Intelligence of Americans	Questionnaire valuation	Ratings
+	+	+	+	5
+	+	+	−	4
+	+	−	+	5
+	+	−	−	3
+	−	+	+	5

American treatment of immigrants	American treatment of DP's	Intelligence of Americans	Questionnaire valuation	Ratings
+	−	+	−	4
+	−	−	+	5
+	−	−	−	0
−	+	+	+	5
−	+	+	−	4
−	+	−	+	5
−	+	−	−	0
−	−	+	+	5
−	−	+	−	0
−	−	−	+	0
−	−	−	−	0

Again, the items are weighted differently depending on the frequency with which a particular "flattering" response was given.

C. The ratings are as follows:

Marginals			
Munich	New York	Total	Ratings
547	317	864	0
154	85	239	3
283	69	352	4
334	25	359	5
762	142	904	No answer on any one or more items

Appendix 15:

Interclass Harm Index

The following is a series of indices each of which is a measure of the harmfulness imputed by respondents to a particular social group with respect to its relations to other social groups and itself.

Each respondent was asked, in questions 2A through 5A of the Strat questionnaire, which of four social groups harmed each of the others and itself. To avoid responses which stressed only the party, this question was asked in two ways:

1. "Which did the most harm?" — a question to which the overwhelming response was, "The party," and
2. "Which was second in this respect?" — the question form upon which this index is based.

Each respondent is scored in terms of the number of groups (up to 4), which he specifies as being harmed by a particular social group. If he says that the intelligentsia harmed no group including itself, he is scored "0"; if in his view it harmed only itself, or one other group, he is scored "1" and so on with the exception that scores three and four are merged.

Since these questions concern four social groups, each respondent receives four ratings, each summarizing his opinion on the extent of harm done by a social group to the three other social groups and itself. Only those respondents who answered all items in terms of one of the four social groups was rated; the No Answers and those who cited the party only are not rated. In addition, those who answered none of the four questions are identified separately.

Munich	*Marginals* New York	Total	*Questions* Interclass Harm Index	
			Harm done by the intelligentsia: Score	
256	86	342	To no groups	0
211	159	370	To one group	1
51	19	70	To two groups	2
202	19	221	To three or four	3
			Harm done by Employees:	*Score*
315	119	434	To no groups	0
205	131	336	To one group	1

	Marginals			Questions	
Munich	New York	Total		Interclass Harm Index	
				Harm done by Employees:	*Score*
47	14	61		To two groups	2
153	19	172		To three or four	3
				Harm done by Workers	*Score*
373	44	417		To no groups	0
172	121	293		To one group	1
52	32	84		To two groups	2
123	86	209		To three or four	3
				Harm done by Peasants	*Score*
515	157	672		To no groups	0
193	122	315		To one group	1
4	3	7		To two groups	2
8	1	9		To three or four	3
108	86	194		D/K, NA to all four questions	

Appendix 16:

Marital Status Profile

The main function of this profile is, simply, to save space by combining on one column data which heretofore had taken two columns. In addition, where pre- and postemigration marital status is relevant to an analytical problem, this profile provides the data in its most convenient form.

The profile is based on the respondent's pre-emigration marital status, on his being single, married, widowed, or divorced. This status is then related to his postemigration status in terms of his marrying, remarrying, or retaining his former marital status. The categories and marginals appear below:

Munich	*Marginals* New York	Total	Marital status profile
			Married in the Soviet Union
586	295	881	No indication of change
114	33	147	Now single
32	6	38	Remarried in emigration
			Widowed or divorced in the Soviet Union
74	54	128	No indication of change
33	10	43	Remarried in emigration
33	8	41	Doubtful emigration status (Claim current marriage but cite date which precedes their emigration)
			Single in the Soviet Union
606	140	746	No indication of change
543	76	619	Married in the emigration
			Other
59	16	75	Profile not ascertainable

Appendix 17:

Material Welfare Profile

This profile combines the responses to the two questions:

V, 10 What was your family's material condition when you were a child? In comparison with the majority, were you better or worse off?

V, 17 What were your material conditions during the last years of your life in the USSR? In comparison with the majority, were you better or worse off? (check list)

The responses to both questions used in the profile were the following:

Better
Same
Worse

Each of the three responses to one question were paired with one of the three responses to the other, thus making for nine response patterns each of which was assigned a code category. Thus the people who said "better" referring to their childhood, were subdivided into three groups depending on their answer to the question referring to their adult experience. The profiles and their marginals appear below:

	Marginals			
Munich	New York	Total	Childhood	Adulthood
367	218	585	Better	Better
47	34	81	"	Same
421	98	519	"	Worse
24	37	61	Same	Better
48	37	85	"	Same
52	26	78	"	Worse
149	45	194	Worse	Better
35	25	60	"	Same
523	62	585	"	Worse
412	56	468	NA to one or both items	

Appendix 18:

The Mobility Code

"Origin" is father's occupation when the respondent was 16 years old. It is used with respondent's steady job (husband's job in the case of housewives) to determine mobility. Where father's occupation at the appropriate time period was not available, it was "inferred" from father's social group membership and such occupational data as were available. If father was under arrest when respondent was 16, and had been arrested not more than 3 years previously, "origin" was considered to be father's last regular job but was double-punched "father in exile." "Upper nonmanual" refers to high managerial and military, business proprietors, intelligentsia, supervisory semi-professional, and graduate students.

"Lower nonmanual" refers to all other nonmanual occupations and undergraduate college students. "Upper manual" refers to foremen, skilled workers, supervisory semiskilled workers, and fathers who were peasants either before the revolution or between 1919 and 1929 and are reported as "dekulakized." "Worker" includes unskilled and nonsupervisory semiskilled workers. "Peasant" refers to peasants who were not subsequently dekulakized and to all who were peasants after 1929, where this time period is relevant.

	Marginals		
Munich	New York	Total	Mobility Code
			Stable (nonmobile)
79	54	133	Upper nonmanual
126	69	195	Lower nonmanual
45	15	60	Upper manual
130	7	137	Worker
103	10	113	Peasant
			Upward mobile (Within manual-labor group)
93	9	102	Peasant to worker or to upper manual; worker to upper manual (Manual to nonmanual)
57	13	70	Peasant to upper nonmanual or to lower nonmanual
66	29	95	Worker to upper or lower nonmanual
97	40	137	Upper manual to upper or lower nonmanual

Munich	*Marginals* New York	Total	Mobility Code
			Upward mobile (Within nonmanual group)
58	65	123	Lower nonmanual to upper nonmanual
			Downward mobile (Within manual-labor group)
117	14	131	Upper manual to worker
100	5	105	Upper manual or worker to peasant
			(Nonmanual to manual)
51	19	70	Upper or lower nonmanual to upper manual, worker, or peasant
			(Within nonmanual group)
74	57	131	Upper nonmanual to lower nonmanual
			Qualifiers
33	23	56	Father in exile when respondent was 16
139	30	169	Origin inferred
			Miscellaneous
873	231	1104	Insufficient information

Appendix 19:

Occupational Satisfaction-Frustration Index

Seven questions were drawn from the Work Section to form a scale. Responses to these questions were scored +, 0, or −, but only the *extreme* responses were scored. A "+" indicates satisfaction and a "−" indicates frustration. *All other responses, INCLUDING DK/NA, were left unscored ("0") as a residual category.* Certain conventions were adopted for special cases, and these are noted below.

Of the seven questions used, three were scored directly and independently. The remaining four were divided into two separate pairs. In each pair, the two items were cross-run and the response *patterns* were then scored in the usual way. Each respondent thus received a total of five separate ratings.

The questions used to form the index and the response categories scored + or − are as follows:

Question:	*Responses Scored:* (*Note: Low Military* classed Semiprofessional. All "Students" were scored 0) *Plus*	*Minus*
II, 1 Respondent's Occupation	Job held *higher* than job chosen	Job held *lower* than job chosen.
II, 6 Free Job Choice		Housewives choosing some standard job. "Other" occupations choosing Intelligentsia level jobs.
II, 8 Career Opportunity II, 9 Career Desire	*Did* have chance for career	Had *no* career chance, but *did want* a career (responses 1–3)
II, 5 Pay Equity re Similar Occupations	*No* "+" *category*	Unequal pay.
II, 4 Pay Equity re Different Occupations	Equal or higher pay.	Unequal or lower pay.
II, 3 Satisfaction with 1940 Job	Satisfied	Not satisfied.

From the five ratings for each respondent, the + and − scores were summed to yield a *net score*. For example, two + and two − had a net value of zero, and one + and three − gave a net score of −2. The full range of possible net scores ran from +4 to −5.

The net scores were then grouped into the following index:

Marginals

Total	Index Score	(Net Scores)
357	Satisfied	(+4, +3, +2)
375	↑	(+1)
527		(0)
499		(−1)
462	↓	(−2)
498	Frustrated	(−3, −4, −5)

Appendix 20:

Political Rights Index

This index is based on a latent distance scaling applied to the following items:

1. What kind of government do you prefer? (IV, 6)
   A government which guarantees personal freedom such as the right to criticize the government, worship freely, etc., but does not assure you of a job (86%);
   A government which guarantees a decent standard of living but does not assure you of these personal rights (14%).

2. Do you think that all people have full freedom to organize political parties without interference by the government? (IV, 19) (This should have read, "*should* have full freedom" but was misprinted on the original questionnaire. Some analysis has indicated that many people interpreted the question as was intended despite the printing error. However, the use of this item in the scale warrants caution in the scale's use.)
   Yes (61%)

3. The state has the right to prevent people from participating in meetings if the purpose of the meeting is to attack the government. (IV, 37)
   Agree (46%)

4. Do you think that people should be permitted to express their opinions openly and say anything they want or should the government forbid certain things from being said? (IV, 24)
   Permit (38%)

The positive responses to these items were combined in such a way as to provide five classes of response patterns. These are discussed more fully in a memorandum from Peter H. Rossi to Alex Inkeles, entitled, "A Latent Distance Scale for Attitudes toward Personal Freedom." In this memorandum, four response patterns are classified as ambiguous. These have been assigned to one of the five classes *and* identified as ambiguous. The procedure used in assigning them to a class was based on the fact that three of these ambiguous response patterns showed a bimodal probability of being recruited from the latent classes; that is, instead of one high probability of being recruited from one of the latent classes, these response patterns showed two high probabilities of being recruited from two latent classes. In three of the cases these two high probabilities straddled an intervening latent class. For example, one pattern showed a high probability of coming from class I and also a high probability of coming from class III. The procedure followed was to assign this pattern to the intervening class II. The same procedure was followed for those response patterns straddling classes III and IV. The last ambiguous response pattern was the most ambiguous, showing a highest probability of coming from class IV, a second highest of coming from class I and so on; this one was assigned to class IV. In using the scale, it is suggested that these ambiguous cases be examined separately with respect to the problem under investigation *before* combining them with the unambiguous cases.

The classes I–V range respectively from a low "score" on personal rights to a high "score." Their marginals are shown below.

	Marginals		
Munich	*New York*	*Total*	*Political Rights Index:*
269	76	345	Class I
402	202	604	Class II
399	118	517	Class III
545	176	721	Class IV
321	44	365	Class V
415	157	572	Ambiguous cases

Appendix 21:

Social Origin Type

This is a summary classification of the data on the prerevolutionary social group of the respondent's father.

These have been classified in the following way: after each classification are the categories on father's prerevolutionary social origin which are combined for each classification.

Following are the procedures used in the case of multiple responses to the question on father's prerevolutionary social group:

1. Those which do not involve more than one of the summary classifications cause no problem.

2. Peasants who are also described as workers or artisans are treated as peasants.

3. Middle class fathers who are also described in other terms are classified according to the latter.

4. All other combinations are not given a summary classification.

Marginals			
Munich	New York	Total	Social Origin Type
374	219	593	Favored nonmanual: Intelligentsia, Civil Servant, Military.
315	162	477	Declasse nonmanual: Nobility, Landowners, Merchants, Clergy, and Middle Class
396	68	464	Workers: Artisans and Workers
876	154	1030	Peasants: Peasants
119	35	154	Nonclassifiable

Appendix 22:

Publications of the Harvard Project on the Soviet Social System

I. Books Published (Russian Research Center Studies, Harvard University Press)

Bauer, Raymond A., Alex Inkeles, and Clyde Kluckhohn: *How the Soviet System Works: Cultural, Psychological, and Social Themes*, 1956.
Berliner, Joseph S.: *Factory and Manager in the USSR*, 1957.
Field, Mark G.: *Doctor and Patient in Soviet Russia*, 1957.

II. Articles and Chapters in Books

Bauer, Raymond A., "The Bolshevik Attitude toward Science," in Carl J. Friedrich, ed., *Totalitarianism*, Cambridge, 1954.
Bauer, Raymond A., "The Implications of the Succession Crisis in the Soviet Union for East-West Relations," *Social Problems*, October 1953.
Bauer, Raymond A., "The Psychology of the Soviet Middle Elite," in Clyde Kluckhohn, H. A. Murray, and D. M. Schneider, eds., *Personality in Nature, Society and Culture*, New York, 1953.
Bauer, Raymond A., "Some Trends in Sources of Alienation from the Soviet System," *Public Opinion Quarterly*, Fall 1955.
Bauer, Raymond A. and David B. Gleicher, "Word-of-Mouth Communication in the Soviet Union," *Public Opinion Quarterly*, Fall 1953.
Beier, Helen and Raymond A. Bauer, "Oleg: A Member of the Soviet 'Golden Youth,' " *The Journal of Abnormal and Social Psychology*, July 1955.
Beier, Helen and Eugenia Hanfmann, "Emotional Attitudes of Former Soviet Citizens as Studied by the Technique of Projective Questions," *The Journal of Abnormal and Social Psychology*, September 1956.
Berliner, Joseph S., "*Blat* is Higher than Stalin," *Problems of Communism*, January–February 1954.
Berliner, Joseph S., "The Informal Organization of the Soviet Firm," *The Quarterly Journal of Economics*, August 1952.
Dicks, Henry V., "Observations on Contemporary Russian Behavior," *Human Relations*, May 1952.
Feldmesser, Robert A., "Social Status and Access to Higher Education: A Comparison of the United States and the Soviet Union," *Harvard Educational Review*, Spring 1957.

Feldmesser, Robert A., "The Persistence of Status Advantages in Soviet Russia." *The American Journal of Sociology,* July 1953.

Field, Mark G., "Alcoholism, Crime and Delinquency in Soviet Society," *Social Problems,* October 1955.

Field, Mark G., "Alcolisme et délinquance en USSR," *Problemes du Communisme,* Mai–Juin 1955.

Field, Mark G., "Drink and Delinquency in the USSR," *Problems of Communism,* May–June 1955.

Field, Mark G., "Former Soviet Citizens' Attitudes toward the Soviet, the German and the American Medical Systems," *American Sociological Review,* December 1955.

Field, Mark G., "Die Pharmazie in der Sowjetunion," *Schweizerische Apotheker Zeitung,* 95:303–311, April 1957.

Field, Mark G., "Russian Medicine: Medical Organization and the Medical Profession." Accepted for publication in *The Transformation of Russian Society since 1861.*

Field, Mark G., "The Professional in Bureaucracy: The Case of the Soviet Physician." Accepted for publication in *Hospital Management.*

Field, Mark G., "The Re-legalization of Abortion in Soviet Russia," *New England Journal of Medicine,* August 30, 1956.

Field, Mark G., "Social Services for the Family in the Soviet Union," *Marriage and Family Living,* International Issue, August 1955.

Field, Mark G., "Socialized Medicine: Soviet Style," *Problems of Communism,* March–April 1954 (a review article).

Field, Mark G., "Some Problems of Soviet Medical Practice: A Sociological Approach," *New England Journal of Medicine,* May 28, 1953.

Field, Mark G., "The Soviet Doctor's Dilemma," *Problems of Communism,* January–February 1957.

Field, Mark G., "The Soviet School: Propaganda and Reality." Accepted for publication in *Problems of Communism* (a review article).

Field, Mark G., "Die soziologische Funktion des Sowjetarztes," *Ost-Probleme,* August 6, 1953 (a translation).

Field, Mark G., "Structured Strain in the Role of the Soviet Physician," *The American Journal of Sociology,* March 1953.

Field, Mark G., "Workday of the Soviet Physician, *"New England Journal of Medicine,* 250:210–211. February 1954.

Friedberg, Maurice, "Russian Writers and Soviet Readers," *The American Slavic and East European Review,* February 1955.

Geiger, H. Kent, "Changing Political Attitudes in Totalitarian Society: A Case Study of the Role of the Family," *World Politics,* January 1956.

Geiger, H. Kent, "Deprivation and Solidarity in the Soviet Urban Family," *American Sociological Review,* January 1955.

Geiger, H. Kent, "Soviet Society Today," *Current History,* January 1956.

Geiger, H. Kent and Alex Inkeles, "The Family in the USSR," *Marriage and Family Living, International Issue on the Family,* November 1954.

Gleicher, David B., "The Professional Soviet Officer." Accepted for publication in *World Politics.*

Gliksman, Jerzy G., "Soviet Labor and the Question of Productivity," *Monthly Labor Review,* June 1957.

Gliksman, Jerzy G., "Terror as Prophylaxis," in Carl J. Friedrich, ed., *Totalitarianism,* Cambridge, 1954.

Hanfmann, Eugenia, "Boris: A Displaced Person," in A. Burton and R. E. Harris, eds., *Clinical Studies of Personality,* Vol. II, New York, 1955.

Hanfmann, Eugenia, and Helen Beier, "The Mental Health of a Group of Russian Displaced Persons," *American Journal of Ortho-Psychiatry,* April 1958.

Hanfmann, Eugenia, "Social Perception in Russian Displaced Persons and an American Comparison Group," *Psychiatry,* May 1957.

Hanfmann, Eugenia and Jacob W. Getzels, "Inter-personal Attitudes of Former Soviet Citizens, as Studied by a Semi-Projective Method," *Psychological Monographs,* Vol. 69, No. 4, 1955.

Inkeles, Alex, "Images of Class Relations Among Former Soviet Citizens," *Social Problems,* January 1956.

Inkeles, Alex, "Social Change and Social Character: The Role of Parental Mediation," *The Journal of Social Issues,* Vol. XI, No. 2, 1955.

Inkeles, Alex, "Social Change in Soviet Russia," in Morroe Berger, Theodore Abel and Charles H. Page, eds., *Freedom and Control in Modern Society,* New York, 1954.

Inkeles, Alex, "The Totalitarian Mystique: Some Impressions of the Dynamics of Totalitarian Society," in Carl J. Friedrich, ed., *Totalitarianism,* Cambridge, 1954.

Inkeles, Alex, and Raymond A. Bauer, "Portrait of Soviet Russia by Russians," *New York Times Magazine,* November 25, 1951.

Inkeles, Alex, Eugenia Hanfmann, and Helen Beier, "Modal Personality and Adjustment to the Soviet Socio-political System," *Human Relations,* Vol. XI, No. 1, 1958.

Inkeles, Alex and Peter H. Rossi, "Multidimensional Ratings of Occupations," *Sociometry,* September 1957.

Kassof, Allen, "The Prejudiced Personality: A Cross-cultural Test," *Social Problems,* Summer 1958.

Kluckhohn, Clyde, "Recent Studies of the National Character of Great Russians," *Human Development Bulletin,* University of Chicago, February 5, 1955.

London, Ivan D., "Contemporary Psychology in the Soviet Union," *Science,* August 31, 1951.

London, Ivan D., "No Comment Necessary!" *American Psychologist,* June 1952.

London, Ivan D., "Psychology in the USSR," *American Journal of Psychology,* July 1951.

London, Ivan D., "Research on Sensory Interaction in the Soviet Union," *Psychological Bulletin,* November 1954.

London, Ivan D., "The Scientific Council on Problems of the Physiological Theory of Academician I. P. Pavlov: A Study in Control," *Science,* July 11, 1952.

London, Ivan D., "Soviet Psychology and Psychiatry," *Bulletin of the Atomic Scientists*, March 1952.

London, Ivan D., "Therapy in Psychiatric Hospitals," *The American Psychologist*, February 1953.

Reshetar, John S., "National Deviation in the Soviet Union," *The American Slavic and East European Review*, April 1953.

Rimberg, John, "The Soviet Film Industry Today," *The Quarterly of Film, Radio, and Television*, Winter 1956.

Rosenblatt, Daniel, "Responses of Former Soviet Citizens to Selected TAT Cards." Accepted for publication in *The Journal of General Psychology*.

Rossi, Peter H. and Raymond A. Bauer, "Some Patterns of Soviet Communications Behavior," *Public Opinion Quarterly*, Winter 1952–1953.

III. Materials duplicated for limited distribution

The list of such materials is too long to reproduce here but may be found in Raymond A. Bauer, Alex Inkeles, and Clyde Kluckhohn, *How the Soviet System Works*, Cambridge, 1956, pp. 252–256.

IV. Publications supported in part by the Harvard Project on the Soviet Social System

Bauer, Raymond A., *Nine Soviet Portraits*, Center for International Studies, Massachusetts Institute of Technology, New York-London, 1955.

Fischer, George, *Soviet Opposition to Stalin: A Case Study in World War II*, Cambridge, 1952.

Reshetar, John S., Jr., *Problems of Analyzing and Predicting Soviet Behavior*, New York, 1955.

Notes

The notes to tables are numbered according to their location within each chapter. To make for easy location the note number is followed by a capital letter and the table number. The questions on which the table is based may be located by reference to the designated section and question number from Appendix 1, "The Written Questionnaires." Sections of the core questionnaire are identified by Roman numerals; otherwise the question number, always given in Arabic numerals, will be preceded by the word "Stratification" or "Job" to identify those two special questionnaires which follow the core questionnaire. Thus, when the table notes identify a question as (I–2), this refers to section I, question 2 of the core written questionnaire: "In what year were you born?"

Chapter I. THE HARVARD PROJECT ON THE SOVIET SOCIAL SYSTEM

1. There is nothing in modern times which comes anywhere near DeTocqueville's classic Democracy in America. The more recent textbooks on American society deal mainly with institutional forms rather than with the details of daily life experience.

2. Frederick Wyle, "A Memorandum on Statistical Data on Soviet Displaced Persons," unpublished report of the Harvard Project on the Soviet Social System, August, 1952. Wyle insists that his figures must be regarded as very approximate. His main sources of information are German wartime statistics and the United Nations survey of postwar refugees.

3. Frederick Wyle, "A Memorandum." As late as 1956, official German sources placed the number of refugees still in their territory as between 80 thousand and 100 thousand, of whom at least half were, however, from the former Baltic States rather than prewar Soviet borders. These last were, however, only a minor remnant of the many times this number who had emigrated to the United States, Canada, Australia and Latin America. See the New York Times, April 10, 1956, p. 12, col. 3.

4. Published estimates of the rate of Soviet postwar defection are virtually nonexistent. Private estimates by Western officials vary considerably, but most officials will say flatly that a precise estimate is impossible since many escapees never pass through official hands. The public tends in general to overestimate the flow of Soviet escapees, confusing this with published estimates of "thousands" of persons fleeing the other Iron Curtain countries as a whole.

5. David I. Dallin and Boris I. Nicolaevsky, Forced Labor in Soviet Russia (New Haven, 1947).

6. Results of these interviews are reported in, Merle Fainsod, "The Komsomols — A Study of Youth Under Dictatorship," The American Political Science Review, Vol. XLV, No. 1, March 1951, and "Controls and Tensions in the Soviet System," The American Political Science Review, Vol. XLIV, No. 2, June 1950.

7. Mr. Raeff is currently Associate Professor of History at Clark University.

8. In the written questionnaire we asked, "Which of the following emigrant political groups do you consider most satisfactory?" For the questionnaire used in Germany we offered a fairly exhaustive list of 18 groups of which we had knowledge. All received some votes. The smallest number, 25 persons, voted for the Hetmanovtsy, a right-wing somewhat extreme, Ukrainian monarchical independence movement of followers of the former Hetman Skoropadsky. The largest number, 608, voted for the ABN or Anti-Communist Block of Nations. The latter was favored in part by its position as first on the list and its resounding name. It also had extremely strong attraction for Ukrainians, Byelorussians and other non-Russians because it claimed to represent all minor nationalities in the USSR. Another large block of votes went to the various Vlasovite organizations: SBONR, the Union for the Struggle for the Liberation of the Peoples of Russia, 339; SVOD, mainly the military arm of SBONR, 161; and the KOV, or Committee of United Vlasovites, 253. Thus, ignoring double voting and the left-right division, there were 753 votes for this block with more appeal to Russians. [See George Fischer, *Soviet Opposition to Stalin* (Cambridge, 1952).]

Only three other groups received more than 100 votes each. The NTS, an extreme Russian nationalist group, received 125 votes. These were balanced by 114 votes for the mildly left-wing League for the Fight for Peoples' Freedom, mainly Russian, and 126 for the URDP, or Ukrainian Workers Democratic Party.

9. A complete list of Project reports is appended to, Raymond A. Bauer, Alex Inkeles and Clyde Kluckhohn, *How the Soviet System Works* (Cambridge, 1956).

10. For a detailed discussion of our interviewing problem, see Alice Bauer, "A Guide for the Interviewing of Soviet Escapees" (unpublished report of the Harvard Project on the Soviet Social System, April 1953).

11. For example, see Mark Field, *Doctor and Patient in Soviet Russia* (Cambridge, 1957), and Joseph Berliner, *Factory and Manager in the USSR* (Cambridge, 1957).

12. Some question has been raised as to the advisability of this procedure as against the more common and methodologically more acceptable one of sending out interviewers who would follow the usual sampling procedures in selecting those to be interviewed. We considered such an approach but were obliged to decide against it. For one thing, the method would have been vastly more expensive, especially since our interview schedule was so long. Where one field agent could get 100 questionnaires in a day we would have needed 100 interviewers per day! Admittedly one of the virtues of the usual procedures is that better sampling enables you to get by with many fewer cases. But we would not have wanted many fewer cases than we got because of the complex types of analysis we anticipated undertaking.

Even if vast sums of money for interviewers had been absolutely no problem, we probably could not have adopted this approach in any event. To be meaningful the procedure requires you know a good deal about the sample characteristics of the population to be studied, and especially about its social ecology. This was not sufficiently well known for the refugee population. In addition, and perhaps most important, the arrival at the door of a pollster, questionnaire in hand, arbitrarily picking out someone in the crowded barracks to interview, was simply unthinkable as a way of getting reliable and valid responses from the refugees.

Our procedure was far from perfect, but we feel it was the most reasonable adjustment to our field conditions of numerous sampling desiderata.

12A. Table 1.

This table differs in certain respects from that given in R. Bauer, A. Inkeles, and C. Kluckhohn, *How the Soviet System Works*, p. 9. The special part of the basic written questionnaire dealing with stratification was there included with 9748 "written questionnaires on special topics." Since it was always given together with the core questionnaire and was completed by the same number of respondents we have included it with 2718 basic questionnaires. In addition several minor specialized questionnaires included in the total of "special topics questionnaires" in *How the Soviet System Works* are not listed here since they do not enter into our analysis in this book.

It is generally but not always the case that those who completed one of the supplementary questionnaires also filled out the core questionnaire. This was least often the case with the family budgets, which were a self-contained unit. Of 1872 who completed that questionnaire, 1439 also filled out the core questionnaire.

Appendix 1 gives the text of the core or basic written questionnaire, the supplement on stratification, and the supplementary questionnaire on ratings of occupations which is there designated "Job." The other questionnaires are not reproduced, but when a question from them is used in a table the question wording is given in the note to the particular table at the rear. These notes are found in order in the notes to each chapter.

In *How the Soviet System Works* the number of postwar Soviet refugees was more stringently defined. The number given here represents all who left Soviet jurisdiction in 1946 and after.

Chapter II. THE SAMPLE

A. Table 2.

In Part 1, of the entire sample of 2718 cases, 2407 are represented. The other 311 cases are accounted for as follows: 2 no answers on the sex question (I–1), 85 male and 40 female no answers to the social group question (I–7), and 132 male and 52 female no answers on the age question (I–2).

In Part 2, the total sample is represented. Social class was assigned by the coder.

1. There was a danger that in a few of the larger camps a homogeneous "camp line" might have developed on Soviet issues. If this were the case such a camp could seriously influence the outcome of our study. In part this was "controlled for" by the fact that our sample included people from a dozen different camps. As a further precaution, however, we made a separate study of the subsample from several of the larger camps. We found that far from being homogeneous and having a "camp line" each camp was marked by great diversity of opinion, whereas people of similar education or occupation tended to see things more alike even when in widely separated locations.

2. *Dostizheniya Sovetskoi Vlasti za 40 Let V Tsifrakh* (Moscow, 1957), p. 11. 2A. Table 3.

Of the entire sample of 2718 cases, only those whose fathers' postrevolutionary social group (V–2) was given as peasant were considered. These cases were further broken down into those whose fathers were dekulakized, 534 cases, and those whose fathers were not dekulakized, 241 cases. Of the 534 respondents with dekulakized fathers only 441 appear in this table, since 6 gave their occupation as student and 87 were housewives or gave no answer on the question concerning their occupation (II–1). Of the 241 respondents with fathers who were not dekulakized, 197 appear in this table, since 5 gave their occupation as student and 39 were housewives or gave no answer on the question concerning their occupation. Job satisfaction was based on II–3.

3. There are two stages of Communist Party membership. The first or "candi-

date" stage is a kind of trial period during which the individual is supposed to be studying the party program and Marxist-Leninist classics. On completing this phase he may be admitted to full membership. Except in periods of rapid growth the membership is predominantly in the full rather than the candidate stage.

4. On the written questionnaire only 36, or little more than 1 per cent, admitted being party members, and 263 acknowledged their membership in the Komsomol. The greater representation of the politically "active" among those who undertook personal interviews may reflect a self-selective bias in that sample. People who had been politically active might be more likely to be the "type" who would volunteer for or undertake a personal interview. It is our opinion, however, that the explanation lies more in what it meant to our respondents to risk admitting *in their own handwriting* — as against in a confidential oral statement — that they had been party members. This assumption is strongly supported by the facts presented in Chapter III with regard to those who both gave a personal interview and filled out the questionnaire. None of the 7 (out of 46) who admitted Komsomol membership in the oral interview acknowledged that fact on their questionnaires.

5. On the American side, much of this information comes from personal conversations with American personnel. Several members of our own staff had been involved in the repatriation. Of particular interest is George Fischer, *Soviet Opposition to Stalin* (Cambridge, 1952).

6. Through at least 1956 the Soviet Union operated a .Repatriation Commission in Germany, directed from East Berlin, with the objective of inducing the return to Soviet authority of those who had not yet succeeded in emigrating. About 330 were in May reported to have returned or "redefected" in the "past year." Most Western observers seem to regard the redefection rate as minor, and felt it was restricted to those who were in quite hopeless situations with regard to employment or emigration prospects. See the *New York Times,* May 9, 1956, p. lx, col. 4; May 10, 4:3; May 15, 30:3; May 16, 29:1.

6A. Table 4.

Of a total of 2718 respondents, there were 1862 men and 854 women with 2 no answers to this question (I–1). Only those 21 and over in 1950 are considered in this table. Of 1862 men only 1694 appear here, since 20 listed themselves as under 21 years old and 148 gave no answer to the question of age (I–2). Of these 1694 men, 1397 are considered in the part of this table dealing with the respondent's occupation, since 51 listed themselves as students and 246 gave no answer to the question on own occupation (II–1). The base for the number of fathers is, of course, the same as for the respondent sons, but only 1448 fathers are considered, since 75 respondents listed their fathers' occupations (V–3) as being "other" and 171 gave no answer. Of the 854 women in the total sample, 792 are considered in this table, since 7 listed themselves as being under 21 years old and 55 gave no answer to the question of age. Of these 792 women, 473 are considered in the part of this table dealing with the respondent's occupation, since 63 listed themselves as students and 256 were housewives or gave no answer to the question on own occupation. The part of this table dealing with the occupations of the respondents' mothers (V–6) reports on only 326 cases, since of 792 relevant women 447 listed their mothers as nonworking housewives, 7 put them in the "other" category, and 12 listed their mothers as working but did not specify the job or type of work.

7. Cf. Robert Feldmesser, "The Persistence of Status Advantages in Soviet Russia," *The American Journal of Sociology,* 59:19–27 (1953). For further discussion, see Chapter IV.

8. Cf. Eugenia Hanfmann and Helen Beier, "Psychological Patterns of Soviet Citizens," Part I, "The Level of Psychological Health of the Total Clinical Group" (unpublished report of the Harvard Project on the Soviet Social System, August 1954), pp. 6–11.

9. See Allen Kassof, "A Comparison of the Attitudes and Experiences of Wartime (Displaced Persons) and Postwar (Recent Defectors) Respondents" (unpublished report of the Harvard Project on the Soviet Social System, July 1954).

10. Ivan D. London and Miriam B. London, "Differential Reactions of Recent and Earlier Defectors to Anti-Soviet Propaganda Themes," *Psychological Reports*, 2:285–292 (1956), report finding some differences in the manner in which recent defectors as against earlier "nonreturners" react to propaganda themes. It was of course precisely the expectation that there might be such differences which had earlier led us to undertake our comparison of the two groups. The fact that for the questions we examined there were no major differences does not, of course, preclude the possibility that on other questions such as those examined by the Londons there would be such differences. Unfortunately, the report by the Londons gives no indication of how many matched cases they have among their total of 425, nor of the nature of the matching, if any, which they made of recent and earlier defectors. It also gives no indication of the precise size of the differences observed. Their material is presumably meant, therefore, to be illustrative and prefatory to a more systematic presentation. Until we have that fuller account we have no alternative but to assume that in the range of questions we investigated the differentiation between early and later defectors is not important. There are, of course, exceptions to this general statement. As we noted earlier in this chapter the postwar refugees did seem to our clinical psychologists to be less well adjusted emotionally.

10A. Table 5.

Of a total of 102 life-history interviews used in compiling this "matched sample" of wartime and postwar refugees, 99 are used in this table, since 3 gave "other" education in response to the question on years of completed formal education (VII–1). The questions used were, in descending order, IV–4B, IV–13, II–8, IV–19, and VIII–2. The differences between figures in parentheses and the original base of 50 wartime and 49 postwar are due to the number not answering the particular question.

In the second portion of the table dealing with all wartime and postwar refugees combined, there were 49 with 0–7 years of education (low) and 50 with 8 or more years (high). The difference between these figures in parentheses and the original base of 49 with low education and 50 with high education are again due to the number not answering the particular question.

11. Cf. Raymond A. Bauer, "Arrest in the Soviet Union" (unpublished report of the Harvard Project on the Soviet Social System, June 1953).

11A. Table 6.

Of a total of 2718 cases, 1664 are represented in this table. The remaining 1054 are accounted for as follows: 785 no answers on the personal arrest profile (Appendix 7); 197 no answers on the question of reliability of the Soviet press (VIII–2); and 72 not classified on education level (VII–1).

12. See Chapter XI where the relation of arrest to hostility and disaffection is discussed.

Chapter III. SOME CONSIDERATIONS OF METHOD AND METHODOLOGY

1. Alice Bauer, "A Guide for the Interviewing of Soviet Escapees" (unpublished report of the Harvard Project on the Soviet Social System, April 1953).

2. Fifteen per cent indicated Lenin did "some good and some harm."

2A. Table 7.

High flattery indicates a score of 4 or 5, and low flattery a score of 0 on the flattery scale (Appendix 14). Moderate flattery (score of 3) was omitted in this table. The five questions on evaluations of Soviet life are, reading from top to bottom, based on III–1, IV–31, IV–29, IV–9, and II–3. Social class is based on I–7.

Of the 1277 cases not considered in this table, the following were omitted on successive sorts, leaving 1441 cases which appear in the table: students (63), other (45) and DK (126) on the social class question; moderate (222) and DK (821) on the flattery scale. The N's used here are the medians of the total numbers, since there were variations in the number of no answers to the five questions in this table.

3. The table given below in this note will suggest the complexity of the relation of flattery scores to other response patterns. It is set up to test the assumption that persons who said extremely favorable things about Americans would also slant the reporting of their other attitudes in the direction they thought Americans

The Relation of Own Attitudes to Expectation of American Preferences

(A comparison of low "flatterers" with high "flatterers.")

Respondents' Opinions	Image of American Opinions				
	(1)	(2)	(3) Difference due to flattery[a]	(4) Difference due to projection[b]	N = 100%
1. FREEDOM OF SPEECH	Against	For			
Against					
Low Flatterers	42%	58%			(460)
High Flatterers	49	51	7%		(490)
For				31%	
Low Flatterers	11	89			(290)
High Flatterers	8	92	3		(339)
2. JOB SECURITY					
Against					
Low Flatterers	60	40			(261)
High Flatterers	61	39	1		(166)
For				26	
Low Flatterers	34	66			(385)
High Flatterers	27	73	7		(478)
3. STATE OWNERSHIP OF TRANSPORT AND COMMUNICATIONS					
Against					
Low Flatterers	83	17			(67)
High Flatterers	87	13	4		(106)
For				41	
Low Flatterers	42	58	12		(565)
High Flatterers	30	70	12		(557)

themselves might prefer. If this is the case, then we should predict that persons who were "flatterers" by the criterion of the "flattery" index would show a greater concurrence between their own expressed attitudes and what they thought Americans wanted, than would persons who were "low on flattery."

The results of our test of this hypothesis are summarized in the table given below. Columns 1 and 2 of this table record the respondents' expectation of what Americans desire. The rows record their own preference on the same issues.

Column 3 records differences which are attributable to "flattery." Column 4 records differences which are attributable to "projection," the tendency to see others in one's own image rather than shape one's own answers to the wishes of others.

Since all these attitudes are related to education in our sample, an initial educational control was employed in the analysis. The figures as presented are a result of averaging the percentages of responses in the high and low educational categories. This gives us in effect a "weighted" average, which treats the data as though there were equal numbers of respondents in each of the educational groups.

A perusal of this table shows that in no instance is our hypothesis violated. The high flatterers show a greater concurrence between their own expressed opinions and what they expect Americans to want than do the low flatterers. Thus, high flatterers who believe Americans are against freedom of speech are 7 per cent more likely to report that they themselves are opposed to it (49 per cent for high flatterers, as compared to 42 per cent for low flatterers). The smallest difference is on the question of job security, where high flatterers who prefer advancement to job security are 1 per cent more likely to see Americans as preferring advancement to security (61 per cent to 60 per cent). The biggest difference is on state ownership of transportation and communications. Of those who see Americans as preferring state ownership, 70 per cent of high flatterers say they prefer state ownership, in contrast to 58 per cent of the low flatterers. The expected differences are obtained in a total of 11 out of 12 possible comparisons when respondents are separated on the basis of high and low education. They are obtained in six out of six instances when the educational groups are collapsed, as in this table. Considering the large numbers of cases with which we are dealing, there can be little doubt but that our hypothesis that high flatterers will show greater concurrence between their own opinions and their expectations of American opinions than do low flatterers is verified in *principle*. But a more careful inspection of this table shows that in *practice* the effect of "flattery" on the reporting of one's own attitudes is virtually meaningless.

There is a far more pronounced tendency for respondents to project their own attitudes onto Americans regardless of whether they are "flatterers" or not. Whereas "flattery" accounted for differences of from 1 per cent to 12 per cent, projection accounts for much larger differences. Even a low flatterer is much more likely to see Americans as favoring freedom of speech if he himself is in favor of it. Only 58 per cent of the low flatterers who are against freedom of speech think Americans are for it. But 89 per cent of those who favor it themselves think that Americans do. This pattern holds for all groups on all questions. The minimum difference is 26 per cent, in the instance of low flatterers on the question of job security. If they are against job security, only 40 per cent think Americans are for it. If they favor job security, 66 per cent see Americans as favoring it. The biggest difference is one of 41 per cent, in the instance of low flatterers on the question of state ownership of transportation and communications. Seventeen per cent of those who oppose state ownership think Americans favor it, but 58 per cent of those who favor it think Americans do. The weight of this evidence is so strong that one can only conclude that our respondents were much more likely to see Americans in the image of their own values and wishes, rather than to report their own attitudes in ways they thought pleasing to Americans.

a. Differences attributable to flattery are derived by subtracting the percentage of low flatterers who give a concurring response from the percentage of high flatterers who do so. Thus, on the question on freedom of speech, 42 per cent of low flatterers who are *against* freedom of speech report that they expect Americans to be against it. However, 49 per cent of high flatterers who are opposed to freedom of speech indicate they think Americans concur with their own opinion. The difference (49 minus 42) of 7 per cent, is assumed to be a reflection of the fact that high flatterers will be more likely to report opinions that concur with the opinions they expect Americans to hold.

b. Differences attributable to projection are computed by subtracting the nonconcurring from the concurring responses for low flatterers. Thus, 89 per cent of low flatterers who favor freedom of speech believe Americans concur in this opinion, while only 58 per cent of low flatterers who are against freedom of speech believe Americans are in favor of it. The difference, 31 per cent, is assumed to be a measure of the extent to which respondents who are low flatterers tend to see others as like themselves. The figures in this column are computed on the basis of the responses of low flatterers. Identical figures can be computed for high flatterers if the total percentage due to "flattery" is subtracted from the difference between concurring and nonconcurring responses. Thus, on freedom of speech, 92 per cent minus 51 per cent — 41 per cent. From this we subtract 7 per cent plus 3 per cent, and get 31 per cent.

4. For a detailed discussion, see David Gleicher, "The Meaning of Distortion: A Note on the Causes and Correlates of Hostility Toward the Soviet Regime," in David Gleicher and Isabel Caro, "Patterns of Ideological and Value Orientation among Former Soviet Citizens" (unpublished report of the Harvard Project on the Soviet Social System, October 1954).

4A. Table 8.

High distortion indicates a score of 2, 3, or 4, moderate distortion a score of 1, and low distortion a score of 0 on the distortion scale (Appendix 11). The response "once in favor" of the Soviet regime is in answer to III–1. Social group is based on I–7.

On successive sorts, 619 cases were omitted from consideration in this table as follows: 63, 45, and 126 were listed as student, other, or DK, respectively, on the social class question; 320 were NA on the distortion scale; 57 were NA and 8 were other on the disaffection question, leaving a base for this table of 2099 cases.

5. The relation between anti-Soviet sentiment as measured on the distortion scale and the reaction to Soviet institutions and life is dealt with in some detail in Chapter XI.

5A. Table 9.

High distortion indicates a score of 2, 3, or 4, and low distortion a score of 0 on the distortion scale (Appendix 11). Moderate distortion (score of 1) was omitted in this table. The three questions on government ownership, reading from top to bottom, are based on IV–31, IV–29, and IV–12. Social group is based on I–7.

On successive sorts, 1058 cases were omitted from consideration in this table as follows: students (63), other (45), and DK (126) on the social class question; NA (342) and moderate (482) on the distortion scale. The N's used here are the medians of the total numbers, since there were variations in the number of no answers to the three government ownership questions, leaving a base for this table of 1660 cases.

6. Babette Whipple, "Munich–New York Comparisons as Validity Tests of the PPQ" (unpublished report of the Harvard Project on the Soviet Social System, September 1954).

7. Students of public opinion have long been struck by the fact that a social group — based on age, occupation, sex or similar criteria — will yield the same *proportion* giving a particular response at two different times despite the fact that many *individuals* in the group will have shifted their opinion over the same span. An interesting exploration of the factors involved will be found in Patricia Kendall, *Conflict and Mood* (Free Press: Glencoe, Ill., 1954).

8. Edward Wasiolek, "Responses by Former Soviet Citizens to a Questionnaire vs. Life History Interview" (unpublished report of the Harvard Project on the Soviet Social System, July 1954).

9. It must be remembered that some of the questions which were part of the personal interview were not actually administered orally, but filled in by the respondent between interview sessions. Hence, the impact of the face-to-face situation would appear also to have carried over to situations in which the interviewer was not physically present, but in which the respondent felt himself to be addressing the interviewer.

10. The most difficult of our processing jobs was that of coding the oral interviews. The final report by Daniel Rosenblatt, "Technical Report on Coding and Reliability Studies," contains an extended discussion of the procedures employed. We note here only that all of the reliability coefficients in those instances in which the code was retained for quantitative work ran between .70 and .83. This means that somewhere between 7 and 8 out of 10 coders could be expected to code exactly alike on every code. We use the word "exactly" because our criteria of reliable coding were extremely conservative. A judgment was counted as unreliable if it did not fit into exactly the same category as the standard of judgment. In many instances errors were of a minor nature. When some questions were coded on a continuum, an answer placed into an adjacent category (i.e., respondent felt "strongly" as compared to "very strongly") would be counted wrong, even though in the process of analysis the two categories might very well be collapsed. In other cases, coders did not discover information, and coded a particular item as "no information" or "not answered." This too was counted as an error, although it would result only in the case being excluded from analysis rather than in a positive error. If such minor errors are discounted, the reliability of coding rises to somewhere in the vicinity of .90.

11. It is an interesting incidental fact that on the two jobs following that of party secretary, the proportion not answering again fell, but remained higher than for any other jobs. There was nothing in these jobs themselves to indicate that the rate of "no answers" was due to their inherent characteristics. It would appear that the conflict produced by passing judgment on the job of party secretary had not been entirely dissipated and persisted to influence the respondents' approach to the final two jobs. This finding is one of the many that makes us skeptical that either indifference or collusion were of such a magnitude as to affect our major conclusions. Most of the seemingly unusual responses we encountered proved to be natural and expected reactions to the particular circumstances.

12. For a detailed presentation of the results and discussion of their probable significance, see Babette Whipple, "Munich–New York Comparisons."

13. After the initial matching on age, residence, education, and social class, the

two samples were checked for congruence on seventeen additional demographic variables. Of these several seemed of minor importance for our purposes, e.g., among the European ("Munich") cases there were more single men and more "only" children. There was one difference which we though might have a major effect on attitudes: a much higher proportion of those in "Munich" than in the United States ("New York") were unemployed at the time they completed the questionnaire. Further controls applied to take account of this difference revealed that employment status did not seem to have a strong influence on the respondents' answers to the questionnaire. See Babette Whipple, "Munich–New York Comparisons."

A qualitative comparison, based on a study of five matched personal interview cases led Mrs. Whipple to suggest further differences between the Munich and New York groups. For example, the group in the United States seemed to have greater facility with words, which would give a more immediate impression of more violent anti-Soviet sentiment; more of the New York people may have been successful in their occupational pursuits while in the Soviet Union; and more of the New York sample may have shown greater degrees of authoritarian belief or personality orientation. Although such differences may have been important in subtle ways, they are very elusive and resisted being brought under systematic control in the analysis.

13A. Table 10.

This table is based on a matched deck of 980 (490 Munich and 490 New York) cases. Only the manual (skilled and ordinary workers and peasants) social classes (I–7) are considered here (216 cases, evenly divided between Munich and New York). The attitude and experience questions, reading from top to bottom, are based on: flattery scale, score 0 (Appendix 14); occupational satisfaction-frustration index, scores 5 and 6 (Appendix 19); distortion scale, scores 3 and 4 (Appendix 11); political rights index, classes I and II (Appendix 20); IV–19, "a little harm" and "much harm" combined; III–1, "leaders, regime opposed to people." The N's given in parentheses reflect the loss of cases from the maximum base of 108 resulting from the differential no answer pattern for the several questions and indices.

13B. Table 11.

A matched deck of 980 (490 Munich and 490 New York) cases is used in this table. Social class is based on I–7. The attitude and experience questions, reading from top to bottom, are based on: II–3; IV–21; VIII–1, C; VIII–2; II–8; VII–3 ("same opportunity as others" and "more opportunity than others" combined), inapplicable cases not included; IV–18. The N's used here are the medians of the total numbers, since there were variations in the number of no answers to the seven questions in this table.

14. Reported in: Eugenia Hanfmann and Helen Beier, "Psychological Patterns of Soviet Citizens: A Summary of Clinical Psychological Aspects of the Soviet Defection" (unpublished report of the Harvard Project on the Soviet Social System, August 1954).

15. For a discussion of the issues raised in this section see Hanan C. Selvin, "A Critique of Tests of Significance in Survey Research," *American Sociological Review*, 22:519–527 (1957).

Chapter IV. OCCUPATIONAL STRATIFICATION AND MOBILITY

1. For discussion of Lenin's role at the Congress, see Isaac Deutscher, *Soviet Trade Union* (London, 1950). Royal Institute of International Affairs.

2. The texts of these decrees are available in English translation in J. H. Meisel and E. S. Kozera, *Materials for the Study of the Soviet System* (Ann Arbor, 1950), Documents No. 21, 31, 40, and 54.

3. See L. E. Hubbard, *The Economics of Soviet Agriculture* (London, 1939), pp. 77–78; and John Maynard, *The Russian Peasant* (New York, 1949), pp. 121–122.

4. Hubbard, *Soviet Agriculture*, pp. 75–76.

5. See Alexander Baykov, *The Development of the Soviet Economic System* (New York, 1957), pp. 39–44.

6. Baykov, *The Development*, pp. 144–145.

7. See Abram Bergson, *The Structure of Soviet Wages* (Cambridge, 1944).

8. Stalin, *Leninism* (New York, 1942), pp. 212–219.

9. *Narodnoe Khozyaistvo SSR* (Moscow, 1956), p. 19.

10. See A. Inkeles, "Social Stratification and Mobility in the Soviet Union: 1940–50," *American Sociological Review*, 15:465–79 (1950).

11. Most studies of the desirability of occupations have included a longer list of jobs. Rather than extend the list, however, we decided to explore more deeply the factors associated with the overall desirability of occupations in the USSR, and asked respondents to rate each of these occupations according to their desirability on each of four dimensions — pay, popular esteem, personal satisfaction, and political safety — in addition to its overall desirability. The contribution of these several dimensions to the overall desirability of various jobs is discussed in Peter Rossi and Alex Inkeles, "Multidimensional Ratings of Occupations," *Sociometry*, 20:234–251 (September 1957).

12. The original scoring scheme in the American study was 5, 4, 3, 2, 1. The proportion in each category was multiplied by the appropriate weight and the sum of the products divided by 5. This leads to the ambiguous outcome of a maximum score of 100 but a minimum score of 20 rather than zero. See "Jobs and Occupations: A Popular Evaluation," in Reinhard Bendix and Seymour M. Lipset, eds., *Class, Status and Power* (Glencoe, III; 1953). We have therefore recomputed the American data on the same basis as the Soviet data. Scores are 100, 75, 50, 25 and 0. The proportion in each category is multiplied by the appropriate weight and the total divided by 100.

12A. Table 12.

Soviet occupations were rated on "general desirability"; American on "general standing." For both countries a five-point scale scored 0, 25, 50, 75, and 100 was used. The ratings represent averages of scores, given by rating populations, using the weights cited. This introduces some changes in the American scores as previously published.

Desirability of Soviet occupations is based on Part A to questions in the Job questionnaire 1–13. Of the 2146 persons who completed the Job questionnaire, the number of no answers to the questions varied and the N given here represents the median of the total numbers answering each question.

The original American figures as published in "Jobs and Occupations: A Popular Evaluation," in Bendix and Lipset, eds., *Class, Status, and Power*, pp. 411–418, are, reading from top to bottom, 93, 89, 84, 86, 81, 80, 78, 60, 76, 50. These scores were originally calculated on a five-point scale with the lowest score 20 rather than 0 as for the Soviet data. Since a range of 0–100 is easier to read, the American scores were recalculated on the same scale used for the Soviet occupations, so that an occupation voted "excellent" by everyone, would have a score of 100, and one voted very poor by everyone would have a score of 0 rather than 20.

13. The distribution of responses with regard to party secretary was markedly bi-modal, suggesting the ambiguity of the stimulus this occupation presented to the refugee group.

14. The same tendency for population subgroups to be in high agreement about occupational rankings has also been observed in similar studies in the United States and Japan. See Alex Inkeles and Peter Rossi, "National Comparisons of Occupational Prestige," *American Journal of Sociology,* 61:329–339 (January 1956).

15. Alex Inkeles and Peter H. Rossi, "National Comparisons." The correlation with the United States is based on scores given in the original United States study, not as here adapted to be more strictly comparable with the Soviet scoring system.

16. *Oktyabr,* No. 10, 1944, pp. 119–121.

17. In 1939, the last census year, it was reported that by occupation 57 per cent of the population were engaged in agriculture, forestry and fishing. See Frank Lorimer, *The Population of the Soviet Union* (Geneva, 1946), p. 106. Fragmentary data for 1955 listed 43 per cent so engaged (*Narodnoe Khozyaistvo,* p. 187).

18. The following table shows an effect of social origin on women's occupational mobility comparable to that given in the text (Table 13) for men only.

OCCUPATIONAL FATE OF DAUGHTERS: BY FATHER'S OCCUPATION [a]

| | Respondent's Origin | | | |
Respondent's Occupation	Profes- sional-ad- ministrative	Semipro- fessional white- collar	All workers	Peasants
Professional	53%	34%	9%	0%
Semiprofessional and white-collar	47	63	44	17
All workers	0	3	41	26
Collective farmers	0	0	6	57
N = 100%	(45)	(74)	(54)	(58)

(a) Of the 357 females (I–1) 21–40 in 1940 (I–2), 231 appear in this table. The remainder were eliminated on successive sorts as follows: other (17) and DK (31) on father's occupation; students (18) and DK (60) on respondent's occupation.

18A. Table 13.

Respondent's origin is based on father's occupation (V–3). Professional-administrative combines the following: political or military administrative positions; economic administrative positions, business, managerial, landowners, etc.; arts; professions and applied science. Semiprofessional includes: semiprofessional; military (below field grade). Skilled worker includes: artisan craftsman, small shopkeeper; skilled worker.

Respondent's occupation is based on II–1. Professional includes: arts; applied sciences; professional; high managerial personnel and all military. Ordinary worker includes: semiskilled worker; unskilled worker.

There were 1325 respondents who were 21–40 in 1940 (I–2) of whom 968 were males (I–1). Only 765 are considered in this table, since on successive sorts the following were omitted: other (42) and DK (86) on father's occupation; advanced students (17) and DK, unclassifiable, or secondary students (58) on respondent's occupation.

19. Estimates developed by Robert Feldmesser in "The Persistence of Status Advantages in Soviet Russia," *American Journal of Sociology*, 59:19–27 (1953).

20. We are indebted to Nicholas DeWitt for these estimates.

21. Data on the United States, France and Germany from Seymour M. Lipset and Natalie Rogoff, "Class and Opportunity in Europe and the U.S.," *Commentary*, December 1954. Soviet data are from a table (not shown) for mobility of *all males* in the sample, according to fathers' postrevolutionary occupations and sons' occupations in 1940.

22. These events are discussed in Raymond A. Bauer, *The New Man in Soviet Psychology* (Cambridge, 1952), especially pp. 112–114.

23. The problem as it has been faced in America is discussed in Byron S. Hollingshead, *Who Should Go to College* (New York, 1952). A local but striking case of the extent to which the fathers' higher status tended to compensate for the lesser intelligence of some of their sons will be found in Elbridge Sibley, "Some Demographic Clues to Stratification," in Bendix and Lipset, eds., *Class, Status and Power*. For a general review of the literature see L. G. Thomas, *The Occupational Structure and Education* (Englewood, 1956).

23A. Table 14.

Educational level is based on VII–1 and includes cases with educational level inferred. Occupational level is based on II–1, and the categories are combined as described in notes to Table 13.

Of the 968 males (I–1) aged 21–40 in 1940 (I–2), 825 are considered here. The remainder were omitted on successive sorts as follows: advanced students (21) and DK, unclassifiable or secondary students (81) on occupational level; graduate work (10) and other (31) on educational level.

24. Thomas, *Occupational Structure*, p. 352.

25. Richard Centers, "Attitude and Belief in Relation to Occupational Stratification," *Journal of Social Psychology*, 27:159–185 (1948).

25A. Table 15.

Respondent's origin is based on father's occupation (V–3). Respondent's occupation is based on II–1, and the categories are combined as described in notes to Table 13, except that here the semiprofessional category includes both semiprofessional and white-collar.

Education is based on VII–1 and includes cases with educational level inferred. High education includes: 10 years; some higher education; completed higher education; graduate work.

Of the 675 respondents aged 21–40 (I–2) of unskilled worker or peasant origin, 583 are considered in this table. The remainder were eliminated on successive sorts as follows: other (22) on education; advanced student (3) and DK, unclassifiable, housewives, or secondary students (67) on respondent's occupation.

26. For details see Chapter VI, especially Table 39.

27. For a review of relevant studies, see Thomas, *The Occupational Structure*, pp. 24–25.

28. Richard M. Stephenson, "Mobility Orientation and Stratification of 1,000 Ninth Graders," *American Sociological Review*, 22:204–212 (April 1957).

28A. Table 16.

Respondent's origin is based on father's occupation (V–3), and the categories are combined as described in notes to Table 13, except that white-collar is included with the semiprofessional category and all categories of workers are combined.

Occupation aspired to is based on V–9. Workers includes: skilled workers; workers.

Of the 374 males (I–1) under 21 in 1940 (I–2), 230 are represented in this table. The remainder were eliminated in successive sorts as follows: other (8) and DK (25) on father's occupation type; other (8) and DK (103) on adolescent job choice.

29. See Genevieve Knupfer, "Portrait of the Underdog," and Herbert Hyman, "The Value Systems of Different Classes," in *Class, Status and Power*, pp. 255–263, and 426–442.

29A. Table 17.

Respondent's origin is based on father's occupation (V–3), and the categories are combined as described in Table 13, except that professional and semiprofessional and white-collar are here combined and all workers are combined.

Respondent's occupation is based on II–1, and the categories are combined as described in notes to Table 13, except that semiprofessional and white-collar are combined as are all workers.

Desire for a career is based on II–9, and "desired" a career includes the first three responses.

Of the 968 males (I–1) 21–40 in 1940 (I–2), 675 are included in this table. The remainder were eliminated on successive sorts as follows: other (42) and DK (86) on father's occupation type; advanced student (17) and DK, unclassifiable, or secondary students (58) to own occupation; other (11) and DK (62) to desire for a career.

29B. Table 18.

Respondent's origin is based on father's occupation (V–3), and the categories are combined as described in the notes to Table 13, except that semiprofessional and white-collar are here combined as are all workers.

Job aspired to is based on V–9. Professional-administrative includes: applied science; medicine; military, naval, aviation, merchant marine; professional.

Fulfillment of aspiration is based on own occupation (II–1). Aspiration is considered fulfilled if: those aspiring to arts had as their occupation — arts; those aspiring to professional-administrative had as their occupation — applied sciences, professional, high managerial personnel and all military; those aspiring to semiprofessional, white-collar had as their occupation — semiprofessional, white-collar.

Of the 968 males (I–1) 21–40 in 1940 (I–2), 315 are represented in this table. The remainder were omitted on successive sorts as follows: other (42) and DK (86) to father's occupation type; other (15), unspecified non-manual (14), and DK (222) to job aspiration; advanced student (13) and DK, unclassifiable or secondary students (30) to own occupation. The remaining 231 cases were eliminated because they aspired to manual jobs, and we here consider only aspiration to white-collar jobs.

30. Richard Centers, "Motivational Aspects of Occupational Stratification," *Journal of Social Psychology*, 28:187–217 (1948). Similar results were obtained in 1937 with the question, "Have you a good chance to get ahead in life and become fairly well off?" See Arthur W. Kornhauser, "Analysis of 'Class' Structure of Contemporary American Society — Psychological Bases of Class Divisions," in G. W. Hartmann and Theodore Newcomb, eds., *Industrial Conflict* (New York, 1939).

30A. Table 19.

Of the 968 males (I–1) 21–40 in 1940 (I–2) in the sample, 232 are not represented in this table. These cases were omitted on successive sorts as follows: other (42) and DK (86) on father's occupation; student (17) and DK (58) on own occupation; DK (29) on chance for a career.

Respondent's origin is based on father's occupation type (V–3). These origins have been combined as described in the notes to Table 13, except that here the worker category includes the combined skilled worker category plus that of ordinary worker.

Respondent's occupation is based on II–1. The occupations are combined as described in the notes to Table 13, except that the skilled worker and ordinary worker categories are here combined.

Chance for a career is based on II–8.

31. See Kornhauser, "Analysis of 'Class Structure,'" especially pp. 239–240.

32. These findings were developed by Alice Rossi and are presented in her report, "Generational Differences in the Soviet Union" (unpublished report of the Harvard Project on the Soviet Social System, July 1954).

32A. Table 20.

Age is based on I–2. Social group is based on I–7, and intelligentsia includes party-Soviet apparatus and intelligentsia. Desire for a career is based on II–9. Those desiring a career gave answers 1–3; those not desiring a career gave answers 4–5. Chance for a career is based on II–8.

Of the 1862 males (I–1) in the sample, 473 are not considered in this table and were eliminated on successive sorts as follows: DK (148) on age; students (29), other (30), and DK (69) on social class; other (20) and DK (155) on desire for a career; DK (22) on chance for a career.

33. Quoted in Y. Marin, "The Proposed Soviet Educational Reform," *Bulletin of the Institute for the Study of the USSR* (Munich), Vol. V, No. 11 (November 1958), p. 31.

Chapter V. MAKING A LIVING

1. Maurice Dobb, *Soviet Economic Development Since 1917* (New York, 1948); Harry Schwartz, *Russia's Soviet Economy* (New York, 1954); Donald Hodgman, *Industrial Production in the USSR, 1928–1951* (Cambridge, 1954).

2. See Warren Eason, "Population and Labor Force," in Abram Bergson, ed., *Soviet Economic Growth* (Evanston, 1953), p. 110.

2A. Table 21.

USSR: Per cent answering "yes" to — "Did you like the job you held in 1940?" (II–3). US: Per cent answering "satisfied" to — "Are you satisfied or dissatisfied with your present job?" (Centers, "Motivational Aspects of Occupational Stratification," *Journal of Social Psychology*, 28:109, 1948). Germany: Per cent who would choose present occupation in response to: "If you were again 15 years old and could start again, would you choose your present occupation or another one?" (from unpublished poll data kindly made available through the courtesy of S. Martin Lipset). Sweden and Norway: Per cent giving satisfied response to question — "Are you satisfied with your present occupation, or do you think that something else would suit you better?" (Cantril, *Public Opinion*, p. 535).

3. Personal communication from S. M. Lipset.

4. *Doxa Bolletino*, Anno viii, No. 20–21 (November 1954). We are indebted to M. Lipset and J. Linz for calling this material to our attention.

5. The relation between indices of hostility to the Soviet system and to the regime, on the one hand, and reported job satisfaction, on the other, are discussed in Chapter XI. That discussion, however, is restricted to the effect of job satisfaction on political orientation.

6. From life-history interviews. All materials based on the life-history interviews, must, of course, be evaluated in the light of the small numbers in each of the occupational groups.

7. See Peter Rossi and Alex Inkeles, "Multi-Dimensional Ratings of Occupations," *Sociometry*, 20:234–51 (September 1957).

8. "Above average" exposure to arrest danger includes the response "one of the most dangerous" and "more dangerous than some" on the question on arrest from Job questionnaire. The per cents are based on the total sample of 2146 who completed questionnaire.

9. Jerzy Gliksman, "Conditions of Industrial Labor in the USSR: A Study of the Incentive System in Soviet Industry" (unpublished report of the Harvard Project on the Soviet Social System, October 1954).

10. In this paragraph we are paraphrasing a memorandum prepared by Mrs. Doris Held.

10A. Table 22.

This table is based on a Sentence-Completion Test administered to 316 of those who took the personal interview. The sentence fragment begins "When the instruments he needed were not delivered in time. . . ." Social group was assigned, not chosen by the respondent, on the basis of occupation and education.

Of the total number of cases (316), 259 are represented here. The remainder were either student, other, or DK on social group or they were other or DK in answer to the sentence fragment.

11. See Joseph Berliner, "Recollected Budgets of Soviet Households in 1940" (unpublished report of the Harvard Project on the Soviet Social System, June 1954).

12. A family budget questionnaire was developed for peasants, and was completed by a substantial number. The complexity of the finances of the peasant, however, coupled with the fact that the mean education of the peasants made it difficult for them to follow the detailed instructions, yielded results too unreliable to permit analysis of the data.

13. The phrasing of the question "Was your pay commensurate (on an equal level) with the pay of people who held other types of jobs in the USSR?" proved, perhaps understandably, ambiguous to a substantial number of our respondents. In addition to 1713 who simply checked off "yes" or "no," 435 wrote in an explanation to the effect that their salary was "higher" or "lower" than that of others. Cross checking these answers against other items revealed that those who said yes almost invariably meant that their pay was equal to or better than that of others. In Table 24 and throughout our analysis we have, therefore, grouped those who answered the question by saying either "yes" or "higher" as satisfied, those who said either "no" or "lower" as dissatisfied.

This ambiguity may have had some impact on the proportions who emerge as satisfied with their pay. We believe, however, that a more important influence on the fact that less than 60 per cent of the top occupational group expressed satisfaction with its pay level was the availability as a reference group of top Communist Party and other officials who made much more.

13A. Table 23.

Data on income was collected through a special questionnaire. Limits of space preclude including the questionnaire form among our appendices, but a full report will be found in Joseph Berliner, "Recollected Budgets of Soviet Households in 1940," (unpublished report of the Harvard Project on the Soviet Social System, 1954).

Of those who completed the budget questionnaire, 983 had also completed the general written questionnaire and we could transfer the data on their income status to other IBM cards to relate income to other variables. Of those 983, only 677 are represented in this table. The remainder were housewives, students, or persons who did not report an occupation. The table is, therefore, based exclusively on those who personally and directly reported their *own* income.

Income data in this table is based on "annual income of subject." This is "annual nominal income" which is the average yearly base pay, net of special bonuses and before deductions at the source. For salaried and fixed wage personnel it is the annual pay rate plus average overtime. For piece-rate workers it is the average annual earnings. Occupation is based on II–1. Professional-administrative includes: arts; applied sciences; professional; high managerial personnel and all military. Peasants are excluded for the reason given in note 12 to this chapter.

14. Data for the United States are from: Richard Centers, "Motivational Aspects of Occupational Stratification," *Journal of Social Psychology*, 28:187–217 (1948), p. 196.

14A. Table 24.

Occupation is based on II–1 and the professional-administrative category is combined as explained in notes to Table 23. Satisfaction with pay as compared with the pay of those holding other types of jobs is based on II–4 — "Was your pay commensurate with the pay of people who held other types of jobs in the USSR?" A satisfied person answered "yes" or "no, had higher pay than most." A dissatisfied person answered "no" or "no, had lower pay than most." Satisfaction with pay as compared with the pay of others holding the same type of job is based on II–5.

Of 2718 cases, 1922 are considered here. There were 704 who were either students, housewives, unclassifiable, or DK on own occupation; the remainder were either DK or irrelevant on satisfaction with pay. Since the number of no answers to the two questions varied, the N's given are the median number answering both questions.

14B. Table 25.

Income is based on "annual income of subject" as recorded in the budget study (see notes to Table 23). Satisfaction with pay compared to other types of jobs is based on II–4, as described in notes to Table 24. Satisfaction with job held in 1940 is based on II–3.

Of 983 cases on which we had income data (see notes to Table 23), only those who had a steady occupation are represented here, eliminating (249) students, housewives, and those who gave no occupation or could not be classified. Of 734 relevant cases, 19 were eliminated because they held jobs as peasants and 38 gave no answer on annual income leaving a base of 677 cases. Since the number of no answers to the two questions varied, the N's given here are the smaller of the two in each case.

15. We are here comparing Soviet data for 1941 and U.S. data for 1949. The job satisfaction reports from the Soviet refugees referred to 1940, and the American study (by Centers) was conducted in 1945. See *Gosudarstvennyi plan*, p. 512, and *Statistical Abstract of the United States* (Washington, D.C., 1950), p. 272.

15A. Table 26.

Occupation is based on II–1, with professional-administrative being combined as described in notes to Table 23. Job satisfaction is based on II–3. Pay satisfaction compared to other types of jobs is based on II–4, as described in notes to Table 24.

Only those who gave a steady occupation and whose answers to the job satisfaction question pertained to this occupation are considered. There were 680 students, housewives, unclassifiable, or DK on own occupation. In addition 72 were eliminated because their answer on job satisfaction did not refer to their steady occupation. Of the remainder 65 were either DK or irrelevant on pay satisfaction, and 38 were DK on job satisfaction, leaving a base of 1863 cases.

16. A similar contrast between the situation of the American worker and the worker in Europe has been made by Seymour M. Lipset and Reinhard Bendix. "Ideological Equalitarianism and Social Mobility in the United States," *Transactions of the Second World Congress of Sociology*, II, 34–54.

16A. Table 27.

Occupation is based on II–1, with professional-administrative being combined as described in notes to Table 23. Reasons for dissatisfaction with job are based on II–3. Only those regularly employed, indicating job dissatisfaction *and* giving a reason for it are represented in this table.

17. Centers, "Motivational Aspects," p. 193.

17A. Table 28.

This table is based on the personal interview (329 cases). The questions on work were open-ended, and the code categories were developed after the interviews were completed.

The N's given represent the total number in each social group whose answers could readily be scored as indicating which quality the informant *most* desired. Each respondent is recorded only once. Those not gainfully employed are also recorded. The number whose answers could not be so scored, from the intelligentsia down, were, respectively, 19, 2, 1, 8, 4. The remainder (18) were miscellaneous or other on social class, leaving a base of 277 considered here.

18. *Ibid.*, pp. 204–207.

18A. Table 29.

Material welfare is based on V–17. Disposable per capita income is based on data drawn from the special budget study (see Note No. 13A above), and represents the disposable income for the household as a whole, divided by the number of persons in the household. Disposable income is *take home pay*, minus other taxes, plus supplementary income. Of 983 cases on which we had budget data, 822 are considered here, 161 having failed to report their material conditions.

Where the respondent was a gainfully employed male the household was classified according to his occupation (II–1); married women's households are classified according to the occupation of their husbands (V–14). Unemployed men (359, including students), and unmarried women (610), were excluded from consideration. Five were excluded because they did not answer the material conditions question, leaving a base total of 1744 for this part.

18B. Table 30.

This table is based on the coding of open-ended questions on the personal interviews. The number who did not comment on the supply of one or another of these goods and services varied with the item, and the N's given are, therefore, the median for the three topics. Social group was assigned by us.

19. In this section we have relied on the memorandum by Carolyn Recht, "The Quantity and Adequacy of Soviet Urban Housing as Viewed by Former Soviet Citizens" (unpublished report of the Harvard Project on the Soviet Social System, June 1953).

20. See, for example, Nicholas DeWitt, *Soviet Professional Manpower* (Washington, D.C., 1955).

21. The two following paragraphs are taken from our earlier study (with Clyde Kluckhohn) *How the Soviet System Works.* We draw heavily here on the analysis by Alice Rossi, "Generational Differences in the Soviet Union" (unpublished report of the Harvard Project on the Soviet Social System, July 1954).

22. Joseph A. Kershaw, "Recent Trends in the Soviet Economy," *Annals of the American Academy of Political and Social Science,* Vol. 303, January 1956, p. 46.

Chapter VI. GETTING AN EDUCATION

1. In the preparation of this chapter we benefited from the analysis of some of the same materials by Irving Rosow and Alice Rossi. See: Irving Rosow, "Educational Patterns in the Soviet Union" (unpublished report of the Russian Research Center, March 1954); and Alice Rossi, "Generational Differences in the Soviet Union" (unpublished report of the Russian Research Center, October 1954).

2. For a succinct description of the school system and its enrollment, see Nicholas DeWitt, *Soviet Professional Manpower* (Washington, D.C., 1955). For more general discussion of Soviet educational history and philosophy, see M. J. Shore, *Soviet Education: Its Psychology and Philosophy* (New York, 1947), and George S. Counts, *The Challenge of Soviet Education* (New York, 1957).

3. This is reflected in our data. The very young children of our respondents, that is those between 6 and 10 years of age in 1940, were almost without exception listed as attending school by parents in both the nonmanual and the laboring classes.

4. *Pedagogika,* A. Kairov, ed. (Moscow, 1948), p. 15.

5. The wording of the question [IV, 32. "What is your opinion of the organization of the system of Soviet education (not about what is taught, but the system itself; for example, the number of school buildings, etc.)? Are you in favor of this or against it? (check one)"] was unusual in that it stressed not the *content* but the *availability* of facilities. This wording was adopted because we wanted to discriminate between individuals, and feared that a question not so "loaded" would bring a global response of rejection of the Communist *content* of education in which all would participate without giving us the opportunity to discriminate *degrees* of approval or rejection. Nevertheless, the question should not be used to assess the absolute levels of support of the Soviet educational system so much as the relative support or rejection among different groups of individuals. The code on the personal interview, which also took account of the evaluation of the *content* of education, showed a lower proportion of each social group approving Soviet education. But the class pattern was preserved.

6. The code was intended to tap the respondents' evaluation of the chances that, given ability, one could get as much education as he desired. It is remarkable that despite the small numbers of persons whose interviews yielded enough information to permit coding this question, the progression is so steady and so steep.

	All Can	Many Can	Few Can	Total	NC
Intelligentsia	22%	49%	30%	(37)	(77)
Employees	17	50	33	(12)	(48)
Skilled Workers	20	30	50	(10)	(24)
Ordinary Workers	17	22	61	(18)	(46)
Peasants	9	18	73	(11)	(28)

NC represents those whose spontaneous comments on this topic during the course of the personal interview were detailed enough to permit coding them.

7. *Naradnoe Khozyaistvo, SSSR* (Moscow, 1956), p. 221.

8. Frank Lorimer, *The Population of the Soviet Union* (Geneva, 1946), pp. 198–199.

9. *Bolshaya Sovetskaya Entsiklopedia* (Moskva, 1948), pp. 1234–1235.

10. A. E. Beilin, *Kadry Spetsialistov USSR* (Tsunkhu, Moscow, 1935), p. 348.

11. Nicholas DeWitt, *Soviet Professional Manpower,* pp. 170–171.

11A. Table 31.

Only those 21 through 40 in 1940 (I–2) are considered (1325). Of these we use only those cases for whom we had educational data on both the respondent *and* his father, if male, or the respondent *and* her mother, if female. For this reason the N's *within* each set are identical. For purposes of obtaining the percentage distributions, the respondents were treated as a separate pool, *as was the same sex parent.* Thus, all fathers were separately distributed by education regardless of the educational level attained by the son, but they entered into consideration only where the son had entered the first column distribution.

12. Based on official Soviet sources as reported in DeWitt, *Soviet Professional Manpower,* pp. 46–67.

13. From *Kul'turnoe Stroitel'stvo — 1940,* as reported in DeWitt, *Soviet Professional Manpower,* p. 54. The enrollment figures are according to the location or classification of the school. The actual proportion of youths of rural residence in the higher grade levels might be higher, since some rural youths travelled to secondary schools in nearby cities. They would nevertheless be listed in this case as part of the *urban* high school enrollment.

14. One of these differences, that of nationality or ethnic group membership, is also related to access to education. Enrollments in the non-Slavic national republics, except for the more advanced trans-Caucasian Georgians and Armenians, have been consistently smaller in proportion to population than has been the case elsewhere. Such minorities do not, however, figure prominently in our study.

15. A fuller discussion and documentation will be found in Robert Feldmesser, "Aspects of Social Mobility in the Soviet Union" (unpublished Ph.D. dissertation, Harvard University, 1956).

16. Robert Feldmesser, "Social Status and Access to Higher Education: A Comparison of the United States and the Soviet Union," *Harvard Educational Review,* Vol. XXVII, No. 2, Spring 1957, pp. 92–106.

17. R. Centers, "Attitude and Belief in Relation to Occupational Stratification," *Journal of Social Psychology,* 27:159–185 (1948).

17A. Table 32.

Social class is based on I–7. Education attained is based on VII–1. We exclude 498 cases whose education had to be inferred, since for this table an exact measure of education seemed desirable.

Of the remaining 2220 cases, 1964 are represented here. There were 190 omitted who were student, other, or DK on social class and 66 eliminated because they indicated "other" in response to the education question.

17B. Table 33.

This table may be read as follows: looking at the first column, we are dealing with respondents whose prerevolutionary social origin or status was upper class. Of those who remained in the upper class after the revolution (see the first two rows of percentages) 82% received over 7 years education, and 50% received over 10 years education. However, if the family moved down a notch after the revolution and became middle class (third and fourth row of percentages) then only 74% of the group received over 7 years of education, and 41% received over 10 years of schooling. The table may also be read across the rows. Thus, taking the third and fourth rows of percentages (respondents of postrevolutionary middle class status), we see that the level of education attained was dependent, in part, on the respondent's prerevolutionary social status, since the proportions completing 7 and 10 years of schooling is higher the higher the prerevolutionary standing of the family.

Only respondents who were less than 13 years of age in 1917 (I–2) were considered (1693).

The social status origin levels for the two periods have been defined according to the following occupational categories:

Parent's Social Group

	Prerevolutionary	Postrevolutionary
Upper	Nobility	Party or Soviet apparatus
	Intelligentsia	Intelligentsia
	Landowners	
Middle	Civil servants	Employees (white-collar)
	Merchants	Skilled workers
	Artisans	Artisans
	Middle class	
	Clergy	
	Military	
Lower	Workers	Rank-and-file workers
	Peasants	Peasants

The figures in parentheses are the bases for the sets of two per cents shown. Thus the first figure (190) indicates that there were 190 individuals whom we knew to be upper class both before and after the revolution and for whom we had educational data. Of these 82% completed more than 7 years of schooling, and only 50% completed more than 10 years of schooling.

Educational level is based on VII–1; prerevolutionary origin on V–1; postrevolutionary origin on V–2.

18. Dael Wolfle, *America's Resources of Specialized Talent*, quoted in J. Kahl, *The American Class Structure* (Rinehart, 1957), p. 283.

18A. Table 34.

Only respondents 21–35 in 1940 (I–2) are considered here (1023). Father's occupation is based on V–3 and is grouped as in Table 13 (note no. 18A of Chapter IV), except that the white-collar category is here included with semiprofessional. Respondent's education is based on VII–1 with "college graduate" being a combination of "completed higher education" and "graduate work."

Of 1023 respondents, 880 are considered here. There were 126 who either were DK/NA or other on father's occupation and 17 who were other on education, which were eliminated.

18B. Table 35.

Only those 11–20 (I–2) in 1940 (643 cases) are considered in this table. Father's occupation is based on V–3 and is grouped as explained in note no. 18A above. Respondent's education is based on VII–1 with "some college" including "some higher education" and "college graduate."

Of 643 cases, 538 are represented here. Eliminated were 98 who answered other or DK/NA on father's occupation and 7 who indicated "other" education.

19. The children 11–20 in 1940 were between 1 and 10 in 1930, when forced collectivization was launched. They therefore felt the full impact of the dislocation

of their families, and the discrimination of the regime, during their early school years. Among the children of ordinary peasants in this age group all but 27 per cent completed the four-year school and went beyond, but among children of kulaks the proportion who got only four years of school or less was 48 per cent.

20. Of these 255 were oldest and 36 youngest children. In order to conserve time and space, these were the only two categories on which we asked a report.

20A. Table 36.

This table reports the education attained by children of our respondents, as reported by the parent respondent. We have combined first-born children (742) and last-born children (384) into one pool. They are sorted by age according to year of birth (Strat. 9B for first children; Strat. 10A for last children), and by education (Strat. 9D for first children; Strat. 10C for last children). Respondent's social class is based on I–7. Nonmanual includes: party-Soviet apparatus, intelligentsia, civil servants. Manual includes: skilled workers, ordinary workers, collective farmers.

Of 1026 children reported by our respondents, 391 are considered here. The other 635 children were excluded from consideration because they did not fall in the age groups considered here (382 first children were either born before 1920 or after 1929; 253 last children were born after 1929).

The age group "over 15" includes first children born 1920–24 and last children born "before 1925." Therefore, it is possible that some among the "last born" children included here were over 20 in 1940.

20B. Table 37.

Only those 15–35 in 1940 (I–1) are considered here (1475 cases). Social origin is based on V–2 (father's postrevolutionary social group). Intelligentsia includes: intelligentsia; party-Soviet apparatus. Skilled worker includes: skilled workers; artisans. Peasants includes both dekulakized and non-dekulakized kolkhozniks. Opportunity for an education is based on VII–3. The first set of totals (to the left) represent all of a given origin who answered the question (6, 6, 4, 16, 55 being DK, from the intelligentsia down, respectively), and the percentages given there represent those who answered "some people had more opportunity to receive an education [than I did]." In the right half of the table, all those who claimed "less opportunity" *and* gave a reason are considered, 20, 24, 36, 78, 116 cases, from intelligentsia down, having claimed less opportunity without giving any reason.

21. A fuller discussion and documentation will be found in Robert Feldmesser, "Aspects of Social Mobility."

22. Those of working class showed a higher proportion satisfied with their educational opportunity, among the *older* people. We have been unable to determine whether this is a statistical artifact or a real fact. During the early years of the regime when the older age group was in school, the regime favored the working class and hindered the middle-class child in his educational aspirations. This may account for the seemingly high enthusiasm the older working-class group shows in evaluating its opportunities to secure an education.

22A. Table 38.

Origin is based on father's occupation type V–3, and is grouped as explained in notes to Table 13, except that white-collar is here included with semiprofessional and all workers are grouped together. Age is based on I–2 and educational opportunity on VII–3 and the percentages here represent a combination of the following two answers: "I had the same opportunity as others." "I had more opportunity to receive an education than others." Only those under 41 in 1940 are considered, eliminating 140 cases over 50 and 205 NA on age. Of the remainder 218 were DK and 120 other on father's occupation; 191 were DK and 67 inapplicable on educational opportunity, leaving a base of 1777 for the table as a whole.

23. See note 22 above.

24. Based on the personal interviews. See Alice Rossi, "Generational Differences."

25. This reversal of the trend, with peasants more often reporting full support in their educational ambitions, is partly due to the tendency of those from kulak homes to have more often experienced such support. Since the kulaks were generally the more ambitious, energetic peasants, they may well have been quicker to realize the value of education. But ordinary peasants also reported they received full support more often than did ordinary workers. It is not clear whether this was because peasant boys and girls had more limited ambitions which could more easily receive full support, but that is unlikely to explain the data. We are inclined to fall back on the more general theory that the greater strength of family ties in peasant than in worker homes more often led the young either to perceive or to actually experience full support in such limited educational drive as they may have had. In Chapter IX, Table 54, it will be seen that peasants, more often than workers, reported their family "grew together" under Soviet conditions. This is offset, however, by the fact that they also more often claimed it "grew apart." Furthermore, on moving to the cities the educational horizon of former peasants was suddenly greatly widened. The parents may well have seemed to these boys to be lagging behind in the support they gave for the pursuit of these new goals.

25A. Table 39.

Only those 15–35 in 1940 (I, 2) are considered here (1475 cases). Origin is based on father's postrevolutionary social group (V–2). Intelligentsia includes: intelligentsia; party-Soviet apparatus. Skilled worker includes: skilled workers; artisans. Peasants includes both dekulakized and non-dekulakized kolkhozniks. Parental support of educational desire is based on V–8 and "utmost support" is based on the answer "supported me completely."

The base for this table is 1190 (781 males; 419 females). The cases not represented were either DK on parental support of educational desire or DK on father's postrevolutionary social group, or were omitted because they reported their father as "other" or disfranchised or because the question was not applicable, their parents having died before 1921.

26. The base N's were: 112, 60, 32, 59, 36 respectively, for intelligentsia through peasant.

27. Based on personal interviews. For discussion see Alice Rossi, "Generational Differences," pp. 64–107.

27A. Table 40.

This table is based on an open-ended question on education from the personal interview, the answers to which were coded by us into the categories cited. Social class was assigned by us. The per cents indicate proportion of "total respondents citing positive reasons" who cited the specific reason indicated. The numbers who gave an uncodable answer were, from intelligentsia on, 4, 3, 2, 8, 9. Eighteen cases were not classifiable on social class.

28. The number of peasant responses to this question was unfortunately extremely small, since it appeared only in the personal interview. Whether this or some other factor accounts for the reversals is not clear. It seems likely that distinctive factors were present in the peasants' orientation toward education. In any event, the reversals do not significantly affect the general patterns shown in the table.

28A. Table 41.

The table represents responses to a sentence fragment, "Education leads to . . . ," responded to by those who completed the personal interview. Social class was assigned by us. Of the total number of respondents who took the sentence completion test (316), 237 are represented here, the others being unclassifiable on social group or having failed to complete the particular sentence stub.

Responses were placed in the three categories as follows.

Personal instrumental: Anything that suggested that education improved the individual or his lot. Includes such utilitarian responses as ". . . a career," ". . . to culture and easy labor"; responses indicating development of the individual either mentally or morally, ". . . the development of mental ability," ". . . the widening of views," ". . . foresight"; or simply such hopeful but ambiguous results as ". . . good things," ". . . happiness," and ". . . a happy future."

Humanistic, social and scientific: All responses which benefit society or mankind in general: ". . . to knowledge of secret of the universe," ". . . to the advancement of knowledge," ". . . to raising the cultural level of a country," ". . . to the civilization and culture of humanity."

Ambivalent and negative: ". . . toward good, maybe toward evil too, bombs, etc.," ". . . happiness, but maybe to just the contrary." "The more you learn, the more you react to all occurrences of life, and there are so many bad occurrences."

28B. Table 42.

The table is based on a matched set (194 cases) of American and Russian interviewees. A total of 97 interviews were conducted with native Americans matched to former Soviet citizens who completed the personal interview. Of those in the matched set, 76 Americans and 87 former Soviet citizens had been given the Sentence Completion Test and responded to the fragment, "Education leads to. . . ." For details on coding see note no. 28A (Table 41).

29. This description of postwar development is based on an unpublished address by Nicholas DeWitt, "Universal Education in Russia," delivered to the 1957 Meeting of the National Education Association, Atlantic City, New Jersey.

30. Article in *Komsomolskaya Pravda* by Shelepin, Secretary of the Komsomol, reported in the *New York Times,* March 21, 1954.

31. Reported by Robert Feldmesser in personal communication.

32. Reported by Jerome Bruner in a personal communication.

33. The birth deficit resulting from the war will, of course, affect this situation. For a period of perhaps a decade from about 1957 to 1967 the age groups eligible for college entrance will be unusually small. If the number of college admissions remains approximately the same or increases, the proportionate chances of these boys and girls will be comparatively better than those prevailing earlier.

Chapter VII. KEEPING UP WITH THE NEWS

1. Some of the material presented in this chapter was earlier reported on in different form in: Peter H. Rossi and Raymond A. Bauer, "Some Patterns of Soviet Communications Behavior," *Public Opinion Quarterly,* 16:653–670 (Winter 1952–53); and Raymond A. Bauer and David B. Gleicher, *Public Opinion Quarterly,* 17:297–310 (Fall 1953).

2. For an extended description of the Soviet communications system and its functioning, see Alex Inkeles, *Public Opinion in Soviet Russia* (Cambridge, 1950).

3. *Narodnoe Khozyaistvo SSSR* (Moscow, 1956) p. 240.

4. F. L. Mott, *The News in America* (Cambridge, 1952).

5. *Narodnoe Khozyaistvo,* p. 184.

5A. Table 43.

This table is based on the open ended questions on communications exposure asked during the personal interview. An individual was scored as using a source if he made any mention of his exposure to it, even if it was infrequent. In the table, however, only media cited by 10 per cent or more were included. The other citations were: books, 6 per cent; foreign radio, 6 per cent; other foreign sources, 3 per cent; films, 3 per cent; and other, 4 per cent.

Of a total of 329 cases, 17 did not answer the question, or did not use any source. Of the 312 who cited a source, 275 gave sufficient information to permit evaluation of which *particular* source was most important.

6. We use the personal interviews here rather than the larger sample on the written questionnaire because only in the former did we inquire as to "most important" source. The relative standing of the roughly comparable media was, however, very similar for the questionnaire sample. Using as a guide the per cent who claimed to use a source "frequently" the order was: newspapers and magazines, 54 per cent; domestic radio, 42 per cent; discussion with friends, 38 per cent (18 per cent cited "rumor"); and agitation meetings, 16 per cent.

7. From "Public Use of the Library," reprinted Daniel Katz *et al.*, eds., in *Public Opinion and Propaganda* (New York, 1954), p. 238.

8. Wilbur Schramm, *The Process and Effects of Mass Communication* (Urbana, 1955), pp. 74–83. In France the figure was only 56 per cent and in Italy 39. Such differences in part reflect differences in literacy and levels of education in the different countries. There is in addition the problem of availability, which may in turn also reflect literacy rates. In any event, the number of copies of newspapers per thousand inhabitants, *published* in the various countries varied with the rates of *use*. Thus, in the United Kingdom the number published was 350, in France 259, Italy 98, the rates of daily use approximately 90, 60, and 40, respectively.

The wording of the question, and the meaning of the terms "regular" or "frequent" also varies from country to country and from study to study. In our more precise written questionnaire, for example, it is only by allowing the answer "seldom" — that is, by excluding only those who said that they "never" read a newspaper — that we can classify close to 90 per cent as using the newspaper as an ordinary source. Those who were "frequent" users, which would suggest daily or near daily reading of the newspaper, were only 54 per cent. This rate will be seen to be lower than that for the United States, England and Scandinavia. This should, however, be of little significance with regard to the main point made in the text, which has to do with the relative importance of the different media for the members of our sample.

9. Materials on the relative importance of the newspaper versus the radio as news sources in the United States are hardly unambiguous in their import. Before World War II the newspaper was generally twice as often cited as a source of news. Apparently the importance of "flash" news in wartime produced a shift in the opposite direction. For a summary of the survey results up to 1946, see Hadley Cantril, ed., *Public Opinion, 1935–1946* (Princeton, 1951), pp. 523–526.

10. Most American surveys report only 5 or 6 per cent citing "talks with friends or other people" as sources of news (see Hadley Cantril, ed., *Public Opinion*, p. 524). The questions put tend to stress sources of "news," however, rather than sources of information or ideas that were important in shaping one's feelings about political issues. There are at least two important American studies which suggest that personal, informal or word-of-mouth communication may under certain circumstances loom as large in the American context as it does on the Soviet setting. Lazarsfeld and his associates asked a question not too different from

ours: "From which sources did you get most of the information or impressions that caused you to form your judgment on how to vote?" In Erie County, Ohio, 56 and 52 per cent of the men and women, respectively, cited some personal contact such as relatives, friends, or associates on the job. (See Paul Lazarsfeld, Bernard Berelson and Helen Gaudet, *The People's Choice,* New York, 1952, p. 171.) In a second study (Samuel Stouffer, *Communism, Conformity, and Civil Liberties,* New York, 1955) a national sample was asked, with regard to unemployment and hard times, whether "you get your information mostly from what you read or hear on the air, or mostly from what you hear in conversations with other people." Fifty-nine per cent cited "other people" as their source.

11. Hostility is here measured by the distortion index. See Appendix 11. The "most" anti-Soviet are those with scores of 4, and the "least" those with scores of 0.

12. The derivation of these types by means of a modification of certain steps of latent structure analysis is discussed by Peter H. Rossi, in the "Technical Postscript" to "Some Patterns of Soviet Communications Behavior," *Public Opinion Quarterly,* 16:666–670 (Winter 1952–53). Peter Rossi developed these typologies.

12A. Table 44.

The exposure to the different types of media is measured according to the Communications Typologies scale described in Appendix 9. These exposure types were developed through Latent Structure Analysis by Peter H. Rossi and described by him in the "Technical Postscript" to Peter Rossi and Raymond A. Bauer, "Some Patterns of Soviet Communications Behavior," *Public Opinion Quarterly,* Vol. 16, No. 4, 1952–53. On official mass media: high is a score of 1; medium, a score of 2 or 3; low, a score of 0. On personalized media (legitimate nonmass media): high is a score of 3 or 2; medium, a score of 1; low, a score of 0. On aesthetic media (entertainment media): high is a score of 2 or 1; low, a score of 0. On covert media (nonlegitimate media): high is a score of 3 or 2; medium, a score of 1; low, a score of 0. Social class is based on I–7, excluding 234 cases who were student, other or DK to this question. The N's given at the bottom of the table represent all those in each social class. *For each of the four exposure types separately,* the figures total to 100 per cent, on the base number given for the class.

12B. Table 45.

As indicated in note no. 5A (Table 43), 275 individuals gave sufficient information to permit specific scoring of their most important source. Of these 16 could not be assigned a class, leaving a total of 259 as the total cases considered in this table. "Other" important sources of information include: magazines, personal observation, and others.

12C. Table 46.

Social group is based on I–7 with students, other, and DK (234 cases) omitted. Anti-Soviet sentiment is based on the Index of that name described in Appendix 5. "Low" indicates a score of 0 or 1; "high" a score of 2, 3, 4, or 5. The per cents indicate the proportion of those of a given social class and a given A.S.S. score who were frequently exposed to the given medium (based on, reading from top to bottom, VIII–1, A, B, C, D, E, F, G, H, VIII–6, VIII–4, VIII–1, I). The base N's are, however, median N's, since for each item there were different numbers who were "no answer" with regard to exposure and these NA's were not included in the base when the percentages were computed.

12D. Table 47.

Occupation is based on II–1 and is grouped as described in notes to Table 13, except that here white-collar is combined with semiprofessional. Students, housewives, "other" (702 cases) are not included. Desire for a career is based on II–9.

"Wanted a career" combines the first three response choices; "did not want a career" combines choices four and five. The last two responses "other" and DK (277 cases) were omitted from consideration. Exposure to media is based on, reading from left to right, VIII–1, parts C, A, E, G, and VIII–6, respectively. In each case, the percentage given represents those who indicated they "frequently" were exposed to the various media. The N's are the median for the five media, since there was some variation in the number not answering for different media.

13. Elihu Katz and Paul F. Lazarsfeld, *Personal Influence* (Glencoe, Ill., 1955).

14. Note that a negatively toned word for "rumor" (*slukhi*) was used. This should have had the general effect of lowering the proportions in all classes who rated rumors as more reliable than newspapers and magazines.

14A. Table 48.

Social class is based on I–7. Anti-Soviet sentiment scores are described in Appendix 5. In this table, "none" indicates a score of 0, "low" a score of 1, "medium" a score of 2, and "high" a score of 3–5. Reliability of rumor is based on VIII–6, C. Only those who reported hearing rumors are considered here. This eliminated 1133 cases who could not pass on their reliability. In addition, on successive sorts, 234 who were students, other, or DK/NA on Anti-Soviet Sentiment were eliminated. Out of the original 2718 cases, this left a base of 1289 cases for this table.

15. See Appendix 5.

16. For a fuller discussion, see chapter 14 of *How the Soviet System Works*.

17. This study was done by John Zawadsky.

17A. Table 49.

Reliability of the Soviet press is based on VIII–2; social class on I–7; and hostility to the Soviets on the distortion index (see Appendix 11). High hostility indicates a score of 3 or 4; medium hostility, a score of 1 or 2; low hostility, a score of 0.

Of 2718 cases, 1957 are represented in this table. The remainder were eliminated on successive sorts as follows: 234 were student, other, or DK on social class; 345 were DK on the distortion index; and 182 were DK on reliability of the Soviet press.

18. The interpretation of news sources by Soviet citizens is discussed by Elena Calas in "Readers' Interpretation of Newspaper Materials in the Soviet Union," *Studies in Soviet Communication*, Center for International Studies, Massachusetts Institute of Technology, 1952. Using similar sources to ours, Mrs. Calas comes to virtually identical conclusions. This section could well have been written exclusively on Mrs. Calas' materials. Our own conclusions on this matter were formed before Mrs. Calas' work was published, and we regard this concurrence of judgment to be a happy circumstance.

19. This particular point is discussed in some detail by Calas, *ibid.*, pp. 59ff.

20. Calas, *ibid.*, p. 63.

Chapter VIII. PATTERNS OF FAMILY LIFE

1. This chapter and that which follows owe much to preliminary work by Alice Rossi, H. Kent Geiger, and Irving Rosow.

2. Frederick Engels, *The Origin of the Family, Private Property and the State, in the Light of the Researches of Lewis H. Morgan* (New York, 1942), pp. 61–73.

3. Available in English translation under the title cited, San Francisco, no date. Quotations are from page 6 of that translation.

4. Vladimir I. Lenin, *Sochineniya* (Works) (2nd ed., Moscow), XIX, 232.

5. Quoted by Vladimir Gsovski, *Soviet Civil Law* (Ann Arbor, 1948), I, 127.

6. William Clark Trow, ed., *Character Education in Soviet Russia* (Ann Arbor, circa 1934), pp. 37–38.

7. Quoted in Gsovski, *Soviet Law*, I, 111. Italics supplied.

8. See Alex Inkeles, "Family and Church in the Postwar USSR," *Annals of the American Academy of Political and Social Science*, 263, May 1949.

9. N. Abramov and K. A. Grave, *The New Law on Marriage and the Family* (in Russian) (Moscow, 1947), p. 25.

10. For citations see Alex Inkeles, "Family and Church."

10A. Table 50.

In both parts of this table we initially considered all Soviet married respondents (1284 cases), that is, those who answered "married" or "other (divorced or widowed)" to V–13. From this base, German spouses (I–4A) and postemigration (1945–50) marriages (I–4) were excluded, leaving 941 cases. Date of marriage is based on V–15.

In the first part of the table, father's occupation is based on V–3 (father's occupation), and spouse's social origin on V–16. Nonmanual occupations of fathers include all those listed under professional-administrative and semiprofessional in notes to Table 13, plus white-collar. Manual occupations of fathers combines all workers listed in notes to Table 13, plus peasants. Nonmanual class origin of spouse consists of: nobility, military, upper bourgeoisie, petit bourgeoisie, and intelligentsia. Manual class origins of spouse include: kulak, peasant or kolkhoznik, skilled worker, worker. There are 778 cases in the upper part of this table, 163 (from 941) having said "other" for father's occupation or "other" or DK/NA on spouse's social origin.

In the second part of the table, nationality of respondent is based on I–3; nationality of spouse on I–4B. Only Russian and Ukrainian respondents with Russian or Ukrainian spouses are included, leaving a base of 633 cases.

11. *Planovoe Khozyaistvo*, No. 5, 1940, p. 19.

12. J. Hajnal, "Differential Changes in Marriage Pattern," *American Sociological Review*, April 1954.

12A. Table 51.

Social class is based on I–7; friendship patterns on VI (number of friends mentioned). Of 2718 cases, 1831 are represented here. There were 234 cases not considered who were DK/NA, other, or students on social class and the remainder were DK/NA to number of friends.

13. Reported by Genevieve Knupfer, "Portrait of the Underdog," in Reinhard Bendix and Seymour M. Lipset, eds., *Class, Status and Power* (Glencoe, Ill., 1953).

13A. Table 52.

Social class is based on I–7. Occupations of three friends is based on VI–3, A, B, and C. Professional includes: arts, applied sciences, and professions. White-collar includes: semiprofessional and white-collar. Worker includes: skilled, ordinary, and unskilled workers. *N's and per cents refer not to respondents but to the total pool of friends cited as first, second, or third friend and identified by occupation.* There were 2235 such friends in all. All friends classified merely as students, housewives, "other" or DK/NA (a total of 3650) were not considered here. Only 2146 (of the 2235) friends are represented in this table, 89 being lost because they were friends of respondents who were students, other, or DK/NA on social class and who were, therefore, not considered.

14. Of almost 500 friends described by our ordinary worker and peasant respondents combined only three were in the professional category. In contrast, of

731 friends described by our intelligentsia respondents 56, or 7 per cent, were peasants or ordinary (as against skilled) workers. Since the numbers in both cases were small, we decided to do a test for significance by x^2. Chi square with Yate's correction equals 32.6. This is highly significant, way beyond the .01 level. Some doubt may be thrown on the result, however, by the fact that the sample of friends is not randomly drawn. We have taken all of the first three friends of our respondents. Thus if a respondent has fallen into our sample, all of his first three friends fall in too. What difference this makes would be hard to say.

15. To test these assumptions in a firm way would require data drawn from a larger and more representative sample than ours, and particularly would require more detailed information than that which we collected. When we take as our base everyone in a given age category, our data suggest that people are getting married later, because the proportions married by age 30, for example, are generally larger among the older generations. This may, however, be largely a function of the proportion who were going to marry at all. Indeed, when we used as a base only those who had gotten married, there was no evidence of any trend in the age at marriage. Unfortunately, our data permitted us to examine this issue in only a restricted part of our sample, including four age classes, each covering a five-year span. The first class contained people who reached the age of 20 between 1916 and 1920 and the last class those who reached the age of 20 between 1931 and 1935. In these age groups we found that among those ever married, the age at marriage was not in any clear-cut way different as one proceeded from the youngest of these "generations" to the oldest. For example, among those in the intelligentsia the proportions married by age 30 were, 73, 74, 79, 74 per cent going from the "youngest" to the oldest generation, respectively. We have no idea whether for age classes after 1935 this trend would hold.

Furthermore, when we examine the length of time which elapsed before the birth of the first child, we find much the same type of stability. Within the same four age groups we found that the proportions who had their first child within the first five years after marriage were relatively steady from age group to age group and certainly showed no clear-cut pattern. It is, of course, possible that a more refined measure than the five year interval would have revealed a trend. It is also very likely that those getting married more recently acted differently, since the effects of industrialization may not have manifested themselves so fully before 1935. But we have no basis for projecting the trend beyond that date.

16. *Narodnoe Khozyaistvo SSR* (Moscow, 1956), p. 243.

17. Frederick Engels, *Origin*, pp. 65–66.

18. Warren Eason, "Population and Labor Force," Abram Bergson, ed., *Soviet Economic Growth* (Evanston, 1953), and Boris Syssoeff, "Women's Participation in the Labor Force of the USSR" (unpublished manuscript, Russian Research Center, Harvard University).

19. Although the proportion of women in the civilian nonagricultural labor force increased from 27 per cent in 1929 to 50 per cent in 1949, this does not necessarily mean that there has been an equally great rise in the proportion of women in the relevant age groups in the urban population who have joined the labor force. A very large part of the rise in the proportion which women constitute in the civilian nonagricultural labor force can be accounted for by the fact that many men have been siphoned out of this segment of the labor force since 1929. In particular the size of the armed forces, almost totally composed of males, has been greatly increased since 1929. In addition, there have been large numbers of persons in slave labor camps, again mostly men, and this number increased greatly after 1929. Finally a much larger proportion of the deaths during World

War II were deaths of men rather than of women. Thus the proportion of women in the age range relevant for potential membership in the labor force has increased. All these factors taken together could plausibly explain a great deal, if not all, of the large increase in the proportion of the civilian nonagricultural labor force composed of women.

Warren Eason in his article "Population and Labor Force," on page 109 of *Soviet Economic Growth* (Abram Bergson, ed.) has this to say:

"In the case of urban females 16–59, the proportion in the labor force (40.1 per cent in 1926) theoretically could have increased by 1939, but there is no way to demonstrate through published data on urban sectors of the labor force that this in fact happened. For example, the marked increase in female workers and employees (the majority of whom are in the urban areas, 1926–1939) does not necessarily reflect any parallel increase in the percentage of urban females in the labor force. That is, the increase in urban female workers and employees could have resulted solely from the large-scale migration of females from rural to urban areas, with 40.1 per cent of migrants 16–59 (and 28.1 per cent of those 60 plus) entering the labor force. On the other hand, if the 1939 proportion is, in fact, much higher than 40.1 per cent it suggests a large number of urban females working full or part-time in private economic activity. Without evidence from Soviet sources that private activity exists on such a large scale, it is assumed that only 40.1 per cent of urban females 16–59 in 1939 are in the labor force."

Frank Lorimer in his written comment on Eason's article, has a contrary opinion. (See page 24 of Abram Bergson, ed., *Soviet Economic Growth*.)

"Mr. Eason assumes no increase from 1926 to 1939 in labor force participation by urban women aged 16–59 years. In view of increased opportunity for employment and decreased responsibilities for children, there is reason to suppose that conditions in the Soviet Union, even in the prewar period, would have led to increased entry of urban women into the labor force."

19A. Table 53.

Occupation of respondent's father is based on V–3 and is grouped as described in notes to Table 13 with white-collar included with semiprofessional and all workers combined into one category. Age is based on I–2; employment of respondent's mother on V–6.

Of 2718 cases, 2104 are represented here. There were 205 NA on age; 375 either other or DK/NA on father's occupation; 34 DK/NA on mother's employment.

20. Limits on the size of the written questionnaire, which is the only instrument with a sufficient number of respondents to pursue this question, did not permit us to ask *explicitly* whether women stopped working after marriage or after they started having children. We asked only whether the respondent, while in the Soviet Union, had a steady occupation. The analysis given in the text is based on the proportions of women who gave such a steady occupation as against those who described themselves as housewives or as not steadily employed. Under the circumstances, it should be clear that we are merely inferring that being married and later having children had some direct influence on whether a woman would work or would continue to work after the event.

On the other hand, the fact that being married or having children appeared to have so slight an effect on whether or not a woman worked may be an artifact of this same question form. That is, women may have answered the question largely in terms of whether or not they had *ever* had a steady occupation, neglecting the fact that they stopped working after marriage or childbirth.

Chapter IX. PATTERNS OF FAMILY LIFE: THE INNER FAMILY

1. For a fuller discussion of these issues, see H. Kent Geiger, "The Urban Slavic Family and the Soviet System" (unpublished dissertation, Harvard University, 1954). Dr. Geiger's work was also of great value to us in dealing with the question of family solidarity. See: H. Kent Geiger, "Deprivation and Solidarity in the Soviet Urban Family," *American Sociological Review*, 20:57–68 (1955).

1A. Table 54.

Respondents were not asked whether in rating their "own" family they were referring to the family in which they had been raised, or to their family of procreation. The sample for this table was selected to minimize this element of ambiguity and to deal mainly with families which were fully active in rearing children during the years of Soviet rule. To this end the base was selected to include only two main groups, which combined to give a base of 985 cases.

Group 1: Those under 40 in 1950 (I–2) who were unmarried while in the Soviet Union (I–4) and who, therefore, must have been referring to the family in which they were reared under Soviet conditions; the social group for those in this category is, therefore, that of the father when the respondent was a child (father's postrevolutionary social group V–2 with categories combined as described in notes to Table 39). Of 1041 unmarried respondents, 530 were under 41 in 1950 and also gave their father's postrevolutionary social group, of whom 494 are represented here, the remainder being NA on family cohesion.

Group 2: Those over 45 in 1950 (I–2) who were married while in the Soviet Union (I–4) and, therefore, raising their families during the years of Soviet rule. Those in this second set of respondents probably, but not certainly, were referring to their "family of procreation" in Soviet times and not to their pre-Soviet "family of orientation." They are listed according to their own adult social identification (I–7). Of 1641 married respondents, 528 were over 45 in 1950 and were also identifiable by social class group, of whom 491 are represented here, the remainder being NA on family cohesion.

This concentration on what would be an approximation of the specifically *Soviet* family was actually not strictly necessary, since controls on age, sex, and marital status revealed that there was a fairly stable pattern of response to this question, with social class being the prime determinant of the pattern obtained.

2. Hostility is measured here by the "distortion scale," with a dichotomization of those who had the lowest score on the scale (zero) as against all the others.

3. For a critical review of the literature on the effects of war, depression and other social crises on the family see H. Kent. Geiger, "The Urban Slavic Family."

4. This study was based on a small subsample of young urban families, described in H. K. Geiger, *ibid*. There were 34 worker and 52 intelligentsia families in the sample.

5. The materials in this section were earlier reported in somewhat revised form by Alex Inkeles, "Social Change and Social Character: The Role of Parental Mediation," *The Journal of Social Issues*, XI:12–23 (1955). The analysis presented here was strongly influenced by Alice Rossi's work on these same materials. See her: "Generational Differences in the Soviet Union" (unpublished report of the Harvard Project on the Soviet Social System, Russian Research Center, 1954).

5A. Table 55.

This table is based on the personal interviews. The prerevolutionary period is based on comments by 125 respondents over 40 in 1950; the postrevolutionary on comments by 92 respondents over 45 in 1950; and the current Soviet period on statements by 146 respondents under 35 in 1950. More than one value was often mentioned by any one respondent. The per cents are based on the sum of responses, that is, on the total number of child rearing values cited by each occupational group within each of the generational groups.

The following are tests of significance to test the differences between values emphasized in the prerevolutionary period and values emphasized in the current Soviet period as presented in Table 55.

Value	*Nonmanual group*	*Manual group*
Tradition	C.R. equals 4.02; P for two-sided test less than .0001	C.R. equals 2.27; P for two-sided test less than .05
Achievement	C.R. equals 2.13; P for two-sided test is less than .05	C.R. equals 0.81; P even for one-sided test is greater than .20
Adjustment	C.R. equals 2.59; P for two-sided test is less than .01	C.R. equals 0.61; P even for one-sided test is greater than .25
Personal	C.R. equals 1.60; P for one-sided test equals .055, for two-sided test .11	C.R. equals 1.21; P even for one-sided test is greater than .10
Political	C.R. equals 2.58; P for two-sided test equals .01	C.R. equals 0.97; P even for one-sided test is greater than .15
Intellectual	C.R. equals 1.67; P for one-sided test is around .047; for two-sided test around .094	C.R. equals 2.02; P for a two-sided test is less than .05

Our information about child rearing in the prerevolutionary or tsarist period is based on the report of those over 40, at the time of interview in 1950, as to how they had been raised. Since the oldest was 70, all of those in this group were born between 1880 and 1910, and with the exception of the very youngest had reached young adulthood, here taken as age 15, by the time of the Revolution of 1917. The social group designation is that of the father when the respondent was a dependent. To learn about child rearing in the postrevolutionary period we have a more direct source of information, since our older respondents, those over 45 when interviewed, raised most of their children from approximately 1920 on, that is, during the main period of Soviet development. Most of them had completed their families and raised the oldest child to young adulthood by 1945. Finally, to learn about current and future Soviet patterns of child rearing in the Soviet Union we can consider the activity as actual parents, or the planned activity as potential parents, of our younger respondents, those under 35. The people in that age group are now raising or will raise the children of the next Soviet generations. In both these last columns the social group is that of the respondent.

There are, of course, some important methodological difficulties facing this effort to explore changes in child rearing patterns in pre- and postrevolutionary Russia. To begin, those who could qualify as representative parents of the tsarist period, that is who raised their children to late adolescence before the Revolution, are not here to speak for themselves but are spoken for by their children, namely those of our respondents who were over 40. Nevertheless, we have evidence that adult individuals report the child rearing values emphasized by their parents not too differently from the way in which they are reported by the parents who reared those same individuals. We tested this by comparing the description given by the older respondents as to how they had raised their children, with that given by the younger respondents as to how they had been raised. Both groups were then referring to roughly the same period. The extremely high correlations of .89

and .95 were obtained. These correlations were obtained separately for manual and nonmanual groups and represent the outcome of the age comparison in each, respectively. The distribution of responses on the full list of ten "flat" code categories characterizing the parents' orientation toward child rearing was used in obtaining the correlations. In each case, i.e., for manual and nonmanual separately, the responses correlated were those given by respondents over 45 in 1950, as to how *they* had raised their children, as against the report of respondents under 35 (1950) as to how their *parents* had reared them. Since those over 45 were not actually the parents of those under 35, the agreement is not strictly one of parent and child, but rather between two groups of representatives of a parental and a children's generation. The ten-year age gap provides an imperfect but adequate generational division, since the median age of the older group was 51 and of the younger 29. In any generational comparison the necessity to use an age criterion creates a situation in which some people who were the *last* children of an older group will be classed in the same generation as others who were the *first* children of a younger group of parents. The age criterion for generational assignment was the only one feasible in this study, however, and seems adequate for our purposes.

This result should serve as well to answer a second methodological objection, namely that the report of those who were parents in the middle period would most likely be a rather glowing and flattering account of how they had raised their children, but one hardly reflecting the true quality of their former behavior as parents. The fact that those who were children in the postrevolutionary period and those who were parents raising children in the same years so closely agree in their description of child rearing values dominant in those years, leads us to believe that our older respondents were honestly reporting at the time of interview the values they had stressed earlier when actually raising their children.

Finally, we must acknowledge the objection that too much weight cannot be assigned to the report of your youngest respondents as to how they were raising their children. In many cases they did not yet have children, hence they were talking of plans and not reality. In any event, their children would be raised not in the Soviet Union but in Germany, the United States, or some other country to which the refugees have emigrated. With reference to this objection we point out that about one third of these younger respondents were between 30 and 35 when we spoke to them, and were already raising children. In addition, in our interview we stressed that we wished our respondents to tell us how they would have raised their children while still in the Soviet Union, rather than how they planned to raise them on the outside. Nevertheless, there is substance to this argument, and we should certainly approach with caution an extrapolation to young parents in the Soviet Union solely on the basis of what our younger respondents reported.

6. See Note 5A to Table 55 above.

6A. Table 56.

The case base for each column in Table 56 was selected on the same basis as those for 55. The four categories of value used represent a collapsing of nine more refined original categories which were combined because of the small "N." Since the total sample was the same and the interview free, it is apparent from the smaller "N's" that our respondents were less likely to discuss the occupational guidance given by their parents, or by themselves as parents, than they were to discuss the broader problems of character formation. Nevertheless, these "N's" are not too small to form a basis for analysis, especially since the direction of the change is so highly congruent with that observed in the general child rearing ethics.

For the nonmanuals we performed significance tests on all four values between the prerevolutionary and postrevolutionary groups and the prerevolutionary and current Soviet groups; for the manuals between the prerevolutionary and postrevolutionary groups, between the prerevolutionary and current Soviet groups, and between the postrevolutionary and current Soviet groups. It did not seem worth while to perform tests of significance between the postrevolutionary nonmanuals and the current Soviet nonmanuals since the differences between these two groups were in all cases so small.

A. Differences among Nonmanuals.
  1. Between prerevolutionary and postrevolutionary.
     a. *Tradition.* C.R. equals 2.91. Two-sided probability is less than .01.
     b. *Rewards.* C.R. equals 1.69. This is significant beyond the .05 level for a one-sided test but the two-sided probability is .09.
     c. *Self-expression.* C.R. equals 2.28. This is significant beyond the .05 level for a two-sided test.
     d. *Political.* By Fisher's Exact Test, the one-sided probability equals .013 and the two-sided probability .027.
  2. Between prerevolutionary and current Soviet.
     a. *Tradition.* C.R. equals 3.07. This is significant beyond the .01 level for a two-sided test.
     b. *Rewards.* C.R. equals 1.38. This is not significant at the .05 level even for a one-sided test.
     c. *Self-expression.* C.R. equals 1.63. This barely misses being significant at the .05 level for a one-sided test.
     d. *Political.* By Fisher's Exact Test, the one-sided probability is .011 and the two-sided probability .023.
B. Differences among Manuals.
  1. Between prerevolutionary and postrevolutionary.
     a. *Tradition.* C.R. equals 2.87. This is significant beyond the .01 level for a two-sided test.
     b. *Rewards.* C.R. equals 0.73. This is not significant even for a one-sided test. One-sided probability is greater than .20.
     c. *Self-expression.* C.R. equals 0.68. Not significant even for a one-sided test.
     d. *Political.* By Fisher's Exact Test, the one-sided probability equals .033 and the two-sided probability .065.
  2. Between prerevolutionary and current Soviet.
     a. *Tradition.* C.R. equals 5.23. Two-sided probability is less than .0001.
     b. *Rewards.* C.R. equals 0.533. One-sided probability is greater than .25.
     c. *Self-expression.* C.R. equals 2.83. Two-sided probability is less than .01.
     d. *Political.* By Fisher's Exact Test, one-sided probability equals 0.28 and two-sided probability .056.
  3. Between postrevolutionary and current Soviet.
     a. *Tradition.* By Fisher's Exact Test, one-sided probability equals .018 and two-sided probability .036.
     b. *Rewards.* C.R. equals 0.18. Even the one-sided probability is greater than .40.
     c. *Self-expression.* C.R. equals 2.15. Two-sided probability is less than .05.
     d. *Political.* C.R. equals 0.18. Even the one-sided probability is greater than .40.

7. For a fuller discussion, see Alex Inkeles, "Social Change and Social Character."

8. Compare David Reisman, *The Lonely Crowd* (New York, 1953).

9. For documentation and discussion, see H. K. Geiger, "The Urban Slavic Family."

Chapter X: THE SOURCES OF SUPPORT: POPULAR VALUES AND ASPIRATIONS

A. Table 57.

Social class is based on I–7. State ownership of transport on IV–12, heavy industry on IV–31, light industry on IV–29. "Keep nothing" includes those respondents who said specifically "keep nothing" in response to IV–20A (What things in the present system would you want to keep in the new one?) or who failed to indicate anything worth keeping. "Keep something" includes all those respondents who, in response to IV–20A, cited one or more aspects of the present system that would be worth keeping in the new one.

Of 2718 cases, 234 are not considered because they were students, other, or DK/NA on social class. Of the remainder of 2484, 557 did not answer question IV–20, and varying numbers failed to answer the state ownership questions. This left 584 who said specifically "keep nothing," and 1239 who named one or more things as worth keeping and who are grouped here under "keep something."

The totals varied slightly depending on the number not answering the particular state ownership question. The N's listed represent the median number answering three questions.

B. Table 58.

Social class is based on L–7, "keep nothing" on IV/20A, and "change everything" on IV–20B. "Change everything" includes all those respondents who said specifically "change everything" in response to IV–20B (What things would you be sure to change [if a new regime were to come to power]?) in contrast to those respondents who indicated specific aspects of the present system which they would favor changing in a new one. The "keep nothing" response is explained in notes to Table 57.

Of 2718 cases, 234 were omitted because they were student, other, or DK/NA on social class, leaving a base for this table of 2484 cases.

1. See David Gleicher, "The Meaning of the 'Keep Nothing' Response," in David Gleicher and Isabel Caro, "Patterns of Ideological and Value Orientation Among Former Soviet Citizens" (unpublished report of the Harvard Project on the Soviet Social System, 1954).

1A. Table 59.

This table is based on those respondents (excluding 234 who were other, student, or DK on social class — I–7) who mentioned some specific institution as worth keeping (1148 cases). That is, it excludes those who were DK/NA on IV–20A (557 cases), those who said "keep nothing" (651 cases), *and* those who said "keep the good things" (128 cases) but failed to cite a *specific* institution.

The base, then, for any social group, is the total in that group who mentioned some institution. The citation of any institution as worth keeping would not occur unless it was salient or highly important to a respondent, since the question was very much "open-ended." Considering these facts it would clearly be unwise to use these per cents as reflecting the *absolute* level of support (as against the relative salience) for any institution. That information is better approached through more direct questions which can be treated in a statistically less ambiguous way.

The headings given stand for our coding categories, as follows: "State ownership" indicates "nationalized planning of economy in general or of strategic parts of it, state ownership of heavy industry, etc." "Social equality and other institutions" indicates "equality of nationalities, race, sex, and class" *and* "institutional forms but different methods of administration and/or really put into practice." "Technical development" indicates "technical development but *no* reference to state ownership." "Arts and science" indicates "cultural-scientific programs, achievements, etc."

1B. Table 60.

This table is based on a matched deck of 980 (490 Munich and 490 New York) cases. The N's given represent the total number of persons citing one or more things to keep, excluding those who said "keep nothing," gave only the vague answer "the good things," or who were DK/NA. Variations in the latter account for the fact that the N's given here are not the same for the Munich and New York samples despite initial matching. The number of peasants who could be matched in New York and Munich was regrettably small, and in this and other manual classes the numbers are further reduced by differences in the "no answer" pattern in the two sets of respondents.

The per cents total to more than 100, since more than one item could be checked by each respondent.

1C. Table 61.

The first part of this table (cradle-to-grave welfare program) is based on the personal interviews. Of a total of 329 cases, 254 are represented here, 16 being unidentifiable by social class and 59 not having answered the question.

The second part of the table is from the written questionnaire. Social group is based on I–7, government guarantee of work on IV–38, age on I–2. Of 2718 cases, 205 were omitted because of DK/NA on age and 208 were eliminated because they were student, other, or DK/NA on social class. Of the remainder (2305 cases), 117 were lost because they were DK/NA on government ownership, leaving a base for this table of 1201 under 41 and 987 who were 41 and over.

1D. Table 62.

Social group is based on I–7, availability of medical care on IV–22, theater and concerts on IV–30, agricultural machinery on IV–21, literacy on IV–34. Because there were variations in the numbers of "no answers" to the various questions, the N's given represent the median number of the given group answering the four questions.

Of 2718 cases, 234 are omitted because they were student, other, or DK/NA on social class.

2. See Mark G. Field, *Doctor and Patient in Soviet Russia* (Cambridge, 1957), especially part III, "The Patient."

3. See Raymond A. Bauer, "Arrest in the Soviet Union" (unpublished report of the Harvard Project on the Soviet Social System, 1953), and Allen Kassof, "Mode of Departure from the Soviet Union" (unpublished report of the Harvard Project on the Soviet Social System, 1953).

3A. Table 63.

This table is based on the personal interviews. Of 329 cases, 16 were omitted because they could not be classified on social class, and 129 were NA concerning their preferred mode of economic organization. This leaves a base of 184 cases considered here.

3B. Table 64.

This table is based on those respondents (excluding 234 who were other, student, or DK on social class — I–7) who mentioned some specific institution as requiring change (1041 cases). That is, it excludes those who were DK/NA on IV–20B (518 cases) and those who said "change everything" (641 cases) or "change everything bad" (284 cases).

The headings given stand for our code categories as follows: "Absolutist state organization" indicates "political form of state in general (institute democracy, etc.)." "Terror and injustice" indicates "introduction of specific freedoms; no reference to political *form* of state" and "organization and practices of state power (eliminate terror)." "Absence of private initiative" indicates "private property, initiative in means of production in general should be instituted; complete change in economy." "Communism and Bolshevik ideology" indicates "abolish Communists and/or Communist Party" and "ideology of Marxism, Bolshevism, Communism."

4. See Samuel A. Stouffer, *Communism, Conformity, and Civil Liberties* (New York, 1955), especially chapter 2.

4A. Table 65.

Social group in the first two sections of this table is based on I–7. Freedom of speech is based on IV–24 and freedom of assembly on IV–37. Freedom of the press data is from the personal interviews and social class in this case was assigned by the coder. Sixteen of the personal interviews were omitted because they could not be classified on social class and 64 were NA on the question, leaving a base of 249 for this column of the table.

In the first and second columns 234 cases were eliminated because they were student, other, or DK/NA on social class. In the first column, 108 were DK/NA on the question and in the second column there were 205, leaving a base for the first and second columns of 2376 and 2279, respectively.

5. For example, the question dealing with the freedom of assembly and describing the aim of the meeting as being "to attack" the government used a Russian word which for many might have suggested physical or armed attack rather than verbal criticism. Under the circumstances we must expect more approval of government intervention than would have been the case had a milder word, such as "to criticize" been used.

6. These comments on conceptions of legality and government authority are not based on statistical analysis of the response to particular questions, but rather on an "impressionistic" or "qualitative" evaluation of a wide range of comments made in the course of our interviews. We have greater confidence in these conclusions because very similar conclusions were arrived at independently by a cultural anthropologist who undertook a "value analysis" of our materials. See Isabel Caro, "Value Patterns of Former Soviet Citizens" in David Gleicher and Isabel Caro, "Patterns of Ideological Orientation Among Former Soviet Citizens" (unpublished report of the Harvard Project on the Soviet Social System, 1954).

6A. Table 66.

Social group is based on I–7, Lenin's contribution on IV–9, Bolsheviks vs. Nazis on IV–18, and fate of Bolshevik leaders on IV–17. The N's given here are the median number in each social class group answering the three questions, since there were slight variations in the N's due to differences in the number of "no answers."

Of 2718 cases, 234 are omitted because they were student, other, or DK/NA on social class.

7. Alice Rossi, "Generational Differences in the Soviet Union" (unpublished

report of the Harvard Project on the Soviet Social System, 1954). There was one seeming departure from this picture. Young people were more inclined than the older to advocate death for the leaders if the regime were overthrown. But as we have earlier noted, an analysis of responses to this question revealed that the people who chose this answer were not the most hostile. The *most* hostile tended to prefer some "other" action, including jail, on the grounds killing was "too good for them."

7A. Table 67.

This table is based on the personal interviews. Social class was assigned by the coder. Of 329 respondents, 16 were omitted because they were unclassifiable on social class, 22 were DK on age, and 53 did not volunteer sufficient comment to be coded on the leadership question. This leaves a base of 238 respondents considered here.

Chapter XI. SOURCES OF HOSTILITY AND DISAFFECTION

1. Some of the materials in this chapter were previously included in Raymond A. Bauer, "Some Trends in Sources of Alienation from the Soviet System," *Public Opinion Quarterly* (Fall 1955).

2. This shift in attitude toward the individual in relation to the state is treated at length in Raymond A. Bauer, *The New Man in Soviet Psychology* (Cambridge, 1952), *passim*.

3. The similarity between the pattern obtained using the distortion scale and that obtained using other measures of hostility is well illustrated in the following table which shows the distribution of "distortion" scores and those on "anti-Soviet sentiment" within the several social groups.

Social class	Distortion Score				Anti-Soviet Sentiment			
	High	Medium	Low	N	High	Medium	Low	N
Intelligentsia	12%	17%	71%	(567)	10%	16%	74%	(632)
White-collar employees	16	25	59	(607)	17	19	64	(670)
Skilled workers	20	26	54	(243)	31	19	50	(277)
Ordinary workers	34	24	42	(410)	37	21	42	(469)
Collective farm peasants	36	24	40	(312)	46	21	33	(372)

The similarity in this pattern does not mean, of course, that in individual rather than group scores the association between different measures of hostility would be so high. But since our analysis is based on trends within groups, this is not a crucial issue here.

4. The "distortion" index, too, has a technical difficulty of which the reader should be aware. Apparently the tendency to "distort," i.e., to express hostility by denial of reality, is related to education regardless of any other factors which may affect it. That is to say that the greater sophistication of the more highly educated respondents seems to make this mode of expression of hostility less acceptable. Therefore, if we were to make a distinction between hostility as such, and the way in which it is expressed, there would be some justification in saying that a college educated man would have to be, in some sense, more hostile in order to give a "distorting" answer than would an illiterate person. To let the case rest there, however, is to miss an essential element in the qualitatively different nature of hostility among the various social and educational groups. Among the lower educated groups, and therefore also those of lower status, hostility — as judged by a variety of criteria — tends to be expressed more directly and to spread over into peripheral areas of opinion. Although the results are not reported here, it was

frequently necessary to employ educational controls in analyzing class differences in manifestation of hostility in order to make sure that we were not measuring *only* different modes of expression of hostility. While such controls invariably reduced the magnitude of the relationships, the relationships nevertheless continued to be manifested strongly in the same direction. In other words, even if one were to contend that the only "true" measure of hostility on the distortion index would be one which compensated for the modes of expression of hostility that are associated with varying degrees of education, all of the *conclusions* which we have drawn would remain unchanged, but the strength of the data on which they are based would be somewhat reduced. In any event, social class and education are so highly correlated that the problem is largely self-correcting. Intelligence hardly has much room to exert "independent" influence in such a situation.

4A. Table 68.

Social group is based on I–7; degree of hostility on the distortion index (Appendix 11). "Least" indicates a score of 0, "medium" a score of 1, and "most" a score of 2–4. The total number of cases considered is 2139, 234 having been omitted because of being student, other, or DK on social class and 345 omitted because they were DK/NA on the distortion index.

4B. Table 69.

Social group is based on I–7; hostility on the distortion index (Appendix 11); and occupational satisfaction on the occupational satisfaction-frustration index (Appendix 19). "Some" hostility indicates a score of 1–4 on the distortion index. High occupational satisfaction indicates a score of 1 or 2; so-so a score of 3 or 4; low a score of 5 or 6, on the six-point scale.

Of 2718 cases, 2145 are represented here. There were 234 eliminated because they were student, other, or DK on social class and 339 were DK/NA on the distortion index.

4C. Table 70.

Social class is based on I–7; hostility on the distortion index (Appendix 11); standard of living on V–17. "Some" hostility indicates a score of 1–4 on the distortion index. Only those respondents saying their standard of living was "better" or "worse" than the majority are considered here (2078 cases). Those citing "average" or DK/NA are omitted.

Further omission of 225 and 180 because of DK/NA on distortion and because of being student, other, or DK/NA on social class, respectively, left a base of 1673 for final consideration in this table.

4D. Table 71.

Social group is based on I–7; hostility on the distortion index (Appendix 11); relationship to the regime on III–1. "No hostility" indicates a score of 0, "some hostility" a score of 1–4 on the distortion index.

Of 2718 cases, 2102 are represented here. There were 10 other and 56 DK/NA on relationship to Soviet regime and 316 DK/NA on distortion. In addition, 234 were omitted because they were student, other, or DK/NA on social class.

4E. Table 72.

Social origin is based on father's occupation type (V–3). Only those of nonmanual or peasant origin are included here, those of worker origin being eliminated. Nonmanual origins include: political or military administrative positions; economic administrative positions, business, managerial, landowner, etc.; arts; professions and applied sciences; semiprofessional; white collar, military. Hostility is based on the distortion index (Appendix 11); respondents' own social group on I–7. An expression of hostility indicates a score of 1–4 on the distortion index.

Of 2718 cases, 1310 are represented here. There were 648 cases of worker origin eliminated at the outset. Also omitted were 418 who were DK or who did not classify their father's occupation type; 131 who were student, other, or DK/NA on social class; and 211 who were DK/NA on the distortion index.

4F. Table 73.

Social class is based on I–7; hostility on the distortion index (Appendix 11); nationality on I–3. Some hostility indicates a score of 1–4 on the distortion index. "Other" nationality includes: Byelorussian, non-Slavic Soviet nationalities, and "others."

Of 2718 cases, 2138 are considered here. There were 234 who were student, other, or DK/NA on social class; 337 DK/NA on distortion; and 9 DK/NA on nationality and were, therefore, eliminated from consideration.

4G. Table 74.

Social class is based on I–7; hostility on the distortion index (Appendix 11); and arrest experience on III–4A. An expression of hostility indicates a score of 1–4 on the distortion index.

The total number of cases considered here is 1652. Of the original 2718 cases, 234 were eliminated because they were student, other, or DK/NA on social class; 227 were DK/NA on the distortion index; and 605 were DK/NA or unclassifiable on arrest.

5. The change from 23 to 36 per cent is a 13-point change; from 33 to 59 per cent adds 26 or an average of 19.5 points for the effect of arrest on groups matched on occupational satisfaction. For groups matched on arrest the changes are from 23 to 33 per cent, or 10 points, and from 36 to 59 for 23 points, an average of 16.5 points.

5A. Table 75.

Occupationally satisfied persons scored 1, 2, or 3 on the occupational satisfaction-frustration index (Appendix 19) and occupationally dissatisfied persons scored 4, 5, or 6 on the six-point scale. To show some hostility persons had to have scores of 1–4 on the distortion index (Appendix 11). No arrest experience indicates no arrest to self or to family. Excluded from consideration are those who indicated arrest experience but failed to specify whether they themselves or their family were involved (see Appendix 7).

Of 2718 cases, 1453 are considered here. There were 234 not considered since they were students, other, or DK/NA on social class (and, therefore, had no occupation). Also 92 were omitted because their arrest experience could not be judged, and 733 were DK/NA on arrest. The remainder, 206 cases, were DK/NA on distortion.

6. This procedure is explained in Note 6A (to Table 76) below.

6A. Table 76.

The percentages given in this table have been weighted to give equal representation to the manual and nonmanual classes. This was accomplished by averaging the percentages for the manual and nonmanual groups. This serves to equalize the greater weight of nonmanuals in the sample as a whole, which is important, when, as in this case, the table gives overall results without separate control by class.

Occupationally satisfied persons scored 1, 2, or 3 on the occupational satisfaction-frustration index (Appendix 19), and occupationally dissatisfied persons scored 4, 5, or 6 on the six-point scale. No arrest experience indicates no arrest to self or to family (Appendix 7). Excluded from consideration are those who indicated arrest experience but failed to specify whether they themselves or their family were involved. Some desire to leave the USSR indicates the response "I wanted to leave the USSR but didn't try to do so." or, "I wanted to leave the USSR very much and tried to do so." to question III–3.

Of 2718 cases, 1233 are considered here. There were 234 eliminated because they were student, other, or DK/NA on social class. Also 92 were omitted because they could not be classified and 733 were DK/NA on arrest. The remainder, 426 cases, were DK/NA on desire to leave the USSR.

6B. Table 77.

Occupationally satisfied persons scored 1, 2, or 3 on the occupational satisfaction-frustration index (Appendix 19) and occupationally dissatisfied persons scored 4, 5, or 6 on the six-point scale. No arrest experience indicates no arrest to self or family (Appendix 7). Excluded from consideration are those who indicated arrest experience but failed to specify whether they themselves or their family were involved. Method of leaving the Soviet Union is based on III–2(1)A. The percentages are weighted simply by averaging those for the manual and nonmanual groups, thus equalizing the greater weight of the nonmanual groups in the sample as a whole.

Of 2718 cases, 1505 are considered here. There were 234 omitted because they were student, other, or DK/NA on social class. Also 92 were eliminated because they were not classifiable on arrest and 733 were DK/NA. The remainder, 154 cases, were either DK/NA or other on mode of leaving the USSR.

6C. Table 78.

Those respondents who indicated in response to question III–1, "I was once favorably inclined toward the regime, but turned against it in . . . (year) before I left the USSR" form the base of this table. Social class is based on I–7 and "reasons for change in relation to the regime" on III–1A.

Of an original base of 791 respondents, those "once in favor" who changed, 707 are considered here. The 84 not represented were either student, other, or DK on social class or failed to indicate a reason for their change in attitude toward the regime.

6D. Table 79.

"Hostile" indicates a score of 1–4 on the distortion index (Appendix 11); "nonhostile" a score of 0. Voluntary departure from the USSR indicates a response to III–2(1)A "deserted (escaped) to the Germans" or "voluntarily escaped with the Germans when the Soviet troops approached." Involuntary departure indicates a response of "taken prisoner by the Germans," or "evacuated forcibly by the Germans."

Of 2718 cases, 2013 are represented here. There were 205 who gave no answer to the question on age (I–2); 344 were DK/NA on the distortion index; and 156 were either other or DK/NA on mode of leaving the USSR.

6E. Table 80.

Age is based on I–2; arrest on III–4(A); mode of departure from the USSR on III–2(1)A. Self arrest includes "respondent arrested once" and "respondent arrested more than once." Voluntary departure from the USSR includes "deserted (escaped) to the Germans" and "voluntarily escaped with the Germans when the Soviet troops approached."

Of 2718 cases, 1770 are represented here. There were 205 no answers to the question on age; and 743 were either unclassifiable or DK/NA on arrest or were also lost because they were DK/NA on mode of leaving the USSR.

6F. Table 81.

Age is based on I–2; arrest on personal arrest profile (Appendix 7). Some hostility indicates a score of 1–4 on the distortion index (Appendix 11). Omitted from consideration are those respondents who indicated arrest but failed to specify whether they themselves or their family were involved.

Of 2718 cases, 1544 are represented in this table. There were 205 DK/NA on age, 69 unclassifiable and 676 DK/NA on arrest, and 224 DK/NA on distortion.

6G. Table 82.

Occupational mobility in relation to father's occupation is based on the mobility code (Appendix 18); arrest is based on III–4A. No arrest indicates no arrest either to respondent or family.

Of 2718 cases, 1206 are represented here. There were 805 DK/NA on arrest and there was insufficient information on the remainder of 707 to warrant their inclusion in the mobility index.

6H. Table 83.

This table is based on a special questionnaire on the wartime occupation. The sample of 902 includes only those respondents, exclusive of western Ukrainians, who lived in Soviet areas occupied by the Germans. Except for 14 cases which were obtained in New York, all the questionnaires were administered in Germany.

Age is based on I–2 and mode of departure from the USSR on III–2(1)A, as given in core questionnaire in Appendix 1. The information on belief in German victory is based on question 16 of the wartime occupation questionnaire, which reads: "Did you think at the beginning that the Germans would win the war?" Possible answers were: "Yes," "No," or "No answer."

Of 902 cases, 690 are represented here. There were 124 DK/NA on age; 49 DK/NA on belief in German victory; and the remaining 39 were DK/NA on mode of departure from the USSR.

Chapter XII. THE PROBLEM OF LOYALTY IN SOVIET SOCIETY

1. Cf. Mark Field, "Alcoholism, Crime and Delinquency in Soviet Society," *Social Problems*, 3:100–109 (October 1955).

2. Cf. the discussion of the early statements of the new leadership in Bertram D. Wolfe, *Six Keys to the Soviet System* (Beacon Press: Boston, 1955), pp. 1ff.

3. The same general problems of adjustment have been described for the more extreme case of inmates in a Nazi concentration camp. Cf. Bruno Bettleheim, "Individual and Mass Behavior in Extreme Situations," reprinted in Guy E. Swanson, Theodore Newcomb, and Eugene Hartley, eds., *Readings in Social Psychology* (New York, 1952).

4. H. Kent Geiger, "The Urban Slavic Family" (unpublished report of the Harvard Project on the Soviet System, 1954). Also see: Alice Rossi, "Generational Differences" (unpublished report of the Russian Research Center, 1954); Alex Inkeles, "Social Change and Social Character," *The Journal of Social Issues*, XI:12–23 (November 1955).

5. The orientation of Soviet families toward this problem is discussed at length in the report of H. K. Geiger, "The Urban Slavic Family."

6. The relationship between loyalty and the stability of the system became clear to us early in our exposure to these data. The essential formulations of this section were presented by us on several occasions in the months immediately following Stalin's death, and well in advance of the dramatic events in Eastern Europe during 1956–57. See Raymond A. Bauer, "The Pseudo-Charismatic Leader in Soviet Society," *Problems of Communism*, 1953, Nos. 3 and 4; "The Implications of the Succession Crisis in the Soviet Union for East-West Relations," *Social Problems*, Vol. 1, No. 2 (October 1953); and "The Social Psychology of Political Loyalty in Liberal and Totalitarian Societies" (unpublished paper read before the American Association for the Advancement of Science, December 1953).

7. The fight of the regime to increase labor productivity reveals the entire range of the phenomenon discussed here. See Jerzy Gliksman, "Conditions of Industrial

Labor in the USSR: A Study of the Incentive System in Soviet Industry" (unpublished report of the Harvard Project on the Soviet Social System, 1954).

8. See Alex Inkeles and Raymond A. Bauer, "Portrait of Soviet Russia by Russians," *New York Times Magazine,* November 25, 1951; Raymond A. Bauer, "The Social Psychology of Political Loyalty"; Clyde Kluckhohn, Alex Inkeles and Raymond A. Bauer, "Strategic Psychological and Sociological Strengths and Vulnerabilities of the Soviet Social System" (unpublished report of the Harvard Project on the Soviet Social System, 1954).

Chapter XIII. SOCIAL CLASS CLEAVAGE

1. Much of the material in this chapter appeared originally in Alex Inkeles, "Images of Class Relations Among Former Soviet Citizens," *Social Problems,* Vol. 3, No. 3 (January 1956). Harvey Fireside assisted in the analysis.

2. Joseph Stalin, "On the Draft Constitution of the USSR" in his *Leninism: Selected Writings* (New York, 1942).

3. Joseph Stalin, "New Conditions, New Tasks in Economic Construction," in his *Leninism.*

3A. Table 84.

Rating group is based on I–7; assessments of fair shares ("less than deserved") on IV–2, A–E. Since the number of "no answers" concerning the rewards of the different classes varied, the N's given here for each rating group represent the median number responding on five "votes." The fifth class rated, the party workers, is not shown in the table. However, the number of persons in each rating group rendering an opinion about the party workers was considered in determining the median N's given in the table. The averages given at the far right represent averages of the row percentages, and therefore give equal weight to each rating group regardless of its actual size relative to the total sample.

Of 2718 cases, 234 are eliminated because they were student, other, or DK/NA on social class and 42 are omitted because they failed to answer the question on fair shares entirely for any social group. Of the remaining 2442 cases, varying numbers were eliminated as no answers on the different questions, leaving an approximate base for the table of 2347 cases.

4. Since the skilled worker rating group had no identical opposite number among the classes evaluated, we decided to simplify the complex presentation in this chapter by including them with those who identified as "ordinary workers" in a single "worker" rating group.

5. Due to an oversight, one possible pair, that of "employees-peasants" was omitted. Because of the regularity of the total pattern of responses to the other pairs it was possible to interpolate values for "employees-peasants." This interpolated column is marked by an asterisk in Table 85. Its inclusion restores the symmetry of the table, but it should be noted that none of the conclusions in this section would be affected in any major way by either the omission or inclusion of the interpolated data.

6. In the case of the peasant-employee relationship, however, the figure is one of those we interpolated.

6A. Table 85.

Rating group is based on I–7; coincidence of interests between classes on IV–4, A–E. Figures given in the row for the pair "Employee-Peasant" are estimates, since inadvertently no direct question was asked pertaining to the coincidence of interests between these two groups. Since the number of "no answers" concerning the coincidence of interests between the pairs of classes varied, the N's given here represent the median number responding on five "votes," each "vote" representing an evaluation of the relations between a different pair of classes. The averages (last col.) represent averages of row percentages, and therefore give equal weight to each rating group regardless of its actual size relative to the total sample.

Of 2718 cases, 234 are omitted because they were student, other, or DK/NA on social class and 323 are omitted because they failed to give a response on coincidence of interest for any pair of classes. Of the remaining 2161 cases, varying numbers are omitted as DK/NA on coincidence of interest between the different pairs of classes, leaving an approximate base for the table of 1783 cases.

6B. Table 87.

There were 2145 respondents who completed a supplementary questionnaire which included job and stratification data. It is these respondents who form the base for this table. Rating group is based on I–7; interclass harm on Strat 2A, 3A, 4A, and 5A (Which group has done the second most harm to a particular social group?). The responses to the question (Strat 2, 3, 4, 5) of which class did the *most* harm are not considered here, since these answers overwhelmingly cited the "party cadres" to the exclusion of any other class group.

Of 2145 respondents, 195 are eliminated because they either did not receive the stratification questions or were student, other, or DK/NA on social class. In addition, those who named the "party cadres" *again* as the group which did the *second* most harm were omitted throughout (400, 395, 393, 402 for table parts A, B, C, and D, respectively). Also omitted were those who did not cite any group as doing the second most harm (370, 376, 265, and 273 for table parts A, B, C, and D, respectively). In some instances, a respondent checked more than one class as being second most harmful which, together with variations in the number of DK/NA responses, accounts for differences in the total N's for each part of the table.

6C. Table 88.

All the figures in Table 88 are drawn directly from Table 87, but in this arrangement the rows no longer add up to 100 per cent. The table is so arranged, however, that the distribution of opinion within any rating group about the harm done to any social class may be ascertained from those four cells each of which is in the same position in the four parts of the table. For example, to find the distribution of opinion among the intelligentsia as to the harm done to the peasant, take the percentage given in the upper right corner cell in each of the four parts of Table 88. It will be seen that 100 per cent of the intelligentsia's opinion about the harm done to the peasant is accounted for. Reading clockwise, we see that 11 per cent said the harm was done by the intelligentsia, 18 per cent charged the white-collar employees with the same harm done, 30 per cent blamed the workers, and 41 per cent said it was the peasantry itself which harmed the peasant.

6D. Table 89.

This table is based on the information presented in Table 87. Each figure in Table 89 represents the average of three figures drawn from Table 87. Those three figures yield the "average" assessment of the harmfulness attributed by any opinion group to *other* social classes, that is, to all *but* itself. For example, take the top figure in the second column, 16 per cent. This is the average of the three per cents (or "votes") by the intelligentsia on the harmfulness of the employees to *other* (non-employee) social groups. This figure of 16 per cent was obtained thus: From Table 87 we take from each part the figure on the first line at the top of the second column. Each of the figures will tell us what proportion of the intelligentsia believed a particular class to have been harmed by the employees. This gives us 12, 56, 17, and 18 from parts A–D, respectively. We then eliminate the 56, since this records the opinion about the employees harming not others but themselves. The remaining three figures average out at 16 per cent. The process is repeated to get the average harmfulness attributed to each of the other classes.

The averages at the bottom of each column are averages of the column percentages. However, since the cells in the diagonal represent a group's assessment of its *own* harmfulness, these assessments are not included in the averaged percentages, which represent the opinion groups had of *each other*. In other words, "average harmfulness to other groups" is arrived at by averaging the three percentages other than the one bracketed.

6E. Table 90.

This table is based on responses to a special questionnaire dealing with experiences under the German occupation, which was completed by 902 respondents. The sample includes only those respondents, exclusive of Western Ukrainians, who lived in Soviet areas occupied by the Germans. All the questionnaires were administered in Germany, except for 14 which were obtained in New York and which are omitted here.

Social class is based on I–7; perception of class adjustment to German occupation on wartime occupation questions 13A, 14A and 8 (Which of the following groups fared best under the German occupation? Which of the following groups fared worst under the German occupation? Which of the following groups were most friendly toward the Germans?).

Of 902 cases, the 14 mentioned above are eliminated as are 94 who were student, other, or DK/NA on social class, leaving a base for this table of 794. This table does not total to 100 per cent in any direction and is not intended to. It should be read as follows: Of 184 respondents in the intelligentsia, 47 per cent felt that the peasants fared best under the Germans, meaning that the remaining 53 per cent must have felt some other group like the "workers" or "party people" fared best.

7. Gabriel Grasberg, "Problems of Stratification" (unpublished report of the Harvard Project on the Soviet Social System, 1954).

7A. Table 91.

This table is based on 2145 respondents who completed a supplementary questionnaire which included job and stratification data. Social class is based on I–7; class leadership most wanted on Strat 7 (see Appendix 1) and least wanted on Strat 7A (see Appendix 1). The N's given here represent the number of respondents in each social group who answered the question on class leadership.

In both parts of the table, of 2145 respondents 195 were omitted because they either did not receive the stratification questions or were student, other, or DK/NA on social class. Also eliminated as DK/NA on the class leadership question were 223 and 272 on the first and second parts of the table, respectively — leaving a base of 1727 for the first part and 1678 on the second part of the table.

8. Some additional evidence for this conclusion will be found in Alex Inkeles, "Images of Class Relations."

8A. Table 92.

The data for the Soviet sample (lines 2, 4, 6) follow Table 84, with the opinion group "worker" separated into "skilled worker" and "ordinary worker." The data for the United States are from Arthur W. Kornhauser, "Analysis of Class Structure," *op. cit.*, table XIV, p. 255, columns 5, 6, and 9. To obtain the American data we simply averaged the percentages given by Kornhauser for the several opinion groups as follows: "Professional-administrative" equals all groups from "major business executives" through "school teachers"; "white collar" equals salesmen plus the three categories of office employees; skilled worker equals skilled worker; ordinary worker equals semiskilled and unskilled worker.

9. From a Fortune poll, reported in Cantril, *Public Opinion*, p. 330.

Chapter XIV. POLITICAL CLEAVAGE IN THE SOVIET UNION: POPULAR IMAGES OF THE PARTY AND THE SECRET POLICE

1. We do not necessarily include in this generalization those in our sample who were party members. Although the proportion of party members in our sample compared favorably with that in the parent Soviet population, the *absolute* number who completed the personal interview was only 11. Eight others had been "candidate" members. This group was too small to permit a systematic comparison of their image of the party with that of the nonparty citizen. On the whole, their description included most of the criticisms and distinctions noted by the nonmember. In any event, our concern here is with the way in which the ordinary citizen saw the party and its members.

2. See T. H. Rigby, "Social Orientation of Recruitment and Distribution of Membership in the Communist Party of the Soviet Union," *American Slavic and East European Review*, 16:275–290 (1957), and Nicholas DeWitt, *Soviet Professional Manpower*, National Science Foundation (Washington, D.C., 1955).

3. Based on written questionnaire.

4. This discussion of popular images of the secret police is based on a detailed study by Dr. Arthur Adams, which constitutes Appendix B of "Political Activism and Social Cleavage in the USSR" (unpublished report of the Harvard Project on the Soviet Social System, 1954).

Chapter XV. THE NATIONALITY PROBLEM

1. In the preparation of this chapter we were greatly aided by the initial work of Sylvia Gilliam, who analyzed the results of the Ukrainian nationality questionnaire, and Irving Rosow, who compared the responses of Russians and Ukrainians on the general questionnaire. We are also indebted to John Reshetar and Michael Luther for their study of the history of Soviet policy toward the Ukraine and popular reactions to that policy by refugee leaders of the national minorities. For further details consult? Sylvia Gilliam, Irving Rosow, and John Reshetar, "The Nationality Problem in the Soviet Union: The Ukrainian Case" (unpublished report of the Harvard Project on the Soviet Social System, Russian Research Center, October 1954).

2. For an authoritative review of these developments, see Richard Pipes, *The Formation of the Soviet Union* (Cambridge, 1954).

3. For a region by region review of these developments see Walter Kolarz, *Russia and Her Colonies* (New York, 1952).

4. For discussion of the complex story of the Ukrainian independence movement in this early period, see Pipes, *The Formation,* and John Reshetar, *The Ukrainian Revolution: 1917–1920* (Princeton, 1952).

5. The number of completed questionnaires was actually 511. Of these, however, 52 were filled out by Ukrainians who had lived in territories ruled by Poland until they were annexed by the Soviet Union in 1939–40. We were, of course, mainly concerned with studying reactions to Soviet conditions as experienced by life-long Soviet citizens. Since most of this group of 52 lived under Soviet rule for less than two years before the Germans swept into the area, they were not included in the analysis presented below. This group is, however, an important seg-

ment of the contemporary Soviet Ukraine since it was largely kept under Soviet control after World War II. Full details may be found in Sylvia Gilliam, Irving Rosow, and John Reshetar, "The Nationality Problem."

6. These and related materials on Soviet policy in the Ukraine are being analyzed and will be reported in separate publications by Dr. John Reshetar and Michael Luther, the members of the Project staff chiefly responsible for the study of the nationality problem with specific reference to the Ukraine. See John Reshetar and Michael Luther, "Aspects of the Nationality Problem in the USSR" (unpublished report of the Harvard Project on the Soviet Social System, 1952).

7. Numerous illustrations of these themes may be found in any one of the various publications of the national minorities organized in the West. See, for example, *The Ukrainian Bulletin,* published semi-monthly by the Ukrainian Congress Committee of America, New York.

8. Many Ukrainians believed, and still believe, that the intensity of collectivization and the famine were arranged by the Soviet regime in order to break the will to resistance of the Ukrainian nation. See John Reshetar, "National Deviation in the Soviet Union," *The American Slavic and East European Review* (April 1953).

8A. Table 93.

This table is based on a subsample of respondents (1269 cases) who were born between 1905 and 1925. Only those of Russian or Ukrainian nationality are considered here.

Origin is based on father's postrevolutionary social group (V–2) or, if the respondent was DK/NA on this question, origin was based on mother's postrevolutionary social group (V–2); nationality on I–3; education on VII–1.

White-collar includes: party-Soviet apparatus; intelligentsia; employee. Worker includes: skilled workers; artisans; rank-and-file workers. Peasant includes both dekulakized and non-dekulakized kolkhozniks.

"More than 10 years" of schooling includes: some higher education; completed higher education; graduate work.

Eliminated from the original base of 1269 were 224 who were of a nationality other than Russian or Ukrainian and 3 who were DK/NA on nationality, as well as 15 who indicated "other" schooling, such as special courses, home education, etc. This leaves a total base considered in this table of 1027 cases.

9. Irving Rosow, "The Relation of Nationality to Experience and Attitude in the USSR" (unpublished report of the Harvard Project on the Soviet Social System, 1954).

9A. Table 94.

Education is based on VII–1; nationality on I–3; occupation attained on II–1. "More than 10 years" of schooling includes: some higher education; completed higher education; graduate work. Professional includes: arts; applied sciences; professional; high managerial personnel and military. Semiprofessional includes both semiprofessional and white-collar. Worker includes semiskilled and unskilled workers.

Of 2718 respondents, 1656 are considered here, since 53 were omitted because they indicated "other" education (special courses, home education, etc.). Also 414 were of a nationality other than Russian or Ukrainian or were DK/NA on nationality and 595 were students, housewives, or DK/NA on attained occupation.

9B. Table 95.

Age in 1950 is based on I–2; nationality on I–3. Occupation is based on II–1, grouped as follows: professional includes arts, applied sciences, professional, high managerial personnel and military; semiprofessional includes semiprofessional and white-collar; worker includes skilled, semiskilled, and unskilled workers. Occupational dissatisfaction indicates a source of 5 or 6 on a six-point scale on the occupational satisfaction-frustration index (Appendix 19).

Of 2718 respondents, 1574 are represented here. There were 205 DK/NA on age and 413 were either of a nationality other than Russian or Ukrainian or were DK/NA on nationality. Also, 526 were either students, housewives, or DK/NA on occupation.

10. Identical proportions of peasants (41 per cent) among Russians and Ukrainians scored high on the political rights index. Among workers the Ukrainians were 1 per cent lower. In the remaining classes more of the Ukrainians scored high. The proportions strong for civil rights, with Ukrainians listed second, were (in per cents) 46–52, 37–43, and 38–47 for intelligentsia, white-collar, and skilled workers respectively. These differences are thus of roughly the same order of magnitude and regularity as those reported in Table 96.

10A. Table 96.

Social class is based on I–7; government guarantee employment on IV–38; government ownership of heavy industry on IV–31; government ownership of light industry on IV–29; government permit/forbid inequality on IV–7, with the responses "inequality should be forbidden" and "there should be limited intervention" combined in the heading "prevent economic inequality."

The N's used as a base for the percentages varied with the rate of DK/NA. The numbers given here are, therefore, approximate for any item but representative for the set of items. Omitted from consideration are 234 who were student, other, or DK/NA on social class and 413 who were either of a nationality other than Russian or Ukrainian or were DK/NA on nationality.

11. There is also some indication that interviewers working in Ukrainian in New York were themselves more sensitive to the nationality problem, and therefore tended more to call it to the attention of those interviewed.

11A. Table 97.

Social class is based on I–7; nationality on I–3; most important factors in marriage on V–18; A-bomb Moscow on IV–28. The percentages given in the second part of the table represent those who answered "Yes, a bomb should be dropped on Moscow now."

Since the number of no answers to the two questions varied, the N given is in each case the *smaller* of the two, i.e., at least that many people in each nationality and social group answered each question. Omitted from consideration were 234 who were student, other, or DK/NA on social class and 381 who were of a nationality other than Russian or Ukrainian or who were DK/NA on nationality.

11B. Table 98.

This table is based on a special wartime occupation questionnaire of 902 cases, not included as an Appendix. It includes only those respondents, exclusive of Western Ukrainians, who lived in Soviet areas occupied by the Germans. Except for 14 cases which were obtained in New York, all the questionnaires were administered in Germany.

Considered in this table are only those respondents who were either Russian or Ukrainian by nationality. The question was: "If you lived in a national republic, how strong were the tendencies toward self-determination, how did they manifest themselves, and what was the attitude of the Germans toward them?" We consider here only those who were in a position to judge the movement. The great majority, whom we do not consider, either did not know about the movement or thought there was none in their region. Taking Russians and Ukrainians together, there were 133 cases, who form the base for the table, who described *both* the strength of the movement and the attitude of the Germans toward it.

11C. Table 99.

Only those respondents whose nationality was Ukrainian are considered in this table.

In the case of the general questionnaire (cols. 1 and 3), nationality is based on I–3, which yielded 947 Ukrainians. Social group is based on occupation (II–1); most important factors in marriage on V–18; least important factors in marriage on V–18B. White-collar includes: arts; applied science; professional; semiprofessional; white-collar; high managerial personnel and military. Workers includes skilled, semiskilled, and unskilled workers. In section A, col. 1 of 947 Ukrainians who filled out the questionnaire there are 605 represented. There were 241 who were either students, other, housewives or DK/NA on occupation, and 101 who gave no answer on most important factors in marriage. In section B there are 565 represented. There were 241 who were either students, other, housewives, or DK/NA on occupation and 141 who gave no answer on least important factors in marriage. (It should be noted that the figures in this table based on the general questionnaire questions on most important factors in marriage differ slightly from those in Table 97. This is due to the fact that in Table 97 social class was used where here occupational group is used.)

The nationality questionnaire (cols. 2 and 4) was administered to 511 Ukrainians (all in Germany except for 32). Excluded from consideration is a group of 52 Ukrainians from Poland, leaving a base of 459. Social class is based on occupation (What was your steady occupation in the Soviet Union?); factors most important in marriage on "Which of the following elements is the most important for a happy marriage?" and factors least important in marriage on "Which element is least in importance for a happy marriage?" White-collar includes: arts; applied sciences; professional; semiprofessional; white-collar. Worker includes skilled, semiskilled, and unskilled workers. In section A, 324 cases are represented. Eliminated are 52 Ukrainians from Poland; 120 who were students, other housewives, or DK/NA on occupation; and 5 who gave no answer on most important factors in marriage. In section B, 312 cases are represented. Eliminated are 52 Ukrainians from Poland; 130 who were students, other, housewives, or DK/NA on occupation; and 17 who gave no answer on least important factors in marriage.

12. All the percentages in the next two paragraphs deal with the sample as a whole rather than on subgroup differences. We have, therefore, used as a base the total number of respondents without exclusion of "no answer" cases.

13. It will be noted that 66 per cent said Ukrainians were more often arrested, yet 44 per cent either named non-Ukrainians or asserted that all were arrested equally. This came about for several reasons: many people cited more than one non-Ukrainian nationality as having "relatively more" arrests; other cited Ukrainians as most arrested but went on to add that all were more or less equally vulnerable or that vulnerability was mainly on grounds of failure to support the regime.

14. The question was actually worded so that it asked whether Ukrainians gave less support than did the Russians. Fifty-seven per cent said explicitly that Ukrainians gave less support to the Bolsheviks. We are assuming that by implication they were saying the Russians gave more support.

15. Respondents often selected more than one group as responsible for the Bolshevik rise to power. This accounts for the fact that the 59 per cent here noted as blaming members of the party, added to those cited in the preceding paragraph as blaming Russians or Jews, total to more than 100 per cent.

15A. Table 100.

This table is based on the 511 nationality questionnaires previously described. Only those respondents who indicated their church membership to be Synodal (147 respondents) or Autocephalous (269 respondents) are considered — providing a total table base of 416.

Since the number of no answers varied with the questions, the N's given are the median N's for the range of items used in the table.

Reading from top to bottom the questions were as follows. "Did Soviet conditions encourage the speaking of Ukrainian?" "From which nationality were there relatively more arrests of the intelligentsia?" "If you answered in the preceding question that the regime exploited certain regions more than others then please indicate which region or regions were more exploited, and which were less exploited." "Which of the following elements is the most important for a happy marriage?" "Which group is most responsible for the Bolsheviks coming to power?" "In general, in comparison with the Ukrainians, the Russians offered greater, less, the same opposition to collectivization?" "In general, certain nationality groups have tended to band together with certain others because of a greater feeling of things in common with these groups and not with others. We would like to know with which of the nationality groups listed below the Ukrainians have felt the most in common and with which of these groups they have had a clash of interests." "Many people say that relations between people of different nationalities are sometimes actually good, sometimes outwardly good but actually bad, and sometimes actually bad. Therefore, we have compiled a list of places where for example, Ukrainians and Russians, or Ukrainians and Jews would most likely work or live together. On the basis of your own personal experience, we should like you to indicate what were the relations between these different groups, in general terms in these different places." [The next item in the table is also in answer to this question.] "Do you feel that the Soviet nationality policy has led to a better understanding, harmony, and friendship between the different peoples of the USSR?" "Did your nationality have any significance for your advancing in your career (at work, in school, in party and state organizations)?" "Has the Soviet nationality policy improved the position of the Ukrainian people?" "In general, did members of the party and Komsomol seek to root out cases of people being offended because of their nationality?"

16. An estimate for 1930–31 distributed church membership in the Ukraine as follows: Autocephalous, 6 million; Synodal (Russian Orthodox), 12 million; and Living Church, 8 million [*Die Religion in Geschichte und Gegenwart,* 5, 1342–43 (Tuebingen, 1931)]. Since about 80 per cent of the inhabitants of the Ukraine were Ukrainians by nationality [*Bolshaya Entsiklopediya* (Moscow, 1948), p. 62, gives this level for 1933] this would mean there were approximately 20 million Ukrainians in the Ukraine, of whom 6 million, or 30 per cent, were Autocephalous.

17. In contrast to the estimated one third of all Ukrainians in the Autocephalous Church in 1930, almost two thirds of those in our sample were members of that church. It is not unlikely that those in the church would be more prone to become nonreturners. In addition, however, we must consider the possibility that many of our respondents switched over to the Ukrainian Church only after becoming refugees. Unfortunately, we neglected to ask whether or not church membership had been the same while the respondent was still in the USSR.

17A. Table 10.

This table is based on the nationality questionnaire, described in notes to Table 99. Occupations are grouped as described in notes to Table 99. Views on separatism are based on the question as given in the text.

Of 511 cases, 52 Ukrainians from Poland are eliminated. Of the remaining 459 cases, 251 are represented here. Eliminated were 130 who were students, other, housewives, or DK/NA on occupation, 47 who were DK on separatism, and 31 who belonged to another church or were DK on religion.

18. The findings reported in this paragraph are based on an informal recording of the personal interviews of Ukrainians undertaken by Miss Gilliam in the course of preparing her report.

19. We have already noted that in answer to the question about what in the system should be changed, references to the nationality policy came predominantly from those interviewed in New York, where émigré organizations were more consistent and better organized in propagating the idea of Ukrainian separatism.

Chapter XVI. THE FUTURE OF SOVIET SOCIETY

1. A major portion of this chapter was included in a statement presented by Alex Inkeles to the Committee on Foreign Relations, United States Senate, February 19, 1958. The content of that statement also appeared in somewhat revised form under the title "The Challenge of a Stable Russia," *The Antioch Review,* 18:133–144 (Summer 1958).

2. See Carl J. Friedrich, ed., *Totalitarianism* (Cambridge, 1954); Carl J. Friedrich and Zbigniew Brzezinski, *Totalitarian Dictatorship and Autocracy* (Cambridge, 1957).

3. "Strategic Psychological and Sociological Strengths and Vulnerabilities of the Soviet Social System" (report of the Harvard Project on the Soviet Social System, October 1954), p. 52; and R. Bauer, A. Inkeles, and C. Kluckhohn, *How the Soviet System Works* (Cambridge, 1956), p. 218.

Index

naire, 356, Table 99; description of, 363–364

NEP (New Economic Policy), 68–69, 252, 274; as preferred mode of economic organization, Table 63; as "golden age" of Soviet development, 246

Newcomb, Theodore, 114n

Newspapers, frequency of use of, Table 11 (Munich vs. New York); types of, 159–160; circulation of, 160, 492; accessibility of, 160; content of, 162; as source of information, 162, 164, 166–169, Table 43; Table 45; exposure to Table 11 (Munich vs. New York), 166–167, 169, 170, Table 44, Table 46, Table 47, 492; in countryside, 171–174; use of by intelligentsia, 174–177. *See also* Soviet press

Nicolaevsky, Boris, 9

NKVD (People's Commissariat of Internal Affairs), 332n.

"No answer" rate, 55, 476; on social class membership, 74; on friends, 199; on state ownership of economy, 243; on collective farm system, 244; on distinguishing between kinds of party members, 327–328

Nonmanual classes, have highest rate of mobility, 82; chance for a career among, 85; educational opportunity of, 86; high job satisfaction among, 103–104, 106, 111; reasons for job dissatisfaction, 117–118, Table 27; quality most desired on job, 117–118, Table 28; educational opportunity among, 134–135; educational attainments of, 137–139, Table 32; reasons for securing an education, 151–153, Table 40; communications behavior, 185; legitimacy of rewards received by, 301–303; conflict of interests with manual groups, 304; feel most harm comes from manuals, 311; class solidarity of, 312. *See also* Social class

NTS, 469

Occupation, generational differences in, 33–34; as criterion of social class membership, 74–75; undesirability of manual, 79–80; education as key to advancement in, 85–86; effect of on saying "had chance for a career," 93–94, Table 19; importance of, 101; arrest and level of, 108; reasons for disliking, 107–112, 117–119, Table 27; politicization of, 107–108, 119–120; income levels of different, 112–114; impact of regime on, 119–120; changes in atmosphere in, 125–127; influence on communications behavior, 165–

168; importance of personal security in, 119–120; political loyalty required in, 288–289; support of regime through, 289–290; influence of nationality on, 343–345, Table 94; as determinant of job satisfaction, 346, Table 95; as determinant of life chances, 347, 380; influence on views on nationality problem, 364–365; influences views on separatism, 367, Table 101.

Occupational aspiration, of Soviet generation, 79–80; effect of social origin on, 86–88, Table 16; realization of, 88–92, Table 18; values in guiding child's, 225–228, Table 56.

Occupational opportunity, equality of, 82–83; determinants of, 84; role of social status in, 85; among manuals, 97–99. *See also* Career: chance for

Occupational placement, of respondents, 33, Table 4, Table 13; influence of education on, 85–87, Table 14, Table 15

Occupational ratings, supplementary questionnaire on, 17, Table 1, Appendix 1; of thirteen occupations, 71–79, Table 12, 478, 479

Occupational satisfaction, effect of kulak origin on, 30, Table 3; effect of Flattery Score on, Table 7; Munich vs. New York differences, Table 11; ratio vs. frustrated, 91–92, 96–97; distortion in reporting, 103; relation to social class, 104, 261; level of, 103–105; national comparisons of, 103–105, Table 21; among women, 105; differentiated from "liking" job, 106; influence of political attitudes on, 106–107; influence of occupational level on, 103–105; income related to, 115–116, 119–120; income satisfaction related to, 116, Table 26; relationship to hostility, 261–262, Table 69, 267–268, Table 75, 507; effect on "voluntary" departure from Soviet Union, 270–271, Table 77; influence of nationality on, 346, Table 95

Ostarbeiter, 8, 32

Parsons, Talcott, 9

Peasants, social origins of, 29–31, Table 3; effects of revolution on, 68; effects of collectivization on, 71, 380; per cent of population in 1939, 73; ranked lowest in occupational realm, 76–78; mobility rate of, 81–83, 347; influence of education in occupational attainment of, 87, Table 15; chance for nonmanual jobs among, 92; occupational frustration of,

RUSSIAN RESEARCH CENTER STUDIES

The Russian Research Center of Harvard University is supported by a grant from the Carnegie Corporation. The Center carries out interdisciplinary study of Russian institutions and behavior and related subjects.

1. *Public Opinion in Soviet Russia: A Study in Mass Persuasion,* by Alex Inkeles
2. *Soviet Politics — The Dilemma of Power: The Role of Ideas in Social Change,* by Barrington Moore, Jr.
3. *Justice in Russia: An Interpretation of Soviet Law,* by Harold J. Berman‡
4. *Chinese Communism and the Rise of Mao,* by Benjamin I. Schwartz
5. *Titoism and the Cominform,* by Adam B. Ulam
6. *A Documentary History of Chinese Communism,* by Conrad Brandt, Benjamin Schwartz, and John K. Fairbank
7. *The New Man in Soviet Psychology,* by Raymond A. Bauer
8. *Soviet Opposition to Stalin: A Case Study in World War II,* by George Fischer
9. *Minerals: A Key to Soviet Power,* by Demitri B. Shimkin
10. *Soviet Law in Action: The Recollected Cases of a Soviet Lawyer,* by Harold J. Berman and Boris A. Konstantinovsky
11. *How Russia Is Ruled,* by Merle Fainsod
12. *Terror and Progress USSR: Some Sources of Change and Stability in the Soviet Dictatorship,* by Barrington Moore, Jr.
13. *The Formation of the Soviet Union: Communism and Nationalism,* 1917–1923, by Richard Pipes
14. *Marxism: The Unity of Theory and Practice,* by Alfred G. Meyer
15. *Soviet Industrial Production,* 1928–1951, by Donald R. Hodgman
16. *Soviet Taxation: The Fiscal and Monetary Problems of a Planned Economy,* by Franklyn D. Holzman
17. *Soviet Military Law and Administration,* by Harold J. Berman and Miroslav Kerner
18. *Documents on Soviet Military Law and Administration,* edited and translated by Harold J. Berman and Miroslav Kerner
19. *The Russian Marxists and the Origins of Bolshevism,* by Leopold H. Haimson
20. *The Permanent Purge: Politics in Soviet Totalitarianism,* by Zbigniew K. Brzezinski
21. *Belorussia: The Making of a Nation,* by Nicholas P. Vakar
22. *A Bibliographical Guide to Belorussia,* by Nicholas P. Vakar
23. *The Balkans in Our Time,* by Robert Lee Wolff
24. *How the Soviet System Works: Cultural, Psychological, and Social Themes,* by Raymond A. Bauer, Alex Inkeles, and Clyde Kluckhohn*
25. *The Economics of Soviet Steel,* by M. Gardner Clark
26. *Leninism,* by Alfred G. Meyer
27. *Factory and Manager in the USSR,* by Joseph S. Berliner*
28. *Soviet Transportation Policy,* by Holland Hunter
29. *Doctor and Patient in Soviet Russia,* by Mark G. Field *
30. *Russian Liberalism,* by George Fischer
31. *Stalin's Failure in China,* 1924–1927, by Conrad Brandt
32. *The Communist Party of Poland,* by M. K. Dziewanowski
33. *Karamzin's Memoir on Ancient and Modern Russia, A Translation and Analysis,* by Richard Pipes

* Publications of the Harvard Project on the Soviet Social System.
† Published jointly with the Center for International Affairs, Harvard University.
‡ Out of print.

Illustrators 35.

DATE			

THE SOCIETY OF ILLUSTRATORS
35TH ANNUAL OF AMERICAN ILLUSTRATION

ILLUSTRATORS 35

From the exhibition held in the galleries of the
Society of Illustrators Museum of American Illustration
128 East 63rd Street, New York City
January 22 - March 26, 1993

Society of Illustrators, Inc.
128 East 63rd Street, New York, NY 10021

ISBN 0-8230-6300-3
Library of Congress Catalog Card Number 59-10849

Distributors to the trade in the United States
Watson-Guptill Publications
1515 Broadway, New York, NY 10036

Distributed throughout the rest of the world by:
Rotovision, S.A.
9 Route Suisse
1295 Mies, Switzerland

Edited by Jill Bossert
Cover design by Daniel Schwartz
Cover painting by Daniel Schwartz
Interior design by Doug Johnson and Ryuichi Minakawa
Layout and Production by Naomi Minakawa

Printed in Hong Kong

Photo Credits: C.F. Payne by Alan Brown/Photonics; Jerry Pinkney by Alan S. Orling; Elwood H. Smith by Doug
Baz; Edward Sorel by Anne Hall

ILLUSTRATORS 35

THE SOCIETY OF ILLUSTRATORS 35TH ANNUAL OF AMERICAN ILLUSTRATION

1/35

Published by Rotovision S.A. Geneva

PRESIDENT'S MESSAGE

Sincere congratulations to all those who are included in this historical edition! *Illustrators 35* continues the tradition of being the only official juried record for excellence in all facets of American illustration.

This year, we've again attempted with great determination to clearly address specific areas of illustration in order to allow an accurate representation of our profession within our Exhibition and Annual.

With the invaluable cooperation of the Chairman of our Annual Exhibition, Hodges Soileau; Assistant Chairman, Steven Stroud; and the Past Chairmen's Committee, I feel that our mission to continue this pursuit of excellence and fair representation has been superbly addressed. Thanks also go to the Publication Committee members for their efforts on behalf of our publishing ventures.

And to the students whose work was selected for our Scholarship Competition Exhibition and appears in the pages of this Annual, I send my heart-felt congratulations. Wishing you, and all illustrators everywhere, continued success and years of prosperity ahead in one of the world's finest professions.

With my warmest regards to all,

Eileen Hedy Schultz
President
1991 - 1993

Portrait by Bernie Fuchs

THE SOCIETY OF ILLUSTRATORS AWARDS: THE ILLUSTRATORS HALL OF FAME, THE HAMILTON KING AWARD, AND SPECIAL AWARDS

Since 1959, the Society of Illustrators has elected to its Hall of Fame artists recognized for their "distinguished achievement in the art of illustration." The list of previous winners is truly a "Who's Who" of illustration. Former Presidents of the Society meet annually to elect those who will be so honored.

The Hamilton King Award is presented each year for the best illustration of the year by a member of the Society of Illustrators. Selection is made by former recipients of this award.

Also, the Society of Illustrators annually presents Special Awards for substantial contributions to the profession. The Dean Cornwell Recognition Award honors someone for past service which has proven to have been an important contribution to the Society. The Arthur William Brown Achievement Award honors someone who has made a substantial contribution to the Society over a period of time. Biographies of the recipients of these awards are presented in the following pages.

HAMILTON KING AWARD 1965-1992

1965 Paul Calle	1979 William Teason
1966 Bernie Fuchs	1980 Wilson McLean
1967 Mark English	1981 Gerald McConnell
1968 Robert Peak	1982 Robert Heindel
1969 Alan E. Cober	1983 Robert M. Cunningham
1970 Ray Ameijide	1984 Braldt Bralds
1971 Miriam Schottland	1985 Attila Hejja
1972 Charles Santore	1986 Doug Johnson
1973 Dave Blossom	1987 Kinuko Y. Craft
1974 Fred Otnes	1988 James McMullan
1975 Carol Anthony	1989 Guy Billout
1976 Judith Jampel	1990 Edward Sorel
1977 Leo & Diane Dillon	1991 Brad Holland
1978 Daniel Schwartz	1992 Gary Kelley

HALL OF FAME COMMITTEE 1993

CHAIRMAN, Willis Pyle
PAST PRESIDENTS OF THE SI

Stevan Dohanos	Alvin J. Pimsler
Diane Dillon	Warren Rogers
Charles McVicker	Shannon Stirnweis
Wendell Minor	David K. Stone
Howard Munce	John Witt

HALL OF FAME LAUREATES 1958-1992

1958 Norman Rockwell	1975 Howard Pyle*
1959 Dean Cornwell	1976 John Falter
1959 Harold Von Schmidt	1976 Winslow Homer*
1960 Fred Cooper	1976 Harvey Dunn*
1961 Floyd Davis	1977 Robert Peak
1962 Edward Wilson	1977 Wallace Morgan*
1963 Walter Biggs	1977 J.C. Leyendecker*
1964 Arthur William Brown	1978 Coby Whitmore
1965 Al Parker	1978 Norman Price*
1966 Al Dorne	1978 Frederic Remington*
1967 Robert Fawcett	1979 Ben Stahl
1968 Peter Helck	1979 Edwin Austin Abbey*
1969 Austin Briggs	1979 Lorraine Fox*
1970 Rube Goldberg	1980 Saul Tepper
1971 Stevan Dohanos	1980 Howard Chandler Christy*
1972 Ray Prohaska	1980 James Montgomery Flagg*
1973 Jon Whitcomb	1981 Stan Galli
1974 Tom Lovell	1981 Frederic R. Gruger*
1974 Charles Dana Gibson*	1981 John Gannam*
1974 N.C. Wyeth*	1982 John Clymer
1975 Bernie Fuchs	1982 Henry P. Raleigh*
1975 Maxfield Parrish*	1982 Eric (Carl Erickson)*

1983 Mark English	1988 Robert T. McCall
1983 Noel Sickles*	1989 Erté
1983 Franklin Booth*	1989 John Held Jr.*
1984 Neysa Moran McMein*	1989 Arthur Ignatius Keller*
1984 John LaGatta*	1990 Burt Silverman
1984 James Williamson*	1990 Robert Riggs*
1985 Charles Marion Russell*	1990 Morton Roberts*
1985 Arthur Burdett Frost*	1991 Donald Teague
1985 Robert Weaver	1991 Jessie Willcox Smith*
1986 Rockwell Kent*	1991 William A. Smith*
1986 Al Hirschfeld	1992 Joe Bowler
1987 Haddon Sundblom*	1992 Edwin A. Georgi*
1987 Maurice Sendak	1992 Dorothy Hood*
1988 René Bouché*	*Presented posthumously
1988 Pruett Carter*	

HALL OF FAME LAUREATES 1993

Robert McGinnis
Thomas Nast*
Coles Phillips*

HALL OF FAME 1993

ROBERT McGINNIS (b. 1926)

It's funny what happens with "time."

It has a curious way of passing very swiftly. No one can predict it. No one. Not even Bob McGinnis's father. Just think about this. Fifty-plus years ago he would sit around the kitchen table with little Bob and show him how to draw "Popeye." That's right, "Popeye." You see, Mr. McGinnis had a penchant for drawing cartoons and his young son, Bob, would sit around this table with the sounds of mother McGinnis, his three brothers and two sisters in the background and watch his dad draw cartoons. Bob was fascinated. His eyes would light up with wonder. He became very good at drawing "Popeye." It came easily to him. Yes, he was convinced that in time he would become a cartoonist. He must.

But, "time," when you least expect it, can play unusual tricks on you. Little did Bob or his dad suspect or predict that in time young Bob would become, not a cartoonist, but one of the most sought-after illustrators of his time. He would produce more than 1,300 paperback book covers for all the leading publishers. His 54 *Guideposts* covers are collectors' items. Many of his illustrations appeared in *The Saturday Evening Post, Good Housekeeping, Reader's Digest,* and *McCall's,* just to name a few.

But his career was not confined to publishing. When he was with Chaite Studio, sitting alongside Frank McCarthy, Bob Peak and Mike Hooks; Sam Brody, the bon vivant of fast-stepping representatives would spring into action and bring to McGinnis many an advertising assignment. He also included movie posters. Did you know Bob completed 35, plus five James Bond ads? Do you remember them? They were great. If you have any, hold on to them tight. They too are collectors' items.

Why was he so successful? I'll tell you why. I know first hand. He produced many covers for me at Bantam Books. When I commissioned him to illustrate a particular title I knew I would receive something superior to what was being done. First of all, the guy could "draw up a storm." Second, McGinnis had, and has, a superior, almost sixth sense about color. I would marvel at this aspect of his art. He had a unique way of using color by not using much color. Yet, strangely, his illustrations always appeared colorful—sensitively, selectively colorful. Obviously he had studied many of the classic, fine artists of the past and observed how they confronted the concept of color. His main medium, like the early Italian masters, has always been egg with powdered tempera.

Another unique aspect of McGinnis was that he could handle any subject. He was the complete artist. He could paint westerns, mysteries, boy-girl, science fiction...you name it, even a still life. I once amused him by giving him a still life assignment. I remember the title, *Look to the Mountain.* It was a gem. I remember when it came in. When the flap was lifted from the painting you should have heard the applause from the art department. A little jewel. I'm serious.

Anyway, the guy was a joy to work with. It was like having a dozen artists rolled into one.

Did Bob ever become a cartoonist? Yes, for a short time. When he was to graduate from high school, his teacher, Mr. Rice, was nice enough to write a rave letter of recommendation to the Disney studios. Much to the delight of Mr. McGinnis and young Bob, he was accepted and worked there for a brief time as an art apprentice. Unfortunately, World War II erupted and the studio disbanded. Bob immediately joined the Merchant Marines. (I often wondered whether "Popeye" was responsible for his going to sea.)

After his sea duty he decided to go back to school and was accepted at Ohio State, combining football and fine arts. He then enrolled at the Central Academy of Commercial Art in Cincinnati, Ohio, where he studied with the teacher who most influenced him, Mr. Gordon Jex.

Soon, and in time, Bob's work became more and more in demand. But it was Mike Hooks who was instrumental in launching Bob's vast paperback career by introducing him to Donald Gelb, Mike's rep at the time.

...And, as time continues to move along, Robert McGinnis does not get older, he just gets better and better. He is very much involved in fine art gallery painting and his highly sought-after work is held in many private collections around the country.

Way back then, sitting around that kitchen table drawing cartoons, I'm sure Mr. McGinnis would never have guessed that some day, this little kid, his son, sitting there, trying to draw "Popeye" would be elected to the prestigious Hall of Fame at the Society of Illustrators. His name would now be included with Norman Rockwell, Howard Pyle, Dean Cornwell, N.C. Wyeth, Frederic Remington...giants, all giants, and now a new giant: Robert McGinnis. He would have never guessed that. Never.

Len Leone
Former Vice President/Art Director
Bantam Books, Inc.

Portraits for cover of *The Ladies' Club*.

"The Coming of Spring," illustration for *Guideposts*, April, 1982.

HALL OF FAME 1993

THOMAS NAST (1840 - 1902)

Thomas Nast regaled the public of the mid- to late-nineteenth century with his piercing observation and unveiling of human folly, greed, and hypocrisy. His illustrations were not intended to be merely amusing, nor a result of a fleeting, impulsive dislike, but quite moralistic, a reflection of his uncompromising expectations of government and its stewards.

This surveyor of America's political system was born in Germany in 1840 and moved to New York five years later with his family. With little formal art training, Nast began to illustrate for *Frank Leslie's Illustrated News* at the age of 15, earning four dollars a week. This was the era of the wood block engraving and his drawings were not reproduced by the photochemical process until the 1880s. Between 1859 and 1887 *Harper's Weekly* was a major forum for Nast's visual polemics, a testimony to his belief in social justice, politicians' accountability to their constituency, and equitable treatment of all people, regardless of race.

By comparison to his later work, Nast's early contributions to *Harper's* are visually conservative, crowded with didactic and literal detail, and marked by an obvious concern with decorative design. The inflamed political climate of the Civil War appealed to the young artist's passions and illustrations of this era utilize a schematic mode of representation. For example, an 1863 illustration, "The Emancipation of the Negroes—the Past and the Future," presents the sufferings of the past on the left side, exhibiting the whipping, branding, and public sale of slaves, while the future is gloriously envisioned to the right, where black children gaily leave for school and a freeman enjoys the liberty of owning his own money.

The use of biblical allusion and allegorical figures typify Nast's work. In "The Union Christmas Dinner" of 1864, he equates the imagined return of the Confederacy to the Union with the return of the prodigal son to his father. Similarly, in an illustration from the following year, Nast parallels the North's victory (which to him was not just a military, but a *moral* victory) with Christ's entry into Jerusalem. One of his most powerful representations of the obstruction of Justice is seen in "Our Modern Mummy" of 1875. Here Justice represents the Supreme Court, immobilized and silenced by bandages which bind her entire body and read "Red Tape." Adding to this insult, she is so neglected that a spider has had time to weave its web from her scales.

The artist often employed literary reference—Shakespeare being one of his favorite sources—to convey a truth about 19th century political life. Horatio Seymour became victim to this form of Nastian attack when he was nominated as the Democratic presidential candidate in 1868. In addition to Nast's fundamental dislike of the Democratic Party, he was particularly disturbed by Seymour's record as Governor of New York, and was quick to revive his dishonorable role in the Draft Riots of 1863. Anticipating the politician's need to erase the incontrovertible evidence of his past wrongdoing, Nast paralleled Seymour's predicament with that of Lady Macbeth. In the cartoon, Seymour stands alone, intent upon his task and rubbing his hands which are marked "New York Riots" while the caption reads, "Out damned spot! Out I say..." Incisive, resonant and unapologetic, this is quintessential Nast.

Nast's forte of course was the bold distortion of his target's physiognomy. In the mid '60s, he began to depict his victims with heads slightly too large for their bodies, thus belittling both their appearance and their political credibility. Rotundity, thinness, long noses, and the like also became easy targets for exaggeration. William "Boss" Tweed, leader of the corrupt Tammany Hall, made frequent appearances in Nast's gallery of caricature and was eventually jailed due in large part to the illustrator's relentless campaign against his manipulation of New York's political machine. Under Nast's pen, Tweed's pear-shaped face became even longer while perfectly round and perfectly blank eyes set in circles of black created a sheep-like visage devoid of intelligence or humanity. In fact, in one of Nast's least visually complicated cartoons (sarcastically title, "The Brains"), Tweed's features are completely eliminated, replaced by a money bag stamped with a dollar sign, which sits atop his bulging corpulence, a further testament to his greed. The image is so direct that the title is almost unnecessary but sarcastically reiterates Tweed's all-consuming motivation and preoccupation: money.

In addition to his political concerns, Nast created a body of work which revealed a man who cherished goodwill, generosity, and domestic concord (the artist married Sarah Edwards in 1861 and together they had five children). The softer, more sentimental Nast was revealed every Christmas season in *Harper's*. Drawing from both European and American traditions, he created our modern version of Santa Claus: a bearded, jovial fellow who lives in the North Pole and bestows gifts to deserving children.

At the time of his death in 1902, Nast had experienced two decades of declining appreciation for his illustration. Although these years were certainly anti-climactic, the fact that his most impressive work is still heralded today is testament alone to his vision and talent.

Clare McLean

Santa Claus plate, Courtesy Thomas Nast Collection,
Macculloch Hall Historical Museum

"Seymour as Lady Macbeth," from *Harper's Weekly*

"Our Modern Mummy. Tammany Tweedledee—'She is going to punish us.'
Canal Tweedledum—'That's the best joke yet,'" from *Harper's Weekly*

HALL OF FAME 1993

COLES PHILLIPS (1880-1927)

Coles Phillips as depicted
by Norman Rockwell in 1921

Clarence Coles Phillips was the creator of that artistic mirage, the "Fade-away Girl." The progenitor for the idea occurred one night in his studio. As the artist described it, "I was lying on the studio couch and a friend was standing in front of the fire. He was fingering his violin, and the firelight shone on him in such a way that although I couldn't see anything of him except his face, the violin, shirt front, cuffs and shoes, I could tell where his arms and legs were by the way the light on his shoes and cuffs shifted. I made a quick sketch of him, then eliminated everything except his face, shirt front, cuffs and shoes. He was still there—as plain as if you had the full figure. I tried the same idea on the figure of a girl, and it seemed as if the more I took out, the easier it was to define her."

Realizing that this could be an effective picture device, he filed away the idea for some future use. That time soon came when the editors of *Life* (then the humorous weekly) wanted to inaugurate their new, full-color covers with a fresh, provocative theme. With this challenging assignment, Coles remembered the idea of the disembodied figures and decided to re-create their counterparts as a beautiful, young woman. His sister was persuaded to pose as a farm lass in a polka dot dress, scattering grain to a flock of chickens. The resulting illustration, titled "Corn Exchange," was a clever combination of visual camouflage with lost and found forms that delighted both the magazine and its readers.

Thus encouraged, the "Fade-away Girl" became a regular feature of Phillips' covers, in multitudinous variations, for nearly two decades for *Life, Collier's, Liberty, The Saturday Evening Post, Good Housekeeping,* and *Vogue* magazines.

Advertisers, too, wanted to take advantage of the popularity of Phillips' beautiful women, and he had a long affiliation with the manufacturers Holeproof Hosiery, Community Plate Silversmith, Palmolive Soap, Willys Overland (automobile) Company, and many other clients.

Phillips always drew and painted from life and his pictures required very careful prior planning. Every area was plotted out in the preliminary stages and each line or shape functioned to carry out the intended idea. Even those shapes to be omitted had to first be drawn in before determining what parts could go or stay. And, although Phillips did not always follow the fade-away formula, his pictures are always distinguished by the originality of his conceptions and his meticulously rendered designs.

"Psi" Phillips—as he was designated by his fraternity brothers at Kenyon College—always knew he wanted to be an artist and created his first published work for the yearbook and the college newspaper. Impatient to pursue his career, he left college after his Junior year and headed for New York.

There he went through a series of part-time jobs, night classes at the Chase School of Art, and a stint as a clothing catalog artist drawing herringbone patterns, buttons, or various other sartorial details in concert with an assembly line-up of other fashion artists, each adding their bit in turn.

This decidedly anonymous endeavor did not hold Psi for long, and he next graduated to an advertising agency as a sketch artist. He quickly proved his resourcefulness and learned the inner working well enough to start his own agency in 1906. However, its success took him increasingly away from the artistic side of the business, and he reluctantly decided to close up the shop and become a full-time, free-lance artist.

He talked a gullible landlord out of the first month's rent for studio space, promising that his completed work would bring a big check to pay for it. He then began to make samples of his wares. It was a pressurized learning period, but his self-defined goal was to create a picture tailored to *Life* magazine. At the end of the month, with only a single completed drawing to show, he convinced *Life*'s editor, John Ames Mitchell, of his talent and made his first sale! (And paid the landlord.)

Mitchell, who had also discovered and nurtured Charles Dana Gibson, became a life-long friend and Phillips worked for that publication regularly for many years, often doing the center double-spread or the covers.

One of his favorite early models was a young nurse from Canada, named Teresa Hyde. Their romance was a tempestuous one, but once wed, the two became a strong partnership, with Tess as the model and studio manager who kept Phillips free to work.

Because his pictures were in so much demand, he was under continual pressure to accept more commissions. In one assignment for a men's clothing catalog, he took on an impossible two months' deadline for completing all the figures in it. The resulting fee made it possible to make the down payment on a house, but the overwork may have contributed to his later ill-health.

His five-year contract to do all the monthly Fade-away Girl covers for *Good Housekeeping* proved to be more than he could handle. After two years, he had to taper off to a few covers a year. By 1924, Phillips began to suffer seriously from kidney problems, and he went abroad for a year to seek help from European specialists. None could help him, and he returned to the States unable to continue his work. His death at 47 terminated the career of an immensely popular artist with a unique ability to mesmerize and delight his appreciative audience.

Walt Reed
Illustration House

"Net Results," *Life* cover, courtesy Illustration House

HAMILTON KING AWARD 1993

JERRY PINKNEY b. 1939

From an interview with Society of Illustrators
Director Terrence Brown

Terrence Brown: Congratulations, Jerry, on the
Hamilton King. Did you think that this would be an
award you would win?

Jerry Pinkney: I have thought about the Hamilton
King Award. Whether I would ever receive it was an
open question. It's a distinguished honor because it's
awarded by one's peers. When I think of the talented
contemporaries in the jury, it makes this award
more meaningful.

TB: The piece was published by Scholastic, but
hadn't it been previously published?

JP: Yes, originally it was an assignment for *National
Geographic*. The subject was slavery and I was able to
do much of the research with the writer,
Charles Blockson.

TB: Is that subject difficult for you?

JP: It does carry deep emotions. It challenges me as a
picture maker to move beyond the anger and
frustration, to create an honest and dramatic image. I
became totally involved in black history, and the
history of slavery. Once you get past the visual
references, something takes over and that's when my
best imagery come out.

TB: The black experience has been a subject of
yours before?

JP: In the seventies there were four calendars on
African-American history for Seagrams, which
presented me with a real sense of artistic freedom.
That was a productive time in my career, both
personally and professionally. And, of course, there
were the nine U.S. Postal issues for the Black
Heritage Series.

TB: We all have Steve Dohanos to thank for the
Citizen Stamp Advisory Committee's appreciation
of illustration.

JP: Yes, he brought the illustrator's point of view to
that committee. Also, I saw those assignments from a
design point of view. I was proud to have been a part
of the Committee ten years.

TB: Your early background was more in design than
illustration, wasn't it?

JP: I was a Design major at the Philadelphia College
of Art and did more design than illustration at
Russcraft Publishing Company in Boston those first
years out of school.

TB: Was the distance from New York at that time
a hindrance?

JP: Not entirely, since my agent, Cullen Rapp, was
representing me in New York. And I made a point to
see the shows and follow the trades.

TB: How do you feel about your earlier work?

JP: I am amazed at the diversity of it then, and by
how far I have come...how much my style had grown.

TB: And growth is important?

JP: I'm always looking inside to see if I can push
myself further. I look at other artists to see their
growth and to see parallels in our work, but never to
just follow trends. There is more freedom outside
trends to develop one's personal style.

TB: Today, you are a star in the children's book field.
What was your development in this market?

JP: I illustrated my first book in 1964. It's still in print
and the modest royalty each year still amazes me. *The
Patchwork Quilt*, in 1984, was my first book in color.
But as an artist active in other markets, I was not at
the top of many publisher's lists in the seventies. Atha
Tehon at Dial Books for Young Readers was the first
to encourage me. She had the insight to nurture
my talents.

TB: The children's book market has changed
dramatically in recent years.

JP: I was fortunate to have had an audience for my
books when it changed. I was in the right place at the
right time.

TB: What do you see as the uniqueness of this market?

JP: You know your audience: children, parents,
teachers, and librarians. It is a market where your
work has longevity. There is always a new audience to
replace young readers who move on to another lever.
A book can become a classic and be around for many
years. Think of such artists as Howard Pyle, N.C.
Wyeth, and Maurice Sendak.

TB: Do you work well with the text and the designers?

JP: My design and production experience comes into
play when working with editors and art directors on
designing the rhythm and format of a book. It is
important, however, for both the text and the art to
provide an open image for the reader.

TB: It is certainly a market well covered by the media.

JP: It does have its awards, shows, and lists, but they
have different audiences in themselves. *The New York
Times* Ten Best Children's Books speaks of aesthetics.
The Caldecott, which is so well known publicly, is
awarded by the American Library Association. And,
there is the Golden Kite Award given by The Society
of Children's Book Writers and Illustrators, and
others such as the AIGA Book Show.

TB: And the Society's juried show, "The Original Art"?

JP: "The Original Art" show is juried by people
sensitive to children's book illustration. I see its
purpose as raising expectations. All of the shows and
awards should serve to inspire us to the extraordinary.

TB: Your family is now grown and your wife, Gloria
Jean, has begun a writing career. Also, Brian, your
oldest son, is a children's book illustrator. And
Andrea, his wife, is a writer.

JP: It's an exciting time for the Pinkney family. You
can imagine the energetic conversation when
we're together.

TB: Do you see yourself in the children's book market
in the years ahead?

JP: Yes, the publishers are giving me exciting projects.
My career is in the right direction...it is limitless.
However, I don't rule out important projects like the
recent *National Geographic* story on the slave trade in
Brazil in the 17th century. That subject was very
emotional but one I wanted. And, there was the
Land's End catalogue cover-these departures are
good for me.

TB: And your personal work?

JP: I came into this business to be an illustrator.
I would like to develop my own ideas with writers.
As an artist, I am always challenging myself...I am
going "out on a limb," or let's say, "I'm creeping out
on a limb."

Hamilton King Award winner, jacket illustration for
"GET ON BOARD, *The Story of the Underground Railroad*"
commissioned by Scholastic Inc.

SPECIAL AWARDS 1993

1993 Dean Cornwell Recognition Award
ROBERT GEISSMANN

Bob Geissmann, who was my good and trusted friend, loved to show off his ability to do one handed push-ups, no matter what his condition. He dressed as a Brooks Brothers artist might, a perfect Rob Roy was his drink, and a good party his game. His fuse could be short at times, but his endless capacity to help and to lead were his long suits.

It was natural for Geissmann, with his great talent and charm, to gravitate to the Society of Illustrators. From the first day of his membership in the Society, through his presidency from 1953 to 1955, to his last day, Geissmann served the Society to the best of his ability. His vision for the Society was total professionalism first, party second—he never lost sight of that vision. He always strove to make the Society and our profession better and he backed up his vision and goals with his brains and brawn.

Geissmann's deep concern for professional standards and practices was felt not only at the Society, but also in his involvement at the Graphic Artists Guild, an organization Bob helped to form, becoming their first president in 1969. His interest in the ethical standards then being practiced in the illustration profession during the late '40s and the concern by members of the Society, the Art Directors Club and the Artists Guild, led to the founding of the Joint Ethics Committee in 1945 and their formulation of the Code of Fair Practice.

Through contacts made during World War II, Geissmann was the driving force behind the Society's participation in the U.S. Air Force Art Program, which was conceived by Lt. Col. Bill Lookadoo and implemented by Lt. Col. George C. Bales. Bob chaired the committee, with John Moodie, from 1954 to 1958.

Geissmann's participation in and enthusiasm for the Society's annual theatrical presentations was legendary. He often helped to write the show, organize the backstage activities, cast for the dancers and, of course, perform center stage.

For Bob Geissmann, there were no unimportant jobs at the Society. He tackled each task as if the very existence of the Society depended on the job being done on time and to perfection. He would have been flattered and very honored to have received this award from his peers.

Jerry McConnell
House Chairman

1993 Arthur William Brown Achievement Award
WALTER HORTENS

A gentle and kind man, rather courtly and refined of manner, reflective perhaps of his Viennese birthplace, Walter Hortens joined the Society in 1958 and thus began an association which was to continue for thirty years until his death in 1988.

He studied at Pratt Institute in New York and at the Academie Julian in Paris with Fernand Léger. An inveterate traveler, his fluency in German, French, and Italian served him well. Characteristically, his involvement with the Society touched many areas, as he was always willing to pitch in where needed. His service included many years as a member of the Board of Directors, as the Society's representative on the Joint Ethics Committee, and as the instigator of the Society's participation in the Police Athletic League's program for New York's disadvantaged youth. Walter's participation at the Society culminated in a two-term presidency from 1985 to 1987.

Soft spoken, acutely considerate in his personal relations, and generous in sharing information with colleagues, Walter's rather benign demeanor masked a steely, even obstinate, determination to rectify many of the injustices found in our profession. Many pay lip service to artists' rights, but Walter had the courage of his convictions and was willing to take on substantial clients in confrontations over issues in dispute, *The New York Times* among them, and to persevere until he won. He knew full well the price to be paid for winning.

Possessed of a sly sense of humor, Walter noted at the President's Dinner, which marked the termination of his term and the election of the Society's first woman President, Diane Dillon, that it was the first time in the Society's 75-year history that the outgoing President and the incoming President had kissed.

Surely if anyone epitomizes the spirit and intent of The Arthur William Brown Achievement Award for many years of service to the Society, it is Walter Hortens.

Dean Ellis
Treasurer

CHAIRMAN'S MESSAGE

The most important ingredient for an outstanding Annual Exhibition is the selection of good juries—all 36 jurors were diligent and conscientious in their deliberations. The relationship of quality of work to quality of jury is evident in the eclectic body of work in this Annual. We are grateful to those responsible for such excellence.

If anyone had suggested that I might someday have the honor of chairing the Annual Exhibition, an event which has meant so much to me and so many other illustrators, I would never have believed it. This is, in my opinion, the most important exhibition of illustration in which anyone can participate. For this reason, I'm extremely proud of the result of this year's effort.

Many dedicated people generously donated their time to make this ambitious undertaking a success. Without their support, it would have been difficult, if not impossible. Many thanks to Eileen Hedy Schultz and Terry Brown and the SI staff: Phyllis, Clare, Mike, Dan, Babe, and Jill. I'd also like to thank my assistant, Steve Stroud, for setting a new standard for the job of Assistant Chairman. He made this challenge easier, but most of all, fun.

Glenn Harrington, one of the many young lions of illustration, created an evocative image for the Call for Entry. Doug Johnson took that image and designed a terrific poster.

Congratulations to all the award winners and to all those who are included in this Annual. This really is quite an elite group when one considers, of nearly 7,000 entires, fewer than 500 were selected. Thank you all for making this a special book.

If the work in this book is any indication, illustration is certainly alive and well.

Hodges Soileau

Hodges Soileau
Chairman, 35th Annual Exhibition

Portrait by Bernie Fuchs

EDITORIAL JURY

WILSON McLEAN
CHAIRMAN
Illustrator

GIL COHEN
Artist/Illustrator

JEFF CORNELL
Illustrator

NORMAN S. HOTZ
Senior Art Editor
Reader's Digest Magazine

BOB LAPSLEY
Illustrator

JIM PLUMERI
Executive Art Director
Bantam Doubleday Dell

MARK SUMMERS
Illustrator

LYNN SWEAT
Illustrator

KENT WILLIAMS
Illustrator

EDITORIAL

AWARD WINNERS

JERRY PINKNEY
Gold Medal

SKIP LIEPKE
Silver Medal

C.F. PAYNE
Silver Medal

JANET WOOLLEY
Silver Medal

Artist: **JERRY PINKNEY**

Art Director: Allen Carroll

Client: National Geographic

Size: 15 x 20 1/4

JERRY PINKNEY
Editorial Gold Medal

"This painting, "Survivor for Sale, The Scramble Auction," was one of the most challenging illustrations of my career, not only because of the research, but also because of the assumptions one has to make with subject matter that has little documentation. Most of all, one feels the emotional demands when dealing as honestly as possible with a history that has so much pain and degradation attached to it. My intent was to show the fear, confusion, and disorientation of the Africans and at the same time convey a sense of resistance to a dehumanizing experience."

2

Artist: **SKIP LIEPKE**

Art Director: Fred Woodward

Client: Rolling Stone

Medium: Oil

Size: 21 ¹/₂ x 14 ¹/₂

SKIP LIEPKE
Editorial Silver Medal

"The Bob Dylan piece was pretty straightforward (as I guess all my work is). I just tried to tap into something that moved me about him, something I hope others can see and feel. It's hard for me to speak eloquently about something that was far better expressed in paint. Without getting too verbose, I guess what I do is paint people, and what I say about them is as open as the human experience."

3

Artist: **C. F. PAYNE**

Art Director: Joseph Connolly

Client: Boys' Life

Size: 13 x 26

C.F. PAYNE
Editorial Silver Medal

"This project was a departure for me and one I looked upon with excitement and great expectations. Then what followed was not expected. Doing a project on a significant figure in a major moment in history was thrilling and a new challenge, but the subject matter regarding this figure had an unexpected effect on me. I was not anticipating those feelings, nor was I prepared. Yet I am proud of the illustration that was produced. I am also proud of *Boys' Life*'s willingness to take on such a subject for their magazine and for giving me this assignment."

Artist: **JANET WOOLLEY**

Art Director: Fred Woodward

Client: Rolling Stone

Size: 19 x 16

JANET WOOLLEY
Editorial Silver Medal

"I was born in Plymouth, England, in 1952. After attending Shrewsbury School of Art until 1970, I went to Brighton College of Art and Design, leaving in 1973 with a B.A. Honors Degree in Graphic Design. Between 1973 and 1976, I attended the Royal College of Art, where I received the Berger Sword for Drawing and a Master of Arts Degree in Illustration. Among the awards I have won are Sainsbury Image of Today, Benson & Hedges Gold, and the Society of Illustrators' Gold and Silver Medals. I have worked mainly in the area of illustration in the U.K. and the U.S.A. and I also lecture at Central Saint Martins School of Art in London."

5

Artist: **MARSHALL ARISMAN**

Art Director: Charmian Carl

Client: Playgirl Magazine

Medium: Oil

Size: 38 x 38

6

Artist: **MARSHALL ARISMAN**

Art Director: Rhonda Rubinstein

Client: Esquire

7

Artist: **STEVE BRODNER**

Art Directors: Jill Armus

Client: Total TV

Medium: Watercolor

Size: 10 1/2 x 16

8

Artist: **KEITH GRAVES**

Art Director: D. J. Stout

Client: Texas Monthly

Medium: Prisma color

Size: 13 x 10

9

Artist: **DAVID M. BECK**

Art Director: Saroyan Humphrey

Client: Guitar Player Magazine

Medium: Mixed media

Size: 16 x 12

5

7

8

9

10

Artist: **ALAN E. COBER**

Art Director: Ron Arnholm

Client: Georgia Review

Medium: Etching, aquatint

Size: 31 x 22

11

Artist: **DAVE CUTLER**

Art Director: A. J. Hartley

Client: The Detroit Free Press

Medium: Acrylic on paper

Size: 16 x 20

12

Artist: **JACK UNRUH**

Art Director: Fred Woodward

Client: Rolling Stone

Size: 14 x 10

13

Artist: **PHIL BOATWRIGHT**

Art Director: Christine Mitchell

Client: Arizona Highways
Magazine

Medium: Mixed media

Size: 16 x 12

14

Artist: **GLENN HARRINGTON**

Art Directors: Pam Powers
Ron Ramsey

Client: Golf Magazine

Size: 15 x 20

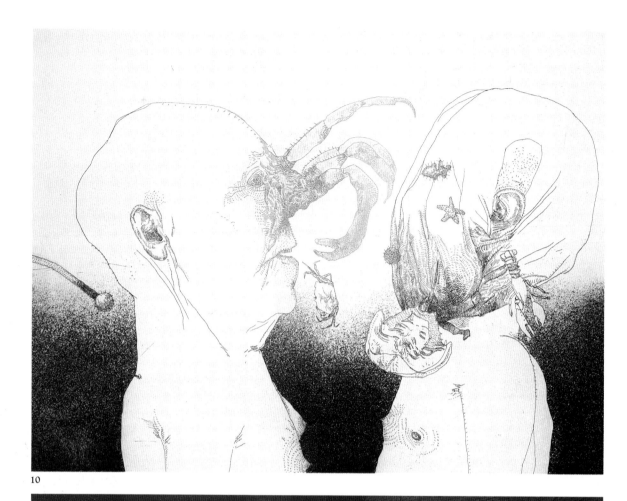

10

11

12

13

14

15

Artist: **KINUKO Y. CRAFT**

Art Director: Kerig Pope

Client: Playboy

Size: 15 x 15 ¹/₂

16

Artist: **ROBERT GIUSTI**

Art Director: Kerig Pope

Client: Playboy

Size: 10 x 10

17

Artist: **BRAD HOLLAND**

Art Director: Hans-Georg Pospischil

Client: FAZ GmbH

Medium: Acrylic on board

Size: 19 x 25

18

Artist: **RALPH STEADMAN**

Art Directors: Michael Grossman
Gregory Mastrianni

Client: Entertainment Weekly

19

Artist: **CHARLES S. PYLE**

Art Director: Rhonda Rubinstein

Client: Esquire

15

16

17

18

19

20

Artist: **DAVE CUTLER**

Art Director: Meg Birnbaum

Client: Natural Health

Medium: Acrylic on paper

Size: 6 1/2 x 5 1/2

21

Artist: **JOHN LABBÉ**

Art Director: A. J. Harrey

Client: The Detroit Free Press

Size: 15 1/2 x 18

22

Artist: **H. B. LEWIS**

Art Director: Karen Siciliano

Client: The Wall Street Journal
  Classroom

Medium: Mixed media

Size: 10 x 17

23

Artist: **RICH BOWMAN**

Art Director: Tom Dolphens

Client: Kansas City Star

Medium: Oil

Size: 17 1/2 x 13

24

Artist: **SUN-KYUNG CHO**

Size: 16 x 12

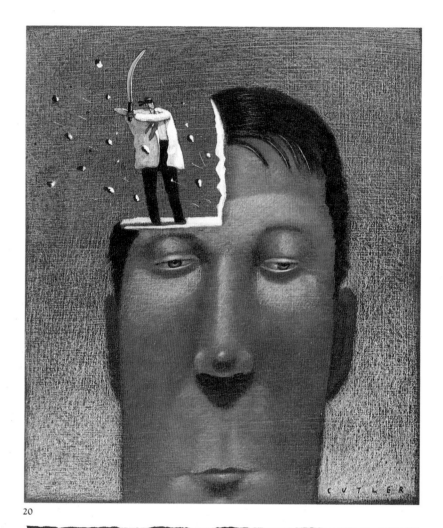

20

21

22

23

24

25

Artist: **JIM SPANFELLER**

Art Directors: Tom Staebler
Kerig Pope

Client: Playboy

Medium: Mixed media

Size: 16 x 16

26

Artist: **JIM SPANFELLER**

Art Director: Robert I. York

Client: Spanfeller Graphics
Group, Inc.

Size: 28 x 30

27

Artist: **HERBERT TAUSS**

Art Director: Allen Carroll

Client: National Geographic

Medium: Oil

Size: 39 x 54

28

Artist: **DAVID JOHNSON**

Art Director: Mindy Phelps Stanton

Client: Times Mirror Magazines

Medium: Watercolor, ink

Size: 12 x 24

29

Artist: **GREG SPALENKA**

Art Director: Elaine Bradley

Client: Vermont Magazine

Medium: Mixed media

Size: 8 x 13

25

26

27

28

29

30

Artist: **KINUKO Y. CRAFT**

Art Director: Rhonda Kass

Client: Forbes

Size: 17 1/2 x 12 1/2

31

Artist: **C. MICHAEL DUDASH**

Art Directors: John Fennell
C. Michael Dudash

Client: Step-By-Step Graphics

Medium: Oil on linen/paper

Size: 24 x 17

32

Artist: **C. MICHAEL DUDASH**

Art Directors: Gary Kelley
C. Michael Dudash

Client: The North American
Review

Medium: Oil on linen/paper

Size: 35 x 27

33

Artist: **GREGORY MANCHESS**

Art Director: Steve Connatser

Client: "D" Magazine

Medium: Oil

Size: 14 x 25

30

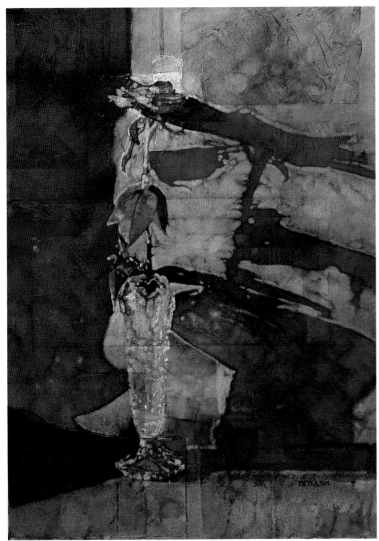

31

32

33

34

Artist: **JOHN COLLIER**

Art Director: Fred Woodward

Client: Rolling Stone

Medium: Pastel

Size: 26 x 21

35

Artist: **BILL NELSON**

Art Directors: Deborah Flynn-
Hanvahan
Robin Gilmore-
Barnes

Client: The Atlantic Monthly

Medium: Colored pencil

Size: 5 x 12

36

Artist: **MATT MAHURIN**

Client: Houston Metropolitan
Magazine

Size: 13 x 10

37

Artist: **GREG SPALENKA**

Art Director: Nancy Duckworth

Client: The Los Angeles Times
Magazine

Medium: Mixed media

Size: 16 $^1/_2$ x 12 $^1/_2$

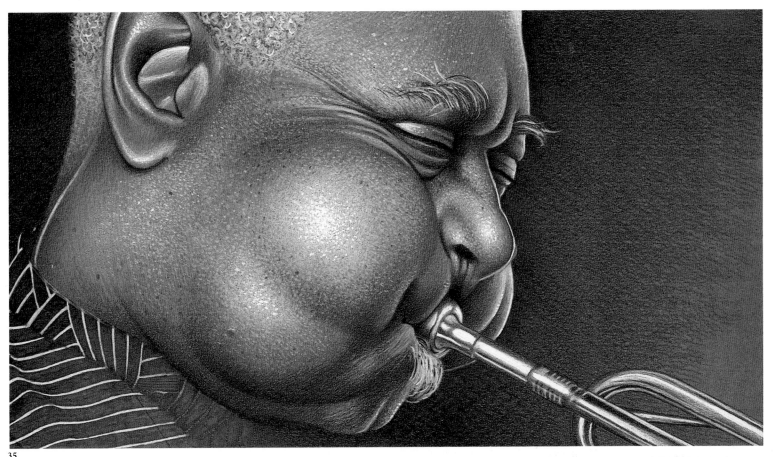

35

36

37

38

Artist: **BLAIR DRAWSON**

Art Director: Fred Woodward

Client: Rolling Stone

Size: 12 x 10 1/4

39

Artist: **ALAN E. COBER**

Art Director: Fred Woodward

Client: Rolling Stone

Size: 9 x 7 1/2

40

Artist: **SKIP LIEPKE**

Client: Eleanor Ettinger Inc.

Medium: Watercolor

Size: 13 1/2 x 9 1/2

41

Artist: **KUNIO HAGIO**

Art Director: Richard Bleiweiss

Client: Penthouse

Medium: Oil

Size: 24 x 18

42

Artist: **SALLY WERN COMPORT**

Art Director: Roy Comiskey

Client: Security Management

Medium: Mixed media

Size: 17 x 13

38

39

40

41

42

43

Artist: **KINUKO Y. CRAFT**

Art Director: Tom Staebler

Client: Playboy

Medium: Egg tempera

Size: 18 x 16

44

Artist: **JAMES CHAFFEE**

Medium: Pen, ink, watercolor

Size: 19 x 19

45

Artist: **JOHN JUDE PALENCAR**

Art Director: J. Porter

Client: Yankee Magazine

Size: 12 x 19

46

Artist: **ERIC DINYER**

Medium: Macintosh Quadra 950

Size: 11 x 8 1/2

47

Artist: **ADAM NIKLEWICZ**

Art Directors: Judy Garlan
Robin Gilmore-Barnes

Client: The Atlantic Monthly

Medium: Acrylic on illustration board

Size: 8 x 6

43

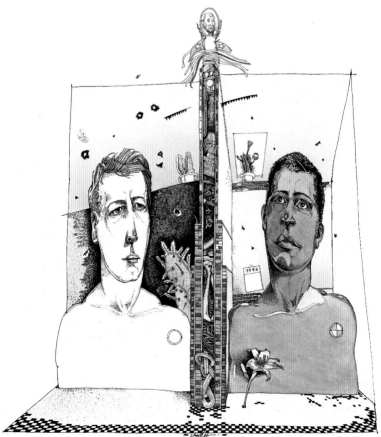

44

45

46

47

48

Artist: **PHIL BOATWRIGHT**

Art Director: Larry Stuart

Client: Discipleship Journal

Medium: Mixed media

Size: 20 x 16 ¹/₂

49

Artist: **KATHERINE LANDIKUSIC**

Art Director: Tom Dolphens

Client: The Kansas City Star

Size: 16 x 23

50

Artist: **PHIL BOATWRIGHT**

Art Director: Christine Mitchell

Client: Arizona Highways Magazine

Medium: Mixed media

Size: 16 x 12

51

Artist: **TIM O'BRIEN**

Medium: Oil on gessoed panel

Size: 18 x 11 ³/₄

49

50

51

52

Artist: **JOEL PETER JOHNSON**

Art Director: Mark Geer

Client: Caring Magazine

Medium: Mixed media

Size: 7 1/2 x 7 3/4

53

Artist: **WILSON McLEAN**

Art Director: Richard Bleiweiss

Client: Penthouse

Medium: Oil

Size: 21 x 23

54

Artist: **PETER FIORE**

Art Director: Roger Dowd

Client: Medical Economics

Medium: Oil

Size: 30 x 20

55

Artist: **MATT MAHURIN**

Art Director: Jane Palecek

Client: Health Magazine

Size: 13 x 10

56

Artist: **MATT MAHURIN**

Art Director: Sandy Chellisto

Client: The Los Angeles Times

Size: 10 x 13 1/4

52

53

54

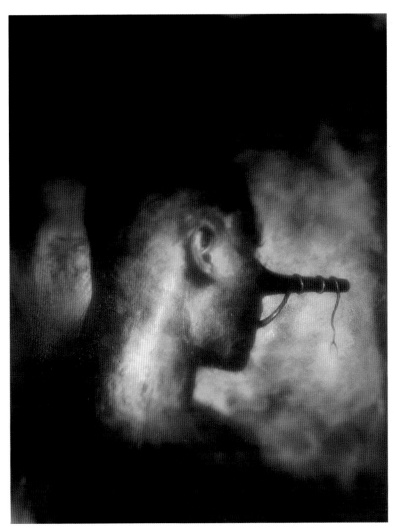

55

56

57

Artist: **ELWOOD H. SMITH**

Art Directors: Kelly Doe
　　　　　　Richard Baker

Client: The Washington Post
Magazine

Medium: Watercolor, india ink

Size: 11 x 10 ¹/₂

58

Artist: **DAVID JOHNSON**

Art Director: John Korpics

Client: Musician Magazine

Medium: Pen, ink, watercolor

Size: 10 ¹/₂ x 9 ¹/₂

59

Artist: **PETER DE SÈVE**

Art Director: Bob Mansfield

Client: Forbes

Size: 12 ³/₄ x 9

60

Artist: **JOHN P. MAGGARD III**

Art Director: Simon Smith

Client: American Legion Magazine

Medium: Acrylic, oil

Size: 23 x 17

61

Artist: **WM. A. MOTTA**

Art Director: Richard M. Baron

Client: Road & Track Magazine

Size: 24 x 26

57

58

59

60

61

62

Artist: **JOHN THOMPSON**

Art Director: Tom Staebler

Client: Playboy

Medium: Oil

Size: 18 x 17

63

Artist: **JANET WOOLLEY**

Art Director: Michael Grossman

Client: Entertainment Weekly

Size: 20 x 16

64

Artist: **C. F. PAYNE**

Art Director: Richard Bleiweiss

Client: Penthouse

Medium: Mixed media

Size: 16 x 20

65

Artist: **DANIEL SCHWARTZ**

Art Director: Fred Woodward

Client: Rolling Stone

Medium: Oil

Size: 13 x 10 1/2

66

Artist: **WIKTOR SADOWSKI**

Art Director: Fred Woodward

Client: Rolling Stone

Size: 15 x 12 1/2

62

63

64

65

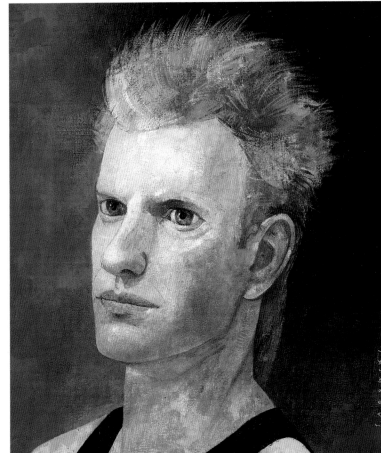

66

67

Artist: **BRALDT BRALDS**

Art Director: Fred Woodward

Client: Rolling Stone

Size: 12 x 10

68

Artist: **JOE CIARDIELLO**

Art Director: Tim Pedersen

Client: Jazziz

Medium: Ink, watercolor

Size: 13 x 10

69

Artist: **BRAD HOLLAND**

Art Director: Fred Woodward

Client: Rolling Stone

Size: 12 x 10

70

Artist: **CHRISTOPHER A. KLEIN**

Art Director: Mark Holmes

Client: National Geographic

Medium: Acrylic

Size: 21 x 11

71

Artist: **JOSEPH DANIEL FIEDLER**

Art Director: Lucy Bartholomay

Client: The Boston Globe Magazine

Medium: Alkyd on paper

Size: 16 x 13 1/4

67

69

70

71

72

Artist: **HERB DAVIDSON**

Art Director: Tom Staebler

Client: Playboy

Medium: Oil

Size: 24 x 20

73

Artist: **MARK SUMMERS**

Art Director: Steve Heller

Client: The New York Times
Book Review

Medium: Scratchboard

Size: 7 x 4 ³/4

74

Artist: **JOHN COLLIER**

Art Director: Fred Woodward

Client: Rolling Stone

Medium: Pastel

Size: 36 x 24

75

Artist: **ARTHUR SHILSTONE**

Art Director: Caroline Despard

Client: Smithsonian Magazine

Medium: Watercolor

Size: 19 ³/4 x 28 ¹/4

73

74

75

76

Artist: **C. F. PAYNE**

Art Director: Sokie Gonzales

Client: U.S. News & World Report

Medium: Mixed media

Size: 15 x 12

77

Artist: **JERRY PINKNEY**

Art Director: Allen Carroll

Client: National Geographic

Size: 14 3/4 x 20

78

Artist: **GARY KELLEY**

Art Director: Martha Geering

Client: Sierra Magazine

Medium: Pastel

Size: 15 x 12 1/2

79

Artist: **BLAIR DRAWSON**

Art Director: Rhonda Rubinstein

Client: Esquire

Size: 15 x 12 1/2

76

77

78

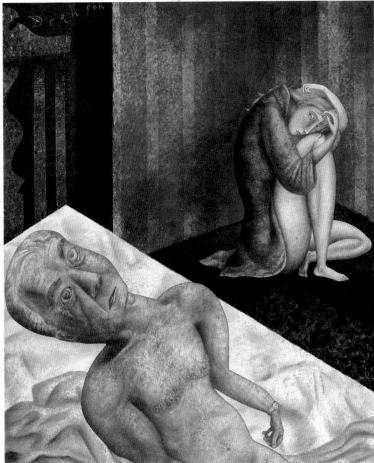

79

80

Artist: **JACK UNRUH**

Art Director: Allen Carroll

Client: National Geographic

Medium: Pen, ink, watercolor

Size: 21 1/2 x 21 1/2

81

Artist: **DAVID WILCOX**

Art Directors: Kerig Pope
Kelly Korjenek

Client: Playboy

Medium: Casein

Size: 21 x 21

82

Artist: **DON WELLER**

Art Director: Don Weller

Client: Park City Lodestar
Magazine

Medium: Plastic overlay

Size: 11 x 15

83

Artist: **MEL ODOM**

Art Director: Tom Staebler

Client: Playboy

Medium: Airbrush, colored pencil

Size: 10 x 7 1/2

84

Artist: **BILL NELSON**

Art Director: Fred Woodward

Client: Rolling Stone

Medium: Colored pencil

Size: 16 x 14

80

81

82

83

84

85

Artist: **BURT SILVERMAN**

Art Director: Peter Morance

Client: American Heritage

Size: 30 x 24

86

Artist: **ROB WOOD**

Art Director: Wayne Fitzpatrick

Client: U.S. News & World Report

Size: 14 x 11

87

Artist: **JOHN RUSH**

Art Director: Tom Staebler

Client: Playboy

Medium: Oil

Size: 31 x 21

88

Artist: **RICHARD SCHLECHT**

Art Director: Allen Carroll

Client: National Geographic

Medium: Watercolor

Size: 19 x 26

85

86

87

88

89

Artist: **DOUGLAS C. KLAUBA**

Art Director: Anthony Ficke

Client: Pension & Investment
Magazine

Medium: Acrylic

Size: 21 x 16

90

Artist: **CAROLE KABRIN**

Art Director: Katherine Dillon

Client: ABC News

Medium: Pastel

Size: 15 1/2 x 18 1/2

91

Artist: **DANIEL MAFFIA**

Art Director: Fred Woodward

Client: Rolling Stone

Size: 16 1/2 x 14

92

Artist: **MARVIN MATTELSON**

Art Director: Richard Bleiweiss

Client: Penthouse

Medium: Acrylic

Size: 13 x 10

93

Artist: **ARTHUR SHILSTONE**

Art Director: Mindy Phelps Stanton

Client: Times Mirror Magazines

Medium: Watercolor

Size: 13 x 15

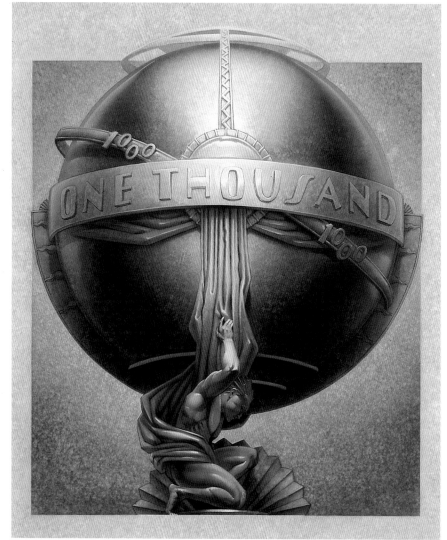

89

90

91

92

93

94

Artist: **MARSHALL ARISMAN**

Art Director: Alfred Zelser

Client: Men's Health

Size: 29 x 23

95

Artist: **WILSON McLEAN**

Art Director: Tom Staebler

Client: Playboy

Medium: Acrylic on canvas

Size: 21 x 25

96

Artist: **JIM PHALEN**

Medium: Oil on board

Size: 18 x 15

97

Artist: **JOHN LABBÉ**

Art Directors: Nicholas E. Torello
Joy Toltzis Makon

Client: Scholastic Inc.

Size: 17 1/2 x 14

94

95

96

97

98

Artist: **C. F. PAYNE**

Art Director: D.J. Stout

Client: Texas Monthly

Medium: Mixed media

Size: 15 x 12

99

Artist: **GUY BILLOUT**

Art Director: Jan Zimmeck

Client: Kiplinger's Personal
Finance

Medium: Watercolor, airbrush

Size: 11 1/8 x 16 1/4

100

Artist: **BURT SILVERMAN**

Art Directors: Nick Kirilloff
Allen Carroll

Client: National Geographic

Medium: Oil

Size: 20 x 18 1/2

101

Artist: **MARK SUMMERS**

Art Director: Steve Heller

Client: The New York Times
Book Review

Medium: Scratchboard

Size: 8 x 7 1/4

98

99

100

101

102

Artist: **SKIP LIEPKE**

Client: Eleanor Ettinger Inc.

Medium: Watercolor

Size: 9 x 12

103

Artist: **SKIP LIEPKE**

Client: Eleanor Ettinger Inc.

Medium: Oil

Size: 12 x 16

104

Artist: **TOM WOODRUFF**

Art Director: Fred Woodward

Client: Rolling Stone

Size: 24 x 19

105

Artist: **FRED OTNES**

Art Director: Jane Polanka

Client: National Academy of
Science

Medium: Mixed-media collage

Size: 25 x 37

102

103

104

105

106

Artist: **JERRY PINKNEY**

Art Director: Allen Carroll

Client: National Geographic

Size: 14 x 9 3/4

107

Artist: **BRAD HOLLAND**

Art Director: Hans-Georg Pospischil

Client: FAZ GmbH

Medium: Acrylic on board

Size: 18 1/2 x 25 1/2

108

Artist: **JOHN MARTIN**

Art Director: Nicole White

Client: Network Computing
Magazine

Medium: Acrylic

Size: 23 x 17

109

Artist: **EVANGELIA
PHILLIPPIDIS**

Art Director: Bob James

Client: The Columbus Dispatch

Size: 15 x 10 1/2

106

107

108

109

110

Artist: **GARNET HENDERSON**

Art Director: Carol Carson

Client: Scholastic Inc.

111

Artist: **KENNETH FRANCIS DEWEY**

Art Director: Dan Hayward

Client: Pennysaver

Medium: Pen, ink, watercolor

Size: 22 x 30

112

Artist: **ARTHUR SHILSTONE**

Art Director: Gary Gretter

Client: Sports Afield

Size: 16 x 11

113

Artist: **ELWOOD H. SMITH**

Art Directors: Robert Lascaro
           Matthew Fernberger

Client: Scholastic Inc.

Size: 12 1/2 x 9

114

Artist: **MARK BELLEROSE**

Art Directors: Nancy Stetler
            Irene Pombo

Client: Patient Care Magazine

Medium: Pastel

Size: 9 x 6 1/2

110

111

112

113

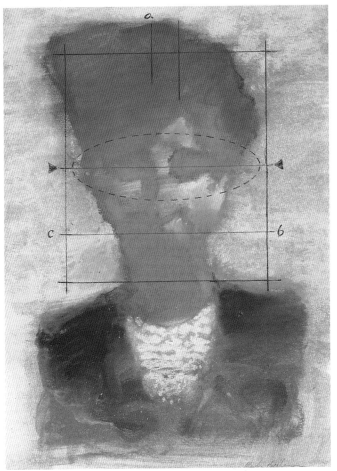

114

BOOK JURY

PETER FIORE
CHAIRMAN
Illustrator

ED ACUÑA
Illustrator

TOM DEMETER
Senior Creative Director
Blazing Graphics

ELAINE DUILLO
Illustrator

LOIS ERLACHER
Art Director
Emergency Medicine Magazine

LEONARD P. LEONE
Designer/Artist/Illustrator

ROBERT E. McGINNIS
Illustrator

NEIL McPHEETERS
Illustrator

STEVEN STROUD
Illustrator

BOOK

AWARD WINNERS

STEVE JOHNSON/LOU FANCHER
Gold Medal

BRYAN LEISTER
Gold Medal

GENNADY SPIRIN
Gold Medal

GARY KELLEY
Silver Medal

JERRY PINKNEY
Silver Medal

SAELIG GALLAGHER
Silver Medal

STEVE JOHNSON/LOU FANCHER
Book Gold Medal

Working as a collaborative team, Steve Johnson and Lou Fancher have spent the last six years producing illustrations for magazines, annual reports, posters, advertisements, and children's books. Because their process is unusual—each painting is created through a back-and-forth joint effort—they've sometimes struggled to explain how they work. Steve says, "You'd have to sit right next to us and watch, which would be pretty tedious, but working together means the ideas and the paintings are better. After six years, I don't think either of us can imagine working without the other person." This painting is from their fourth children's book, *Up North at the Cabin*.

JOHNSON/
NCHER

ancher

e & Shepard

n paper

2

116

Artist: **BRYAN LEISTER**

Art Director: Doris Borowsky-Straus

Client: St. Martin's Press

Medium: Oil

Size: 14 1/2 x 10

BRYAN LEISTER
Book Gold Medal

"This painting was done for a book about a plot to assassinate Queen Elizabeth. The assassin was to hide in the eye of a gigantic dragon float. Doris Borowsky-Straus, the art director, had come up with this idea of the Queen with the dragon in her lap. I had just seen Leonardo's "Lady with an Ermine" at the National Gallery in Washington, D.C., which inspired me to render the dragon in this pose. I combined several versions of the Queen's portrait in order to come up with the most ideal."

117

Artist: **GENNADY SPIRIN**

Art Directors: Atha Tehon
Amelia Lau Carling

Client: Dial Books for Young
Readers

Medium: Watercolor

Size: 8 ¹/₂ x 15

GENNADY SPIRIN
Book Gold Medal

Spirin, a native of Moscow and product of the Russian art education system, which recognizes special talents and trains children at an early age, began his career in the former Soviet Union. He moved to the U.S. for a six-month visit but enjoyed the conditions and remained. Of his work he said, *"Snow White and Rose Red* is a classic tale by the brothers Grimm. It is a story I loved as a child, set in a part of Northern Europe that is very familiar to me. There are many dramatic, magical incidents that lent themselves to my style."

118

Artist: **GARY KELLEY**

Art Directors: Tom Peterson
Louise Fili

Client: Creative Education

Medium: Pastel

Size: 19 x 12

GARY KELLEY
Book Silver Medal

Finally they found on the dock one of those old nocturnal coupés that one sees in Paris after nightfall, as if they were ashamed of their misery by day.
"What a treat it is for an illustrator to be asked to visually interpret an entire book of words like these from Guy de Maupassant. *Merci beaucoup!*"

119

Artist: **JERRY PINKNEY**

Art Director: David Tommasino

Client: Scholastic Inc.

Size: 14 x 15

JERRY PINKNEY
Book Silver Medal

"I have long been interested in the Underground Railroad and especially the heroine, Harriet Tubman. This painting represents the triumph and survival of an enslaved people over their enslavers. One can only wonder about this woman's courage and resolve, to risk her life over and over again to secure the freedom of others."

120

Artist: **SAELIG GALLAGHER**

Art Director: Michael Farmer

Client: Harcourt Brace Jovanovich

Medium: Oil

SAELIG GALLAGHER
Book Silver Medal

"To infuse an inner life into an image, into a character and its settin
this is what a fairy tale calls upon us to do as we work with it and
attempt to find its visual counterpoint. One of the most compelling
things about fairy tales, I find, is the way the mind receives them, th
naturalness with which we dismiss the authority of rationality and e
the dreamscape. That we shift our awareness to recognize in them
poetic truth is perhaps equivalent to what we value most in painting
the recognition (in physical fact) of a state of being."

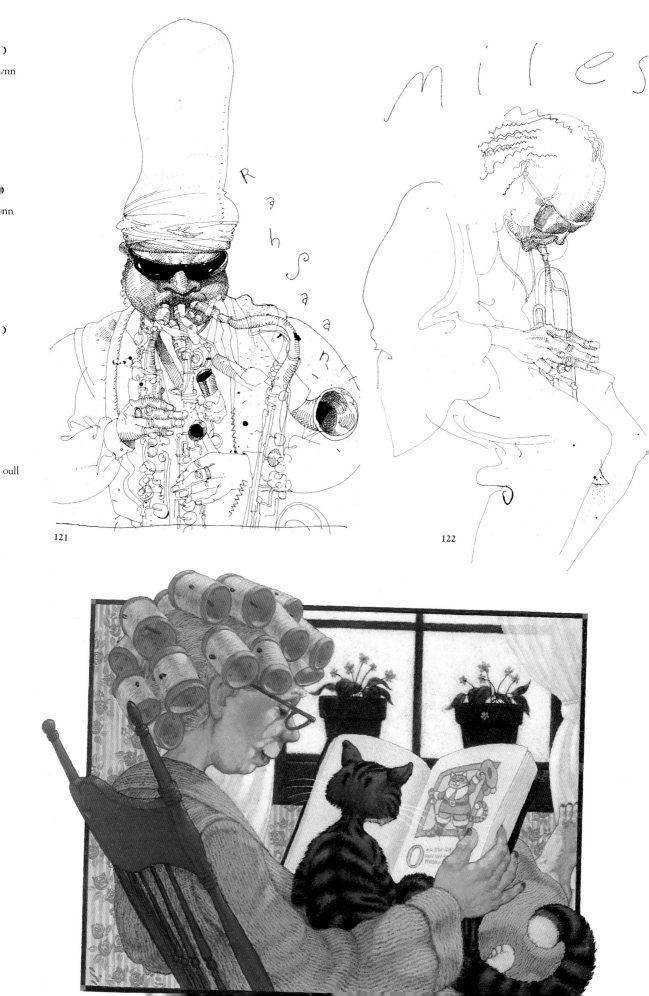

121

122

124

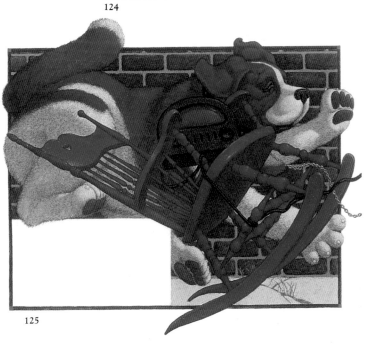

125

126

Artist: **GARNET HENDERSON**

Art Director: Michaela Sullivan

Client: Houghton Mifflin

Size: 6 x 6

127

Artist: **JOE CIARDIELLO**

Art Director: Patrick J.B. Flynn

Client: Spanfeller Press

Medium: Pen and ink

Size: 11 x 12 ¹/₂

128

Artist: **STEVEN ASSEL**

Art Director: Yook Louie

Client: Bantam Books

Medium: Acrylic

Size: 37 x 51

129

Artist: **WARREN CHANG**

Medium: Oil

Size: 15 x 11

130

Artist: **STEVEN ASSEL**

Art Director: Yook Louie

Client: Bantam Books

Medium: Oil

Size: 24 x 20

126

127

128

129

130

131

Artist: **JEFF CORNELL**

Medium: Graphite

Size: 10 x 12

132

Artist: **PATRICIA ROHRBACHER**

Size: 11 ¹/₂ x 12

133

Artist: **GARY KELLEY**

Art Directors: Tom Peterson
Louise Fili

Client: Creative Education

Medium: Pastel

Size: 18 ¹/₂ x 23 ¹/₂

134

Artist: **JOHN THOMPSON**

Art Director: Larissa Lawrynenko

Client: Reader's Digest General Books

Medium: Oil

Size: 14 x 9

135

Artist: **DAVID SHANNON**

Art Director: Michael Farmer

Client: Harcourt Brace Jovanovich

Medium: Acrylic

131

132

133

134

135

136

Artist: **KAZUHIKO SANO**

Art Director: Hiroko Kodama

Client: Shincho-Sha Publishing

Medium: Acrylic

Size: 18 x 13

137

Artist: **KAZUHIKO SANO**

Art Director: Chihiro Takahashi

Client: Shincho-Sha Publishing

Medium: Acrylic

Size: 23 x 17

138

Artist: **MARK SCHULER**

Art Director: Soren Noring

Client: Reader's Digest

Medium: Watercolor

Size: 13 x 9

139

Artist: **ELAINE DUILLO**

Art Director: James Harris

Client: Ballantine Books

Medium: Acrylic

Size: 18 x 25

137

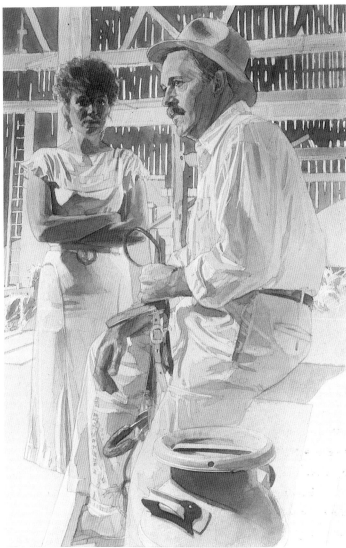

138

139

140

Artist: **DORIAN VALLEJO**

Art Director: Tom Egner

Client: Avon Books

Medium: Oil on illustration board

Size: 23 x 15 1/2

141

Artist: **DORIAN VALLEJO**

Art Director: Jamie Warren Youll

Client: Bantam Books

Medium: Oil on illustration board

Size: 24 x 15

142

Artist: **MICHAEL J. DEAS**

Art Director: Elizabeth Parisi

Medium: Oil

Size: 23 x 19 1/2

143

Artist: **JEFFREY TOMAKA**

Medium: Pastel, oil

Size: 11 x 20 3/8

141

142

143

144

Artist: **PETER DE SÈVE**

Art Director: Paul Elliot

Client: Rabbit Ears

Size: 14 x 13

145

Artist: **ELAINE DUILLO**

Art Director: Gerald Counihan

Client: Dell Publishing Company

Medium: Acrylic

Size: 17 ½ x 16 ½

146

Artist: **STEPHEN YOULL**

Art Director: Jamie Warren Youll

Client: Bantam Books

Medium: Acrylic, oil

Size: 27 x 37

147

Artist: **LISA FALKENSTERN
MILTON CHARLES**

Art Director: Milton Charles

Client: Delphinium Press

Medium: Oil

Size: 11 ½ x 8 ½

148

Artist: **STASYS
EIDRIGEVICIUS**

Client: Viking Penguin

Size: 15 x 18

144

145

146

147

148

149

Artist: **PETER SCANLAN**

Art Director: Susan Newman

Client: Macmillan Publishing
Company

Medium: Acrylic

Size: 17 x 17

150

Artist: **JOHN COLLIER**

Art Director: Alex Jay

Client: Viking Children's Books

Medium: Pastel, gouache

151

Artist: **JERRY PINKNEY**

Art Director: Atha Tehon

Client: Dial Books for Young
Readers

Size: 12 x 19 ³/₄

152

Artist: **LISA FALKENSTERN**

Art Director: Milton Charles

Client: Delphinium Press

Medium: Oil

Size: 11 ¹/₂ x 9

153

Artist: **TOM CURRY**

Art Director: Kym Abrams

Client: Scott Foresman

Medium: Acrylic

Size: 14 x 11

149

150

151

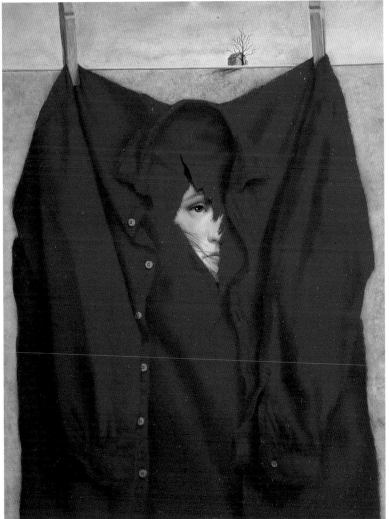

152

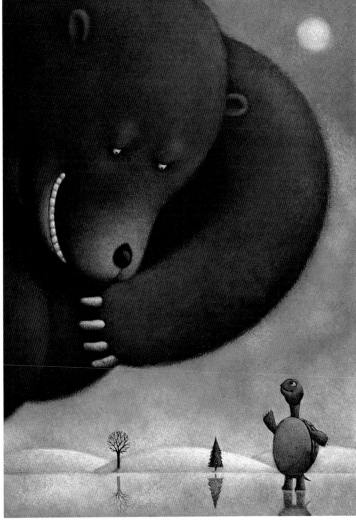

153

154

Artist: **DELANA BETTOLI**

Art Director: Linda Huber

Client: Silver Press/Simon & Schuster Books

Medium: Gouache

Size: 10 x 7 7/8

155

Artist: **LOIS EHLERT**

Art Director: Harriet Barton

Client: HarperCollins

Medium: Cut paper

Size: 12 1/2 x 14 3/4

156

Artist: **CHRISTOPHER MOELLER**

Art Director: George Broderick

Client: Innovation Corporation

Medium: Mixed media

Size: 25 1/2 x 15 1/2

157

Artist: **BRYAN LEISTER**

Art Director: Racquel Jaramillo

Client: Henry Holt and Co. Inc.

Size: 15 x 10

158

Artist: **ANTHONY CARNABUCI**

Art Directors: Cecilia Yung
Barbara Henessey

Client: Viking Children's Books

Medium: Oil

Size: 9 x 16

154

155

156

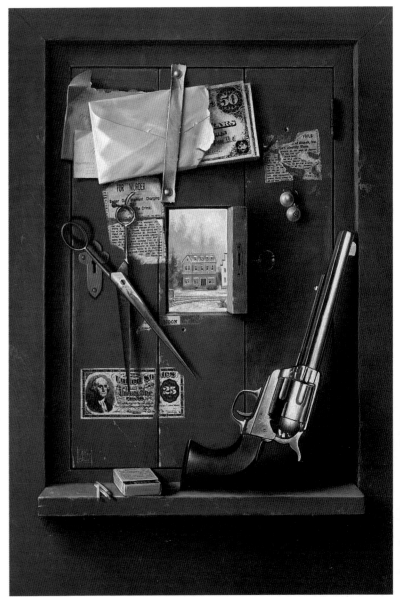

157

158

159

Artist: **HEIDE OBERHEIDE**

Art Director: Tom Egner

Client: Avon Books

Size: 26 x 16

160

Artist: **C. MICHAEL DUDASH**

Art Director: Gerald Counihan

Client: Delacorte Press

Medium: Oil on linen

Size: 31 x 20 1/2

161

Artist: **C. MICHAEL DUDASH**

Art Director: Gerald Counihan

Client: Dell Publishing Company

Medium: Oil on linen

Size: 27 x 18

162

Artist: **CHRISTOPHER MANSON**

Art Director: Marc Cheshire

Client: North-South Books

Size: 13 1/2 x 25 1/2

159

160

161

162

163

Artist: **RICK LOVELL**

Art Director: Tom Egner

Client: Avon Books

Size: 18 1/2 x 12

164

Artist: **JEAN-FRANCOIS PODEVIN**

Art Director: Judith Murello

Client: Berkley Publishing

Size: 19 x 11 3/4

165

Artist: **JOHN JUDE PALENCAR**

Art Director: David Saylor

Client: HarperCollins

Medium: Watercolor, acrylic

Size: 22 x 16

166

Artist: **BARRY MOSER**

Art Director: Christine Kettner

Client: HarperCollins

Size: 9 x 19

163

164

165

166

167

Artist: **MANUEL GARCIA**

Art Director: Michael Farmer

Client: Harcourt Brace Jovanovich

Medium: Acrylic

Size: 17 x 13 1/2

168

Artist: **JOHN THOMPSON**

Art Director: Angelo Perrone

Client: Reader's Digest Condensed
Books

Medium: Acrylic

Size: 30 x 40

169

Artist: **BOB LARKIN**

Art Director: Whitney Cookman

Client: Doubleday

170

Artist: **JOEL PETER JOHNSON**

Art Directors: Bob Aulicino
Bob Scudellari

Client: Random House

Medium: Mixed media

Size: 9 x 7

167

168

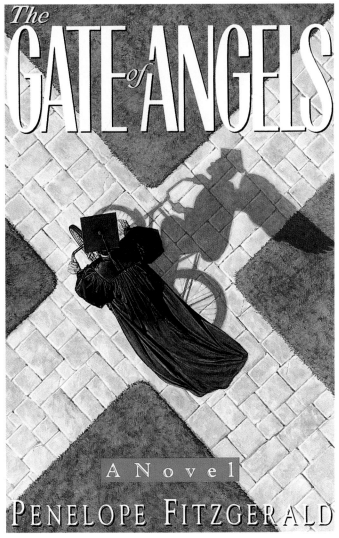

169

170

171

Artist: **PAUL MORIN**

Art Director: Michael Farmer

Client: Harcourt Brace Jovanovich

Medium: Oil

Size: 26 1/2 x 21 1/2

172

Artist: **JOHN JUDE
PALENCAR**

Art Director: Judith Murello

Client: Berkley Books/Ace Books

Medium: Watercolor, acrylic

Size: 17 x 21

173

Artist: **DAVID JOHNSON**

Art Director: Larissa Lawrynenko

Client: Reader's Digest

Size: 14 x 9 1/2

174

Artist: **JIM DEAL**

Art Director: Gerald Counihan

Client: Dell Publishing Company

Medium: Acrylic

Size: 14 x 9

171

172

173

174

175

Artist: **ROBERT HYNES**

Medium: Acrylic

Size: 12 x 9

176

Artist: **MITCHELL HOOKS**

Art Director: Lorraine Paradowski

Client: Harlequin Books

Medium: Oil

Size: 19 x 14 1/2

177

Artist: **MARK RYDEN**

Art Director: Catherine
                Vandercasteele

Client: LA 411

Medium: Oil

Size: 10 1/2 x 16

178

Artist: **TED COCONIS**

Art Director: Tom Egner

Client: Avon Books

Medium: Oil on canvas

Size: 24 x 36

175

176

177

178

179

Artist: **MICHAEL J. DEAS**

Art Director: Barbara Leff

Medium: Oil on panel

Size: 20 x 13

180

Artist: **JIM BURNS**

Art Director: Ruth Ross

Client: Ballantine Books

Medium: Acrylic

Size: 25 x 17

181

Artist: **TOM SCIACCA**

Art Director: Jamie Warren Youll

Client: Doubleday

Medium: Acrylic

Size: 10 x 7

182

Artist: **PETER DE SEVE**

Art Director: Paul Elliot

Client: Rabbit Ears

Size: 10 1/2 x 16

179

180

181

182

183

Artist: **DENIS BEAUVAIS**

Art Director: Judith Murello

Client: Berkley Publishing Group

Size: 36 x 26

184

Artist: **JIM BARKLEY**

Art Director: Larissa Lawrynenko

Client: Reader's Digest General Books

Medium: Oil

Size: 19 x 14

185

Artist: **ROBERT CRAWFORD**

Art Director: David Bamford

Client: Berkley Publishing Group

Medium: Acrylic

Size: 16 ¹/2 x 10

186

Artist: **ROBERT HYNES**

Art Director: David Seager

Client: National Geographic

Medium: Acrylic

Size: 11 x 13 ¹/2

183

184

185

186

187

Artist: **LIANA SOMAN**

Medium: Oil on illustration board

Size: 15 1/2 x 12

188

Artist: **GARY HEAD**

Medium: Oil

Size: 13 1/2 x 17 1/2

189

Artist: **STEPHEN T. JOHNSON**

Art Director: Donna Martin

Client: Andrews and McMeel

Medium: Pastel, watercolor

Size: 21 x 16 1/4

190

Artist: **ADAM NIKLEWICZ**

Art Directors: Doris Borowsky-
          Straus
          Michael Accordino

Client: St. Martin's Press

Medium: Acrylic

Size: 12 x 7 1/2

187

188

189

190

191

Artist: **ROBERT McGINNIS**

Art Director: Marva Martin

Client: Bantam Books

Size: 16 x 11 1/2

192

Artist: **KEN LAAGER**

Medium: Oil

Size: 18 x 24

193

Artist: **FRED OTNES**

Art Director: Kazko Nogouchi

Client: The Greatest Illustration Show of America

Medium: Collage

Size: 14 x 11 1/2

194

Artist: **DAVID SHANNON**

Art Directors: Gunto Alexander
Nanette Stevenson

Client: G.P. Putnam Sons

Medium: Acrylic

Size: 17 x 13

191

192

193

194

195

Artist: **JEAN PIERRE TARGETE**

Art Director: Diane Luger

Client: Berkley Books

Medium: Oil

Size: 25 x 17

196

Artist: **MURRAY TINKELMAN**

Medium: Pen and ink

Size: 20 x 16

197

Artist: **PHILIP SINGER**

Art Director: Jackie Merri Meyer

Client: Warner Books

Size: 8 1/2 x 7

198

Artist: **CATHERINE HUERTA**

Art Director: Al Cetta

Client: HarperCollins

Size: 19 1/2 x 18

196

197

198

199

Artist: **RICK BERRY**

Art Director: Arnie Fenner

Client: Mark V. Ziesing

Medium: Oil

Size: 29 1/2 x 19

200

Artist: **TONY O. CHAMPAGNE**

Art Directors: Trent Angers
William 'Buz' Carter

Client: Lou Ana Gardens

Size: 19 x 14 1/2

201

Artist: **TOM TAGGART**

Art Director: Tom Peyer

Client: DC Comics

Medium: 3-D, mixed media

Size: 20 1/2 x 13 1/2

202

Artist: **KIRK REINERT**

Art Director: Gene Mydlowski

Client: Harper Paperbacks

Medium: Oil

Size: 29 1/2 x 18

203

Artist: **WENDELL MINOR**

Art Director: Al Cetta

Client: HarperCollins

Medium: Watercolor, gouache

Size: 10 x 7

199

200

201

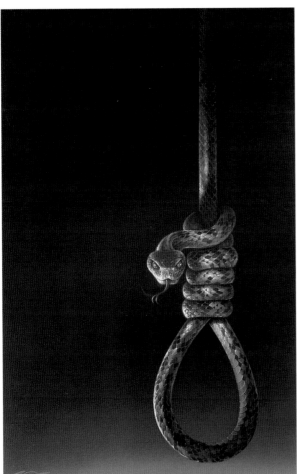

202

203

204

Artist: **KEVIN HAWKES**

Art Director: Audrey Bryant

Client: David R. Godine Publisher

Size: 13 3/4 x 11 1/4

205

Artist: **DEREK JAMES**

Art Director: Hollie A. Rubin

Client: Scholastic Inc.

Medium: Oil

Size: 17 x 10 1/2

206

Artist: **DANIEL SCHWARTZ**

Art Director: Don Owens

Client: American Jury Trial
Foundation

Size: 20 x 16

207

Artist: **ROBERT ANDREW
PARKER**

Art Director: Cecilia Yung

Client: Viking Children's Books

Medium: Etching, aquatint

Size: 8 x 6

208

Artist: **DAVID STIMSON**

Art Director: Tom Egner

Client: Avon Books

Size: 18 1/2 x 13

204

205

206

207

208

209
Artist: **KEN LAAGER**
Art Director: Yook Louie
Client: Bantam Books
Medium: Oil
Size: 24 x 16

210
Artist: **LANE SMITH**
Art Director: Molly Leach
Client: Viking Children's Books
Medium: Oil
Size: 12 1/2 x 10 1/4

211
Artist: **JOHN H. HOWARD**
Art Director: Jackie Merri Meyer
Client: Mysterious Press/
    Warner Books
Size: 24 x 18

212
Artist: **KEN LAAGER**
Art Director: Yook Louie
Client: Bantam Books
Size: 18 x 24 3/4

209

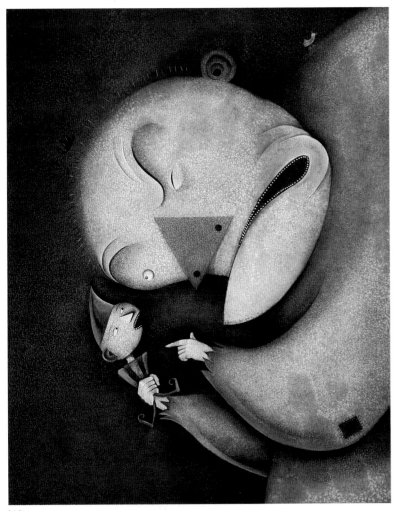

210

211

212

213

Artist: **LIANA SOMAN**

Art Director: Elizabeth Parisi

Client: Scholastic Inc.

Medium: Oil on illustration board

Size: 18 x 12

214

Artist: **MICHAEL J. DEAS**

Art Director: David Saylor

Client: HarperCollins

Size: 21 x 14

215

Artist: **DAVE CUTLER**

Art Director: Tom Mack

Client: Macmillan Publishing
Company

Medium: Acrylic

Size: 14 x 11

216

Artist: **ERIC DINYER**

Art Director: Anne Twomey

Client: Warner Books

Medium: Oil

Size: 11 x 14

217

Artist: **ERIC DINYER**

Art Director: Anne Twomey

Client: Warner Books

Medium: Oil

Size: 12 $^1/_2$ x 8 $^3/_4$

213

214

215

216

217

218

Artist: **ROBERT HUNT**

Art Director: Charlotte Bralds

Client: Earth Island Institute/
Graphis

Size: 43 x 40

219

Artist: **FRED OTNES**

Art Director: Kazko Nogouchi

Client: The Greatest Illustration
Show of America

Medium: Mixed-media collage

Size: 24 x 32

220

Artist: **JOHN JUDE
PALENCAR**

Art Director: Sheila Gilbert

Client: Daw Books

Medium: Watercolor, acrylic

Size: 20 ¹/₂ x 21

221

Artist: **PHIL PARKS**

Art Director: Ann Spinelli

Client: Putnam Publishing

Medium: Acrylic

Size: 18 x 12

218

219

220

221

222

Artist: **TOM NACHREINER**

Medium: Watercolor, gouache

Size: 23 x 31 1/2

223

Artist: **DAVID CUNNINGHAM**

Art Director: Karen Campbell

Client: Albert Whitman & Company

Medium: Gouache

Size: 6 1/2 x 6

224

Artist: **JEFF CORNELL**

Medium: Charcoal

Size: 28 x 18

225

Artist: **STEPHEN T. JOHNSON**

Art Director: Donna Martin

Client: Andrews and McMeel

Medium: Pastel, watercolor

Size: 21 x 16 1/4

226

Artist: **WILLIAM JOYCE**

Art Director: Christine Kettner

Client: HarperCollins

Size: 7 1/2 x 11

222

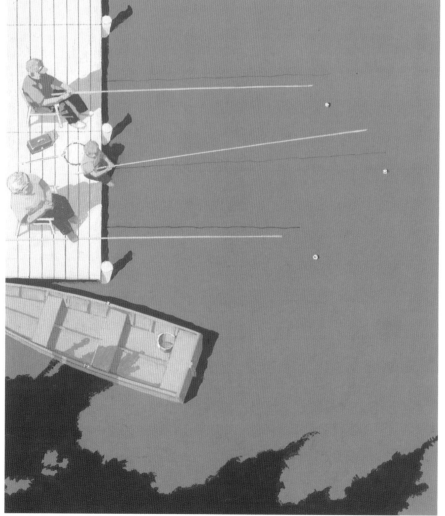

223

224

225

226

227

Artist: **FRED OTNES**

Medium: Mixed-media collage

Size: 21 x 22

228

Artist: **BRUCE JENSEN**

Art Director: Jamie Warren Youll

Client: Bantam Books

Medium: Acrylic/CG

Size: 14 x 11

229

Artist: **JERRY PINKNEY**

Art Director: Atha Tehon

Client: Dial Books for Young
          Readers

Size: 12 x 19 ³/4

230

Artist: **JOHN COLLIER**

Art Director: Paul Buckley

Client: Penguin USA

Medium: Oil pastel

Size: 28 ¹/2 x 20 ¹/2

231

Artist: **BOB RAFEI**

Medium: Oil

Size: 36 x 24

227

228

229

230

231

232

Artist: **SHANNON STIRNWEIS**

Medium: Oil

Size: 36 x 24

233

Artist: **RICHARD SPARKS**

Art Director: Michael Baldyga

Client: Easton Press

Medium: Oil

Size: 20 x 14

234

Artist: **RICHARD SPARKS**

Art Director: Michael Baldyga

Client: Easton Press

Medium: Oil

Size: 21 x 16

235

Artist: **TOM NACHREINER**

Medium: Watercolor

Size: 22 x 29 1/2

233

234

235

236

Artist: **MICHAEL J. DEAS**

Art Director: Hollie A. Rubin

Client: Scholastic Inc.

Medium: Oil

Size: 16 x 11

237

Artist: **ALEX SCHAEFER**

Medium: Oil

Size: 24 x 15 ¹/2

238

Artist: **MARC ERICKSEN**

Art Director: James Harris

Client: Ballantine Books

Size: 40 x 35

239

Artist: **TRACI HAYMANS**

Medium: Pastel with linseed

Size: 10 x 11

240

Artist: **CATHLEEN TOELKE**

Art Director: Jackie Merri Meyer

Client: Mysterious Press/
Warner Books

Size: 9 x 6

236

237

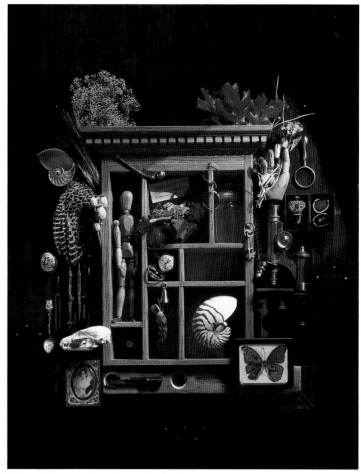

238

239

240

241

Artist: **ED LINDLOF**

Art Director: Neil Stuart

Client: Dutton Books

Medium: Pen, ink, Rotring Artist Color

Size: 14 x 12

242

Artist: **C. BRUCE DUPREE**

Medium: Colored pencil, watercolor

Size: 15 x 10

243

Artist: **TED COCONIS**

Medium: Oil

Size: 30 x 39

244

Artist: **PAUL BACHEM**

Art Director: Elizabeth Parisi

Client: Scholastic Inc.

Medium: Oil

Size: 32 x 22

245

Artist: **JIM BARKLEY**

Art Director: Larissa Lawrynenko

Client: Reader's Digest General Books

Medium: Oil

Size: 14 1/2 x 19 1/2

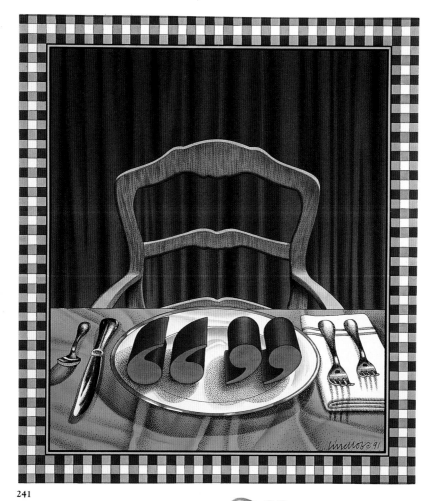

241

242

243

244

245

ADVERTISING JURY

JOHN WITT
CHAIRMAN
Creative Director/Illustrator

TINA ADAMEK
Executive Art Director
McGraw-Hill Healthcare

DAVID BLOSSOM
Illustrator

JOHN COLLIER
Illustrator

ALAN E. COBER
Illustrator

MICHAEL GARLAND
Illustrator

ENID V. HATTON
Illustrator

BURT SILVERMAN
Illustrator/Painter

ATHA TEHON
Associate Publisher/Art Director
Dial Books for Young Readers

ADVERTISING

246

Artist: **KINUKO Y. CRAFT**

Art Director: Clay Freeman

Agency: May & Company

Client: May & Company/
Washington Opera

Size: 22 x 15 1/2

KINUKO Y. CRAFT
Advertising Gold Medal

"The best moment in the creation of one of my illustrations is when I can begin to see the image forming in the board, almost as if it were an empty box, before I have ever touched the surface. At that moment, it is most full of hope and dreams, and all things are possible."

247

Artist: **MICHAEL J. DEAS**

Art Director: Jim Cotton

Agency: Jim Cotton
       Communications

Client: Ghurka Luggage

Medium: Oil on panel

Size: 16 x 24

MICHAEL J. DEAS
Advertising Gold Medal

"This painting, done on panel for Ghurka Luggage, was a complete campaign image used in many ways, shapes, and sizes from stamps to posters. The objective in this advertisement was to give the product a classic, timeless look—it could be 1933 or 1993."

248

Artist: **WIKTOR SADOWSKI**

Art Director: Wiktor Sadowski

Client: Polish Film

Medium: Oil

Size: 23 x 16

WIKTOR SADOWSKI
Advertising Gold Medal

This poster for the movie by Peter Greenaway, *The Draughtsman's Contract*, was assigned by the distributor of this movie in Sadowski's native Poland. The atmosphere is full of insinuation; it is magical and mysterious and allows one to create a visual image, free from literal translation.

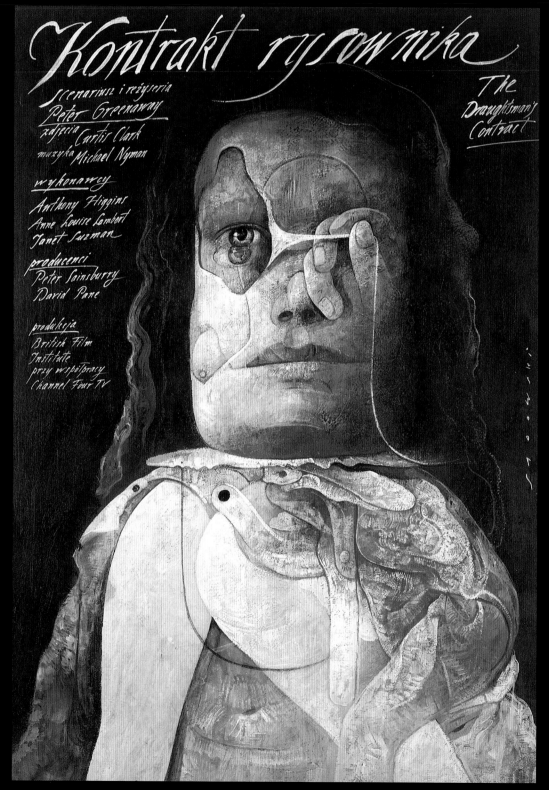

249

Artist: **WILLIAM LOW**

Art Director: Drennan Lindsay

Client: Eddie Bauer

Size: 20 x 20

WILLIAM LOW
Advertising Silver Medal

" 'Orcas Island Ferry' is my second Eddie Bauer catalog cover illustration and my first assignment since moving from New York where I have always lived. Now I'm living and painting in a suburban, semi-rural sprawl. Because my paintings are about light, many people assume that I have a sun-drenched studio. In reality, it is in the small damp basement of my house without sunlight but full of spiders and fluorescent lights. To overcome these problems, I use a lot of imagination, some photographic reference and inspiration from many artists: Fairfield Porter, Isaak Levitan, Richard Diebenkorn, Claude Monet, and Edward Hopper. I understand from letters responding to the Eddie Bauer cover that Orcas Island *is* a beautiful place and that I've captured the feeling of these islands. It sounds like it could make for a lovely vacation. Maybe one day I can experience this feeling for *myself*."

Artist: **MARK SUMMERS**

Art Director: Michael Fountain

Agency: Ice Communications, Inc.

Client: Remington Steel

Medium: Scratchboard, watercolor

Size: 9 x 8

MARK SUMMERS
Advertising Silver Medal

This ad for Remington Steel, makers of quality shotgun shells, was the first piece Mark did in his new home in Ontario. Rumor in the community had it that he was an artist...and that the neighbors weren't quite sure what to expect. Mark saw a big guy jogging past one day, stopped him, and asked if he wouldn't mind modeling for an advertisement. It turns out the guy was a cop and once he saw the layout, he got enthused. Word spread that the new artist was not a "weirdo type" and soon he was accepted in the neighborhood.

251

253

251

Artist: **ROBERT HUNT**

Art Director: Chuck Stern

Agency: Foote Cone & Belding

Client: Baykeepers

Medium: Oil

Size: 33 x 24

252

Artist: **PATRICK D. MILBOURN**

Medium: Oil

Size: 30 x 15

253

Artist: **CHRIS HOPKINS**

Art Director: Bill Sweeney

Client: Silver Creek Farms

Medium: Oil

Size: 14 x 22

254

Artist: **BRALDT BRALDS**

Art Director: Arnie Arlow

Agency: TBWA

Client: Carillon Imports

Medium: Oil

Size: 24 x 20

255

Artist: **BRALDT BRALDS**

Art Director: Arnie Arlow

Agency: TBWA

Client: Carillon Imports

Medium: Oil

Size: 24 x 20

256

Artist: **RICH BOWMAN**

Art Director: George Kaufman

Agency: Kuhn & Wittenborn

Client: Baskin Robbins

Medium: Oil

Size: 20 1/2 x 10

257

Artist: **MARY GRANDPRÉ**

Art Director: David Bartels

Agency: Bartels Associates

Client: GDS

Medium: Pastel

Size: 13 x 24 1/2

254

255

256

257

258

Artist: **KATHERINE LANDIKUSIC**

Art Director: Martha Swords

Client: Prince of Whales Polo Cup

Medium: Pastel

Size: 36 x 22

259

Artist: **FRANCES JETTER**

Art Director: Taras Wayner

Agency: Mad Dogs & Englishmen

Client: Audubon

Size: 18 x 11

260

Artist: **JOHN JUDE PALENCAR**

Art Director: Diane Stegmeier

Client: Steelcase

Medium: Watercolor, acrylic

Size: 16 1/2 x 14

261

Artist: **CHARLES SANTORE**

Art Director: Bernie Hogya

Agency: Bozell, Inc.

Client: Merrill Lynch

Medium: Watercolor

Size: 11 x 8

262

Artist: **CRAIG FRAZIER**

Art Director: Craig Frazier

Client: Mill Valley Film Festival

Medium: Cut paper

Size: 14 1/2 x 11

258

259

260

261

262

263

Artist: **BERNIE FUCHS**

Art Director: Drennan Lindsay

Client: Eddie Bauer

Medium: Oil

Size: 26 x 26

264

Artist: **JOEL PETER JOHNSON**

Art Director: Suzanne Adrian

Client: Koch International Classics

Size: 6 x 6

265

Artist: **WILLIAM LOW**

Art Director: Peter Schaefer

Client: The New York Times

Size: 10 x 15 ¹/₂

266

Artist: **JOYCE PATTI**

Art Director: Becky Connell-
Swanson

Agency: DMB & B

Client: LaSalle Banks

Medium: Oil

Size: 17 x 11

267

Artist: **JOYCE PATTI**

Art Director: Becky Connell-
Swanson

Agency: DMB & B

Client: LaSalle Banks

Medium: Oil

Size: 17 x 11

263

264

265

266

267

268

Artist: **CARY AUSTIN**

Art Director: Randy Smith

Agency: Randall Smith Associates

Client: Pioneer Theatre Company

Medium: Acrylic

Size: 18 x 15 3/4 .

269

Artist: **FRANCIS LIVINGSTON**

Art Director: Chris Knight

Agency: Macy's

Client: Macy's

Size: 24 x 24

270

Artist: **CATHLEEN TOELKE**

Art Director: Shuzo Hirata

Agency: Hakuhodo Inc.

Client: Cecilene

Medium: Gouache

Size: 19 x 14

271

Artist: **PAUL ROGERS**

Art Director: Robert Upisandi

Agency: Saatchi & Saatchi

Client: Toyota

Medium: Acrylic

Size: 30 x 20

272

Artist: **F. XAVIER PAVY**

Art Director: Frank Olinsky

Client: Sire/Reprise Records

Medium: Oil

Size: 24 x 24

268

269

270

271

272

273

Artist: **LAURA PHILLIPS**

Art Director: Claude Prettyman

Client: Red Robin Restaurants

Medium: Acrylic, airbrush

Size: 24 x 22

274

Artist: **MARY JO PHALEN**

Art Director: Mary Jo Phalen

Client: San Diego Zoo Wild
Animal Park

Medium: Mixed media

Size: 28 x 36

275

Artist: **BART FORBES**

Art Director: Rich Burk

Client: The Fred Meyer Challenge

Medium: Oil on canvas

Size: 18 1/2 x 27 1/2

276

Artist: **TIM LEWIS**

277

Artist: **BERNIE FUCHS**

Art Director: Helene Sigman

Client: Ameritech

Medium: Oil

Size: 35 x 24

273

274

275

276

277

278

Artist: **DUGALD STERMER**

Art Director: Melanie Doherty

Client: DFS Group, Ltd.

Medium: Pencil, watercolor on Arches

Size: 20 x 12

279

Artist: **DUGALD STERMER**

Art Director: Greg McGough

Agency: SlaughterHanson Advertising

Client: Southern Natural Gas

Medium: Pencil, watercolor on Arches

280

Artist: **TRISTAN A. ELWELL**

Art Director: Dick Calderhead

Agency: Calderhead & Phin

Client: Willis Corroon

Medium: Oil on gessoed paper

Size: 12 x 9

281

Artist: **WARREN LINN**

Art Director: Stephen Byram

Client: JMT Productions

Medium: Acrylic, collage on plywood

Size: 36 x 24

282

Artist: **MIKE REAGAN**

Art Director: Albert Chiang

Client: Islands Magazine

Medium: Watercolor, ink

Size: 16 x 21

278

279

280

281

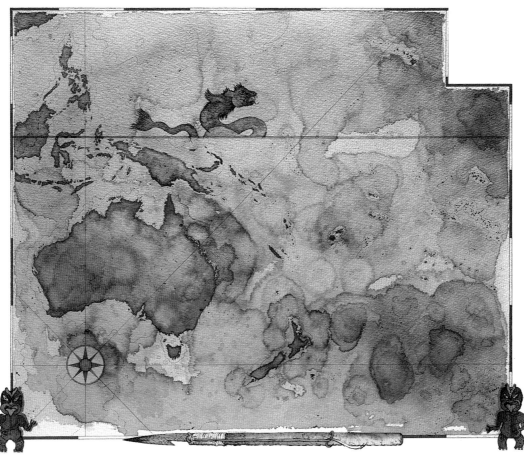

282

283
Artist: **JERRY LOFARO**

Art Director: Woody Litwhiler

Agency: Bozell, Inc.

Client: Minolta

Medium: Acrylic

Size: 26 x 20

284
Artist: **GERALDINE CONEY**

Medium: Paper sculpture

Size: 18 x 18

285
Artist: **PAUL MICICH**

Art Director: Randy Messer

Client: Perfection Learning

Medium: Alkyd

Size: 25 x 20

286
Artist: **MILAN KECMAN**

Art Director: Sue Monahan

Agency: Glazen Advertising

Client: National City Bank

Medium: Scratchboard

Size: 9 x 6

287
Artist: **MARVIN MATTELSON**

Art Director: June Robinson

Agency: McCaffrey & McCall

Client: A & E

Medium: Oil

Size: 10 x 8

283

284

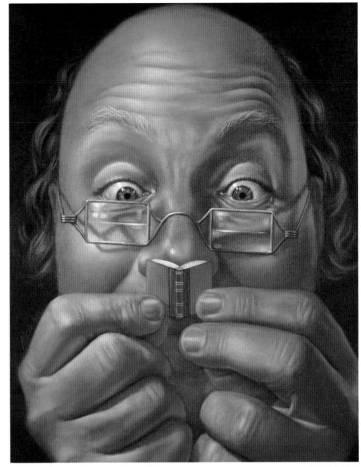

285

286

287

288

Artist: **WILLIAM C. BURGARD**

Art Director: Susan Pollay

Client: Ann Arbor Summer
Festival

Medium: Pastel, collage

Size: 45 x 30

289

Artist: **CAROLYN RIE**

Art Director: Matthew Schille

Agency: Hammond-Farrell, Inc.

Client: Integrated Network
Corporation

Medium: Tempra, gouache

Size: 12 x 14

290

Artist: **STASYS
EIDRIGEVICIUS**

Art Director: Laurie Churchman

Agency: Hewson, Berlin

Client: Commerical Risk Partners

Medium: Masks, cardboard, pastels,
guache

291

Artist: **JOHN BURGOYNE**

Art Director: Rudy Banny

Agency: Grant Jacoby

Client: Wilson Sporting Goods

Size: 35 x 18 1/2

292

Artist: **NATSUMI KAWAKAMI**

Medium: Oil

Size: 24 x 12

288

289

290

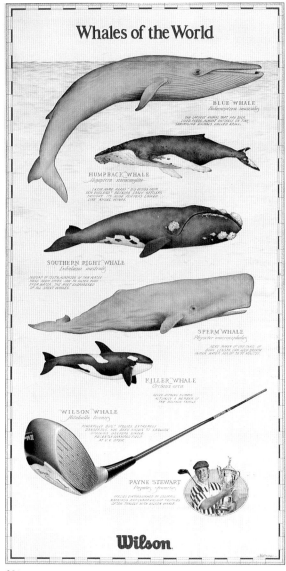

291

292

293

Artist: **ALEX MURAWSKI**

Art Director: David Bartels

Agency: Bartels Associates

Client: Gator Lager

Medium: Ink, acrylic

Size: 12 x 13

294

Artists: **GRIESBACH/ MARTUCCI**

Art Director: Doug Klein

Agency: Rapp-Collins Marcoa

Client: Rapp-Collins Marcoa

Medium: Oil on masonite

Size: 15 x 12

295

Artist: **MARVIN MATTELSON**

Art Director: Geoff Hayes

Agency: TBWA

Client: HIP

Medium: Oil

Size: 11 x 17

296

Artist: **PETER SIU**

Art Director: Gary Larsen

Agency: Larsen Colby

Medium: Oil, pen, ink on paper

Size: 7 1/2 x 6

297

Artist: **JAMES McMULLAN**

Art Director: Jim Russek

Agency: Russek Advertising

Client: Lincoln Center Theater

Medium: Watercolor

Size: 10 1/2 x 5 1/2

293

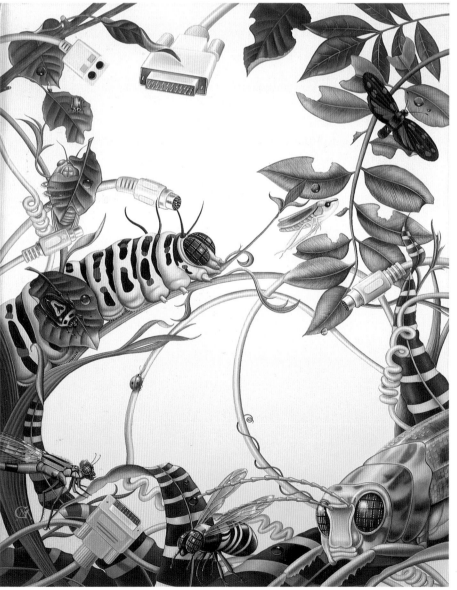

294

295

296

297

298
Artist: **TIM JESSELL**
Art Director: John Norman
Client: Nike
Medium: Pastel, mixed media
Size: 26 x 18

299
Artist: **SCOTT SWALES**
Medium: Pastel, acrylics
Size: 10 x 8 1/2

300
Artist: **PAUL DAVIS**
Art Director: Eric Baker
Client: The Body Shop
Medium: Acrylic on board
Size: 17 x 11 1/2

301
Artist: **ROBERT HUNT**
Art Directors: Henry Lehn
              Tony Seiniger
Agency: Seiniger Advertising
Client: Amblin Entertainment
Medium: Oil
Size: 38 x 24

302
Artist: **DANIEL SCHWARTZ**
Art Director: Daniel Schwartz
Client: Mobil Corporation
Medium: Oil
Size: 18 1/2 x 15

298

299

300

301

302

303

Artist: **LAURA PHILLIPS**

Art Director: Gary Larsen

Agency: Larsen Colby

Client: Austin Computer Systems

Medium: Acrylic, airbrush

Size: 12 x 14 1/2

304

Artist: **J.W. STEWART**

Client: PolyGram/Island Records

Medium: Mixed media

Size: 12 3/4 x 15 1/2

305

Artist: **BART FORBES**

Client: Dallas Arts Jazz '92

Medium: Oil

Size: 14 x 38

306

Artist: **PAUL DAVIS**

Art Director: Janice Brunell

Agency: Russek Advertising

Client: Big Apple Circus

Size: 19 1/2 x 14 1/2

307

Artist: **PAUL DAVIS**

Art Director: Janice Brunell

Agency: Russek Advertising

Client: Big Apple Circus

Size: 20 x 15

303

304

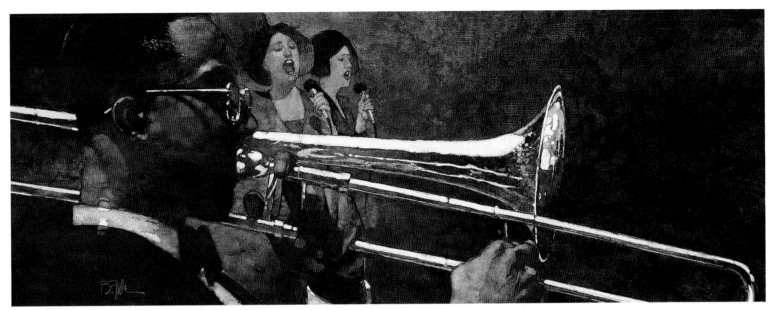

305

306

307

308

Artist: **JERRY LOFARO**

Art Director: Woody Litwhiler

Agency: Bozell, Inc.

Client: Minolta

Medium: Acrylic

Size: 26 x 20

309

Artist: **JERRY LOFARO**

Art Director: Woody Litwhiler

Agency: Bozell, Inc.

Client: Minolta

Medium: Acrylic

Size: 29 1/2 x 24 1/2

310

Artist: **ROBERT G. STEELE**

Art Director: Richard Mantel

Client: New York Magazine

Medium: Watercolor

Size: 15 1/2 x 12

311

Artist: **MARK A. FREDRICKSON**

Art Director: John Vitro

Agency: Franklin Stoorza

Client: Thermoscan

Medium: Acrylic

Size: 14 x 23

308

309

310

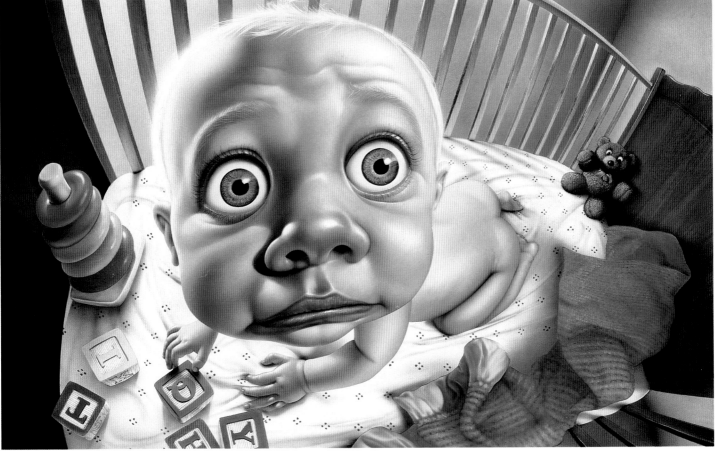

311

312

Artist: **FRED HILLIARD**

Art Director: Clay Turner

Agency: Ackerman McQueen

Client: Wiltel

Medium: Pen, ink, gouache

Size: 10 x 10

313

Artist: **MARK RYDEN**

Art Director: Melanie Penny

Client: Private Music

Medium: Oil

Size: 15 1/2 x 15 1/2

314

Artist: **BERNIE FUCHS**

Art Director: Karen Lothan

Agency: Hal Riney & Partners

Client: Nuveen

Medium: Oil on canvas

Size: 24 x 36

315

Artist: **JOEL NAKAMURA**

Art Directors: Nancy Donald
David Coleman

Client: Sony Music

Medium: Mixed media

Size: 27 x 13

316

Artist: **REGAN DUNNICK**

Art Director: Don Sibley

Client: Ameritrust

Medium: Pastel, oil

Size: 11 x 7 1/2

312

313

314

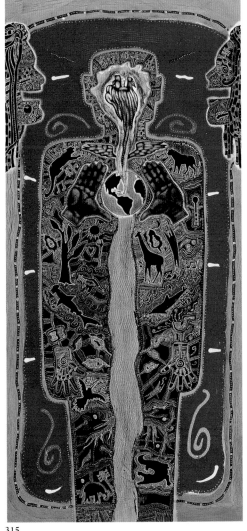

315

316

317

Artist: **MARK RYDEN**

Art Directors: Nancy Donald
Mark Ryden

Client: Sony Music

Medium: Oil

Size: 20 1/2 x 20 1/2

318

Artist: **PAUL DAVIS**

Art Directors: Paul Davis
Jim Russek

Agency: Russek Advertising

Client: WNCN

Medium: Acrylic on board

Size: 3 1/2 x 28

319

Artist: **GREGORY MANCHESS**

Art Directors: Gregory Manchess
Stan Thomas

Client: Homewares, Inc.

Medium: Oil

Size: 21 x 25 1/2

320

Artist: **VIVIENNE FLESHER**

Client: New York Magazine

Medium: Pastel

Size: 18 x 14

321

Artist: **CATHLEEN TOELKE**

Art Director: Carol Chen

Client: Sony Music

Medium: Gouache

Size: 9 1/2 x 6 1/2

317

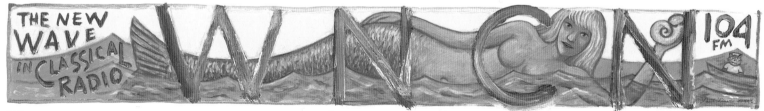

318

319

320

321

322

Artist: **SKIP LIEPKE**

Art Director: Harry Kramp

Agency: J. Walter Thompson/
PPGH

Client: Heineken, Netherlands

Medium: Oil

Size: 31 1/2 x 24

323

Artist: **MARK ENGLISH**

Art Director: Jim Plumeri

Client: Bantam Books, Doubleday
Dell, Audio Publishing

Size: 21 1/2 x 13

324

Artist: **KAZUHIKO SANO**

Art Directors: Charles Davis
John Grimaldi

Agency: Davis & Grimaldi

Client: Saul Zaente Company

Medium: Acrylic

Size: 35 x 22 1/2

325

Artist: **CAROL WALD**

Art Director: Susan Russo

Client: Dennos Museum Center

Medium: Oil

Size: 72 x 216

322

323

324

325

326

Artist: **JOHN PIAMPIANO**

Medium: Acrylic

Size: 9 1/2 x 9 1/4

327

Artist: **TERRY RAVANELLI**

Art Director: Grady Phelan

Client: H.J. Heinz

Medium: Ink, watercolor

Size: 13 x 13

328

Artist: **PAUL DAVIS**

Art Director: Fran Michelman

Client: Mobil Mystery!

Medium: Acrylic on board

Size: 16 1/2 x 11

329

Artist: **RUSS WILSON**

Art Director: Russ Wilson

Client: Aslan House

Medium: Pastel

Size: 20 x 13

330

Artist: **DORI SPECTOR**

Medium: Oil

Size: 25 x 29

326

327

328

329

330

331

Artist: **BRALDT BRALDS**

Art Director: Jack Frakes

Agency: Ross Roy Advertising

Client: Alfa Romeo

Medium: Oil on masonite

Size: 12 x 10

332

Artist: **CORBERT GAUTHIER**

Art Director: Brent Boyd

Agency: CMF & Z

Client: Pella Windows

Medium: Oil

Size: 19 x 13

333

Artist: **ALEX MURAWSKI**

Art Director: Bruce Campbell

Agency: KSK

Client: V.M. Systems

Medium: Ink, acrylic

Size: 9 x 6

334

Artist: **JOHN THOMPSON**

Size: 8 1/2 x 11 1/2

331

332

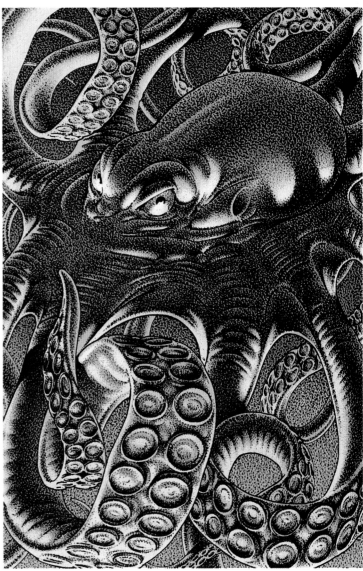

333

334

335

Artist: **JOEL SPECTOR**

Art Director: Tom McManus

Agency: TBWA

Client: Absolut Vodka

Medium: Pastel

Size: 16 x 21

336

Artist: **GERRY GERSTEN**

Art Director: Gerry Steijn

Client: Intermediair

Size: 17 x 14

337

Artist: **WIKTOR SADOWSKI**

Art Director: Wiktor Sadowski

Client: Polish Film

Medium: Oil

Size: 15 x 21

338

Artist: **RAFAL OLBINSKI**

Art Director: Alane Gehagen

Agency: Ziff Marketing

Client: New York City Opera

Medium: Acrylic on canvas

Size: 20 1/2 x 14 1/2

339

Artist: **C. MICHAEL DUDASH**

Art Director: Robin Bray

Client: Time-Life Music

Medium: Oil on gessoed gator foam

Size: 18 x 14

335

336

337

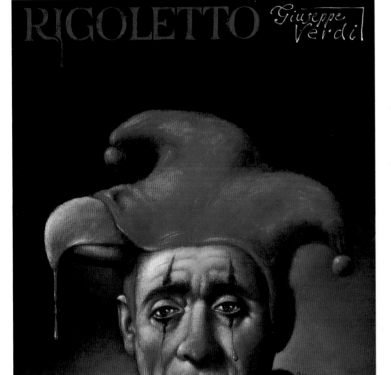

338

339

340

Artist: **ETIENNE DELESSERT**

Art Director: Steven Doyle

Agency: Drenttel-Doyle

Client: World Financial Center, NY

Medium: Watercolor

Size: 11 x 8

341

Artist: **ETIENNE DELESSERT**

Art Director: Rita Marshall

Client: Creative Education

Medium: Watercolor

Size: 11 1/2 x 8

342

Artist: **ELWOOD H. SMITH**

Art Director: Steve Curran

Client: Gametek

Medium: Watercolor, india ink

Size: 10 x 8

343

Artist: **ADAM MATHEWS**

Art Directors: Scott Fixari
Kurt Hill

Client: Responsible Dog Owners Assoc.

Medium: Acrylic

Size: 15 x 12

344

Artist: **PAUL MICICH**

Art Director: Randy Messer

Client: Perfection Learning

Medium: Alkyd, photo silkscreen

Size: 31 x 24

340

341

342

343

344

345
Artist: **VICTOR LEE**

Medium: Acrylic

Size: 14 x 11

346
Artist: **DANIEL MARK DUFFY**

Size: 30 x 46

347
Artist: **GLENN HARRINGTON**

Art Director: Glenn Harrington

Client: Artefact

Size: 9 x 7

348
Artist: **ERNEST NORCIA**

Art Director: Robin Bray

Client: Time-Life Music

Medium: Oil paint on cotton board

Size: 17 x 12 ^{1}/2

349
Artist: **LINDA DEVITO SOLTIS**

Art Director: Linda DeVito Soltis

Client: The Stephen Lawrence Company

Medium: Oil on canvas

Size: 18 x 23

345

346

347

348

349

350

Artist: **DAVID LESH**

Art Director: Jeff Larson

Client: Boeinno Assoc.

Medium: Mixed media

Size: 7 1/2 x 7

351

Artist: **SALLY WERN COMPORT**

Art Director: Dan Hooven

Agency: White, Good & Co.

Client: Mechanicsburgh Rehab System

Medium: Mixed media

Size: 14 x 16

352

Artist: **KAREN CHANDLER**

Medium: Oil

Size: 26 1/2 x 39 1/2

353

Artist: **RON FINGER**

Art Director: Carol Poulson

Client: Travellers Express

Medium: Gouache, pastel

Size: 22 x 16

354

Artist: **RAFAL OLBINSKI**

Art Director: Alane Gehagen

Agency: Ziff Marketing

Client: New York City Opera

Medium: Acrylic on canvas

Size: 20 x 30

350

351

352

353

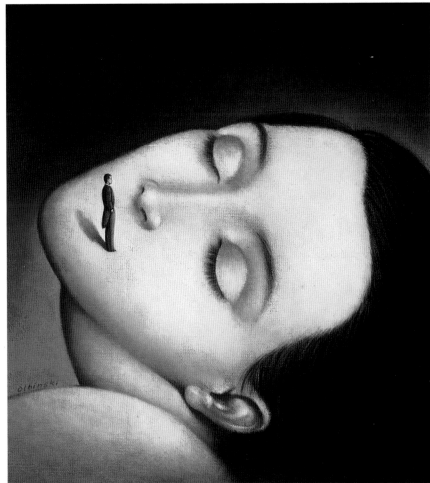

354

355

Artist: **TIM O'BRIEN**

Medium: Oil on gessoed panel

Size: 27 1/2 X 17 1/2

356

Artist: **RON FINGER**

Art Director: Mike Fazande

Agency: Fallon McElligott

Client: Aveda

Medium: Watercolor

Size: 18 1/2 x 13

357

Artist: **CAROLINE MICHAUD**

Art Directors: Sharon Jacobs
Carla Miller

Client: International Jugglers
Association

Medium: Pastel

Size: 38 x 24

358

Artist: **WILLIAM MATTHEWS**

Art Director: Steven Whatley

Client: Warner Western Records

Medium: Watercolor on handmade
paper

Size: 24 x 19

359

Artist: **WILLIAM MATTHEWS**

Art Director: Steven Whatley

Client: Warner Western Records

Medium: Watercolor on handmade
paper

Size: 23 x 19

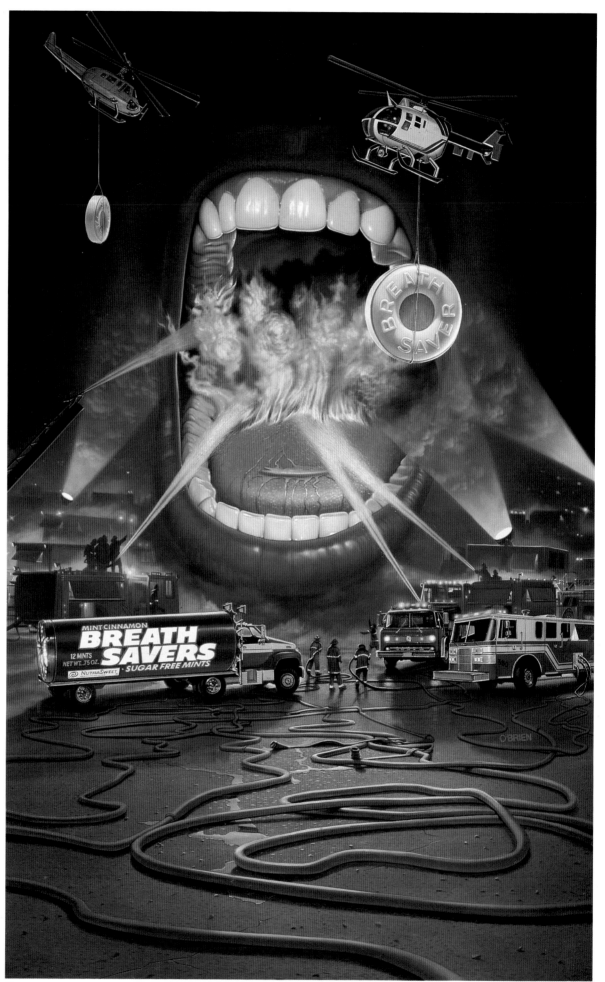

356

357

358

359

360

Artist: **MAURICE LEWIS**

Art Director: Hunter George

Agency: Johnston/George & Breslau

Client: Sterling Electronics

Medium: Oil

Size: 22 x 27

361

Artist: **PAUL SCHMID**

Art Director: Judy Dolim-Shafer

Agency: Nordstrom

Client: Nordstrom

Size: 9 1/2 x 9 1/2

362

Artist: **MIKE SCANLAN**

Art Director: Mike Scanlan

Agency: CS & A

Client: CS & A

Medium: Acrylic, colored pencil

Size: 7 x 6

363

Artist: **FRANCIS LIVINGSTON**

Agency: Corporate Graphics

Client: St. John's Hospital

Size: 11 x 8

364

Artist: **RICHARD SPARKS**

Medium: Oil on linen

Size: 30 x 40

360

361

362

363

364

365

Artist: **WIKTOR SADOWSKI**

Art Director: Alane Gehagen

Agency: Ziff Marketing

Client: National Actors Theatre

Medium: Oil

Size: 29 x 25

366

Artist: **CURTIS PARKER**

Art Director: Brad Ghormley

Client: Childsplay Theater

Size: 17 x 17

367

Artist: **JAMES McMULLAN**

Art Director: James McMullan

Client: Michael Di Capua Books/
HarperCollins

Medium: Watercolor

Size: 9 1/4 x 8

368

Artist: **STEFANO VITALE**

Client: Pantheon/Random House

Size: 12 x 9

369

Artist: **GREGORY MANCHESS**

Art Directors: Gregory Manchess
Stan Thomas

Client: Homewares, Inc.

Medium: Oil

Size: 18 x 30

365

366

367

368

369

370

Artist: **LELAND KLANDERMAN**

Art Director: Steve Olson

Agency: Ryan Co.

Client: Home Savings of America

371

Artist: **JOSH GOSFIELD**

Art Director: Kim Champagne

Client: Capricorn Records

Size: 50 x 34 x 9

372

Artist: **RON FINGER**

Art Director: Sally Wagner

Agency: Martin Williams Advertising

Client: Minnesota Orchestra

Medium: Acrylic

Size: 14 x 9

373

Artist: **RICHARD SPARKS**

Medium: Watercolor

Size: 30 x 22 ¹/₂

374

Artist: **BILL MAYER**

Art Director: Shirley Fee

Size: 8 ¹/₂ x 18

370

371

372

373

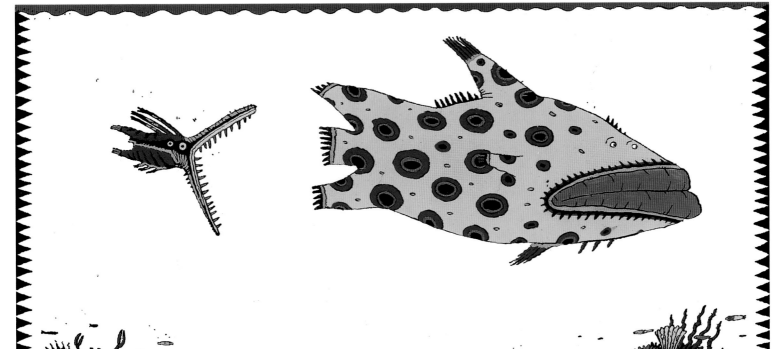

374

375

Artist: **MICHAEL GARLAND**

Art Directors: Larry Rosler
Tim Gillner

Client: Boyds Mills Press

Medium: Oil

Size: 14 x 11

376

Artist: **ELIZABETH TRAYNOR**

Art Director: Stephen Jones

Agency: Tucker Wayne Luckie
Company

Client: Reynolds Metals Company

Medium: Handcolored scratchboard

Size: 7 x 9

377

Artist: **CHERYL COOPER**

Medium: Oil

Size: 48 x 36

378

Artist: **ETIENNE DELESSERT**

Art Director: Rita Marshall

Client: Centre Design Uqam,
Canada

Medium: Watercolor

Size: 4 ³/4 x 6

375

376

377

378

379

Artist: **ROBERT GIUSTI**

Art Director: Joann Tansman

Agency: BBD&O

Client: General Electric

Medium: Acrylic on canvas

Size: 14 x 14

380

Artist: **MIKE REAGAN**

Art Director: Larry Bennet

Agency: McKinney & Silver

Client: Bahamas Ministry of Tourism

Medium: Watercolor, ink

381

Artist: **DOUG STRUTHERS**

Art Director: Ted Whitby

Agency: KPR

Client: Syntex

Medium: Computer

Size: 19 x 15 1/2

382

Artist: **VIVIENNE FLESHER**

Art Director: Vicki Morgan

Client: Rabbit Ears

Medium: Pastel

Size: 16 x 22

379

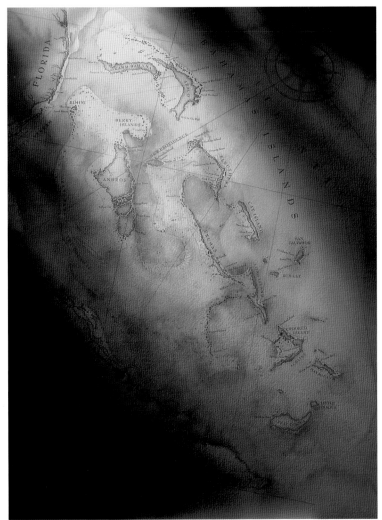

380

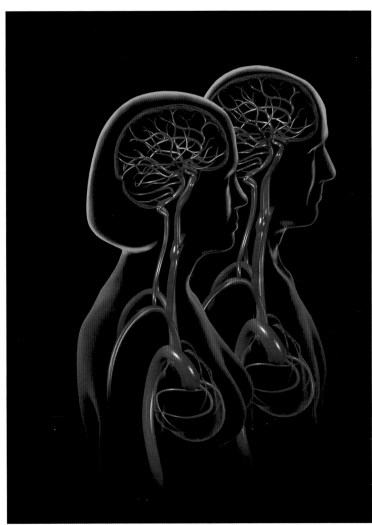

381

382

383

Artist: **MIKE BENNY**

Art Director: Bob Beyn

Agency: Seraphein Beyn

Client: Shanley's

Size: 17 x 18

384

Artist: **LIN H. SHEN**

Medium: Oil

Size: 13 x 15

385

Artist: **JAMES McMULLAN**

Agency: Russek Advertising

Client: Lincoln Center Theater

Size: 10 x 5

386

Artist: **PAUL MICICH**

Art Director: Randy Messer

Client: Perfection Learning

Size: 34 x 26

387

Artist: **ROGER DE MUTH**

Size: 5 ¹/₂ x 8

383

384

385

386

387

INSTITUTIONAL JURY

DENNIS LYALL
CHAIRMAN
Illustrator

DAVID BARTELS
President, Bartels & Company

NICK DI DIO
Art Director
Golf Digest

H. TOM HALL
Illustrator

ROBERT HUNT
Illustrator

CHARLES KADIN
Director, Graphic Art,
Harlequin Books

HIRO KIMURA
Illustrator

ELWOOD H. SMITH
Illustrator

JOSEPH STELMACH
Senior Director
Art & Design, BMG Classics

INSTITUTIONAL

AWARD WINNERS

TRAIAN FILIP
Silver Medal

ALBERT LORENZ
Silver Medal

EDWARD SOREL
Silver Medal

HERBERT TAUSS
Silver Medal

388

Artist: **TRAIAN ALEXANDRU FILIP**

Medium: Oil, mixed media on carhood

Size: 43 x 54

TRAIAN FILIP
Institutional Silver Medal

Born in Romania, Filip holds an MFA from Grigorescu Institute of Fine Arts in Bucharest. He has lived in the U.S. since 1989, pursuing his career as a painter, etcher, and graphic artist working in a diversity of media. The award winning work "From Door to Door," was painted on a car hood. Says Filip, "Art is magic and has its own life. Sometimes when I'm working it seems like a painting is creating itself without me. I can't explain what I'm doing until I'm finished. Then I see things I wasn't conscious of before and I understand myself better, because painting comes from the deepest part of your soul."

389

Artist: **ALBERT LORENZ**

Medium: Pen, ink with watercolor

Size: 21 x 37

ALBERT LORENZ
Institutional Silver Medal

Albert Lorenz holds degrees in Architecture from Pratt Institute and Columbia University and is a Ph.D. Candidate in Anthropology at Princeton University. He has illustrated for architects, publishers, ad agencies, and editorial venues since 1969 and has authored and illustrated a number of instructional volumes about drawing and architectural illustration. His work has been included in professional exhibitions and journals including the Art Directors Show, the Society of Illustrators Exhibitions and Annuals, and *Pictorial Maps* by Nigel Holmes.

EDWARD SOREL
Institutional Silver Medal

"This appeared on a poster for an exhibition of children's book art. Dorothy and her friends from Oz are exiting at 63rd Street because that's where the exhibit was held. Illustrating posters is quite different from illustrating children's books—with posters you never get semi-annual statements informing you how much money you still owe from your advance."

391

Artist: **HERBERT TAUSS**

Art Director: Peter Fiore

Client: Society of Illustrators

Medium: Oil

Size: 36 x 26

HERBERT TAUSS
Institutional Silver Medal

Growing weary of posing, she stepped from the platform, holding close her robe. Approaching his easel she saw with horror how he had maligned her. She struck him—not once but over and over again, until the stretchers could no longer support the canvas. He fell to the floor. But then her hands, ever so slowly, rose to her lips in recognition. The sight of him froze her still. The paint had darkened his hair and he wore an expression of a time forgotten. Of a time long gone. She went to him and cradled him in her arms. And being the bastard that he was, he could only think, "Sargent was right. 'A portrait is a picture in which there is just a tiny little something not quite right about the mouth.' "

392

Artist: **GEORGE ANGELINI**

Art Director: Jeff Palmer

Client: American Showcase

Medium: Oil

Size: 34 x 24

393

Artist: **GEORGE Y. ABE**

Art Director: Monte Dorman

Client: KCI

Medium: Acrylic

Size: 11 x 14

394

Artist: **MIKE BENNY**

Client: ASPCA

Medium: Acrylic

Size: 12 x 9

395

Artist: **ROBERT M. CUNNINGHAM**

Client: Lustrare

Medium: Acrylic on paper

Size: 18 x 27

392

393

394

395

396

Artist: **PHILIP BLISS**

Art Director: Philip Bliss

Client: American Showcase

Size: 10 x 8

397

Artist: **RON FINGER**

Art Director: Richard Lawrence Baron

Agency: Quest Business Agency

Medium: Pastel

Size: 23 x 41

398

Artist: **PHIL BOATWRIGHT**

Art Directors: Phil Boatwright David Spurlock

Client: Society of Illustrators of Dallas

Medium: Mixed

Size: 12 x 9

399

Artist: **ETIENNE DELESSERT**

Art Director: Etienne Delessert

Client: Musée Des Arts Décoratifs, Switzerland

Medium: Watercolor

Size: 7 x 5

396

397

398

399

400

Artist: **DAVID BOWERS**

Medium: Oil on gessoed masonite

Size: 14 1/2 x 10 3/4

401

Artist: **KERNE ERICKSON**

Size: 28 x 32

402

Artist: **ALLEN GARNS**

Art Directors: Brad Ghormley
Steve Smit
Art Lofgreen

Client: Messenger Graphics

Medium: Oil

Size: 34 x 26

403

Artist: **W. B. PARK**

Medium: Ink, watercolor

Size: 13 x 10

400

401

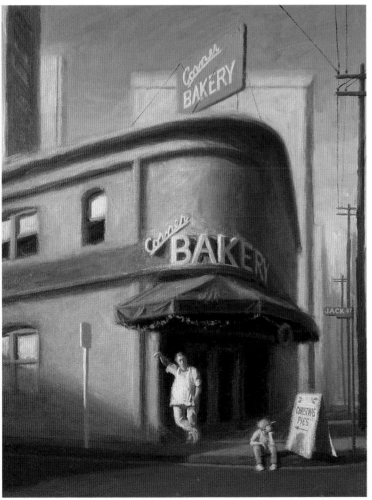

402

403

404

Artist: **DANIEL CRAIG**

Art Director: Dave Peterson

Client: Children's Museum

Medium: Oil

Size: 28 x 23

405

Artist: **ALLEN GARNS**

Art Directors: Brad Ghormley
Steve Smit
Art Lofgreen

Client: Childsplay Theatre

Medium: Oil

Size: 18 x 18

406

Artist: **MARK A. FREDRICKSON**

Art Director: John Vitro

Agency: Franklin Stoorza

Client: Thermoscan

Medium: Acrylic

Size: 12 x 19

407

Artist: **M. JOHN ENGLISH**

Art Director: Kevin Pistilli

Client: Raphael Hotel Group

Medium: Oil on canvas

Size: 18 x 24

404

405

406

407

408

Artist: **FRED HILLIARD**

Client: Olympus Press

Medium: Pen, ink, gouache

Size: 24 x 18

409

Artist: **JACK UNRUH**

Art Director: Danny Kamerath

Client: Triton Energy Corporation

Size: 13 x 12

410

Artist: **RICHARD WEHRMAN**

Art Director: Jeff Gabel

Agency: Hutchins Y&R

Client: Dresser-Rand

Medium: Acrylic

Size: 11 x 22

411

Artist: **CARLOS TORRES**

Medium: Acrylic, airbrush

Size: 19 x 14

412

Artist: **C. F. PAYNE**

Art Directors: Fred Woodward
Harold Burch

Agency: Pentagram

Client: Applied Graphic
Technologies

Medium: Mixed media

Size: 17 1/2 x 13

408

409

410

411

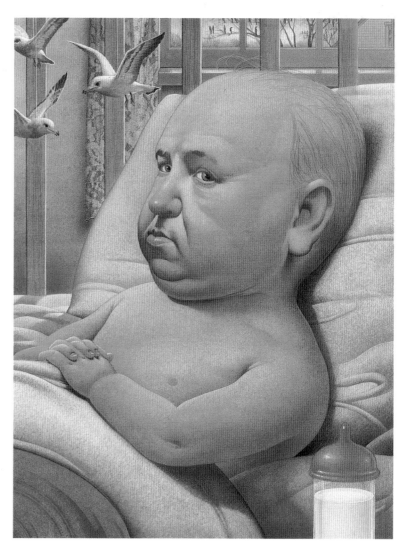

412

413

Artist: **PAUL ROGERS**

Art Director: Brad Stone

Client: Wherehouse Entertainment

Medium: Acrylic

Size: 36 x 22

414

Artist: **WILL WILSON**

Art Director: Sean Delonis

Client: The John Pence Gallery

Medium: Oil

Size: 19 x 14

415

Artist: **EDWARD SOREL**

Art Director: Marcus Ratliff

Client: Susan Conway Galleries

Medium: Pen, watercolor

Size: 13 1/2 x 10

416

Artist: **MARK SUMMERS**

Art Director: Pat Levy

Agency: Hudson Health Care
    Communications

Client: Wyeth-Ayerst Laboratories

Medium: Scratchboard, watercolor

Size: 6 1/2 x 8 1/2

414

415

416

417

Artist: **WILL WILLIAMS**

Medium: Oil

Size: 51 x 34

418

Artist: **GREG HARGREAVES**

Client: Hellman Associates

Medium: Acrylic, colored pencil

Size: 16 x 11

419

Artist: **SALLY WERN COMPORT**

Art Director: Tom Nujens

Agency: Robin Shepherd Studio

Client: Blue Cross & Blue Shield of Florida

Medium: Mixed media

Size: 15 x 12

420

Artist: **JOHN H. HOWARD**

Art Director: Bob Dinetz

Client: Metaphor

Medium: Acrylic on canvas

Size: 2' x 6'

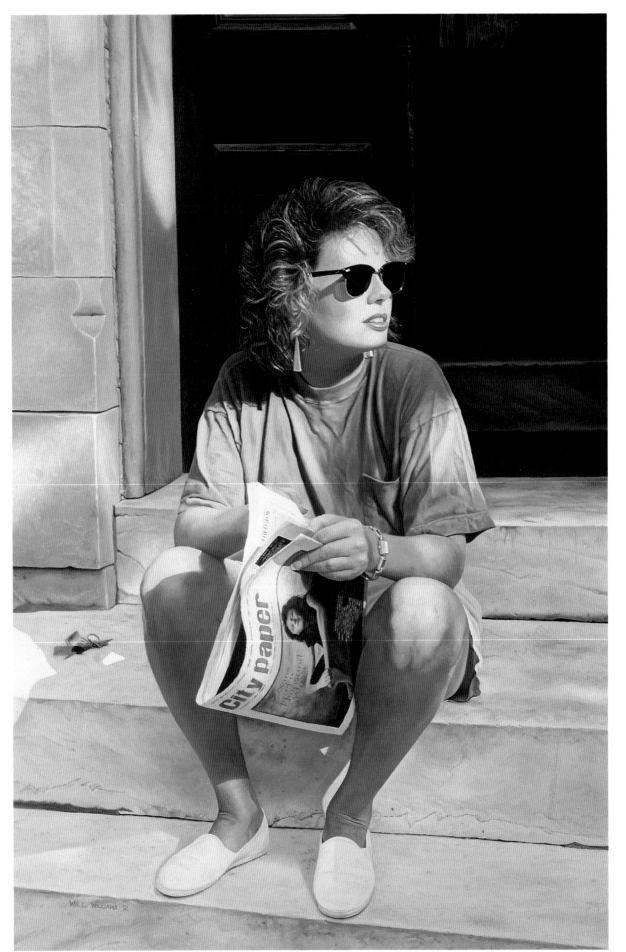

417

418

419

420

421

Artist: **SARAH WALDRON**

Size: 10 x 10

422

Artist: **BILL MAYER**

Art Director: D. J. Stout

Client: Texas Monthly

Medium: Airbrush

Size: 15 x 15

423

Artist: **JEFF MEYER**

Art Director: Bill Cook

Agency: William Cook Graphics

Client: Republic Capital Group
Inc.

Medium: Pastel, charcoal

Size: 18 1/4 x 11 1/2

424

Artist: **STEVE JOHNSON
LOU FANCHER**

Art Director: Karen Geiger

Client: Employee Benefit Plans

Medium: Acrylic on paper

Size: 16 x 13

425

Artist: **RICHARD
HARRINGTON**

Art Director: Kathy Cairo

Agency: Buck & Pulleyn

Client: AD Council of Rochester

Size: 13 x 21

421

422

423

424

425

426
Artist: **CHRIS HOPKINS**
Art Director: Chris Hopkins
Client: Fairy Tale Mail
Medium: Oil
Size: 15 1/2 x 11

427
Artist: **MAXINE BOLL**
Art Directors: Maxine Boll
Melanie Paykos
Client: Los Angeles County
Museum of Art Council
Size: 21 x 30

428
Artist: **MATT MYERS**
Art Director: Bryan Winke
Client: Florida Winefest
Medium: Oil on board
Size: 36 x 24

429
Artist: **GARY LOCKE**
Art Directors: Matt Key
Jeff Jansen
Client: Summer Stage
Size: 23 x 14

430
Artist: **BILL MAYER**
Art Director: Steve Russo
Agency: Russo Assoc.
Medium: Airbrush
Size: 8 1/2 x 11 1/2

426

427

428

429

430

431

Artist: **MARK ENGLISH**

Art Director: Bruce Hartmen

Client: Johnson County
Community College

Medium: Oil pastel

Size: 21 x 32

432

Artist: **MARK ENGLISH**

Art Director: Bruce Hartmen

Client: Johnson County
Community College

Medium: Oil pastel

Size: 17 x 23

433

Artist: **MARK A. BENDER**

Art Directors: Vance Wright Adams
Karen Burns

Agency: Vance Wright Adams &
Assoc.

Client: Consolidated Natural
Gas Co.

Medium: Gouache

Size: 31 x 6 ¹/₂

434

Artist: **JOHN F. MARTIN**

Art Director: Les Mintz

Medium: Oil

Size: 17 x 13

435

Artist: **ALAIN MOREAU**

Client: National Park Academy of
the Arts

Medium: Prismacolor

Size: 20 x 15

431

432

434

433

435

436
Artist: **TIM O'BRIEN**
Medium: Oil on gessoed panel
Size: 18 1/2 x 17 1/2

437
Artist: **LARRY MOORE**
Art Director: Larry Moore
Client: Central Florida Press
Medium: Pastel
Size: 12 x 12

438
Artist: **ALEX MURAWSKI**
Art Director: Akiva Boker
Client: Lasky Printing/Murawski
Medium: Ink, acrylic
Size: 9 x 10 1/2

439
Artist: **BILL MAYER**
Art Director: Don Smith
Agency: Adsmith
Medium: Airbrush
Size: 13 1/2 x 10 1/2

440
Artist: **DAN JONES**
Client: Richard Salzman
Medium: Pencil drawing, airbrush
Size: 15 x 8 1/2

436

437

438

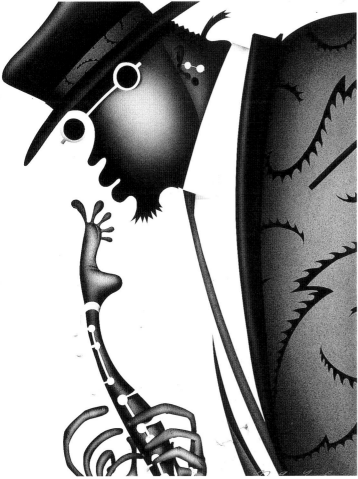

439

440

441

Artist: **JACK UNRUH**

Art Director: Brian Boyd

Size: 17 x 20

442

Artist: **JON ELLIS**

Size: 16 x 19

443

Artist: **RAFAL OLBINSKI**

Art Director: Alane Gehagen

Agency: Ziff Marketing

Client: New York City Opera

Medium: Acrylic on canvas

Size: 32 1/2 x 26

444

Artist: **JOHN P. THOMPSON**

Client: Hellman Associates

Medium: Scratchboard, acrylic

Size: 12 x 9 1/2

445

Artist: **VITO-LEONARDO SCAROLA**

Art Director: Vito-Leonardo Scarola

Client: American Red Cross,
Orange County,
CA Chapter

Medium: Oil on illustration board

Size: 16 x 23

441

442

443

444

445

446

Artist: **WILSON McLEAN**

Art Director: Roy Comiskey

Client: Security Management

Medium: Oil

Size: 25 x 20

447

Artist: **LELAND
          KLANDERMAN**

448

Artist: **MARY GRANDPRÉ**

Size: 18 x 10 ¹/₂

449

Artist: **TOM CURRY**

Client: James Conrad

Medium: Acrylic

Size: 14 x 11

450

Artist: **JOHN CRAIG**

Art Director: Dave Willett

Agency: Rhea & Kaiser
          Advertising, Inc.

Client: Temik

Size: 12 x 9

446

447

449

448

450

451

Artist: **FRANCIS LIVINGSTON**

Client: Open Hand Program

Size: 19 x 24

452

Artist: **PAUL ZWOLAK**

Art Director: Paul Marince

Agency: SlaughterHanson
Advertising

Client: Omni Plan/Sungard

Medium: Oil

Size: 14 x 14

453

Artist: **GARY KELLEY**

Art Director: Pat Levy

Agency: Hudson Health Care
Communications

Client: Wyeth-Ayerst Laboratories

Medium: Pastel

Size: 22 x 28

454

Artist: **CHARLES ROWE**

Medium: Oil, collage

Size: 16 x 12

455

Artist: **FERNANDO RANGEL**

Art Director: Marvin Mattelson

Client: School of Visual Arts

Medium: Oil

Size: 18 x 13

451

452

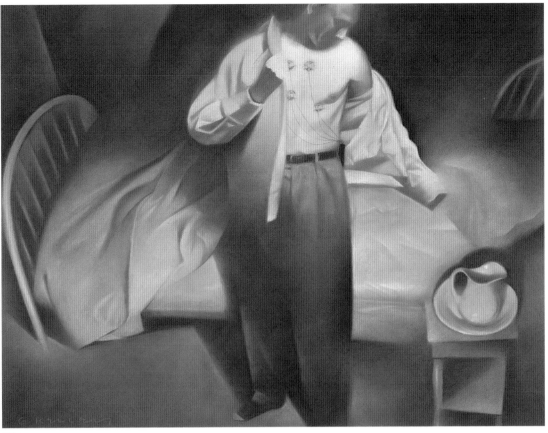

453

454

455

456

Artist: **KAZUHIKO SANO**

Art Director: Kazuhiko Sano

Client: Society of Illustrators
of San Francisco

Medium: Acrylic

Size: 20 x 16

457

Artist: **SUE ROTHER**

Client: Jerry Leff Associates

Size: 15 x 15

458

Artist: **FRANK A. STEINER**

Art Director: Michael Turner

Client: Harleysville Life
Insurance Co.

Size: 19 ^{1}/$_2$ x 25 ^{1}/$_2$

459

Artist: **DAVID GROFF**

Art Director: Michele Edwards

Client: World Watch Institute

Medium: Mixed media

Size: 15 x 12

460

Artist: **GREG HARGREAVES**

Client: Hellman Associates

Medium: Acrylic, colored pencil

Size: 24 x 20

456

457

458

459

460

461

Artist: **LONNI SUE JOHNSON**

Art Director: Chris Passehl

Client: Wolf Color Print &
         Goodspeed Opera House

Medium: Watercolor

Size: 17 x 15

462

Artist: **PAUL ZWOLAK**

Art Director: Paul Marince

Agency: SlaughterHanson
          Advertising

Client: Omni Plan/Sungard

Medium: Oil

Size: 13 x 13

463

Artist: **FRANCIS LIVINGSTON**

Art Director: Bill Dunn

Client: Freda Scott

Medium: Oil

Size: 12 x 11

464

Artist: **STEVEN POLSON**

Medium: Oil

Size: 14 x 12

465

Artist: **C. F. PAYNE**

Art Director: Will Hillenbrand

Client: Butler Manufacturing

Medium: Mixed

Size: 11 x 11

461

462

463

464

465

466

Artist: **GREG RUDD**

Art Director: James Helzer

Client: Unicover Corporation

Medium: Oil on gesso and board

Size: 15 x 12

467

Artist: **GREGORY LOUDON**

Medium: Acrylic

Size: 12 ¹/₂ x 18 ¹/₂

468

Artist: **MARK RYDEN**

Art Director: David Bartels

Agency: Bartels Associates

Client: GDS

Medium: Acrylic

Size: 11 x 23

469

Artist: **KEN HAMILTON**

Medium: Watercolor

Size: 9 x 14

470

Artist: **PAUL RATZ DE TAGYOS**

Medium: Oil on masonite

Size: 8 x 12

466

467

468

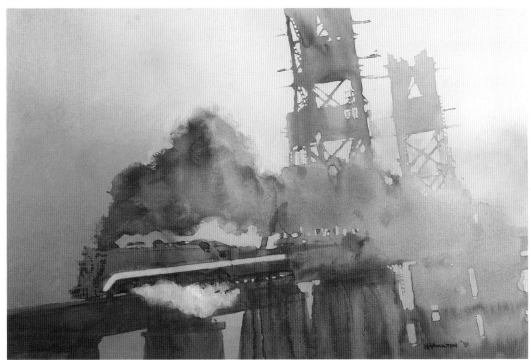

469

470

471

Artist: **BUD KEMPER**

Art Director: Carl Hermann

Client: Maritz, Inc.

Medium: Oil

Size: 24 x 22

472

Artist: **MARK ENGLISH**

Art Director: Bruce Hartmen

Client: Johnson County
　　　　Community College

Medium: Oil, pastel

Size: 20 x 17

473

Artist: **GARY KELLEY**

Art Director: Pat Levy

Agency: Hudson Health Care
　　　　Communications

Client: Wyeth-Ayerst Laboratories

Medium: Pastel

Size: 22 x 28

474

Artist: **JOHN COLLIER**

Art Director: Richard Solomon

Medium: Oil pastel

Size: 36 x 40

475

Artist: **DANIEL SCHWARTZ**

Art Director: Richard Solomon

Medium: Oil

Size: 82 x 64

471

472

473

474

475

476

Artist: **SCOTT HUNT**

Art Director: Ed Giganti

Client: The Catholic Health
Association

Medium: Charcoal

Size: 11 x 13

477

Artist: **PAUL MELIA**

Medium: Ink, gouache, watercolor

Size: 38 x 42

478

Artist: **LARRY WINBORG**

Art Director: Larry Winborg

Client: Sage Publishing

Medium: Oil

Size: 24 x 30

479

Artist: **ROBERT MEGANCK**

Art Director: Robert Meganck

Client: Communication Design,
Inc.

Medium: Scratchboard

Size: 24 x 15 ¹/2

480

Artist: **BUD KEMPER**

Art Director: Carl Hermann

Client: Maritz, Inc.

Medium: Oil

Size: 24 x 22

476

477

478

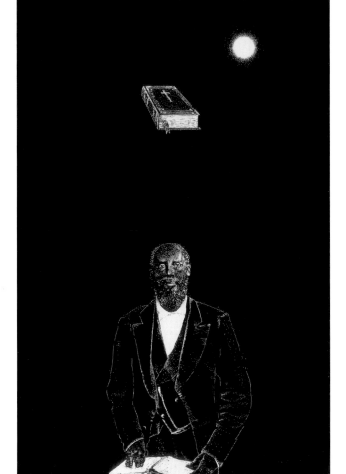

479

480

481

Artist: **DEBORAH L. CHABRIAN**

Art Directors: Lynn Hollyn
Marty Roelandt

Client: Gibson Greetings Inc.

Medium: Watercolor

Size: 11 x 13

482

Artist: **GLENN HARRINGTON**

Art Director: Doug Johnson

Client: Society of Illustrators

Medium: Oil

Size: 22 x 24

483

Artist: **PAUL LACKNER**

Client: Hellman Associates

Medium: Watercolor

Size: 14 x 21

484

Artist: **BRAD HOLLAND**

Art Director: Albert Leutwyler

Client: Joint Ethics Committee

Medium: Acrylic on board

Size: 14 x 11

485

Artist: **RAFAL OLBINSKI**

Client: Andre Zarre Gallery

Size: 31 x 24

481

482

483

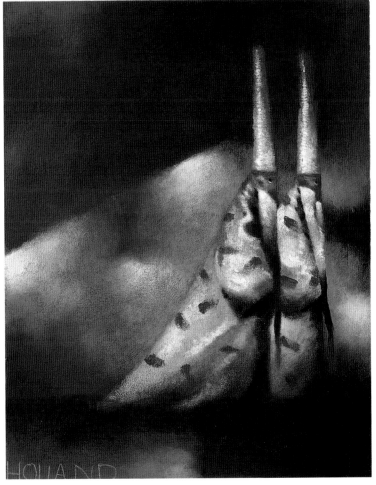

484

485

486

Artist: **DAVID BOWERS**

Medium: Oil on gessoed illustration board

Size: 12 x 10 ¹/₂

487

Artist: **JOHN JINKS**

Art Directors: Elena Foundos
Robin Presslaff

Client: New York University/SCE

Medium: Acrylic

Size: 19 x 17

488

Artist: **BERNIE FUCHS**

Art Director: Jack Scharr

Client: '92 Olympics

Medium: Oil

Size: 28 x 40

489

Artist: **WILL HILLENBRAND**

Art Director: Bart Crosby

Client: Champion International

Medium: Oil on linen

Size: 20 x 28

486

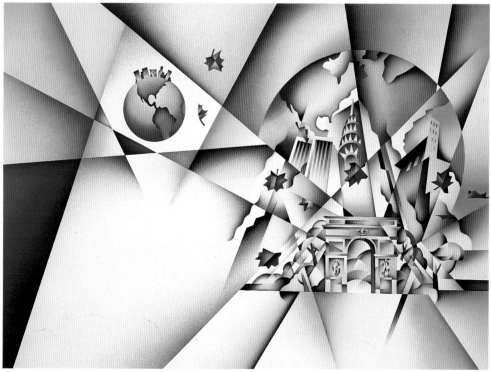

487

488

489

490

Artist: **ROBERT McGINNIS**

Medium: Oil

Size: 11 x 8

491

Artist: **WILSON McLEAN**

Art Director: Bill Shin

Agency: Barton Gillete

Client: University of Michigan
Medical Center

Medium: Oil

Size: 25 1/2 x 18

492

Artist: **ROBERT HUNT**

Client: Barbara Gordon Associates

Size: 31 1/2 x19

493

Artist: **JOEL SPECTOR**

Art Director: Kari Voldeng

Client: St. John's Hospital

Medium: Pastel on canvas

Size: 41 x 72

490

491

492

493

NEW VISIONS

NEW VISIONS

The future of illustration lives in the young artists who test their new-found skills, break away from tradition, and create their own visions. The Society of Illustrators is again pleased to reproduce the catalogue of its Annual Student Scholarship Competition in this year's Annual Book so that you may see illustration from the perspective of these talented young artists.

From the over 5,500 entries received from 100 accredited institutions nationwide, 121 works by young artists were selected by a prestigious jury. Again, Beverly Sacks was instrumental in the crucial fund raising for awards and Alvin Pimsler, Chairman of the Education Committee, guided the jury through the lengthy selection process. The original works were exhibited at the Society of Illustrators Museum of American Illustration.

The technical proficiency and level of problem solving is again exceptional in these young people. It is not difficult to imagine students from across the country entering the marketplace with the tools necessary to achieve success.

We hope you will enjoy the promise of the future in New Visions.

Congratulations to all those involved in the 1993 Student Scholarship Competition.

Those students whose work has been accepted into this exhibition can be *very* proud of their great accomplishments, and those who are award winners can be doubly proud. It's an exceptional achievement. A special commendation to the families of these students for their unequaled and invaluable support. This is a great tribute to you as well.

Congratulations also go to the colleges who continue to uphold their highest standards and to their instructors who inspire, encourage, guide and share their professional expertise with the students through their formative years.

Special thanks go the Hallmark Corporate Foundation for its truly generous funding over the years and to those sponsors who continue to encourage students with their invaluable support, including The Starr Foundation, The Reader's Digest Association, Jellybean Photographics, The Franklin Mint Foundation for the Arts, Dick Blick Art Materials and Hachette Magazines; and plaudits to Alvin Pimsler, Chairman of our Education Committee for his superb work on behalf of the students, the 16 judges who also devoted so much of their valuable time and efforts in this undertaking; and to Beverly Sacks, Chairperson of our Annual Christmas Auction, which brings in major funding for our scholarship programs each year.

Supporting our future generation is one of the most rewarding and gratifying efforts one can possibly make and so our gratitude goes out to all involved in this endeavor.

And finally, there's a long, hard road ahead of you, students, but the rewards are great and the profession is one of the finest and most satisfying in the world.

Continued success and prosperity to you all.

Eileen Hedy Schultz
President

Each year the scholarship exhibition, sponsored by the Society of Illustrators, continues to provide fresh, new talent for the professional field of illustration. This year is no exception. The work on display in the exhibition gallery at the Society, and in this catalogue, is as usual at the highest standard.

The students who came through the trial of submitting, selection and the awards, should be justifiably proud; as should their parents and teachers who gave them sincere and solid support. The Society of Illustrators is pleased to be the conduit presenting the marketplace the opportunity to view the new and promising work offered by these young people.

Congratulations to these future professionals and their parents and teachers. The Society's special thanks to the jurors, who worked so hard and fairly, and gave so freely of their time.

Alvin J. Pimsler
Chairman, Education Committee

▶
Sean Beavers
Marvin Mattelson, Instructor
School of Visual Arts
$2,000 Robert H. Blattner Award

▶
Tonya Fisher
Susanne Spann, Instructor
Ringling School of Art and Design
$1,500 Dick Blick Art Materials Award

▼
Ian Graham
Joel Nakamura, Instructor
Art Center College of Design
$1,500
The Reader's Digest Association Award

▲
Michael Fadollone
David Mocarski, Instructor
Art Center College of Design
$1,500
The Reader's Digest Association Award

▶
Dean Kube
Mark Langeneckert, Instructor
Kansas City Art Institute
$1,500 The Starr Foundation Award

▼
Steven Knotts
David Mocarski, Instructor
Art Center College of Design
$1,500 Jellybean Photographics Award

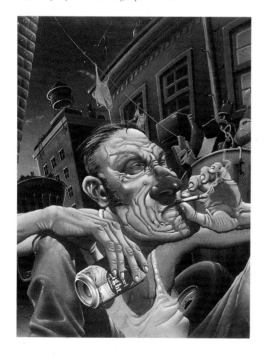

▲
Nicole Tortoriello
Phyllis Purves-Smith, Instructor
University of the Arts
$1,500
The Franklin Mint Foundation
for the Arts Award

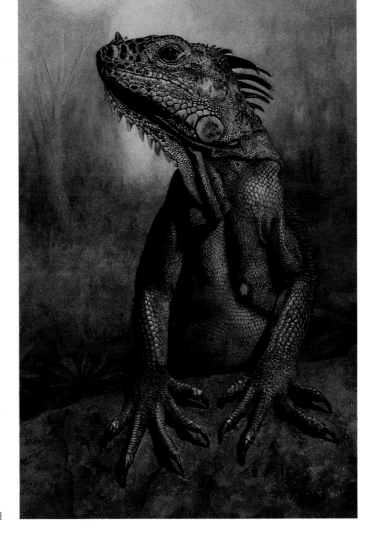

◄
Kosal Kong
Paul Kratter, Instructor
Academy of Art College
$1,500 The Starr Foundation Award

►
Krista Wallhagen
Jack de Graffenried, Instructor
Sacred Heart University
$1,500 Jellybean Photographics Award

▼
Joan Costello
Peter Caras, Instructor
duCret School of the Arts
$1,000
Norma and Alvin Pimsler Award

▲
Maria Somma
Rosemary Torre, Instructor
Fashion Institute of Technology
$1,000 The Starr Foundation Award

Kimberlee Lynch
Jon McDonald, Instructor
Kendall College of Art & Design
$1,000 The Starr Foundation Award

▼
Victor Zavala
Larry Johnson, Instructor
California State University
at Fullerton
$1,000
The Reader's Digest Association Award

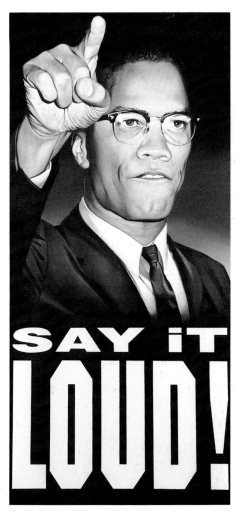

▼
Daisuke Takeya
Frances Jetter/Linda Benson,
Instructors
School of Visual Arts
$1,000 Hachette Filipacchi
Magazines, Inc. Award

◄
David Dedman
John Falato, Instructor
Paier College of Art
$750
The Reader's Digest Association Awa

►
Paul Lachapelle
Benton Mahan, Instructor
Columbus College of Art & Design
$750 Phillips/Rodewig Award

▲
Scott Hall
Richard Young, Instructor
Boise State University
$750 Award
in Memory of Harry Rosenbaum

▲
Wendy Mersman
Jon McDonald, Instructor
Kendall College of Art & Design
$750 Award
in Memory of Robert Anthony

▼
Craig Pennington
Jon McDonald, Instructor
Kendall College of Art & Design
$750 Kirchoff/Wohlberg Award
in Memory of Frances Means

▼
Christopher Petrocchi
Courtney Granner, Instructor
San Jose State University
$750 Award
in Memory of Meg Wohlberg

▲
Charles Wren
Peter Caras, Instructor
duCret School of the Arts
$750 Award
in Memory of D.L. Cramer

▲
Mari Lou Smith
Barbara Pearlman, Instructor
Fashion Institute of Technology
$750 Award
in Memory of Jim Dickerson

▲
J. Chadwick Cameron
Durwood Dommisse, Instructor
Virginia Commonwealth University
$500 Award

▲
Michael Petit
Charles Rowe, Instructor
Univeristy of Delaware
$500 Award

▲
Nanci Geideman
Roy Waits, Instructor
ACA College of Design
$500 Award

▼
Robert Sullivan
Marvin Mattelson, Instructor
School of Visual Arts
$500 Award

▲
Matt Manley
Jon McDonald, Instructor
Kendall College of Art & Design
$500 Award

▼
Gwenda Kaczor
Chris Polentz, Instructor
Art Center College of Design
$500 Award

▲
Cyndi Grill
Jon McDonald, Instructor
Kendall College of Art & Design
$500 Award

▼
David Gianfredi
Jon McDonald, Instructor
Kendall College of Art & Design
$250 Award

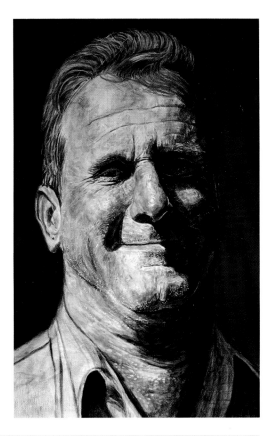

▶
Tony Terrell
George Fernandez, Instructor
Long Island University at C.W. Post
$250 Award

▲
Robert Moody
Thomas Sgouros, Instructor
Rhode Island School of Design
$250 Award

▶
Joel Parod
Eve Page, Instructor
San Jose State University
$250 Award

▼
Brian Blood
Craig Nelson, Instructor
Academy of Art College
$100 Award

▲
Laura Cronin
Jack Endewelt, Instructor
School of Visual Arts
$100 Award

◄
Julia Lundman
Rich Kryczka, Instructor
American Academy of Art
$100 Award

◄
Randsom Owens
Glen Edwards, Instructor
Utah State University
$100 Award

▲
Eric Nava
Craig Nelson, Instructor
Academy of Art College
$100 Award

THE EXHIBIT

3

5

1

2

4

9

10

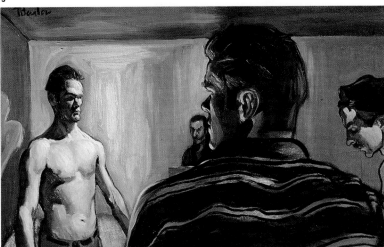

6

8

7

11

Addiction

12

20

15

17

16

18

14

19

13

21

24

22

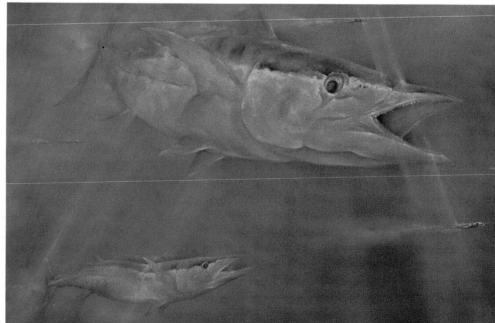

25

23

26

29

27

30

28

31

33

38

40

34

35

39

37

32

36

41

42

49

45

47

51

50

43

48

46

44

56

53

62

54

57

58

59

52

60

61

55

THE EXHIBIT

65

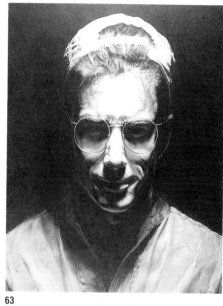

71

63

68

70

66

64

69

72

67

73

77

76

75

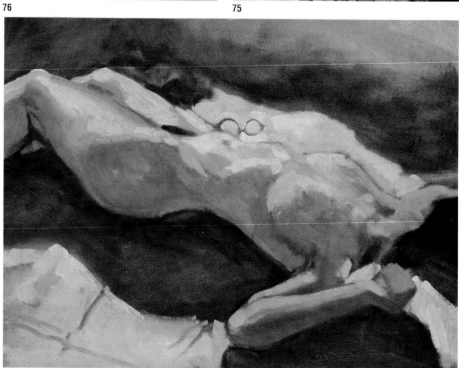

74

78

82

81

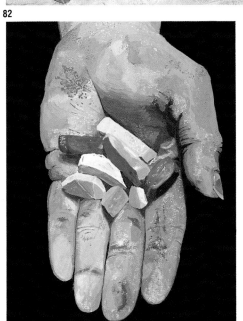

79

83

80

ARTIST INDEX

ART DIRECTORS, CLIENTS, AGENCIES

PROFESSIONAL STATEMENTS

GERALD & CULLEN RAPP

Illustration

RAY AMEIJIDE
EMMANUEL AMIT
GARY BASEMAN
LOU BORY ASSOCIATES
MICHAEL DAVID BROWN
LON BUSCH
JOSE CRUZ
JACK DAVIS
BOB DESCHAMPS
BILL DEVLIN
LEE DUGGAN
THE DYNAMIC DUO
JACKI GELB
RANDY GLASS
THOMAS HART
CELIA JOHNSON
LIONEL KALISH

LASZLO KUBINYI
SHARMEN LIAO
LEE LORENZ
BERNARD MAISNER
ALLAN MARDON
HAL MAYFORTH
BRUCE MORSER
ALEX MURAWSKI
MARLIES NAJAKA
BOB PETERS
SIGMUND PIFKO
JERRY PINKNEY
CAMILLE PRZEWODEK
MARC ROSENTHAL
DREW STRUZAN
MICHAEL WITTE
CRAIG ZUCKERMAN

ROMEO EMPIRE DESIGN

FREE TALENT PORTFOLIO

Illustration Buyers-Write to us on your company letterhead and we'll send you our wire-bound talent portfolio. It has over 50 full color pages featuring America's most talented illustrators and photographers. Outside USA/Canada send $10.00 int'l postal money order for shipping.

108 EAST 35 STREET (#7) NEW YORK, NY 10016
PHONE (212)889-3337 FAX (212)889-3341

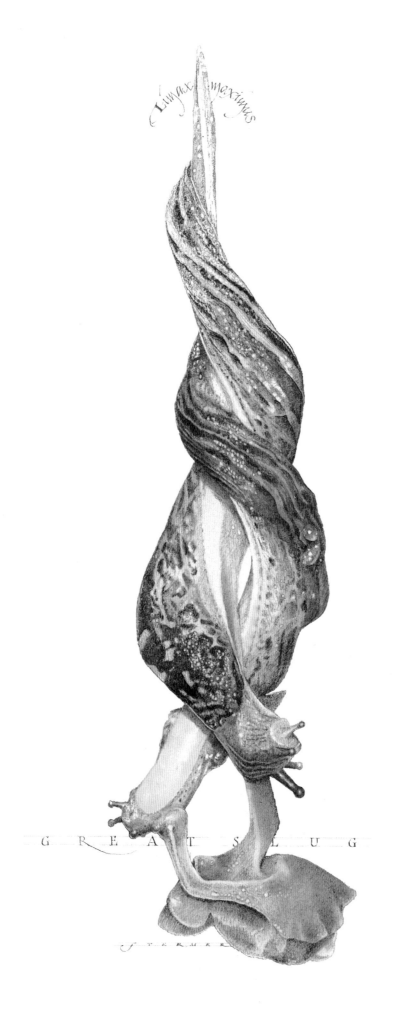

Limax maximus

G R E A T S L U G

Stermer

D U G A L D S T E R M E R
Represented by Jim Lilie   415-441-4384

Tim O'Brien

LOTT REPRESENTATIVES
212·953·7088

Illustrators

NAME	COLLEGE	NAME	COLLEGE	NAME	COLLEGE
Kelly Alder	School of Visual Arts	John Genzo	School of Visual Arts	Gary Paolillo	School of Visual Arts
Kelynn Alder	School of Visual Arts	Roy Germon	School of Visual Arts	Michael Paraskevas	School of Visual Arts
Dale Allen	School of Visual Arts	Bill Gibbons	School of Visual Arts	Lisa Peet	School of Visual Arts
Ray Alma	School of Visual Arts	Roby Gilbert	School of Visual Arts	Francesca Pelaggi	School of Visual Arts
Matthew Archambault	School of Visual Arts	Lucy Gould-Reitzfeld	School of Visual Arts	Donna Perrone	School of Visual Arts
Gil Ashby	School of Visual Arts	Alexa Grace	School of Visual Arts	Patrick Pigott	School of Visual Arts
Beth Bartholomew	School of Visual Arts	Julie Granahan	School of Visual Arts	Brian Pinkney	School of Visual Arts
Jill Batelman	School of Visual Arts	Cheryl Griesbach	School of Visual Arts	Leticia Plate	School of Visual Arts
James Bennett	School of Visual Arts	Bob Guglielmo	School of Visual Arts	Joel Popadics	School of Visual Arts
Winston Berkel Jr.	School of Visual Arts	Russell Gundlach	School of Visual Arts	Katherine Potter	School of Visual Arts
Rose Mary Berlin	School of Visual Arts	Joseph Gyurcsak	School of Visual Arts	Joe Quesada	School of Visual Arts
Drew Bishop	School of Visual Arts	Kenneth Harrison	School of Visual Arts	Joyce Raimondo	School of Visual Arts
John Boppert	School of Visual Arts	Edward Heck	School of Visual Arts	Chris Reed	School of Visual Arts
Joseph Borzotta	School of Visual Arts	Garnet Henderson	School of Visual Arts	Richard Rehbein	School of Visual Arts
Robert Brennan II	School of Visual Arts	Kingman Huie	School of Visual Arts	Missy Rehfuss	School of Visual Arts
James Cardillo	School of Visual Arts	Richard Hunt	School of Visual Arts	Denise Rettmer	School of Visual Arts
Roger Caruana	School of Visual Arts	Clifford Jackson	School of Visual Arts	Kurt Ritta	School of Visual Arts
Robert Casilla	School of Visual Arts	Donald Jones	School of Visual Arts	Sandro Rodorigo	School of Visual Arts
Andrew Castrucci	School of Visual Arts	Rodney Jung	School of Visual Arts	Barbara Roman	School of Visual Arts
Joseph Cipri	School of Visual Arts	Holly Kaufman-Spruch	School of Visual Arts	Pres Romanillos	School of Visual Arts
Howard Coale	School of Visual Arts	Thomas Kerr	School of Visual Arts	Joseph Rutt	School of Visual Arts
Alan E. Cober	School of Visual Arts	David Klehm	School of Visual Arts	Amantha Samatis	School of Visual Arts
Paul Cozzolino	School of Visual Arts	Norman Kraig	School of Visual Arts	Melinda Saminski	School of Visual Arts
Janelle Cromwell	School of Visual Arts	Mark Lang	School of Visual Arts	Barbara Samuels	School of Visual Arts
Peter Cunis	School of Visual Arts	Russell Lehman	School of Visual Arts	Peter Savigny	School of Visual Arts
Dave Cutler	School of Visual Arts	Marie Lessard	School of Visual Arts	Thomas Sciacca	School of Visual Arts
Joseph Danisi	School of Visual Arts	David Levinson	School of Visual Arts	Mary Servillo	School of Visual Arts
Paul Davis	School of Visual Arts	Mirriam Lippman	School of Visual Arts	Maurice Sherman	School of Visual Arts
William Denoyelles	School of Visual Arts	Missy Longo-Lewis	School of Visual Arts	Susan Sherman-Jackson	School of Visual Arts
Lisa DePolo-Passen	School of Visual Arts	Janie Lowe	School of Visual Arts	Phillip Singer	School of Visual Arts
Diana Deutermann-McKee	School of Visual Arts	Joanne Maffia-Pampinella	School of Visual Arts	Brigitte Sleiertin	School of Visual Arts
Grace DeVito	School of Visual Arts	Kam Mak	School of Visual Arts	Jeffrey Smith	School of Visual Arts
Linda DeVito Soltis	School of Visual Arts	John Mandato	School of Visual Arts	Mark Sparacio	School of Visual Arts
Susan Diehl-Marx	School of Visual Arts	Richard Martin	School of Visual Arts	Dalia Spina	School of Visual Arts
Steve Dininno	School of Visual Arts	Emily Martindale	School of Visual Arts	John Stadler	School of Visual Arts
Eric Dinyer	School of Visual Arts	Sam Martine	School of Visual Arts	Steven Stankiewicz	School of Visual Arts
Maria Dominguez	School of Visual Arts	Stanley Martucci	School of Visual Arts	Deborah Steins	School of Visual Arts
Deborah Dorton	School of Visual Arts	Deborah Max	School of Visual Arts	Dan Stern	School of Visual Arts
Erin Dwyer	School of Visual Arts	Kevin McCloskey	School of Visual Arts	Bruce Strachan	School of Visual Arts
Masako Ebata	School of Visual Arts	Patrick McDonnell	School of Visual Arts	John Stundis	School of Visual Arts
Timothy Ebneth	School of Visual Arts	Lisa McLeod	School of Visual Arts	James Sullivan	School of Visual Arts
Tristan Elwell	School of Visual Arts	Diane Merkel-Shanian	School of Visual Arts	Thomas Thorspecken	School of Visual Arts
Jack Endewelt	School of Visual Arts	Randi Meyerson-Adler	School of Visual Arts	Jeffrey Tomaka	School of Visual Arts
Joanne Farkas	School of Visual Arts	Frances Middendorf	School of Visual Arts	Dorian Vallejo	School of Visual Arts
Teresa Fasolino	School of Visual Arts	Arthur Miller	School of Visual Arts	Eric Velasquez	School of Visual Arts
George Fernandez	School of Visual Arts	Elizabeth Montalvo-Meletiche	School of Visual Arts	Damon Von Eiff	School of Visual Arts
James Forman	School of Visual Arts	Alison Moritsugu	School of Visual Arts	John Ward	School of Visual Arts
Lynne Foster	School of Visual Arts	David Moyers	School of Visual Arts	Lisa Weinblatt	School of Visual Arts
Christine Francis	School of Visual Arts	Joel Naprstek	School of Visual Arts	Joanna Whitney	School of Visual Arts
Douglas Fraser	School of Visual Arts	Emilya Naymark	School of Visual Arts	Mick Wieland	School of Visual Arts
Drew Friedman	School of Visual Arts	Jose Ortega	School of Visual Arts	Joe Wilkonski	School of Visual Arts
Frank Frisari	School of Visual Arts	Felix Padron	School of Visual Arts	Marc Yankus	School of Visual Arts
Patricia Garafano	School of Visual Arts	Richard Pagano	School of Visual Arts	Jonathan Zack	School of Visual Arts
Cynthia Garrett-Maurice	School of Visual Arts	Donna Pallotta	School of Visual Arts	Lynn Zollin	School of Visual Arts
Lee Gaskins III	School of Visual Arts			Darryl Zudeck	School of Visual Arts

Illustration Alumni

School of Visual Arts

①②③ A COLLEGE OF THE ARTS • 209 EAST 23RD STREET • NEW YORK, NEW YORK 10010-3994 • (212) 679-7350 • FAX (212) 725-3587

San Francisco Ballet/Nutcracker

Work in Progress

Minolta/Maybe the Best Way to Handle Risk is to Avoid it Altogether

GTE North Classic/Giants of Golf - Ray Floyd

JERRY LOFARO

57 Laight St. 4th Flr. N.Y., N.Y 10013   (212) 941-7936   Represented By American Artists: (212) 682-2462

For Additional Work, Please See American Showcase 14-17, Society of Illustrators 29, 32- 35 and Communication Arts Annual 34.

These images were photographed using the patented lighting system of Gamma One Conversions Inc. which insures full tonal response at the same contrast as the art. Textural details and brush stroke information are recorded with unprecedented accuracy. Jerry LoFaro uses Gamma One Conversions exclusively for reproduction.Gamma One Conversions Inc. We Make Photographing Art an Art. Contact Maia Nero/212 925-5778

ROSEKRANS HOFFMAN

TOM LEONARD

COLIN BOOTMAN

Kirchoff/Wohlberg, Inc. • 897 Boston Post Road • Madison, CT 06443 • (203) 245-7308

TROY VISS

DANIEL MORETON

KIRCHOFF
WOHLBERG

Artists Representatives

866 United Nations Plaza
New York, NY 10017
(212) 644-2020

Les Paul & Mary Ford in home Studio
Circa 1954

JOE CIARDIELLO   **(718) 727 - 4757**

Right after you get it, it starts to turn yellow.

No wonder. Every art director in the business looks for artists in the same place. They turn to the yellowed pages of Showcase Illustration.

A M E R I C A N   S H O W C A S E

We are proud to introduce a very simple way to look at a few of our award-winning illustrators from around the planet. Since words alone can't describe their stellar work, we had to go about showing it in our own colorful way. One that you'll appreciate the first time you open our new 1994 annual. When you do, you'll be at a loss for words, too. Call us at 212-682-1490.

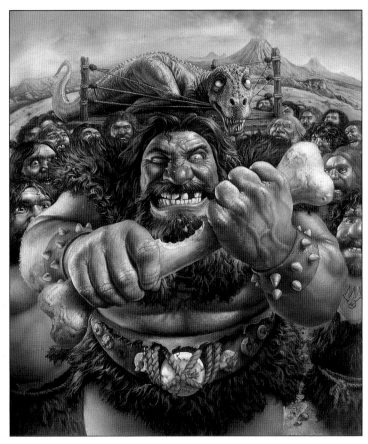

MARK FREDRICKSON

6 0 2 • 7 2 2 • 5 7 7 7

Kazuhiko Sano
Studio (415) 381-6377   Fax (415) 381-3847

New York: Renard Represents Inc.
(212) 490-2450
Fax (212) 697-6828

The Best of Illustration

Tom Nachreiner

New Artists

TRACY SABIN

PAUL COZZOLINO

MARC MONGEAU

WALDEMAR SWIERZY

MARLENA TORZECKA • 211 EAST 89 STREET • SUITE A-1 • NEW YORK • NEW YORK 10128 • TELEPHONE 212 • 289 • 5514

So the world isn't beating a path to your door

just because you have tha

wonder okay, how do I get from here to actually

being

Cindy Sandro| *illustrator*

That's where we come in.

some of

the brightest young art directors

Sarah Kennedy| *illustrator*

the country. It's real world experience, taught b

Ruth Mitchell| *illustrator*

program designed to help you create a seasoned,

professiona

Margaret DeNeergaard| *illustrator*

Barb Hogan| *illustrator*

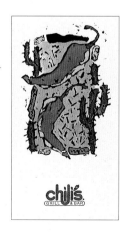

chili's.
GRILL & BAR

ard-earned BFA. And you're  starting to

Robin Sawyer| *illustrator*

 n 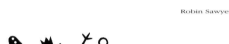 illustrator instead of someone who can draw.

Jack Meacham| *illustrator*

Sheryl Southern| *illustrator*

At Portfolio Center we'll put you to 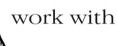 work with

Barbara Hogan| *illustrator*

graphic designers,  photo- graphers and writers in

Jack Meacham| *illustrator*

nationally-known, working professionals. A two year

Cindy Sandro| *illustrator*

 portfolio. To make you an illustrator.

David Kacmarynski| *illustrator*

PORTFOLIO CENTER

125 Bennett Street
Atlanta, Georgia 30309

CALL 1-800-255-3169 FOR OUR FREE CATALOG

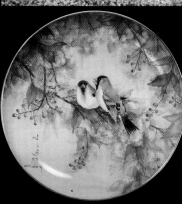

Jim Spanfeller

(914) 232-3546

60 Mustato Road, Katonah, NY 10536

"Best of Saki"
 H.H. Munro
Franklin Library
A.D. Michael Mendelsohn

Linotype Machine Promotion Art for The Spanfeller Press
Brewster, New York *A.D. Robert I. York*

"An American Original . . .
You can tell a Spanfeller from across the
room. I think it is hard not to be alter-
nately charmed and dazzled by the
work of this gifted artist. The quality is
there, the originality, the impact.
He is distinctive."
Peter Dzwonkoski. Head, Department
of Rare Books and Special Collections,
University of Rochester Library.

Self Portrait

Impossible Vacation, by Spalding Gray • Playboy Magazine • *A.D. Tom Staebler, Kerig Pope*

fiat & associates
312 464 0964 *
312 554 1729 *

j o h n k l e b e r

martha productions inc
310 390 9744
310 390 3161 *

the mccann company
214 526 2252
214 526 5565 *

* fax

THE SOCIETY OF ILLUSTRATORS 35TH ANNUAL OF AMERICAN ILLUSTRATION

SI Society of Illustrators
Museum Shop

The Society of Illustrators Museum of American Illustration maintains a shop featuring many quality products. Four-color, large format books document contemporary illustration and the great artists of the past. Museum quality prints and posters capture classic images. T-shirts, sweatshirts, hats, mugs and tote bags make practical and fun gifts.

The Museum Shop is an extension of the Society's role as the center for illustration in America today. For further information or quantity discounts, contact the Society at TEL: (212) 838-2560 / FAX: (212) 838-2561

NEW!

* ILLUSTRATORS 35 *
320 pp. Cover by
Dan Schwartz
Contains 420 works of art.
Included are Hall of Fame
biographies and the
Hamilton King interview.
Our most recent annual,
the most contemporary
illustration. $55.00

ILLUSTRATORS ANNUAL BOOKS

These catalogs are based on our annual juried exhibitions, divided into four major categories in American Illustration: Editorial, Book, Advertising, and Institutional. Some are available in a limited supply only.

In addition, a limited number of out-of-print collector's editions of the Illustrators Annuals that are not listed above (1959 to Illustrators 28) are available as is.

Also available for collectors are back issues of The Art Directors Club annuals and GRAPHIS Annuals.

Contact the Society for details...

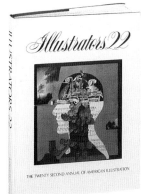
ILLUSTRATORS 22
$20.00
limited number remaining

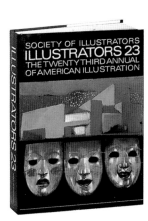
ILLUSTRATORS 23
$20.00
limited number remaining

ILLUSTRATORS 24
$20.00
limited number remaining

ILLUSTRATORS 27
$40.00
limited number remaining

ILLUSTRATORS 29
$45.00
limited number remaining

ILLUSTRATORS 31
$49.95

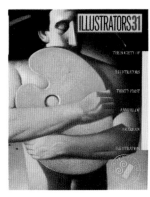
ILLUSTRATORS 32
$49.95

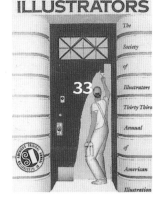
ILLUSTRATORS 33
$49.95

ILLUSTRATORS 34
$49.95

ART FOR SURVIVAL
248 pp, full color, 150 images
by contemporary illustrators
commenting on the Environment.
Introductions by Tom Cruise
and others. $40.00

**THE ILLUSTRATOR IN
AMERICA** (1880-1980) -355 pp.
Compiled by leading authorities
on illustration. Contains 700
illustrations by 460 artists.
$40.00

SOCIETY OF ILLUSTRATORS • 128 East 63rd Street • New York, NY 10021

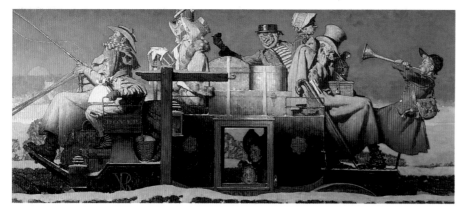

"The Dover Coach" by NORMAN ROCKWELL, 1935
$12.00

"Blond at a Filling Station" by MEAD SCHAEFFER, 1938
$12.00

"Horse Race" by HAROLD VON SCHMIDT, 1939
$12.00

"The Blue Cloak" by LYMAN ANDERSON
$12.00

MUSEUM QUALITY POSTERS

Posters of classic works from the Society's permanent collection.
Reproduced on glossy stock in a 20" x 30" format.
Suitable for framing. $12.00 per poster; $38.00 for the set of four.

EXHIBITION POSTERS

Posters created for exhibitions in the Society of Illustrators Museum of American Illustration. Suitable for framing. $10.00 per poster; $27.00 for the set of three.

"Recycled Ideas"
"The Illustrator and the Environment "
by FOLON $10.00

"Science Fiction" by JOHN BERKEY, 1984
$10.00

"Wizard of Oz", The Original Art by EDWARD SOREL, 1991
$10.00

EXHIBITION CATALOGS

These volumes have been created for exhibitions in the Society of Illustrators Museum of American Illustration. They focus on specific artists, eras or subjects.

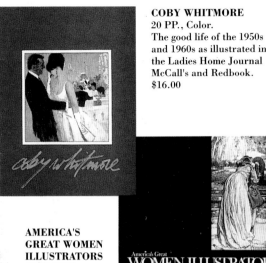

COBY WHITMORE
20 PP., Color.
The good life of the 1950s and 1960s as illustrated in the Ladies Home Journal McCall's and Redbook.
$16.00

AMERICA'S GREAT WOMEN ILLUSTRATORS
(1850-1950)
24 pp, B&W.
Decade by decade essays by important historians on the role of women in illustration.
$5.00

THE BUSINESS LIBRARY

Each of thesee volumes is a valuable asset to the professional artist whether established or just starting out. Together they form a solid base for your business.

The set of three volumes. $42.00

GRAPHIC ARTISTS GUILD HANDBOOK PRICING AND ETHICAL GUIDELINES - Vol. 7
Includes an outline of ethical standards and business practices, as well as price ranges for hundreds of uses and sample contracts.
$22.95

THE LEGAL GUIDE FOR THE VISUAL ARTIST
1989 Edition.
Tad Crawford's text explains basic copyrights, moral rights, the sale of rights, taxation, business accounting and the legal support groups available to artists.
$18.95

HEALTH HAZARDS MANUAL
A comprehensive review of materials and supplies, from fixatives to pigments, airbrushes to solvents.
$9.95

NEW EDITION

150 pages in full color of Children's books from 1992. This volume contains valuable "how-to" comments from the artists as well as a publishers directory. A compilation of the exhibition, "The Original Art 1992 - Celebrating the Fine Art of Children's Book Illustration."
$29.95

GIFT ITEMS

The Society's famous Red and Black logo, designed by Bradbury Thompson, is featured on the following gift items:

SI LAPEL PINS
$6.00
Actual Size

SI BASEBALL CAPS
Blue or red corduroy, adjustable back strap and the logo in white
$15.00

SI PATCH
White with blue lettering and piping - 4" wide
$4.00

SI TOTE BAGS
Heavyweight, white canvas bags are 14" high with the two-color logo
$15.00

SI CERAMIC COFFEE MUGS
Heavyweight 14 oz. mugs are white with the two-color logo
$6.00 each, $20.00 for a set of 4

SI T-SHIRTS

Incorporating the Society's logo in three designs (large SI, words and lines, multiple logo). Orange shirts with black lettering. Blue shirts with white lettering. White shirts with two color lettering. $10.00 each.
SIZES: Small, Large, X-Large, XX-Large.

Also special heavyweight white cotton, four-color T-shirts featuring classic images from the Society's Permanent Collection $20.

"Easter" by **J.C. LEYENDECKER**
The Saturday Evening Post 1934

"The Black Arrow" by **N.C. WYETH**
Frontispiece for the Scribner's Classic by Robert Louis Stevenson

SI SWEATSHIRTS

Blue with white lettering of multiple logos. Grey with large red SI. $20.00 each.
Sizes:
Large,
X-Large,
XX-Large.

SI NOTE CARDS

Norman Rockwell greeting cards, 3-7/8" x 8-5/8", inside blank, great for all occasions. Includes 100% rag envelopes

10 cards - $10.00
20 cards - $18.00
50 cards - $35.00
100 cards - $60.00

ORDER FORM
Mail to the attention of:
The Museum Shop, SOCIETY OF ILLUSTRATORS, 128 East 63rd Street, New York, NY 10021

35

NAME _____

COMPANY_____

STREET_____

CITY_____

STATE_____ ZIP _____

DAYTIME PHONE ( ) _____

Enclosed is my check for $ _____
Make checks payable to Society of Illustrators
Please charge my credit card:
❑ American Express ❑ Master Card ❑ Visa
Card Number _____
Signature _____ Expiration Date _____
*please note if name appearing on the card is different than the mailing name.

Qty	Description	Size	Color	Price	Total
# of items ordered		Total price of item(s) ordered			
		*Shipping/handling per order			3.50
		TOTAL DUE			

* Foreign postage additional